Praise for Doug Wead's *New York Times* bestseller
ALL THE PRESIDENT'S CHILDREN

"[A] must-read for students . . . for politicians who try to rear children, and for the publishers and writers who may try to exploit them."

—*Weekly Standard*

"Good fun to read. . . . *All the Presidents' Children* [will] amuse and inform White House watchers and students of political history."

—*Kirkus Reviews*

"[A] definitive work on the subject."

—*The Washington Times*

"Doug Wead's compelling book captures the human side of presidential history. It also shrinks presidents down to the rest of those who can identify with Woodrow Wilson's lament: 'From my daughters I have learned what every parent knows of himself—that I do not know how to raise children.'"

—*Saturday Evening Post*

"Perfect! This is the perspective that has been missing. One sees the presidents through a whole new light."

—Dave Weldon, U.S. congressman, Florida

All the Presidents' Children is available in paperback from Atria Books.

ALSO BY DOUG WEAD

All the Presidents' Children

THE RAISING OF A PRESIDENT

The Mothers and Fathers of Our Nation's Leaders

—— ★ ——

DOUG WEAD

ATRIA BOOKS

NEW YORK LONDON TORONTO SYDNEY

ATRIA BOOKS

1230 Avenue of the Americas
New York, NY 10020

First Atria Books trade paperback edition January 2006

10 9 8 7 6 5 4 3 2

ATRIA BOOKS is a trademark of Simon & Schuster, Inc.

Manufactured in the United States of America

For information regarding special discounts for bulk purchases, please contact
Simon & Schuster Special Sales at 1-800-456-6798 or business@simonandschuster.com

To my wife, Myriam,
who shared the adventure

Contents

——— ★ ———

★

PART ONE

FOUNDING FATHERS AND MOTHERS

—— ★ ——

ONE

How the Presidents' Parents Shaped Their Sons and Influenced the Nation

God bless my mother, all I am or ever hope to be I owe to her.[1]
—Abraham Lincoln

This is the first book written about the presidents' parents. That fact will come as a surprise to many students of history, for there are numerous books devoted to the lives of the presidents' mothers and several written exclusively about the presidents' fathers, but not a single study that treats them both. "Our relationship with our parents is the 'original' relationship of our lives," writes Dr. Dale Atkins, "the template for all other connections."[2] How can one consider the development of these complicated lives without a thorough examination of both parents interacting together with the sons they raised?

Can one really understand Franklin D. Roosevelt without considering the role of his domineering mother, a woman who wouldn't let him take a bath without her until he was nine years old and who sat there, silent in the background, when he gave his first radio fireside chat to the nation? Or how would history read if one considered only the mother of John F. Kennedy, who, according to his wife, Jackie, never once told her president son that she loved him? Imagine trying to understand Kennedy without examining the role of his father, Joe, who as Kennedy himself admitted, made it all happen.

It was not just the presence of an affirming, loving mother that motivated young Abraham Lincoln to read his books, but also the ominous presence of an ignorant, sometimes abusive father described as "cold and inhumane"[3] in his treatment of his son. Lincoln, the boy, may have read his books to escape the angry man, who sometimes hit him so hard that he knocked him to the ground, as much as to impress the woman who nurtured and protected him.

It is curious that no psychologist has taken on this subject, connecting the dots by comparing the parents of the various presidents, searching out any possible common denominators, and extracting any lessons to be learned. Are there things these parents said or did that sparked high achievement in their offspring? Are there patterns to be applied for the rest of us?

It's a difficult and unwieldy subject, to be sure. There are so many variables of time and circumstances, so many generations to cover. And psychologists insist that much of a parent's impact comes in the first five years. There is so much esoteric data demanded. It would be helpful to know if our subjects were breast-fed or bottle-fed. But while we may have studied the lives of our presidents with insatiable and unbridled curiosity, even to the point of exploring their sex lives, there is not much available on the subject of presidential breast-feeding.

Still, we have clues about those early years of nurturing, clues that are based on the things the presidents and their parents have said and done. Thanks to a growing body of sociological data, we can get a picture, even though sometimes blurry, of those early relationships and a feel for how they impacted the lives of our chief executives.

THE POSITIVE IMPACT OF A NURTURING MOTHER

Not surprisingly, a number of presidents' mothers seem to have done everything right. We know that the tender early love of a mother or surrogate creates deep reservoirs of self-confidence throughout one's life. Studies coming out of the former Soviet Union showed that children of the state who were denied physical contact and affirmation— even those who were well fed and otherwise cared for—had difficulty learning to speak and walk. A nurturing, reassuring, calm mother figure successfully satisfies what psychologists refer to as *the intimacy drive* of the infant. This leads to a strong attachment between a mother and child. Drawing on the security of this attachment, the child will more quickly explore his environment and thus realize his separate identity. This process is called *separation and individuation*.

When a child experiences the parent as a safe base, the child's range of exploration will increase. Picture a baby crawling away from his mother and then pausing to look back to see if she is still there. Eventually, the child will internalize this sense of security and consider "the self" as a safe base as well. He or she will begin to feel secure even when alone or away from the parent. The greater the sense of security, the greater the child's autonomous functioning. Thus, there is an essential intertwining among what psychologists refer to as *the intimacy drive, the internal location of control,* and the *need for achievement,* all three of which are psychological necessities of life.

Thanks to our open society and thanks to the strong two-party system, we have a virtual banquet of detail on the adult lives of our presidents, including unflattering inside accounts of their personality flaws, as well as their successes. Drawing on such descriptions, we can work backward to an understanding of their early parental relationships.

In studying the presidents, one trend is hard to ignore. Many had very strong relationships with their mothers. As former *New York Times* reporter Doris Faber discovered in her study, they are "almost without exception mama's boys."[4]

President James Madison considered his mother to be his most trusted adviser. They were close throughout their lives and never seemed to have an argument. Nelly, as she was affectionately called, was often sick with malaria, but she lived to be ninety-six. In her old age, friends said she looked younger than her son. She was lucid and active, and until her dying day she did not need reading glasses.

"Mother McKinley," parent of our twenty-fifth president, was a nurturing parent, observed cuddling her baby for hours at a time. The ultimate break came when her son defied her wishes and rejected a career as a preacher. But the disappointment did not last. Her son's great success brought her quiet pleasure, and the president became so dependent on her prayers that he set up a special wire to her home in Ohio so he could talk to her daily. When she lay dying, he took his presidential train, the *Air Force One* of its day, and rushed to her side. A few years later, absent the protection of his mother's prayers, William McKinley was felled by an assassin's bullet during an exposition in Buffalo, New York.

"I was a mama's boy," said Woodrow Wilson, "no question about it, but the best of womanhood came to me through those apron strings."[5]

Sara Delano Roosevelt nursed her baby, Franklin, for a full year. A friend at a dinner party once asked what she was feeding him, and she answered, "Nature's own food."[6] Sara recorded her son's every move and could report, "Baby very well and laughing all the time."[7]

Hannah Milhous Nixon was a calm, understated woman who, as in the case of so many other presidents' mothers, was deeply religious. Unpretentious and nonjudgmental, she was a stark contrast to her choleric, loud husband. When Richard M. Nixon was in political trouble, he would call her and she would say, "I will be thinking of you." It was her signal that she would be praying, for as a humble Quaker she took literally the admonition not to pray publicly or make a pretense of one's prayers. In 1974, when Richard Nixon gave his tearful farewell to the nation, he declared, "My mother was a saint."[8]

In 1918, a German pediatrician, Ernst Moro, made the observation that a baby's first and most powerful instinct was to hug, and that when taken from the womb a baby would immediately reach out with both arms in an attempt to grasp his mother.[9]

Moro's observation brings to mind the relationship between President Andrew Jackson and his remarkable mother, Elizabeth Hutchinson Jackson. "Betty," as she was called, was an Irish beauty with an indomitable spirit who found it easy to express love to her children. But Betty was born in troubled times. According to legend, she was a patriot who juggled raising her fatherless sons and nursing wounded soldiers during the American Revolution. Then she contracted cholera from a patient, turned deathly sick herself, and suddenly died.

Betty Jackson insisted that her children stay by her bed as she passed from this life, and she used what strength she possessed to give each one of them special words of advice. Her last comments to Andrew were obviously etched deep: "Don't lie or steal, and don't rely on the courts to solve your problems, settle them yourself."

Psychologists who were consulted on this project suggest that America's seventh president, Andrew Jackson, spent his whole life seeking to become one of those very war heroes for whom his mother had sacrificed herself. During the Indian Wars and the War of 1812, and in numerous duels of honor, Jackson was frequently in mortal danger. When he died in his bed in 1845 at the age of seventy-eight, he still carried several bullets in his body, including one that had lodged close to his heart. Throughout his life, Andrew Jackson had sought to be as worthy as those men his mother had nursed, the soldiers who had taken his mother from him. It was a lifelong journey back into his mother's arms.

Andrew Jackson became one of America's greatest military and political leaders and one of its most beloved public figures. Even when he was in retirement, crowds would line the road when he passed by on horseback. He never met his father, described by some historians as an Irish linen weaver and farmer. Andrew Jackson would be one of three American presidents whose fathers would die before their sons were born—Rutherford B. Hayes and William Jefferson Clinton being the others—but his mother's short life would greatly impact him. Her dying admonition became part of his core beliefs, and thus it was that the last words of a poor young Irish widow helped inspire and frame the great political philosophy of a whole generation of Americans and define its era in our nation's history.

In a sense, part of the Jacksonian years and the popular so-called Jackson Doctrine belong to Elizabeth Hutchinson Jackson, a widowed mother of three whose birth date and birthplace in Ireland have been forever lost to history. Nursing the wounded, she was willing to take on a humble servant's role in helping her young nation's birth, never knowing that the small son at her side would rise to lead those very United States and become the most powerful and popular president in its early history.

Some of the most remarkable mothers of the presidents demonstrated a resilience and cunning beyond their times. Abigail Adams, responsible for her family's sustenance during her husband's years of absence in service to his country, sold pins, coffee, sugar, handkerchiefs, and other hard-to-find commodities that John Adams sent home from Philadelphia and Europe. Sometimes she bartered the goods for hard currency and necessities.

A young, widowed Sophia Hayes, mother of our nineteenth president, devised a clever way to avoid almost certain financial ruin: she came up with a complicated formula that involved renting out parts of her farm in exchange for food, which she then bartered for other goods. She not only held her frightened family together but even prospered in a difficult situation.

Herbert Hoover's mother, Huldah, a devout Quaker, was a tower of strength after the death of her husband. She raised her family with stern values, refused charity, sewed for food, and became a popular minister in the Quaker Church. Huldah refused to spend a single penny of her husband's life insurance, saving it instead for her children's education. One night, exhausted after preaching a sermon, she walked twenty miles home in a cold rain, caught pneumonia, and died. Herbert Hoover was suddenly an orphan at the age of nine, but he was empowered with a remarkable heritage.

In 1907, heading into his presidential campaign, William Howard Taft was tapped by his friend President Theodore Roosevelt to make a goodwill trip around the world. With his mother sick and close to death, Taft decided to cancel his trip to be with her. In a trembling, dying hand, Louise Torrey Taft wrote the last words he would ever receive from her, a statement that reflected six generations of one of America's greatest families: "No Taft, to my knowledge, has ever yet neglected a public duty for the sake of gratifying a private desire." [10] He went.

As a volunteer midwife to poor, black tenant farmworkers, Lillian Carter outraged her segregationist neighbors. Brilliant and sassy, she joined the Peace Corps at age sixty-eight, serving in India. She returned a hero to that country during her son Jimmy Carter's presidency. Lillian lived for months at a time in the White House, where she was often shamelessly fawned over by visiting dignitaries and heads of state. When King Hassan of Morocco presented her with yet another gift of "rare" perfume, Lillian retorted, "Oh, you foreigners are all alike." The king laughed uproariously, and a relieved President Carter laughed with him.

FATHERS OF POWER

Not surprisingly, most presidents were the sons of very powerful fathers, some inspirational by example and some abusive. Of course, the father of John Quincy Adams was a president himself, as was the father of George W. Bush. And the father of George Herbert Walker Bush was a U.S. senator and millionaire businessman. William Henry Harrison's father signed the Declaration of Independence and went on to become governor of Virginia. President Benjamin Harrison was the son of a congressman who was himself the son of a president. John Tyler's father was a governor of Virginia.

Zachary Taylor's father was a Revolutionary War hero. "My father contributed much more than words to my life," Taylor said, "He provided the example of a man who did not know the word surrender."[11]

During the years of the American Revolution, Benjamin Pierce, father of the fourteenth president, heard about the Battle of Lexington and left his plow in the middle of the field to head out and fight for independence. He was involved in most of the major engagements of the Revolutionary War, suffering through Valley Forge and eventually rising to brigadier general. He later became governor of New Hampshire. Even after becoming president, the son was in awe of his father's career.

Alphonso Taft, the millionaire father of William Howard Taft, was the secretary of war under Ulysses S. Grant and an ambassador under Chester A. Arthur.

In more modern times, FDR's father was a successful businessman who, among other investments, owned coal mines. He himself had come from a prominent patrician family, once turning down a dinner invitation from the Vanderbilts, considering them to be nouveau riche and beneath the social standing of the family.

Joseph P. Kennedy was a millionaire by age thirty-five and a leading public figure. In the 1960s, when the presidential helicopter lifted off from Hyannis Port, Massachusetts, the young president, John Kennedy, waved to his father below and said to a nearby assistant, "There's the man who did all of this."[12]

Three fathers of presidents were clergy. Both fathers of Grover Cleveland and Woodrow Wilson were Princeton seminary graduates, pastors, and denominational leaders in the Presbyterian Church. William Arthur, father of the twenty-first president, was a fiery Baptist preacher, so quarrelsome that he was run out of five different congregations. But the son rebelled and was never baptized. As president he attended St. John's Episcopal Church on Lafayette Square, within walking distance of the White House. His mother was mortified that her son had abandoned the family's cherished Baptist faith, but, according to biographer Steven Alcorn, this rebellion may have been at the heart of his drive to succeed.

Many of our presidents sprang from humble origins, but some of their fathers had the most powerful holds on their sons. In some cases the parent was an inspiration, whose integrity and character far surpassed their poverty or diminished social standing. Some were organizers who gave their children a sense of structure and discipline that allowed them to succeed. And others were not only poor; they seemed to lack any discernible parenting gift at all, except for a great love of their children. In some cases, the son rose to vindicate the father.

Nathaniel Fillmore, the first presidents' father to actually visit his son in the White House, was a tenant farmer who sometimes lived off the charity of others. His son's rise is attributed by his biographer to "his father's blunders."

Herbert Hoover's only memory of his father was that of a strong, laughing man, lifting him out of the mud and shaking him off. The boy was only six when his father—the sunny, eternal optimist and town blacksmith—fell dead of heart disease. His mother, Huldah Hoover, was so poor and their budget so strictly enforced that she often had to forgo correspondence. Even postage stamps were out of reach.

"He was not a talker," Harry S. Truman said of his farmer father, "he was a doer."[13] Dwight Eisenhower's father was humiliated by poverty and forced to declare bankruptcy. Nixon's father was a grade school dropout who struggled financially all his life.

Orphaned at six years of age, Jack Reagan, father of a future president, spent his life as a modest shoe salesman, forever struggling with alcohol. In a scene out of a Frank Capra movie, he was once handed his dismissal notice on Christmas Eve.

Recently released KGB documents show that in 1980 the Soviet Union developed a dossier on Jack Reagan and his struggles. They leaked the information to American journalists during the son's presidential campaign, hoping to derail his candidacy. Jack Reagan, mercifully, was gone long before the Soviet smear campaign. He had lived just long enough to see his son, future president Ronald Reagan, star as George Gipp in the film about the football legend Knute Rockne of Notre Dame University. He would never know that he had been the father of the American president who was credited with ending the Cold War.

Ronald Reagan, meanwhile, would have an enduring obsession with the character he played in the movie. It was his last link to his father. In one of his last public appearances before Alzheimer's disease set in, Ronald Reagan sat backstage and talked to friends about George

Gipp: "Some day, when the team is down and there doesn't seem to be much hope, remember me, and tell the boys to win one for the Gipper." [14]

Some presidents rose from very dark and abusive relationships. They might have easily succumbed to the bouts of self-hatred and guilt that plague most victims of abuse. Rather, in each case they discovered a device—a way out—that enabled them to triumph. Some reacted to their experience by a conscious *counteridentification* with the parent. That is, they determined that they were the opposite personality of the despised father or mother. This is most surely the example for America's greatest president.

Abraham Lincoln's father, Thomas, could be abusive, sometimes striking out with his fists at the future president. Many respected experts on Lincoln discount these episodes, suggesting that Thomas was only acting within the norm of his times. Albert Ellis makes the point with Rational-Emotive Therapy that we behave according to the truth as we perceive it, and Abe would not have seen such treatment as abuse. Or so it is reasoned.

But Abraham Lincoln saw many things ahead of his time; it is part of his enigma, part of the mystery of his spectacular rise from ignorance and poverty, without any seeming stimulation or trigger to cause it. I focus on the incidents of abuse because they are the most powerful images of his youth, the most conflicted and frightening. Perhaps he was able to achieve enough objectivity to realize the injustice of his situation, especially given the fact that his father did not strike his cousin or his sister or his mother.

Lincoln was nine years old, living in the wilds of Indiana, when his mother died. A few months later his father departed, leaving a grieving Abe, his teenage sister, and a cousin alone in a log cabin in the middle of the woods. A friend who finally sought out the youngsters found them caked with mud and skeletal from months of malnutrition. They were surviving on a diet of dried berries and an occasional squirrel. Although working in Elizabethtown, Kentucky, less than a seven-day trek away, Thomas Lincoln finally showed up a half a year later, with a new wife in tow. Young Abe Lincoln ran to the strange woman and hid himself in her skirts.

Nurtured by his new stepmother, Abraham Lincoln's emotions healed sufficiently to function and his intellect was awakened, but years later he would not bother to attend his father's funeral. Friends joined his wife, Mary Todd Lincoln, in convincing him that he should finally name one of his sons after his father. Lincoln, in perhaps a moment of guilt, complied, naming his fourth son Thomas. But he could never bring himself to actually speak his father's name. The boy was called simply "Tad."

As is often the case in an abusive relationship, Abraham Lincoln may have unintentionally passed the pain on to yet another generation. Psychologists suggest that it is common for a child to *counteridentify* with a flawed parent on a conscious level, while *identifying* completely on an unconscious level.

His son Robert Todd Lincoln always felt estranged from his father. After the assassination of Abraham Lincoln, the son vented his rage on his mother, using her money to hire doctors to declare her insane. For her part, Mary wrote him a letter confirming what he had always feared, saying that his father never really "liked" him.

Robert Todd named his second child Abraham Lincoln II but refused ever to use the name, calling him "Jack" instead. He told the boy that he would be called "Abraham" only when he was finally worthy. But young Abe II would never be "worthy." He died at sixteen, and so ended the Lincoln family name.

A more successful escape from the cycle of abuse was experienced by Leslie Lynch King, Jr. His father, King, Sr., was a wool trader from Omaha, Nebraska, who conducted a whirlwind courtship of a twenty-year-old Illinois coed named Dorothy Ayer Gardner. Leslie L. King, Jr., was born the next year.

But the father was a violent man, taking out his rage on his wife and beating her frequently. Fearing for her baby, Dorothy left town one night, never to return. She eventually obtained a divorce and married a gentle paint salesman from the Midwest. If Abraham Lincoln needed a stepmother to nurture him back to emotional health, Leslie Lynch King, Jr., found a stepfather who made the difference in his life. The paint salesman from the Midwest gave the young boy direction and a sense of belonging. Years later he formalized the process, adopting him as his own and wiping out the pain of the past by giving him his own name as well. The little boy would become Gerald Rudolph Ford, Jr., the thirty-eighth president of the United States, and he would help heal the nation after the trauma of the Watergate scandal.

HOW PRESIDENTS HAVE "RECONSTRUCTED" THEIR PARENTS

So many presidents lost their fathers and mothers at an early age that it has been hard for historians to ignore the connection. George Washington was eleven when his father died; Thomas Jefferson fourteen, James Monroe sixteen, William Henry Harrison eighteen, Andrew Johnson three, James Garfield only one, and Grover Cleveland just sixteen when they lost their fathers.

Teddy Roosevelt was nineteen when his father died and only twenty-five when he lost his mother and his wife within hours. His distant cousin Franklin was eighteen when his father died. Herbert Hoover was six when he lost his father and nine when he lost his mother. John Tyler lost his mother at the age of seven, and Calvin Coolidge was only twelve. Andrew Jackson, Rutherford B. Hayes, and Bill Clinton were not yet born when their fathers died. Jackson would lose his mother, as well, at age fourteen.

Psychologists have long argued that there was a connection between revolutionaries and the early deaths of their fathers. Washington and Jefferson are cited, but also Hitler, Stalin, and Mao Zedong. Is it because of an unconscious rage at authority, represented by the father who abandoned them?

In one sense, a parent isn't really dead until his or her children are gone as well, for each child will retain an internalized concept of that parent until his or her last breath. We are told that children modify, distort, and reconstruct the image of their parents as an ongoing part of their internal thought life. This process is especially critical to a child whose parent dies early. Such a child has greater freedom to reconstruct a father or mother and then identify or counteridentify with that parent.

Abraham Lincoln's famous quote "God bless my mother, all that I am or ever hope to be I owe to her," or, in some historical accounts, "my angel mother," is almost an obligatory cliché for a biographical account of any one of the presidents' parents. But the psychologists I consulted all agreed that even if Lincoln's mother had been an angel, the son would not have remembered. Nancy Hanks, the mother of the sixteenth president, died when young Abraham was nine years old. Psychologists suggest that a more accurate version of Lincoln's experience should be "All that I am or hope to be, I owe to my own internal, reconstructed, idealized version of my mother." Perhaps more daunting to such theories is the conclusion of Dr. Thomas Schwartz of the Illinois State Historical Society, who warns that we cannot be sure that Lincoln ever made the statement.[15]

A parent doesn't have to die to be successfully reconstructed by the child. One sees this process at work in the life of Ulysses S. Grant, the eighteenth president. Some historians suggest that Hannah Grant, the president's quiet, religious, Methodist mother, was mentally disturbed. Others say that she was a simpleton. The family carefully shielded her from the public. She never granted an interview and never once joined her husband on his many visits to see their son in the White House. This story of her mental incapacity was so publicly pervasive that the family made a special point of trying to contradict it by releasing a statement the day she died, saying that she had read the newspaper *as usual* that morning before passing away peacefully in the afternoon.

Whatever the problem, President Grant, who died two years after his mother, idealized her from a distance. He did not see her once during his eight-year presidency and made her only a single visit during his retirement and then only so she could see her grandchildren.

Meanwhile, Grant's father, who was boastful, stubborn, and rich from the tanning business, was always available and stayed at the White House for long periods. Yet Grant consistently attributed his success to his enigmatic Methodist mother, who disdained all glory, never set foot in Washington, and was hidden by the family from public view. His biographer referred to an "uncommon detachment" between the president and his mother. It is a bit of a puzzle to historians, but psychologists who have reviewed the president's letters have their own explanation. They say that he worshiped another person—the reconstructed image of his mother—and thus preferred not to encounter the real one.

Bill Clinton's biological father, William Jefferson Blythe, was a tall, handsome traveling salesman from Sherman, Texas, who epitomized the central figure of so many traveling salesman jokes. He was a serial husband and actually married Virginia Cassidy seven months before his divorce from his fourth wife. It would be his last marriage. Blythe was in a freak auto accident a few months before the future president was born. His car turned upside down, and, trapped inside, he drowned in a puddle of water only inches deep.

If a stepparent would be the salvation for Abraham Lincoln and Gerald Ford, it would be a great trial for Bill Clinton. In 1950, his mother, Virginia Cassidy Blythe, married Roger Clinton, a Buick salesman from Hope, Arkansas. He would eventually give his stepson a new name but not much else. Roger Clinton was an alcoholic and wife beater who once fired a gun at his wife inside his own home. Bill Clinton was only a few feet away.

So what inspired young Bill Clinton to seek a better life? His mother, who would eventually marry five times, was a habitual gambler who worked by days and haunted area nightclubs by night. Could she have provided the example he needed? Not likely, says psychologist Chet Sunde. Rather, Clinton would be susceptible to seduction and flirtation by the opposite sex, and at some deep level of his psyche he would always be looking for a woman of adventure like Mom.

Bill Clinton's success was probably born out of his internal reconstruction of his dead father. Clinton openly pined for his "real" dad, the one who had died before his birth: "I thought about it all the time." The experience spoke to him of the fragility of life and gave him an urgency to move quickly. It was not unlike the experience of George Washington, who was eleven years old when his father suddenly died and who was constantly plagued by premonitions of his own death. It was the driving force for Washington, whose beloved stepbrother and surrogate father died young as well. And it prompted Bill Clinton to move quickly, to take chances. By age thirty-two he was called "the boy governor" of Arkansas and he was on his way.

BREAKING AWAY:
THE PROCESS OF INDIVIDUATION

Notwithstanding the popular view that the presidents sprang from good soil, a striking number of these families were clearly dysfunctional, and some of the revered presidential mothers were, in fact, emotionally disturbed women. Psychologists write of the "opportunity for trauma or empowerment" when a child eventually breaks from his mother—that is, assuming that the child is able to do so. The stronger the bond, psychologists say, the more traumatic the break for both mother and child. This very process may have been the defining moment for some presidents and a trigger for their ambition.

James Buchanan's mother was a brilliant, self-educated woman who could quote John Milton at length and who argued with her son "about everything." The president suggested that the habit contributed to his political skills. Early in his government career, she adamantly demanded that he refuse appointment as minister to Russia. When her campaign failed, she employed guilt as a device, claiming that if he left her she would die before he returned. For the first time in his life Buchanan publicly defied his mother's will. He went to Russia, whereupon she promptly died. Eight years later he became the fifteenth president.

But if American presidents reared by obsessive or even abusive parents are able to triumph anyway, there is ample evidence to show that they are not immune to the same traumas experienced by the rest of us. Things can go wrong when the separation from one's mother and the process of one's own *individuation* does not occur properly. The result is either *detachment* or *dependency*. For a surprisingly long list of American presidents, this very moment of crisis led them on to greatness.

Dwight D. Eisenhower's mother, a deeply religious woman, was a pacifist who openly wept when her defiant son left home for West Point and his rendezvous with history.

Sara Roosevelt, the mother of FDR, dominated her son to the point of obsession. FDR sought independence by marrying his cousin Eleanor, but Sara easily crushed the spirit of his new bride, who finally capitulated and allowed Sara to raise her children. FDR defied his mother by seeking a political career against her wishes, only to be crippled by polio and fall back into her clutches again. "Please don't make any more arrangements for my future happiness," Franklin Roosevelt once wrote to his interfering mother.

According to Kerry Little, a licensed mental health counselor in Fort Lauderdale who has studied the Roosevelt family, the process may have turned one of America's greatest presidents into an unconscious misogynist, leading him to ultimately betray and humiliate the women in his life.[16] But it was also a key to his powerful energy and strength of leadership.

George Washington was openly embarrassed and irritated by his controlling, egocentric mother, who lived to be eighty-one. In his thousands of papers he rarely mentions her name. And Thomas Jefferson allegedly despised his mother, who died while he was writing the Declaration of Independence. Commenting on the fact that Jefferson's voluminous writings seldom mention her name, his biographer Merrill Peterson suggests that the president's mother represented a "zero quantity"[17] in her son's life.

The mother of Franklin Pierce was an alcoholic who suffered from deep depression and grew senile while still in her fifties.

Some psychologists suggest that a "disturbed" mother can become obsessed with her newborn baby, who is dependent and nonthreatening. The same smothering attention that irritates the child when he is older may provide comfort and security during infancy. Notwithstanding the nervousness or irrationality of such a mother, in some rare instances the early, obsessive attention may actually empower the child. This may be just the formula at work in one of the most controversial and perplexing relationships of all the presidents and their parents, the relationship between Mary Ball Washington and her son, the father of America, George Washington. When he was a youth, Mary was obsessively protective, and when he was grown she constantly sought his attention. Indifferent to his successes and absorbed in her own fears of impending poverty, she persisted in her demands, but George Washington kept coming back for more.

The point is that whether the mother was nurturing or abusive, she was strong-willed. This more than any other factor is the common denominator of presidents. Washington may have been irritated by his mother and she may have been too selfish to often express her love, but she was certainly very strong and stubborn, unwilling to bend or retreat or listen to reason. None of her great son's towering achievements intimidated her in the slightest.

Lincoln's mother was so physically strong that she wrestled with men and beat them. The locals in Elizabethtown, Kentucky, would take sucker bets from strangers, suggesting that they could not even beat one of their own women, and then persuade Nancy Hanks to fight for the town's honor.

I found this trend so predictable that even when there was an exception, the pattern was close at hand. For example, John F. Kennedy's mother, Rose, was certainly not a possessive, powerful figure in the tradition of a Mary Washington or a Sara Roosevelt. But Joe Kennedy, the president's father, had all the dynamics at work in his own life. His mother, Mary Augusta, referred to her firstborn son as "my Joe." She was a large, imposing woman who was bigger than her husband, P. J. And she was highly ambitious for her son, shunning the Catholic schools in favor of Boston Latin and later Harvard. Joe was on the track to becoming president himself. One of the nation's richest men, he was ambassador to the United Kingdom when his political misjudgments ended any White House possibilities. Joe transferred his ambition to his sons and minutely orchestrated and financed their political rise.

Dorothy Walker Bush and Barbara Bush are examples of modern, strong-willed mothers of presidents, and both, like Sara Roosevelt, were themselves daddy's girls. "We have some strong women in our family," says Jeb Bush.[18]

WAITING IN THE WINGS

Next to the power of nurturing mothers and reconstructed idealized fathers, the most consistent and powerful dynamic in the raising of a president is what one could refer to as the second-choice syndrome; that is, the president is often the second choice of siblings within a family. Francis Bacon spoke of this phenomenon: "A man shall see, where there is a house full of children, one or two of the eldest respected, and the youngest made wantons; but in the midst some that are as it were forgotten, who many times nevertheless prove the best."[19]

This is certainly not a universal law among presidents, but it does happen frequently enough to bear mention. After the death of Augustine Washington, it was firstborn Lawrence who carried his father's hopes on his powerful shoulders. Little eleven-year-old George would not even have his education provided for. Yet the young child by his bedside, standing in the shadows, would achieve glory and power beyond all that the striving, ambitious father could have dreamed.

This story persists into modern times. The spotlight was on Milton Eisenhower, the high-achieving baby brother in the family, who held several different midlevel government positions and could hold the family spellbound at Thanksgiving reunions with stories of White

House receptions. The third son, Dwight, was on a treadmill in the military bureaucracy. In 1939, he was a major in the army and an assistant to a general; only three years later he was the commander of the Allied forces and ten years later the president of the United States.

Joe Kennedy expected his firstborn son Joe, Jr., to have a public career but never Jack, the sick one, too shy to speak publicly, the writer. There was a moment when Jack first ran for Congress when Joe Kennedy sat in a car with a longtime colleague, watching his skinny, frail, shy son Jack shaking hands with factory workers. Joe would tell his friend that he had never thought he would see such a scene in a thousand years. He hadn't thought his son had it in him.

As you will read in later chapters, the spotlight was on George W. Bush, the eldest son in the family of President George Herbert Walker Bush, but he chafed under the heat of expectations, developed a drinking problem, and finally disqualified himself from any significant public career by his reckless behavior. The spotlight shifted to Jeb, the second son, with the father, George H. W. Bush, openly proclaiming that he would have a national career. But with the spotlight off, George W. thrived and came roaring back, beating his brother into a gubernatorial slot. Within a ten-year period, starting at a point of financial desperation, George W. Bush became a millionaire, was elected governor of Texas, and became president of the United States.

PIECING THE PUZZLE TOGETHER: HOW THIS BOOK CAME ABOUT

By the end of my four-year study of presidents' parents, I had developed a new appreciation for the American presidents themselves, how some of them overcame abusive fathers or neurotic mothers, how they avoided becoming victims. During a fifteen-year study of presidents' offspring, which resulted in my book *All the Presidents' Children,* I had seen the worst side of many of America's chief executives.[20] Even the great ones stumbled in their parenting roles, even those august men on Mount Rushmore. George Washington was so remote to his stepchildren that they stopped speaking when he entered a room. Jefferson penned an awful letter to his daughter, listing the ways she could be "worthy" of his love. Lincoln was indulgent to the point of the absurd and passed on his estrangement with his own father to his third-born son. And Theodore Roosevelt, who initially struck me as the ideal parent, who romped with his children on the grass, also often pushed them beyond endurance. Three of his children died far too young, one by his own hand.

Still, when one considers the emotional baggage they carried into their parenting roles and the relationships they had with their own parents, these presidents were remarkable men. Again and again the lesson is brought home that circumstances and events that would destroy most children were often the very things that sparked greatness in our presidents.

Several psychologists and licensed family counselors advised me in the analyses and preparation of these stories. All concluded that available biographical sketches of presidential parents tend to be idealized by history. Some of the accounts are pure political fiction. Most of the stories were told during the president's lifetime, when no contemporary observer seemed willing to say anything too critical of a president's mother and father. And the story of Lincoln's childhood, written in earnest after his assassination, when he was already headed for historical sainthood, is only myth. Still, the stories emerge from the swamp of presidential correspondence and papers, and, if one is patient, the parents can be seen more clearly, both their good points and their flaws.

In the final part of this book, the reader will find biographical sketches of all the presidents' parents, appearing in chronological order. But most of this study will focus on six important stories that are representative of the whole. Writing an account of George Washington's parents was problematic. Few documents survive, and the sources are often contradictory. But Washington's powerful personality, formed in his youth, set the nation in motion and established much of its traditions. For similar reasons I devoted several chapters to the story of Abraham Lincoln's presidency. While much of his story cannot be told with certainty, the myth itself impacted the culture of the nation and, in so doing, influenced the presidents who followed.

The four great political family dynasties of American history—the Adamses, the Roosevelts, the Kennedys, and the Bushes—were chosen for the obvious reason that in each case the family formula resulted in the emergence of multiple public figures and national leaders. Something was at work here, and I wanted to know just what it might be.

The James Roosevelts were chosen because they are a classic example of the familiar threads that weave their way through so many of these stories. The Kennedys were included for the opposite reason. Their story brazenly contradicts so many of the others—a strong, engaged, father instead of a strong mother, for example. Finally, the Adamses' and the Bushes' stories are compelling, each with different lessons to impart. Yet, even though those stories are separated by almost two hundred years, one can eerily recognize many of the same dynamics at work in both.

As you will discover in the following pages, some of the parents of the presidents, either by accident or design, stumbled onto modern secrets of raising a high achiever. But more often than not, these are the stories of ordinary families—often dysfunctional, abusive ones—who produced children who soared to greatness anyway. Many times, these are the stories of parents who did the wrong things and got the right results, for sometimes surprising reasons.

—— ★ ——

TWO

A Magnificent Obsession:
George Washington's Parents

Upon all occasions and in all companies I am left in great want.
—Mary Washington, mother of the president

The story of Augustine Washington and how he may have unintentionally provoked his son to greatness is a story that transcends generations. In seventeenth-century England, the Washington family was on the cusp of nobility. It had been a long, tedious climb, a complicated series of carefully negotiated marriages and ruthless land acquisition. But with one blow—the rise of Oliver Cromwell and the temporary end of the Crown—the efforts of generations came tumbling down. Any family that had anything to do with the hated King Charles was anathema. Like so many scions of other families of marginal nobility, the brothers John and Lawrence Washington left for the New World and settled in Virginia.

But if the Washington family expected to find in the backwoods of colonial America the social status that had so narrowly slipped away from them in their civilized and wealthy mother country, they were destined for disappointment. Successive generations of Washingtons would race to their death on the treadmill of rapid land acquisition, only to have it divided among copious offspring, thus diluting a lifetime of effort. Three descendants would serve in the Virginia House of Burgesses. They would have moments of success in their ongoing family preoccupation with expansion, but they could never quite break into the closed, tightly knit upper tier of Virginia society.

By 1694, when Augustine Washington was born into the third generation of this Virginia family, they had all but forgotten their old English roots. Even so, their instincts remained remarkably the same. Augustine was yet another Washington imbued with the obsessive spirit of ambition and sense of "nobility denied" that had characterized each successive generation before him. It was as if their personalities defied the actual circumstances of their lives and came exclusively through the bloodline.

If each had a desire to increase the family estate, it had been a losing battle for years. Their tens of thousands of acres had now been reduced to only thousands. The Washington family, who had risen slowly and painstakingly to their peak in old England, had been ratcheting downward ever since, and seemingly no generation could stop the descent. Augustine, along with two older siblings, inherited the unenviable task of trying to beat the odds and work his way up out of this downward cycle and build an estate that would not be critically diminished by its division among his heirs. There was something desperate about Augustine's ambition, as if the trait had accelerated through the family bloodline to reach its most hysterical manifestation.

Augustine was a man of great physical strength and ferocious determination. His son, George Washington, described him as "tall, fair of complexion, well proportioned and fond of children."[1] But Augustine did not make decisions easily, and the more important the issue, the more likely he was to procrastinate. If not quick-tempered—a fact that gave him some degree of pride—he was far too prone to litigation, which often only complicated his life unnecessarily.

Augustine was four years old when his father, Captain Lawrence Washington, died. The captain was one of the more successful family members, having made quite a run at breaking into the old Virginia aristocracy. There is no better way to illustrate the futility of these efforts than to review the impressive résumé of this Captain Lawrence, who not only served in the House of Burgesses but had at one time been the acting governor of Virginia. All of that was not enough for the stuffy old English families that lorded over the society of the Virginia colony. Even in colonial America, the Washingtons were on the outside looking in.

Augustine's mother, Mildred Warner Washington, inherited substantial assets but legally transferred them all to a new husband, a Mr.

George Gale. Only a few months later, they moved to England, where Mildred promptly died, leaving behind a six-year-old orphan and a messy, ongoing legal battle over the estate. Augustine was enrolled in the Appleby School in Westmoreland, England, until the age of nine, when he was returned to Virginia to live with a cousin named John Washington. Perhaps at the knee of his cousin he developed his fondness for litigation, for John was deep into the contest with George Gale, hoping to recapture the assets he had taken out of the family.

In 1715, twenty-one-year-old Augustine Washington married Jane Butler, the fifteen-year-old daughter of a successful Virginia tobacco planter. They would have four children. "Gus," as he was called, is described as a man totally committed to his work and relentlessly focused on improving his lot. He and his family would scrimp and even live poorly if the money could be used to expand his estate. He served as a justice of the peace and sheriff, probably only for the additional 1,000-plus pounds of extra tobacco it earned him each year.[2] He never wrote or made any memorable comments about community service. Gus also served as a church warden, but probably only to advance the family socially. There are no great letters with Gus questioning the meaning of life. There is no remembrance among friends and relatives of long philosophical talks or any curiosity about theology or history or science.

The exception was when something related personally to his ambition for advancement. When iron was discovered on his land, Gus came alive with interest. He insisted on understanding the whole process and arranged for the Principio Company to develop a mine on his property at Accokeek Creek with him owning shares in the ironworks that came out of it. He conspired and dreamed with the developers of the Ohio Company, even to the point of involving himself in Virginia politics. But it was all to advance his own interests. He was certainly not a visionary seeking to see the interior of the continent developed for its own sake, as an act of science and geography. He was clearly motivated by the huge land share reward that was at stake.[3] All of this is not an indictment of Gus; he was an accomplished and hardworking man, but his expectations were excessive, and that set him up for disappointment.

One can get a sense of the climb necessary for Augustine Washington and what drove him so furiously when one considers the other landowners of his time. Robert "King" Carter controlled more than 330,000 acres. The Harrison family owned 125,000 acres. William Byrd II had 187,000. Augustine, as the third child in the family, had started with only 1,750.[4]

It is quite possible that Augustine entertained the idea of someday returning to England in triumph. This would account for his shameless willingness to live so poorly among his Virginia neighbors, to save his money for expanding his estate. It would explain his one great extravagance. Sometime around 1725, his first two sons, Lawrence and Augustine, Jr., were sent back to his old alma mater, the Appleby boarding school. "There is no success without a successor," the well-worn English homily claimed. And to succeed him, Gus decided that his sons needed a proper English gentleman's education in the mother country.

The ongoing, tireless effort to advance the Washington name appears to have been somewhat contagious within the family. The following year, Augustine's sister, Mildred, deeded to him a tract of land called Little Hunting Creek. She was comfortably married, she said, and didn't need it. It would be the future site of Mount Vernon, the beloved plantation of Augustine's son, George Washington.

Yet the best efforts of Gus Washington were not enough. The ironworks could not produce a profit. Most of his acquired land lay desolate and undeveloped for lack of capital. The tobacco crop, which required many slaves and much labor, barely covered its own expenses. His numerous odd jobs, which kept him away from his wife and family, provided only a pittance. In 1730, after a business trip to England, he returned home to learn that his twenty-eight-year-old wife had died the previous November.

Gus Washington was in a desperate situation. With his tenuous empire built of cards, with farms to run and a small daughter at home, it is not hard to understand his attraction to his neighbor, the widow Mary Ball.

In Mary Ball, Gus found a soul mate, a woman who knew how to live frugally and carefully while her husband gave himself over to the task of provider. He would never have enough land and status, and she, dominated by her fears, would never have enough security. Her "love language" was work, and Gus could pour it on. To sweeten the deal, with Mary Ball came several thousand additional acres. They were married on March 6, 1731, less than a year after Gus had learned of his first wife's passing.

Gus and Mary had much in common. Both had lost their fathers as toddlers. And both had lost their mothers at an early age as well. According to one story, they met in England. Gus was on a business trip, and Mary was visiting a stepbrother. She was sewing, looking out the window at a handsome man struggling with his horse. The man was finally thrown from the mount, injured, and brought into the nearest house, where a dutiful Mary Ball nursed him back to health. When they learned that they were not only both Virginians but neighbors, they knew at once that destiny had brought them together.

Like most Washington family tales, this story is not to be trusted. But in any case, the marriage was arranged quickly and Mary would soon come to dominate the Washington household with her brooding, fearful insecurity, while Gus would travel the countryside working his heart out in an attempt to sate his inexhaustible ambition.

On February 22, 1732, George Washington was born, to be followed by six other children, four boys and two girls. For three years the family lived on Pope's Creek; then, in 1735, they moved to a modest home on Little Hunting Creek Farm. There, on the spot of the future Mount Vernon, they lived for three years—idyllic memories in the mind of the first American president—before moving to the 260-acre Ferry Farm, across the river from Fredericksburg, Virginia. It would be Augustine's last move.

On a stormy, chill, April day in 1743, Augustine Washington was caught in the open in a downpour. He rode his horse back to the farmhouse but was soon in bed with a severe cold. On April 10, experiencing what doctors called gout, he took a turn for the worse. His son George, away on a visit with cousins, raced back home and saw his father alive for the last time. Again, according to legend, as Augustine lay dying, his thoughts turned toward the hereafter. He allegedly thanked God that he had never used his remarkable strength to hit a man in anger, for if he had he would surely have killed him and the blood would have lain heavily on his soul. "As it is, I die in peace with all men."[5]

Young George Washington must have been in great turmoil. The death of his father surely meant an end to his most ambitious goals. There would be no English education. And it meant that he would now fall further into the grasp of his domineering mother. Some scholars see significance in Washington's faulty memory of that day; he writes of his father's death occurring when he was ten years old, when in fact he was eleven. Washington's mistake, they suggest, indicates that he felt younger than he was and thus even more cheated by the experience.

There is great irony at the deathbed of Augustine Washington. He had spent his whole life struggling to achieve status, wealth, and social standing. As he lay dying, he still cherished hopes for his eldest son, Lawrence. But those dreams would not bear fruit, for Lawrence would be struck down only a few years later.

Yet at Augustine Washington's deathbed was an eleven-year-old boy who would one day redefine success. He would help launch a movement that would change the rules that Augustine and his ancestors had labored under for generations. When a distinguished member of the English aristocracy would later write a letter to George Washington to propose a genealogical study of his family, Washington would brush him off, replying in his majestic tone that his country had no agency or office to record such information.[6] It was anachronistic and irrelevant. This was a new world, where what one accomplished was far more important than one's family crest. It was a world where titles were won and lost by personal merit, not dispensed as favors from the powerful, a world where each generation had to struggle for its own, with no guarantees. It was a place where a man like Augustine could start at the bottom and soar to the top in one lifetime, without dying young from exhaustion.

The little boy who knelt in grief at the deathbed of Augustine Washington would one day be offered the job of ruling that new world. He would command armies, inspire hero worship, and eventually serve as president of a new nation, but he would not sully the sacred ideal of such a society by becoming its king. Even so, there would be cities named after him and monuments and glory beyond anything that Augustine Washington would ever imagine.

But on that day, April 12, 1743, when the rain had finally stopped and the weather had mocked the scene by turning gloriously warm and sunny, Augustine "Gus" Washington died, oblivious to the greatness that lingered nearby and the legacy that was trailing behind.

MARY BALL WASHINGTON,
MOTHER OF GEORGE WASHINGTON

Douglas Southall Freeman describes the relationship between George Washington and his mother, Mary Ball, as a "strange mystery."[7] James Flexner writes that the "relationship was always stormy."[8] Many historians believe that the mother was "mad." Some suggest that she exhibited classic symptoms of neurosis or paranoia, but such diagnoses did not exist in her time and such terms are much too clinical to convey the lively essence of this woman. It is easier for writers to just say that she was "mad"—an egocentric, choleric woman who lived in ignorant anxiety most of her life.

Washington biographer Noemie Emery sees her as too self-absorbed to relax and enjoy the achievements of her great son.[9] Ralph Andrist agrees, writing that she "evidenced not the slightest pride in her illustrious son's accomplishments."[10] She might easily have become the "mother figure" of our nation, a woman of history, but throughout her son's greatest years she could never see far beyond the front porch of her modest rambling house in Fredericksburg, Virginia. At least that is the legend.

We know that George Washington spent most of his adult life avoiding his mother, though he made a few, calculated attempts to reconnect with her, especially in the latter years of her life. After long, shameful absences, he would visit her home and spend a night or share a breakfast. Perhaps he was inspired by the relationships of other sons and their mothers, and no doubt he was reinventing her from the safe distance of time and separation. He may have concluded that the estrangement between them could not be solely laid at the feet of his angry, eccentric mother but was partly his own fault. In earlier years, on a few occasions, the separations were broken by her initiative. She would suddenly descend on him like a summer storm. But almost always the reunions were regretted and over quickly, sometimes after a single meal together. When he returned to Fredericksburg for the Christmas of 1769, for example, he spent only minutes with her before leaving to enjoy a week of lodging and dining with nearby friends, showing up for "Mother" only the day after Christmas and spending only one night before moving on. His diary shows that he frequently slept in Fredericksburg—at someone else's house. During his visits home he would apparently appreciate anew the reasons for their estrangement and, repentant of his effort to reconnect, steel himself for an even longer hiatus.

Till her last days, Mary Ball Washington would aggressively lash out in a combination of anger and fear, always sure that poverty and abandonment, those evil twins of her tormented mind, were looming on her doorstep. Her acid personality would guarantee the latter, but as convinced as she was that abject poverty was imminently upon her, it never really gained a foothold except in her fertile imagination.

There are varying accounts about Mary Ball's own mother, Mary Johnson. We are told that she married young and that her first husband died soon after the wedding.[11] She was later rumored to have been the housemaid of one Joseph Ball, a distinguished Potomac tobacco planter pushing sixty years of age.[12] According to the story, when Ball's wife died he took this young housemaid, Mary Johnson, as his new bride.

Virginia society was properly outraged by the union. Ball, a distinguished member of the gentry, had married a shy, illiterate commoner young enough to be his own daughter. Ball's children and other family members rejected the marriage in spite of the old man's extravagant attempts to buy them off with generous parcels of land.[13]

According to most sources, this marriage produced only one child, Mary Ball, Washington's mother, born in 1708, but she would play a singular role in the destiny of America. When Mary was three years old, her illustrious father died, leaving her 400 acres, fifteen cattle, and three Negro slaves.[14] Her mother, Mary Johnson Ball, inherited much of the rest of the estate, including thousands of acres of land, but if Joseph Ball had left his new young wife and child with some measure of material wealth, he had left them with very little knowledge of what to do with it.

The vulnerable widow, Mary Johnson Ball, was quickly surrounded by savvy, sly, greedy advisers and soon learned to her frustration that no one could be trusted. No longer the housemaid, she had land, wealth and with it even a measure of social status, but she knew that it could all be lost in short order. Her child Mary, Washington's mother, would absorb this attitude, and it would define her life.

After the death of Joseph, Mary Johnson Ball made an attempt to establish a cordial relationship with her late husband's family, including his siblings, to little avail. During those early years, they would have nothing to do with her. She then reportedly married a third time, this husband soon dying as well.

The daughter, little Mary, the mother of our first president, would be raised by an illiterate woman of common birth, confronted by a world that she did not understand and surrounded by people ready to exploit her ignorance. Mary would lose two fathers in quick succession, and then, unexpectedly, when she was only twelve years of age, she would lose her mother as well. Now, truly an orphan, she inherited thousands of acres of land, her mother's china sets and teacups, mirrors and fancy silk clothes, and with them her mother's terrible anxieties about the future.[15]

Mary Ball was raised by one George Eskridge, a friend of the family. While not much is known of this relationship, it was at least positive enough for her to give his name to her own firstborn son. Or perhaps, as one psychologist suggested, her guardian was only a father figure she was trying to please, hoping that this honor would win her the love she felt was missing.

There is some indication that Mary was a willful young lady. The many early deaths in her family had left her with much land. She had a fine wardrobe, and when she took to a horse she rode on a fancy silk saddle.[16] But her fears and insecurities combined with her strong will, prompting erratic and unreasonable behavior. She could be inactive and brooding for days, then suddenly oddly aggressive, apparently convinced that if some immediate action were not taken, all would be lost. It was an odd combination, making for an unpredictable personality, and, as is often the case, it grew more pronounced and eccentric with advancing age.

Mary Ball was twenty-two years old when her neighbor Augustine Washington showed an interest in her. According to some historians, she was "plump" and "domineering," not the greatest catch.[17] Augustine, who was exceedingly ambitious, had hoped for a second marriage that would advance him even further socially and financially, but nevertheless this union represented a step in the right direction. When he sat down to review their combined assets, he learned that Mary had more land than he.

At twenty-two years of age, Mary Ball was already considered past the marrying age. So, however fearful she might have been of the intrusive changes that marriage represented to her, the interest of Gus Washington was likely viewed as her last chance. They were married on March 6, 1731. The firstborn arrived the following year, on February 22, 1732.[18] The baby was named George, presumably after George Eskridge, Mary's guardian. Eventually, the marriage would produce six children.

George Washington would never speak or write much about his childhood. From the accounts we have and from his later actions, historians are fairly certain that it was a stressful time for him. Mary Ball Washington was very possessive of her brood, keeping her children back from the riverbanks for fear of drowning long after other children their age could play there with abandon. Even when George was a young man, she arranged for servants to ride with him on horseback so he wouldn't be injured by a runaway. Her constant anxieties over her children, even into late adolescence, made her a fearsome presence. A friend of the family would later recall that her control of her children was relentless and that even as a grown adult she intimidated him: "[I was] ten times more afraid than ever I was of my own parents."[19]

In 1743, when a forty-nine-year-old Augustine "Gus" Washington died, leaving eleven-year-old George without a father, his mother's obsessive control increased. Historian Richard Ketchum writes that he "found his mother a powerful, strong willed, demanding and extremely difficult parent."[20]

George found refuge with his older half brother Lawrence, who had inherited Little Hunting Creek Farm, one of the family's old homes, where George had played as a child. It had a spectacular view of the Potomac River. Lawrence was on the verge of becoming everything their father had wanted for the family. He was a respected planter and a partner in the hugely important Ohio Company, the great business and exploratory adventure of its time, and was already considered a bit player in the political life of the colony.[21]

Two years before Augustine's death, Lawrence had received the king's commission as a captain and sailed away to fight the Spanish. He returned to the Potomac region of Virginia a hero, covered in glory, his resplendent uniform an inspiration to young George, who would become addicted to such trappings. He would one day wear his French and Indian War uniform to the Continental Congress, despite the fact that the war had been over for nearly twenty years.

On his inherited land Lawrence built a new two-story home on top of the old foundation. He named it Mount Vernon, in honor of his commanding officer.

Some historians glibly ascribe to Lawrence a fatherly role in the life of his younger half brother. But he was surely not a father in the sense of the time. He did not heap stern and pompous admonitions on young George, as fathers were expected to do. Sensitive to how oppressed young George was by his mother's stern control, Lawrence introduced him to Virginia society, including his illustrious neighbor, Lord Fairfax. Lawrence even encouraged the romantic idea of George joining the king's navy and sailing to distant ports. It must have been an intoxicating idea for a teenager struggling to break out of his protective shell. For Mary, obsessively worried about her children, such notions were seen as a great betrayal.

In typically erratic fashion, she arrived at this conclusion late. First, she actually toyed with the notion of seeing her eldest son in uniform. George was never around anyway and, she reasoned, could benefit from the discipline of the English navy. Most of all, it would mean a salary of hard English currency to support her and his siblings. It was a temptation. In the end, her possessiveness trumped her greed and she demanded that any notion of the adventure be scuttled.[22] A famous letter to Mary from one of her long-lost stepbrothers in the Ball family warned against young George going to sea. The letter railed on about the excessive ambition the youth was exhibiting. There was no need to try to get rich quick, the uncle warned. It wouldn't work.

The fact was that George had nothing. His two older half brothers had inherited most of the land and been given the best of English educations. George, as a child of his father's second marriage, had very limited prospects. Formal training was now out of the question. He had been only self-taught, with some sporadic, limited opportunities from nearby schools. It had been a distinctly elementary education. His inheritance consisted of the Ferry Farm on the Potomac near Fredericksburg, but his mother was living there. It belonged to him only on paper. She had the authority to administer the farm till he reached legal age, but George realized very early that it would never come to him without an undignified fight. Mary had been well provided for by her husband, with dozens of other properties, but she had already begun her descent into a tormented state of anxiety, persisting in the

notion that she was destitute. She would not relinquish the land until
Washington was in his thirties, already famous and successful.[23] By
then his mother must have calculated that it was worth more in his
hands, leveraging the bequest into even greater financial support from
her powerful son.

Yet there was something else besides land that Gus Washington
left young George, something that would change his destiny and the
destiny of the continent. In a storage shed on Ferry Farm, a teenage
George Washington found a collection of surveyor's instruments. At
first they were just another escape mechanism from an omnipresent,
possessive mother. But within a year Washington had developed a
profitable craft, one that eventually took him into the forests and
mountains alone and away from his mother's reach. At fifteen years of
age, George Washington was a proficient surveyor. By the time he was
eighteen, he had traveled deep into the wild territory of western Virginia, much of his work being done on behalf of Lord Fairfax and his
family. With his income he purchased almost 1,500 acres for himself.

In 1752, when George Washington was twenty years old, his half
brother Lawrence died. It was the most difficult blow of his life. After a
period of deep grief, the tragedy jolted George to even greater ambition. To the scorn of his mother, who felt that her son was neglecting
his duties on the farm, the young man called on leaders across the
colony, campaigning for Lawrence's old position as an adjutant for the
militia of his local Virginia military district. It was a bit of a stretch for
one so young and so poor, but his grace and poise in conducting the
campaign attracted favorable attention. Perhaps the Fairfax family decided that his defeat would be interpreted as their own. In any case,
though being declined the military leadership in his own district, he
was rewarded with another. It was in one of the more remote districts
of the colony, but with the appointment came the rank of major.

Striving to live up to his idealistic vision of his half brother
Lawrence, George now set his sights on the Mount Vernon estate,
home to so many happy memories. His half brother's widow could not
romanticize the death of her husband, nor could she take the time to
luxuriate in grief. For the sake of survival she had already started a new
life, with a new man, in another place. So she rented the Mount Vernon plantation to young Major George Washington. He would eventually buy the place and till his dying day would never let it go. The

stage was set for one of the more dramatic and memorable moments in the life of a mother and son.

By 1754, the French and Indian War was well under way, with western Pennsylvania serving as the critical theater of action. English investors in the Ohio Company were agitating in London, concerned that the French had encroached on their land.[24] Washington, who knew the region well as a surveyor, was tapped to deliver a message of warning. After the French engaged in several months of scattered battles with Washington's ragtag militia, the English Crown decided to settle the issue once and for all: it would send in the professionals.

In 1755, a British military expeditionary force was slated to drive deep into the Pennsylvania wilderness. They would push all the way to Fort Duquesne. No one in the proper colonial English society knew the wild forests as well as Washington, and thanks to a civility cultivated by long hours with Lawrence at the Fairfax dinner table, there was hardly a colonial around who could better comport himself as a proper gentleman. George Washington was invited along as a glorified scout and volunteer aide-de-camp to the famous General Edward Braddock, who had arrived in force from England. The British had no respect for the colonial militia, and Washington's record was mixed at best, embarrassing at worst, so he would be given no rank. But otherwise the young, dashing colonial was the perfect fit for Braddock's task, and he was thus accorded the honor of a posting to the general's personal staff.

News of her son's latest adventure angered Mary Ball Washington to the core. She appeared unannounced at Mount Vernon at the worst possible time, just as her son was preparing to ride off to his first meeting with the British general. What was he doing, she asked incredulously, involving himself in affairs that were none of his business? What kind of person would neglect his own land and mother and siblings? She later wrote a relative of his pitiful attempts to portray his mission as duty to king and country and friends, and a moment of glory. But what of his duty to his mother? she asked. While he sought glory, should she and his own siblings starve?

Washington patiently listened to her diatribe, which he probably could have recited himself. He carefully explained his actions, hoping to assuage her anxiety and maybe to use the occasion to bring her up out of her misery and enjoy the drama of stepping with him onto the world stage. The minutes turned to hours, and it was apparent that he was missing his appointment. On this occasion Washington stubbornly waited her out, letting her launch her arguments again and again.

When it was clear that he had indeed missed his appointment and had perhaps ruined his relationship with the important general, she had no further interest in staying. Mary terminated the meeting herself and stormed out of the house, leaving Washington behind her, drained and exhausted.[25]

Still, in spite of her best efforts, Mary Ball Washington could not disrupt the charmed destiny of her firstborn son. General Braddock would accept Washington's apology for the snub, and they would travel together into the wilds of Pennsylvania, where the British army would be ambushed and massacred by the Indians. Braddock would die from his wounds. Washington would survive and become immortalized by colonists. Hungry for a local hero, they would embellish his role, touting the survival of the colonial youth and declaring he had outshone British professionals in the murderous Indian ambush.

Washington's stormy relationship with his mother made him extremely shy with the opposite sex, but in time, with a confidence won from his public exploits, he reinvented himself as a young man of dignity and poise. He proposed to one Betsy Fauntleroy twice but was rejected, Betsy's father finding the young soldier unsuitable.

His great teacher was Sarah Cary Fairfax, the wife of his neighbor and best friend. Sally, as she was called, was an impetuous flirt and tease who would lead young, inexperienced Washington to the brink, only to reverse herself and express indignant surprise at his dishonorable intentions, whereupon she would initiate the process all over again. She would teach him much about women and much about patience and restraint.

In 1755, while deep in the forests with Braddock, he found the courage to begin his romantic correspondence with her. At twenty-six years of age, he wrote openly of his love. Between 1768 and 1773, Washington carefully recorded in his diary dozens of dinners and visits at the Fairfax table. And when he was sixty-six, in retirement, only two years away from his death, he wrote her a letter suggesting that she return to the area and visit nearby. His wife, Martha Washington, was still alive and living at Mount Vernon.

After his exploits began to spread, his reserve morphed into a graceful and powerful presence that made women weak at the knees and soon earned him the sobriquet "the stallion of the Potomac."[26] Washington's sexual appetite and power over women sometimes exceeded his grasp. "If you don't let go of my hand, sir," one woman told him at a dinner in his honor, "I'll tear out your eyes and the hair from your head, even if you are a general."[27]

In succeeding years, George Washington would marry the widow Martha Custis. He would expand his acreage around Mount Vernon. He would rise to international fame as a statesman and soldier. He would fight and win the Revolutionary War. But his mother would not be inspired to make a single comment on any of it. Her only correspondence to him during these years would be a reminder of his neglect and her abject poverty, notations on how much corn was left and what dire things were happening to the animals.[28] When Washington and his men were suffering at Valley Forge she sent not a word, neither to him nor to anyone else, nor is it recorded that she ever asked about or ventured a comment on any of his deprivations and accomplishments, even later, when there was time to reflect.

For his part Washington wrote voluminous letters to his brothers and sisters, with warm reassurances that he was safe, but he could not spare a single moment to write his mother. On one revealing occasion he mentioned her in a letter to a sibling, asking that they not dispatch to her news of a recent defeat in battle.[29] At the time Washington was already a dynamic figure. French military officers wrote back glowing accounts of his poise and stature. Newcomers from Europe, already aware of his reputation, were nonetheless rendered speechless by his "sense of greatness" and elegance. They would always note their surprise that such power of presence could radiate from a despised colonial. John Adams, who nominated Washington as commander in chief of the American armies, indicated in a letter to Abigail Adams that he was "one of the most important characters in the world."[30] When Abigail met Washington later, she thought her husband had "not said half enough in praise of him."[31] But for all his worldly wisdom and stature, and for all his feigned indifference toward his mother, Washington still obviously cared about her opinion and apparently longed for some approbation. At some deep level, Washington, the little boy, still harbored a deep need for approval from the powerful, willful, emotionally disturbed woman who had owned his childhood and still ruled some part of his psyche.

There is clear evidence that Mary began cashing in on her son's fame by receiving "gifts." Washington wrote his siblings, urging her to stop it. But Mary apparently continued, justifying any gift that she herself did not solicit. Again, Washington, whose integrity was cherished like burnished silver, pleaded with his siblings to help rein her in.

In 1780, one year before the English defeat at Yorktown and while the future of the colonies lay in the balance, Mary took public action. In what some historians see as a purposeful, willful attempt to discredit her son and force him to recognize her needs, she petitioned the Virginia legislature for a pension as the mother of the commander in chief, on the grounds that her children had neglected her to the point of poverty. The general was easily able to show that his mother was not destitute, that he and his siblings had provided abundantly for the old woman. The petition was quashed, but Washington's political enemies throughout the colonies rejoiced in this public humiliation.

In 1784, after the Revolutionary War and after a long separation, George Washington visited his mother in Fredericksburg, Virginia. It was finally impossible for her to ignore his public persona. Enthusiastic townsmen turned the visit into a communitywide event. The mayor made presentations; veterans of the war came from miles around and thronged the streets to cheer. Thirteen toasts were offered, each accompanied by a round of cannon fire. There was a public dinner at the local coffeehouse. Washington, no doubt pleased to bask in such admiration in the presence of his own mother, could speak only of her. He told his hometown audience that any honors given to him were due to a benevolent Providence and his courageous army. And then he went on to talk of his "revered mother, by whose maternal hand, early deprived of a father I was led to manhood." [32] It was about as sentimental as Washington would ever get about his mother, but Mary, for her part, made no comment at all.

After another long absence, Washington made an attempt to get her to move into the home of one of her children, although he was careful to make it clear that he did not mean his own home at Mount Vernon. It was too noisy there, he pointed out, and there were too many guests coming and going. At her age she should have more calm. In Fredericksburg, away from the excitement of her famous son's dinner table, Mary took long, solitary walks, lingering at a rock near the Lewis mansion where she would pray and meditate.

There is insufficient information to break into the enigmatic relationship between this famous mother and son. It is quite possible that George Washington's love of military life and soldiering was not only inspired by the colorful uniform and adventures of his half brother Lawrence but developed as a challenge to his mother's protective nature. Indeed, some see his whole leadership role in the American rebellion as an extension of his fight with this authority figure from childhood.

Yet in other ways, even with the best of intentions, Washington sometimes slipped into his mother's mold. James C. Rees, executive director of the Mount Vernon Ladies' Association, sees both mother and son as strong, no-nonsense kinds of persons, with very demanding personalities.[33] Neither had many close friends, and both were hard workers till the last days of their lives. Washington's letters to the Continental Congress, complaining of want and dire circumstances, are an eerie echo of her own letters to him.

But while both mother and son saw themselves as victims, each dealt with the perceived crisis differently. Mary was petty; George was visionary, a big thinker. She was an erratic egocentric; he was a disciplined soldier. She was miserly; he was generous, housing and feeding anyone who came to his door at Mount Vernon. By one count, in 1798, more than 677 guests were entertained at Mount Vernon.[34] She was a pessimist, always in need of more; he did the impossible with what he had.

Washington, the boy, stung by his controlling, fearful mother, may have longed for some admission from her that he was indeed a mature, sensible person who could take care of himself and others. If so, Mary would never offer him such satisfaction, insisting in the face of overwhelming evidence to the contrary that he had failed at his most basic responsibility, the eldest son of the family taking care of his own widowed mother. And for her part, before the ugliness of her neurosis completely consumed her mind, it is likely that her exaggerated cries for help were purposely deceptive, a device to force him home to conduct his own investigation, a contrivance to see her son. But if so, her internal torment was her own worst enemy. Each meeting turned bitter and further separated them.

Washington's tactless description of life at Mount Vernon and why it would not suit her needs must have hurt her bitterly. She was not wanted. Historian George Nordham suggests that "George did not love his mother and most observers have concluded that he did not even like her."[35] But the psychologists I consulted during this project dispute that. If he had not loved her, there would have been no conflict. As in all relationships, especially relationships between mothers and sons, each was looking to the other for reassurance that they were loved. All their desperate efforts to find such reassurance were woefully misspent. Each clumsy effort to win over the other only drove them further apart. Mary, who lived so close by, would not visit Mount Vernon during the last thirty years of her life, and no record exists that her son ever complained about it.[36]

On April 30, 1789, George Washington was inaugurated the first president of the newly created United States of America. His mother had no comment for the visiting journalists and curious people descending on her home. Four months later, with the eyes of the infant nation riveted on bustling New York City, where the busy work of Congress and a new government led by George Washington made history, Mary Ball Washington, the mother of the president, quietly passed away in Virginia. At her request, she was buried alone near the rock by the Lewis mansion in Fredericksburg where she had paused every morning to offer her prayers.

——— ★ ———

THREE

John Adams and the
First American Dynasty

You will comply with my desires.[1]
—Deacon John Adams

In 1638, Henry Adams and his wife, Edith Squire Adams, dissenters from the Church of England, gathered together their only daughter and eight sons, along with a few necessary possessions, and climbed aboard one of the many small, dangerous sailing ships bound for the New World.[2] Adams was seeking a place in the American colonies where he and his family could worship freely and practice their Puritan principles without ridicule or harassment.

It was a good time to leave. England was ripe for religious war. For years, Puritans had been assailed for their spiritual beliefs, driven from pillar to post. By 1642, King Charles I would be stripped of his power and, in a shocking development for the monarchy, would be executed for treason in 1649. War would rage for years.

Family legend has it that Henry Adams and his family embarked with Reverend Thomas Hooker, who would eventually help found Connecticut. A century later, John Adams would write graphic descriptions of his ancestors' harrowing journey across the wild North Atlantic, with lightning striking the foremasts and storm-driven waves nearly carrying passengers and sailors overboard. Many of those creaking wooden vessels never made it, but Henry Adams's ship, as well as others carrying the great surge of Puritan migration, survived the passage.

When the family reached the rocky Massachusetts shore, they settled in the new coastal town of Braintree, which they pronounced "Bran-tree." The little town, located twelve miles south of Boston and approximately thirty miles up the coast from Plymouth Rock, was a frontier wilderness. There were trees to hew, rocks to clear from the fields, shelters to build, and gardens to plant to stave off certain starvation.

One priority was to build the church meetinghouse, the keystone of the community. Its spire would call its citizens to mandatory worship twice each Sunday. "What has preserved this race [or family] of Adamses in all their ramifications in such numbers, health, peace, comfort and mediocrity?" John Adams would later hypothesize to his friend Dr. Benjamin Rush. "I believe it is religion, without which they would have been rakes, fops, sots, gamblers, starved with hunger, or frozen with cold, scalped by Indians . . . been melted away and disappeared."[3]

Early pioneer living tested the endurance of every man, woman, and child. Nobody could sit on his hands. Everyone had to work or starve. They were all farmers, but, during the fallow winters, they were forced to work at trades to obtain "hard money" for necessities. There were gunsmiths and blacksmiths, coopers and carpenters, millers and seamstresses, tailors and tanners. All trades were valued and respected, and essential. Henry Adams and many of his descendants worked as maltsters, brewing the malt required for the production of beer and the baking of bread.

Henry and Edith Adams's eight sons provided their parents with a remarkable eighty-nine grandchildren. Large families were needed to shoulder the unending labor of coaxing crops from the rocky, intransigent soil. But hard land makes tough people, and the stubbornness it took to wrest a livelihood was bred into all the Adamses, as well as many of their neighbors. Henry was well respected in his community, even though, like most others of his time and place, his material possessions were not great. At his death, his estate consisted of forty acres of land, a three-room house, a barn, a cow and calf, some pigs, and fodder for the animals. In that tiny house were kitchen utensils, three beds, a few old books, and one silver spoon.[4]

Their one daughter, it is thought, never married but apparently stayed at home, caring for Henry and Edith. Eventually, all of their sons except Joseph, the seventh son, went elsewhere to live. One went back to England. Another, Captain John Adams, became a mariner and grandfather to revolutionary firebrand Samuel Adams.

Toiling on the family farm in Braintree, Joseph Adams had a son he also named Joseph, who grew up to marry a woman named Hannah Bass. Hannah's grandparents had been John Alden and Priscilla Mullins of Plymouth Colony, whose apocryphal romantic adventures were made famous to generations of American schoolchildren in Henry Wadsworth Longfellow's classic poem "The Courtship of Miles Standish." When John sought her hand for another man, the feisty Priscilla is said to have spoken her mind, giving us those immortal words: "Speak for yourself, John." He did, and the rest is Adams's history.

The Adamses dug in, and for four generations, they lived perfectly ordinary, simple lives, farming and mostly brewing malt for a livelihood. They lived modestly, even passing clothing on for others to use. In one diary entry, it is written that "A hat would descend from father to son, and for fifty years make its regular appearance at meeting."[5] One Adams male after another served as selectmen in Braintree's town councils, bearing responsibility for managing town business and the evolving community needs. Two future American presidents, John Adams and John Quincy Adams, were both proud of the simplicity, virtue, and independent spirits of their forefathers.[6] John Quincy would write that his ancestors had been noted only for their "industry, sobriety, and integrity."[7] They were qualities that both men would multiply exponentially in their own lives, carrying them further than anyone could have expected—even to impossible standards.

In 1691, one of twelve children was born to Joseph and Hannah. This son, too, was named John, and in later years, he would be called Deacon John, in honor of his position in the church and to distinguish him from his famous president son.

Deacon John Adams fit the mold of his father—sober and industrious, taciturn, fiercely independent, and, like the land of New England itself, granite hard when it came to living by his principles. Deacon John was a farmer, cordwainer (shoemaker), lieutenant in the local militia, collector of tithes and taxes, and selectman for Braintree, all the while dreaming of better things for his family. In his autobiography, John Adams wrote of Deacon John's "admiration of learning," probably received from his mother, "which remained with him, through life, and which prompted him to his unchangeable determination to give his first son a liberal education."[8]

Deacon John vowed that his firstborn son would attend Harvard, as had the deacon's older brother, no matter the financial cost or the physical burden caused by the loss of an able body on the farm. He was looking to the future. John Adams, as an adult, would echo his father's vision: "I must study politics and war that my sons may have the liberty to study mathematics and philosophy. My sons ought to study geography, natural history, naval architecture, navigation, commerce and agriculture, in order to give their children a right to study painting, poetry, music, architecture, statuary, tapestry, and porcelain."[9]

DEACON JOHN AND SUSANNA ADAMS: PARENTS OF A PRESIDENT

In a time when most men married in their early twenties, Deacon John Adams remained single into his early forties. When he finally decided to wed, he would "marry up." It has been said that he established a pattern for the men of his family. John Adams, too, would "marry up" when he later took Abigail Smith to be his wife.

In October 1734, when he was forty-three, Deacon John married Susanna Boylston, a woman almost twenty years his junior. The daughter of Peter Boylston, she was a scion of a medical family from Brookline, Massachusetts, whose grandfather, Thomas Boylston, was a prominent émigré surgeon from England, and whose uncle, Zabdiel Boylston, participated in introducing vaccination against smallpox into America.[10]

Some historians say that she taught her son, John Adams, how to read at the age of five.[11] Others add that he was the only one of her brood to inherit her love of books.[12] Still others contend that this is all an invention that we must lay at the feet of early, idealistic historians. Since nothing written in Susanna's handwriting survives, the more recent wisdom holds that she was illiterate.[13] Indeed, during John Adams's eight-month stay in Philadelphia during the 1777 Continental Congress, he is known not to have sent a single letter to his mother.[14] Historians fault the mother's inability to read rather than any estrangement.

Illiterate or not, Susanna created her own cultural treasure that she willingly and proudly passed on to her son: the heirloom seal of the Boylston family. On signing the two peace treaties with Great Britain, John Adams would solemnly affix the Boylston seal beside his name.

John Adams wrote little about Susanna, other than that she was his "honored and beloved mother."[15] Biographer David McCullough notes that "she was a highly principled woman of strong will, strong temper, and exceptional energy, all traits he shared though this he did not say."[16] When he was a youngster, young John had noticed that all of his friends' homes were ruled by "reason," while his own was ruled by "passion." For him, it was not an attractive quality. His parents, both strong and forceful figures, "bickered to an unusual degree."[17] Even though his own personality would exhibit the same tendencies, John Adams would write in his diary that his mother "frets, squibs, scolds, rages, raves" until she gets her way.[18] Still, all evidence points to Susanna's generally loving spirit, and, later, Abigail Adams would find her a beloved companion, as well as mother-in-law.

A few months after the wedding, Susanna told Deacon John that she was going to have his baby. As time grew close for the birth, he and Susanna both undoubtedly worried. Deaths in childbirth happened too frequently in their time. But exactly one day before their first wedding anniversary, on October 30, 1735 (by the new calendar), Susanna gave birth to a healthy, squalling baby, John Adams. He was followed in 1738 by a brother, Peter Boylston Adams, and in 1741 by another brother, Elihu.

By all accounts, young John Adams spent a blissful childhood. His writings are full of tales of exploring beaches, woodlands, fields and creeks, "of making and sailing boats . . . swimming, skating, flying kites and shooting marbles, bat and ball, football."[19] He learned to smoke at age eight, a talent that would come in handy years later, when he awed a Turkish ambassador by blowing smoke rings throughout an entire diplomatic session.[20] He loved going fowl hunting and "running about to quiltings and frolics and dances among the boys and girls."[21] Historian Peter Shaw notes that Deacon John and Susanna gave John Adams "the gift of freedom" and that the atmosphere of the home was "moralistic but not unbending."[22] Indeed, one day, after John's first schoolteacher complained that the boy had skipped school, spending the morning shooting birds, young John audaciously begged his parents for the rest of the day off; he was planning to swim in the marshes and shoot more birds. They let him go.[23]

John Adams detested school and despised his teacher, declaring him to be "lazy, indifferent and malevolent."[24] When Deacon John scolded the ten-year-old for squandering his opportunities for education, warning that if he were not more disciplined he would lose his opportunity to go to college, young John announced that he had no desire for college anyway.

"And what do you want to do with yourself?" his father asked.

"Be a farmer," the boy replied.

To which Deacon John responded with restrained amusement, "Well, I will show you what it is to be a farmer."

The following day, a confident Deacon John, "with great good humour," took young John to work with him in the marshes to cut thatch, the roofing material of rushes and reeds. It was a long, hot day. There were mud and bugs to contend with, and abrasive reeds that cut the hands and arms.

That night at home, Deacon John quizzed his boy: "Well, John, are you satisfied with being a farmer?"

"I like it very well, Sir," the boy answered defiantly, apparently willing to invest another grueling day in the contest of wills.

"Aye, but I don't like it so well," his father answered, deciding to extend this lesson in life no further. "You will comply with my desires."[25] And John Adams went back to school—although, as he later wrote, he was "not so happy as among the creek thatch."[26]

Deacon John Adams joined confidently in the community debate over issues that affected the colonies, and young John listened with some degree of wonderment. American militiamen, eager to help defend their British colonial borders from the French and allied Indian tribes, were deemed inferior and incompetent soldiers by haughty English officers. It was a source of irritation for the colonies, who claimed that their militia was treated with abuse and contempt and delegated the "most distasteful" duties.

In 1745, New England militiamen, on their own initiative and without the aid of British officers or soldiers, attacked and captured the French fortress of Louisbourg on Cape Breton Island in Nova Scotia. The fortress had been considered impregnable and was a great irritant to the Americans and their ocean fishing grounds. As the expedition to Cape Breton progressed and reports trickled back to Braintree, ten-year-old John Adams listened "with eagerness to his [father's] conversation with his friends . . . and I have received very grievous impressions of the injustice and ingratitude of Great Britain toward New England in that whole transaction."[27] The formal declaration of war with the French and Indians would come eleven years later, but the unfolding crisis would provide the dramatic introduction for young John Adams to the great events that ebbed and flowed beyond their Braintree homestead.

In time, Deacon John and Susanna discovered that it wasn't an education their son was avoiding as much as his manipulative and spiteful teacher. When the boy begged his father to let him study privately with a Master Joseph Marsh, Deacon John complied and the boy soon thrived. John seemed to be especially talented at Latin, a requirement for entrance to Harvard, and by the time he reached adolescence, he had made up for any earlier lapses. At the age of fifteen, John Adams was on an equal footing with other young students his age and deemed ready for college the following year. When the invitation came to take the Harvard entrance exam, young John's tutor declared him ready and able.

It was a challenging experience for any boy, but for John Adams, with his lower social standing and uncertainty about his abilities, it was terrifying. On the day he was to ride to Cambridge to appear before the panel of robed and bewigged professors, John was horrified to learn that his teacher, Master Marsh, had come down ill and was unable to accompany him. "You'll be fine," Master Marsh assured him, but John's horse clopped more and more slowly the closer he got to Harvard. John strongly considered turning around and going home, but thoughts of facing his furious parents killed that notion.

To his great surprise, John passed the test easily, and he galloped home joyously to tell Deacon John and Susanna. "I was as light when I came home, as I had been heavy when I went,"[28] he later wrote.

Deacon John and Susanna were, of course, ecstatic. Not only had their son won acceptance, but he had been awarded a partial scholarship on the strength of his testing. His education would be a staggering economic hardship, but one that Deacon John and Susanna had anticipated from John's birth and one that they would gladly shoulder.

The deacon had always taught that land was the only enduring investment, the only treasure that wouldn't break or run away, and in the family it was immutable law that once land had been purchased, it was never to be sold.[29] Deacon John broke that rule only once in his life, selling off ten acres to pay for John's college.[30] His son knew what that meant and respected it. Once when Susanna and John's aunt came to visit him at Harvard, they were appalled to see the boy's room rigidly spartan, nearly bare. He had been "loath to burden my father with the expense," he explained.[31]

John Adams's time at Harvard was a fond memory, a time that "invigorated my body, and exhilarated my soul."[32] The curriculum and expectations were exacting, but his love affair with books blossomed, and the range of available subjects was staggering. Deacon John applauded his son's voracious intellectual appetite, appreciating John's "relaxation of my zeal for my fowling piece."[33] No more shooting birds until duty was done.

Harvard had been founded primarily to train ministers, and when John Adams left home to pursue his studies, it was, by the good deacon's expectations, to become a preacher. But John soon had different ideas. Not only was his outspoken personality poorly suited to the pulpit, he feared that the ministry would not offer enough intellectual stimulation—he found among the clergy the "pretended sanctity of some absolute dunces."[34] There were too many rules and too many people to please to suit John Adams. He'd rather have time with his books than have to counsel depressed people and dun the poor souls who were behind in their tithes. The ministry would, he said, "involve me in endless altercations and make my life miserable, without any prospect of doing any good to my fellow men."[35]

Perhaps John was discouraged by the hypocrisy. His own father had a fondness for telling off-color jokes in company but had once helped remove a minister whose conduct was deemed "light if not immoral."[36] He suspected that the ministry would challenge his innate sense of honesty. He would have to be dogmatic, he said, and say what people wanted to hear or "never get a parish, or getting it must soon leave it."[37]

Still, his parents had made sacrifices to send him to Harvard, and John could not easily slam the door on their dream. He spent two miserable years as a schoolmaster, vacillating between his father's desires and his own, teaching "little runtlings, just capable of lisping A.B.C. and troubling the master."[38] He was simply marking time. "Although my Father's general expectation was that I should be a Divine, I knew him to be a man of so thoughtful and considerate a turn of mind, to be possessed of so much candor and moderation, that it would not be difficult to remove any objections he might make to my pursuit of physick [medicine] or law or any other reasonable course." [39]

His preference was for a career in law, a profession—his father had warned—full of the sorts of persons who would "sacrifice all, to their own advancement" [40] In John's inner dialogue he reached for integrity between the two dreams, the man of higher, spiritual ideals—the preacher that his parents wanted him to be—and the earthly desires that burned in his bosom. As he neared his twentieth birthday, John Adams had to confront the realization of his ambition—that he was, after all, seeking to become a "great man," [41] someone who would rise above the fate of "the common herd of mankind, who are to be born and eat and sleep and die, and be forgotten." [42] But he would strive to reach his goals within the boundary of pure motives. It would be a struggle that would consume him for the rest of his life.

On August 21, 1756, John Adams finally came to terms with his decision and signed a contract to study for two years under James Putnam, the foremost lawyer in Worcester. For his sustenance, he would continue teaching the children by day and study at night, but at the end of it, if he remained true, he would be admitted to the bar. "I set out with firm resolutions," he vowed, "I think never to commit any meanness or injustice in the practice of law." Pursuing his favored profession would "not dissolve the obligations of morality or of religion." [43]

Two years later, after successfully completing his contract with Putnam, John Adams received wonderful news: Deacon John had invited him home to begin his practice near the family. After an absence of eight years, John joyfully accepted. He spent his first weeks catching up on old times, helping his father with chores, and preparing for the bar. His diary boasts that he chopped wood and translated Justinian with equal doggedness. [44]

On November 6, 1759, John Adams was admitted to the bar in Boston, an occasion of great joy, his attainment of the family dream. While young John had pursued his studies, his brothers, Elihu and Peter, had stayed at home working the farm, alternately admiring and resenting their brother's advantages as the eldest son. The entire family had sacrificed much for John's education, and all had pinned their hopes on the golden boy. A few weeks later, the whole enterprise would be tested.

Two Braintree neighbors, Luke Lambert and Joseph Field, had been feuding for years. One day, two of Luke Lambert's horses broke into Field's pasture, apparently causing considerable damage—at least according to Field's claim. Field seized the horses, planning to have them impounded until he could force Lambert to pay the damages.

But Lambert saw what was happening and ran in, waving his hat and yelling at the horses, scaring them out of the pasture and illegally removing them from Field's custody. Litigious as ever, Fields headed straight for the court. This wasn't the first time Lambert's horses had trampled his crops, but an earlier case had been thrown out on a technicality. If he could help it, that was not going to happen again.

Joseph Field came to young attorney John Adams for help. John was disinclined to get involved. Brand-new baby lawyer that he was, all his training had been in theory, not in actual preparation of writs. He would be rushed to get the papers filed by the deadline but influenced by what he later wrote as the "cruel reproaches of my Mother," and entirely against his better judgment, John Adams decided to look into the case.[45]

His fears were well founded. By omitting one critical word, "county," in the directions of the writ, John's case was thrown out. The other town lawyers and judges—not to mention Luke Lambert—smirked behind their hands; that fool Adams didn't even know how to prepare a writ. John was made to look the simpleton in the eyes of his hometown and his own family. He had taken his first case and lost. In his home court. Baldly. Glaringly. Humiliatingly.

And if Joseph Field's "wrath waxed hot," John Adams's anger was volcanic.[46] What happened when he returned that evening is conjecture, but some historians speculate that young Adams erupted defensively, pouring out his frustrations. Adams thought himself ruined before he'd even had a chance to get started.

The following day his mother, Susanna, went into one of her famous rages. The outburst appeared unrelated to her son's failure, but there is little doubt that his humiliation triggered the crisis. Perhaps she thought the incident boded ill for the family's fortunes. Tensions had been brewing even before John's return from court. Now they came out into the open.

Deacon John, as part of his selectman's duties, was an overseer of the poor. When the town could find no other place for them, the deacon apparently brought home young women who required shelter, at his own expense. On this memorable day, Susanna Adams exploded. "I won't have all the town's poor brought here, stark naked, for me to clothe for nothing," she raged at Deacon John. "I won't be a slave to other folk's folk for nothing," she scolded. "You want to put your girls over me, to make me a slave to your wenches," she raved. She had endured enough, she said; he would have to resign as selectman and do so immediately.

Deacon John rose to the occasion, steadfastly refusing his wife's entreaties. "His temper roused at last," but without uttering a "rash word," the man of the house "resolutely asserted his right to govern."[47]

Judah, one of the young girls in question, began to cry, adding to the general furor. Brother Peter, apparently sympathizing with the poor girl, entered the fray. Young John Adams, fresh from his court defeat, upbraided him, whereupon Peter exploded as well. John was so shaken by the whole fiasco that he "quitted the room, and took up [his book of] Tully to compose" himself.[48] Ironically, years later when John Adams would marry Abigail Smith, his mother, Susanna, would send them a young lady to help set up housekeeping. It would be Judah.[49]

With the mortifying loss of his very first case, John Adams focused on mastering law with renewed obsession. Never again would he allow himself to be caught unprepared legally. "I have read Gilberts 1st Section, of feuds, this evening but am not master of it," he wrote in his diary. The next night, he scribbled his remarkable day's work: "Rose about sunrise. Unpitched a load of hay. Translated two leaves more of Justinian . . . and am now reading over again Gilbert's section of feudal tenures." For twelve straight nights, Adams reread the Gilbert section. "This small volume will take me a fortnight, but I will master it."[50] He was as good as his word.

John Adams read everything he could get his hands on and castigated himself for not reading more. He buttonholed local attorneys on point after point of law and wrote letters to former classmates from Harvard, posing other legal questions as fast as he could conjure them up. He interviewed tradesmen to seek hard knowledge. "Let me inquire of the next Master of a Ship that I see, what is a Bill of Lading, what [is] the Purser's Book. What Invoices [do] they keep. What Account[s] [do] they keep of Goods . . ." [sic].[51] Later, after the Revolution's first battles at Lexington and Concord, he would ride to the towns and listen, utterly absorbed, as citizens recounted the day's terror. It was a pattern John Adams would retain his entire life—an "organized effort to master the world."[52] The young man who had lost his first case and humiliated himself and his family would soon be considered one of the best lawyers in Boston.

Deacon John Adams would not live to see his son reach his full potential. Susanna's Uncle Zabdiel, the man who had helped introduce inoculations against smallpox to America, had no such defense against influenza. In the spring of 1761, an epidemic struck Braintree, killing seventeen of its elderly citizens. Both Deacon John and Susanna would become desperately ill. On May 25, 1761, when Deacon John Adams started to fail, Susanna roused herself and came to his bedside, joining John, Peter, and Elihu. The father of America's second president died at the age of seventy, his wife and children gathered around his bed. Susanna remained too ill to attend her husband's funeral.

John scribbled the eulogy on the back of his father's last will and testament, praising his noble spirit and love of family. He would write nothing else about his father's death, either in letters or in his diary, but he would later pay anonymous tribute to his father's life in one of his revolutionary newspaper essays. The passion of the essay would reveal not only how John Adams loved his father but also his need to reinvent the man he was following. John Adams would come to see his father as a man of committed character and integrity and also a man of colonial patriotism. It would justify his own growing patriotism and attendant ambition.

FOLLOWING IN THE DEACON'S FOOTSTEPS

Deacon John's estate was valued at 1,330 pounds, nine shillings, and eight pennies—sixteen times that of the first patriarch, Henry Adams.[53] John's inheritance was a bit of acreage and a small house near his beloved father's farmhouse. It was, at first, an emotional burden he could hardly bear. He sank into a deep depression, plagued by thoughts of unworthiness and of the sacrifices his father had made for him and doubts about his own life choices. Deacon Adams had been the principal force in his life. And no matter how contentious their discussions about education and career had been, John held enormous respect for his father. He was "the honestest man I ever knew," he wrote, and, comparing him to other men in the community, John said he had never found any man his father's superior.

In the months following Deacon John's death, his mournful son revisited many of the old man's admonitions and desires. The father was the lodestone that would guide the son, in matters of faith and in service to his country. In the Adams family, the two were indistinguishable. Deacon John and Susanna had always striven to live by the Puritan tenets bequeathed by their ancestors. An integral part of the church structure, the elder Adams had served *fourteen* terms as deacon, earning his sobriquet. His many responsibilities had included the collection of tithes, but far more imperative than any physical duty of the congregation was the responsibility to live in integrity with God, not only in deeds but in motive. John Adams would inherit an intensified manifestation of this burden.

Historian Peter Shaw notes that the "distinction of being an Adams involved not so much rising in the world as satisfying one's own standards of duty."[54] Deacon John had served proudly and with great loyalty as a lieutenant under Colonel Josiah Quincy in the Braintree militia. In a blatant example of the patronage abuse that would one day incense the colonists, Colonel Joseph Gooch replaced Colonel Quincy, offering Deacon John a captaincy. The elder Adams refused in a huff; loyalty to others was more important than loyalty to oneself. It was a story-lesson that two American presidents, John Adams and his son John Quincy Adams, would remember all their lives.

For months John Adams processed his grief and guilt, and then finally coming through the tunnel on the other side, he awakened to a life of extraordinary activity and accomplishment. With the deaths of his father and of his own youthful rebellion, he would spend the rest of his life surpassing his reconstructed ideal of Deacon John's desires.

With his father's demise and the inheritance of real estate, John Adams became a freeholder, eligible for public office. In this, too, he would follow his father's guiding light. Deacon John had served for nine annual terms and, "by his industry and enterprise," had managed "for twenty years together almost all the business of the town."[55] John Adams would succeed his father as selectman in the Braintree town meeting.

Like his father, freshman selectman John would initially be saddled with the onerous tasks that no one else wanted. As surveyor he grumbled, but he performed diligently and improved the local roads, then devised ways to finance them. Because of his superior service, he received an unprecedented formal vote of thanks from the city. It was a moment that would have made the elder Deacon John Adams proud. But it was only the beginning. Already the disquieting murmurings of revolution were being heard, and it was calling for uncompromising men of both courage and intellect. Ever curious and involved, he was listening and watching intently.

On October 25, 1764, twenty-eight-year-old John married nineteen-year-old Abigail Smith in Weymouth, Massachusetts. If the age spread was not quite the same as that of his parents, it was close enough for his mother to identify with the new bride. Susanna and Abigail would get along famously and perhaps forge a bond closer than mother and son. Historian David McCullough wrote, "To Abigail, her mother-in-law was a cheerful, open-minded person of 'exemplary benevolence,' dedicated heart and soul to the welfare of her family, which was more than her eldest son ever committed to paper, even if he concurred."[56]

There is historical speculation that Adams, like Washington and Jefferson, was somewhat estranged from his mother, but all evidence points to a poignant devotion. Other than her famous choleric nature, history offers us surprisingly little on Susanna. In her book *Women Forgotten in Time,* Mary Ann Wilcox describes her as able to outwork and outtalk any of the Adams men, but she also paints the portrait of a mother who insisted on listening to everything her children had to say, making them reconstruct their day and taking an interest in every detail.[57] John was her clear favorite, and he thrived under her attention.

Years later, when the name of Farmer John Dickinson, the man who had fought against the Declaration of Independence, was raised, Adams would blame it all on the pacifist Quaker women in Dickinson's family. Dickinson could not serve his country and his family at the same time, John hypothesized. John would use the occasion to brag about his own women. "If I had had such a mother and such a wife," he concluded, "I believe I should have shot myself."[58] Both Susanna and Abigail had created family atmospheres of inner strength, ingenuity, resolve, and patriotism that had allowed him to absent himself from Braintree for months and sometimes years on end, and give his life to the creation of America.

A PUBLIC MAN OF HONOR

In 1765, the year after John and Abigail's wedding, England enacted the infamous Stamp Act. Parliament decreed that every official paper and license in the colonies was to be taxed, even newspapers. Saddled with an unimaginable debt of £137 million from the French and Indian War, Parliament had determined that the colonists would have to pay up. While the tax itself wasn't particularly burdensome, it ignited fires of revolution across America. Why should colonists, who had no members in Parliament and no means of determining policy or law, be forced to pay taxes? Colonial courts closed down as judges rebelled and refused to use the stamps on court documents. John Adams's once lucrative law practice dwindled overnight. For years he had struggled against poverty, and now, as he was finally building a career, events beyond his control were stopping him cold.

Personally conflicted over the raging issues, John Adams nevertheless agreed in principle with the colonists and wrote the Braintree Instructions, detailing the opposition and noncompliance with the Stamp Act. When they were published, forty other towns promptly adopted them. By request, John appeared in court in Boston and argued that the Stamp Act was invalid. "No taxation without representation," he stoutly and famously asserted. The words would resonate throughout the thirteen colonies.

Feeling the emotions running through the colonies, John Adams found his voice in revolutionary newspaper essays. In a series signed anonymously as "Clarendon," he based his writings on a historical English Lord Chancellor. This was the man who had proposed a lenient religious settlement for the Puritans during the very English Civil War that had driven his ancestor Henry Adams to the New World. As Clarendon, John Adams speaks of a father who represents "both love of his son and love of country."[59] He is, of course, embodying Deacon John and what historian Peter Shaw called his "unimpeachable public character."[60]

"And I charge you, on my blessings," Adams has the father telling his son, "never to forget this nation, but to stand by the law, the constitution, and the real welfare and freedom of this nation vs. all temptations."[61]

John Adams, driven by his sense of responsibility and personal guilt, indebted to his parents and siblings, who had sacrificed their own futures to let him make something of his life, would be the very kind of man the newborn nation would need. Like his father, he would be a man of ambition constrained by deep moral conviction, a man who would be forever questioning motives as well as actions. He would inherit his mother's passion and her work ethic and be empowered by her attention to and interest in his every move. The birth of the nation would not happen overnight, and it would not happen easily. But men such as John Adams, focused on the highest principles of government, would slowly, painfully forge the path. Deacon John would have proudly affirmed that John Adams had "complied with my desires."

FOUR

Sacrificed on the American Altar

The habits of a vigorous mind are formed in contending with difficulties.
Great necessities call out great virtues.
—Abigail Adams to her son John Quincy Adams

As John Adams grew older, he became a portly, balding man with none of the charisma of the majestic George Washington, who loomed six feet, four inches in his resplendent Continental uniform and awed everyone who stood in his presence. Adams was hindered by his explosive temper, inherited from his mother, and was sometimes mocked with the name "His Rotundity." In today's media, with its emphasis on appearance, John Adams wouldn't have stood a chance.

Even in his own times, he was not perceived by other members of the Continental Congress as their leader. But they knew him as a man of unbending principle and courage and would unfailingly turn to his focused, brilliant legal mind whenever studies on vital issues were required, begging him to write crucial document after crucial document. Congress named him, along with Thomas Jefferson and Benjamin Franklin, as part of the committee to draft the Declaration of Independence. Though Jefferson did the writing, John Adams defended it before Congress with eloquence and power. Fellow patriots called him the Atlas of Independence, as he shouldered a staggering load of duty. John Adams was a builder of a new nation, a union based on law. No "sunshine patriot," he would give his entire life, fortune, and family to the process.

Three generations later, John Adams's grandson Charles Francis

Adams would say, "The history of my family is not a pleasant one to remember. It is one of the great triumphs in the world but of deep groans within, one of extraordinary brilliancy and deep corroding mortification."[1] It is a devastating admission about a remarkable family, and the deep groans he invoked would be felt through two presidencies and four generations.

The Adams family kept copious, lifelong diaries and virtually every letter written. Because of that, we are able to peer into their private thoughts, doubts, fears, strengths, and weaknesses. Historians have waded through the mountains of papers and speculated endlessly about the "truth" about the Adamses. And most of them disagree.

What is beyond disagreement is that John Adams lived a life of private torment while striving to give public excellence to his country. The teachings of Deacon John and Susanna Adams, garnered from their Puritan ethos, engendered perpetual, constant self-examination for purity of motive. It was like picking at a sore, never allowing it to heal. It caused a lifelong, unresolved tension punctuated by volcanic rages and explosive outbursts. More than anything, John Adams wanted to be a great man yet clubbed himself for the desire. He yearned for the recognition and appreciation of his work from his country but wanted it to come voluntarily, without his having to seek it. He was prone to deep depressions and debilitating exhaustion, usually after overcoming some great crisis in his life or in his country's— his duties had to be completed before he could have a breakdown. One historian has noted, "In another era, John Adams would have needed Prozac."[2]

There is a famous pastel portrait by Benjamin Blyth drawn when John Adams was about thirty-one years old. His face is unlined, untested, wholly unremarkable. Indeed, his face looks like a bowl of vanilla pudding. When he was almost eighty-nine, John Adams posed a last time for Gilbert Stuart. He is nearly bald, with wisps of fine white hair curling about his ears. Toothless, his face is wrinkled with great age. But his eyes are blazing fiercely, still full of vibrant fire and purpose, with no diminution of intellect, gazing steadfastly at the viewer. It is the face of a man whose life has been well lived, almost everything used, nothing wasted, and yet with much still unresolved.

The point of reference for John Adams was his wife. Abigail Smith was a remarkable woman for any time but certainly an extraordinary woman for her century. She was well read, with a strategic mind and a keen sense of people. She affirmed her husband, argued with him, and tested the logic of his theories and decisions. And it was a two-way street. John Adams welcomed her partnership, something a bit uncommon for a man of his time, and because of it she, too, grew intellectually and emotionally. It is doubtful that John Adams would have had the courage to soar so high, breaking free for long periods from his bouts of inner self-flagellation, had it not been for the perspective and sense of shared adventure that he held in common with his "dearest friend."

Though John Adams would never speak about the issue, it was likely the familiarity of his mother's intrusive and argumentative spirit that allowed John Adams the freedom to develop such an open-ended intellectual relationship with Abigail. As a child he had experienced the power of having an active woman in his life, challenging and encouraging him and serving as a sounding board to his every thought. Notwithstanding his manly complaints about his mother's temper and interference in his life, he clearly sought to re-create a more perfect version of the same arrangement with Abigail.

ABIGAIL SMITH ADAMS, MOTHER OF JOHN QUINCY ADAMS

Family legend holds that when John Adams wedded Abigail Smith on October 25, 1764, her minister father gave a homily based on Matthew 11:18, "For John came neither eating nor drinking, and they say, 'He hath a devil.' "[3] Those of us with modern sensibilities would cringe at such an inappropriate slap during what, to the young lovers, was their supremely happy moment. To a young man already conflicted about his qualities and abilities, it would have been yet another scornful public humiliation. One wonders about his reaction.

While the scripture is, ironically, about the dangers of making judgments on the actions and motives of others, the incident is recorded in Abigail's *Memoir* by her grandson Charles Francis Adams, who insisted that the text was about the Yankee aversion to the relatively new profession of lawyer.[4] Abigail's mother, Elizabeth Quincy Smith, was adamantly opposed to the marriage, not only because of John's profession but also because he came from a lower class. Elizabeth

Smith sprang from "the bedrock of the Bay Colony's Puritan theocracy."[5] The family pointed proudly to the fact that one of their ancestors had traveled with William the Conqueror to conquer England in 1066 and that a Quincy had been on hand when King John was forced to sign the Magna Carta.

Elizabeth's father was Colonel John Quincy (which they pronounced "Quin-zee"), descended from Edmund Quincy, one of the founders of the colony. Colonel John was known as a man who was not easily impressed. "He did not often speak evil," John Adams wrote, "but he seldom spoke well."[6] Abigail adored him. In a few short years, she would name her eldest son after him, and in 1792, the part of Braintree where the Adamses lived would be renamed Quincy, in honor of Colonel John.

The paternal side of Abigail's family was equally proud. As far as her father was concerned, even if Henry Adams *had* arrived first, the Smiths were from the "respectable" merchant class, prospering from both seafaring and a butcher's business in Charleston. Reverend Smith himself was a graduate of Harvard, with a reputation, it is said, "for piety and a fondness for recording rather tasteless jests in his journal."[7] He and his wife disliked the idea of their daughter marrying the son of a farmer and shoemaker—no matter that the farmer in question had the sterling character of Deacon John.

John Adams, for his part, didn't much care for Abigail's father at first, perceiving him as a "crafty, designing" fellow, "given to the ostentatious display of wealth."[8]

Born on November 22, 1744, and hailing from the nearby coastal village of Weymouth, Abigail Adams was sister to one brother, William, and to Mary and Elizabeth, sisters to whom she would remain devoted for her entire life.[9] The unfortunate William would live a life of deceit and weakness and die of alcoholism, dissolute, after abandoning his wife and six children. It would cause his sister to vow, as historian Paul C. Nagel put it, that "no child of hers would come to maturity only casually disciplined."[10]

Whereas the Adamses of necessity had to be thrifty, the Smith family was comfortably supported by revenue from two farms, so they were not dependent on a clergyman's paltry income. That didn't preclude the Smiths from being frugal, however; Abigail's mother insisted on "the importance of saving an apple paring."[11]

Interestingly, considering her father's profession and Abigail's later stance on slavery, the family owned two slaves.[12] She recognized the incongruity of fighting for one's own independence while holding a whole race in slavery. In September 1774, Abigail would write to John Adams, "You know my mind on this subject. I wish most sincerely there was not a slave in the province. It always appeared a most iniquitous scheme to me—fight ourselves for what we are daily robbing and plundering from those who have as good a right to freedom as we have."[13] She would not live to see her son John Quincy Adams fight to the death against the "iniquitous scheme."

Abigail's parents taught their family the precepts of kindness and compassion. One of her mother's favorite sayings was "We should never wait to be requested to do a kind office, an act of love."[14] Reverend Smith would repeatedly caution his daughters "never to speak ill of anybody . . . to make things rather than persons the subjects of conversation," Abigail wrote. Before his daughters would leave the house, even "if it was but for an afternoon," the Reverend Smith would restate the rules.[15] No gossiping, girls.

Abigail grew up high-spirited and obstinate, and her despairing parents consoled themselves with Grandmother Quincy's adage that "wild colts make the best horses."[16] Abigail was even once scolded: "You will either make a very bad or a very good woman."[17]

At home, her elder sister, Mary, and their mother taught Abigail a mixed bag of literature, with some French thrown in. Unlike her brother, William, who was expected to go to Harvard, she was not allowed to study Latin, as it was a subject considered scandalous for women to learn. But she was free to use her father's extensive parson's library and to learn from him not just the words but the ideas behind them.[18]

When Richard Cranch entered the family sphere to court sister Mary, the hodgepodge learning style changed. He began tutoring Abigail in earnest and opened to her the world of great minds, teaching her to "love the poets and [putting] into my hands, Milton, Pope, Thompson and Shakespeare."[19] He urged her to look beyond the usual intellectual expectations of women, saying that "the true female character consisted not in the tincture of the skin or a fine set of features."[20] Abigail became inordinately fond of poetry, which she would quote in letter after letter, from memory. It would be a lifelong path of learning, one she would walk, at her own pace, beside John Adams.

One day, Richard came to visit Mary accompanied by his friend John Adams. The young sister, Abigail, with her wit and intelligence, stole his heart. Soon John was riding his horse up the coast road to Weymouth at every opportunity. Their love letters are a voyeur's treat of eighteenth-century amorous yearning. Hearkening to his law professor's warning not to wed until his practice was well established and he could actually afford a wife, John struggled to control his passionate feelings toward Abigail, pushing back the date of their wedding until she insisted that *now* was the time.

The day finally came, and John Adams lived through the insulting wedding sermon. After a long reception where the gentlemen told ribald eighteenth-century wedding-night stories, John took Abigail home to Braintree, to the house he had inherited from his father, mere yards from the home where he had been born and in which Susanna still lived. He was twenty-nine; in less than a month, his new bride would turn twenty.

By Christmas, Abigail knew she was expecting their first child. On July 14, 1765, baby Abigail came into the world. Everyone would call her Nabby, and she would live a tragic and unhappy life, be serially deserted by an irresponsible husband who was off chasing ephemeral fortunes, undergo breast surgery without anesthesia, and die of the cancer that continued to eat away at her body.

But for now, she was a loved and treasured baby daughter, soon to be followed on July 11, 1767, by her first brother, John Quincy Adams, and, later, by frail Susanna, whom they nicknamed "Suky," and brothers Charles and Thomas Boylston Adams. Sometime before the birth of John Quincy, the loathsome Stamp Act would be proclaimed, and John Adams would be thrust into the role of revolutionary.

A PATRIOT'S BREW

In the thirteen years that followed the wedding, John Adams was often absent from home. The family would move from Boston to Braintree and back again, depending on John's law practice and political activity. To drum up legal business, he was obliged to "ride the circuit" of courts in one town after another. It became more commonplace for him to be gone than to be home. One of Abigail's letters described a dejected Nabby, sorrowfully rocking baby John Quincy and singing, "Come, pappa, come home to Brother Johnny."[21] It must have ripped his heart out.

Letters from John were frequent and filled with fatherly advice. Like Deacon John before him, John Adams deemed it crucial to instill in his children the moral imperatives of hard work, patriotism, and virtue. "The education of our children is never out of my mind," he wrote home on his way to Philadelphia. "Train them to Virtue, habituate them to industry, activity and Spirit." Letter after letter followed, containing similar upward urgings.

Unlike young John Adams, John Quincy and the other children were not given the guiltless freedom of playing hooky or romping in the woods. They did play, but it wasn't guiltless. When John Quincy was ten years old, he wrote to his father a famous and poignant letter. "Dear Sir," he scribbled, "I love to receive letters very well, much better than I love to write them. I make but a poor figure at composition, my head is much too fickle. My thoughts are running after birds' eggs, play and trifles till I get vexed with myself. I have but just entered the 3d volume of Smollett, tho' I had designed to have got it half through by this time. I have determined this week to be more diligent." John Quincy goes on to beg his father, "I wish, Sir, you would give me some instructions with regard to my time, and advise me how to proportion my studies and my play, in writing, and I will keep them by me and endeavor to follow them."[22] Such letters amaze historians and prompt some to suspect that Abigail herself dictated them, not only in the hope of pacifying John Adams's mind as he rushed from meeting to political meeting, but as part of her sense of responsibility for raising a son worthy of his country.

John Adams's reply was just as focused. He wished for ten-year-old John Quincy to read Thucydides' history of the Peloponnesian War—in the original Greek. The reason, he said, was that "the future circumstances of your country may require other wars, as well as councils and negotiations," he wrote his son, presciently. "I wish to turn your thoughts early to such studies as will afford you the most solid instruction and improvement for the part which may be allotted to you to act on the stage of life."[23]

As the children grew older and John Adams's political activity increased, they would gather around as Abigail read his letters aloud, listening with wide eyes to the messages from their revolutionary hero father. The whole family was well aware that if the British ever captured him, his likely future would be in chains to the Tower of London, or even the gibbet. The thought made it easier for his children to comply with his lofty desires and, as we shall see in the adulthood of John Quincy, to push them to extremes.

In June 1774, John Adams was chosen as a Massachusetts delegate to the first Continental Congress. In other colonies, opposition to British rule was considerably milder. But Boston was already in a virtual state of rebellion. The port was still closed. No courts were open for trial. In this atmosphere, John Adams and the other delegates left for Philadelphia, and Abigail took her little family home to Braintree, where they would spend the rest of the Revolution.

Whereas he had once questioned every acquaintance about legal writs and shipping invoices, John now sought out information on the character of his fellow delegates and what coalitions they might seek. In Philadelphia, John Adams and the other Massachusetts delegates would at first tread softly, understanding that they were perceived as political firebrands and that belligerence on their part would frighten off a consensus for liberty. When a coach is driven, he wrote, "the "swiftest horses must be slackened and the slowest quickened, that all may keep an even pace."[24] It was a tentative time. About a third of the colonists were for liberty, a third wanted to remain tied to England, and a third were neutral. It could go either way. Through it all, for the sake of unity, John Adams would cajole, flatter, conciliate, debate, convince, hammer out statements of rights, and plant the seeds of independence among his more timid colleagues. It was a very different strategy than he would employ when he returned to wage war. Then, he would push, pull and prod, thunder and explode.

The Continental Congress was due to adjourn in October, but before they left, the delegates sent a final appeal to King George, urging his justice and pledging loyalty. It would do no good.

On October 26, 1774, Congress adjourned and John Adams hurried home to his family. But back in Braintree, there was little time for rest. John Adams would continue to work and write and plan for the war that was now sure to come. Six months later, the hammer fell.

In April 1775, British redcoats marched through the Massachusetts countryside, headed toward Concord. Their target was the colonial military depot at Concord. Warned by outriders such as Paul Revere and William Dawes, the Minutemen grabbed their rifles and headed into action, many passing the Adams's farm. It was the beginning of the Revolutionary War.

John Adams left quickly for the Continental Congress, this time not to conciliate but to pursue war. Abigail and the children lived in terror. John Quincy would later write that in "the space of twelve months, my mother with her infant children dwelt, liable every hour of the day and of the night to be butchered in cold blood, or taken and carried into Boston as hostages." [25] Despite her fear, Abigail had already plotted her own course. Just two months before Concord and Lexington, she had written to her friend Mercy Otis Warren and mused, "Is it not better to die the last of British freemen than live the first of British slaves?" [26]

Patriots to the core, Abigail Adams and her children contributed all they could to the cause. John Quincy, seven years old, carried water to the passing soldiers. Abigail opened her house to refugees from Boston and scrounged sanctuary for the rest in other Braintree households. She fed and sheltered soldiers in her attic and barn, writing to John in Philadelphia that it was such "a scene of confusion . . . you can hardly imagine how we live." [27]

One day, as family legend tells it, some ragged American militiamen knocked on her door, begging for any metal to make bullets. Abigail promptly hooked a huge iron kettle over the crane in the kitchen fireplace and stoked the fire. Surrounded by Minutemen and aided by John Adams's brother Elihu, she filled the kettle with the Adams's treasured store of pewter. It soon began to bubble and melt, ready to be poured into the bullet molds.

Young John Quincy Adams pushed through the soldiers to see what was going on. "Why, uncle, what are you doing?" he asked. "What strange soup."

Uncle Elihu answered tersely, "Bullet soup." [28]

Less than two months after the Battles of Lexington and Concord, Abigail and the children were awakened at three o'clock on a Saturday morning by thunder, not the booming of a spring rainstorm, as they first thought, but of cannon. The Battle of Bunker Hill and Breed's Hill had begun.

True to her role as republican mother rearing a son for public service, Abigail took John Quincy by the hand and led him through the orchard and up Penn's Hill, where they could see, far in the distance, the smoke and flashes of explosions. The British attack was relentless, with cannon fire throughout Saturday and Sunday. Abigail wrote to John Adams in Philadelphia, "The constant roar of the cannon is so distressing that we cannot eat, drink or sleep." [29]

On Sunday came the heartbreaking word that their friend Dr. Joseph Warren had been killed—shot in the face, his body brutalized by British bayonets. His death brought the war home to the seven-year-old boy, for Dr. Warren was a close family friend, much beloved, who had earlier saved John Quincy's finger from amputation. Abigail taught the children a poem as a memorial to their beloved doctor. Years later, at the end of his own life, JQA could still quote the words.

Abigail and the children started living a divided life, dealing with the needs of the war, on the one hand, and trying to keep the farm running and the family fed, on the other. As it would be for the rest of her years, John's absence was her greatest burden. Living without him had not been in the plan. Abigail had chosen the life of a wife and a mother but had seen herself become a public servant, without acclaim or recognition. This, she concluded in sad resignation, would be her anonymous, patriotic sacrifice, at least for the years of the Revolution. In fact, her life and that of her family would be an ongoing sacrifice for years to come.

Due to the crush of work, John Adams could not write as often or as much as his wife needed. Even so, Abigail kept up a steady stream of letters, pouring out her heart and keeping John advised of news about the farm, as well as reporting on the local war efforts. She became his political eyes and ears in Massachusetts. He valued her careful observations, often sharing them with other delegates.

Abigail's letters would end with requests for scarce items such as pins and coffee, handkerchiefs and sugar. These were not selfish wishes for luxuries. It was a matter of survival. Abigail could sell them for hard money or barter them for necessities. Little by little, Abigail was becoming the sole parent, breadwinner, and decision maker for the family in Braintree, freeing up John Adams to play his role on the national stage. Like women everywhere, from time immemorial, she did what had to be done.

During one of John's infrequent visits home, Abigail became pregnant. Alone, she suffered a difficult pregnancy, and alone, she suffered through a painful labor. Astonishingly, she wrote to John throughout the process, and when the pain became unbearable and the baby was coming, she wrote, "I must lay my pen down this moment, to bear what I cannot fly from." When the baby was delivered, she continued her letter to her husband without even a comma, "and now I have endured it I reassume my pen."[30] She had delivered a stillborn daughter.

In August 1775, an epidemic of dysentery swept throughout the Boston area. The battlefields' filthy, unsanitary conditions endangered not only the soldiers but civilians as well. John Adams had long fumed against the conditions. "Dirty frying pans slayed more than swords," he told Abigail.[31]

Captain Elihu Adams, John Quincy's thirty-four-year-old "bullet soup" uncle, succumbed to dysentery on the battlefield while commanding American troops. His death was only the beginning. No sooner had Uncle Elihu been buried than his widow lost her infant daughter. And finally disease struck the Braintree home. Isaac, a hired hand, fell ill, and for a week, Abigail wrote her husband, there was no place in the house to escape from "his terrible groans."[32] Abigail fell violently ill at the same time, and then two servants, Suzy and Patty, did so as well. Little Thomas Boylston Adams was next. Fortunately, the other children had been sent to safety while they were still well. Through it all, the responsibilities for everyone else's care fell to the still weak Abigail. The nauseating stink of the house with so many people sick at once was overpowering. "A general putrefaction seems to have taken place, and we can not bear the house only as we are constantly cleansing it with hot vinegar."[33] Another week passed.

A messenger arrived with devastating news: Abigail's aging mother, who had also been caring for dysentery victims, had contracted the disease and died. There was no time or strength to grieve. Others in the household may have been slowly recovering, but Patty was dying, horribly, and she knew it. Patty begged Abigail to stay with her for the short time she had left. Finally, mercifully, after an illness of five weeks, Patty died as well. The epidemic had taken its last victim. As the crisis passed, grief and depression set in and Abigail collapsed with fatigue.

John Adams sent Abigail letter after comforting letter, praising her courage. But he did not come home. Paradoxically, his own health improved. He wrote a friend during the crisis at Braintree, "How it is I know not—but I am very happy." [34] Historian John Ferling postulates that his family's afflictions enabled "him to see his service in Congress as all the more sacrificial and virtuous, and to view his grief as the equivalent of the cares borne by those who soldiered." [35]

During a later outbreak of disease, when a smallpox epidemic threatened the area, Abigail took her children to Boston to be inoculated, a procedure that had its own dangers—without asking for John's advice or presence. He was attending the official signing of the Declaration of Independence.

Indeed, as her confidence in her skills grew, her requests for his advice lessened. Immediately after the first battles of the Revolutionary War, when friends and family were escaping Boston and Abigail was helping them find temporary shelter in Braintree, she ran up against one of her tenant farmers, a man named Hayden. His sons were all in the army, and he lived alone in one of the Adams's houses. A friend of John had fled to Braintree with his pregnant wife. All the other houses were filled to capacity, so Abigail had the brilliant idea that the couple might be able to stay with Hayden. Christian charity demanded as much. He refused her request out of hand, announcing that no one from Boston would inconvenience him. Further infuriating Abigail was the fact that Hayden hadn't even paid his rent or done his share of the farm work. When confronted, he announced that John Adams, the man of the house, was the boss and only he could give such orders, not Abigail.

Seething, Abigail fired off an angry letter to John, who backed her up in no uncertain terms, enclosing an order evicting Hayden. But the loutish Hayden refused to budge. The contest endured for months, defying John's legal abilities, till Abigail hit upon a method he couldn't resist: she paid the man to get out.

In Philadelphia, John Adams continued his formidable labors. His grandson Charles Francis Adams wrote that he "was a member of ninety, and chairman of twenty-five committees." From congressional documents and diaries, scholars have pieced together a staggering list of administrative work churned out by the deacon's son. [36] Beginning in June 1776, even while serving on the committee tasked with the writing of the Declaration of Independence, John Adams was appointed to direct the Board of War and Ordnance. He transformed the assignment into a one-man War Department. "Ships! Ships!" he demanded, knowing that the new country was doomed without naval power.[37] Later in the war, when mediocre generals continued to lose battles, John suggested that each be evaluated once a year and the incompetent ones sent home. It might even be a good idea once in a while to "shoot a General," he said. It just might get their attention.[38]

Early on, it had become apparent that the war could not be won without help from at least one other major power. The obvious choice was France or even Spain, historic enemies of England. But no country would be willing to enter the conflict as long as there was the slightest possibility of colonial reconciliation with the mother country. For that, there needed to be a clear break, a declaration of independence. And following that, no substantial military aid could be expected until there was at least some hope that America could win its war.

The year 1777 was the nadir of the Revolution. The exhilarating days of patriotic fervor were over. Congress was facing years of drudgery. The paper money issued by the Continental Congress was valueless. "Not worth a continental" became an expression that entered the colonial vernacular. It was hard to get supplies to the troops and harder still to keep the troops from going home. Battle after battle was being lost. When British General William Howe took Philadelphia, Congress was forced to flee north to Yorktown, Pennsylvania.

On October 17, 1777, the colonials received a miraculous reprieve. American troops forced the complete surrender of General John Burgoyne's army at Saratoga, New York. It was a decisive victory—some say a turning point in the war. The victory would give the fledgling new nation enough credibility to warrant international intervention. Congress needed a representative in Paris, someone to follow up on the victory by making the case for the colonies.

The victory at Saratoga coincided with John and Abigail's thirteenth wedding anniversary. She and Nabby rode to Boston to celebrate, without John. He was in Philadelphia, tending to new law clients. If they were to have their long-awaited domestic life together, he would have to resume his dormant law career. He had been gone much during their first thirteen years of marriage, but if Abigail could be patient a little longer, her fondest hopes would come true; John would be home to stay.

John enjoyed two weeks of hearth and home upon his return to Braintree, surrounded by his Abigail and his laughing, noisy children. Then he was back in the saddle, this time heading for Portsmouth, New Hampshire, to represent a new client in some maritime litigation. When he'd been gone only a few hours, urgent letters arrived. Thinking they might contain messages that John would need to see immediately, Abigail ripped them open to read stunning news. Although he had just been granted an extended, indefinite leave of absence, John Adams was once more Congress's choice. If he would accept, he would join Benjamin Franklin and Arthur Lee as the representatives of the Continental Congress in Paris, France. Abigail's dream was over.

Her feeling of pride was soon overwhelmed by feelings of panic and betrayal. She knew that it meant another sacrifice of years. Perhaps he would never return, captured by the British or drowned in some raging North Atlantic winter storm. She fired off an enraged letter to James Lovell, a Massachusetts congressional delegate and friend of her husband. How dare he "contrive to rob me of all my happiness?"[39] Her fury tempered into heartache in a few short paragraphs. "Can I, Sir, consent to be separated from him whom my heart esteems above all earthly beings, and for an unlimited time?"[40]

Abigail had several days to stew and brood before John returned from Portsmouth. There is no record of the emotional exchange that ensued. We know that the couple soon agreed that John would accept the appointment. There was really never any question. But then Abigail pressed the case that *she* should go as well. John quickly nixed that idea. It was simply too dangerous for a woman, even one as tough as the self-reliant, hard-headed Yankee patriot Abigail Adams, who had already overcome extraordinary ordeals for her family—and her country. It would, however, be appropriate for him to take his ten-year-old son, John Quincy. It would be a good education for the boy, his father insisted. Reluctantly, grudgingly, with a heavy, fearful heart, Abigail came to the same conclusion. It was best for her husband, it was best for her son, it was best for her country—but her heart was broken.

On February 13, 1778, father and son, both future presidents of the United States, boarded the twenty-four-gun American frigate *Boston* to begin their life-changing adventure together. It was a journey that would be a bonding experience between father and son, one that would empower John Quincy Adams and give him a confidence that would turn a patriotic family into a political dynasty. Abigail, who sensed it was an important moment for her two men, would not, could not go down to watch them sail away.

THE INITIATION OF JOHN QUINCY ADAMS

The British ruled the seas, and they knew that Mr. Adams would be trying to sail to France. Stealthily, to avoid British spies, a small boat rowed them out to the frigate on a secluded stretch of coast. The Atlantic crossing was a swashbuckling tale, full of danger and courage—and seasickness. Violent winter storms threw passengers and crew about the cabins, forcing father and son to clasp "each other together in our arms" and to brace "our feet against the bed boards and bedsteads to prevent us from having our bodies dashed against the plants and timbers of the ship."[41]

With one storm barely over, Captain Samuel Tucker spied three British ships on the horizon. Thinking them to be merchant vessels, he headed in their direction, eager to capture at least one of them as a prize of war. Closer, he realized with dawning horror that the three were not merchantmen but warships. He turned tail and ran, outsailing two of them. The third followed hard on their heels for three long, desperate days until the *Boston* was swallowed up by the night.

The whole affair represented a dangerous enterprise. John Adams's diplomatic pouch had been weighted to toss overboard. The British, of course, had been advised of his appointment and were looking for him all over the ocean. There was no diplomatic immunity; indeed, John's status as a representative of the rebellion only increased his danger. If captured, he would almost certainly face imprisonment at Newgate. As an infamous rebel, he would be denied "the honor of an apartment in the Tower [of London] as a State Prisoner."[42] Very possibly, the Crown might send him to a traitor's gallows. However, as historian David McCullough has noted, John Adams "remained enough of a Puritan to believe anything worthy must carry a measure of pain."[43] Because he was utterly convinced of the efficacy of his mission, despite the rigors and danger John Adams was in very good spirits indeed.

Through it all, ten-year-old John Quincy's behavior gave his father great happiness. "Fully sensible of our danger," John wrote to Abigail, "he was constantly endeavoring to bear it with a manly patience."[44] John Quincy would need it, for now the frigate was hit with another storm. Lighting split the mainmast, above and below decks. Twenty seamen were hurt, and one man, struck in the head by lightning, would die "raving mad."[45] The raging winds blew currents against currents, creating "a tumbling sea, vast mountains of water, sometimes dashing against each other,"[46] threatening to submerge the frigate and send it to the bottom. "The shrouds and every other rope in the ship exposed to the wind became a chord of very harsh music," John Adams vividly recounted. "Their vibrations produced a constant and hideous howl."[47]

When the storm finally vented, the *Boston* was several hundred miles off course. The crew spent the interlude hammering the battered frigate back into seaworthiness. John Adams, the one-man Department of War, took the opportunity to hammer the captain into seaworthiness, as well. The ship had to be cleaned up, he insisted, with more discipline and order. John had already lost one brother to dysentery, and he had seen more men die from disease than wounds. However much of a royal pain John might have been, Captain Tucker tolerantly obliged his wishes. Patients were brought up on deck for clean air, while below decks, seamen scrubbed everything clean. "This ship would have bred the plague or jail fever, if there had not been great exertions since the storm to wash, sweep, air and purify clothes, cots, cabins, hammocks and all other things, places, and persons," John wrote.[48] A respect and even fondness grew between the two wildly dissimilar men. At a Navy Board hearing, Captain Tucker would compliment John Adams: "I did not say much to him at first, but damn and bugger my eyes, I found him after a while as sociable as any Marblehead man."[49] High praise from a sea dog.

A few days away from France, another British ship hove into sight. It was the *Martha,* and it was a heavily armed merchantman. Captain Tucker ordered John and John Quincy belowdecks as firing commenced. In the midst of battle, Tucker looked around to find Mr. Adams dressed as one of his marines and firing away, just as a cannonball whizzed by, narrowly missing his head. "Why are you here, sir?" he yelled.

"I ought to do my share of the fighting," Adams snapped.

Captain Tucker replied angrily, "I am commanded by the Continental Congress to carry you in safety to Europe, and I will do it!"[50] In the years to come, the captain would affectionately tell the story and acknowledge "the bravery of my venerable and patriotic Adams."[51]

No sooner had John Adams arrived than he learned his job had already been done. Even before he and John Quincy had left Massachusetts, the French had agreed to a treaty with the United States. John Adams did not put details in his diary, only noting his dismay.

Fearful that his undertaking would become the subject of ridicule, Adams cast about for a way to justify his presence in Europe.[52] The American Commission in Paris was in shambles. His immediate task was clerical. Papers and financial records at the mission were in disorder. John set about to reform the system, effectively demoting himself from diplomat to bureaucrat. But it was work that had to be done.

Helplessly choleric, within weeks he was deeply into the messy politics of the mission. Benjamin Franklin and Arthur Lee despised each other, and Silas Deane was being recalled for financial irregularities. French favorite Franklin spent his time making the social rounds, staying up late at night and sleeping late in the morning. Franklin made a good case that he was playing an indispensable role, but John Adams suspected that the famous American was only lazy and untrustworthy. Suspicious and perhaps even a little jealous of Franklin's popularity in Paris, Adams soon determined that the French goal was to keep America a subservient French vassal state. Spies—both British and French—floated throughout the city. Vergennes, the French foreign minister, conscious that Adams's agenda was scrupulously American, detested the man and did whatever he could to undercut his efforts, a situation that would grimly deteriorate after Adams was appointed to negotiate peace and commercial treaties with the English. To a man who desperately needed to be needed, "to shine in use,"[53] John Adams's time in Paris was utter frustration.

Always conscientious, John Adams fired off a memo to the Continental Congress, suggesting that there were too many commissioners. One would do. He recommended Benjamin Franklin, but he was hoping that someone would have the good sense to compare letters home and realize John Adams would do better. But the Continental Congress agreed. One commissioner would do, and that one would be Benjamin Franklin. It was another blow to his pride and, he felt, a slap at his honest contributions. To make matters worse, he was not called home. He wasn't even mentioned in the official communiqué from Congress. John Adams was being left in Paris to sit.

If the political arena of Paris was maddening for John Adams, his time with his son John Quincy was a blessing. Quincy was attending one of the best French schools and learning more French in a day than his father could learn in a week, much to John Adams's pride—and chagrin. Everywhere they went, the French people loved John Quincy. One night at a dinner party, John Adams had ventured that sometimes it was a citizen's duty to sacrifice everything for the good of his country. Marie Grand, the wife of the French banker for American funds, was taken aback. Surely, she replied, the love of family would be more powerful than love of country. When John Adams assured her that his wife felt exactly the same, Mme. Grand wrote to Abigail to express her admiration for father and son. She praised John Quincy, saying that he "inherits the spirit of his father." [54]

The Adams father and son began haunting the French theater—which facilitated John Quincy's comprehension of the language—and operas, which John Quincy relished, although his first love would always be theater. Together, they passionately ferreted through bookshops and toured the beautiful French countryside. John Adams cautioned his son, however, that when writing home to Mother he should rein in his enthusiasm for French culture. Abigail was excessively anxious about the moral decadence of Europe.

Eventually, John Adams had had enough. His Puritan nature asserted itself. He would not stay indefinitely, enjoying France and living off the congressional purse. He and John Quincy packed their bags and took the next ship home. They landed near the same secluded spit of land where they had weighed anchor eighteen months earlier. It was deserted. No one knew they were coming.

If the beach was deserted, it would not be so at the Adams home. Nabby, Charles, and Thomas Boylston were eighteen months taller, with eighteen months of catching up to do. Stories flowed between father and children, and John Quincy astounded everyone by showing off his French. Old friends hurried to the home to embrace the world travelers. And heart-weary Abigail likely hummed the words of an old Scottish ballad she had written to John in Paris: "His very foot has music in 't, as he comes up the stairs." [55]

John Adams was soon astonished to learn that, no matter how insignificant and unappreciated he had perceived his foreign service, he had not returned in ignominy. Within two months of his arrival home, letters arrived from the Continental Congress, asking him to go back to Paris as minister plenipotentiary to negotiate treaties of peace and trade with England. The war appeared to be a stalemate; the only way to induce Britain to end the war was to dangle the carrot of commerce before them. A brilliant, hardheaded legal mind was needed, or so it was presumed.

This time, apparently, Abigail was resigned. Not only would John Adams go, but he would take with him John Quincy and their nine-year-old son, Charles. John Quincy, now twelve years old, favored staying home to prepare for Harvard, but Abigail, in a remarkable farewell letter from a mother who was surely already grieving for the impending loss of husband and two sons, eloquently changed his mind. "It is not in the still calm of life, or the repose of a pacific station, that great characters are formed," she wrote her son. "The habits of a vigorous mind are formed in contending with difficulties. Great necessities call out great virtues. When a mind is raised, and animated by scenes that engage the heart, then those qualities which would otherwise lay dormant, wake into life and form the character of the hero and the statesman." [56]

In the years to come, John Quincy would grow resentful of the repetitive flow of his mother's letters urging him ever upward toward virtue, purity, chastity, and all the highest ideals, and warning him against weakness and immorality, chiding him on his dress and appearance. He would eventually forbid his wife, Louisa Catherine, even to mention grooming. But for now, the message of her farewell letter spoke to the man John Quincy Adams would become. Contending with difficulties and great necessities, he would form the character of a hero and a statesman. Observing his beloved father's travails and his betrayals by colleagues, John Quincy Adams would overcome his own problems in the only way he knew how—by single-handedly mastering and controlling his world. He would take his father's "organized effort to master the world" [57] and drive it to an extreme degree. Whereas his father would excoriate himself endlessly and examine his motives after one of his famous explosions of temper, John Quincy would openly court hatred, living life on his own terms, beholden to no one, free to act according to his inner iron chord. It would make

him an implacable foe to evils in American life, such as slavery and the
"gag rule," as we shall see, but it would also make him a singularly odi-
ous person to countenance.

THE RISE OF JOHN QUINCY ADAMS

According to some historians, the best part of John Adams's public
service was over. For the next twenty years he would draft treaties and
obtain critical Dutch loans to finance the Revolution, be appointed as
the first U.S. minister to Britain (this time with Abigail at his side),
twice serve as George Washington's vice president (and be ignored),
and become the second president of the United States—then be sum-
marily booted out of office because of his obstinate and unpopular efforts to keep the United States out of a disastrous war with France.
The years would be marred by contention, intrigue against him both
at home and abroad, and a veritable sacrifice of himself and his family
upon the altar of his country's best interests.

On March 4, 1801, having lost reelection to his popular rival
Thomas Jefferson, an embittered John Adams would depart the White
House at 4:00 A.M. and head back to Massachusetts, refusing to attend
his successor's inaugural. At age sixty-five, he was convinced that his
life was finished. His entire identity had been stripped from him by the
Jefferson political onslaught, and all he had sacrificed for was being
perceived as hollow—and, worse, as unpatriotic. Back in Braintree—or
Quincy, as it was now called—John Adams holed up in his house, staring out the window and refusing to see visitors. He would spend the
next decade attempting to vindicate his public service—writing, ever
writing, day after day.

When a letter from Benjamin Franklin surfaced from the time of
his "disgrace" during the debacle with French Foreign Minister
Charles Vergennes in 1780, an enraged John Adams took up his pen to
denounce "this dark transaction to posterity."[58] Historians would
eventually vindicate his motivation and political insight, if not his people skills. But vindication would not come sufficiently in his lifetime.

When Mercy Otis Warren published her history of the Revolutionary War in 1805, both John and Abigail were devastated. Mercy
had been a dear friend to Abigail throughout her personal struggles
with John's absence in service to his country, and now Mercy was fla-

grantly attacking John and denigrating that very service. Indeed, Mercy accused him of betraying the Revolution. He had lived too long in Europe, she claimed, and had come home corrupted and enamored of all the splendor of courts and "beclouded by a partiality for monarchy."[59] Much of this criticism was based on the scandal that had ensued when Congress was attempting to decide on titles for the new chief executive. To bring dignity and respect to the office of the president and thus strengthen the union, John's unfortunate suggestion had been that George Washington should be called "His Majesty the President." It was too close to a monarchy for the other congressmen to bear. John became a universal butt of jokes. In retirement, John again picked up his pen and rambled and raged through ten letters, attempting to clear his name and reputation.

Adams answered charges of other historians and sent off letters to newspapers. He started on his autobiography, quit—saying it was too painful—picked it up again, and laid it down for good. Eventually, it all became too much. Nothing he could say was going to change anyone's mind. And people were tired of hearing about it. John Adams mostly let it go. After all those years of absence and preoccupation with duty, it was a time for family and a time to observe the ascending star of his son John Quincy. The parallels in their careers were already uncanny.

Both John Adams and John Quincy credited the father's stern supervision for the latter's success. John Quincy would apply the same principle to the rearing of his own children—with disastrous results. It is more likely that the bonding between father and son that took place during their first trip to France led to the self-confidence behind John Quincy's rise to power. There they were, two future American presidents, a father and his young boy, living in a foreign country where they could not speak the language or trust their colleagues. They had only each other. They had likely shared thoughts and ideas a father and son would never ordinarily share.[60] It was likely love, not lectures, that had led inexorably to a statesman's career.

At age fourteen and already fluent in French, John Quincy Adams had gone to Russia as Ambassador Francis Dana's personal secretary. Two years later, he would travel alone from Russia through Scandinavia back to his father's side, getting his first intoxicating taste of personal independence. It would be the overarching goal of his entire life. He would choose to return to the United States and attend Harvard, just as his father had done. He would start his own law practice, hating every minute of it, then turn to political journalism, as had his father. This time around, however, the goal of the political journalism would be to defend that hero father from Thomas Jefferson's charges of Adams's political "heresy."

John Quincy would soon be appointed minister to the Netherlands. After his father, John Adams, was elected president, he thought to bring his son home, an idea much to the liking of Abigail. However, George Washington made the point to the father that John Quincy's talents should not be wasted simply because he was a son. He was the brightest and best, Washington told his father. The letter could not have meant more to John Adams. He appointed his son minister to Prussia.

After his return to the United States, John Quincy would be elected to the U.S. Senate, then break with the Federalist Party when he supported Thomas Jefferson's Embargo Acts. The embargo would prove to be a colossal disaster for the United States, but, as always in his life, John Quincy would vote as he saw fit, no matter what party politics had to say about it. Just as they had his father, the Federalists labeled him a traitor and sought to get rid of him. An irate, independent John Quincy resigned rather than submit to their machinations. He was soon back overseas as minister to Russia—appointed not out of gratitude by Thomas Jefferson but by President James Madison. Later, as minister to England, following his own parent's path to the Court of St. James's, he would negotiate the peace treaty after the War of 1812.

John Adams was watching his firstborn son with inordinate pride and no small trepidation. Would it all end with his son ascending to the presidency? He would most certainly be wounded and attacked like the father. Would he be strong enough to withstand the political and personal battering? John Adams needn't have worried. John Quincy had grown a very tough skin indeed.

★

FIVE

A Private Grief

There is no passion more deeply rooted in my bosom
than the longing for posterity to support my father's name.[1]
—John Quincy Adams

For eight years, the mystique of George Washington held the fledgling country together. When Washington left office, astute political observers knew that no other president would receive the kind of support and loyalty he had engendered. "The President is fortunate to get off just as the bubble is bursting, leaving others to hold the bag," Jefferson wrote to James Madison. "Yet, as his departure will mark the moment when the difficulties begin to work, you will see that they will be ascribed to the new administration."[2]

Ideas about how the country should be run were becoming viciously polarized. The Federalists, including John Adams, felt that the country had to have a strong central government in order to survive. The Republicans, including Thomas Jefferson, were insistent that states' rights were the overriding principle; a strong federal government would be too close to the monarchy they had just battled to defeat. Both John Adams and Thomas Jefferson knew that whoever the next president was, he would be in for a bumpy ride.

John Adams won the election by three electoral votes over Jefferson. And although they were of different parties, by the rules of the day Jefferson became the vice president. But if John Adams had loyally supported George Washington as his vice president, he would not receive the same allegiance from Jefferson. Nor would he receive fidelity from his own Cabinet. In the first major miscalculation of his presidency, John Adams agreed to keep on Washington's Cabinet, not knowing the extent of their philosophical bond to Alexander Hamilton, a brilliant man of ruthless ambition, in league with the Bank of England. The Cabinet members would report to super-Federalist Hamilton and undercut John Adams at every opportunity. Believing that his responsibility was to the country and not to party politics, John Adams was soon caught in the middle of a fierce national political storm, taking heat from Federalists and Republicans alike.

John Adams was inaugurated on March 4, 1797. Within two weeks, he learned that the Directory, the government of the French Revolution, had refused to receive the official U.S. diplomat, General Charles Cotesworth Pinckney, forcing him to flee to Amsterdam and send for further instructions from his government. Worse, the Directory had launched an undeclared war on American ships. "My entrance into office is marked by a misunderstanding with France," he wrote to John Quincy in a sublime understatement, "which I shall endeavor to reconcile."[3] For the next four years it would be the principal preoccupation of his government.

As he had during the American Revolution, John Adams insisted on "wooden walls," his term for naval defense, building up the U.S. Navy from virtually nothing to fifty ships in just two years. Jefferson and his Republicans would scream that Adams was warmongering, but the naval strength would prove his major bargaining chip for peace.

When some French officials tried to extort money from American ministers for a treaty, they responded, "Not a sixpence," and wrote home to Adams for instructions. He attempted to keep the scandal under wraps, thinking it would lead straight to war, but the secret leaked, and the new capital city of Washington, D.C., was buzzing with rumors that something was amiss. When Congress insisted on knowing the full story, John Adams, who had nothing to hide, turned over the letters. The Republicans were aghast—incredulous that the French, whom they admired, could have resorted to such treachery. The Federalists were ecstatic. The crisis turned the love of all things French to ashes. Overnight, war fever reigned.

But John Adams would not be moved. He knew that a war at this critical juncture would cripple and most likely destroy the new nation. Now the Federalists lambasted him. He was weak, they said, and for-

saking the nation's honor. Not until the final days of his presidency
would a peace treaty be signed. Through it all, John Adams withstood
the Federalists, the Republicans, Jefferson, Hamilton, his faithless Cabinet, the Bank of England, the French Directory, and, finally, Napoleon
Bonaparte. Abigail wrote, "I suppose they want him to cringe, but he
is made of oak instead of willow. He may be torn up by the roots, or
break, but he will never bend."[4]

John Adams fully understood the magnitude of the gift he had
given to his country at such a terrible personal price. He would later
write to a friend, "I desire no other inscription over my gravestone
than: 'Here lies John Adams, who took upon himself the responsibility
of peace with France in the year 1800.' "[5]

In an ironic twist, in 1803 Napoleon Bonaparte gave President
Thomas Jefferson the opportunity to purchase the Louisiana Territory,
thereby doubling the size of the United States with a stroke of his pen.
Had not John Adams made peace with France, it would likely not have
happened.

A PERSONAL STORM

John Adams's presidency would be a period of great personal crisis and
pain for the family. And the death of his mother, Susanna, a mere
month after his inauguration was a harbinger for all that would be
coming. Five years after Deacon John's death, Susanna had married a
man named John Hall, whom she also outlived. Thereafter, she had
lived with her son, Peter, not far from John and Abigail's house in
Braintree. Both Abigail and John had begged her to move in with
them, but she was accustomed to her own life. Still, Susanna visited
regularly, even tromping through deep snow to see Abigail. The two
women remained remarkably good friends, with Abigail taking good
care of her mother-in-law and encouraging other family members to
remember her with little gifts. When a letter arrived from Abigail and
John while John was serving as minister to Great Britain, saying they
were doing well, Susanna tersely said, "Aya, I'd just as soon hear she
was coming home."

Susanna Adams had lived long enough to hear that her son had
been elected president of the United States. On March 4, 1797, he was
inaugurated in a ceremony held in the Chamber of the House of Rep-

resentatives in Philadelphia. He did away with the courtly trappings of George Washington's celebration, riding instead in a simple, elegant black coach with two horses. "They shall have a republican President in earnest," he wrote to Abigail.[6] It was a slap at all the furor engendered after he had suggested that George Washington be referred to as "His Majesty the President."

Shortly after the inauguration, Abigail had been ready to leave Quincy to join her husband. But her departure had been delayed by a late-spring snowstorm. The weather sent Susanna's health into a tailspin. On April 17, 1797, as her son was serving his first month as president, Susanna Adams died. She was ninety-eight. Abigail had been with her until the end.

Abigail made all the preparations for Susanna's funeral in the front parlor of the family home. The Boston newspapers wrote that the president's mother had "afforded the present generation a living example of that simplicity of manners and godly sincerity for which the venerable settlers of this country were so justly esteemed."[7] Abigail wrote to John on April 26, telling him, "Our aged parent has gone to rest," and that she "fell asleep, and is happy."[8]

John would respond with grief. "Our ancestors are now all gone, and we are to follow them very soon to a country where there will be no war or rumor of war, no envy, no jealousy, rivalry or party."[9] Nor would Susanna's death be the last family grief of his presidency.

During the last months of 1800, President John Adams was under bitter political attack from all sides. Especially galling were the criticisms of Thomas Jefferson, his own vice president, who had once called himself a friend. There was a very real possibility that Adams would be rejected by the voters and lose reelection.

In November came the bitter news that his son Charles had died of cirrhosis of the liver. All his life Charles had struggled with the incessant family demands for excellence. Whereas John Quincy would harden himself and carry the burden to new heights, Charles seemed to break beneath the load of the excessive expectations. It would be a dreaded replay of the life of Abigail's alcoholic brother William, which she had vowed never to allow to happen to her own sons.

Earlier, John Adams's Puritan temper had led to estrangement with Charles. Learning that his son had descended into an alcoholic stupor and abandoned his wife and church, he declared his son to be "a mere rake, buck, blood and beast . . . a madman possessed of the devil." Finally, Adams had written, "I renounce him." [10] After his death, Abigail would write of her son, "He was no man's enemy but his own. He was beloved in spite of his errors." [11]

Three months later, in February 1801, the electoral votes were opened in Congress. Thomas Jefferson and Aaron Burr had tied. They had both beaten President John Adams, the incumbent. It was a bitter blow. Congress would select Thomas Jefferson, and he would be one of America's most popular presidents. In retirement, John and Abigail Adams would have to watch from the sidelines in painful silence.

THE HEALING OF HEARTS

In April 1804, troubling news came to Quincy. Thomas Jefferson's youngest surviving daughter, Polly Jefferson Eppes, had died following childbirth. It brought back memories of a time when Adams and Jefferson had been on friendly terms, the former serving as the American minister to Great Britain, the latter assigned to Paris. Abigail remembered receiving the news that Polly, the nine-year-old daughter of Thomas Jefferson, accompanied by her black slave girl, had arrived in London on their way to France. Abigail had insisted that they be her personal guests. She remembered the little motherless child who had run wild, how she had taken her to get new clothes and restored her manners. Polly had captured Abigail's heart. When Jefferson's aide had come to take Polly to Paris, Polly had clung to Abigail and cried, "O, now I have learned to love you, why will they tear me from you?" [12] And now the news came that the little girl she had hosted in London, the president's daughter, was dead.

Abigail didn't write Thomas Jefferson for a month. There had been too many painful events since that lovely time of friendship between the two families. Finally she picked up her pen and expressed her sorrow and sympathy. "The powerful feelings of my heart have burst through the restraint," she wrote. "The attachment which I formed for her, when you committed her to my care, has remained with me to this hour." It was her first letter to Jefferson in seventeen years, and it would spark a correspondence that would only begin to draw off the political venom that had poisoned their relationship.

Abigail had intended to write only one letter of condolence, but

Jefferson's response, after remarking on their long friendship, ended with the comment "I can say with truth that one act of Mr. Adams's life, and only one, ever gave me a moment's personal displeasure. I did consider his last appointments to office as personally unkind." [13]

Near the end of John Adams's administration, his long-cherished dream of a strong, independent judiciary had been furthered by a bill expanding the circuit courts and adding twenty-three new judges. Before he had left office, John Adams had appointed them all. Jefferson and the Republicans had decried the "midnight judges," creating a public image of a bitter John Adams hunched over his desk the night before he was to leave the President's house. In fact, virtually all had been nominated by February 20, with the rest completed by February 24, a week before the inauguration.

It was like waving a red flag in front of Abigail. Why shouldn't John Adams appoint the judges? That was his duty as president. She fired back a letter to "freely disclose to you what has severed the bonds of former friendship and placed you in a light very different from what I once viewed you in." [14] First there had been the issue of the spurious journalist named James T. Callender, she told him. Jefferson had paid Callender to defame John Adams. Abigail delicately refrained from mentioning that it had also been Callender who had later published the scandal that Thomas Jefferson had fathered children by Sally Hemings, the same black slave girl who had accompanied Polly to London and then on to Paris years before. She simply noted, "The serpent you cherished and warmed, bit the hand that nourished him." [15]

Seven letters were to pass between Abigail Adams and Thomas Jefferson. She eventually got to the point that really mattered. It had to do with her son. To save face, John Adams had recalled John Quincy from his service as ambassador to Prussia before he left office, and it had been a lean time as John Quincy struggled to build a law practice at home. A district judge had appointed John Quincy as commissioner of bankruptcy in Boston. The small income from the sinecure would have made all the difference. As president, Thomas Jefferson had rolled back the judiciary and replaced the judges. John Quincy was out, too. It was a slap in the face. Jefferson struggled to convince Abigail that he had not known how the decision had impacted her son's life and he had never planned for the young man to be caught up in his purge.

That was the end of their letters. Only after this seventh letter did

Abigail let John see the bulk of the correspondence. On November 19, 1804, he wrote at the bottom of her copy, "Last evening and this morning at the desire of Mrs. Adams, I read them whole. I have no remarks to make upon it at this time and in this place."[16] It would be eight more years before he would be ready to write his own letter of reconciliation.

As time passed, the old former president began to correspond again with old friends whose relationships, for one political reason or another, were estranged. Even the break with Mercy Otis Warren was healed, much to the relief of everyone concerned. In 1805, John wrote to Dr. Benjamin Rush, his deepest friend, who had also been distanced by politics. "It seemed to me that you and I ought not to die without saying goodbye," he said, opening the door to a renewed correspondence that would give both old men the greatest enjoyment.[17] Mrs. Rush would comment that the two were acting like schoolgirls. They would talk of many things, including the grief John was feeling while rummaging through old papers, trying to write his autobiography. There was such "an immense load of errors, weaknesses, follies and sins to mourn over and repent of," he said.[18] But he had learned to rejoice in all things, as the Apostle Paul had taught. "This phrase 'rejoice ever more' shall never be out of my heart, memory or mouth again as long as I live, if I can help it."[19]

After four years of happy correspondence with his old friend, Dr. Rush sent the first fateful letter. Although he'd been a personal friend of John Adams for a lifetime, Rush was politically closer in thought to Thomas Jefferson, and he admired both men. It grieved him that the two old friends were still estranged. He thought the time was right for forgiveness and reconciliation. He'd had a dream, he told John Adams, about a history book, written far in the future, which reported that the two old presidents had renewed their correspondence and friendship. According to Rush's dream, it was Adams who had initiated the reconciliation. "This letter," he described, "did great honor to Mr. Adams. It discovered a magnanimity known only to great minds. Mr. Jefferson replied to this letter and reciprocated expressions of regard and esteem. These letters were followed by a correspondence of several years."[20] John Adams loved the dream and begged for more. But still he wrote no letter.

The year 1811 was the "most afflictive" the Adamses had ever known. Their youngest son, Thomas, was thrown from his horse and nearly crippled for life. Charles's widow, Sally, began spitting up blood, and it was obvious that she was dying of consumption. Abigail's favorite tutor and John's lifelong friend, Richard Cranch, died, followed only two days later by John's wife, Abigail's, sister Mary. But it was the death of their daughter Nabby that changed everything. Nabby had lived a painful, unhappy life, and now she had discovered a hard lump in her breast. Dr. Rush ordered a mastectomy as soon as possible. Four surgeons performed the operation in the family home in Quincy, without the benefit of anesthesia. In the next room, hearing his daughter scream out in pain would cause a life change for John Adams. There would be no more temper, no more outbursts. He was ready to forgive and be forgiven.

At Christmas, John received another letter from Dr. Rush, reminding him of a visit the previous summer from a couple of young Virginians. John Adams had told them, "I always loved Jefferson and I still love him."[21] When the young men returned to Virginia, they conveyed the words to former president Jefferson, who was living in retirement at Monticello. Upon hearing this message, Jefferson wrote Dr. Rush, "I only needed this knowledge to revive toward him all the affections of the most cordial moments of our lives."[22]

The moment was at hand. On January 1, 1812, John Adams sat down and wrote to his old friend Thomas Jefferson. It was exactly as Dr. Rush had dreamt. Their correspondence, however feeble and shaky the handwriting, brought great joy to both. Jefferson would keep a bust of John Adams beside his desk at Monticello for the rest of his life.

THE PASSING OF A GREAT WOMAN

Deaths continued. In April 1813, word came that Dr. Rush had died. Thomas's young daughter died, and then John Quincy and Louisa Catherine's daughter perished in Saint Petersburg, Russia, on the same day that Moscow surrendered to Napoleon Bonaparte. On July 26, Nabby arrived so frail that she had to be carried into the house. The cancer had returned and was eating up her body. She suffered until August 15, 1813, passing at the age of forty-nine.

Abigail, though frail and in ill health, continued to care for her family. There were a lot of them, gathered around the parents at the home in Quincy. Charles's widow and his children lived there, as did Louisa Smith, the daughter of Abigail's alcoholic brother, William. Grandchildren roamed about, with many fewer expectations placed on them than on their parents. Abigail even allowed them to blow bubbles in one of John's pipes, leading her to declare that the bubbles were as "fleeting as life's hopes and ideals." [23]

As Abigail grew older, she feared she would become senile. It was a humiliation her pride would not have to endure, but her body, susceptible to illness during her entire life, finally had enough. On October 28, 1818, just shy of her seventy-fourth birthday, she succumbed to typhoid fever. Her final words were that if she could not be useful, she did not wish to live.[24] John, her "dearest friend," was there, too, visibly shaken and wishing he could lie down beside her and die, too. But characteristically, when he noted that Louisa Smith, the niece who had been like a daughter, was even more distraught, he crossed the room to console her tenderly.

When Abigail's remarkable last will and testament was read, her lifelong devotion to other women became ever more apparent. There were no bequests to men, but each woman in her life was gifted with clothing or jewelry, real estate, stocks in bridge companies, or cash. She overlooked no one. Even in death, Abigail would micromanage her estate.

John Quincy's wife, Louisa Catherine, had never been comfortable around Abigail. Their relationship had been strained from the first, when Abigail had thought her too frail and fancy to be a good wife to her son. After Abigail's death, Louisa and John Quincy began reading Abigail's voluminous correspondence. Louisa discovered a remarkable mind and an extraordinary character. Abigail's forthright views on women's issues and the evils of slavery impressed the soon-to-be first lady who, because of changing social mores, was expected to be a mere ornament and often felt as confined as a slave herself. "If particular care and attention is not paid to the ladies," Abigail had written to John Adams in the year of the Declaration of Independence, "we are determined to foment a rebellion, and will not hold ourselves bound by any laws in which we have no voice, or representation." [25] Louisa Catherine, who would be an outstanding first lady herself, was saddened that she had not had a closer relationship with her mother-in-law.

RECLAIMING THE WHITE HOUSE

John Quincy Adams, in the shadow of a giant, had forged a remarkable career. He had served as a diplomat, as a senator, and finally in 1817, as secretary of state for President James Monroe, where he had crafted the enduring Monroe Doctrine. In 1824, in a bitterly fought presidential election, he had lost the popular vote but won the White House when the contest had been thrown into the House of Representatives. The loser, Andrew Jackson, would grow in national popularity and haunt John Quincy's four years in power, much the same way that Thomas Jefferson had affected his father. It would in some respects be a bitter replay.

Yet, at his inauguration, for a moment in time, the Adamses' ambition could take some satisfaction in the turn of events. For the first time in American history, a son of a president had been elected. No one in the family could miss the sense that this represented an astounding vindication for them all. Thomas Jefferson sent a letter of congratulations to John Adams, and John replied that his "kind congratulations are solid comfort to my heart." [26]

The second Adams White House tenure was a repeat in personal dimensions as well as political. John Quincy and Louisa Catherine began to pay the same price their father had paid, with a toll on their children. Two of their sons were battling alcoholism. Old John Adams thought that the "affliction" had been "visited on the family to check its pride." [27] Perhaps regretting some of his own decisions, he would write his president son John Quincy, counseling him that "children must not be wholly forgotten in the midst of public duties." [28] But the warning would come too late.

In the last months of his life, John Adams would develop a bond with his grandson, George Washington Adams. He had been a bit offended to see one of his own named after Washington, whom he respected but felt wholly unworthy of the unrestrained hero worship of the nation. George Washington Adams had sought him out, and the grandfather had responded, sensing that the pressure on this young man, whose father and grandfather were both presidents, was taking a toll.

As the fiftieth anniversary of the signing of the Declaration of Independence neared, John Adams and Thomas Jefferson grew too frail to keep up their renewed correspondence, except by dictation. "The little strength of mind and the considerable strength of body that I once possessed appear to be all gone," John wrote, "but while I breathe I shall be your friend."[29] Both old statesmen were determined to live to see the anniversary of the declaration. It would be touch-and-go.

On June 30, some local dignitaries called on John, asking for a toast that they could read in his name at the local celebrations. "I will give you 'Independence forever!' " John exclaimed. Was there anything more he'd like to add? "Not a word," he replied.[30]

The following day, John Adams was too weak to rise and could barely speak. His family tried to make him more comfortable. On July 4, he awakened and was told that it was the Fourth of July. In a clear voice, he said, "It is a great day. It is a *good* day."[31] Late in the afternoon, he roused and whispered, "Thomas Jefferson survives." He was wrong.

A similar scenario had been taking place at Monticello. Thomas Jefferson drifted into and out of consciousness, periodically awakening to ask, "Is it the Fourth yet?" He died about one in the afternoon on July 4, 1826.

It had been raining in Quincy all throughout that momentous afternoon. Just as John Adams died peacefully at 6:20 P.M., there was a clap of thunder and the sun broke through the clouds. "Bursting forth," John Marston would write to President John Quincy Adams, "with uncommon splendor at the moment of his exit."[32] The grandson, George Washington Adams, was at the former president's side, sobbing in grief.

The nation would rejoice in rather than mourn the deaths of the two great statesmen. The manner of their passing, countrymen said, proved the benediction of God on a grateful United States of America. John Adams, in life always desiring recognition and gratitude for his great sacrifices, received it in full measure at his death.

COMPLETING THE TASK

In time, John Quincy's son, George Washington Adams, would be claimed by the same devils that had destroyed his uncles—the inability to live up to expectations and the bottle. In 1828, John Quincy Adams would be defeated for reelection. Andrew Jackson would sweep to a landslide victory. The Adams White House was packing its boxes for the move back to Massachusetts when word came that the body of

George Washington Adams had washed up onshore in New York, an accident or more likely a suicide.[33] Meanwhile, John Quincy's other brother, Thomas Boylston Adams, also fought his own demons. He had detested law, wanting to go into business and even seriously contemplating going off to the frontier with John Quincy. But law it was, and he had become a judge—and like his brother a raging alcoholic. He would disappear for days on drunken binges, then return as if possessed, threatening his wife and children. Charles Francis Adams, John Quincy's son, thought him one of the most unpleasant people in the world, "a brute in manners and a bully in his family."[34] Eventually, in March 1832, Thomas, too, died of alcoholism.[35]

John Quincy Adams determined not to follow his father to a bitter retirement. In 1830, against all advice from family and friends, the former president returned to the fray and a second career as a U.S. congressman from Massachusetts. He would serve a remarkable seventeen years, tying up many loose ends of the Adams legacy. One of the more remarkable stories would result in the birth of the Smithsonian Institution. John Quincy, grandson of Deacon Adams, a man committed to education, and son of John, who had written the idea of "encouragement of literature" into the Massachusetts State Convention, would play a pivotal role.

The family had long recognized that the people of a country— both men and women—must be educated in order to be truly free. One of John Adams's great fears about the French Revolution—rightfully so, as it turned out—had been the fact that so many French citizens were illiterate. In later years he had written to Thomas Jefferson about the matter, "The first time that you and I differed in opinion on any material question was after your arrival from Europe; and that point was the French Revolution. You were well persuaded in your own mind that the nation would succeed in establishing a free republican government. I was as well persuaded, in mine, that a project of such a government over 25 million people, when 24.5 million of them could neither write nor read, was as unnatural, irrational and impracticable as it would be over the elephants, lions, tigers, panthers, wolves and bears in the Royal Menagerie at Versailles."[36]

Now, years later, serving in the House of Representatives, the old former president John Quincy Adams would wade into an uproar over money bequeathed to the United States to promote education.

In 1829, an Englishman named James Smithson died in Genoa,

Italy. The illegitimate son of the first duke of Northumberland and a widow of royal blood, Smithson had been educated in the best English schools and had inherited a fortune when his mother had died. Highly talented, he had become a noted scientist and researcher in chemistry, mineralogy, and geology. But even with riches, intelligence, and talent at his disposal, he could never escape the social stigma of being a bastard. "The best blood of England flows in my veins; on my father's side I am a Northumberland, on my mother's I am related to kings, but this avails me not," he wrote. And then he vowed, "My name shall live in the memory of men when the titles of Northumberlands and the Percys are extinct and forgotten." [37]

When he died, his last will and testament exacted what would be a fitting, ironic retaliation. After settling a life estate on a nephew, "nameless like himself," [38] his will read as follows: "I bequeath the whole of my property to the United States of America, to found at Washington, under the name of the Smithsonian Institution, an establishment for the increase and diffusion of knowledge among men." Scholars claim not to know why Smithson chose to gift his estate to America. He had never visited, nor did his papers reflect any particular admiration for, the country. It is, however, interesting to note that his half brother (the legitimate one, no doubt), Lord Percy, was the officer who had attempted to relieve British troops on their bloody, disastrous retreat from Lexington and Concord.

In July 1835, the news of the bequest caused an uproar in the United States. Jacksonian Democrats were outraged that the United States would have to become a claimant in an English Chancery Court. Some, like Henry Clay, thought it was "beneath the dignity of the United States to receive presents of this kind of anyone." [39] As one might imagine, John Quincy Adams took an entirely different tack. Intrigued, he made inquiries at the British Legation about Smithson's life and was "coldly received." [40] Never one to take no for an answer, John Quincy did precisely as his father would have done: he interviewed every English visitor he could find until he knew all there was to know about James Smithson. Adams saw enormous possibilities.

Soon, former president John Quincy Adams was in the U.S. House of Representatives, serving as chairman of a select committee tasked with considering the bequest. John Quincy proposed a bill authorizing the president to prosecute a suit in Chancery Court for the legacy, based on an "imperious and indispensable obligation" to Smithson's wishes.[41] With his usual unflagging, bulldog tenacity, he finally wore down the opposition. Andrew Jackson appointed Richard Rush as special agent to go to England and get the money. When he returned, Rush had in his possession $508,318.46 in gold. Later, $54,165.38 was added to the pot.

Now the question was, What to do with the money? Everyone had a favorite theory. Richard Rush begged for an institution that would distribute free garden seeds. Others wanted a great public library or an agricultural experiment laboratory. Some people wanted another university. John Quincy favored the establishment of an astronomical observatory and lobbied hard for its acceptance. The former president was met with ridicule for his idea of a "lighthouse in the sky." In no event, he told President Van Buren, should there be "jobbing, no sinecures, no monkish stalls for lazy idlers."[42] It was John Quincy's dogged persistence that kept the project focused and saved the Smithsonian fund from being frittered away and lost forever. He relentlessly introduced bills in the House that were voted down. He tried to hold committee meetings when there was often no quorum. He wrote, delivered, and published lectures to expose the threatened betrayal of the bequest, the danger that politicians would slice away big pieces of the funds in pork-barrel schemes.

Finally, in 1846, an act was passed providing that the Smithson money be placed on permanent loan to the United States and that only the interest be used for the support of the "Smithsonian Institution." James Smithson, whose name now lives "in memory," got his wish. John Quincy Adams, in his wildest imaginings, could never have dreamed that his perseverance would one day produce the modern Smithsonian.

In a humorous aside, John Quincy got his revenge, as well. By the time of the Smithsonian act, a government observatory had also been established, although he would derisively note that the funding for it had been "clandestinely smuggled into the law, under the head of a depot for charts."[43]

The legacy of Abigail Adams was just as powerful for John Quincy. Throughout his lifetime he would reread her letters, and they would solidify his opposition to slavery. In the House of Representatives, he would relentlessly, mercilessly use the powers of his enormous intellect to fight, badger, confound, and thwart the proponents of slavery. He had tirelessly fought against the "gag rule," which made it impossible for citizens—mostly women—to present petitions against slavery, and against the Mexican War, which he had perceived as a ploy to add more slave acreage to the United States.

On February 21, 1848, at eighty years of age, he entered a ringing vote of "No!" to a bill of thanks to generals of the Mexican War. Immediately thereafter, he suffered a stroke at his desk in the House. He would never return home again, dying in the speaker's office two days later, still in service to his country. John Quincy Adams, too, had complied with—and exceeded—the desires of his father.

On November 2, 1800, the day after John Adams had moved into the mansion that would come to be known as the White House, he wrote Abigail a letter: "I pray heaven to bestow the best of blessing on this house, and on all that shall hereafter inhabit it. May none but honest and wise men ever rule under this roof!"[44] Many years later, President Franklin D. Roosevelt would have the words lettered in gold in the marble over the fireplace in the State Dining Room.

The children of Deacon John Adams and his choleric Puritan wife, Susanna, had given much to the nation, and the nation had often misunderstood and rejected them. Most of the children had suffered for it. But there was a singular line of exception, starting with John and Abigail and reaching on past John Quincy Adams into future generations. This line had fulfilled the most optimistic expectations of Deacon John and Susanna. "You will comply with my desires," he had ordered the stubborn little boy who had wanted only to be a farmer, and he had birthed a great American political dynasty.

PART TWO

———— ★ ————

THE ENIGMATIC RISE
OF ABRAHAM LINCOLN

——— ★ ———

SIX

Forged in a Crucible:
Abraham Lincoln and His Father

My early history is perfectly characterized by a single line of Gray's Elegy: The short and simple annals of the poor.[1]
—Abraham Lincoln

According to legend—and almost anything written about this young man is shrouded in unreliable legend—Abe Lincoln took a canoe down the Sangamon River in the summer of 1831.[2] He was a twenty-two-year-old, wide-eyed, gangly oddity from the backwoods of Illinois, and he took his canoe to the dock of the small village of New Salem. Lincoln had left behind family and home, striking out on a life of his own.

As the good people of New Salem would later tell the story, they had seen their fair share of peculiar creatures emerge from the woods, but all would later insist that this one had been a bit more alien than most. He was exceptionally tall for the times and suffered from a sunken chest and an ugly face, prematurely lined with wrinkles.[3] His worn, patched pants barely reached mid-ankle, showing a good six inches of his shins. This young fellow wasn't just poor, he was *wretchedly* poor. And, again according to the legend, he was dirty from his travels.[4] The pretty girls on the street openly laughed at him. But the stranger didn't seem to mind; he actually carried himself with dignity, and he exhibited a self-confidence that belied the absurdity of his appearance. Abraham Lincoln had worked his whole life for his father, dutifully turning in every penny. Now he was finally free. Nothing and nobody would spoil the pure pleasure of his newfound independence.

Young Lincoln was looking for Denton Offutt, a man who had promised him a job. So he asked around town in his shrill, singsong, soprano voice that was such a mismatch with his grave, lined face that it sometimes startled people. It so happened that Lincoln's first day in New Salem, Illinois, was election day and the entire county was out on the streets.[5] Lincoln joined right into the conversations, telling a funny story about a lizard that had crawled up a preacher's pants in the middle of his sermon.[6] The story was not remarkable as Lincoln's went, but there was something in the telling that so amused the listeners that the story and the report of the young man who told it became a delightful nugget of gossip for a sleepy town. Forty years later, townspeople could still recount the tale and their first impressions of the dirty, lanky, poor youth. When he had stepped off the dock and walked into town, he had been openly ridiculed for his appearance, but before the day was over he had morphed before their eyes into an enigmatic figure of fascination. And that, according to legend—reconstructed after Lincoln's assassination, when the nation revered him as a secular saint—was only his first day.

Within a week, Lincoln's boss, Denton Offutt, was bowled over by his new employee. During the day he would leave Lincoln alone at the store and slip away to talk to anyone who would listen. This newly hired, backwoods oaf was a virtual walking library, he told them. He could quote scriptures and literature verbatim. He knew just about any fact one could ask, and every spare minute the boy was reading another book. People soon saw Lincoln in public so engrossed in a book that he would read while he walked down the street, sometimes stopping to chuckle at what he was reading, oblivious to man and beast around him.

It didn't take the young men of the region long to test the tall, awkward-looking newcomer, as young men will do, but there was great surprise at his strength and tenacity in a fight. His sunken chest and tiny, shrill voice could throw a man off. He had swung an ax since the age of eight, and there were powerful rippling muscles on the shoulders and arms underneath his shirt. Within weeks, there materialized a veritable cottage industry of gambling, with new feats of superhuman strength spurring on new challenges, and money flying back and forth, with the smart ones always putting their bets on Abe. He quickly became the recognized town champion. Men came from fifty miles around to wrestle him. They always lost, but he always ended the match with some good-natured story and gentle smile to his opponent. Before the summer was over, Lincoln had demonstrated that he could outrun, outwrestle, and outwork any other man in the county. Denton Offutt was publicly telling people that Abraham Lincoln would one day be the president of the United States.[7] And this about a young man who was so poor he still didn't own a decent pair of shoes or even his own bed to sleep on. In the backroom of Offutt's store, Lincoln was sometimes forced to share a cot with complete strangers passing through town. When one turned over in the night, they both had to turn over.

Lincoln's famous reputation for honesty was supposedly established early during his time in New Salem. When a woman was accidentally overcharged six cents, he dutifully walked six miles after work to return her money.[8] People quickly crowned him with the sobriquet that he would carry all the way to the White House: "Honest Abe."

For all the interest he had aroused, Lincoln was still a loner. According to later testimony from neighbors and friends, he didn't drink whiskey or play cards with the boys, but there was no doubt that he was trusted and had found a new home. Increasingly, he was asked to judge their horse races and chicken fights and use his astounding "country wisdom" to settle their personal arguments.

When New Salem formed a debating society for the cultured class and anyone wanting to better himself, Abe Lincoln joined and gave his first public speech. James Rutledge, the president of the society, was very impressed. This was more than a young man with amusing tales to tell. There was something profound, even great, coming from some reservoir deep inside the lad. All he needed was some refinement and culture, but that was inevitable with a mind like his. He was a twenty-two-year-old youth on his first experience away from home, yet a complete stranger could sense his greatness.

Later, when he traveled to Springfield to inquire about a new job, the wife of a prospective employer was horrified. She asked her husband about the gawky, gangly, poorly dressed young man who had just been in their home. "He is a freak," she said, "downright ugly."

"Yes," her husband admitted, "But don't be fooled by his appearance. There is nothing common about this man."[9] Indeed, in 1831, there was a growing sense throughout the community of New Salem,

Illinois, that the young man, Abraham Lincoln, was only passing through, that he had a unique destiny.

What had brought Abraham Lincoln to this point? Though Lincoln scholars stress that any of the early references to his life and character is pure conjecture—including his own politically expedient, autobiographical accounts—there is hardly a testimony from a neighbor or friend that does not comment on how out of place he was, as if he were from a different planet. And most testimony would insist that the seeds of greatness were already apparent. Even derogatory comments from his impish cousin Dennis Hanks, such as the charge that Lincoln was so lazy he would spend a whole day reading a book, affirm what legend persists in telling us. And what Lincoln was apparently appeared very early in his life.

The people of New Salem insist that when they encountered him, the package was almost complete. In fact, parts of his first speech in that community are so sophisticated and so mournfully philosophical that they are sometimes confused with things he would later say as a lawyer and president. He had no formal education, no material resources, no wise and accomplished mentors. How had his character developed? Where had he found such maturity, patience, and integrity? Where had he developed his intellectual strength? Was it in the blood? What role had his parents played? Lincoln himself often pondered those questions.

THE DARK SIDE OF THOMAS LINCOLN

Thomas Lincoln was reportedly a dull man but considered by his neighbors to be honest and a steady plodder.[10] Using Hardin County neighbors as his sources, historian Louis Warren described him as "a worthy Kentucky citizen and devout Christian."[11] Most early historians described him as poor, as Lincoln himself did, but revisionists challenge that. In 1814, he owned enough land to be ranked fifteen out of ninety-eight in Hardin County.[12] Much is made of the fact that he was always being cheated out of his farm. Carl Sandburg, whose works on Lincoln have become literary classics, called him a "careless man."[13] But Kentucky land titles were uncertain. Wealthy outsiders who could afford the hated lawyers were always stealing a man's land. Thomas Lincoln's frustration and poverty were endemic to the time and place.

Even so, there was a dark side to Tom Lincoln that could not fully be justified by his circumstances. One wonders about his constant "bad luck." He sold his Kentucky farm for twenty dollars and forty barrels of whiskey. Currency was worthless; barter was everything. When he moved his belongings upriver to Indiana, his flatboat allegedly capsized, sending household goods, tools, and valuable whiskey, the precious currency of the frontier, to the bottom of the river. Only a small part of it was recovered.

There is no doubt that Tom Lincoln could sometimes be rough on his son. Dennis Hanks, the cousin who later lived in the same cabin, referred to Tom's "cold and inhumane treatment"[14] of young Lincoln. According to Dennis, the father sometimes knocked his boy to the ground.[15] This happened in front of visitors and sometimes before complete strangers, whenever Abe would ask questions.[16] It was apparently embarrassing to Tom. Either he felt his son was disrespectful for speaking out of turn—children were to be seen and not heard—or he felt demeaned that he didn't have all the answers to his son's endless inquiries. Of course, the Lincoln boy was also routinely thrashed for various offenses by both the father and the mother. The biblical admonition "Spare the rod and spoil the child" was a philosophy that conveniently covered a multitude of parental sins of anger. Lincoln accepted the whippings as the right of a parent, and he never spoke of his father's beatings. We have only the record of Dennis Hanks, who says that Lincoln never answered back or reacted in any way other than quietly weeping alone.[17]

Over the years, hundreds of books have been written about our sixteenth president, and just about every kind of theory has been postulated and challenged, but few seem to dispute Dennis Hanks's statement that Thomas would "sometimes knock him over."[18] Rather, historians have differed on the significance of the incidents, whether they were severe enough and frequent enough to offset Thomas Lincoln's good qualities, and whether they were out of the norm of the violence of frontier life. David Herbert Donald, Benjamin Thomas, and Michael Burlingame, highly respected Lincoln historians, move quickly through this testimony, as does Charles Strozier, a pioneer in psychohistory. Still, they all include the account. If it is true, there may be something unique to these incidents, unique in that they never happened to Dennis Hanks, an illegitimate nephew who for a long time lived under the same roof, nor to Sarah, Abe's older sister, who was called Sally, nor to any of Tom's stepchildren by his second wife.

Some historians suggest that Thomas Lincoln occasionally yielded to doubts about the paternity of his son. There were such rumors throughout the community. Even the mother's devout religion was used against her. After all, this Nancy Hanks, mother of young Abe, was in fact a bastard herself, it was said, the product of a wanton relationship. Didn't the worst sinners later become the most religious, the most grateful for their redemption? Even today, there is debate about her lineage.[19]

The rumors were fed by the physical differences between the father and son. Thomas was supposedly five feet, nine inches tall; Abraham was six feet, four inches. Thomas, at 185 pounds, was considered heavy.[20] His son was described as skinny. And then, after his own namesake died at the age of two, Thomas could have no other children. Even when he later married the fertile Sarah Bush, there were no further offspring.

Tom and Abe were famously opposite in personalities. While both men were honest, had incredible strength, and could tell a good story, Abe was a lover of books and people. Thomas, on the other hand, disdained what he called "eddication" and usually had no time for small talk. As they grew older, the son seemed to make a point of being different, rejecting the two most important philosophical expressions of his father's life, his religion and his politics.[21]

Though many of the great Lincoln biographers are satisfied that Thomas Lincoln was indeed the father of our sixteenth president, William Herndon, Lincoln's law partner, suggested that Tom actually caught Nancy in adultery with Abraham Enloe, the man who was whispered to be Lincoln's true father, and that it helped provoke the move to Indiana. I mention it here only because some revisionists have provided the times and places that make Herndon's story physically possible and the same authors who reject Herndon on this accept many of his other early accounts of Lincoln's life. As has often been pointed out, there would be no biography of Lincoln's childhood without Herndon. And so one must, at least, include his suspicions on this matter as well.

After the assassination of Abraham Lincoln, when his deification was in full bloom and people who knew him were still living, biographers and journalists tracked down the various rumors of Nancy Hanks's infidelity and debunked them one by one. Their work was good enough for most historians, and it was generally accepted until the 1960s, when other studies began to relentlessly chip away, showing that the "facts" about dates and places that had been used to discount the theories were sometimes bogus. One rumor, which was rampant during the Lincoln presidency, held that the true father was Abraham Enloe. A Kentucky neighbor, the infamous Mr. Enloe would have been only a teenager at the time of conception, but that was certainly no disqualifier. Enloe reportedly resembled Lincoln and had his large ears and nose and extralong arms. As an old man, Enloe publicly denied the story, but he privately told close relatives that he was likely the father. In fact, Lincoln himself acknowledged that he was named not only after his grandfather but after this very Abraham Enloe, as well.[22] He explained that the family had owed much to the neighborly Enloes. If so, there was soon a falling-out, with a great ruckus between Tom Lincoln and the Enloe family. Supposedly, this was one of the reasons why old Tom gave up his fight for his land and moved across the Ohio River into Indiana.

Historians William Barton and Louis A. Warren probe this issue ad nauseum, with Warren making an effective case against the Enloe theory. More convincingly, Lincoln authority David Donald believes that the evidence for Enloe is slight.[23] For our purposes, it doesn't really matter whether Thomas Lincoln was the biological father of Abraham Lincoln or not. What matters is that there were seeds of doubt, and if Tom was a dull, angry, primitive sort of man, he may well have been tormented by them.

Other historians, wanting to put Tom's parenting style into context, remind their readers that the frontier itself was violent. There was a public whipping post in Elizabethtown, Kentucky, where white men as well as black men were whipped on their naked backs.[24] In 1805, Tom Lincoln had taken a job in Hardin County and been paid six cents an hour for "catching and whipping recalcitrant slaves."[25] When, as a rash youth, Abraham Enloe actually made a public boast that he was the father of Abraham Lincoln, Thomas supposedly fought him viciously, biting off a piece of his nose and afterward, according to one dramatic account, spitting blood and Enloe's nose out of his mouth.[26]

In 1819, after his wife, Nancy Hanks, died, Thomas Lincoln returned to Kentucky, leaving little nine-year-old Abe and his eleven-year-old sister alone in the wilds of the Indiana woods. The journalist Ida Tarbell saw nothing significant in this absence, and historians all point out that he went to find a new wife, but the trip back to Elizabethtown took only seven days.[27] Tom Lincoln was gone six months. When Tom returned with a new wife, Sarah Bush, Abe Lincoln ran to this strange woman and hid himself in her skirts, ignoring his father, who had been away for half a year.

There is a poignant story that Lincoln told about leaving home and heading out to live a life of his own. He was walking past a farm when he heard shouting and screaming. A woman was beating her children. Young Abraham Lincoln approached the farmstead to see a father cowering on the side while an angry woman thrashed away. Lincoln, perhaps hoping that his interruption might change the mood, asked if he could help, but the woman—understanding his intention full well—was only enraged further.[28] Lincoln walked away sadly. It is revealing that this particular story, an account of parental abuse, would be Lincoln's most persistent memory from his very first day away from his father and out on his own.

Lincoln's own parenting style may provide further evidence of the abuse he suffered. He was indulgent to an extreme, even to the point of absurdity. His law partner, William Herndon, complained that Lincoln's children would come into the office on Sundays and pull all the law books off the shelves, but Abe would only laugh and carefully rebuild his library each Monday morning. The two men were once engrossed in a close game of chess, reaching the breaking point, when one of Lincoln's boys tipped over the whole tray, sending chess pieces scattering. Lincoln only laughed. Cabinet officers were outraged when Lincoln would leave a meeting suspended while he escorted his young son on a promised carriage ride around Washington. Lincoln, the wise man who led the nation in its bloodiest war, didn't have the heart to discipline his own children.

Finally, there are the few letters Lincoln sent home, usually to his stepbrother and always ending with a request that his love be passed on to "Mother" while pointedly ignoring his father. When all of these stories and pieces are added to his refusal to attend his father's funeral, they add power to the argument that he had been affected by any abuse he might have received. As an adult he would say, "I know what it is like to be a slave."[29] Psychologists I consulted during this project suggest that it is likely such beatings occurred before Dennis Hanks started living with the family. A father who felt free to knock his son to the ground in front of witnesses, they argue, would feel even less inhibition when alone. Nor would the severity and frequency of such events have been a factor. Even one such occasion could traumatize a child, and Dennis Hanks was apparently a witness on a number of occasions.

Regardless of how one characterizes Thomas Lincoln—as an abuser or a disciplinarian appropriate for his times—all historians agree that there was an estrangement between him and his son. Such an estrangement would not be attractive for a man in public life, so Lincoln, the politician, ignored it for the most part. Still, he would offer nothing positive about his father. When historians promoted the idea that Thomas Lincoln had moved to Indiana partly because he opposed slavery in Kentucky, an argument well documented by the testimony of neighbors and friends, Lincoln broke his silence on the subject of his father, openly discounting the idea. Normally a magnanimous man who had little interest in personal glory, Lincoln was not willing to allow his father even that small moment of history.[30]

Yet very little has been written about how the bouts of abuse—or discipline—shaped the life of the sixteenth president. It is widely accepted that his famous melancholic personality stemmed from the early loss of his beloved mother and then his older sister, who died young in giving birth to a child. But certainly those losses were more keenly felt when they left him alone with his unaffectionate father. And how does an abused son feel about himself? Lincoln's backwoods cousin Dennis Hanks may have made the best observation of all, simply saying that after a thrashing young Abe was "quiet and sad."

A MAN OF THE SOIL

Who was Thomas Lincoln, the father of our greatest president? And what motivated him? He was born to Abraham and Bathsheba Lincoln on January 6, 1778, in Rockingham County, Virginia. Young Tom was one of five children, the third son in the family. It was a dangerous time: the Revolutionary War was on, and parts of Virginia were still experiencing raids by infuriated Indians.

In 1782, still seven years before George Washington would be

sworn in as president, the Lincoln family moved to what they expected
to be greener pastures in Kentucky. But this new land in Kentucky was
covered with forests. Clear land and pastures were wrested from nature
only with great effort. It was in those woods, at the age of six, that
Thomas Lincoln experienced the defining moment of his life. He had
tagged along with his father, Abe, and his brother Mordecai to help
clear a plot of land. A lone Indian brave, moving stealthily through the
woods, took a clean shot and killed the father. According to family
lore, the Indian brazenly stepped into the clearing, picked up young
Thomas as his prize, and started off. But his brother Mordecai responded coolly, running to a nearby cabin, where he picked up his
rifle, took careful aim, and felled the Indian with a single, well-placed
shot, thus saving the life of the future father of America's sixteenth
president.

One can only speculate on the impact of such violence. Tom spent
his formative years being passed from the home of one relative and
friend to the next. By the age of sixteen, he was on his own, fighting
Indians, hunting for runaways slaves, and taking on odd jobs, while
learning the craft of cabinetmaking.[31]

It is common for early historians to describe Thomas Lincoln as
shiftless and lazy. Sandburg describes him more diplomatically, saying
that he was a man who lacked initiative.[32] In recent years he has gone
through a rehabilitation of sorts. It is pointed out that in 1803, at the
age of only twenty-five, Lincoln bought a 238-acre farm on Mill
Creek in Hardin County, Kentucky. And he paid cash.

Now established, young Tom felt sufficiently confident to march
into nearby Elizabethtown, Kentucky, to find himself a wife. For years
he had had his eye on one Sarah Bush, but she turned him down flat.
She would marry Daniel Johnston, a man who had once worked for
her father.[33] But Tom's second proposal succeeded. Nancy Hanks, a
local seamstress, agreed. And so Tom Lincoln and Nancy Hanks were
married and settled on the Mill Creek farm. Their first child, Nancy
"Sarah" Lincoln, was born February 10, 1807. Their second child,
Abraham Lincoln, was born two years later.

It is very likely that the tension between the father and son played
a role in Abraham Lincoln's intellectual development, the reading of
books, and the pursuit of knowledge, a trait that is almost exclusively
credited to his mother, Nancy Hanks, and to his stepmother, Sarah

Bush, who would follow. Some psychologists theorize that Lincoln was likely pursuing his books not only to better himself but also to escape his painful life. And then there was the chance to "break" from his father, for one of Thomas Lincoln's few philosophical gifts to his son was his lifelong conclusion that "eddication" was worthless. It would be an ongoing contest between the two men. Thomas would insist that it was all a waste of time; Abe would pursue it relentlessly. It was a soft rebellion on the young Lincoln's part and a soft rejection of the father who "knocked him over."

As a boy, Lincoln, the future great debater, was choosing safe ground on which to fight back. If the ignorant backwoods farmer, who had three times miscalculated on the ownership of his own land, rendering worthless the years he had spent clearing and plowing and laboring to build something, wanted to insist that reading and writing had no merit, well, that was ground the young Lincoln boy would fight on. The whole of society and his mother would back him up. According to this theory, with every book he read, he was spitting in the face of the father who was beating him and who thought such activity frivolous, only an escape from reality and hard work.

There is more. The whole issue of "reading books" was an equally appropriate device for Nancy Hanks to vent her frustration at her husband and escape the poverty that was all around her. Poverty was endemic to the frontier life, but Thomas could reportedly carry it to absurd lengths. One story has her reduced to using thorns to hold her dresses together, buttons being beyond the reach of their pocketbook, even while Tom wore silk suspenders, purchased on credit at a store in Elizabethtown.[34] She once said, "I would rather my son would be able to read the Bible than to own a farm, if he cannot have but one."[35] It may have been a mild rebuke for her husband, who was constantly losing the ownership of his farms, and she did not talk just about "reading" but rather "reading the Bible," which ratcheted up the moral level of the argument. What could Thomas say?

The debate over education worked both ways. If, as a boy, Lincoln used it to distinguish himself from his father and to mock him, later, when Lincoln was an accomplished adult, the father would use his ignorance to mock the son. Old Thomas Lincoln, ever stubborn and convinced of his own opinion, would go backward, regressing, and, in so doing, belittle Abraham's achievements. As a young man, Thomas

Lincoln could read and write—at least according to some sources—while his "intelligent" wife, Nancy, could only read, but in latter years he began making his mark with an X, stressing the point that learning to read and write had been a waste of time. One could do just fine without it. He too could have pursued education with the best of them, but he had learned that it was all a sham. This regression would cause historians no end of confusion. Many authoritative accounts make the claim that Thomas Lincoln had always been illiterate.

There are great irony and frustration in this father-and-son relationship. Old Tom, like any other father, must have longed for admiration and respect from his son, and he must have concluded very early on that he would never get it. Education had been the enemy. Education had taken his son. How could he compete with the heroes in Lincoln's books? How could he be more honest than Parson Weems's idealized, false characterization of George Washington or more Christian than the protagonists in John Bunyan's *Pilgrim's Progress*?

Meanwhile, young Abe had been elected to the U.S. Congress. There were rumors that he would make a good president, rumors that would have been enthusiastically carried deep into the forests, to the front door of his father's cabin. But for all his acclaim, Abraham Lincoln, like any other son, needed his father's approval. Thomas, on the other hand, would never get the respect he needed from Abe, and so he would never acknowledge that his son's pursuit of a better life had borne fruit. It was the only weapon left in his arsenal to hurt the little boy who had defied him by hiding behind his mother's skirts and reading books for hours.

For his part, Abraham Lincoln had not just become educated. He had become a lawyer. He had joined the enemy. This was the very class of people who had again and again robbed his father and friends of their lands, destroying their dreams, rendering worthless their years of labor. He had rejected his father's politics and religion, as well. For both Thomas and his son, this was not just a debate on the merits of education or books or learning or shirking work, this was about power.

When Abe Lincoln finally slipped out of his father's clutches and left home, his father supposedly told a visitor, "I s'pose Abe is still fooling hisself with eddication. I tried to stop it, but he has got that fool idea in his head, and it can't be got out. Now I hain't got no eddication, but I get along far better'n ef I had. Take bookkeepin'—why, I'm the best bookkeeper in the world! Look up at that rafter thar. Thar's three straight lines made with a firebrand; ef I sell a peck of meal I chalk a black line across, and when they pay, I take a dishcloth and jest rub it out; and that thar's a heap better'n yer eddication."[36] The visitor was deeply impressed with Thomas Lincoln's homespun wisdom. But old Tom's "wisdom" had long before been discarded by the son. Young Abe had had enough.

When twenty-two-year-old Abraham Lincoln walked out of his father's house to head out to New Salem, Illinois, and a life of his own, Thomas must have known that it was too late. He had lost the debate, and he had lost his son as well. Life was a puzzle for Thomas Lincoln. When the old man turned deathly ill, Abraham Lincoln, the lawyer, former congressman, and renowned public figure, would not come back to his father's bedside. He had made an earlier visit, and it had been painful. After ignoring numerous letters, Lincoln finally wrote his stepbrother, admitting that he had received the correspondence but just hadn't taken the time to answer. "Say to him that if we could meet now, it is doubtful whether it would not be more painful than pleasant."[37] Only days later, Tom Lincoln would die. His famous son would not attend the funeral. Lincoln may have privately determined that he would no longer let his father hurt him, but it is almost certain that even from the grave, Thomas continued to strike out at his son again and again, till the end of Abraham Lincoln's life.

———— ★ ————

SEVEN

Nancy Hanks:
A Mother of Mystery

*"Be kind to each other and to your father
and live as I have taught you."* [1]
—The dying words of Nancy Hanks Lincoln

If the story of Thomas Lincoln is elusive, at least there are occasionally documents to offer parameters. The story of Nancy Hanks, the mother of the president, is absolute myth. And it is a legend altogether different from that of her husband. Historians find it almost impossible to define this woman. She was both tender and tough, a good girl and a bad girl—or was it a bad girl turned good? We know that as a young woman she had a questionable reputation, that she was accused of "pushing the envelope" of propriety. It was a trait that helped attract Tom Lincoln, who had no time for etiquette any more than he did for "eddication." At the same time, she was known as deeply religious, always reading her Bible and only occasionally venturing into the pages of a newspaper.

Most intriguing was her young experience as a wrestler.[2] It was said that she could throw a man in a fair fight, a trick that inspired locals to take sucker bets from strangers passing through. The clerk of the Grayson court was said to have fought her repeatedly, losing almost every time. One must suspect that if it were true, the clerk probably enjoyed his bouts with the backwoods dominatrix or he would not have been willing to relive the humiliation again and again.

If she wrestled with men, she could hardly have been squeamish about their anatomy. Thus there were dozens of rumored affairs, which sprang up like crabgrass when her son became a candidate for president. Some of the stories were authenticated by respected locals, including some by the country judge. There is, of course the issue of Abraham's paternity.

If Herndon was right, if Nancy sometimes sought tenderness and intimacy she was not finding at home—if there was an affair with the famous Abraham Enloe, for example—she would have surely carried that fact to her grave. For all his faults, Tom Lincoln was a much better man that the worthless, shiftless Enloe, who lived with his sister, a notorious prostitute.[3] A life with Enloe would have likely meant living in a brothel with two prostitutes instead of one. And if Abe were the son of another man, there may have been times when the fanatically religious Nancy would have resented him as a reminder of her sins, a source of anger or denial. But we are told that she was only loving to Abraham, and if that cannot be proved there is certainly no other contrary evidence or examples of inconsistency.

One of Lincoln's most famous quotes, and one that appears earlier in this book, states touchingly, "All that I am or ever hope to be I owe to my angel mother."[4] The statement was made to William Herndon, Lincoln's law partner, as they traveled to the circuit court in Menard County, Illinois, to argue a case involving paternity. The case supposedly included arguments about identity and the inherited qualities of a bloodline, such as temperament and intelligence.[5] Lincoln was solemn and quiet on the trip, and when he spoke up, it was to announce that his success in life was likely the accident of a complicated genealogy. His mother, Lincoln said sadly, was a bastard, born out of wedlock, the result of a union between a wealthy, educated Virginia planter and his own poor, uneducated grandmother. Lincoln, who often wondered how he could have turned out so differently from his father, credited this bloodline with his success, and that was behind his famous statement that all he was or ever hoped to be he owed to his mother. "God bless her," he added. Then he asked Herndon, "Did you ever notice that bastards are generally smarter, shrewder, and more intellectual than others? Is it because it is stolen?"[6] He was speaking of his mother.

The problem with this famous story, which is so important in the life of Lincoln that some of the most famous biographies open with its telling, is that it may not have happened at all. Like so many other early Lincoln tales, there are inconsistencies waiting in the wings to run it off stage. In this case, researchers at the Abraham Lincoln Presidential Library have recently made the point that no such case was ever on the docket of Menard County in the first place. Could it have been lost? In another county? An exaggeration? A real conversation reconstructed wrongly by faulty memory? Pure Herndon fiction? So we are back to telling the early Lincoln story the only way it can be told—by pure faith. It is an American presidential myth.

According to the myth, Nancy Hanks was born in Virginia out of wedlock, her mother, Lucy, a promiscuous young girl who had allegedly once caught the eye of the great General Lafayette while he was visiting the Burton Parish in Williamsburg as the guest of the local hero, George Washington. If it happened, it was her one moment of glory, for it was apparently downhill ever after. Lucy allegedly had an affair with a distinguished tobacco planter, a Washington neighbor, but when she became pregnant he refused to marry her. Nancy was born out of wedlock and immediately passed on to her grandparents. Lucy, unencumbered by her baby, was apparently unrepentant and more provocative than ever. Fornication was an indictable offense, giving birth to a bastard a misdemeanor.[7] When the community became aroused, the grandfather—the patriarch of the Hanks family—deemed it wise to move them all west. We cannot prove this story, but this is the popular legend.

It was not an easy feat, moving a whole family, but the strenuous move and the new environment were wasted on the unquenchable Lucy Hanks. Nancy's wanton mother was involved in further fornication, this time in the new community. When it became a public issue, with demands for legal action, they all moved even further west, deep into the Kentucky frontier. Finally, one Mr. Henry Sparrow put Lucy Hanks out of her misery, agreeing to marry the infamous nonvirgin from Virginia. Lucy dutifully settled down to the role of frontier motherhood. Nine babies came in quick succession, with enough work to exhaust her passion.

Meanwhile, her illegitimate daughter, Nancy Hanks, lived with her grandparents until the grandfather died, when she was passed onto Lucy's sister Elizabeth, who had conveniently married another member of the very same Sparrow family. According to some disputed accounts, this was when Nancy grew tall and strong and sometimes found herself in wrestling matches with other women and men.[8] It was indeed the wild frontier. But her aunt Elizabeth Sparrow allegedly helped break the cycle and start the ball rolling toward greatness when she took the time to teach Nancy to read the Bible. It was a source of great comfort to Nancy Hanks. Years later, when she saw her son lonely and in pain, she would know the solution. Yet another vocation sent Nancy on the path toward Thomas Lincoln. Lucy's sister also taught her how to sew, to earn her own way as a seamstress, and it was through this work that she encountered the man she would marry.

Thomas Lincoln had learned some of his carpentry skills at the feet of one Joseph Hanks, Nancy's uncle, and so the two had seen each other in the little frontier towns and knew each other by reputation. Thomas Lincoln did not often drink or curse, meaning that there were occasional exceptions to this self-discipline. Nancy was known as a bright, kind, and religious young woman, who was also no pushover when aroused, as witnesses to her exploits of wrestling could attest. The physical descriptions of her are contradictory. Some local residents remember her as being five feet ten inches and weighing in at 140 pounds; others insist that she was "small, dark and pretty." [9]

Nancy Hanks was working as a seamstress for Richard Berry in Washington County, Kentucky, when Tom Lincoln stopped by to ask for her hand in marriage. He had already broached the subject with Sarah Bush, the daughter of his former slave patrol captain, but she had turned him down flat. So a great deal of emotional energy was riding on Nancy's decision. [10]

The fact was that she had few options. If we accept the story as is, there was no father to give her away or quiz the prospective groom. She probably had no dowry. Yes, by some accounts she could read and sew, and she could wrestle, whatever value that represented. But that was about it. Thomas Lincoln was not a bad catch. He had just purchased a 238-acre farm on Mill Creek in Hardin County, Kentucky. And so they were married in the log cabin of her boss, Richard Berry, on June 12, 1806. Thomas was twenty-eight; Nancy was twenty-three.

The next February Nancy "Sarah" Hanks became their first child. They called her "Sally." Since she appeared before the requisite nine months, rumors spread that the wedding had been a necessity and that Tom's wife took after her mother. Worse would come; some people would later suggest that good ol' Christian Tom had married her only to cover up someone else's mess. Such was life in a small community.

THE BIRTH OF A PRESIDENT

In 1809, the family moved again, this time to the 300 acres of the so-called Sinking Spring Farm, named for the spring bubbling from a cave on the property. The water was convenient, but the land would eventually prove unfit for farming. While living off wild game that he would kill and Nancy would clean and cook, Tom built a log cabin. It was eighteen by sixteen feet with no windows and only a dirt floor. It was built just in time, for Nancy was pregnant again. According to neighbors and relatives, she rested on a mattress of corn husks on a bed held up by poles, a necessary protection from the rats and snakes. It was on this bed, on a snowy, cold Sunday morning, February 12, 1809, that Nancy Hanks, the illegitimate seamstress from the backwoods of Kentucky, gave birth to America's greatest president. Witnesses said that the wind whistled and snow blew through the cracks in the log cabin walls, but Nancy and the baby were buried beneath a warm bearskin blanket. Periodically, the weakened mother would reach out to brush the snow from the bearskin.

Abraham Lincoln had little recollection of his years in Kentucky. A younger brother, Thomas, was born but died two years later. When Abe was seven, his mother sent him to his first school. Even Tom was apparently pleased with the idea. The teacher, Zachariah Riney, was a Catholic, but Abe had permission to leave the cabin when religion was discussed.[11] School lasted three months.

If we know little of the details of the life of Nancy Hanks, we know much about the lively culture of her frontier region. During the Kentucky years, friends and relatives remember seeing Tom and Nancy at the Methodist camp meetings, which could attract as many as a thousand people in the middle of the wilderness. People issued down from the little trails in the wooded hills like streams pouring into an ocean. Each cabin had its favorite singer and each region its star banjo picker. There were famous cooks and famous preachers, but only the best were featured at these grand gatherings. The performers, who had exhausted their pies and cakes and sermons and banjo songs on the locals, rose to the occasion, suddenly invigorated by a new audience and stimulating competition.

According to later eyewitnesses, these were great experiences for Nancy Hanks, a short relief from a life of incessant work. Most people had never heard more than two banjos playing together at the same time, but according to witnesses, the old Methodist camp meetings could boast an "orchestra" of hundreds. The very earth and trees would vibrate to the rhythm. And when a mass of people broke into singing, it sent chills down the spine. Nancy Hanks Lincoln, by all accounts, had a beautiful voice and must have thrilled at letting it go, hearing her own lusty sounds, embraced and protected by a choir of so many others. They sang inspiring songs of the hereafter, songs of immortality, where even death was fearlessly dismissed with bravado.

During these Kentucky years, Thomas Lincoln had been deeply impressed with the arguments and passion of an antislavery Methodist preacher named Jesse Head.[12] This man had local roots, hailing from nearby Springfield in Washington County. And perhaps best of all, Jesse was a cabinetmaker on the side, which Thomas admired. Perhaps Tom was tormented by his days hunting runaway slaves, men whom he had been required to beat with a whip after capture. So at first the Lincolns leaned toward the Methodist faith and the antislavery preacher. But it was exhausting, the endless reexamination of their lives and the fear of eternal damnation. Eventually the Baptist doctrines proved seductive. The Baptists preached a version of John Calvin's ideas—that, once "saved," one could be forever assured of salvation. The world was preordained, and nothing could interfere. Nancy became devoted to this concept. It brought comfort and some relaxation to her life to think that she could not change its outcome. Their poverty, if one accepts the argument that Tom was poor, was not his fault. And the rumors that spread about her promiscuity were a burden she must bear.

The doctrines of John Calvin, revised and amended for use in the frontier state of Kentucky, would have their ultimate test in the issue of slavery. The Baptists argued that the slaves too, were preordained for their plight. Hadn't Paul told slaves to work hard for their masters and masters to treat their slaves kindly? This was too much for the Lincolns, who joined a small, persecuted branch of Baptist Separatists who opposed slavery. There were things ordained by God that could not be changed by man, they agreed. But who was to say that God himself could not ordain the change? They had opened a small crack in the rigid wall of Calvinism, one that would soon prove useful to Nancy. And so, in 1816, they determined to move away from the slave state of Kentucky to the newly planned free state of Indiana, where they wouldn't have to compete with landowners who owned slaves and where the ownership of the land was guaranteed by the local government. They would make a new beginning—but poverty would pursue them across the river.

When Tom went ahead of his family to make his claim and prepare a place to live, Nancy took Sally and Abe to visit the grave of his little brother. The picture of his mother, mourning quietly over the child she would be leaving behind, was a memory etched deep in Abe's mind.[13]

Young Abe Lincoln would spend the next fourteen years of his life in Indiana, most of it clearing land. He would be wielding an ax by the age of eight. But fight as they would, the Lincolns could never create quite enough farmland to make it work. As in Kentucky, survival depended on the hunting of wild game. Life was lived one day at a time, and if Tom got sick, even for a day, they might not eat.

Life in America was not easy. Some convicts in England who had been offered the choice "Hang or be sent to America" had simply shrugged. "Hang me."[14] And the thickly wooded, newly declared state of Indiana was the frontier at its most harsh. Settled after Kentucky, Indiana had a population of fewer than three persons per square mile. Those first years were unexpectedly cruel. Tom built a three-faced camp into the side of a hill, with two sturdy trees and log poles to hold up a roof of sticks covered with brush. There was no floor and no need of a window or door, for the entire third side was open. It would be their home until he could build a cabin.

Throughout the winter of 1816–1817, claimed by one historian to have been the worst on record, they would be exposed to all the elements, wind, rain, snow, sleet and hail.[15] They would sleep on beds of leaves and bearskins, curled up in the two corners of their open shed "like dogs," as someone said, listening to the cry of the wild animals, and always, fearfully, feeding the important fire that burned at the entrance.[16] If the fire grew too hot or the wind shifted fiercely, it could consume their three-sided shack of sticks and take their lives, but if it died out they would freeze or be food for the bears and wolves that prowled the woods all around them. Years later, offering an interview to a journalist, Abraham Lincoln still marveled at the dangers they had faced during those years.

Historians differ on how long they suffered in the three-sided shack. Sandburg insists that it was a year, but he is almost certainly wrong.[17] It was surely the low point in the life of a very poor family. Nancy Hanks resorted to a variety of devices to escape her misery. She took refuge in her faith, invoking favorite verses of scripture, which she quoted over and over. Young Lincoln memorized entire portions of the Bible this way, catching the verses from his mumbling mother like secondhand smoke. She cooked and planted and hoed. She made candles and clay lamps and clothes and blankets. One never really finished work; one only stopped and slept for a while before beginning another day.

Years later, Abraham Lincoln, the lawyer, traveled to a small town in Illinois to help a dying old woman write her will. When the woman asked him to read a few lines from the Bible for her, he launched into several verbatim quotes, later explaining to his law partner that he had learned them from his mother, who had recited them over and over during those early years in Indiana. He quoted the Twenty-third Psalm and then repeated his mother's mantra. "You believe in God," Lincoln quoted, "believe also in me. In my father's house are many mansions. I go to prepare a place for you."[18] Afterward, Lincoln became very misty-eyed in speaking to his friend of those miserable years in Indiana, saying that just by reciting the verses he could bring his mother back to life and feel her presence.

But life with Nancy Hanks was not all tender and motherly. When young Abe fell into a creek and almost drowned and worried about his reception at home, facing his parents with wet clothes, he was more afraid of his mother than his father. She was firm, providing structure to his life. When he was wrong, she thrashed him too, as any God-fearing parent did in those days. It was considered an act of love to the children. But mostly, Nancy was remembered for her long Bible story sessions. According to some sources, she read the four gospels over and over till Sally and Abe could practically recite the words.

Sometimes, on long winter nights, when the loneliness and boredom were oppressive, Nancy would depart from the Bible to tell her children fireside tales that had been passed to her by rote and stories from the War of 1812, when, she said, she had tended the wounded. Lincoln remembered that she stressed the idea that there were no limitations in America, that a person could be or do whatever he or she wanted. This, from a woman living in abject poverty.

Nor was Nancy's great singing voice limited to hymns or the

catchy gospel melodies learned from the Kentucky Methodists. Sometimes the "religious" Nancy Lincoln would kick back and wail a bawdy tune, passed on from her wayward mother, Lucy. It was all she really had from her flesh-and-blood mother, the only connection to her roots. There were no glasses or plates or blankets or jewelry, just a few songs. Typical was the ballad of a fair maiden who inherited lands of gold. So, while the Lord was her shepherd for weeks on end, while she mindlessly labored and worked for her family, mumbling her scriptural hymns, there were times when she would open the door to a less religious past.

There was one song that breached the gulf between both worlds. Nancy would sing it at the end of her repertoire, perhaps making sure that the children were not too enthused by her irreligious entertainment. It was the mournful ballad of wicked Polly, the story of a wayward young girl, who ran wild and rejected the best advice of her parents.

> *I'll turn to God, when I get old,*
> *And He will then receive my soul.*

But wicked Polly was struck down in her youth without a chance of repentance. She called her parents to her side and lamented her horrible fate:

> *When I am dead, remember well,*
> *your wicked Polly screams in hell.*[19]

Was Nancy's song a retelling of the story of her own mother? Was it only a warning to her own children, advice, packaged in good humor, from a devout woman who in spite of vicious gossip to the contrary had actually kept her faith intact since those youthful days when she had found such comfort in reading the Bible? Or was she boisterously celebrating her own life and her own narrow escape from perdition, thrilling in the knowledge that she had beaten the odds and was now a Baptist, assured "a mansion yonder."

Amazingly, the malicious rumors about Nancy Hanks eventually found their way onto the desolate little trails deep in the wooded Indiana wilderness. There was no escaping. After the assassination of Lincoln, when biographers descended on those isolated cabins to harvest every scrap of information, one Laurinda Lanman, a Lincoln contemporary, told an interviewer, "My mother liked [the Lincolns] but she always said that not only was Nancy Hanks an illegitimate child herself but that Nancy was not what she ought to have been herself."[20]

Regardless of the theory, whether she was wicked Polly turned nice Nancy or nice Nancy surviving with good humor and optimistic faith the cruel sentiments of the wicked society around her, she was a very strong woman. Either journey required a remarkable and resilient personality. Tom Lincoln was muscular, tough, and ignorant and dominated his son, but if Nancy Hanks Lincoln stood her ground, Tom Lincoln surely would have heard warning bells in his head and backed down.

So in 1817, during the worst winter of her life, Nancy Hanks was poor and hopeless, living in a three-walled shed, working tirelessly, day after day. Her Baptist Separatist belief allowed no dancing, drinking, or cursing. It warned her that life was capricious and did what it would. Weak humans were moved by God like pawns on a chessboard for reasons they would learn only in the life hereafter and maybe not even then. But when she was told that a new school was opening, only nine miles away from them, she was uncharacteristically roused to action. Was this not fate too? And did not God expect some action on the part of his own creation? If a slave could become free, could not the ignorant become wise?

According to legend, this was her moment. Nancy Hanks Lincoln, we are told, seized the leadership from her stubborn, abusive husband and announced that Sally and Abe, both of them—the daughter, too— would be going to school. Thomas, who had approved of schooling in Kentucky, now sneered at the folly of sending his kids eighteen miles a day for nothing. Both Sally and Abe were big enough to work, and he complained about it often but, rightly sensing Nancy's passion, backed down and let her have her way.

It was called a "blab school" because learning was achieved through public recitation. The students learned to spell or define new vocabulary words or learn their multiplication tables by repeating the facts aloud, over and over, all at the same time. It was a tumultuous din of noise, but a fearsome teacher with a whip could know who was working and who was not. It was as if the children's minds were turned inside out and the teacher could hear them thinking aloud and memorizing their work.

Having lost the battle, Thomas Lincoln may have allowed himself a vicarious thrill at seeing his son march off to school, for on that first day he is remembered as saying "You're a gettin a real eddication. Your a–goin' to larn readin writin and ciperhin." But his enthusiasm did not last. His boy was lazy, he told neighbors. School was a ruse to get out of work, he told his wife.

The legend insists that Nancy remained steadfast. As long as the school operated, she would send her children—which, as it turned out, wasn't very long at all. According to Abraham Lincoln's own account of his life, his combined lifetime education both in Kentucky and Indiana amounted to one year. But this modest experience represented a window of hope for Nancy's children and through them for herself. It offered a change in the rhythm, a chance to break out of the endless cycle of poverty and misery that smothered any dream of a better life. Abraham would remember his mother preparing him for school, scrubbing his face and behind his ears, building his excitement with her own enthusiasm: "You larn all ye kin, Abe." She would kiss him, and he would take his big sister's hand and begin the nine-mile walk through the forest.

NANCY HANKS LINCOLN GOES HOME

There is debate about just when the new Lincoln cabin was finished. Some accounts suggest that the family moved into it unfinished and extrapolate from Abe's own autobiographical account to "prove" it. At the latest, they would have moved into the place shortly after the opening of the school. It was one room, eighteen feet by eighteen feet, with a dirt floor, no windows, and a bearskin hanging as a front door, but, added to the exciting prospect of an education for her children, it must have seemed to Nancy that her life was showing some signs of God's goodness.

Then came the biggest surprise of all. Again, reader, beware. The timing is suspect, and there are a dozen different versions, some with the event happening earlier and some later. Nancy was at the door of her new cabin one day when a family on a wagon appeared in the clearing, only a few yards away. There were cows trailing along behind. During these years no one passed by the Lincoln cabin. It was the end of the line. The trail into the desolate farm was not made for wagons and represented a grueling engineering feat to navigate. These people could only be coming to visit the Lincolns.

Tom and Elizabeth Sparrow were Nancy's closest living relatives and her dearest friends. This was the aunt who, according to family history, had taken her in as a girl, teaching her how to read and sew. It is hard to think of anything that could have brought more joy to her lonely life. The Sparrows were bringing along their adopted son, Dennis Hanks, Elizabeth's seventeen-year-old illegitimate nephew.[21] Dennis had lived near the Lincolns in Kentucky and had been in their cabin, at Nancy's side, the very day that young Abe had come into the world.

The Sparrows had suffered the same land title problems that Thomas Lincoln had and had decided to start over in Indiana. It had to be better than Kentucky. They settled into the three-sided shed that the Lincoln family had just abandoned. They would build their own cabin and farm and the two families would be neighbors and there would be milk to drink! As it turned out, the milk would almost kill them all.

There flourished in that part of Indiana a tall, lush, poisonous plant called white snakeroot. The cows feasted on it, passing its venom on through their milk. For many years, even into modern times, the origin of the so-called milk sickness defied explanation. All that was known at the time was that some people fell ill to the disease and others escaped. There was speculation that it had something to do with cows and their milk, but this was a vague notion and no one could imagine the connection to the luscious weeds growing in the woods all around them.

By the late summer of 1818, the wife of the nearby bear hunter Peter Brooner fell ill. Nancy Hanks made the trek up to their cabin, saw the telltale white mucus on her neighbor's tongue, and then nursed the woman for a week. Mrs. Brooner endured sharp pains to her stomach and vomited so violently that she collapsed in exhaustion afterward. Nancy was with her to the end, when her eyes rolled up into her head and she lapsed into coma. It was not an easy death. Watching her neighbor die must have made Nancy conscious of her own mortality and how much her children needed a healthy mother. If she were to die, what would become of them all?

There was an evil omen before the end of that summer. Abe Lin-

coln was kicked in the head by a mule and lay bleeding and unconscious. He would later claim that he had been "killed for a time."[22]
For several hours he could not speak, but he soon recovered. His
mother, bracing herself against the pain of such a loss, was philosophical about it all, leaning deeply into the comfortable embrace of her
Calvinist instincts. God would do what he would do, and nothing
could change it. "It was not your time, Abe," she said when he recovered, and life went on.

In the fall, the milk sickness struck Tom and Elizabeth Sparrow.
The dreaded white secretion was detected on their tongues, and the
sharp pains to the abdomen began soon after. They were both dead
within a week. Tom Lincoln dutifully crafted two crude coffins while
young Abe carved the pegs that would hold the boards together.

They were buried in a clearing on a beautiful hillside, a quarter of
a mile from the cabin, in the middle of a deer run where the animals
raced by to a watering hole at the end of a meandering creek. Nancy
would have to have felt great shock and pain at the loss. It would have
been much better to have heard of their death in Kentucky, far away,
than to have had them come here, brighten her lonely days, laugh with
her for a few months, and then practically die in her arms. In her pain,
she likely thought ahead to the summer, when there would be a break
in the weather and the work and she would have the time to return
to the graves of her surrogate parents and pursue the mystery of
God's providence. But God's providence would quickly choose another direction.

There are numerous accounts of when and how Nancy discovered
her own illness. Some suggest that she was literally taken on a sled
from the deathbed of Mrs. Brooner, the bear hunter's wife.[23] Most have
it occuring immediately after the loss of her aunt and uncle. In any
case, she was soon in her bed of leaves and corn husks, buried in
bearskins, crying out for water as her stomach burned. She knew what
was coming, and she knew that mercifully it would be over within a
week. She retched and suffered, sweating in between her worst fits. She
whispered Bible verses until she was too weak and then asked the children to read them for her. "Yea, though I walk through the valley of
the shadow of death, I will fear no evil."

Nancy knew from her experience with the disease that her ra-
tional moments would be limited, that her life could now be counted

in hours. So she asked the children to come close to her bed. She ran her clammy fingers through Abe's hair and offered barely audible words of motherly advice. She told them to be kind and good to each other and to their father. She told them to live as she had taught them and to "worship God."[24] She dipped into and out of coma during those last days, her bodily functions shutting down. The "milk sickness" was predictable. The patient always died on the seventh day. Sally and Abe hoped for a miracle. They cried over their mother and prayed for recovery, seizing on any murmur or groan as good news. But just as in the case of all the others, on the seventh day of her illness, October 5, 1818, Nancy Hanks Lincoln passed on. Tom put copper pennies on her eyes to hold them shut and immediately started working on her casket.

Years later, Dennis Hanks told interviewers that the misery in that cabin had been indescribable. The children, Sally and Abe, had cried out, "Mammy, mammy," clinging to her cold, lifeless body, but there was no reply. They had heard their mother describe death in her Bible stories. They had seen it come to their animals and most recently to their uncle and aunt. Shortly after moving into their new cabin, Abe Lincoln had pointed a rifle between the log slats and shot a turkey unwittingly wandering nearby.[25] It had made him sick, he later said. He would never kill a large animal again. He took no pleasure in death. "An ant's life to it was as sweet as ours to us," he once lectured a playmate.[26] But nothing prepared him for this loss.

Charles Strozier sees guilt and Oedipal tension in Lincoln's telling of the turkey story, pointing out that it comes awkwardly and seemingly unrelatedly in his short autobiographical sketch, right before the death of his mother.[27] It suggests that Lincoln felt somehow responsible for her death and carried this burden for some time.

His mother had been the only tenderness in a harsh world where wolves and bears sought to devour men and giant trees and rocky soil yielded their treasure, only to brute force. His father had knocked him to the ground when he had asked a question of a stranger passing by, but his mother had been his window to a life beyond the horizon, to places and people he could imagine only from her fireside stories. As much as he could understand, that window was now closed forever. There was only the darkness of the forest.

Years before, in the summer after the birth of her baby Abraham,

Tom and Nancy had taken their family to a Methodist camp meeting. One or two banjo players had begun picking a familiar tune. Soon dozens of others had recognized the verse, joining in, strumming all at once, while a blend of hundreds of voices gently lifted the melody into the nighttime sky. She had been young then, and not yet so worn by her work. According to the testimony of neighbors who saw her there, Nancy was joyously abandoned to song, either because she believed that God had forgiven her sordid past or because he knew the truth of her innocence. And when they had reached the chorus and the words that the whole crowd could all easily remember, words they had hummed alone to themselves over fires and cooking pots all year long, they broke into a giant choir, the volume renting the heavens with their voices:

> *You may bury me in the east,*
> *You may bury me in the west,*
> *And we'll all rise together in that morning.*[28]

The story of Nancy Hanks Lincoln, however true or false it may be, has become an important tale in our national history. It may reveal more about us than her. Bewildered by the spectacular rise of such a great and brilliant man from such remote and limited circumstances, early witnesses and historians distorted the story of this woman far beyond our ability to reconstruct it accurately. Even the exact location of her grave is debated, though most accept that thirty-four-year-old Nancy Hanks Lincoln was buried without a funeral or gravestone in the grassy knoll next to Tom and Elizabeth Sparrow.

After burying his mother without a word or any fanfare, an angry, grieving, nine-year-old Abraham Lincoln sat down and wrote an eloquent letter to an old Kentucky preacher who had admired his mother's saintliness and sagacity. Days afterward, nine-year-old Abraham Lincoln could be seen sitting on his mother's grave, weeping at his loss.[29]

A few weeks later, a letter from David Elkins arrived, announcing that he would come to hold a service for the departed Nancy Hanks Lincoln. Word spread through the woods that a preacher was coming, and on the appointed Sunday, a rather sizable crowd of almost two hundred people arrived from the surrounding region. According to

Carl Sandburg, Elkins was an elder in the Methodist Church.[30] Other historians insist that he was a Baptist preacher.[31] In any case, regardless of his denominational pedigree, David Elkins rose to the occasion, describing with feeling the spirit and saintliness of Nancy Hanks.

According to witnesses, at the end of his sermon the audience fell to their knees, a tribute far more appropriate than any of them could have realized. Nancy Hanks Lincoln had given birth to the greatest figure in American history. She had inspired him with her stories of a world beyond the poverty and ignorance that would eventually suffocate every other childhood figure around him. She had worked and toiled, and he had felt her pain and would use his power to free 10 million slaves with the stroke of a pen. So passed from this life, unheralded and unacknowledged by the powerful and the mighty of her generation, the "angel mother," the woman who had helped shape and inspire the life of Abraham Lincoln.

— ★ —

EIGHT

A Wonderful Stepmother: Lessons in Love

She has been my best friend in this world and
no one could love his mother more than I love her.[1]
—Abraham Lincoln

The only intimate witness to life in the cabin after the death of Nancy Lincoln is the famous cousin Dennis Hanks. And while there are plenty of reasons to doubt him, much of what he would later tell hungry writers would be confirmed by Lincoln's stepmother. According to Hanks, after the death of Nancy, the light went out of her children's lives. As desperate as they had been before, they were soon reduced to living like animals. Not only was Abe deprived of his mother's tenderness, but, having lost her role as protector, he was subject to the whims of his boorish, hard-driving father. Sally grew so lonely that in the night she could be seen sitting by the fireplace, rocking back and forth and sobbing.

The Lincoln cabin turned into a mother's worst nightmare. Sally and Abe made an effort but were soon overwhelmed. One historian, drawing on descriptions of other cabins in similar straits, described it as dark and foul, swarming with vermin, the beds of corn husks and bearskins filled with fleas.[2] The workload for nine-year-old Abe and his eleven-year-old sister was unrelenting, but their very survival depended on it. Tom and Dennis Hanks had to hunt to keep them alive, but Abe and Sally kept the water coming and did all the skinning and cleaning and cooking and mending. Eventually, even Tom could not endure the filth. He washed himself in a creek, put on his silk suspenders, and left his two young children behind, heading out for Kentucky to find something better, maybe a new wife to bring home.

Many historians have offered descriptive accounts of the frightful and desperate life lived by the two youngsters, but aside from Dennis Hanks, there was only one known visitor who spoke of that period. A neighbor made the trek up to their cabin and found them living in squalor, skeletal, caked with dirt, and existing on dried berries they had picked earlier in the year. As the months passed, the children concluded that they had been abandoned. Young Abe Lincoln said later that he had been convinced they were dying.

In the cold days of late December 1819, six months after he had left, Thomas Lincoln returned to the Indiana cabin with a wagon led by four horses. There was a woman in the wagon, and she had three children. Tom had returned to Elizabethtown, Kentucky. There he had learned that a young lady to whom he had once proposed marriage, Sarah Bush Johnston, was now a widow living with three young children in a modest cabin. According to her granddaughter, Harriet Chapman, Sarah was tall, attractive, and vivacious, with a mischievous sense of humor. She had rejected Tom as a youth, but he had apparently never forgotten her.

According to the carefully reconstructed story of his courtship, Tom Lincoln had gone straight to the point: "Mrs. Johnson, I have no wife and you no husband. I came a-purpose to marry you . . . I've knowed you from a gal and you've knowed me from a boy. I've no time to lose; and if you're willin' let it be done straight off."[3]

Sarah explained with sadness that such an arrangement would have to wait. She had debts, and she would need to resolve them first. It might take some time. But Tom had apparently been working and saving money during his summer away from Indiana. He asked for the list, marched around town paying them all off, and on the next day, December 2, 1819, an impressed Sarah Bush Johnston became Mrs. Thomas Lincoln.

There was a telling moment at the arrival of Tom Lincoln with his new family in Indiana. Abe did not run out to greet his father, the man he had known all his life and whom he had not seen for six months. Instead, the now ten-year-old boy buried himself in the skirts of the strange woman, Sarah Bush Johnston. Starving for warmth and womanly tenderness, he would call her "Mama." And she would return his affection. It was practically love at first sight.

Christmas 1819 was a time of wonder for Abe and Sally. Their new mother had brought with her a wagonful of luxuries. There was a walnut bureau that had cost the staggering sum of forty-five dollars.[4] There were a table and chairs, a spinning wheel, sets of matching dishes and glasses, and complete sets of silverware. Most remarkable of all were the pillows and plush bedding and blankets. Various historians offer descriptive accounts of young Lincoln sleeping for the first time in such softness, but it is not likely that Sarah laid out her clean bedding immediately. Sarah's later narrative of those first days confirms Dennis Hanks's description of a filthy cabin with a dirt floor.

Off and on, Tom had nurtured a lifelong infatuation for the widow Sarah Bush, and she was shrewd enough to exploit it while it lasted, perhaps leveraging his ardor for practical changes. She knew that he was a carpenter, so she demanded a proper wooden floor and a door, as well as a window, which would be covered with greased paper. She wanted a loft where her son, John, and Abe and Dennis Hanks would sleep separately from Sally and her girls, and she wanted a headboard for their bed. Tom accomplished it all in short order.

Sarah Bush, meanwhile, organized the Lincoln cabin into a harmonious unit. It is said that she treated her new stepchildren and her own birth children fairly, and as a result no jealousies or resentments developed, at least not immediately. She had obviously determined and planned to make the arrangement work, even before meeting the children. She had likely grilled Tom about Dennis and Sally and young Abe, the baby of the family, for she seemed to know just what to say and what to do.

The most meaningful gift to young Abe was the small library of books she unpacked. Though some historians challenge the literacy of Nancy Hanks, there was no doubt about Sarah. She could not read a word. Yet she had brought with her six new books. They could have easily been sold before she left Elizabethtown, but, hearing that Abe was a struggling reader, she had added them to their traveling inventory. The books included three volumes that were national best sellers, the popular literature of many generations, and they would forever influence and shape the character of Abraham Lincoln. There was

Aesop's Fables, which Lincoln would absorb so deeply that he would make them his own, recycling the principles in his own anecdotes, with quaint characters from the frontier and fresh plots but coming to the same conclusions. There was John Bunyan's best seller, *Pilgrim's Progress,* which helped inspire in Lincoln a knack for a well-honed allegory. And finally, there was Parson Weems's apocryphal *Life of Washington.* There is wonderful irony in the fact that the pontificating embellishments of Weems's fiction, including his imagined story of Washington admitting to his father that he had cut down the cherry tree, became inspiration for the young boy in the Indiana cabin. In a curious example of reality mimicking art, if one could call Weems's huckstering account of Washington's life "art," Lincoln would one day bring to life Weems's idealized version of the first president by becoming scrupulously honest. This honesty made for some awkward moments, but it was reinforced by the attention he received. His stepmother would later say that "he never lied to me."

Sarah Bush Lincoln faithfully fed her stepson's voracious appetite. Other books followed. She found another Washington biography and used precious money to purchase a copy of *The Life of Henry Clay* that helped set his political orientation.[5] She borrowed books from neighbors or distant schoolmasters. As long as he was willing to read them, she would try to keep them coming. When another "blab school" opened up, about a mile from the cabin, Sarah insisted, like Nancy before her, that the children attend. All four of them were enrolled, but it lasted only three months.

As a boy, Lincoln was apparently a slow reader—but then in the winter there was plenty of time. David Donald, one of Lincoln's most respected biographers, quotes a cousin describing young Abe as being "somewhat dull . . . not a brilliant boy—but worked his way by toil: to learn was hard for him, but he worked slowly but surely."[6]

Sarah Bush, ever positive, saw his ability to focus as an asset, a secret of his intellectual success. "He must understand everything—even to the smallest thing—minutely and exactly. He would then repeat it over to himself again and again—sometimes in one form and then in another and when it was fixed in his mind to suit him he never lost that fact or his understanding of it."[7]

According to Herndon, Lincoln described the subsequent years as the happiest in his life.[8] He not only recovered from the emotional

scars of his childhood, he absolutely flourished, with his stepmother
as his one-woman audience. He would call her his best friend, and he
would say that no man ever loved a mother more. Nothing seemed
to be able to disturb their mutual admiration. "I never gave him a
cross word in all my life," Sarah would later say. "His mind and mine—
what little I had—seemed to move together—move in the same
channel."[9]

Meanwhile, Abe's physical stature matched his emotional and intellectual growth. Tall and skinny, he towered over his parents. His father ominously remarked that he needed to be smoothed out with a
jack plane, but Sarah teased the boy, saying that she could tolerate his
tracking mud into the cabin but he had better wash his head because
she was not about to scrub her newly whitewashed ceiling. Shortly
after, with Sarah away from the cabin, a mischievous Abe found two
young neighborhood urchins, had them stomp through the mud near
a horse trough, and then held them upside down as they walked across
the ceiling of the Lincoln cabin. When Sarah saw the muddy foot-
prints on the ceiling, she laughed for an hour.[10] Abe then dutifully
cleaned up the mess. Such was their relationship.

In the one-room cabin that held eight persons, Sarah maintained
family harmony through her scrupulous sense of fairness. But when
Tom Lincoln began to openly criticize his son Abe for his laziness and
then began to show overt favoritism to her own son, John D. Johnston,
Sarah may have felt freer to give attention to the rejected stepson.
Years later, after she had outlived all three of the men, she would venture an opinion on her two sons: "Both were good boys, but I must
say—both now being dead that Abe was the best boy I ever saw or
ever expect to see."[11]

THE LINCOLN FAMILY SCATTERS

There was obvious sexual tension in this coed cabin of adolescents.[12]
In 1821, the population shrank by two. Dennis Hanks married Sarah's
thirteen-year-old daughter, Elizabeth, and moved to his own homestead nearby. Meanwhile, young Lincoln grew as strong as an ox.
When a farmer hired Abe and three others to move a chicken coop,
the Lincoln boy got tired of waiting, hauled the coop up on his shoulder, and moved it himself. When wielding an ax, it was commonly

known, he could do the work of two men. Legends about the Lincoln boy spread around the county. The chicken coop supposedly weighed 600 pounds.

Thomas Lincoln was thrilled with his son's strength. This was something he could respect. When the local wrestling champion of Cumberland County began hearing stories of Tom's boy, he sent over a challenge. Thomas Lincoln himself insisted that the bout take place. Young Abe beat the Cumberland tough in four straight fights.[13] Nobody had ever beaten the champion before, and he was furious. For a while it looked as if the whole mob would erupt into fighting. Thomas was at the scene, trying to whip his son into a fury as well, but if young Abe had inherited his father's strength, he had not inherited his attitude. Abe only laughed, made some good-natured comments, and shook the man's hand. The tension was broken, and the champion became one of Lincoln's great admirers.

Tom Lincoln began hiring his son out to farmers and other settlers in the area. But every penny came back to the father. Abe was big enough and strong enough to defy old Tom's wishes, but tradition, habit, and his growing sense of his own integrity kept him bound to his family.

Young Lincoln developed a satirical irreverence during these years that was a subtle challenge to the hard-core Christian theological beliefs of his father. He was circumspect about the emotional displays at the various camp meetings, which had eventually crossed the river into Indiana. Fifty years before the Pentecostals would appear in America, Abe Lincoln encountered an itinerant faith-healing preacher who mumbled unintelligible words as he prayed for the sick. On a Sunday afternoon, when a Baptist preacher stretched the emotional limits of his audience, a row of young women began to shake and dance and finally swoon from exhaustion and had to be laid out on the grass to cool off.[14] Lincoln was amused but much too respectful of his stepmother to say anything.

Only later, away from the meeting or church, would he offer his own satirical version of the service to small audiences of neighboring farmers, who would howl with delight. Many would later say that Lincoln's sermon had been better than the original. Thomas, who had grown more tolerant of Abe's stories and jokes, was often outraged by these displays, worried that the boy's antics bordered on blasphemy.

But there was always a point to what his son said, and his satire was clearly aimed at hypocrisies and inconsistencies that others vaguely sensed but could not quite define. They were laughing precisely because they recognized young Abe's questions and feelings within themselves, so when Tom upbraided his son, the neighbors would defend him.

When Abe was seventeen, his sister, Sally, married and left home. She would die in childbirth two years later, and Abe would deeply feel the loss. Some historians would insist that its cumulative impact on the young man would make it a more damaging blow than the loss of his mother and would be the mechanism for his mounting melancholia.

Shortly after Sally left, Sarah's youngest daughter, Matilda, was married. The cabin of eight was down to four. Tom was losing his sight and failing in health, depending more and more on Abe and John D. Johnston to keep the farm afloat. But Abraham Lincoln was yearning to be on his own.

In 1828, young Abe was hired out on a trip down the Mississippi River to New Orleans. It would be one of the most important early adventures of his life. New Orleans boasted a population approaching 10,000. By 1852, it would be the third largest city in the United States, and its bustling port, swelled by the slave trade, was already ranked fourth in the world. New Orleans had hosted its first Mardi Gras the year before Lincoln's arrival, and he came back filled with profound impressions from the streets of the city. Among other experiences was his exposure to slave auctions. Both fascinated and repelled, young Lincoln lingered and watched, his senses violently shocked by the scenes of inhumanity. He would occasionally refer to the experience for the rest of his life.

In 1830, at the urging of Dennis Hanks, who, with his new bride, was determined to find better land, the Lincoln family made one last move across another river, to another state. Abe, now a young adult, dutifully went along, but he was counting the months until he would be of legal age and free to strike out on his own. There is no record that Sarah Bush Johnston Lincoln wept or fretted or followed him to the river when he launched his canoe down the Sangamon River. Perhaps she loved him too much to cling to him. According to legend, when the day came, Abraham Lincoln wrapped all of his meager earthly belongings in a handkerchief, tied it to a long stick over his shoulder, and headed onto his destiny in New Salem, Illinois.

A LAST TRIP HOME

In 1842, Abraham Lincoln married Mary Todd, the highly respected daughter of a socially prominent banker in Springfield, Illinois. Neither of his parents attended the wedding, and it is doubtful that Lincoln invited them. Closing the door on his childhood meant extinguishing the light on the people he loved as well as the people who had hurt him. Throughout his life, he studiously avoided conversations about his parents and his early years in Kentucky and Indiana. When he won the Republican nomination for president and journalists and campaign handlers insisted that he fill in some of the blank spots in his brief biography, he offered his now-famous quote: "My early history is perfectly characterized by a single line of Gray's Elegy: The short and simple annals of the poor." [15]

John Locke Scripps, the senior editor of the *Chicago Press & Tribune,* was one of several seasoned writers who traveled to Springfield, trying to discover a little bit about Lincoln's youth. The *Tribune* was a Republican paper and Scripps a sympathetic ear, but he found little cooperation from Lincoln. "The chief difficulty I had," he said, "was to induce him to communicate the homely facts of his youth." [16] As I have pointed out, some of the more respected Lincoln historians debunk his one-line autobiographical claim of poverty, suggesting that Lincoln's lifestyle was typical or even above average for a family on the frontier. But that makes his claim all the more intriguing. Was Lincoln viewing his past in the context of his own spectacular ambition and thus it was poor in comparison? This is exactly the view of some historians. Or is it a rejection, an indictment of his father and his lifetime of effort as a provider, as well as an effort to repress a painful period of his life?

Years later, when Abraham Lincoln was a married congressman, with two children of his own, his father and stepbrother, the favored son, John D. Johnston, sent him a letter begging him for twenty dollars to save the farm. Thomas had an old debt that he had forgotten, Johnston explained. At first, Lincoln was appalled that the farm would be jeopardized by such a paltry sum, but then he concluded that it was more likely a scheme hatched by his stepbrother, the man so admired by Tom for his industry but rightly divined by Lincoln as a bit of a scoundrel. He sent the twenty dollars, adding the note "give my love to mother" without any expressions of affection for his father. [17]

In the winter of 1850, Abraham Lincoln's youngest son, Eddie, died. He and his wife, Mary Todd Lincoln, went into deep mourning. According to William Herndon, it was a defining moment, a turning point in Lincoln's life. The following year, on January 17, 1851, Thomas Lincoln, the father of the sixteenth president, died in Cole County, Illinois. He had just turned seventy-three years old. Sarah Bush Lincoln, his wife, was at his side, as well as John D. Johnston. Abraham, however, was still in mourning over the loss of Eddie and did not attend the funeral.

When we think of Abraham Lincoln, we think of him as a figure of history; we see him in the White House or standing with his generals in the place of honor on an army parade grounds. But when Lincoln looked at himself, what did he see? Lincoln's entire life in the White House consisted of slightly more than four years, while his life in the one-room cabin in Indiana lasted fourteen.[18]

In the 1840s, after serving as a U.S. congressman, Lincoln made a quick journey to the old Indiana neighborhood. He peeked inside the cabin and touched the carved graffiti on the logs and the nearby trees. He remembered a family that could not afford buttons or paper to write on. Sarah said he had often used charcoal for a pen and wood slabs for paper. He stood by his mother's grave. Overcome by the sensations of nature and the memories they triggered, he composed a poem:

My childhood's home I see again,
And sadden with the view:
And still, as mem'ries crowd my brain,
There's pleasure in it too.[19]

In 1860, President-Elect Abraham Lincoln made his last journey home. He visited the humble grave of his father and noticed that there was no marble stone marking the spot. Perhaps for the sake of witnesses, he announced that he would immediately correct the oversight. It was one promise that Honest Abe would not keep.

The real reason for this journey, he explained to a companion, was to visit his stepmother, Sarah Bush Lincoln. She was his last living family member, his only link to his long life in the woods. She was living with her daughter in a remote part of Illinois. To find her, the president-elect had to transfer from a passenger train to a freight train to a horse and buggy.

He and his mother had a long talk. And when he started to leave, Sarah uncharacteristically burst into sobs. She had a premonition, she told him. She had not cried when he had left for New Orleans or when he had struck out on his own down the Sangamon River. She cherished his love of adventure and would never hold him back. But this time, she said, she had a feeling that he was going to get hurt. She had carried this feeling for a long time. She admitted to him that she had prayed daily that he would lose the election. Here was a woman who loved Abraham Lincoln—the person, not the symbol of ideas or as the great hope for the future of the country. She had seen him as a little boy, likely suffering from malnutrition, caked with dirt, and emotionally devastated. She had scrubbed him clean—"to make him look human," she explained in a later interview. For Sarah, what he had achieved could not compare to who he was, and perhaps Lincoln, only days away from his inauguration, had come back home, away from the office seekers, just to experience that love one last time. He consoled her at the door of the humble cabin, telling her to trust in God and invoking all the clichés of the religion she had lived by, but nothing would stop her flow of tears.[20]

On April 14, 1865, John Wilkes Booth fired a bullet into the head of her little boy as he sat in the president's box at the Ford Theatre. Abraham Lincoln died early the next morning. By midafternoon, his body was scrubbed and cleaned in preparation for burial, just as Sarah had long ago scrubbed and cleaned it for life. Sandburg's classic account, often challenged for its factual flaws but brilliant in capturing the spiritual poignancy of the Lincoln story, describes the rolling tide of church bells that began to mournfully ring across America. A train carrying the president's body and filled with visiting dignitaries was already heading back to Illinois when someone, deep in the woods of a remote part of Cole County, Illinois, carried the message to the cabin door of Sarah Bush Lincoln: Your son is dead. Stoic and without tears, she nodded her thanks to the messenger. She had seen it coming.

Sarah Bush Johnston Lincoln, arguably one of American history's most influential figures, lived to hear of the impeachment trial of Andrew Johnson and the inauguration of Ulysses S. Grant. But national events had little meaning to a woman who lived a simple life. She had once loved a devastated, frightened, and broken little boy living alone with his sister in a cabin in the woods of Indiana. That love had changed the course of history. She died on April 10, 1869, just a few days before the fourth anniversary of her son's murder. She was eighty years old.

PART THREE

— ★ —

THE ROOSEVELTS: AMERICA'S GREATEST FAMILY

───── ★ ─────

NINE

James Roosevelt:
An American Aristocrat

My father was no snob.
—Franklin Delano Roosevelt

If there were ever American elitists—families that hid behind the veil and pulled the strings, families that remained at the pinnacle generation after generation, using their influence to pave the way for each succeeding generations and perhaps using that influence to lob the challengers off the mountain—they were not the Rockefellers, darlings of conspiracy lore. They were certainly not the Kennedys. Nor would they be the Adamses or Bushes, whose successes in public life came from in-your-face persistence by the former and a combination of feigned inadequacy and lower expectations in the latter.

The real elitists of American tradition do not exist, at least not as constituted by the mythmakers, but surely the closest thing that we have ever seen has been the Roosevelts. Although not now in the news and somewhat dormant as public figures in recent generations, they have consistently been at the top of American society and stayed there the longest of any other family in American history. By almost any definition, they are America's greatest success story.

One of the early patriarchs of the clan was an ambitious American colonial named Nicholas Roosevelt. In 1664, when Nicholas was only six years of age, the bustling village of New Amsterdam was ceded by King Charles II to his brother the duke of York. Young Nicholas Roosevelt found himself living at the very center of frontier commerce and at the birth of what would become New York City. By the time Nicholas was a young man, many fortunes had already been made in fur trading along the Hudson River and enterprising adventurers were pushing west. But Nicholas Roosevelt found no need to be original in his quest for riches. Wearing moccasins and a leather jacket, he began following the same well-established trail of success, trading with a new generation of Indians along the very Hudson River that had enriched earlier Dutch entrepreneurs.[1] In due time, Nicholas established his fortune and retired to enjoy the life of a colonial gentleman.

Nicholas Roosevelt would be the ancestor of two great American presidents. From his lineage would come both the Oyster Bay Roosevelt clan of Long Island, family of the famous Theodore Roosevelt, and the rival Hyde Park clan, family of the thirty-second president, Franklin Delano Roosevelt.

One of the more distinguished ancestors of the Hyde Park clan, Isaac Roosevelt, was born in 1752. By this time, the colonies had grown impatient and the American Revolution was imminent. Isaac had established a sugar refinery, the first in the city, and made his headquarters in a four-story building that rivaled the church steeples on the New York village skyline.[2] He helped found the first hospital, the chamber of commerce, and eventually the Bank of New York.[3] Isaac's work put him into direct competition with British-owned sugar manufacturers working in the Caribbean, and that likely contributed to his sympathies for independence. Regardless of his motivation, Isaac courageously helped organize resistance against the British and served in numerous positions in the emerging independent local government. As a result, he earned the moniker "Isaac the Patriot" and incurred the wrath of vengeful Redcoats, who were encouraged to ransack his residence and business during the war.

Isaac's achievements and personal investments were so shrewd and wound so tightly that the next three generations could afford to unravel slowly, enjoying the life of gentlemen farmers and luxuriating in eccentricity, only occasionally spurred to some successful venture to test their mettle and affirm that the Roosevelt touch was still available if it needed to be called forth.

Isaac's son James would sell much of their Manhattan real estate to John Jacob Astor and retire to farming upriver. He would build Mount Hope on the Hudson River and help establish one of the most imposing of the new American aristocratic communities. James would return the favor and have a son named Isaac, who would be even more unconventional and less ambitious than his father before him. Only after devoting years to his medical training at Princeton and winning his diploma did he conclude that his aversion to the very sight of blood would rule out such a noble profession. He intermittently worked the farmlands inherited from his father, James, and preoccupied himself with the insoluble theological mysteries of his precious Dutch Reformed Church. And finally, Isaac would marry and have a son, again named James, this one the father of our thirty-second president.

JAMES ROOSEVELT,
THE FATHER OF THE PRESIDENT

James Roosevelt, the father of the thirty-second president, was born in Hyde Park, New York, on July 16, 1828, and raised in the reclusive, suffocating atmosphere of this eccentric father. Tutors went to and fro from the grim mansion on Mount Hope. Isaac the Saint, consumed with his own righteous deliberations, fretted over his son's every decision. When James was finally sent away to school, as all young sons of gentlemen eventually were, he flourished, but his worldly interests continued to irritate and concern the father. None of the schools was completely satisfactory. First there was Poughkeepsie Collegiate and then, at age thirteen, a private school that specialized in unruly boys, located in Lee, Massachusetts. At first Isaac was impressed with the serious religious regimen of the later school. Prayers services were conducted twice daily, and the Sabbath was strictly observed to the point of fasting the whole day.[4] This benefited the school budget, and it gave literal meaning to "breakfast" on Monday morning. Still, Isaac fretted over the worldliness of the new generation.

When he learned that his son was reading fiction, he was roused to action, writing to the superintendent to complain. Isaac longsufferingly allowed that some fiction, such as John Bunyan's allegorical *Pilgrim's Progress,* had moral value, but in general he shared the legalistic conclusion of a few Dutch Reformed theologians who saw the whole new emerging genre of popular fiction as ungodly. It was by its very definition false, literature flagrantly based on the telling of a lie. James was sent to another school upstate with a headmaster who was famous for mastering recalcitrant sons of gentlemen. But regardless of the school, James continued to find outlets that shocked his serious, dourly religious father.

When James insisted on enrolling at what is today New York University, there were stern lectures and hand-wringing despair from Isaac Roosevelt at Mount Hope. An uncle from the city, sympathetic to Isaac's frustration, warned that James "will become a Dandy and will walk Broadway with his cane." Isaac finally relented, but only on condition that James live with the uncle. The arrangement lasted only one semester, and James was apparently not sober for much of it.

When he was transferred to Union College in Schenectady, New York, James joined the Delta Phi, then a newly organized secret society with headquarters in a tavern. A visitor to James Roosevelt at Union College found him and a friend laid out on the floor in a stupor, too drunk even to offer a drink to a guest.

This was the last straw. Isaac, who had been watching his son like a hawk, dutifully wrote his son a warning letter but privately despaired.

Notwithstanding his vigorous pursuit of worldly pleasures, James Roosevelt managed to graduate in 1847 and leveraged his immense popularity with teachers and classmates to offer the class oration at summer commencement.

Isaac, still scrambling to find some device to shake up his son's direction in life, decided to send him on a trip abroad. At the time many considered such an adventure the educational equivalent of a year at a university and an important passage of maturity for a young gentleman. Isaac, at his wits' end over his worldly son, decided that it was worth risking. And so James Roosevelt and his friends set out for the journey of a lifetime, traveling to Europe and the Holy Land, away from his father's eyes and ears, tasting life for himself. Isaac Roosevelt offered his departing son a scriptural warning: "We know not what a day may bring forth."[5] After seeing his son leave, Isaac wrote a reflective note to a relative, saying that the boy was now in the hands of God.

Predictably, James Roosevelt's time abroad did not provide the curative and corrective medicine Isaac had wanted for his son. There is no doubt that it achieved the purpose of scrambling things up. During one hectic summer month, James and his friends donned red shirts as soldiers of fortune in the famous army of Giuseppe Garibaldi, the

Italian liberal idealist then on his heroic quest to unite all of Italy. It is very likely that these heady weeks, packed with danger, prompted James to confront the reality of his own mortality and ask questions about what he wanted to do with his life. Garibaldi's forces were even then laying siege to Naples.[6] One thing, decided quickly, was that he did not want to die young in Italy, however noble the cause. After a short month, he and his friends wisely obtained discharges from Garibaldi's army.

In 1849, an older and decidedly more mature James Roosevelt returned to the United States, ready to take up his mantle as a member of a grand American family.[7] The Rockefellers, the Mellons, the Morgans, the Henry Fords were all yet to come. Andrew Carnegie was only a thirteen-year-old boy. But the Roosevelt family, however eccentric, had already experienced five generations of great wealth and material success.

James completed a law degree at Harvard University without incident and joined the law firm of his uncle and Hudson River neighbor Benjamin D. Silliman. In a move that would weigh heavily on his financial future, Silliman arranged for James to serve on the founding board of directors of one of the firm's new clients, the Consolidated Coal Company of Maryland. James would watch the development of this company with keen interest and later apply the lessons learned to his own enterprise.

Bored with law, James Roosevelt was soon occupied with his investments and his escalating social role among a new generation of American Protestant elitists. He moved with ease in the rarified circles of Boston, Hyde Park, and New York City. He was elected to the prestigious Porcellian Club, visited frequently at the home of Mrs. Astor, and began to court some of New York's most socially prominent debutantes.

In 1853, at the age of twenty-five, he married his cousin Rebecca Brien Howland. She not only hailed from a prominent family with the pedigree of a *Mayflower* descendent but was the daughter of a wealthy shipping magnate as well. They honeymooned at Niagara Falls, and then, after setting his investments in order, James took her to Europe for an extended time. In a cycle that would be repeated with his second wife, Sara, James and Rebecca returned from Europe expecting a child. In 1854, their son was born. Bearing the cumbersome Dutch aristocratic appellation of James Roosevelt Roosevelt, he would be known in the family as "Rosy."

The political evolution of the Roosevelt family, and James in particular, would eventually have a profound impact on the nation. The family had been Whigs for several generations. The Oyster Bay Roosevelts—Theodore's family—would graduate to the Republican Party, as would most other Whigs, including the young congressman from Illinois, Abraham Lincoln.

But James Roosevelt, perhaps sensitized by his Garibaldi experience, had no interest in noble causes—even the end of slavery—and the strident, passionate propaganda of northern abolitionists was seen by respectable socialites as being in poor taste. Mostly, James worried over his investment interests, including various potential projects in southern states. James became an open Democrat, one of the few of the Hudson River gentlemen to do so, and within time became a friend of the 1864 Democratic presidential nominee, General George McClellan. While the Oyster Bay Roosevelts agonized over hiring stand-ins for their service in the Union Army, a common practice for the rich, James Roosevelt had no qualms about it at all. He saw no great glory in risking his life for a Republican administration, however noble the cause.

When his father, Isaac, died a natural death in the middle of the Civil War years, James inherited the bulk of the estate, including the magnificent Mount Hope. A few years later, it burned to the ground, taking generations of memories with it into the ashes.

James and Rebecca bought a 110-acre estate nearby, which they named Springwood but soon began calling Hyde Park, after the nearby town. It would become the Mount Vernon of Franklin D. Roosevelt, not only as the home of his childhood but as the scene of world summits and a Shangri-La for his marathon years as president.

MAKING HIS OWN MARK

Each generation of what would become known as the Hyde Park Roosevelts had put their own unique stamp on the history of the family. Isaac the Patriot had created the wealth that had started it all. His son James, who had sold their interests in burgeoning, over-crowded New York City, had moved upriver to help establish a slice of English domesticity on the Hudson. Visiting English aristocrats were in awe of the rituals and finely re-created Yorkshire lifestyle. And James's son Isaac had more than held his own, winning the respect of the greater community for his lifetime of philanthropic Christian deeds. Isaac, who devoted much of his life to theological studies, could claim that he was pursuing interests far more important than the temporal preoccupations of the two generations that had passed before him.

James Roosevelt, son of this last Isaac, needed to find his place on this wall of imposing family portraits and do so realistically. There was more than a dash of self-denial in the conventional history of the family. His father enjoyed the luxury of practicing good deeds and pursuing unanswerable spiritual questions only because his vast inheritance afforded him the time. And his grandfather namesake, the dashing squire of the Mount Hope estate, had actually squandered the family's chance to become wealthy on a par with the Astors or even the recent upstart Vanderbilts by foolishly trading businesses and prime Manhattan real estate for the quieter life of the gentleman farmer on the Hudson. The family had not really seen the equal to Isaac the Patriot in more than three generations.

James Roosevelt set out to become rich on a truly grand and ambitious scale. The superwealthy of the Industrial Age and the so-called Gilded Age that followed were the celebrities of their time. Movie stars were yet to come, and the stage was despised as being only one step away from burlesque. Motivated to hero worship by the exploits on Civil War battlefields, the American public demanded celebrities and followed the wealthy and socially prominent families of their country as teenagers of a later era would track their favorite rock stars. They strained for newspaper and magazine glimpses inside their opulent homes and private railroad cars. They read with a vicarious thrill the details of their dinner parties and cheered or suffered with the rise and fall of their social standing. Wealth was synonymous with fame and greatness in America. The rich were rich because they worked hard and were smart or even because they were "chosen."

Teaming up with an uncle, James Roosevelt relied upon his experience in the coal industry to found the Consolidation Coal Company. It was a name quite similar to that of the start-up Maryland firm he had worked with as a young lawyer. But the plan for this enterprise called for no less than a monopoly on coal in the rich Cumberland Mountains of Kentucky and Tennessee. By 1868, Consolidation had become the largest bituminous coal company in America.[8]

His railroad holdings likewise prospered, and from them emerged an equally ambitious scheme. The mammoth Pennsylvania Railroad and other smaller New York and Connecticut companies invested millions of dollars in a project that called for a virtual rail monopoly in the reconstructed South. One by one, southern cities were linked by rail. Roosevelt, on his annual European jaunts, conspired with his old friend George McClellan. By 1872, James had been elected president of the Southern Railway Security Company and the company had successfully locked up an exclusive network of southern rails. James Roosevelt was poised to achieve superwealth on a scale of the Astors and Carnegies. It was not to be.

In 1873, America experienced a judgment of almost biblical proportions: a severe drought ravaged the Midwest. Farming was still the nation's greatest industry. By some estimates, more than 80 percent of the population lived in rural America. Not only were many farmers ruined, but thousands of the attendant service industries in rural America were forced into bankruptcy. The drought was followed by a plague of millions of grasshoppers that produced a truly strange phenomenon. The insects were crushed on the railroad tracks, creating an oozing grease that threatened rail safety and in many cases brought both passenger and freight traffic to a halt. None of this stopped the powerful James Roosevelt machine.

But in September, an overvalued stock market, burdened by a summer of natural disasters, came crashing down, taking with it Consolidation Coal and the Southern Railway Security Company. It would be called the Panic of 1873. For ten days the New York Stock Exchange was closed. America was in the throes of a full-fledged depression. In 1875, a humiliating stockholders' revolt forced Roosevelt out of his own company, Consolidation Coal, and the following year, still reeling from the setback, his beloved wife, Rebecca, died of heart trouble at the age of forty-eight. The dream was over.

THE GENTLEMAN AND HIS ESTATE

If a bad throw of dice had ended James Roosevelt's game of monopoly, there was a by-product to his work of a lifetime. After four generations of amassing great wealth without provoking public scandal, the Roosevelts had proven themselves to the elite scorekeepers of New York and New England society. Driven by Mrs. Astor and other "old-wealth" society dames, the rules that governed America's aristocratic class were as arbitrary and personal as those of any schoolyard playground. Indeed, they were not meant to be understood, lest they be exposed for their hypocrisy. It was not so much that the socialites personally favored James Roosevelt as much as the fact that they favored themselves. The reworked Victorian rules they used to justify their own social preeminence just happened to coincide with his own lifestyle and experience. The James Roosevelt family was "in."

After marrying Rebecca, James had abandoned the quaint version of the Dutch Reformed faith practiced by his father, Isaac, and had become an Episcopalian, the religion of choice for Manhattan millionaires. His annual trips to England and France always included Sundays in Anglican churches, important watering holes for the New York society herd. On November 19, 1878, his son Rosy married Helen Schermerhorn Astor, the daughter of Caroline Webster Schermerhorn Astor and the great-granddaughter of the legendary John Jacob Astor himself. A front-page article in *The New York Times* enthusiastically described the splendor of the bride's reception at the home of the Astors.[9] Coaches full of finely dressed gentlemen and ladies virtually closed down Fifth Avenue.[10] The Astors bestowed a $400,000 trust fund on their bride. For the time, in preinflation dollars, it was a fortune.

If snobbery was the norm in this world of excess and seeming regality, there were many who noticed an unattractive side to James Roosevelt's life as a denizen of society. He struck many as pompous and arrogant, riding around his estate in imported English tweeds, sporting muttonchop sideburns, and brandishing a rider's crop. Behind his back his friends laughed, saying that he was playing the role of an English lord but in fact managed only to look like an English lord's coachman. There were rumblings of mistreatment among his servants. Indeed, when Mount Hope was burned to the ground while James and Rebecca were away in Europe, investigators suspected that it was likely the result of arson by a disgruntled servant.[11]

There was a much-touted story that James and his second wife, Sara Roosevelt, had once turned down an invitation to dinner by the famous Cornelius Vanderbilt. Sara had actually looked forward to seeing the impressively decorated mansion, but James had gently explained that if they accepted the invitation to dine with the tacky nouveau riche Vanderbilts, they would be obligated to return the favor. And the idea of having the Vanderbilts for dinner at their own house was simply intolerable.

Peter Collier, in his epic account of the Roosevelt family, suggests that James Roosevelt "may have shared McClellan's bitter hatred of Abraham Lincoln and blacks."[12] Even charitable historians question James's apparent selfish indifference to the Civil War and the tumultuous issue of slavery that reached its climactic resolution right before his eyes, prompting hardly a comment or thought other than concern for his investments.

Just as disappointing are the stories of anti-Semitism in the early Roosevelts of Hyde Park. Jan Pottker's well-researched tome *Sara and Eleanor* describes one of James and Rebecca's trips to Europe aboard the Cunard Line. Rebecca's sole complaint was that they were accompanied by "the greatest number of Jews."[13] Some historians dismiss this attitude as indicative of the ignorance of the class and the age. There was a period in American history when Jews and Catholics were both routinely prohibited from the best clubs and golf courses in America, as blacks would experience long after. This was an unseemly characteristic of the White Anglo-Saxon Protestant culture, dominant in the nineteenth century and part of the partisan line of the evolving aristocracy that James Roosevelt embraced. Yet all of that does not explain its absence among the Oyster Bay Roosevelts, the family of Theodore Roosevelt.

Depressed by his failing business schemes and grieving over the loss of his wife, whose ghost called to him from every corner of his beloved Hyde Park estate, James Roosevelt began to reach out to family and friends far beyond his home. This included frequent candlelit society dinners in Manhattan and encounters with members of the Oyster Bay Roosevelt clan. He had the time for such forays. James had always wisely diversified his assets. He had never bet the ranch on any of his ambitious projects. He had developed the habits that had kept the family wealthy for four generations.

In the process of reaching out, he had developed a friendship with Bamie, sister of Theodore Roosevelt, who, as is often the case of young ladies befriending older gentlemen, was aghast when she discovered that his obsessive interest in her was more than casual. Historians often see Bamie, who was handicapped and in danger of permanent maidenhood, as a much more likely match for James than the beautiful Sara Delano, but such stories seldom burrow very deeply into his biography.

Sara was seen as haughty and imperious. Those characteristics had driven away other suitors. Though much is made of her father's exploits, her mother was equally impressive. When she was a child, her family had entertained John Quincy Adams, Daniel Webster, and Ralph Waldo Emerson. Together, her mother and father could name an astonishing thirteen different family lines that could trace their lineage back to the *Mayflower*.[14]

Nor could she be defined only as a child of good breeding. Sara had experienced the world in a way that few her young age ever had. She had been entertained in the sumptuous court of Houqua, a Chinese businessman–state official of eclectic talent and wealth, a figure worthy of a James Clavell novel. Many years later, a reminiscing Alice Roosevelt, daughter of the first Roosevelt president, would talk about Sara's early experiences in China with a tinge of jealousy, noting her tales about the great Houqua. At the time, none of the Oyster Bay clan could boast such an exotic experience.

When Bamie sat the confident, very proper, young Sara Delano at the same table with James Roosevelt, the two were almost immediately smitten. What others saw as arrogance, each saw in the other as dignity and poise. What others believed to be selfishness and egocentricity, each saw in the other as good taste and an appropriate sense of protocol. Theirs was an understanding that spanned generations.

Historians puzzled by this enigmatic romance see it as simply one between a rich old man on the prowl and a young lady in need of a father figure. Certainly, all of that was in the equation. Sara adored her father. James Roosevelt and Warren Delano II were both men of substance, both squires of the Hudson River fraternity, both directors of many of the same companies, and practically the same age. If this were only about finally clinching the adolescent Oedipal contest with her rival sisters, Sara had surely won.

But there was much more. Sara's father had won a fortune twice. In between, the family had lived on the brink of frightful, abject ruin. The insecurity of that roller-coaster ride made the Roosevelts of Hyde Park with their unspectacular but seemingly permanent wealth reassuring. Four times the torch had been passed in the Roosevelt family, covering the entire history of the United States, and always a new generation had risen to the task and maintained or increased the family estate. Sara's devotion to decorum, etiquette, and all the minutiae of their society was an affirmation of the choices and commitments James had already made in his life. Divided by a generation, this match was, nevertheless, a perfect fit for two oddly eccentric individuals with exacting tastes.

Years later, when they awakened on board a sinking ship in the North Atlantic with water streaming into their cabin, Sara calmly announced, "It appears we are going down."

Without the slightest trace of anxiety, James sighed and answered dryly, "So it appears." Whereupon Sara roused herself to assist their baby, Franklin.

"Poor little boy," Sara said. "If he must go down he's going down warm." [15] And then she wrapped him in her fur coat.

The ship eventually rode out the storm, but the dignity and stoicism with which they confronted death is instructive. What James and Sara each found in the other was a mirror of their most heroic and admirable selves, and there is no love so intoxicating as that injected with a healthy dose of narcissism.

So it was in 1880, at a dinner party hosted by the mother of Theodore Roosevelt, that Sara Delano and James Roosevelt were brought to the same table. Sara's girlfriend Bamie was uniting two soul mates for life. Throughout the evening James Roosevelt could not take his eyes off Sara Delano. [16]

They were married at Algonac, the Delano estate on the Hudson River, on October 7, 1880. After the wedding ceremony the couple was taken halfway to nearby Hyde Park in a Delano coach that stopped at the midway point, allowing the couple to disembark and enter a second coach, this one belonging to the distinguished groom. As a young wife, Sara would demonstrate a remarkably generous spirit, not only living without complaint in the home of her husband's first wife but bragging about the decor and pronouncing everything to be perfectly to her taste. Even the servants who lined up at the front door to greet them were kept, without exception. Nothing was touched or changed. And the more she impressed James, the more he doted on her.

During their first years together James and Sara led a life of quiet luxury. Beyond the sprawling 1,000-acre estate at Hyde Park, there was an apartment in New York City. Though touched by Sara's respect for the memory of his deceased wife, James bought his bride her own summer place, a hideaway off the coast of Maine on the idyllic island of Campobello in New Brunswick. When they traveled, they traveled like royalty, occupying the finest cabins on the most luxurious ships and staying at the most famous hotels in Europe. In the United States they traveled in their own railway carriage with sleeping compartments, dining quarters, and servants in attendance.

But there was obviously more to this highbrow American couple than a self-satisfied sense of their own rank. Sara was a young woman with a firm commitment to living honorably. And James could be an affectionate and caring man when his attentions were focused. He had written sentimental love letters to Rebecca throughout their marriage and was now proving to be just as tender with Sara. He was a loving father to both Rosy and Franklin. Though separated by almost a generation, the two boys could claim similar childhood memories. James was a spent man when Franklin came along, but he taught both young men how to swim and ride horses and took each of them in turn on sleigh rides in the winter and European trips in the summer.

Franklin obviously loved his father—"Popsie," he called him. Later, when the son became president, he fought for James Roosevelt's place in history, peeling off some of his own equity to buy a better image for the old man. There was no need for such a campaign other than FDR's tender affection for the person who had raised him. It stands as a stark contrast to Abraham Lincoln, who refused the chance for eager and willing journalists to cast his own father in a more favorable light.

Franklin Delano Roosevelt once said, "My father was no snob." FDR's defense of his pompous father was dutifully accepted by an adoring press and continues to be promoted by uncritical historians today, but there appears to be good political reason behind FDR's comment.

Stung by criticism that James Roosevelt had been self-absorbed and indifferent during the Civil War, FDR tried to advance the idea that his father had worked on a sanitary commission, aiding sick and wounded soldiers. The president was sufficiently popular during his lifetime to sell this idea to a fawning media. Later historians doubt the truth of the claim, and there is no record by which it can be substantiated.[17]

Likewise, Roosevelt was sensitive to his father's perceived anti-Semitism. Sara, who could be politically shrewd when it was necessary, insisted that James had said that if he were a Jew, he would be proud of it—although she would carefully add each time she told the story that there was not a drop of Jewish blood in the family.

Today, there is increasing speculation about how the prejudices of the father might have infected the son who became president. Recent declassified papers used by historian Michael Beschloss confirm that in the last years of World War II the White House became fully aware of the systematic mass murder of the Jews in Nazi Germany.[18] First Lady Eleanor Roosevelt supposedly lobbied her husband to order the bombing of the Auschwitz camps, as did Secretary of the Treasury Henry Morgenthau, Jr., himself a Jew. It was felt that the risk of collateral damage was worth interrupting the process of mass murder and might not only save the lives of thousands of people en route to the camps but give the current inmates a chance to escape to the countryside. FDR reportedly dismissed the idea with a derogatory comment about international Jewry.

Apparently, FDR felt at liberty to unload all of his Jewish phobias on Morgenthau. He reportedly warned that the Jewish admissions at Harvard should be arbitrarily limited to 5 percent and made the point about Jewish immigration that no American community should be expected to put up with the arrival of more than one Jewish family.

Meanwhile, publicly, when anti-Semites suggested that the Roosevelt family name was actually of Jewish ancestry, FDR decided that it was in his political interest to allow the idea to spread. On several occasions he made comments about the likelihood that there was both Jewish and Catholic blood in his background. Actually, the Roosevelts knew their genealogy full well. As president during a time when the discussion of race was reaching its terrible climax in Europe, outsiders and experts investigated his ancestry with impish delight, following every trail for the slightest trace of Semitic blood. The family name and ancestry were clearly Dutch and could be traced back hundreds of years. As one in-law described it in parody of the early strict religious devotion of the Roosevelt ancestors, they were "Dutch deformed."[19]

The point is that FDR loved his father, and while other presidents cut and ran when family skeletons tumbled out of the closet—rightly justifying to the family that what is good for me is good for us all—this president fought for his father's name. It was evidence of the relationship they had. Yes, Sara ran the show with her son, and yes, the father was old and fighting for his very life during Franklin's adolescence, but the early times and words they shared were sufficient to communicate a kindhearted love that would sustain the son long after the father was gone.

The birth of Franklin Delano Roosevelt was a watershed in the life of the family. After a difficult labor, Sara was warned not to have other children. It was no great sacrifice for Sara, who years later told her grandson, "We were Victorians. I knew my obligations as a wife and I did my duty."[20] In an age before effective birth control, the couple's sex life was at an end. The mother turned her affection to her newborn son. James briefly considered a public career. Indeed, for years his name had been bandied about as a congressional candidate. It had taken his active intervention to stop it.

Meanwhile, his cousin Theodore Roosevelt caused a minor scandal in the family by jumping into the fray, running successfully as a Republican for the state legislature. During the presidential contest of 1884, James raised money for the Democrat nominee, Grover Cleveland, and, when offered a concession, passed it on to his son Rosy, who received a diplomatic appointment to Vienna.

One of Franklin's earliest memories was riding with his parents in their private train car to Washington, D.C., where they were greeted by President Grover Cleveland at the White House. Incredibly, Cleveland ended the conversation by taking the hand of five-year-old FDR and announcing soberly, "My little man, I am making a strange wish for you. It is that you may never be the President of the United States."[21]

James had one last hurrah, one last business enterprise that offered a chance of immortality and stratospheric wealth. For years, engineers had contemplated a canal across Nicaragua, uniting the Atlantic and Pacific Oceans. As early as 1567, King Philip II of Spain had ordered a study of the possibility. It was not as farfetched as a look at the map of Central America might suggest. There was a well-worn route up the San Juan River and across Lake Nicaragua. In the 1850s, prospectors on their way to the goldfields of California followed this very trail. The U.S. military was considering the practicality of the idea, and with Roosevelt's investors behind the effort it just might have happened. However, in 1890 the world of James Roosevelt would be dramatically changed by events beyond his control.

LIFE WITHOUT FATHER

Franklin was eight years old when his father had his first heart attack. Historians suggest that it was an early defining moment in the life of the future president.[22] Fearful that he might upset his father and exacerbate his decline, Franklin assumed the role of a cheerful, positive, dutiful son. It would become one of the more prominent characteristics in his personality and one that would be carried into adulthood. The day would come when the voice of a calm, positive FDR would soothe and reassure the nation. "We have nothing to fear," FDR would say in his inaugural address, "but fear itself."

Concentrating on maintaining his health for the sake of his family, James took Sara and Franklin on frequent European jaunts in search of yet another health spa. Like many other people of the nineteenth and early twentieth centuries, James Roosevelt was convinced of the curative powers of mineral springs. He almost never quarreled with Sara and Franklin. Perhaps he remembered the inefficacious lectures of his sainted father, Isaac, and, anyway, life was too precious now for the slightest rancor. Every extra day together was a gift. When on very rare occasions Sara insisted that Franklin needed correction, James would intone, with feigned seriousness, "Franklin, consider yourself spanked."

Parallel to the ten-year decline of James Roosevelt was the ascendance of his famous cousin from the Oyster Bay clan. In 1897, Theodore Roosevelt was appointed assistant secretary of the navy. When an international crisis developed with Spain, Theodore resigned the post to organize a volunteer cavalry that became immortalized as the Rough Riders.

Before the year was out, Theodore Roosevelt had led the heroic charge up Kettle Hill in San Juan, Puerto Rico, bullets buzzing all around him. Hardened journalists whooped and hollered at his bravery, one calling it the greatest moment that any man had ever experienced. The United States had won the Spanish-American War, and Theodore Roosevelt, with his uncanny instinct for publicity, had become a huge international figure and an icon for American youth.

Only a few months later, Franklin and his parents were among the masses on the streets of New York, cheering themselves hoarse as Theodore Roosevelt and the heroic Rough Riders paraded past. In 1898, Franklin and his father abandoned their beloved Democratic Party to vote for their cousin's election as governor of New York. It was a grand time to be a Roosevelt.

While his father was fading, Franklin began to identify more and more with his famous but distant uncle. Schoolmates teased him for trying to look and sound like the charismatic Theodore. By 1889, he was announcing to James and Sara that he was planning a career in the U.S. Navy. Sara was mortified: it was so common. He would later boast that he would climb to the presidency using the same steps as his esteemed uncle, including a stint as an assistant secretary of the navy.

But when he told his father that he wanted to enroll at the U.S. Naval Academy, James sternly rejected the idea out of hand. Franklin would be inheriting a large estate, he was told, and he would have to be close by to watch his interests. What he needed was a law degree, James said, repositioning his son to follow in his own footsteps rather than the romantic trail being blazed by that other Roosevelt from Oyster Bay.

By the summer of 1900, James Roosevelt was too weak to make the annual trek to Campobello and was ensconced instead in his rooms at Hyde Park. His dutiful son Franklin had forsaken his navy dreams and obeyed his father, enrolling at Harvard University for the fall semester, planning to follow the path laid out for him, not wanting to be the catalyst that would send the old man to his grave.

Still, even as the world was falling apart around the Hyde Park Roosevelts, the other clan, the Theodore Roosevelts, saw their star continue to climb. That summer, a national Republican nominating convention, filled with power brokers determined to bury the idealistic Governor Theodore Roosevelt, nominated him for the vice presidency. It would, they hoped, be his ticket to oblivion. The vice presidency, they all agreed, was a dead-end proposition for most men.

By November, James Roosevelt's ambitious plan for a canal across Nicaragua was finally squelched. Panamanian lobbyists in Washington, with dire forecasts of destructive volcanoes in rival Nicaragua, were already winning the day, and James would not be around to fight them.

Then came news that Franklin, away at Harvard University, was struggling. His grades were average, at best, and though he had been elected captain of the freshman football team, it was the last of eight freshman teams. Then he had been rejected outright for the first pass of membership in the prestigious Porcellian Club.[23] This was a cruel disappointment. Membership had become a Roosevelt rite of passage. James and Rosy and cousin Theodore had all been members. Still, there would be another chance the following year.

As the Thanksgiving holidays approached, Sara abandoned her plans to take her husband to South Carolina for the winter and had him moved instead to their New York City apartment to be closer to his doctors. She wrote Franklin daily with blow-by-blow accounts of his decline: "He has had this time more flatulency than I ever knew him to have, and also much bowel trouble which causes weakness."[24]

While James Roosevelt's gastronomical performances were the big news in the shrinking world of the once proper and dignified Hyde Park family, the name of Theodore Roosevelt was constantly in the nation's headlines. In the national elections that month, James, a lifelong Democrat, cast his ballot for one of the most conservative Republican presidential nominees in American history, William McKinley, because his vice presidential running mate, Theodore Roosevelt, was in the family. When the Republican ticket won, Franklin was ecstatic, proudly participating in a Republican torchlight parade at Harvard and calling home from Massachusetts to report on all of the excitement.

But Sara was much too distracted to enjoy the moment. Convinced that James would die within days, she insisted that both Rosy and Franklin come to Manhattan to be at their father's side for Thanksgiving. It was the last time the family would be together. James roused himself slightly, donning a velvet robe and summoning all his energy to enjoy his progeny. But no sooner had Franklin arrived at Harvard after the holiday than Sara called him back to New York again. She was so afraid that James would die before their son reached his bedside that she asked him if he had any last words for the boy. "Only tell Franklin to be a good man," James said.

Both sons were in the room on December 8, 1900, when James Roosevelt had one last massive heart attack. He died, holding the hand of his young wife, before a doctor could arrive. Franklin noted that he would be nineteen in a few days and that it was the same age that Theodore Roosevelt, the new vice president, had been when he had lost *his* father.

Sara was inconsolable and in deepest anguish. She lamented that their twenty years together had been far too short. "All is over," she wrote in her diary. "At 2:20 he merely slipped away. As I write these words I wonder how I lived when he left me." Sara had her two sons accompany her back to Hyde Park, but for a time there was little consolation. "I see him every minute," she wrote in her diary. "I hear his voice at every turn."

★

Sara Roosevelt:
A Formidable Presence

Whatever Franklin achieves must be largely due to you.[1]
—Eleanor Roosevelt to her mother-in-law

The mother of Franklin Delano Roosevelt is an imposing, complex figure in American history. She is often described as a domineering, possessive presence in the life of her presidential son, a cliché that is fiercely disputed by some historians and family members. But if she is not the caricature of popular history, one can only blame those closest to her, for no matter how much they insisted that FDR was his own man and his mother's relationship with his wife, Eleanor, was really loving, and no matter how fondly they speak of her playful repartee as a grandmother, it is *their* stories and *their* quotes that paint the picture we have of this powerful woman.

The Delanos were descendants of one Philippe de Lannoy, who hailed from a courageous French Protestant Huguenot family of the seventeenth century. The de Lannoys fled the Catholic persecution in their home country, finding a safe life in the Netherlands. But Philippe, who had actually been born in Leyden, watched with regret as friends of the family sailed off to the New World on the historic *Mayflower*. Only a teenager, Philippe secured passage on the next ship, surviving the harrowing sea adventure across the Atlantic and settling in the famous Plymouth Colony.

Almost from the beginning, the Delanos were a seafaring clan. By the time Sara's father, Warren Delano II, was born, three generations had sailed the seas and the wharf they sailed from in Fairhaven, Massachusetts, bore their family name.[2] In 1833, Warren II set sail for China, where he worked for a famous Boston tea-exporting company, Russell and Sturgis. Reliable and bright, Warren stayed for nine years in the midst of one of the most tumultuous and dangerous periods for American seamen in the orient. The great opium wars were on.

For many years the insatiable British demand for Chinese tea had been depleting Her Majesty's gold reserves. Opium grown in the British Indian colony seemed to be the answer. But the exchange of opium for tea had proven to be too effective. The Chinese demand for the drug became inexhaustible, and the world's most populous nation began to reel under the weight of massive addiction. The Chinese government, slowed to action by endemic corruption, finally began fighting back, trying to protect its people by passing laws to outlaw the ubiquitous opium dens. The British were in the morally indefensible position of demanding the right to traffic in a drug that was destroying a country. Warren Delano II eventually became the "commission merchant" for Russell and Sturgis, running its tea and opium operations in Canton, Macao, and Hong Kong.[3]

By 1843, thirty-three-year-old Warren Delano II returned to the United States a wealthy man many times over. Handsome, rich, and erudite, he married Catherine Robbins Lyman, an eighteen-year-old beauty from a socially prominent Massachusetts family with a long tradition of political involvement. The Lymans were bowled over by the dashing Delano, who took his bride right back to China, where he put in three more years of accumulating capital. When they returned to New York City, the Delanos were a wealthy family buying a grand house in Manhattan, right next door to John Jacob Astor, the richest man in the United States.

The Astor family would be a recurring seam throughout the history of the Delanos and the Roosevelts, bringing the two great families close to each other long before the marriage of James and Sara sealed the union. While James Roosevelt's son Rosy would eventually marry an Astor, Franklin, the brother of Warren Delano II, did the same thing a generation earlier. His marriage to Laura Astor made headlines, and although Franklin Delano's newfound wealth and status as an Astor in-law meant that he would miss all the fun in China, he would play a role in history because of his namesake.

By 1851, New York City had grown into one of America's greatest cities. A number of prominent families were building estates further north on the Hudson River, quickly accessible to the city by rail. Warren and Catherine Delano, who had a houseful of children, quickly settled on a stunning property overlooking the river. To help him rebuild and expand his estate, Warren hired the renowned Andrew Jackson Downing, the architect who had designed the grounds of the White House and Capitol. The Delanos christened their mansion Algonac, meaning "hill and river."[4] It was in this sprawling mansion of forty rooms that Sara Delano was born on September 21, 1854. She was their seventh child, and she would not be the last.

In her later writings, Sara idealized her life at Algonac. Relatives visited often, showering the children with gifts. Franklin, the rich uncle, was such a frequent guest that he soon built his own magnificent estate nearby. Sarah, the maiden aunt, actually moved in for a time, prompting the family to identify the little Sara as "Sallie," a nickname that stuck. When they visited Fairhaven in the summer, the same family cast would reassemble.

Sara, or "Sallie," adored her father. Warren Delano II was her hero, and when he was forced by events to return to China yet again, she cherished each postage stamp from his letters home. It would be the beginning of a lifelong hobby as a stamp collector and one she would pass on to her president son.

On August 8, 1857, one of the nation's most important financial institutions, the Ohio Life Insurance and Trust Company, collapsed with consequences that rippled through the economy. Almost five thousand companies were plunged into bankruptcy. Warren Delano II was ruined. His New York property was sold, and Algonac was put on the auction block, saved only at the last minute because the banks could find no buyers.

Warren Delano II was fifty years old. It was much too late in life for a spectacular comeback. Opium, the familiar road to riches, was now firmly closed. And the import-export game in China had shifted to Hong Kong, with new players, new rules, and the doors closed to outside competition. Still, Warren instinctively sensed that his path back from bankruptcy would be a long, circuitous route that would pass through China. Rejecting loving advice from his brothers, he called for his wife and children to join him in the Orient. To hear Sara describe it, the family was in for a great adventure.

For the rest of her life, Sara Delano would display her experiences in China as if they were grand trophies. Though many Englishmen of her class could tell tales of India, which was after all a British colony, China was different. Not many people of her time, other than sailors, had a reason to travel so far. The world's largest nation was an enigma, closed to outsiders, who were labeled barbarians. Yet China was a very important trading partner, guardian of the world's supply of tea, the drug of the Western world. Sara's stories of wealth in China were the envy of her cousins. As a grown woman she could drop an exotic tale at a dinner party that would top just about anything anyone else had to say. And there was no one to contradict her. In the privacy of her own home she would sing jaunty songs of the sea to her young Franklin, claiming that she had learned them on board the family ship on route to the Orient.

In fact, this great and seemingly important part of her life took all of two years, and several months of that was spent going and coming aboard the ship, with only her family and the crew as companions. While in China the family were virtual prisoners in their compound; they left the grounds rarely and only when accompanied by elaborate security.[5]

Indeed, Sara and her family missed the great epic of their times, the dramatic duel of Grant and Lee as the American Civil War raged to its climax. While Americans and Europeans followed the clash with avid interest and horror, the Delano children were far away, isolated, missing it all, the exception being Warren Delano II, Sara's father. He had found a new client, the U.S. government.

The Union Army, in its war of attrition against the South, was experiencing staggering casualties, and opium became the medicine of choice for the wounded. The Civil War, far removed from the Delano family, saved their father's business and made them all millionaires. Yet an inventive Sara Delano recast her two years in China as the center of the world and the greatest experience in her life.

As the family slowly transitioned back to Algonac, Sara lived for a time with her grandparents in Fairhaven and then reunited with her parents and siblings in Europe. Her seemingly uneventful time on the continent was far longer than her years in China and was marked by some amazing moments. In 1866, while staying in a luxury apartment in the Bois de Boulogne, Sara watched from her balcony as royalty passed beneath her. Count Bismarck, the king of Prussia, Empress Carlotta of Mexico, and the French Empress Eugénie all passed by on their way to the Universal Exhibition.[6] From her perch, Sara waved joyfully at the parade of royal carriages and guards. By the time the family resettled on the Hudson River, Sara Delano was a well-traveled, beautiful young lady, fluent in French and German, and hailing from an old American family now fully restored to wealth. The Delanos had come full circle.

Life at Algonac was idyllic. The five girls immersed themselves in reading and art and pursued the whole gamut of outdoor sports from archery to horses. The family worshiped at the Unitarian Church of Our Father in Newburgh, where for years Warren had been a major contributor.

One of the sisters married young, and there were numerous suitors for Sara, who by all accounts was a regal beauty, standing an imposing five feet, ten inches tall. One early romance was squelched by her fearsome, respected, larger-than-life father, Warren Delano II.

The young man in pursuit of Sara was one Stanford White, the dashing son of a Shakespearean scholar and a promising young architect with a seemingly limitless future. White would eventually design Madison Square Garden, the Washington Square Arch, and the New York Herald Building. He would move with ease among the socially prominent of his day, designing summer homes for the Vanderbilts and the Astors. And he was apparently avidly pursuing the last of the Delano daughters. But Warren Delano II, Sara's astute father, could spot a cad when he saw one and fiercely nixed the romance.

It would be a prescient decision. Stanford White would become a notorious womanizer, bedding teenage chorus girls, one of whom would provoke a jealous rival to take a pistol and plug Stanford White in the head, shooting him dead in the midst of a lively evening at a New York rooftop restaurant.[7] It would become the scandal of the age, with all of White's sordid past spilling out onto the front pages of the newspapers.

By then, thanks to her wise and authoritative father, Sara Delano was far away, mercifully spared the humiliation of any association with White, comfortably married to another man, and nursing her little baby, the future president of the United States.

Content with her life at Algonac, Sara had been in no hurry to leave home. The years soon passed. Her older namesake aunt had never married, and Sara began to accept that it would be her lot as well. She noted in her diary that she was a "contented spinster."[8] Her own reminisces of this time are deceptively self-deprecating. According to her account, she was practically an old maid when her ancient husband, a man twice her age, finally put her out of her misery. Writing of the society dinner where she'd met James Roosevelt, she told her son, Franklin, "If I had not come then, I should now be 'old Miss Delano,' after a rather sad life."

In fact, a society writer described the five Delano daughters as stunning beauties, and there are early pictures of Sara that should end any speculation.[9] She was an attractive young woman of extraordinary self-confidence but with tastes so exacting that they drastically limited the marriage pool.

Sara Delano was twenty-six years old when Bamie invited her to that fateful dinner party in New York City where she met fifty-two-year-old James Roosevelt. Sara learned something about herself that night. She learned that she preferred a man of substance over a man with a future, and not just a man of material substance but of social standing, intellectual strength, and spirituality. She decided that she had found them all in James Roosevelt.

Not long after the dinner, a second event was arranged by James Roosevelt at his spectacular estate on the Hudson River. As squire of the domain, James asked Sara to arrange the flowers for the evening. In their insular, privileged society that apparently signaled his profound interest in the young beauty. Sara picked up on it instantly, expressing not even the slightest concern over their different ages, and so the romance was on.

After her father, Warren Delano II, recovered from the shock that one of his own business colleagues was his future son-in-law, the march to the altar moved forward at a brisk pace. They married in the splendor that only a rich older man can shower on a young bride. They honeymooned in Europe for a full year.

The marriage between James and Sara was obviously romantic, and there were many common interests. If she was a trophy wife, it was not in the conventional sense of an old man demonstrating virility, but rather an old man demonstrating that he still had relevant and impeccable taste. And if Sara only sought security, she had other younger, wealthy suitors from which to choose. She, too, saw it as a union in good taste, an advance for them both. While for some young people, marriage is an escape from home, the union with James Roosevelt represented for Sara a chance to replicate the familiar. It was a chance for a second life at Algonac, only this time on the other side of the river at Hyde Park.

THE BIRTH OF A PRESIDENT

The birth of Franklin Delano Roosevelt on January 30, 1882, signaled strongly that Hyde Park would not be another Algonac, a house full of children, echoing with the boisterous sounds of rough-and-tumble. Sara's labor was long and difficult. Her baby weighed a hefty ten pounds. The doctors, who ordered Sara to bed for a month, ruled out any more children. Franklin would be the first child and the last. James and Sara, conscious of the danger to her life, would forgo sex for the rest of their lives.

Typically, Sara rallied to her new reality. Just as she had made exile to China the adventure of a lifetime, to be envied by cousins and friends alike, she would become an ardent evangelist for the advantages of raising an only child. She would say that large families always turned the older siblings into bullies. And when that didn't happen, they tended to reduce themselves to the intellectual level of the youngest. Without data to corroborate her views, she would pontificate with great conviction about the advantages of an only child. The fact is, she had no choice.

Sara had hoped to name her newborn son after her father, Warren Delano II. Her husband, who was at the end of a long line of Roosevelt men playing leapfrog with the names Isaac and James, felt no compunctions about calling an end to the tradition. Sara was low emotional maintenance and a comfortable fit for an older husband set in his ways. She had hardly rearranged a chair at Hyde Park. She grandly delighted in his first wife's china and left her portrait proudly staring back at them from the wall. Without hesitation, she had left the Unitarian faith to worship with James as an Episcopalian. There was nothing insecure about Sara Delano.

So the request to name their newborn Warren was met with loving approval by James Roosevelt. But there was a complication: Warren Delanos tended to die. Her father and mother had named one of their early children after the father, but he had died an infant in 1851. When they had tried it again, Warren Delano III survived to adult-hood. But soon after the birth of Sara's child, his own four-year-old Warren Delano IV died of scarlet fever.

The Roosevelts discreetly inquired about the idea of using the name for their own baby, but the brother-in-law indicated that it would be too painful. And so Sara chose the name of her rich uncle Franklin Delano, the one who had married the granddaughter of the richest man in America.

Sara's baby became the focus of her life. She breast-fed Franklin for the first year, and, having made that choice, she promoted the idea for others ever after.[10] She lectured that even women who had servants and nursemaids available would be well advised to learn everything they could about caring for their own children.[11] But some of Sara's other parenting techniques were more controversial. She kept Franklin in dresses until he was six and took baths with him until he was nine.[12] "Mama has left this morning and I am going to take my bath alone," Franklin proudly wrote his father, marking the historic milestone in his life.[13] She feared that he would become too hard and insensitive, so she read him sentimental stories, sometimes weeping over the pages. "What's wrong, Mummy?" Franklin would ask, trying to comfort her.

Later on, as her son entered public life and journalists began the tedious business of reconstructing his biography, including his child-hood years, Sara was savvy enough to know that some of her methods would appear controversial. She wrote her own books and magazine articles, artfully blaming herself for any excesses and defending against the notion that her son was a "sissy," an idea that persisted within the wider Roosevelt family. Franklin was a stamp collector and a bird-watcher, Alice pointed out. And while the Theodore Roosevelt family all rowed, the James Roosevelt family all sailed, suggesting the manli-ness of the former. But Sara shrewdly took the blame on her own shoulders. "We mothers had daintier ideas [for] apparel than was pop-ular with our sturdy offspring," she said.[14]

Reluctantly, defensively, but out of her sense of political need, Sara later admitted that Franklin had sometimes chafed under her supervi-sion. He had been embarrassed by his Little Lord Fauntleroy suits and his long, girlish curls, which Sara had grudgingly cut, preserving each precious lock for her own memories and later for posterity. In a revealing moment she spoke of him one day sighing sadly and rhetorically announcing to the room how unhappy he was and how he longed for "freedom!" [15] But after her initial panic and her earnest efforts to make sure the child had more room, Sara convinced herself that Franklin had not been serious; it had been a false alarm, a passing mood. Sara bristled at suggestions that her son had been lonely and deprived.

ON HIS OWN

Young men in their society went to boarding school at age twelve. But James had waited two more years, and so had his son Rosy. And Sara could not bear to part with Franklin. So the boy was held back two years before arriving at Groton preparatory school at the age of fourteen. The motto at Groton, the school of choice for the entire Roosevelt family, was *Cui servire est regnare,* "To serve is to rule." [16] But even then, Franklin could count on his mother's careful, persistent attention.

Not long after leaving him at Groton, she left with James on a trip to Europe, hoping that the waters at the Bad Nauheim spa would help him. "Nothing but James' health would induce me to cross the ocean without Franklin," she said. But when she learned that the boy had contracted a case of scarlet fever, and remembering well how Warren Delano IV had died of the dreaded disease, Sara raced back to the United States and descended, unannounced, on the Groton campus. Finding her son under strict quarantine, she requisitioned a ladder from nearby workers and unceremoniously climbed to his floor, tapping on his window with her gloved hand. The reinforcements had arrived.

Not surprisingly, Franklin's first years away from home were a rude shock to his system. He had some major readjusting to do, and it would not happen overnight. He had lived in the sophisticated, subtle world of adults, who adored him, and now he was open to the cruel ridicule and vulgar directness of his peers. He was hazed and teased but wouldn't complain about it. His father's health was precarious, and Sara lost her mother that year. His instincts told him that his parents didn't need any more disappointment in their lives. Anyway, he couldn't bear the thought that his parents might think less of him.

Franklin loved sports, but games with paid servants had not really tested him. A local Hudson River resident later recalled that he had failed to make the neighborhood baseball team and that boys from other privileged families felt sorry for him. At Groton he was cha-grined to discover that he was perhaps the worst player at the school. He once swung at a pitch that hit him in the stomach and, having the wind knocked out of him, fell to the ground in panic.

At Hyde Park, his mother would often break into sobs when pass-ing his empty room. She wrote him letters, mourning his absence, and he wrote back sad missives telling of his hope that sickness would cause the headmaster to send him home.

To survive, Franklin had to shelve his more pristine tastes and in-terests. But Sara—and to some extent James—had unconsciously gifted Franklin with something far more powerful than an ability to relate to peers. Both parents were unflappable by, even superior to, trouble and troublesome people. And Sara was an unabashed optimist, supremely self-confident regardless of the circumstances. Franklin had absorbed these characteristics himself.

Franklin, confronted with the fact that he was seen by classmates as a fastidious prig, responded with equal calm and patience. He refused to play the victim. Without dissolving into emotional defeat, he set about the long task of winning the acceptance of his classmates, with-out compromising his own sense of self. It would be an ongoing strug-gle to adulthood and the harbinger of his political talent to come.

Franklin's immediate salvation was his famous relative Theodore Roosevelt, who sometimes visited his old alma mater to speak at chapel services. On one occasion in 1897, he singled out Franklin in the audience, and for days thereafter the young man was a hero to his classmates. Occasionally Franklin received invitations to events at Sag-amore Hill, the Theodore Roosevelt estate at Oyster Bay. And al-though it meant suffering a gauntlet of teasing and abuse from his sports-minded, high-achieving cousins, it was worth it all just to be able to talk about it later to his classmates at Groton. When his mother declined an invitation for him to attend a Fourth of July Sagamore Hill celebration, Franklin was irate, ending a letter with a stern rebuke: "Please, don't make any arrangements for my future happiness." [17]

The year 1898 was an eventful one for the entire Roosevelt family, a year of tragedy and glory. Warren Delano II, Sara's beloved father, died, leaving her a fortune that made her even richer than her hus-band. And it was the year that Theodore Roosevelt soared into the stratosphere as the hero of the Spanish-American War.

Franklin was now a sixteen-year-old student at Groton. In the fall, he carefully followed the successful Roosevelt campaign for governor of New York. That Christmas, when he received an invitation to a family party at the home of Corrine Roosevelt, Theodore's sister, he was ecstatic. Franklin danced several times with fourteen-year-old Alice Roosevelt, Theodore's oldest daughter, who was already fast becoming the pouting, acerbic beauty of legend. Alice would later say in a reproach to Franklin's softness that she preferred men more like her father's Rough Riders.

But during the dance, Alice inadvertently set into motion an alliance that she would come to regret. She suggested that Franklin offer a dance to the other, more awkward fourteen-year-old cousin in the room, the one with the buckteeth and funny-looking clothes. Sitting on the sidelines was the uncomfortable and lonely Eleanor Roosevelt. Franklin gallantly offered her his hand.

The last year at Groton was Franklin's best. He was now six feet one, his emotional and intellectual growth running parallel. His grades had improved, and he won the Latin Prize. Perhaps his most bizarre pleasure came from breaking the school record in the unique "high kick" contest.[18] A tin pan was suspended from the ceiling and raised higher and higher each time a student was able to kick it. It was suspended well over seven feet, with Franklin kicking each time and falling heavily to the floor, bruising his neck and side.[19] It was, perhaps, an indication of how deeply his classmates' rejection hurt him and how willing he was to suffer to gain recognition from his peers.

Franklin's first year at Harvard University was undistinguished both in and out of the classroom. He thought of himself as a good writer but was denied a coveted spot on *The Harvard Crimson,* the school newspaper. Told that anyone who persevered would be guaranteed a place on the football team, he tried out and was given a position on the very last of the eight freshman teams.

Three months into Franklin's first year at Harvard, his father, James Roosevelt, died of cardiac arrest. The elder Roosevelt had been losing strength for ten years, fully half of the time of his married life to Sara. It had been a long good-bye. She had thought long about what life would be without him. Even so, she had been shocked by the suddenness of his final passing and was caught by surprise at the degree of grief that now engulfed her.

James Roosevelt stated in his will that his wife would be Franklin's sole guardian and that "I wish him to be under the influence of his mother." The parting admonition was superfluous. For Sara, the death of her beloved James meant a total transfer of energy and attention to the surviving son. She promptly moved to an apartment in Boston, close to the Harvard campus, where she would be available for a few months, on a standby basis, just in case of need.

There is some evidence to suggest that Sara's periodic multimonth visits to Boston made a difference. The second time around, Franklin was given a position on the school newspaper. Before his graduation he would become the editor. But his academic record was still mediocre, and his role in football games was reduced to usher and sometimes cheerleader. The Porcellian Club, which had claimed James and Rosy and his esteemed cousin, Theodore Roosevelt, would remain resistant to the end, issuing to him "the greatest disappointment in my life."[20]

On September 6, 1901, an anarchist shot President William McKinley at the Pan American Exposition in Buffalo, New York. The president lingered for several days and then died on September 14. Theodore Roosevelt was promptly inaugurated the twenty-sixth president of the United States. For the next few years, Franklin watched the dramatic events in Washington with avid interest and fascination. At Harvard he was sometimes confused for the president's son. Some of the ridicule for his aristocratic and priggish mannerisms passed. He was nominated for class chairman and lost but as consolation won a post as the permanent chairman of the Class Committee. Franklin was sufficiently cocky to ask his classmates if they thought he would make a good president of the United States. His mother played to this newfound sense of confidence. When she read a biography of Theodore Roosevelt, she learned that his father's last words to the boy had been to be a good man. Those had also been the last words of the dying James Roosevelt to his son, Franklin, she enthused, as if it were a sign from God that he was destined for great things.[21]

Unknown to his mother, there was a new source of empowerment in Franklin's life: he had fallen in love with a cousin, a young lady even more awkward than himself, yet someone who shared his fascination with the shifting sociopolitical dynamics of their time. Perhaps just as important, she was the niece of the president and cousin he so idolized. Franklin assiduously protected the privacy of his relation-

ship with the girl, referring to her in code names, instinctively knowing that if given half a chance his mother would kill the relationship—
indeed, *any* relationship with the opposite sex. But if he now had a
bounce to his step, if he now radiated Sara's own self-confidence, there
was a reason.

A MARRIAGE OF THREE

On Thanskgiving 1903, at a Delano family event in Fairhaven, Massachusetts, a twenty-one-year-old Franklin D. Roosevelt pulled his
mother aside and gave her the news: he was getting married to Anna
Eleanor Roosevelt, his cousin.[22] It was a done deal, no discussion. He
wanted her to know and to be happy with his momentous decision.

Sara Roosevelt's reaction to this news and her subsequent role
leading up to the marriage of Franklin and Eleanor have been the subjects of great speculation and conjecture. She was obviously stunned
and hurt. Did this mean that Franklin didn't really love her or value
her judgment? Was he now so removed from her that she would not
even be consulted when he made the most important decision of his
life? Did it mean that she was not trusted by her own son? Did he fear
that she would not respect his right to make a decision for himself?
This was so unlike Franklin. Had Eleanor put him up to this? Was this
her idea? Or had her son presented her with a fait accompli because at
some level he knew his decision was a wrong one and he didn't want it
exposed to the withering, critical analysis of one who really loved
him? And finally, was this only immaturity and youth? Was it only a
mistake? That evening, she simply recorded in her diary, "Franklin
gave me quite a startling announcement."[23]

In time, when her son became president and her every word and
action would be revisited, Sara, the perpetual optimist, would insist on
the latter reasons for her exclusion. She would not be the victim. She
would take the offense. Franklin was too young. Indeed, she would
raise the issue at her next meeting with the couple. She would ignore
the absurd notion that she was jealous of Eleanor. She understood that
her son would marry one day. She wanted his happiness. It was far too
painful to contemplate any of the other possibilities, but, that being the
case, the situation now called for her tenacious involvement.

Franklin made every effort to appease her. "I know what pain I must have caused you," he wrote, "and you know I wouldn't do it if I really could have helped it—mais tu sais, me voilà!" Then he showed her some of the fortitude and stubbornness she had instilled in him: "That's all that could be said—I know my mind, have known it for a long time, and know that I could never think otherwise: Result: I am the happiest man just now in the world; likewise the luckiest—And for you, dear Mummy, you know that nothing can ever change what we have always been & always will be to each other—only now you have two children to love & to love you—and Eleanor as you know will always be a daughter to you in every true way."[24]

But the battle had only begun. Sara controlled the considerable family fortune, and the small allowance that Eleanor received from her parents' trust was minimal. Franklin was only a senior at Harvard, with plans to pursue a law degree. How would they survive? He lived in a world of butlers and cooks and gardeners and chauffeurs. He and Sara still traveled in their own private railroad car, *The Monon,* with porter and attendant.[25] When he was roped into doing some charitable chores for Eleanor and one errand took him up the stairs of a tenement building, he was shocked: "My God, I didn't know people lived like that!"[26] He talked about it long after, as if it had been an exotic experience to a foreign land, as indeed it was.

Within days of his surprise announcement in Fairhaven, Franklin's mother arranged for a meeting of the three of them in New York City. Her great concern, she told the couple, was their youth. Eleanor was only eighteen, she insisted (actually she was now nineteen), and Franklin was only twenty-one. Her father, who was the measure of all things excellent and wise in manhood, had been thirty-three when he married and already established with a great career. With Franklin still in school, how could they possibly make it? Implied was the threat that they would need her money to survive. But such threats were always implied, never spoken; Sara did not dare force a showdown between herself and Eleanor. To lose Franklin was unthinkable. And how could they even know they were in love? Sara continued. Any reasonable couple would put their feelings to a test of time and separation. She would give her consent, she said to the anxious, unbelieving young couple, who felt that this was too good to be true, if they would agree to her terms. They must wait a full year, to see if their love was real. And they must keep the engagement secret. Franklin must go on his

summer trip with her as usual so nothing would look suspicious. A relieved Franklin and Eleanor agreed. They were confident that their
love could endure. And Sara had just bought herself a year. The fact
that the engagement would be secret obviously offered the assurance
that there would be no family embarrassment when the break came.

From what both women later recounted, Sara felt that this was a
mismatch, that her son was getting the bad end of the bargain. She
could understand the poor girl's attraction for Franklin but was puzzled over what Franklin saw in her. Sara later made fun of Eleanor,
mimicking her buckteeth and shrill voice. It was a cruel act that their
esteemed cousin Alice, the daughter of President Theodore Roosevelt,
would one day make famous.

But Sara was not alone in sensing that the arrangement was out of
balance. "I shall never be able to hold him," Eleanor confided to a
cousin during the engagement. "He is so attractive." [27] Later, after she
became a respected first lady and a beloved figure in her own right,
Eleanor disingenuously claimed that the Lady of Hyde Park would
have preferred "a more worldly and social match" for her son.

The magnetism of Eleanor and Franklin's attraction to each other
has remained beyond history's ability to divine it. Sara would certainly
never understand it. Eleanor speculated that both of them knew what
it was like to be ridiculed and left on the outside, and so each reveled
in the unrestrained, genuine affection of the other. They hungered for
the respect and recognition of their peers, and through their relationship they each uniquely provided it to the other.

Then there were the deep emotional needs. Psychologists suggest that Franklin was looking for a woman who would be shrewd
enough to help him break from his mother, yet too weak to dominate
him as his mother had and to keep him from going back home when
he needed.

There was also his relationship with James. At some unconscious
level, feeling abandoned by a father who had died when he was nineteen, Franklin had transferred his hero worship to his noble cousin,
now the president of the United States, Theodore Roosevelt. The
Oyster Bay Roosevelt clan was now at the top of its game. Each
family member was becoming a world-class celebrity. Franklin was
desperate for entrée into it, yet he was openly ridiculed by his cousins,
the president's children, who referred to his initials, FDR, as "Feather

Duster Roosevelt." Eleanor, the president's niece, was his ticket to enter the circle.

Eleanor's needs were just close enough to Franklin's to give them a common bond. When she was a child, her beautiful mother openly ridiculed her looks, calling her "Granny" in front of visitors. Eleanor would later say that the remarks had cut so deeply she wanted to "sink through the floor in shame."[28] Awkward and self-conscious, the orphaned young lady was beginning to manifest her own deep emotional scars in her courtship with Franklin. She was now calling him pet names that she had once reserved for her beloved father and signing her letters to Franklin with long-forgotten pet names her father had once called her.

As Sara rightly suspected, the fearful and shaky Eleanor was nonetheless conspiring with Franklin in the campaign to win her over. "I know just how you feel & how hard it must be," she wrote to Sara that December, "but I do so want you to learn to love me a little. You must know that I will always try to do what you wish for I have grown to love you very dearly during the past summer.

"It is impossible for me to tell you how I feel toward Franklin, I can only say that my one great wish is always to prove worthy of him.

"I am counting the days to the 12th when I hope Franklin & you will both be here again & if there is anything which I can do for you [sic] you will write me, won't you?"[29]

Sara did not take the bait. Instead she focused on the propriety of their actions and the danger of being seen together. It soon became apparent that keeping the engagement a secret was a device that Sara planned to use.

While Franklin was busy at law school during the week, each hour of the weekends was a morsel to be fought over by the two women. Sara tried to keep the battle on her turf, invoking fear of scandal, that they would be ruined if seen together too often. In this way she could appear to be fighting in their own interest by keeping them apart. After all, they were not publicly engaged. Letters flew back and forth, pressing the case on why it was important for him to spend a weekend without Eleanor at Hyde Park and how dangerously close they would be to irreparable scandal if they were seen again by this person or that.

And often, after Sara and Eleanor had parsed every argument, they would press Franklin to choose between them. Would it be a rendezvous with Eleanor in New York City, with the danger that a scandal would ruin them both and spell an end to their marriage prospects altogether and perhaps—although it was never said—force Sara, reluctantly, to disinherit them? Or would it be Sara and the security and privacy of Hyde Park?

Though Eleanor's letters to Franklin were sometimes written as if she hoped he would share them with Sara, filled with praise for the woman and proclaiming her complete understanding of what might just as easily have been dismissed as outrageous maternal possessiveness, she knew full well that she was in a fight and that if Franklin did not help her, they could both be swamped by his mother's unrelenting emotional onslaught. "I realize more and more how hard it is for her & we must both try always to make her happy," Eleanor said in a letter to Franklin, but then she added pathetically to show how cruel the woman was, "I do hope some day she will learn to love me."[30]

As part of the deal, Sara and Franklin went on their annual trip together. It was, at Franklin's suggestion, a Caribbean cruise. Sara was exultant. She would have him all to herself and could press her arguments without the pathetic, self-pitying counterpoints of her underestimated rival. But Franklin came home exhausted by his mother's relentless advocacy and more in love with Eleanor than ever.

Eleanor, racing to the finish line, wrote Franklin sweetly, "Don't let her feel that the last trip with you is over. We three must take them together in the future. . . . Someday I hope that she really will love me and I would be very glad if I thought she was even the least bit reconciled to me now."[31]

Sara was desperate. She took Franklin to Washington and arranged a meeting with the American ambassador to the Court of St. James's, asking him baldly to take Franklin back as his secretary. The ambassador declined.

Sensing that Franklin was susceptible to the maudlin appeals of Eleanor, she tried them herself. In an uncharacteristic mood of self-pity, she wrote him from Hyde Park, "I am feeling pretty blue. You are gone. The journey is over & I feel as if the time were not likely to come again when I shall take a trip with my dear boy, as we are not going abroad, but I must try to be unselfish & of course dear child I *do* rejoice in your happiness, & shall not put any stones or straws even in the way of it. . . . Oh how still the house is."

In March 1905, only two weeks before the wedding, Sara Delano Roosevelt took Franklin and Eleanor to Washington to witness the inauguration of their "esteemed relative," Theodore Roosevelt. Having assumed the presidency after the assassination of William McKinley, TR had rashly promised not to seek another two full terms in office. He was already fulfilling much of McKinley's second term, he pointed out to the nation, and that called for a disciplined gesture to honor the tradition of George Washington. It would be a promise he would much regret. So Sara stressed the fact to Franklin and Eleanor that this would be the last time any of them would ever witness the inauguration of a Roosevelt and they should be a part of the historic moment for the family.

On March 16, 1905, a defeated Sara wrote in her diary, "This is Franklin's last night at home as a boy."[32] The following day, Eleanor and Franklin were married before two hundred invited guests in a private ceremony at her cousin's town house on Seventy-sixth Street in Manhattan. Her uncle, President Theodore Roosevelt, gave the bride away. When Eleanor first appeared, family on her mother's side gasped, surprised by her beauty and saying that she almost reminded them of her mother, Anna. But cousin Alice, one of a bevy of gorgeous brides-maids, thought Eleanor had made a mistake in having so many girls prettier than herself in the ceremony. Alice, whose own White House wedding would soon fill the front pages of the nation's newspapers, would take the lesson to heart and have no competition at her own wedding.

Eleanor and Franklin paid a price for inviting the president. Because of his schedule, he had been given a virtual veto on the date. They had finally selected Saint Patrick's Day, when the president would be in New York for a political speech anyway. That worked fine for Eleanor. It had been her mother's birthday. And then the ceremony had to begin promptly when the president arrived because he would have to leave soon after. It seemed to be a small price to pay.

But as soon as the ceremony ended, the president jovially slapped the groom on the back and announced for all to hear, "Well, Franklin, there's nothing like keeping the name in the family," whereupon he promptly disappeared to the adjacent parlors to taste the food. Within minutes, the crowd moved as one body into the next rooms, pawing and bantering after the star of the hour, Theodore Roosevelt.

For a brief moment, Franklin and Eleanor were left standing entirely alone. The line of well-wishers who were greeting them had simply evaporated. For a moment they were outsiders at their own wedding, before the eyes of their own invited relatives and guests. As the crowd sensed that the president was going to leave and each person had his or her little prepared speech for him or urgent advice to pass on, there was a mood of panic. Alice Roosevelt thought it was all rather funny and would later declare, "My father wants to be the corpse at every funeral, the bride at every wedding and the baby at every christening."[33]

But with time, as he brooded about it, Franklin would not be amused by the memory. With great irony, Alice would one day remark about the fall of the Oyster Bay Roosevelts and the rise of the Hyde Park Feather Duster, "The joke was on us."

At some level Franklin and Eleanor knew that their marriage would not put an end to Sara's manic involvement in their lives. The same leverage that had given her such control during their year of secret engagement was still in play. Nothing had really been changed by the wedding ceremony. But such blackmail worked both ways. If Sara had any real power to punish, she would also have to demonstrate her power to reward. What was the threat of loss unless there was something to lose?

When Franklin and Eleanor professed their need of a town house in New York so he could finish his law degree, she generously rented one near her own place and had it elegantly furnished with her selections, down to the pots and pans and the hiring of the servants. In late summer, when Franklin and Eleanor returned from their delayed honeymoon in Europe, many hours of which were consumed by Eleanor's blow-by-blow, handwritten accounts to Sara of every word and action, the town house awaited them.

And at Christmas of the following year, Sara seemingly outdid herself by presenting them with the plans for two *new* town houses on East Sixty-fifth Street, one for herself and one for her beloved children. They would both be spacious brownstone mansions, six stories tall, but there was a caveat: they would have adjouining parlors and dining rooms, a common vestibule, and a connecting door in the private fourth-floor bedroom area.

The move was three years away, and Eleanor was able to put it out of her mind, but when the day finally came and they moved into their New York town house mansion, Franklin found his wife alone, crying to herself. "This is not my house," she sobbed. "I did not help plan it, and it isn't the way I want to live."[34] Franklin was flabbergasted. Where had this come from? Hadn't they gone over the plans together? Why hadn't she said something before?[35]

The connecting doors on the bedroom floor sealed the verdict on Sara Delano as far as many historians were concerned. That was unforgivable. Years later, at the height of her popularity and power and without Sara around to contradict her, Eleanor would vent her feelings to a sympathetic biographer, milking the arrangement for all it was worth: "You were never quite sure when she would appear day or night."[36]

The house on Sixty-fifth Street was certainly a metaphor for their life together. But the door on the fourth floor swung both ways. Eleanor was, by her own admission, an inadequate wife and mother. She didn't know how to run a household, arrange meals, or plan a budget. She was totally dependent on Sara and her servants. She was with her mother-in-law constantly, taking a pass on invitations from old friends and relatives and missing her weekly Bible classes. When babies started coming, she was so clumsy and inept that they all preferred their nannies or Sara to their real mother. Her feeble attempts to do things on her own often resulted in humiliation. After reading that babies needed fresh air, Eleanor put her firstborn, Anna, in a wire contraption and hung her out on the front porch. When the baby turned blue, the neighbors threatened action and Eleanor quickly took her back inside.

She would later complain that her mother-in-law had fostered her sense of helplessness, that she had encouraged the servants to take the children, for example, when she, Eleanor, had wanted to care for them. "Franklin's children were more my mother-in-law's children than mine," she later admitted.[37] Once, the eldest daughter, Anna, packing for a European trip with Granny, found Eleanor weeping alone in a room. She had very much wanted to take the youngsters to Europe herself, she told her daughter, but she hadn't the money to do so.

Sara, who almost always used the kindest of language in her correspondence and conversations with Eleanor, could be quite cruel in her own proper way. She continually, openly expressed her great love to the children, telling them, "Your mother only bore you." [38]

Yet this relationship between Sara and Eleanor was clearly a co-dependent one. Sara no longer complained about Eleanor. She now defended her to Franklin and shielded her ineptitude. For her part, Eleanor drank deep from the dregs, allowing Sara to co-opt her marriage and her own children. Even her devotion to good deeds was squelched; she could no longer visit seedy tenement houses to help the poor, she was told. It could be disastrous. She might inadvertently bring back communicable diseases to the children. And so, for a while, the mother practically co-opted the wife.

There was, of course, one weapon the wife could wield that the mother could not, but there is every reason to believe that Eleanor was inadequate in this regard as well. When Eleanor was a young girl, her saucy cousin Alice Roosevelt had explained the reproductive process to her, using stories from the Bible to prove her points. Eleanor had been horrified and had shrieked that Alice was blasphemous.

After a trip to Europe she wrote her mother-in-law, telling in horror of what respectable people let their daughters do outside the sanctity of marriage. "Your hair will curl as mine did." [39] When Eleanor's daughter Anna was three, she tied her hands to the bedposts at night to keep her from masturbating. Later, when the daughter was a grown adult, Eleanor confided to her that "sex was an ordeal to be borne."

But if his wife was in the process of being possessed by his mother, Franklin was flourishing. He was admitted to the bar in 1907 and then promptly taken into a reputable firm. The boys at Groton and Harvard may have had their moments of hazing and tormenting him, but they were all on *his* turf now.

In 1910, good-natured and imbued with his mother's optimism and good looks, Franklin was visited by a delegation of Democratic politicians urging him to run for the New York State Legislature. Franklin hesitated, saying he would have to ask his mother. Taken back, the gentlemen patiently explained that the voters and the press would not be impressed by a man who could not make his own decisions, whereupon Franklin immediately agreed; he would be their man.

Sara was aghast at the impropriety of it all. It was a clear deviation from the successful pattern of Warren Delano II, her esteemed father.

It was even a deviation from Franklin's father, James Roosevelt, who, although a Democrat, was a gentleman who properly limited his public service to his own home turf and his own kind. It was not the life she had envisioned for her son. When Eleanor cheered him on, Sara, unwilling to relinquish an inch of her status with Franklin, went along too, even when victory meant that she would lose them both for weeks at a time at the state capital in Albany, New York.

★

ELEVEN

FDR's Break with Mother

Franklin doesn't know everything.[1]
—Sara Delano Roosevelt, mother of FDR

In the national election of 1912, Theodore Roosevelt, out of power, had attempted a comeback, trying to take the presidency away from his own designated successor, the Republican incumbent, President William Howard Taft. It split the Republican Party, and the Democrat candidate, Woodrow Wilson, was elected. The Oyster Bay Roosevelts had now—temporarily, they hoped—fallen from power.

In 1913, the new President Wilson appointed Franklin Delano Roosevelt, a lowly New York Democrat state legislator, to the post of assistant secretary of the navy. It was a position he had coveted for a long time, the very position that former president Theodore Roosevelt had held before he had resigned to organize the Rough Riders and charge into history. Just as the Oyster Bay Roosevelts were in decline, the Hyde Park Roosevelts were in ascendancy. Theodore Roosevelt had been thirty-nine when he got the job, Franklin crowed to his close friends, while he was still a young thirty-one.

As Sara may have feared, Franklin's political career slowly began to take him away to a life of his own. As the new assistant secretary of the navy, he had to move his family to Washington, where in time both he and Eleanor developed an expertise beyond Sara's own interests. Eleanor was especially transformed, beginning to manifest a remarkable streak of independence from both Franklin and Sara, discounting her mother-in-law's advice and pouring herself into a plethora of public causes.

Sara visited often, and when she came, she sat opposite Franklin at the breakfast table, Eleanor demurely shifting to a side chair with the children. Sara also still ruled at Hyde Park, on which the family descended for long holidays. And she was still an unremitting presence at their summer homes at Campobello Island off the coast of Maine. A formal family portrait of the time showed Franklin and Eleanor with their six children surrounding them and Sara sitting snugly between the couple. But there was no doubt that she was losing her grip, that Franklin and Eleanor were slipping away. Then a troubling marital crisis erupted, bringing her back as a powerful force in their lives.

In the summer of 1917, using the polio epidemic as his rationale, Franklin shipped his whole family off to Campobello Island while he stayed behind in Washington and worked. Eleanor was suspicious. The following year she quietly informed her mother-in-law that Franklin was having an affair with her own former social secretary, the beautiful and accomplished Lucy Page Mercer. Though she had suspected it and it had played its part in her new, reinvented self, Eleanor was shattered by the actual confirmation. All of her feelings of inferiority came rushing back. She immediately demanded a divorce.

But Sara was not so accommodating. Mounting her own nonstop, interfamily campaign, she made clear what had been only veiled threats during their courtship. Everything was now openly on the table: Sara was prepared to disinherit her son if he left his marriage. And he could say good-bye forever to his beloved Hyde Park. She would simply not countenance such a humiliation for herself and the family name.

And, although no expert, she felt certain that he could count his political career as done. Franklin backed down. His relationship with Lucy receded deep into the shadows. A few years later, Lucy would marry another. But in the catharsis of 1918, a reborn, toughened Eleanor seized the moment, closing her bedroom door on Franklin forever. That "ordeal," at least, was ended.

In the politics following the death of Theodore Roosevelt, many pundits were hailing Franklin as the heir to his uncle's mantle. Democrats were attempting to steal his name for their own purposes, saying that Theodore had always been more of a Democrat than a Republican and his young cousin was proof. The year 1920 was turning into a showdown between the Oyster Bay Republican Roosevelts, led by Theodore, Jr., and the Hyde Park Democrat Roosevelts, led by Franklin. The acrimony was bitter. At the Democratic National Convention, Franklin was chosen as the vice presidential running mate of the Democratic nominee, James Cox of Ohio. Franklin pointed out to his mother that their esteemed cousin TR had been forty-one when nominated as vice president, one of the youngest in history, yet now Franklin was only thirty-eight. Thousands of people descended on Hyde Park to cheer the surprise candidate.

Sara, originally shocked by the idea that politics involved entertaining persons of every station in life, fairly beamed with pride as the crowds cheered her boy. The Democrats were trounced in the general election, but Sara turned it all around, referring to it in her diary as no more than a rainy day and saying that Franklin was relieved to have lost the vice presidency. In fact, he emerged from the defeat unscathed, with a reputation within the party as a proven politician with an undiminished future.

In 1921, Sara returned home from her annual European trip to the startling news that Franklin had taken ill at Campobello. He had been diagnosed with polio and was virtually paralyzed from the chest down. He was unable even to perform his own toilet. Eleanor had bravely taken on the task of using a catheter to void his bladder and giving him enemas to help empty his bowels. Sara learned that her daughter-in-law had risen powerfully to the occasion, changing his sheets and massaging legs she hadn't touched since the news of Lucy Mercer had severed her sexual relationship with her husband.

Franklin experienced bouts of intense depression during his illness when he wondered aloud if God had abandoned him, only to finally conclude that his crisis was a chastisement and that God would not bother with such a correction unless some great unfinished task still lay ahead. Eleanor worked to exhaustion for the man who had betrayed her and sometimes wondered to what end. Her children once stumbled onto her, sobbing with exhaustion in a room by herself.

But those were rare occasions. Mostly, Franklin's room resounded with laughter and bravado as Franklin and Eleanor made great fun of his situation. And to Sara, he kept up a good front. He had not shared with her his humiliation at Groton, where as a boy he had been an object of ridicule, and he would not allow her to see anything but optimism now.

Sara was not fooled. Even as her son was proclaiming that he would regain the use of his legs, she was having the mansion at Hyde Park refitted for a wheelchair. And she renewed an intense but ultimately doomed campaign to convince him to retreat to Hyde Park as a gentleman. Surely in these circumstances he could see the wisdom of doing so. But Franklin was more determined than ever not to fall back into his mother's clutches. While Eleanor spent more and more time with her newfound liberal female friends, Nancy Cook and Marion Dickerson, whom Franklin derided as "she-males," he embarked on his own self-made holistic regimen for recovery, taking to a boat in warm Florida waters accompanied by friends, including a devoted, worshipful secretary in her twenties named Marguerite "Missy" LeHand.

Eleanor may or may not have been physically intimate with her friends. Historians have researched the subject obsessively.[2] Her own companions insist that she was not and was much too prudish even to discuss the subject. But there is no doubt that they inspired her and that there was a deep emotional bonding that gave her the confidence that she was loved. Eleanor would build her own cottage at Hyde Park, which she would dub Val-Kill, and there she and her newfound sisters would live away from Sara and her own children. The doilies on the table would bear the three ladies' initials. Eleanor and her friends would devote themselves to political issues and make the needs of women a relevant subject for the Democratic Party.

Meanwhile, Franklin may or may not have been intimate with young Missy LeHand. Some Roosevelt historians insist that their relationship was never consummated. Eleanor and the children accepted the relationship, which speaks for its innocence. Sara spoke favorably of Missy's family and upbringing. Years later, only Elliott, of all the children, would declare that it had not been as benign as historians liked to believe.

On the Florida beaches, away from doctors with their depressing diagnosis, Missy would join Franklin on his program of holistic healing, slithering together along the beaches in the sand and mud, Franklin dragging his dead legs behind him, convinced that he was somehow imparting life to his limbs. It is hard to imagine that during the long, moonlit nights on his houseboat, on trips that lasted for months at a time and involved much alcohol, they did not at least experiment. Later, in Warm Springs, Georgia, where FDR would bathe in the mineral water, looking for a cure, they would spend three years together. One of FDR's biographers estimates that during a seven-year period he was away from his children half the time, with Eleanor averaging visits of only two weeks a year, usually in March, near their anniversary. When Eleanor was hospitalized in New York, Franklin did not send a note or a flower. But Missy was at his side year after year, with only an annual monthlong visit home to spend time with her parents.

We do not know for certain the intimacies of these respective relationships. But twelve years later in the White House, Eleanor and another close female friend would each have her own private bedroom, across the hall from the other in the upstairs family quarters. Historians would eventually read some of their letters, containing heartfelt avowals of love to each other but also an explanation from Eleanor justifying her unwillingness to give herself completely. And Franklin would still have his Missy, at least for those first years in the White House. She sometimes roamed the halls of the private quarters in a robe, and when Eleanor was gone, she could be seen sitting jauntily on the president's lap, even in front of the visiting grown children.

The dysfunctional Roosevelt marriage offers further evidence of the powerful role his mother played in his life and how it inadvertently shaped his political career. Certainly, Sara's possessiveness put FDR in what today's family therapists would call a double bind. On the one hand, she made it clear that an affair with another woman was out of the question for her son; on the other, she bragged about the upbringing and pedigree of Missy LeHand, the other woman at his side. Sara was obviously conflicted. At some level she may have been pleased that her son and his wife were not sleeping together. Such an arrangement had worked for her and James. This led her to tolerate, sometimes even encourage, Eleanor's female friends. And it led to mixed signals about her son's potential paramours.

According to one family therapist, Kerry Little, the victim of the so-called double bind often develops an emotional resiliency, while creating a protective shield to hide his or her true feelings. This is a classic description of FDR. His emotional resiliency helped him fight

"Father, I cannot tell a lie. I cut the tree." Parson Weems's apocryphal story of George Washington and his father was widely accepted as true. Ironically, young Abraham Lincoln read the parson's book and later personified many of Washington's idealized virtues. *Courtesy of the Mount Vernon Ladies' Association*

Mary Washington was a possessive, domineering woman who tried to keep her son from wandering far. He loved his early work as a surveyor, probably because it took him far away from her. *Courtesy of the Mount Vernon Ladies' Association*

George Washington and his mother. Some historians say that he did not even like the woman, but he sought her approval to the end. After losing in battle early in his military career, he wrote a sibling, telling him not to mention the event to their mother. *Courtesy of the Mount Vernon Ladies' Association*

Mary Washington's house in Fredericksburg, Virginia. The first president provided well for his mother, but she was constantly plagued by fears of impending poverty. *Library of Congress*

Artist's depiction of George Washington and his mother at their last meeting, March 11, 1789. He had written her a letter urging her to live with one of her children but made it clear that she should not come to Mount Vernon. *Courtesy of the Mount Vernon Ladies' Association*

Mary Ball Washington was a domineering, irritating presence in her son's life. She seemed to take no pleasure in his many accomplishments. *Library of Congress*

Abigail Adams, wife and mother to presidents, wrote her husband: "If particular care and attention is not paid to the ladies, we are determined to foment a rebellion, and will not hold ourselves bound by any laws in which we have no voice, or representation." *Library of Congress*

Benjamin Franklin, John Adams, and Thomas Jefferson working on the Declaration of Independence. If Jefferson was the author, Adams was the voice who effectively argued its wisdom before the Continental Congress. *Library of Congress*

Stuart's official portrait of President John Adams. His father broke the family rule, selling land to pay for his Harvard education, while his siblings were denied any educational opportunities themselves. It made John keenly conscious of his responsibility to succeed. *Library of Congress*

John Quincy Adams at twenty-one years. He was an extreme version of his father, who had already idealized and exaggerated the grandfather's principles. The same sort of evolution would be in play in the last three generations of the Bush family. *Library of Congress*

Slave-state supporters were constantly bedeviled by John Quincy Adams's tactics. He was way ahead of his time on the problem of slavery, and sensing that history would vindicate him, he fought to the death against the gag rule and for the petitioner's right to speak up on the issue. *Library of Congress*

John Quincy Adams, the first son of a president to win the White House for himself, actually lost the popular vote. He was extremely independent and hated partisan politics, feeling he should be the president of the people, not a party. His self-righteous commitment to duty made enemies. *Library of Congress*

John Quincy Adams died in the Capitol building. The eighty-year-old former president was serving in Congress, where he was ardently leading the effort against slavery. He was on the floor of the House when he suffered a stroke and was carried to the chamber of the speaker, where he died two days later. *Library of Congress*

Thomas Lincoln, father of the sixteenth president. Old Tom sometimes knocked his boy to the ground, said Dennis Hanks, the cousin who lived for years in the same cabin. Hanks referred to Tom's "cold and inhumane treatment" of young Lincoln. *Library of Congress*

Some enterprising Kentuckians claimed that this was the actual log cabin in which Abraham Lincoln was born. When the family moved to Indiana they lived for a winter in a three-sided shed, with one side open to the elements and heated by a constantly burning fire. *Library of Congress*

Some historians trace the Lincoln family to the Shenandoah Valley. This drawing supposedly represents the homestead where Lincoln's father was born. The family was attacked by Indians and a young Thomas saw his father murdered. *Library of Congress*

Lincoln was supposedly given an ax at the age of eight and spent most of his life clearing land and splitting rails, but much about Lincoln's early years is unproven. "The chief difficulty I had," said John Locke Scripps of the *Chicago Press & Tribune*, "was to induce him to communicate the homely facts of his youth." *Library of Congress*

Harry Dayton Sickles's portrait of Lincoln on the Sangamon River. Lincoln was twenty-two when he arrived in New Salem, Illinois. Citizens of the town said he was always reading a book. *Library of Congress*

Sarah Bush Johnston was the wonderful stepmother. When she first saw him he was caked with dirt and "looked like an animal." She said, "I never gave him a cross word in all my life. His mind and mine—what little I had—seemed to move together—move in the same channel." *Courtesy of the Abraham Lincoln Library and Museum*

"Take it quietly UNCLE ABE and I will draw it closer than ever"!!

"A few more stitches ANDY and the good old UNION will be mended"!

THE "RAIL SPLITTER" AT WORK REPAIRING THE UNION.

A political cartoon of the era depicts Lincoln repairing the union. Historian-psychologist Charles Strozier saw Lincoln as resolving his personal conflicts with his father through public events. The president became famous for his biblical quote "A house divided against itself cannot stand." *Library of Congress*

Elizabeth Irwin Harrison, mother of Benjamin Harrison, was one of a long line of deeply religious presidential mothers. She died giving birth to her tenth child. She once wrote Benjamin that she was praying for him daily, that he would avoid "straying from the paths of duty." *Courtesy of the President Benjamin Harrison House*

James Roosevelt and son, Franklin. The father stated in his last testament, "I wish him to be under the influence of his mother." It was a wish that would be granted. *Courtesy of the Franklin D. Roosevelt Library*

FDR and his patrician father, James Roosevelt, on horseback at Hyde Park. Sara is holding the dog's leash. James once turned down an invitation to dine at the home of the nouveau riche Cornelius Vanderbilt, explaining to Sara that if they accepted they would have to return the invitation, which was intolerable. *Courtesy of the Franklin D. Roosevelt Library*

Young Franklin and his mother off Campobello. When he was a small boy, she wrote, he once startled her by sighing sadly and declaring, "Oh, to be free." *Courtesy of the Franklin D. Roosevelt Library*

James Roosevelt and his wife, Sara Delano Roosevelt. When they met, he was fifty-two and she was twenty-six, but they were a match. "All is over," she wrote in her diary. "As I write these words I wonder how I lived when he left me. . . . I see him every minute, I hear his voice at every turn." *Library of Congress*

FDR landed a spot on the Harvard school newspaper and by his senior year won some grudging respect. Raised in an aristocratic family, he was a bit of an oddball throughout his school days and was rejected for admission to the prestigious Porcellian Club. *Courtesy of the Franklin D. Roosevelt Library*

Sara Roosevelt with her son at Fairhaven, Massachusetts. She was a formidable presence in his life. Franklin had his first bath by himself when he was nine years old. *Courtesy of the Franklin D. Roosevelt Library*

Sara Roosevelt standing between Franklin and Eleanor. The picture is a metaphor for their lives. Sara gave the newlyweds a New York brownstone mansion that adjoined her own. The two homes were connected in the vestibule and on the bedroom floors. *Courtesy of the Franklin D. Roosevelt Library*

FDR on his houseboat in Florida, where he and his wife's attractive secretary, Missy LeHand, spent several years off and on, vacationing and in rehabilitation. FDR was struggling with the emotional demons of polio. *Courtesy of the Franklin D. Roosevelt Library*

FDR with sons Elliott and James and their grandmother Sara. "Your mother only gave birth to you," Sara Roosevelt told them. "I raised you." *Courtesy of the Franklin D. Roosevelt Library*

Eleanor, Franklin, and Sara with Mr. and Mrs. James Roosevelt, the president's firstborn son and his wife. Eleanor would say, "I looked at my mother-in-law's face after she was dead and understood so many things I'd never seen before. It is dreadful to have lived so close to someone for thirty-six years and feel no deep affection or sense of loss." *Courtesy of the Franklin D. Roosevelt Library*

The president and his mother, Sara Roosevelt. "When you read history," she once said, "it seems as if most of the presidents didn't have mothers." She would change that. In her last letter to her son Sara wrote, "I think of you night and day." *Courtesy of the Franklin D. Roosevelt Library*

When new president Harry Truman brought his mother back to Washington, there was a huge airport greeting. "If I had known this would happen," she harrumphed in good humor, "I wouldn't have come." An ardent southern Democrat, she refused the Lincoln Bedroom at the White House and found the high bed in the Queen's Room too pompous, settling for a single bed in an adjacent room for the maid. *J. Sherrel Lakey, courtesy of the Harry S. Truman Library*

David and Ida Eisenhower with their family. Future president Dwight, age twelve, is on the upper left, followed by Edgar, Earl, Arthur, and Roy. Milton is the little boy up front. When young Dwight contracted septicemia, the doctors wanted to amputate his leg, but the father heeded his son's plea and they prayed for a miracle instead. *Courtesy of the Dwight D. Eisenhower Library*

back from polio, and his protective shell became the most pronounced characteristic of his political persona. Even members of his own White House staff would later write about the difficulty of seeing behind the president's sphinxlike smile, to know what he was really thinking.

THE POLITICAL RESURRECTION

In 1924, Franklin Delano Roosevelt, confident and beaming with optimism, appeared onstage at the Democraticic National Convention, standing with the help of painful leg braces and propped up by the podium. The place broke into waves of cheering and tears. FDR's speech rang out with clarity, urging the nominating convention to vote for his candidate, "the Happy Warrior," New York Governor Al Smith. FDR's man would not win the nomination, but the thunderous approval that followed the end of his speech and the very sight of him sent journalists scurrying to their typewriters to knock out positive stories on his apparent courageous road back from the near-death grip of polio. No one knew that it was a bluff, that Franklin had rehearsed for weeks the intricately choreographed "walk" to the podium, using his own son as a crutch and carefully arranging for shills to appear to stop him and talk, to cover for his slow pace. And when it was over, no one outside his inner circle knew what it had taken out of him. He was both exhilarated and exhausted by the performance.

Four years later he was back at the Democratic National Convention with another speech, an even more sophisticated shuffle to the podium, and another tumultuous reception. This time his candidate for president, Al Smith, won the nomination, and he had a role for Franklin to play. Smith was in a tough general election contest against the Republican nominee, Herbert Hoover, a man of towering popularity and integrity. It was essential to carry the nation's most populous state, and having the admired FDR atop that state's ticket would certainly help. Smith wanted Franklin to run for his old spot as governor of New York and promised that the state Democratic political machine would help make it happen.

Franklin's doctor said no, and Sara was adamant, speaking directly to party officials—her son would not be a candidate. Franklin and Missy discussed it together in their cottage in Warm Springs, Georgia, and decided that he should decline. But the pressure was unrelenting, and Missy's fervent pleas for him to defer probably sealed the case; Franklin was not about to be possessed by yet another woman.

Reluctantly, against the orders of doctors who questioned whether his precarious health would allow such a test, he signaled back to the party bosses, some of whom were waiting him out in hotel rooms in Warm Springs, that he would be a candidate for governor. And then he added the warning "But don't let my mother know about this."[3]

In New York, out of the loop and busy with their own many political and social causes, Eleanor and Sara learned about Franklin's decision in the newspapers. Sara took the next train to Georgia. In an ad hoc meeting with Democratic Party political operatives gathered in Warm Springs, Sara opened fire, saying that she could not fathom why anyone even wanted governmental office, and that if the campaign cost her son's life, she would never forgive them and would personally hold all of them responsible. Having thus vented, she returned to New York and committed her money, time, and tireless energy to her son's campaign.

On election night, November 6, 1928, Al Smith and the Democrats went down to ignominious defeat. Herbert Hoover was projected to be the new president-elect, and, while the contest for governor of New York was close, Franklin Roosevelt seemed to be losing to Albert Ottinger. The Roosevelt family and campaign supporters stayed up late at their Biltmore Hotel headquarters in Manhattan, waiting for some confirmation one way or the other. But as midnight approached and it was apparent that there would be no celebration, the crowd began to slip away. When all the next morning's newspapers arrived declaring a Republican victory from top to bottom and confirming that Ottinger had indeed beaten Roosevelt in the gubernatorial race, Franklin and Eleanor said good night to their supporters and were whisked back to their brownstone house on East Sixty-fifth Street.

Sara Delano Roosevelt was not so easily defeated. She had uncharacteristically abandoned Hyde Park, waiting with the faithful at the Biltmore Hotel campaign headquarters in New York City. Shortly after the candidate left, most of the remaining crowd had evaporated. By 1 A.M. the ballroom lights were turned off and Sara moved into a small corridor where a tight-knit core of political operatives maintained the death watch over the rapidly disintegrating Roosevelt campaign.

When a discernible trend emerged showing that Franklin was at least running better than Al Smith in New York, there was a brief rally of spirits among the less savvy and a phone call was finally placed to Franklin, waking him up to pass on the meaningless message. The rural votes always went predominantly Republican and they were the largest share still outstanding, so the outcome still looked bleak. Franklin took the news, a bit annoyed at their having bothered waking him with such a report, and promptly went back to sleep.

Over the next few hours, several courteous staffers offered to escort Sara Roosevelt home. But the candidate's mother refused to budge. Her son had chosen this contest in spite of his health, against her wishes and better judgment, but if that was his choice, he had better win. A little after four in the morning, just before sunrise, Franklin Delano Roosevelt barely pulled ahead. It was finally clear. He would win the election by a razor-thin margin.

A weary seventy-four-year-old Sara Delano Roosevelt stood in the dimly lit hotel corridor, sighed with deep satisfaction, and joined the faithful few who were still awake in a toast to her son, the newly elected governor of the state of New York. She had milk in her glass. Taking a taxi across the empty streets of Manhattan, she arrived at her connecting brownstone mansion. Though she was tempted to walk into her son's room and wake him with the good news, her motherly instincts prevailed: her boy, the new governor, needed all the sleep he could get.

As the sun broke over Manhattan and the New York newspapers busily rewrote their second editions, Sara finally retired, pleased that the good citizens of the state had the sense to know who should lead and who should follow.

The victory only complicated the life of Eleanor Roosevelt, now first lady of New York. "I am not excited about my husband's election," she bitterly snapped to a reporter from the *New York Post*. "I don't care."[4] In planning the sleeping arrangements for the governor's mansion, she assigned Missy LeHand to the first lady's bedroom.

On October 24, 1929, the New York Stock Exchange collapsed and the American economy began its descent into what would be called the Great Depression. Sara, whose effortless ability to manage her financial affairs and her seemingly endless source of money are mysteries to historians, was hardly affected. FDR was more intrigued by the political ramifications of the disaster. The Republicans controlled the White House and were sure to bear the brunt of the political fallout. Franklin's 1930 reelection tested this dynamic. As expected, he rode to an easy victory. In 1932, as an admired governor of the nation's most populous state, a Democrat, and a Roosevelt, he was almost certain to be elected the president of the United States.

In 1931, during a trip to Europe, Sara contracted pneumonia and was hospitalized in Paris. As the mother of the presidential front runner she was shocked and a little pleased by the attention it triggered. Front-page newspaper stories followed her progress.

As a boy, young Franklin had suffered from scarlet fever at Groton Academy, and Sara had raced home to be at his side. Now it was Sara's turn to give her son a scare. Accompanied by one of his sons, he took passage on the *Aquitania,* traveling across the ocean, hoping to arrive in time to see his mother one last time. As it turned out, Sara was in good spirits, well on her way to recovery, being feted in her hospital room by national leaders and celebrities. After Franklin's visit she revived sufficiently to be moved into a suite at the George V hotel.

THE PINNACLE

As expected, after a marathon of political wrangling in the summer of 1932, the Democratic National Committee finally nominated Franklin Delano Roosevelt for president. When he appeared at the door of her Hyde Park home as the Democratic nominee for president, a deeply moved Sara Delano Roosevelt embraced her polio-stricken boy and wept openly. Beneath all her protestations and put-downs of public life, she had wanted greatness for him as much as he wanted it himself, maybe more. Still, even after his election she tried to cushion the blows that she knew were coming, telling reporters, "Never did I think that my son would be president. That was the last thing I should ever have imagined for him, or that he should be in public life of any sort. My only ambition was that he grow to be a fine, upright man like his father, straight and honorable, just and kind, an upstanding American."[5] More than a successful presidency, she wanted his happiness, and her lowered expectations guaranteed that he would always surprise her by doing better.

At his inauguration, Franklin used the old Roosevelt family Bible for the swearing-in ceremony. It had belonged to Isaac the Patriot. Sara talked of James all day and telling any who would listen how proud he would have been.

The week of the presidential inauguration, it was not the face of Franklin or Eleanor that graced the cover of *Time* magazine but rather the proud and proper visage of the chief executive's mother, the first woman in American history to vote for her own son as president. In May, NBC had her address the nation for Mother's Day. In the fall, *Newsweek* ran a cover story praising her role. The next year, a magazine article she had started for *Good Housekeeping* was transformed into a best-selling book, *My Boy Franklin.* And a year later there was another best seller written on her life. She was feted at banquets and charity events, with thousands in attendance and orchestras striking up as she dramatically entered the ballroom. At the White House the domestic staff treated her like visiting royalty and snapped to attention when she arrived. The government issued a stamp with her picture on it and it sold briskly. Sara Delano Roosevelt was turning out to be the most popular presidential mother in American history, and she was taking it all in stride.

Still, she was perhaps the only one with the nerve and know-how to push her son's buttons. She agreed with his handlers to be interviewed for a series in a national magazine, but when she saw her name used in commercial advertising promoting the piece she promptly broke off the relationship. She would not abide such impropriety. When her son ignored her protests and ordered the official recognition of the Soviet Union, she declared her complete boycott of the White House. And indeed she stayed away for two whole weeks. When her president son visited Hyde Park, she would often eavesdrop on his important telephone conversations. "Mama, will you *please* get off the line," he was heard saying desperately on one occasion. "I can hear you breathing. Come on, now."[6] She once announced to the visiting press corps that she was not going to allow Franklin to attend church the next Sunday because he was too far behind on his correspondence. And America loved it all.

Both Sara and Eleanor had been changing dramatically as circumstances had demanded. Eleanor finally hit her stride, establishing her own identity, taking on lost causes, and championing the rights of the poor and disenfranchised. It was the beginning of what would be a spectacular rise and an independent career, which grew even more stellar after the death of her husband. She now began to champion the causes of black America and eventually became one of the most powerful advocates for the cause of the Jews, at a critical time in their history.

Sara's evolution was just as remarkable. The woman who had refused to accept an invitation to the Vanderbilts' now turned Hyde Park into an extension of Eleanor's activities one week and the White House public relations office the next. She entertained hundreds of people with just a few hours' warning from either Franklin or Eleanor.

She had virtually raised the Roosevelt children. Jimmy Roosevelt had once said, "We were fortunate to have a grandmother who would do for us when we had a mother who could not and a father who would not."[7] Now she took on the great-grandchildren as well, juggling marathon summers at Hyde Park and spectacular Christmas celebrations that started in Washington at the White House and inevitably ended up with midnight train rides to Hyde Park for sledding and snowball fights, lasting through the holidays.

But she was getting older, and she was finally beginning to feel it. In 1934, she made only seven trips to the White House. And there was that nagging reality that Franklin had slipped away, that he had outgrown her. To keep up, she called in specialists to try to help her understand the complex economic issues with which her son was grappling, and she invited her own servants to explain to her how their own savings and pensions worked and how they would live in retirement.

On her eightieth birthday, the whole clan gathered around her, including the grandchildren. They would be a tormented generation, the children of Franklin and Eleanor. The five would have nineteen marriages between them. Two of the in-laws would commit suicide, and another would attempt and fail. Living in this family was not easy. Sara would lament that it was because they had never been taught to know right from wrong, a slap at her own troubled Franklin and Eleanor. Her grandchildren presented her with a scroll that said that Hyde Park was their only real home and that Hyde Park meant her and all the fun she gave them there.

Much of Franklin's great strength came from his lifetime struggle to break from her. "Oh to be free," he had wistfully said to her at the age of five. She had duly recorded the moment in her book. And although she had explained it away, she must have known, at some level, what she was doing. The mystery of her riches was the secret of her power, and her discretion was flawless. She could have given Franklin a piece of the Hyde Park estate early and let him go free, but she held it all close to the breast, without ever letting a scrap of information out. There is no question that she was generous. When he won the governor's mansion and had to take a cut in pay, she promptly told him on the side that she would make up the difference. Her largesse extended into the White House, where she subsidized large parts of the entertainment budget. But she was not so generous as to lose control. Never.

Once a reporter had asked a question in her presence about the national debt and the budget, and in a senior moment she had misunderstood. "The budget? The budget?" She seemed alarmed. "Franklin knows nothing of the budget." She was referring to her own carefully controlled family finances.

There is no greater testament to her business acumen than the fact that nineteen years after her death the seemingly inexhaustible Delano wealth, which had been sustained by succeeding generations for almost two hundred years, had been totally spent by her self-indulgent descendents. During the Depression, when it might or might not have been jeopardized, during her son's political rise she had divested herself of many investments, just to avoid any possible charges of conflict of interest. She didn't want Franklin's decisions as governor and president to have an undue impact on her estate. And through it all she had never shared a single bit of information to her son about her finances. No wonder she had tolerated Eleanor's stretch toward feminism. Many of its tenets she understood instinctively and had experienced personally.

In the early years of his presidency, Franklin used his mother as an important surrogate. She sometimes took the political lead and was applauded by White House handlers, as when she put down the controversial Senator Huey Long. "Who is that dreadful man sitting next to my son?" she had asked Eleanor, loudly enough for the whole dinner table to hear. During his first year as president, Franklin used the occasion of her annual European trip to bring back private messages from world leaders.

Now, older and increasingly unable to keep up with fast-moving events, Sara's strong-arm attempts to weigh in on policy became a nuisance. She wrote him letters from a latter European trip, praising Franco and bragging about the order and efficiency of Mussolini's Italy. Over cocktails, Franklin read the missives aloud to his staff, and with his encouragement they all laughed uproariously at his mother's expense. There was something primitive about Franklin's triumph. It was like a dog rolling over the carcass of a fresh kill. There was no reason to involve his staff in his mother's humiliation, and it must have been an awkward moment for them, wondering how far to be drawn in and how the president would feel about it later. But it was clear that she was out of her depth. He was free.

In 1939, eighty-four-year-old Sara Roosevelt hosted the king and queen of England at a formal dinner party at Hyde Park. At first, when Franklin had said he would need the New York estate to host the royal couple, a humbled, failing Sara had graciously suggested she leave. But he had said no, they would be visiting three days, she was the mistress of Hyde Park, and she should stay. The formal dinner would be all hers. There ensued a muted turf war as a somewhat revived Sara tried to muscle Eleanor out of having a picnic with American hot dogs. They were not good enough for royalty, she sniffed. They were now back on her turf. But Eleanor gently explained that the visitors from England would hardly be impressed if everywhere they went society mimicked the English, that there would be much more to talk about of their visit back at Windsor if they experienced *real* American culture.[8]

More than a hundred thousand people lined the roads as the king and queen of England were driven from the railroad station to the Roosevelt Hyde Park estate. The picnic was a hit.

But Sara's meticulously planned formal dinner involved a number of mortifying mishaps, including a butler who took a tumble and an improvised table that tipped over, sending stacks of valuable china crashing to the floor. Eleanor was amused and wrote it up for her newspaper column, which had to pass Franklin's veto. At first Sara's son questioned the motives of his wife's piece, but then he decided that a little family self-deprecation might help balance the scales of public opinion after such an imperial visit. So the story ran in newspapers around the country and was picked up by the foreign press, as well.

Some historians see it as a bit of Eleanor's sweet revenge on her flagging tormentor. Sara complained to her children that the White House had insisted on using its own butlers at her dinner and that if she had been allowed to use *her* staff, it would never have happened. Eleanor would later play to that comment as well, pointing out that Sara's staff was all white while most of the White House staff was black, implying for history that the president's mother was a bigot, an unfair accusation.

"I THINK OF YOU NIGHT AND DAY"

If Sara Roosevelt was growing old and losing some of her equilibrium and her ability to hold her own against her emboldened and brilliant children, she was still her son's biggest fan. She went to the movies every week just to see him in the newsreels. When he gave the first of his famous fireside chats on national radio, she was asked to be at his side, and thereafter, year by year, she carefully listened to every one of his speeches from her library in Hyde Park, talking back to the radio as if he were with her in the room. Sometimes Franklin would tease her by sending her outrageous and hateful anti-FDR editorials, which would inspire a shrill letter back in his defense, pointing out to him the flawed logic of his enemy's argument. The president still needed her reassurance. "I think of you night and day," she wrote him in the last letter of her life.[9] When she ignored his request to hire a nurse and he upbraided her for it, she rushed to apologize. Realizing that she had unintentionally been the cause of worry and a distraction from his important work, she did a complete about-face and hastily responded, "Of course, you were right to have a nurse. I am sorry you got alarmed."[10] She would take a nurse—if not for herself, then to please her boy.

The outbreak of World War II in Europe and the initial role the United States played as a neutral country, sympathetic to the English and French, was a balancing act that consumed her son's total attention. It was not just a question of diplomacy; America needed time to reinvent its economy, to get onto a war footing without retarding a recovery that had just begun after the greatest depression in world history. Sarah, herself, followed the disheartening accounts of German blitzkrieg as Hitler overran Europe. She plunged into numerous charities and activities, including projects to help persecuted Jews fleeing

Nazi Germany. At the end of 1940, Franklin Roosevelt addressed the nation from the White House, defining for the public America's role in the encroaching world crisis. Sitting at his side were key members of his cabinet and his eighty-six-year-old mother.

By the spring of 1941, Sara's health was failing rapidly. She delivered her annual Mother's Day radio broadcast to the nation, but her charity work and her prolific letter writing slackened. During the summer, First Lady Eleanor Roosevelt was in the middle of a complicated political battle over American war readiness and the organization of its civil defense program. But during a telephone conversation she could sense that her mother-in-law was in trouble. Eleanor helped Sara make the annual trip to Campobello, where the president's mother expected the cool waters to refresh her as they had done so often in the past. But she was so weak that she barely left her bedroom.

Eleanor was waiting to welcome Sara back to Hyde Park that September and, after taking a good look at her mother-in-law, telephoned Franklin and told him to take the presidential train home in a hurry.

The year 1941 was a consuming one for Franklin D. Roosevelt and the nation. Hitler's armies turned east, overrunning the Balkan countries and Greece. That summer, at the same time as Sara had been convalescing in Campobello, Germany had invaded the Soviet Union. Her president son had met Winston Churchill in a rendezvous on board a ship in the North Atlantic. The Second World War was entering a new and dangerous time, with America's neutrality difficult to maintain. And at the same time, the president's personal life was in transition. By most accounts he had become infatuated by the exiled Crown Princess Marthe of Norway, who had replaced Missy LeHand at his side on long drives into the surrounding Virginia fox country. The rejected Missy had collapsed at a White House dinner party and two weeks later suffered a major stroke.[11]

By September, when Sara returned exhausted to her Hyde Park home, German armies had surrounded Leningrad and were within a hundred miles of Moscow. There was a very real fear that America would be brought into the war. And of course, the Japanese were planning to do just that. Their surprise attack on Pearl Harbor would take place that December.

When a Canadian journalist asked for an interview, Sara consented in spite of her waning strength. He asked about the dangerous times and where they might lead. Unfailingly optimistic, she offered that "there is nothing to fear on that score. We don't know where the times are taking us, but if we all do the sensible things and have brave hearts, a better world is bound to come."[12]

On September 4, a German submarine fired torpedoes at an American ship in what the United States insisted was a neutral zone off Iceland. The president had been moving a reluctant country toward war against the Nazis for many months, and so he had publicly exposed the incident and was planning to address the nation on the crisis when the call came through from Eleanor. The president immediately canceled his national radio address and took his private train overnight to Hyde Park.[13]

When she heard that the president was coming to see her, Sara revived. She put on her finest bed jacket, tied a blue ribbon in her hair, and moved to the chaise lounge in her bedroom. They talked all morning and much of the afternoon, Franklin telling her about his meetings with Winston Churchill. Sara, forgetting how ill she was, expressing petulantly how she wished he had brought the English prime minister to Campobello, which after all, was so close.

At 9:30 in the evening she developed a blood clot in her lung and fell into a deep coma. The president sat by her side throughout the night and into the next morning, taking small naps and staring intently at the woman who had raised him and had given birth to him on the very bed where she now lay. At noon, on Sunday, September 7, 1941, Sara Delano Roosevelt, one of America's greatest mothers, passed away. She was only two weeks shy of her eighty-seventh birthday. As word of the death of Mrs. Roosevelt began to spread to servants and presidential aides throughout the house, outside, a giant oak tree, the tallest on the entire Hyde Park estate, cracked at the trunk and came crashing down with a thunderous roar. The president was wheeled out onto the yard to stare at the scene and marvel at the coincidence. Sara was gone. "When you read history," she had once said, "it seems as if most of the Presidents didn't have mothers."[14] She had changed that.

Eleanor Roosevelt would write a friend, "I looked at my mother-in-law's face after she was dead & understood so many things I'd never seen before. It is dreadful to have lived so close to someone for

36 years & feel no deep affection or sense of loss. It is hard on Franklin however."[15]

The funeral was held in the library of the Roosevelt home on the Hyde Park estate. At the end, the St. James Episcopal choir stood and sang one of Sara's favorite hymns, "Abide With Me." It had been sung at the wedding of the English king and queen she had once entertained in that very room. To the words "Heaven's morning breaks, and earth's vain shadows flee; In life, in death, O Lord, abide with me," some of the same servants who had carried the coffin of James Roosevelt forty-one years before now lifted the coffin of his wife and carried her to the waiting hearse.

At the St. James churchyard, the president's vehicle was driven right up to the open grave, which was positioned next to the resting place of James Roosevelt and his first wife. Sara had often come to this very spot to meditate and remember the man she had married and the father of the boy who had consumed her life. The president stood out of respect, in spite of the effort involved, propping himself up on the car door. Surrounding the grave were Eleanor and most of the children, members of Sara's dwindling family, and local staff and invited villagers. As her casket was lowered into the grave, the group began to recite the Lord's Prayer.

In July 1944, the president's former secretary and companion, Marguerite "Missy" LeHand went to a movie theater in Boston with her sister. A newsreel came on, showing the president's pallid face. He was suffering from arteriosclerosis. Concerned, Missy returned home and pulled out old photo albums, comparing the pictures and confirming the appearance of his declining health. That night, after reliving the joy and sorrow of her private relationship with a dying man who had once loved her and then rejected her, she suffered a number of strokes and was taken to a nearby hospital, where she died at the age of forty-five. Eight months later and only a little more than three years after the death of his mother, President Franklin Delano Roosevelt died of a cerebral hemorrhage in Warm Springs, Georgia. His old sweetheart Lucy Mercer Rutherfurd was at his side. He was sixty-three. Eleanor would live another seventeen years and establish a career of her own, serving as President Harry Truman's ambassador to the United Nations. She is consistently ranked by historians as one of the greatest of America's first ladies.

★

TWELVE

The Ruthless Ascent
of Joseph P. Kennedy

*The measure of a man's success in life isn't the money he has made
—it's the kind of family he has raised.*[1]
—Joseph Patrick Kennedy

The Kennedy family of Massachusetts, one of America's greatest political dynasties, sprang from humble Irish roots. Indeed, much about their early history is shrouded in Irish mist, for they were common folk and no one thought to keep a record of their early lives. We know that in the mid–nineteenth century they lived as a family of nine in a four-room cottage with a dirt floor and a thatched roof of grass and straw on twenty-five acres in County Wexford.[2] It was not a grand existence, but it was better than that of others, who died all around them in the seemingly never-ending series of potato famines that ravaged the land. Yet, for a while, they lost even the little they had, finding themselves evicted from their land, sitting at the side of the road and hiring themselves out to other farmers before new laws ended the abuse of absentee landlords and restored them to their modest home and farm.

In 1848, when James Roosevelt, the father of future President Franklin Delano Roosevelt, was returning from his youthful, carefree graduation fling in Europe, one poor, young Irish immigrant, Patrick Kennedy, was taking a ship to America, hoping to find a better life. There are numerous graphic accounts of the terrible conditions aboard the "coffin ships" from Ireland to the New World. By some estimates, only a third of the emigrants survived the voyage.[3] The fact that so many Irish were nevertheless willing to risk such a passage, all for the dream of a better life, is an indication of the despair and hopelessness that characterized their existence.

Patrick Kennedy, this first family pilgrim, survived the foul, cramped steerage quarters of the ship and found romance in the shape of a lovely fellow passenger, one Bridget Murphy. The fact that she, too, hailed from County Wexford was a source of wonder for both of them. On the rare occasions when they were allowed up on the deck to see the glorious starlit skies and feel the salty breezes of the dark ocean, they would seize on this coincidence as a sign from God that their destinies were foreordained to intertwine and that it had taken this great adventure to make it happen.

In America, Patrick and Bridget married and struggled with poverty, bringing five new Kennedys into the world, including one John Kennedy, who died in infancy a year later. Patrick had brief moments of success. Working as a cooper, he earned an annual wage of $300 in 1852, almost grasping the dream that had fueled such hope so far away in his home country. In the end the American dream eluded him.[4] Patrick found only cholera. On November 22, 1858, a date that would have solemn and tragic significance in the years to come, Patrick Kennedy died at the age of thirty-five.

Earlier in the year, his wife, Bridget, had given birth to their last child, a boy named Patrick Joseph Kennedy. He would be called "P. J." to distinguish him from his father. Now widowed, with an infant and a house full of other young children, she would have to carry on alone, always haunted by the specter that if she too were to succumb to sickness and death, it would mean a life of unfathomable misery for her orphaned babies.

The story of the Kennedy family is full of resilient women who courageously stepped into the vacuum of departed husbands and brothers. Bridget Kennedy was a remarkable early example of that tradition. "Irish need not apply" was a common sign posted in the shop windows of Boston during those years. The mounting mass of Catholic immigration posed a threat to the ruling white Anglo-Saxon Protestant brahmins. Limited by such bigotry and unable to hide her transparent Irish lilt, Bridget used what cunning she had to survive. She packed her family into one small room on Liverpool Street and rented out the rest of her apartment to boarders. She cleaned houses—

those that would accept an Irish maid—and worked at a fancy stationery and notions shop in East Boston, near the waterfront.

Under the industrious, disciplined hand of Bridget Kennedy, the children, including young P. J., pooled their resources and bought the very notions establishment that had employed her. With the package came a three-story building in the heart of East Boston. Driven by the privations that had almost swamped her and her babies and inspired by the lifestyles she had witnessed as a housekeeper, Bridget immediately expanded her notions store by adding to the stock. She was soon selling groceries and liquor as well. She had learned the power of delayed gratification. It was a trait that would have little resonance with future generations of Kennedys, but it would be the secret of her son's success.

As a young man, P. J. Kennedy studied his mother's business and quickly concluded that liquor represented the greatest moneymaking opportunity. It generated the most reliable repeat customers and earned the greatest profits. At the same time, P. J. had seen its devastating consequences. He vowed early to be a teetotaler, a promise that he occasionally relaxed when business or political reasons demanded. At fourteen he dropped out of school to work the docks, plowing money back into his mother's enterprise. She later returned the favor, saving enough to help him buy a saloon on Haymarket Square. By age thirty, P. J. was the proprietor of three Boston taverns and a whiskey-importing business, all the while remaining sober himself. Before he reached forty, he would help found a bank, the Columbia Trust.

At least some measure of P. J.'s early success was owed to his colorful Irish bartending charm. He knew how to spin a good tale when the occasion demanded, and, more important, he knew how to listen. It was the latter gift that eventually built his clientele and led naturally to his career as a politician. In 1884, urged on by friends, he ran for the Massachusetts State Legislature, where he would eventually serve five terms in the lower house, followed by three more as a state senator.

In 1887, Patrick Kennedy took Mary Augusta Hickey as his bride. She was the daughter of a fellow saloon owner and a sister of the mayor of Brockton, Massachusetts. The next year would be one of the most eventful for the family. In the summer, P. J. would leave a pregnant Mary to travel to Saint Louis, Missouri, to attend the Democratic

National Convention and offer a seconding speech for the presidential nomination of Grover Cleveland. The family had come a long way.

On September 6, 1888, P. J. and Mary presented Bridget Kennedy, the family matriarch, with her first grandson, Joseph Patrick Kennedy. But Bridget's health would fail rapidly. Only a few days before Christmas, she died of a cerebral hemorrhage, never knowing that the grandbaby she had kissed would one day become the father of America's greatest political dynasty. He would own banks and real estate and motion picture distribution companies. He would be a friend of and sometimes an enemy to many of the world's leaders. In spite of his poor Irish roots he would reach the social summit, serving as his nation's ambassador to the Court of St. James's. And it would be through his unrelenting and sometimes ruthless efforts that his own son would be elected president of the United States.

P. J. and Mary Augusta Kennedy were nurturing parents who indulged their firstborn son. Mary had a mischievous, irreverent spirit that refused to acknowledge defeat. This buoyancy would manifest itself as a dominant trait in a future generation of Kennedys, but it would be sorely tested with the loss of their second baby, Francis, who died of diphtheria at the age of two.[5] Time allowed Mary little chance to adequately grieve; a baby daughter arrived that same year.

Suffering over the loss of Francis, P. J. and Mary poured their love even more earnestly into their firstborn, Joe Kennedy. Father and son were inseparable, making the rounds together at P. J.'s business enterprises, playing baseball in the yard, and taking in Red Sox games on the weekends. Mary gave birth to a second baby girl in 1898, but, according to historian Doris Kearns Goodwin, neither sister challenged her older brother's primacy.[6] Joe was loved by his parents and worshiped by his sisters. It was a formula that would created consummate confidence in the young man.

There was much about her husband that Mary Augusta resented. This was picked up like secondhand smoke by the son. P. J. was a kindhearted Irishman. It was part of the formula that had built his successful saloon business and segued so easily into running a political machine. There was an endless stream of needy people who knocked on Kennedy's door, and P. J. never turned one down. It was the way of old-fashioned ward politics. The local politico took care of his people, and on election day they delivered him the votes. But Mary and young

Joe were not convinced that it was a fair trade. Both were suspicious that the same faces kept showing up.

P. J. was a weak legislator.[7] Serving in a political machine meant taking orders from superiors, which P. J. accepted as part of the bargain but which made Mary Augusta bitter. A plaque hung above the desk of P. J. Kennedy. "I shall pass through this world but once," it read. "Any kindness I can do, or goodness show, let me do it now—for I shall not pass this way again."[8] But his wife and son were not buying.

If P. J. kept the Irish lights a-glowin', Joe's mother, Mary Augusta, taught her son how to shake off the stigma of his immigrant roots. If asked for his name, she told him, he should simply answer "Joseph" and never "Joseph Patrick," which was practically an announcement that they had only recently disembarked. She was the force that insisted he get into the Protestant upper-class schools. While other teenagers were satisfied by East Boston's Xavier High School, she moved him over to Boston Latin. And upon graduation, while other ambitious Catholics submitted to the Jesuits at Boston College or Holy Cross, she encouraged him to enroll at Harvard. But all through his life he would carry his Irish identity like a chip on his shoulder. Years later when a newspaper identified him as Irish, he exploded, "Goddam it! I was born in this country! My children were born in this country! What the hell does someone have to do to become an American?"[9]

It is a mistake to assume that Joe Kennedy rejected out of hand all that his father had so laboriously built. He shared his mother's resentment of the bosses who lorded over them, and he agreed that his father's generosity and constituent services were often misspent, that the family should come first. But he was mesmerized by the workings of his father's neighborhood political machine. Joe would never forget a breathless campaign worker bragging to his father on election day that he had already voted 128 times.

But what was the value of his father's muscle-bound network if it remained untapped for the family? And beyond arranging a low-paying government job for a cousin, how could it be put to more practical, personal use?

THE MAKING OF A BUSINESS TYCOON

Joe Kennedy demonstrated a knack at making money early in life. At first he took on odd jobs like many other young people his age, but he soon showed an extraordinary ability as an entrepreneur, with a talent for both organization and promotion. He devoured the popular Horatio Alger series, which promised great rewards to common people with uncommon desire and commitment. At fifteen he formed a neighborhood baseball team, raising money to buy the uniforms, renting the fields, and making a profit in the process. When the players asked to share in the spoils, Joe turned them down flat. It was his enterprise, he had taken the risk, and he would enjoy the results. P. J., his father, would have eagerly given it all away, seeing it as another generous device to further expand his neighborhood network of friends. Joe Kennedy was taking a different course.

There is an instructive story that reveals how Joe's belief system was evolving. His love of baseball carried over into his years in high school, where he became an accomplished hitter, winning the city-wide batting average championship his senior year at Boston Latin. The great Irish icon Boston Mayor John "Honey Fitz" Fitzgerald presented the Kennedy boy with his award. Joe must have fantasized about a major-league career and breaching the short but deep chasm that separated the baseball diamond at Boston Latin from the nearby Huntington Avenue Grounds of the beloved Red Sox. But if he harbored such dreams, they were dashed at Harvard. Riding the wave of his hot bat, he made the freshman varsity team but, by his senior year, nagged by chronic injuries, he was assigned a permanent spot on the bench.

On the last day of the season, two men in business suits showed up just before the start of the game, cornering the team captain, pitcher "Chick" McLaughlin. It was known around campus that McLaughlin wanted to open a movie theater after graduation. The strangers suggested that helping Joe Kennedy earn his varsity letter in baseball might not be a bad move. His father had clout at City Hall, they said, and might help clear the way for the requisite permits. Late in the game McLaughlin petitioned the coach to put Joe Kennedy in the lineup for the last inning. It would guarantee Joe's coveted letter. As it happened, the last play of the game was a grounder to the mound, which McLaughlin fielded and tossed over to Joe for the final out. The baseball itself would have been a wonderful keepsake, a souvenir representing the Harvard pitching career of "Chick" McLaughlin, but "Kennedy stuffed it in his pocket and left the field."[10]

During his years at Harvard, Joe Kennedy and a friend launched a business for tourists. First they bought a bus from a failing company, and then they traded on P. J.'s political clout to talk Boston Mayor "Honey Fitz" into granting them a license for a bus stand at a prime downtown site. As is so often the case in business, the location was the key. By the end of the second summer they had parlayed a $600 investment into a $10,000 gain, a small fortune at the time.[11]

If Franklin Roosevelt was an awkward fit for Harvard University, young Joe Kennedy took the place in stride. He was only a fair athlete and a passing scholar, but he exuded confidence and had many friends. Still, the best clubs eluded him. This included the snobbish Porcellian Club. It had blackballed the nerdy Franklin Roosevelt years before, but its exclusion of the brassier Joseph Kennedy represented something uglier. Kennedy had two strikes against him: he was Irish, with only one generation separating him from his immigrant ancestors, and he was Catholic. But there would be time for payback later.

Upon graduation, Joe Kennedy began his working career as a modest clerk at the Columbia Trust, the small bank his father and friends had founded in 1895. Kennedy declared that banking was a basic business that related to all others. If he could learn it, all the other doors would open. Even so, he would not stay in place very long. One of his employers spotted his drive and natural talent, taking him under his wing and then urging him to pursue a position as a bank examiner. Once more, Joe Kennedy traded on his father's political influence, and, once more, he pressed his case to Boston Mayor John "Honey Fitz" Fitzgerald. New York State had no Irish Catholic bank examiners, Kennedy argued, and if the mayor could convince the governor to appoint one, well, it would surely be remembered on election day. Historians offer differing accounts about who was really behind the appointment, with Kennedy himself diminishing the mayor's role in favor of his mentor at Columbia Trust. But in any case, regardless of the messenger, the argument carried the day and young Joe Kennedy was soon traveling the state of New York, learning the finer points of the banking industry from a totally unique vantage point. It was an education that would come none too soon.

The very next year his old employer, the Columbia Trust, found itself in a fight for survival. A large Boston bank was making a takeover bid, and the stockholders at Columbia were vulnerable to the offer. A youthful Joe Kennedy sprang into action. He had played on his Irish roots to get his job as an examiner; now he played the card again in the contest over the Columbia Trust. He warned the Boston Irish community that it was about to lose *its* bank. The publicity worked. Another large Boston financial institution took notice of Kennedy's cleverly waged campaign and decided to back the young man's plan. The Harvard graduate, who had come close to flunking courses in economics, who had begun his career as a financier only two years before, a complete novice to the banking fraternity, now returned to Columbia Trust as its savior and new president. He was twenty-five years old.

The story of Columbia Trust helped spark the legend of Joe Kennedy, the brilliant young financier, and the legend had its own exponential power, for with the publicity and attention came increased deposits and further loans to the community. The bank quickly grew into an important Boston institution, and its young president was heralded a hero among Irish Catholics. Kennedy had learned the power of the press, that what was perceived by the public as truth was sometimes self-fulfilling. It would be a formula he would return to again and again.

Joseph Kennedy, a wealthy, socially acceptable bank president who had marched into Mayor Fitzgerald's office many times before, now marched back in once more, this time to ask for the hand of his daughter. At the mayor's great receptions, his lovely daughter, Rose Fitzgerald, had been an elegant fixture on his arm. She dazzled his guests. For years, she and Joe had been thrown together by their parents' collaborative political interests, but if someone had suggested that the two were a match, Honey Fitz, as the mayor was called, would have recoiled. He had been holding his beautiful daughter in reserve for a truly worthy man, one who would advance the station of the family, which was already perched atop the quaint Boston Irish society. But in 1913, Honey Fitz ran into some personal and political trouble, forcing him to back down from a mayoral reelection bid. Reluctantly, himself diminished in stature, Honey Fitz gave his blessing to the couple. Joe Kennedy may have been a pushy social climber, but he possessed something no other suitor could claim, the promise of a limitless future.

Joseph Kennedy and Rose Fitzgerald were married on October 7, 1914. Rose would later say that she could not actually remember ever having been asked. In his confidence Joe had simply passed over that process, moving directly to the negotiation of the date. Joe would remember, "I was never seriously interested in anyone else." [12]

Their firstborn son arrived the next summer. Joe's father-in-law made no secret of his ambition to be the child's namesake. The newspapers, no doubt fed from the mayor's office, predicted as much, but none of that influenced Joe Kennedy, who knew perfectly well how the newspaper game worked. The new baby was christened Joseph Patrick Kennedy, Jr., after his father.

None of that stopped the mayor from holding forth in gushing pride at the arrival of his grandson. "He is going to be the President of the United States," Honey Fitz declared. [13] He would be wrong, of course, but not by much. A second child, born to Joe and Rose on May 29, 1917, would finally bear the mayor's name, John Fitzgerald Kennedy. Although this new Kennedy would indeed become president, Honey Fitz had used up all of his superlatives on the first grandson. Young John F. Kennedy would live much of his early life in the overbearing shadow of his older brother. Eight more children followed. The mayor joked that his son-in-law needed to buy a bus.

In 1917, on the same day as the birth of the future president, his father was elected to the board of the Massachusetts Electric Company, making him "one of the youngest trustees of a major corporation in America." [14] Before the year was finished, he was spotted by the legendary Charles M. Schwab and hired on the spot to run the giant Forge River Shipyards of the Bethlehem Steel Company. Kennedy and Schwab, though separated by years, culture, and religion, had much in common as businessmen. Before founding Bethlehem Steel, Schwab had risen to the top of the corporate world, serving as president of United States Steel, the largest company in the world, and all at the fresh young age of thirty-nine. His admirers described him as a great motivator, and, like Kennedy, he had a dark side. Winning was everything, and Schwab was known to employ a bribe or two when it moved a project along. Thomas Edison called him "the master hustler." [15]

Though World War I inspired great patriotism among Kennedy's old Harvard alumni, Joe was much more cynical. He saw America as a willing dupe in an essentially European fracas. He personally stayed out of the war, justifying his patriotism to those who questioned it by concentrating on building ships for Bethlehem Steel. There was a revealing encounter during these years with Franklin Roosevelt, the young assistant secretary of the navy. Roosevelt, imitating the jawbone tactics of his famous cousin, who years before had preceded him in the same office, demanded that Bethlehem Steel release two ships to the Argentine government for the war effort. Kennedy refused, demanding that the Argentines first pay their bill. Roosevelt ordered in armed troops and won the day. Kennedy publicly insulted Roosevelt during the quarrel and privately admitted that the man had driven him to tears of frustration.[16]

Joe Kennedy's first millions came in the next decade. Through his contacts at Bethlehem Steel, he linked up with the successful investment banker Galen Stone, who promised to teach the young business sensation how to make a profit on the stock market. In 1922, Joe opened an office with Hayden, Stone and Company, learning quickly how to turn insider information to his advantage and coordinating team purchases into windfall stock deals. The following year he opened his own office, making millions of dollars and purchasing properties, including theaters along the East Coast and a Hollywood production company. For all he had accomplished, Joe Kennedy was still an Irish Catholic to the white Anglo-Saxons who were desperately clinging to their stranglehold on American commerce. And if the times were changing, it was not fast enough for Kennedy. He was still rebuffed at country clubs.

For a summer vacation in 1926, he had his chauffeur drive the family to Hyannis Port in a Rolls-Royce. There he rented a two-and-a-half-acre estate overlooking the harbor. His growing family spread out in the big house and were so happy at the summer retreat that Joe eventually bought the place, transforming it into a second palace for the clan with fourteen bedrooms, nine baths, a swimming pool, tennis courts, and a private theater wired for talking motion pictures. The family would move to New York and back to Boston, but the summer residence in Hyannis Port and later a winter retreat in Palm Beach would remain as welcome constants in the long history of this volatile family, places to put down roots.

Joe Kennedy's magic as a businessman was often in his timing. Some historians have long suspected that he imported liquor during Prohibition, and there is no doubt that when the laws were finally changed he was ready to cash in. He made his fortune on Wall Street while the making was good, commenting to a friend that they had better hurry up before new laws closed the mile-wide loopholes they were trading through.[17] When the stock market crash, precursor of the Great Depression, finally hit, Kennedy was already substantially divested of his stocks. While the rest of the world suffered and many great fortunes collapsed, he only made more money. His children later said that they had hardly been aware that the greatest depression the world had ever seen was happening on their doorstep.

THE GLORIA SWANSON AFFAIR

With their great success, all was not happy in the Kennedy household. Committed to her faith, Rose gravitated to conservative priests, who righteously insisted that sex was a sacred act reserved solely for procreation, a concept that Rose, with nine children, had no problem comprehending. There is some evidence that Joe sought to contest this theology and thus fight for his marriage. Historian Doris Kearns Goodwin tells of Joe occasionally confronting the issue in the presence of weekend friends. "Now, listen, Rosie," Joe would say. "This idea of yours that there is no romance outside of procreation is simply wrong. It was not part of our contract at the altar, the priest never said that and the books don't argue that. And if you don't open your mind on this, I'm going to tell the priest on you."[18] It was an invitation for the friends to weigh in, but Rose was not moved. Later, after the birth of Teddy, the baby of the family, she allegedly closed her bedroom door forever.

On some level Joe probably continued to smart from the earlier judgment by Rose's father. The old mayor, Honey Fitz, had once declared that the boy was not good enough for his daughter. For years he wouldn't even let the Kennedy youth enter his house. Joe Kennedy did not take kindly to snubs of any sort. In any case, now as the head of his own household and denied his wife's bed in Boston, he turned to Broadway and Hollywood, where there were willing paramours ready to offer the praise and affection a movie mogul and financier of international fame should expect.

In a letter to Arthur Houghton, a theatrical manager in New York, Joe suggested that he "have all the good looking girls in your company looking forward with anticipation to meeting the high Irish of Boston because I have a gang around me that must be fed on wild meat."[19]

Joe Kennedy's most notorious conquest was the movie legend and sex goddess, Gloria Swanson. She came to him in New York in 1927, a supplicant in need of financing but also a huge star at the peak of her game and a gorgeous woman at twenty-eight. There was more at play here than Kennedy's libido. Swanson was a self-made woman, with hard-won business skills and an intimidating presence. When producer Mack Sennett had promised he would make her into a second Mabel Normand, she had replied, "I won't be a second anyone!"[20]

There was a minor complication. Both were married. Gloria Swanson's marriage to the Marquis Le Bailly de La Falaise de La Coudraye had been a public sensation. She had officially become what her fans had thought all along she was, a member of a royal family. Her arrival back in the United States, with her marquis husband at her side, drew tens of thousands of well-wishers to the dock. When they took the train across the American heartland to California, it became a sensational victory lap, dominating headlines and drawing sensational crowds at every stop along the way.

But supplanting royalty would have been, at some level, only a further attraction for Joe Kennedy. Snubbed for a lifetime by the WASPs of Boston, nothing could mollify his bruised ego more than crushing a member of the European elite—someone from the exclusive families to which the Brahmins of Boston so slavishly pretended. And then the marquis, for all his breeding, was virtually penniless, a circumstance that soon became problematic.

Not long after their first meeting, Joe Kennedy invited the couple to Palm Beach. When the train pulled into the station, the marquis went to arrange the luggage, giving Kennedy the opening he wanted. Storming into Swanson's compartment, he mumbled excitedly, pushed her back onto the train seat in her drawing room, and kissed her twice. When he stood he hit his head on the luggage rack, losing his glasses. Disheveled, with lipstick smeared on his face, he dropped to his hands and knees scrambling on the compartment floor on all fours, looking like a child, chasing his runaway glasses. In spite of herself, Gloria

Swanson laughed. It was not the movie star entrance Joe Kennedy had likely rehearsed.[21]

The story of the early Palm Beach visit was a metaphor for the relationship. Swanson, hurt many times before and savvy in the ways of love and powerful men, would remain cautious. She may have known where Joe was headed even before he knew himself. First he arranged to have the marquis win a lucrative job back in France. And then he talked business, drawing the actress deep into the planning stages of several long-range movie projects.

For all his worldly wisdom, including his bouts of casual infidelity, Joe Kennedy fell hard. He begged the movie star to have his child and gave huge donations to the Vatican, seeking to find a way out of his marriage with Rose. Anxious to have her meet his whole family, he brought her back to Hyannis Port, where the local papers followed her every move as if she were a head of state. Rose, descending into deep denial or performing a good imitation of it, entertained her husband's mistress gallantly and graciously.

At the very height of the charade, Joe and Rose took the movie star along with them on a trip to Europe. When they returned late in 1929, Swanson was asked to a meeting in a Manhattan hotel room, where she was confronted by none other than William Cardinal O'Connell, the archbishop of Boston.[22] "I am here to ask you to stop seeing Joseph P. Kennedy," he said. "Each time you see him you become an occasion of sin for him."[23] The Church had its own marriage with the Kennedys to protect. The movie star said that she would consider the advice.

When the Kennedy-Swanson affair ended, it was in scenes eerily reminiscent of her final days with the other men in her life. Her first husband, actor Wallace Beery, was fourteen years her senior, her second husband eighteen years older. Both had been bad experiences. According to Swanson, Wallace Beery had become inebriated on their wedding night and raped her. When she had later become pregnant, he had offered her "medicine" that caused an abortion. Her second husband had turned vicious during the divorce proceedings, winning the war of the financial settlement and becoming stridently vindictive. The break with Kennedy would have similar overtones.

Early in the affair she had signed away her power of attorney to her ardent tycoon, and only when the break came did she discover the fine print of the contracts. If a movie made a profit, she would share with Kennedy fifty-fifty, she learned, but if it lost money, it was only hers to lose and Kennedy would be untouched.

But if Joe was too experienced to lose money, there is clear evidence that Swanson was able to beat him in the emotional contest. Friends said that he was depressed. And right in the middle of the unraveling affair, news came that his father, P. J. Kennedy, was dying. Joe was too preoccupied with untangling his romantic and business affairs in Hollywood to make it back to his father's bedside or even to attend the funeral, an omission comprehensible only in light of his great personal trauma. Tormented by stomach pains, which he self-diagnosed as cancer, he was convinced that he, too, was dying until a long period of testing proved otherwise.

The affair with Gloria Swanson came to an end, but Kennedy's insatiable thirst for conquest had only been awakened. There would be a steady stream of starlets and chorus girls. There would be permanent pads maintained at major hotels around the country, love nests for his use. But never again would Joe Kennedy allow himself to become so emotionally involved, and never again would his marriage be so publicly threatened by another woman.

Joe Kennedy's break from Gloria Swanson paralleled his divestiture of his movie industry holdings. He had re-created and conquered untamable Hollywood, and it had left him millions of dollars richer. But he had reached a point in his life where more money alone would move him no closer to the social preeminence that drew him.

JOE KENNEDY'S QUEST FOR POLITICAL POWER

In 1932, the presidential election between the incumbent, Herbert Hoover, and Franklin D. Roosevelt captured the attention of the nation. The contest transcended Joe Kennedy's romanticized drama of the film world and overshadowed the heroes of the corporate realm. Kennedy found both Hollywood and Wall Street limiting. The Great Depression was changing America. The role of a central government was going to be more powerful, and the persons involved in this transition would be the new celebrities. As Joe Kennedy's friends would later explain, he began to see national political power as a means of achieving an end run around the society cliques that had excluded his family and his religion.

Politics was a dangerous game for a man who had much to hide. The historian Ted Schwarz, in his biography *Joseph P. Kennedy,* convincingly demonstrates a long-running connection between Joe and organized crime in New York, Chicago, and Hollywood.[24] In some situations it was the price of doing business in America during Prohibition. In others instances it was more collaborative.

To gain access to the popular new president, Kennedy began to build a relationship with FDR's son Jimmy Roosevelt, angling to help him make money in a new life insurance career. But even while helping the Roosevelt kid, Joe could not resist picking off another fortune for himself. Just before the repeal of Prohibition, he took young Roosevelt with him to England for meetings with distillers. Just the presence of the president's son on his team helped Kennedy land critical liquor-importing franchises worth millions of dollars. Some sources insist that young Roosevelt was initially offered a percentage of these lucrative contracts. It would have made him financially independent for life. But Kennedy artfully reneged on any deal, claiming that such an arrangement would prove to be a political embarrassment to Jimmy's father, FDR.

By 1934, Joe Kennedy had ingratiated himself sufficiently with the White House to be named by President Roosevelt as the first chairman of the Securities and Exchange Commission. His career in government was off and running. It was a highly controversial appointment, and some major newspapers were outraged. It would be like putting a fox in the henhouse. But the president, who anticipated a storm over the appointment, asked who better to police the crooks on Wall Street than someone who knew the system inside and out?

To the surprise of many in the Roosevelt administration, Joseph P. Kennedy acquitted himself well as SEC chairman and played a historical role in reorganizing the rules governing Wall Street. But he learned hard political lessons in the process. Many liberals were unimpressed. It was too soon for them to know how well he had done his job, and they would never forgive him or trust him after he had made his fortune so ruthlessly and, they suspected, so unscrupulously. Conservative business leaders instantly saw what he was doing to them and labeled him a traitor. He stayed only long enough to define the problems, offer solutions, and organize the follow-up work. When he left, his public reputation, trampled during the time of his announced appointment, was restored.

Joe Kennedy had given a masterful, marathon, nonstop working performance that would have translated immediately into an even better assignment except for what would happen with Jimmy Roosevelt, the president's son. Kennedy had arranged for the twenty-seven-year-old college graduate to become president of the National Grain Yeast Corporation, a New Jersey company planning to manufacture industrial alcohol. Kennedy was no novice to public relations. He allegedly had a number of journalists on his payroll, including a columnist for *The New York Times.* But he was still learning just how intrusive and thorough the press could be with government public figures. Advertising dollars and backroom deals could turn a business story fairly easy. Political news was tougher to manage.

Unfortunately, a story broke that showed a link between the New Jersey alcohol company and organized crime. Jimmy Roosevelt was depicted as a front man for the operation and forced to resign. The president finally rescued his firstborn son, installing him as a lieutenant colonel in the Marine Corps and having him stationed at the White House. Out of trouble and out of Kennedy's clutches, the president hoped, he would make a comeback.

If a political career meant greater public scrutiny, Joe still could not resist a shady deal when he felt certain he could get away with it. One rumored scam involved a kickback from the Catholic Church. According to the plan, Joe would donate $1 million to the Vatican and receive a receipt. The Vatican would later return $500,000 of it, perhaps to another nonprofit entity controlled by Joe. Everyone would be a winner. The Church would receive a half-million dollars it wouldn't have otherwise collected, and Joe would receive a $1 million tax write-off. But thanks to a rare indiscretion inside Kennedy's tightly run team, the IRS was apparently onto the scheme.

Joe Kennedy needed to shake the investigation and once more jump-start his political career. He wrote to Missy LeHand, the president's secretary, saying that he was available if needed. There was no response. Desperate, fearing that the door to the White House was slamming shut forever and he should get what he wanted quickly, he wrote Missy a series of brazen letters asking for autographed pictures of the president for key friends and handwritten presidential notes for his children. His great public career seemed to be at an end.

Good politicians run scared; it is why they win. And there has seldom been a better American politician than Franklin D. Roosevelt. Although headed toward a massive reelection landslide in 1936, Roosevelt was nervous about the visceral anger his New Deal had provoked in the conservative business community. Just as Kennedy was despairing of his own public career, the election year provided an opening. Joe began his own ingratiating public campaign in the president's defense. He raised thousands of dollars from his Wall Street friends and declared that as a businessman with traditional free enterprise sentiments, he had seen the light; that the emergency of the Great Depression called for a rethinking of government's role. Kennedy employed his media contacts to get the message out effectively and had a ghostwriter help him knock out a 150-page book entitled *I'm for Roosevelt*.[25]

Kennedy's book has been much disparaged by historians. It is alleged that his friend Arthur Krock was the true author and that the book is in fact a poorly written, shameless vanity piece. Actually, except for its sycophantic title, the book compares quite well with other political tomes of the time. It has Joe Kennedy's direct, somewhat brassy style, which lends it an air of authenticity, and it includes many wonderful and cogent arguments that must have thrilled Roosevelt to the core. Most amazing of all, the clothbound book was conceived, written, and published in a matter of months, an astounding accomplishment for the times.

After the election, in 1937, the president finally responded. Kennedy was appointed chairman of the Federal Maritime Commission. But he was not happy. He wanted more, and he let the president know it.

In 1938, Joe Kennedy went back to the well, once more petitioning the president's son Jimmy Roosevelt for help and mounting a stubborn insider Washington campaign for the ambassadorial post to Great Britain. President Roosevelt considered it quite a reach for the Irish Catholic and laughed so hard when he first heard the idea that he almost fell out of his wheelchair. But he had hardly recovered from his amusement a few days later when he reconsidered. It might indeed serve his purposes. Roosevelt was incensed by Prime Minister Neville

Chamberlain's arrogant refusal to consider an invitation to the United States. Perhaps sending them the obnoxious and irritating Irishman would return the favor. Besides, Roosevelt determined that he would fire Kennedy "the first time he opens his mouth and criticizes me."[26] No one in the White House or State Department expected that to take too long.

Franklin Roosevelt, unusually burdened by a hectic month of meetings, decided to have a little fun with the outlandish appointment, insisting that his prospective ambassadorial nominee and Jimmy come in together to see him at the White House. One account has the self-confident Kennedy holding his own. The president allegedly told Kennedy that he would have to give up his mistress, Gloria Swanson. And Kennedy, who could have explained humbly that the affair was over and past, instead snapped back that the president should set the example and give up his *own* mistress, Missy LeHand.[27]

Then Roosevelt expressed his grave reservations about the appointment owing to widespread rumors to the effect that Kennedy was bowlegged. As ambassador to Great Britain, the president explained, he would be required to wear knee breeches and silk stockings at formal events, and the United States could not be the laughingstock of the diplomatic corps in London. The president ordered Kennedy to drop his pants so he and his son could have a look. A brief expression of pain crossed the proud tycoon's face, but after a moment of reluctance he obeyed orders, dropping his pants and standing before the president and his son in his shorts while they examined his legs. It was all a ruse, of course, a moment of cruel presidential hazing, perhaps a moment of revenge for the humiliations his son had experienced at the hands of the arrogant Kennedy. And perhaps it was a morbid reassurance to Roosevelt that even if he suffered from polio and was reduced to a wheelchair, he could still humiliate powerful men who had the legs to stand before him. The president had his moment, a story that would be relished by history. He eventually pronounced Kennedy qualified, after all. Joe Kennedy left the White House, his pride bruised but his prospective title intact. For the rest of his life he would be called "Mr. Ambassador."

THE AMBASSADOR'S AMBITION

Considering the humble origins of the Kennedy family, it was an extraordinary achievement and, in spite of Roosevelt's casual treatment of the posting, a moment for the history books. Not only was he the ambassador to the Court of St. James's, the most socially prominent position in the American government, a role that had been played by John Adams, John Quincy Adams, and other presidents, he was an Irish Catholic, the first ever to hold the post. The irony was not lost on Irish communities the world over. Having considered themselves victims of generations of British tyranny, they now had one of their own representing the very nation the British might need most for their immediate survival. Speculation abounded that with Kennedy's wealth, the presidency was indeed within his reach.

Joe Kennedy's first days in London signaled that he was going to be more than a caretaker ambassador. Almost immediately, he made it known that he sided with Prime Minister Neville Chamberlain's assertion that there must be some accommodation with the Germans. A strict isolationist, Ambassador Kennedy was often accused of seeing the world selfishly, with his own business interests in mind. But World War I had left many Americans cynical. Many concluded that thousands of their sons had died to help settle an essentially European dispute. And most people in England and France were in no mood to have another war. Privately at least, many statesmen were quite willing to admit that the Treaty of Versailles had been unfair to Germany and that Hitler could be allowed to nibble away a bit to get some of the lost territory back.

For a brief moment in time, Ambassador Joe Kennedy hung suspended in the stratosphere. Everything worked. Almost anything seemed possible. On one of his first golf games in Britain, he hit a hole in one on the second tee. When he brashly broke protocol and rushed across a ballroom floor to claim the first dance with the queen of England, she was actually amused. Old, resurrected controversies seemed only to add to the public interest. His reputed underworld connections gave him a roguish charm. Even his philandering—now rampant with his irresistible label of "Millionaire Ambassador"—only prompted titters. And if Roosevelt were to decline an unprecedented third term, American polls listed Ambassador Kennedy as being among the top five Democratic presidential hopefuls. Celebrated members of English society jockeyed to get close.

The Kennedy children only added to the charm. The London press followed their exploits as if they too were celebrities. "His bouncing offspring make the most politically ingratiating family since Theodore Roosevelt's," gushed a *Life* magazine piece.[28] Firstborn Joe, Jr., made it clear to friends that if his father didn't make a run for the White House, he himself would be the first Catholic president. Meanwhile, the baby of the family, Teddy, played elevator operator at the embassy, asking each person who entered, "What floor, please?"[29] But the party did not last.

Many in the White House and State Department regretted the Kennedy appointment as soon as it was made. Roosevelt promised his secretary of state that he would have people watching Kennedy every hour on the hour and reporting back. But it was not enough. Joe Kennedy slipped his leash again and again. There are those who suggest that Franklin Roosevelt, not one to leave a rival standing, had purposely knocked the props from under his ambassador. If so, it was hardly necessary. As Hitler's intentions in Europe became plain and as the brutality of his personality became more and more manifest, anyone associated with the earlier appeasement was hopelessly discredited. Prime Minister Chamberlain was humiliated before the world, and Ambassador Kennedy, who had been vigorously pushing an accommodation with the Germans, saw his popularity fall with him.

Things could have been even worse. Declassified documents and personal testimony from this period show that the ambassador played an ugly, defeatist role behind the scenes. When Chamberlain made his last-minute rendezvous with Hitler at Berchtesgaden, Kennedy sent a report to Washington suggesting that in the event of war the German Luftwaffe would destroy London and Paris with impunity. Publicly professing to be an isolationist, he privately told the German ambassador that Jews were not allowed in Boston clubs either, a shamefully cruel remark with potentially devastating consequences. The Hitler regime needed little encouragement in its repression of the Jews.

Kennedy family apologists, some of them otherwise credible historians, always make the point that the Holocaust had not yet begun, that the full horror of Hitler was still unfathomable. Even so, Joe Kennedy's cold analysis of the unfolding drama, given to Hitler's ambassador, was

seen as an American response to the Nuremberg Laws, which prohibited Jews in Germany from even attending a motion picture in a public cinema. The fact is that German Jews were already being randomly
murdered and thousands of them were in full flight, leaving behind
generations of work. Within a year, the trap would spring shut in Germany and later in Poland. Inexplicably, Kennedy failed to mention to
the German ambassador that the same Boston clubs that prohibited
Jews had long excluded the Irish, as well. Today, some historians are
calling the Kennedy sojourn in London the worst diplomatic appointment in the history of the United States.[30]

What was then public was bad enough. A British newspaper
quoted him on the subject of the Spanish Civil War, calling FDR's
policy "a Jewish production."[31] Kennedy's two oldest sons, Joe, Jr., and
"Jack," as he was called, gamely tried to defend their father's motives as
an isolationist. Jack took up the controversial argument in *The Harvard
Crimson,* the campus newspaper, suggesting that if Hitler disarmed, he
should probably be given back some of his overseas colonies, as well as
the territory he had already taken.[32]

But the old man knew that his days as an ambassador were num-
bered and any future public career was beyond resuscitation. An
honorary doctorate from Harvard, once in the works, was quickly
withdrawn on the grounds that an ambassadorship was insufficient
merit. Adroitly, still struggling for his own emotional survival, Joe used
his media contacts to plant the story that he had turned it down. At
the White House, FDR could easily spot a Kennedy-planted newspaper story. Howling with laughter, he asked his aides, "Imagine Joe
Kennedy turning down an honorary doctorate from Harvard?"

Now all of Ambassador Kennedy's extraneous baggage added to
the weight that was dragging him down. The stories about his womanizing seemed less funny. Embassy staffers talked about the young
ladies he escorted into and out of his private office for quick one-on-
ones. Jokes were made of his prolific use of a personal bomb shelter,
each visit accompanied by a different beautiful young lady. There were
stories that he was using his insider knowledge as ambassador to make
money, that he had sold Czech securities short just before Hitler decided to occupy the rest of the country, and that he was using special
space on shipping routes to export his liquor to America.[33]

Congressmen began calling for his resignation. Kennedy floated the idea that he be brought back to the United States as the chairman of the Democratic National Committee. But for all the money he would bring to such a post, it couldn't offset his negatives.

There is some evidence to suggest that Kennedy vacillated in his ambition to achieve higher office and that in order to cushion a fall he often told himself that he really didn't want to go further. On the eve of the trip to London, he had said as much to a close friend. "Don't go buying a lot of luggage," he told a member of his personal staff, "We're only going to get the family in the *Social Register*. When that's done we come on back and go out to Hollywood to make some movies and make some money." [34]

But that plan had obviously changed when his star had ascended so rapidly. Now bitten by the presidential bug, imagining that he had been within reach, he could never return to Hollywood and the mundane world of making money. His career was in shambles, but there was another way back. It was time for the son. He had been grooming Joe, Jr., all along, thinking that it was much more realistic to plan a generation ahead. Now that the ultimate prize had finally been denied him, he fell back on the original idea. He would revive the plan for the son. If Joe Kennedy's political future was at an end, Joe, Jr.'s, future was only beginning. There was still time for a Kennedy.

Many years later, when historian Michael Beschloss spoke with the publisher and Republican activist Clare Boothe Luce, he was told that Joe Kennedy had made a deal with Roosevelt. "We agreed that if I endorsed *him* for president in 1940," Kennedy had reportedly said, "then *he* would support my son Joe for governor of Massachusetts in 1942." [35]

★

THIRTEEN

Survivor:
The Mother of John F. Kennedy

His mother really didn't love him. . . . History made him what he was.[1]
—Jacqueline Kennedy Onassis,
speaking of her late husband, John F. Kennedy

Rose Elizabeth Fitzgerald, referred to within the Kennedy family as "the glue that held it all together," was born to John F. Fitzgerald and Mary Josephine Hannon on July 22, 1890.[2] Her father was a legendary Irish politician with the nickname of "Honey Fitz." A hero to the Boston immigrant community, he served in the Massachusetts State legislature and in the U.S. House of Representatives before being elected mayor of the city.

From the very beginning Honey Fitz showered Rose with attention and affection. "He seems to have regarded me as a miracle," Rose later reflected, "an impression from which he never really recovered."[3] As she grew into a beauty, Rose was often seen on the mayor's arm at receptions or political gatherings, supplanting her mother as the hostess and soon acquiring an education in the smarmy world of Boston politics. By Irish immigrant standards, the Fitzgeralds were wealthy and successful, and while a certain amount of restraint was necessary for a politician in Boston, Rose felt truly free to enjoy those privileges on frequent foreign trips. The pleasant memories of such travels would lead to a continuous cycle of travel—an addiction, really—all through her life until, eventually, at the very end, her advanced age brought the excursions to a halt.

Rose Fitzgerald and Joseph P. Kennedy were often thrown together at political events or working vacations. P. J. Kennedy, Joe's father, was seen as one of the important cogs in the Massachusetts Democratic political machine. By the summer of 1906, eighteen-year-old Joe Kennedy and sixteen-year-old Rose Fitzgerald were in love.[4] But Mayor Honey Fitz had much higher plans for his daughter. He wouldn't allow her to go with Joe to the Boston Latin dance or, years later, to the Harvard junior prom. Rose was frequently packed off to Europe or sent on an errand out of town just to keep her away from Joe and interrupt his plans. Young Kennedy was forbidden even to enter the house, a rule that Joe would not forget nor forgive and for which old Honey Fitz would be repaid many times over with Joe's pointed barbs, dripping with sarcasm. After Joe became one of America's rich and famous, the good-natured Honey Fitz would try to sneak by the house and visit his grandchildren with Joe away, thus avoiding the humiliating verbal hazing.

In January 1911, Mayor Fitzgerald presented his Rose to Boston Irish society. It was a grand event with 450 distinguished guests, including the governor of the state, two congressmen, and the entire city council. Rose would later speak of the night with more precise detail and praise than the day of her own wedding. The house in Dorchester was filled with roses, and the debutante was wearing an embroidered gown of white satin. But if Honey Fitz was holding out for a better man for his daughter, the inexorable attraction between Joe and Rose only thrived under the opposition. It was only a matter of time before the ambitious Joe Kennedy would find his opening.

In 1913, rumors began to spread that Mayor Fitzgerald was having an affair with Elizabeth Ryan, a cigarette girl at the Ferncroft Inn, who just happened to be the same age as his daughter, Rose, but who was a woman of some ill repute. "Toodles" Ryan, as she was called, was on intimate terms with quite a number of the powerful men of Boston. While most Fitzgerald family historians suggest that there was insufficient evidence to prove the charge, it was undeniable that the two *had* been seen together—and often. The mayor openly kissed his Toodles and danced with her. It did little for his defense to point out that he kissed and danced with all the young pretty girls in Boston, one legend claiming that he had danced with five thousand ladies in his first two years as mayor.[5] Both his wife, Mary, and his daughter, Rose, rejected the rumors out of hand. Rose, in particular, urged her father to fight the charges, but the mayor knew well the political winds of war. Innocent or guilty, he decided to stand down and take a sabbatical from Boston politics.

With the mayor diminished and young Joe Kennedy, a new bank president, proving to be an enterprising businessman, Honey Fitz reluctantly allowed the couple to be married. On October 7, 1914, seventy-five special guests were invited to a grand breakfast at the Fitzgerald house. Later in the day, the couple was married in the private chapel of William Cardinal O'Connell, with the archbishop of Boston himself presiding.

Joe and Rose honeymooned in Greenbrier, West Virginia, before returning to their impressive seven-room, two-story house in Brookline, Massachusetts, an upscale Protestant enclave of Boston. And then the children started coming. Between 1914 and 1932, Rose was pregnant for 40 percent of her life. Joseph Patrick, Jr., was born in 1915, John Fitzgerald, called "Jack," in 1917, Rosemary in 1918, Kathleen "Kick" in 1920, Eunice Mary in 1921, Patricia in 1924, Robert Francis in 1925, Jean Ann in 1928, and finally, Edward Moore "Teddy" in 1932.

Although Joe provided nurses and servants, the large number of children demanded disciplined organization and systemization. Rose invoked techniques she had learned from the Ursuline nuns of the Sacred Heart Academy.[6] She kept card files on her children's health, meticulously tracking the various symptoms, illnesses, doctor's appointments, and vaccinations. Friends remember that "she would leave any party to be home in time for a baby's feeding."[7] She was described as a "tough, constant, minute disciplinarian with a fetish for neatness."[8] But it was a juggling act. "If you can keep your head about you when all about you are losing theirs," Rose said, paraphrasing Rudyard Kipling, "it's just possible you haven't grasped the situation."[9]

Even the vacations were regimented, *especially* the vacations. At the summer home in Hyannis Port, Rose partitioned her porch so she could expose the children to the outdoor salty sea air but still keep them separated in little pens so they couldn't hurt one another.[10] As they grew older, she bought different-colored bathing caps to keep track of the girls while they were swimming in the surf and put clocks in every room to try to keep the clan on time for meals.[11] Ignoring the family's Irish roots, Rose took excursions to historical sites up and down the East Coast, imbuing the children with a love of American history.[12] If a child was sick, Rose would read to him or her in bed. From the age of three, young Jack Kennedy, the future president, was perpetually sick with bronchitis, chicken pox, the measles, mumps, scarlet fever, and whooping cough. When he was at boarding school, Rose corresponded with the headmasters, walking them through the signature ailments of her sickly son.

Reflecting on those years, she would later write, "I looked on child rearing not only as a work of love and duty, but as a profession that was fully as interesting and challenging as any honorable profession in the world and one that demanded the best that I could bring to it."[13]

By the time their third child, Rosemary Kennedy, was five years old, it was clear that something was wrong. They would never know if her mental disability was a genetic anomaly, due to the clumsy use of forceps during her birth, or even related to a flu epidemic at the time of her birth. Rose saw the problem as a gift from God, a blessing to teach the whole family lessons it needed to learn. She poured her life into the young child, and at times the other siblings picked up on her spirit and pitched in and helped. But as the work became more consuming, requiring hands-on, high-maintenance home schooling sessions and learning therapy, Rose shuttled the two oldest sons, Joe, Jr., and Jack, out to various private schools.

In September 1917, the family moved to New York. Joe and Rose were disgusted with the anti-Irish, anti-Catholic bigotry of old Boston. With his corporate interests on both coasts, the move made a lot of sense for Joe Kennedy, but it turned out to be a devastating sojourn for Rose. Away from familiar friends and places, she described the move as a "blow to the stomach."[14] But the real pain came with the news of Joe's infidelities. In 1920, the couple was briefly separated, Rose packing her bags and returning to her father, old Honey Fitz, the man who had sounded early warnings about the brash, uncouth Joe Kennedy.

But after a few short days in the bosom of her own family, Rose realized that she could not escape her responsibilities as a wife and mother. Surprisingly, her father refused to cooperate with her return home, insisting that her duty as a Catholic lay with her husband and family. If she needed a bigger house, she should ask for it. If she needed time alone to survive the stressful marriage, she should take it.

ESTRANGEMENT FROM JOE

Rose Kennedy's is one of the most elusive biographies of modern presidents' mothers, in part because of her own political instincts to show the best possible face to the public and her clever ability to dilute or contradict even the smallest negative about herself and her family. Rose's own autobiography, *Times to Remember,* written when she was an amazing eighty-one years old, is filled with wonderfully crafted themes and anecdotes. Her advance from Doubleday publishers was a cool $1 million. But the propaganda effect for the family was immeasurable. Early biographical sketches slavishly draw on this material, creating an idealized version of a matriarch. Indeed, that was likely the purpose of her book, for Rose would conspire for days on end with her writer, discussing how to position a thought or contradict an unflattering anti-Kennedy theme. More recent accounts of her life reveal a figure far more complicated and ambitious than the dutiful wife and mother in denial over her marriage to Joe and suffering stoically through the grievous deaths and loss of her sons. The truth is no less stunning, revealing a more calculating personality, but with an even greater self-discipline than her most ardent admirers would have dared ascribe to her.

Rose Kennedy returned to her family in 1920 with a new sense of perspective. Striving for balance, she developed a lifelong regimen of physical exercise, intellectual stimulation, and spiritual devotion. If her children and family would not follow, she would set the pace alone. Within time, nothing would be allowed to interrupt her rituals, not even the sudden tragedies that began to rain down on the family. She spent long hours alone on golf courses, always walking, never resorting to a golf cart, going for a swim every day, and, at the family homes in Hyannis Port and Palm Beach, taking long, solitary walks along the beaches. The rugged physical exercise was surely part of the chemistry for maintaining her emotional equilibrium. By remaining physically strong and rested, she was able to better endure the emotional assaults that came with time.

The counterbalance to this active outdoor life was her renewed devotion to the Church. Following the brief hiatus at her parents' house, she committed herself to a number of religious retreats and bought a series of books reviewing the obligations of a good Catholic wife and mother. She began paraphrasing scripture with little philosophical tidbits. "Make sure you never, never argue at night," she would lecture her children. "You just lose a good night's sleep, and you can't settle anything until morning anyway." [15]

If she had been a devout believer all her life, her faith now took on even more importance and would remain the one constant to the last moments of her life. She attended Mass almost every day. At Hyannis Port she had her own little house built on the beach so she could pray and enjoy devotional readings. Experiences would come that would shake the conviction of the most faithful believer, but they would be endured by Rose with few moments of hesitation.

Yet there were yawning contradictions in Rose Kennedy, even in the practice of her faith. Her marriage to Joe became a great trade-off. According to friends, she knew of his infidelities but chose to look the other way, not as a means of redeeming their marriage but simply to continue to enjoy the lifestyle. [16] When she read a *Fortune* magazine account of their wealth, she was shocked, never having imagined that they were worth so much. She began to display an extravagance that would last well into the late years of her life, abandoning herself to frequent shopping excursions to Paris, contending smartly that it was her wifely duty to look her best, all the more so since her husband's work in Hollywood exposed him to the most beautiful women in the world.

Meanwhile, as the years wore on, she would quibble over bonuses to servants, cut back on coffee for nurses attending her invalid husband, and attempt to cheat the country clubs out of greens fees by replaying the same holes several times over. It didn't work. Kennedy children consulted with family trust lawyers behind her back to take care of loyal staffers, and the country clubs in Massachusetts and Florida were onto her eccentricities from the very beginning, billing her for the appropriate amount while leaving her blissfully unaware.

During the Hollywood years, Joe was rarely home. Rose faithfully lined up the children on Sunday to await their father's weekly telephone call. She called him "the architect of our lives" and taught the children—whatever her own feelings—to respect him. [17] On those rare occasions when he was there, she and Joe took long walks, hand in hand, with the children following behind like so many ducks. Yet even then, hardened by his infidelities, she shut her bedroom door to his embraces.

If her husband was often gone, a newly reinvented Rose Kennedy decided to hit the road herself, traveling the world and leaving the children to the servants, the nannies, and the eldest son, Joe, Jr. Young Jack was especially saddened by his mother's constant departures, sometimes openly crying, which angered Rose and made her even more distant. In 1923, only five-year-old Jack openly confronted her, asking what kind of mother would leave her children alone.[18] She was not amused by the encounter. The future president later confided to a friend that a Kennedy learned at a very young age that you got much more out of Joe and Rose if you accepted defeat stoically.

Joe, Sr., who had once longed for a new life with movie star Gloria Swanson, was reduced to accommodating a newly independent wife, even providing her with a suite at the Plaza Hotel to ease the burden of her Manhattan shopping excursions. When Joe retired from Hollywood and became a ubiquitous presence at home, Rose increased her travels and was gone for weeks at a time. By one estimate she made seventeen trips abroad during the first six years after Joe's return from California.

An unwritten rule promised the absent parent that he or she would not be burdened by the worries of home. Away in California, Rose was not told when her children were all in bed with the measles. And when Joe once called in, Rose calmly took his call without mentioning the fact that she had just had an automobile accident. After hanging up, she had a servant drive her to the hospital.

By some family accounts, Rose could be cold and distant to the children. Kennedys were expected to take their falls without sympathy. In an interview with a renowned historian, made public only in recent years, Jackie described her mother-in-law as enjoying her role as mayor's daughter and talking about her years as the ambassador's wife, but caring little for her son Jack. "History made him what he was," Jackie said, speaking of her late husband, the president. "This lonely sick boy. His mother really didn't love him."[19]

Almost instinctively, Jack Kennedy struck back where it hurt his mother the most, by playfully questioning her Catholic faith. Rose once asked the children to pray for a happy death. Young Jack said he would rather wish for two dogs instead.[20] As a young man, returning from a trip to the Middle East, Jack declared that he had seen "the rock where our Lord ascended into Heaven in a cloud, and [in] the same area, I saw the place where Mohammed was carried up to Heaven on a white horse, and Mohammed has a big following and Christ has a big following, and why do you think we should believe Christ any more than Mohammed?"[21] In 1942, angry at his parents for their role in his breakup with a girlfriend, he threatened to join a Protestant Bible class.[22] When Joe and Rose threatened to disown their daughter Kathleen "Kick" Kennedy for marrying an English nobleman—who naturally belonged to the Church of England—Jack sided with his sister.

Though Rose became famous for her well-publicized theories on child rearing, the Kennedy children slipped quickly beyond her reach. Subscribing to the biblical admonition "Spare the rod and spoil the child," she would grab a wooden spoon or the nearest weapon and thrash away at a recalcitrant child. But as the children grew older her tirades became pitifully inadequate. Rose mustered no fear and little respect. Disciplinary episodes were out of touch with reality and laughed off by the children. Years later, with her children all graduating from college, she toyed with the idea of writing a book about her world travels but warned a potential writer-collaborator not to mention it to her children as they would only make fun of her idea.

Though resigned to rejection by her children, Rose shared her husband's longing for social acceptance and held a burning ambition for herself, as well as her family. She once famously asked one of Jack's friends at Harvard, "When *will* the nice people of Boston accept us?"[23] She actually kept copies of the hated little newspaper messages, "No Irish Need Apply," which she pasted in a family scrapbook. Society matrons, threatened by the upstart Kennedys, could be cruel. A visitor recalled that Rose was a lovely person but had an appalling voice.

Rose constantly made a pretense of never being ambitious for herself, only her sons, but years later she confided to a friend, "If I had grown up in today's world, without hesitation I would have become a politician," adding provocatively, "Who knows, I might have become the first woman President of the United States."[24]

Nothing was more puzzling than her relationship with her daughter Rosemary. By 1939, the mentally disabled daughter had begun to turn violent. As a youngster, she had exhibited the sweetest nature of all the children and had fought her disability with an endearing spirit. As pictures attest, she was the prettiest of the girls. But as she developed into a woman and began to realize that her siblings were passing her by, she became frustrated, sometimes using her fists to hit and bruise her attendants. While at a Catholic convent in Washington, D.C., Rosemary disappeared from the compound, only to be found in the middle of the morning walking the streets. Rose was worried.

In 1941, without consulting his wife, Joe Kennedy had doctors perform a prefrontal lobotomy on Rosemary. For a brief, brutal period in the history of surgery, this operation was thought to hold the key for the disabled in Rosemary's situation. But the operation did not go well. Rosemary was reduced to the mental state of a five-year-old. Joe had her institutionalized at St. Coletta's, a Catholic home for mentally retarded people in Jefferson, Wisconsin, where he had a small house built for her on the grounds. According to Kennedy legend, Rose was told that Rosemary needed a life of her own and that visits would set her back. Supposedly, Rose did not know of Rosemary's condition until Joe himself was struck down with a stroke. Then, when she visited the home in Wisconsin, she lashed out at friends and family, asking why she hadn't been told about the operation. They replied that none of them had known it had happened. Rose had worked with her disabled daughter for twenty years and was incredulous about Joe's decision. "He thought it would help her," she said at ninety years of age, reflecting on this most mysterious story within the family, "but it made her go all the way back. It erased all those years of effort I had put into her. It was all gone in a matter of minutes."[25]

In light of emerging stories and historical data, revisionists find Rose somewhat disingenuous in her biography and are now questioning her whole life, including making a reexamination of the role she played with her disabled daughter. No matter how sophisticated Joe's ruse—apparently he had arranged for letters from the sisters at the home directing Rose away—why had the mother refused to visit Wisconsin and see Rosemary for herself? Why had she waited so many long years, till her husband's stroke? She had the independence to travel the world, sometimes by herself.

The traditional explanation holds that Rose had refined her

mother's tendency toward self-denial into an art form and that at some unconscious level she knew something was terribly wrong. But could it have been a conscious sleight of hand from a tough, disciplined woman, famous for her view that "neither comprehension nor learning can take place in an atmosphere of anxiety"?[26]

If anything, the passing of time has led historians to enlarge her political abilities and her strategic sense, honed at the feet of her father, the mayor of Boston. "There's nothing I like less than bad arguments for a view that I hold dear," she once said. After Joe Kennedy had humiliated himself as ambassador to the United Kingdom and suffered endless backroom betrayals at the hands of the Roosevelt White House, he was prepared to endorse FDR's political opponent, Wendell Willkie, for president. On the trip down to Washington for a tête-à-tête with FDR, Rose warned her husband to look at the big picture. As grievous and painful as the White House petty political games had been, the public wouldn't understand them. They would see only that FDR had appointed Joe Kennedy ambassador to the Court of St. James's and he had bitten the hand that had fed him. Joe would have to stay loyal to the Democrat Party, if not for his own future, then for his sons'.

Rose would employ the same cold logic in her personal relations with her husband. No matter how bitter her private actions might be, Rose would only say publicly that she loved him and always had. "I've had an exciting time; I married for love and got a little money along with it."[27] Years after her son's presidency, she spotted Gloria Swanson in a restaurant in Paris and walked over to give her daughter and granddaughter a Kennedy half dollar.

Yet, for all the negative things that would come to light, Rose triumphed by simply surviving, not only physically but in her spirit. To those who criticized her personal extravagances, she would say, "It's our money, and we're free to spend it any way we please."[28]

To some who thought she should never be photographed smiling or enjoying life after the death of her sons, she answered that no matter how much sorrow we encountered in life, God expected us to go on living. Even so, with all the public bravado, her sorrow was very real and the tragedies took their emotional toll. Long after the deaths of Joe, Jr., and Kathleen, after the assassinations of Jack and Bobby, after the death of her own husband, a peaceful Rose Kennedy and her daughters gathered again at Hyannis Port for a summer. They sat at the dinner table where so many memories had been made and were soon in animated, boisterous discussion. "What more could you have, Mother?" Jean asked, over the laughter. "Your daughters all around you like this and all of us laughing and having such a good time."

The conversation suddenly turned very quiet. "My sons," Rose finally said, very softly. "My sons."

★

FOURTEEN

The Rise of Camelot

I have no political ambitions for myself or for my children.[1]
—Joseph Patrick Kennedy

There is no doubt that with all of their failings Joe and Rose Kennedy loved their children dearly. Joe, especially, made an effort to redeem his early absence from their lives. During his years in Hollywood he showered them with thoughtful gifts: autographs to the girls from Gary Cooper and letters to the sons from famous Hollywood cowboys.

If Rose was the driving force behind their love of sports and the outdoors, Joe was certainly the one who instilled their sense of competition on the playing field. "We want winners," he insisted. "We don't want any losers around here."[2] After the Hollywood years, with Rose gone much of the time, Joe drilled them out on the lawn at Hyannis Port. He encouraged friendly family competition but looked for opportunities for them to compete with outsiders. The children were entered in public swimming races, each in a different category so they would not be competing with their siblings. "And if we won," remembered daughter Eunice, dryly, "he got terribly enthusiastic."[3]

Joe, Jr., the firstborn, was obviously his father's favorite, but such a privilege came with a price: he was expected to set the example for the whole brood. If Joe disciplined his son, he expected the lesson to be passed down. For all his bravado and pride as the chosen one, Joe, Jr., was desperate for his father's attention. Joe, Sr., had missed his son's confirmation, a fact that Junior never forgot. But if the firstborn, the heir apparent, the chosen one, had insecurities, one wonders how deeply the absent father inspired insecurity in the others.

Aware of his overpowering, domineering personality, old Joe encouraged independence and even a measure of impertinence in his two oldest sons. When Joe, Jr., returned from a summer of study in Russia, spouting the advantages of socialism, old man Kennedy was not troubled and actually delighted in his independence. As it turned out, Joe, Jr.'s, flirt with socialism turned out to be a passing fancy.

The second son, Jack, felt some of the pressure of the comparison to his older, favored brother. He talked with friends about how Joe, Jr., was a better dancer, was smarter, made better grades, and was better at football. But Joe, Jr., still apparently felt threatened. He bullied Jack and physically hurt him when family play gave him the chance.

The competition is seen in their effort to win their father's approval. In a letter to Joe, Sr., in November 1929, Jack wrote, "Joe came home he was telling me how strong he was and how tough. The first thing he did to show me how tough he was [sic] to get sick so that he could not have any Thanksgiving dinner. Manly youth. He was then going to show me how to Indian wrestle. I threw him over on his neck."[4]

But Jack's victories were rare. When Joe, Jr., graduated from the university in 1933, he won the coveted Harvard Trophy, awarded to the single student combining the best scholarship and sportsmanship. Jack could not begin to compete for such an honor. In 1931, Jack Kennedy failed the Latin segment of his entrance exam at Choate. He was a reasonably bright young man, scoring a 119 on his IQ test. But both facts came to light only recently. The Kennedy machine would foster the idea that the president's raw intelligence had always registered outstanding scores, even when he was a youth, and had consistently measured at genius or above. An uncritical press, which favored Kennedy, never really probed into the claims. Officials at Choate suggested that he had finally been accepted at the school, in spite of his Latin scores, simply because he was a Kennedy. At times, Joe, Sr., despaired over his second son. Writing to the headmaster at Choate, Joe complained, "I can't tell you how unhappy I was in seeing and talking with Jack. He seems to lack entirely a sense of responsibility."[5]

Joe Kennedy, Jr., had it all. When their father's isolationist stand landed him in trouble with President Roosevelt, he started speaking publicly about staying out of the war and leveraged his way onto the Massachusetts delegation to the Democratic National Convention, where he cast one of the very few votes against FDR for nomination to a third term.

When, with his father's help, Jack turned a senior thesis into a best-selling book, *Why England Slept,* Joe, Jr., dismissed it as so much intellectual masturbation. "It seemed to represent a lot of work but didn't prove anything."[6] He later poked holes in JFK's acclaim as captain of *PT-109.* After congratulating him on all the publicity, he asked the hard questions that Kennedy detractors would ask years later, trying to debunk the heroics; "Where the hell were you when the destroyer hove into sight, and exactly what were your moves, and where the hell was your radar?"[7] Joe, Jr., openly talked about running for president someday. They both agreed that Jack was much too shy. It was thought that he would be a writer or journalist.

Rose continued to offer her two oldest sons advice, some of it nagging. During their time in London, she wrote young Joe letters, urging him to pray daily and to go to Mass. And she was quite protective of the younger children. When the Lindbergh kidnapping flashed into the news, she asked publisher friends to lower the profile of the family, a rare request coming from Rose. Ever the organizer, when back in the United States she insisted that the whole household be up by 6 A.M., with the day's war news posted for discussion at breakfast.

But Joe and Jack, the two oldest sons, had bonded completely with their father. Though Rose was offended by the slightest off-color joke, the boys helped their father recruit lovers and one-night stands.[8] During his years in London, the ambassador would prowl the halls of the embassy at night, looking for a lady with an unlocked door. Jack liked to tell the story of his father suddenly standing at the bedside of one of his daughter's overnight girlfriends, disrobing and whispering to the shocked young lady that she was going to have an experience she would always remember.

In fact, Joe's pursuit of women was so ravenous that it was the one issue that sometimes trumped his sons'. One night in Florida, Jack and a girlfriend were heading out to a movie, saying good night to old Joe. Putting down his son, whose health was flagging, Joe flirted with the girl: "Why don't you get a live one?" A friend shook his head at the old man's cruelty, but Jack upbraided him, saying, "Everybody wants to knock his jock off but he made the whole thing possible."[9]

The example was set, and both Joe and Jack followed suit. Later, while serving in Congress, Jack Kennedy ran rampant through the women of Georgetown. Historian Doris Kearns Goodwin concluded that something far deeper than the male hunger of conquest was at work. Jack, she concluded, had a problem with intimacy.

Joe showed no alarm over his son's relationships with women. There are no known lectures on the subject other than one about the political danger Jack once posed when an early girlfriend was targeted by the FBI as a possible spy, and a later one warning that Jack was probably not suited for marriage and that he should not delude himself into thinking he could be monogamous. Perhaps Joe felt impotent and hypocritical to suggest restraint. Perhaps he felt reaffirmed by his son's life choices.

There was no question that he took great pride in his sons' accomplishments and never hesitated to boost their status, even as his own star was waning. During his posting in London, he greedily snatched every incoming letter from Joe, Jr., and carried them around, once reading them aloud to guests at a formal diplomatic dinner party. At one point he planned to make a book out of them.

With the crisis in Czechoslovakia ongoing and Hitler making his demands to occupy the remaining parts of the country, Joe risked the wrath of the whole U.S. diplomatic community to arrange for his second son, Jack, to make a visit to that country. He wanted him to get a feel for the culture in a soon-to-be Nazified nation and to garner material for his senior thesis.[10] And although Jack was almost always ill and unable to follow up on his accomplishments, his father was patient, never tiring of tracking down the top doctors, sometimes resorting to leverage learned as a businessman to secure the best hospital bed and medical team.

It was the senior-thesis-turned-book by younger brother Jack Kennedy, more than anything else, that changed the paradigm with his older brother. His father had arranged for privileged interviews and ordered staff to run down the documents Jack needed. Editors were hired to rewrite the chapters. A distinguished journalist suggested changing the title to *Why England Slept,* although one of JFK's professors privately dubbed it "Why Daddy Slept," for it was indeed an impassioned defense of Ambassador Kennedy's opinions, recast with a cleverly updated interpretation of events. But the fact remained that it was Jack Kennedy's name on the jacket. And it was second son Jack Kennedy who had crafted the widely read apologetics of their father's almost indefensible positions. The newly empowered Jack Kennedy advised his father on what to say when he resigned as ambassador in December 1940, and how to neutralize the charges of appeasement that were being noised about in the press.

On August 2, 1943, Jack Kennedy's torpedo boat, *PT-109,* was rammed by the Japanese destroyer *Amagiri,* and young captain Kennedy, risking his life, helped save members of his crew. The story, along with the best-selling book, made him a national hero. He sometimes told fellow navy men, "When I become President, I will take you to the White House with me."[11] But Joe, fearful for his son's life, began a campaign to get him home. Furious that his boy was being kept in the war in spite of his chronic health problems, the former ambassador began telling friends that if he were still an FDR protégé his son would be home by now. Eventually, Joe's efforts succeeded, and, with Jack safely ensconced in the Mayo Clinic, Joe flew in to be at his side.

In August 1944, with the war winding down, Joe Kennedy, Jr., no doubt feeling the heat, volunteered for a very risky mission. He was to fly a plane full of explosives to help take out a German missile site. It was a poorly planned, desperate task, and it was ironic that a son of the isolationist Ambassador Kennedy was taking it on. Before leaving, Joe told a friend staying at the Claridge's Hotel, "I'm about to go into my act. If I don't come back, tell my dad . . . that I love him very much."[12] Joe Kennedy, Jr., perished in the mission. At the death of his brother, Jack was dispirited, believing that in death Joe was forever established as his father's favorite. He told a friend that it was like shadowboxing and that the shadow was always going to win. Joe, Sr., was inconsolable. He told a friend, "You know how much I had tied my whole life up to his and what great things I saw in the future for him."[13] He told others that he had a premonition: that he too would die soon.

THE PURSUIT OF POWER

The one thing that had always energized Joe Kennedy, Sr., whether in public or private life, had been the chase, the pursuit of a goal, a dream. This applied to both money and women, and frustrated though he was by his ill-fated journey into public life, he could not easily walk away, leaving that dream unrealized.

Just as he had used his father's network to pursue a totally different life for himself, he insisted that his own sons use his wealth to pursue yet another. Joe didn't want them being compared to himself—thinking it would hurt them. In any case, he had earned all the money the family would need for years to come, and he didn't want them to repeat the same story all over again. At times he had worked twenty-hour days, sleeping in his clothes at a desk and taking all his meals in an office. And he was somewhat disappointed that he had lingered in the business world too long, that he had made too many enemies, that his public career had hit a ceiling too quickly and he was running out of time. His sons, he reasoned, should pick up the mantle where it was and not retrace the same old steps.

His new heir apparent, Jack Kennedy, was trying. After the war, convinced that he should pursue journalism, he made an effort to get an article published, but it was turned down by all the major magazines. Typically, Joe stepped in and arranged for his son to win an assignment to cover the United Nations conference for the *Chicago Herald-American*. But Joe was not buying the idea of journalism as an end in itself. He told the family that if the new president, Harry Truman, offered him a position, he would ask for one for Jack instead, probably for the post of assistant secretary of the navy. It was the slot that Theodore Roosevelt and FDR had both used as a stepping-stone to the White House.

"I got Jack into politics," Joe, Sr., later declared bluntly. "I was the one. I told him Joe was dead and that it was therefore his responsibility to run for Congress."[14] JFK told a friend that his father had "demanded" his entry into politics. Relaxing with a friend at the Kennedy compound in Palm Beach, Jack saw his father hustling across the lawn and said, "God, there goes the old man! There he goes figuring out the next step. I'm in it now, you know. It's my turn. I've got to perform."[15] In a letter to Rose, a friend said of Jack, "I am certain he never forgets he must live Joe's life as well as his own."[16]

As Jack's political star ascended, he and his staff agreed that his father was a liability. A revisionist campaign was launched, with the father's full cooperation, to downplay Joe Kennedy's role in advancing his son's career. There were fears that the old man's isolationism and performance in London would hurt the son, but most of all, there was the fear that Jack would appear less of a leader, less his own man. Joe told reporters he had done nothing more to advance his son than make phone calls, something that any father raised in a political family would do for a son. Later, as Jack pursued the presidency, Kennedy staffers would indignantly and angrily insist on this revised history, intimidating journalists into adhering to their line, but the preponderance of facts buries that idea.

Joe Kennedy was intimately involved in the process from the beginning and all the way to the White House. His money and influence helped move the pieces and arrange for the right congressional district to open. At first, Jack played his part, reluctantly and only as a shill for his departed big brother, telling a reporter that "I'm just filling Joe's shoes. If he were alive, I'd never be in this." [17]

Some Massachusetts politicians were outraged at Joe Kennedy's arrogance. When a delegation favoring another congressional candidate sat down to make a deal, suggesting that if Joe's young son dropped out of the race and kept out of trouble they would promise him a job in the new congressman's Washington office, Joe shot back, "You fellows are crazy. My son will be president in 1960." [18]

Joe helped plant a national account of Jack's heroics in the *PT-109* incident, financed the distribution of a 100,000 copies of a *Reader's Digest* version of the story, and ended up spending close to $300,000, at the time an unprecedented amount for a lowly congressional campaign. One old political hand declared that Joe could have gotten his chauffeur elected with that kind of money. But Joe Kennedy saw this as only the launch of something bigger. He was taking no chances. Three days before the election, Joe and Rose hosted an elaborate formal reception for 1,500 guests in the Irish community. Almost the entire Kennedy brood was on hand and pitched in to greet guests and campaign for their brother.

Joe even provided the personal emotional support for his son. Trying to overcome his shyness and struggling as a public speaker, young Jack would visit his father and pour out his despair and sense of failure.

Eunice remembers how tenderly and skillfully old Joe would turn things around, claiming that he had heard glowing reports on the same speech. After rebuilding his son's flagging spirits, he would circle back around and ask the son what *he* thought could be improved. Later, when Jack was dispirited over widespread political rejection of his suggestion of support for Algerian independence, his father boosted his morale by calling it a bold move, telling his son not to be discouraged, that he was in fact lucky beyond his dreams. Within a few months, he would be proven right.

When Jack Kennedy won his congressional seat, Joe immediately began preparing for the next step. First he called in favors and pulled strings to help his son win a seat on the House Education and Labor Committee. Then he hired a publicist to promote the new congressman, sparking a series of positive articles and later earning young Jack Kennedy his place as one of the chamber of commerce's ten most outstanding young men of 1946.

Jack repaid FDR for hurting his father, voting with Republicans in favor of the Twenty-second Amendment to the Constitution. Limiting a president to two terms, the amendment was a slap at Franklin Roosevelt, who had sought the office four times.

But sometimes there was tension. When Jack once voted his own way on a bill, Joe sarcastically told a friend that he had given each of his children a million dollars so they could feel free to spit in his eye whenever they wished. "I guess Dad has decided that he's going to be the ventriloquist," his congressman son retorted, "so I guess that leaves me the role of the dummy." [19]

In Congress, Jack Kennedy slowly began to gain a measure of independence from his father. Old Joe's international views were influenced by his instinct to protect his own personal financial empire. In the past this had sometimes led to outrageous positions, such as his backing appeasement with Germany before the outbreak of the war had proven to be a disastrous position. Now he was suggesting that Greece and Turkey should be allowed to fall into the Soviet orbit. It would overburden the Communist bloc, Joe contended, and force its economic collapse. But an aggressive Soviet Union, with complete control of the Black Sea and Greece to use as a launching pad, would pose a dangerous threat in the Mediterranean, and the increasingly important, oil-rich Middle East would be in jeopardy. The more outrageous Joe's suggestions, the more his son Jack gained confidence, realizing that his own view of the world was more realistic.

After Jack Kennedy's reelection to the House, when a decision was finally made for him to make a run for the Senate, Joe immediately went to work. Notwithstanding the later revised family history, contending that the father was out of the loop, Joe was in fact into everything. He helped coordinate the speechwriting, scheduling, policy, and advertising, as well as tapping the best advisers and critics in the country. He not only hired but fired as well, which sometimes infuriated Jack's own inner circle.

At Joe's insistence, his younger brother Bobby was brought in to help run the organization. At first Bobby seemed overwhelmed and underqualified, but Joe knew that in politics, loyalty and self-interest were the principal ingredients. As a trained talent hunter, he must have seen something in Bobby that the son didn't even see in himself. The younger Kennedy's gift at organization soon asserted itself. Bobby became the surprise of the whole campaign, his disciplined, methodical approach impressing the hired veterans who had earlier dismissed him.

Joe spent huge amounts of money, putting it where it would speed up the process and forge needed allies. It is unlikely that the full extent of his expenditures will ever be known, but some examples have tumbled out into the open. In the fall of 1952, John J. Fox, owner of the *Boston Post,* met with the Republican Senate candidate, Henry Cabot Lodge. In a face-to-face meeting, Fox told Lodge that his paper would endorse him for the Senate. It was a critical promise of support worth thousands of votes since the *Post* was one of the few papers that made such endorsements. But two weeks before the election, the paper threw its support to Jack Kennedy. It just so happened that Fox and his paper were in deep financial trouble, and Joe Kennedy had just made them a $500,000 loan to help bail them out.

Even so, there were public avowals that the father was not behind the scenes pulling strings. In public appearances Jack kept insisting to older voters that he, not his father, was running for the Senate. It was a critical message for Jewish voters, who had not forgotten the ambassador's pro-appeasement policies. In November 1952, Jack Kennedy was elected to the U.S. Senate in a narrow election. It would never have happened without his father.

Upon taking his seat in the U.S. Senate, John F. Kennedy was immediately seen as a powerful political figure with an unlimited future. Only thirty-five years old and handsome, a war hero, hailing from one of America's richest families, Kennedy was immediately mentioned in the press as a potential Democratic presidential candidate, although most journalists could never have dreamed how quickly the story would unfold.

It seemed that the only piece missing was a wife. Then came the news of Jack's engagement to Jacqueline Lee Bouvier, a stunning twenty-four-year-old. She was the product of a cultured upbringing, having studied for a year at the Sorbonne in Paris before graduating from George Washington University. Jacqueline was an art collector and linguist who more recently had worked as a photographer-reporter for the *Washington Times-Herald*. The two became instant magic to the Washington press corps.

At first, the Kennedy family felt threatened by Jackie Bouvier. At Hyannis Port, the sisters succeeded in getting her into a family touch football game, where she promptly broke her delicate ankle. Rose was incensed that Jackie always slept late, missing the important family time at breakfast. It was, she reasoned, an indication of other vices.

But Joe Kennedy was impressed. The longer he and Jackie knew each other, the closer their bond would become, forging a tender, loving father-and-daughter-in-law relationship. Though quite young, she was every bit as educated and refined as the WASPs whose attitudes had so intimidated him all his life. Joe was fascinated. His concern lay with his son. Would the playboy, second-born Senator Jack Kennedy be able to make a marriage work? During the Senate campaign Joe had followed behind, using money to help clean up his son's promiscuous trail.[20] But it was one thing to keep stories out of the press, something altogether different to win the cooperation of an aggrieved spouse. What if his son fell in love with another woman? Joe likely hearkened back to his own fling with Gloria Swanson, when he had been willing to lose everything, all the pieces, just to have her. The family had come too far and had too much riding on this one son to lose it all over a failed relationship. Divorce for an elected public servant was, in that era, the kiss of death.

John F. Kennedy and Jacqueline Bouvier were married on September 12, 1953, in St. Mary's Roman Catholic Church in Newport, Rhode Island. A crowd of almost three thousand people waited outside.

The most immediate threat was not to Jack Kennedy's marriage. It was his health, which was still precarious. Doctors warned that he would lose his ability to walk without a complicated spinal operation. It was risky, he was warned, and it could easily go wrong. After his experience with his daughter Rosemary, Joe Kennedy had limited faith in surgeons and their solutions. Joe begged his son not to have the operation, and when that failed, he begged Jackie to intervene. He pointed out how effective FDR had been from a wheelchair. After surgery, when his son went into a coma, Joe collapsed, his whole body shaking with fear and rage, sobbing uncontrollably, sure that he had lost his son. But Jack recovered. And in February 1955, he went back under the knife again.

This time, Joe took him back to Palm Springs to recover under his watchful eye. As Jack grew stronger, he used his convalescence to pen a new book on the history of courageous members of the U.S. Senate who had risked their careers to do the right thing. Joe produced writers and researchers to develop first drafts of the chapters and later employed the loyal journalist Arthur Krock to help promote the book. It was entitled *Profiles in Courage,* and it would become a national best seller. The saga of one of America's greatest political dynasties was only beginning to reach its climax.

As Joe had suspected, Jackie was totally unprepared for marriage to a Kennedy. She was stunned when they went to parties and Jack would escape into a room with a pretty young staffer. Eventually, he simply left her home alone and went to the parties by himself. In 1956, with Jackie pregnant, Jack was living the life of a playboy on an extended vacation in the Mediterranean. He and a companion were enjoying one young woman after the other at various ports of call. When the news came that Jackie had lost the baby, Kennedy's revelry continued unabated until his friend warned that if his wife divorced him he could kiss his presidential ambitions good-bye.[21] Jack raced back to her side.

On September 24, 1955, Republican President Dwight Eisenhower suffered a heart attack during a visit to Denver, Colorado. Rumors spread that the popular incumbent president could not possibly run for reelection in 1956. If a Democrat won the presidency and held it for eight years, Jack would be able to run for office in 1964. He would be forty-seven years old.

To get into position, he and Joe decided that they needed to move quickly, promoting their own man for president now in return for a pledge to take Jack onto the ticket as vice presidential running mate. Serving as vice president for eight years would put Jack Kennedy into pole position for the race for the White House in 1964. Joe Kennedy still had lots of money and influence and, more important, had shown a willingness to use it to help his son. He finally decided to back the Democrat leader in the Senate, the rascally, powerful Lyndon B. Johnson of Texas.

Johnson was just as crude and wily as Joe Kennedy, and the two would have more than one important conversation of national consequence. In his negotiations, Joe told the Texas senator that he would finance a presidential campaign if Johnson would agree to take his son onto the ticket. But Johnson demurred, and eventually the popular Eisenhower recovered, deciding to run for a second term after all. The game would have to wait.

Convinced that the Democrats would go down to defeat in 1956 and sure that his son need not play an important role in the upcoming Democratic National Convention, Joe was relaxing on the Riviera in the south of France when the news came through that his son Jack was being touted as a vice presidential running mate for Adlai Stevenson. Joe was furious. Stevenson had already been decisively beaten by Eisenhower in the 1952 election. The replay was expected to be a slaughter. A second landslide defeat, Joe reasoned, would be blamed on the fact that Jack Kennedy, the vice presidential running mate, was a Roman Catholic. His son would forever be branded a loser, and a Catholic would not be on another presidential ticket in his lifetime. Or so Joe Kennedy reasoned.

While the Kennedy family was maneuvering stateside to get Jack onto the presidential ticket, others were pressuring Stevenson to name the popular Tennessee Senator Estes Kefauver to the ticket, or the up-and-coming Senator Hubert H. Humphrey of Minnesota. In a move that was seen as a rebuff of the Kennedy effort, Adlai Stevenson decided to let the convention make the decision itself. He announced publicly that he was not going to name a running mate. The convention would be open.

It was exactly the sort of game the Kennedy family knew best. But their master strategist and the one with all the money was in Europe. Joe, Sr., was fuming, still arguing against the idea of Jack going onto the ticket. When younger brother Bobby called to ask for advice, he received an earful, with Joe calling his son Jack an idiot.

Then daughter Eunice got on the phone. Eunice Kennedy Shriver was one of the more remarkable members of the family, often a mature and wise presence in the middle of the storm. She had married Robert Sargent Shriver, Jr., in May 1953, even before Jack had married Jackie. She patiently explained to her father that the dynamics were shifting. Some in the media and the party were enamored of other players. Kefauver had a big following, but even more threatening was the up-and-coming Hubert Humphrey. Without a highly visible campaign at some point, Jack could never be president.

As would often happen in the Kennedy saga, Eunice would prove to be prescient. Estes Kefauver finally won the vice presidential nomination, but Jack Kennedy came so close that he became a national celebrity. When he graciously urged the convention to make the nomination of Kefauver unanimous, he won kudos from the media and the nation across the board. Joe Kennedy returned to the United States pleased and surprised by the positive outcome. Not only was the dream alive; it had been advanced.

★

FIFTEEN

Shattered Dreams

Birds sing after a storm; why shouldn't people
feel as free to delight in whatever remains to them?[1]
—Rose Fitzgerald Kennedy

In the immediate afterglow of Jack Kennedy's near brush with national power, he grew depressed. By Thanksgiving he was admitting to his father that the whole idea of a Catholic being elected to national office in the United States was untenable. Joe, ever the cheerleader, continued to prop him up. There was a new generation coming of age, he pointed out; there were many sons and daughters of immigrant families ready to support someone who embodied their own aspirations. But Jack continued to worry, shifting his concern to his chronic health problems, which were known to only a few people and which he felt comfortable talking about only with his father. Getting elected might be a moot point, Jack concluded. He wasn't sure things would get even that far.

As long as the door was not finally closed, Joe continued to busily lay the groundwork for his son's promotion. That Christmas he was furious with Bobby, who was serving as counsel for a Senate investigating committee looking into racketeering in the unions. Jack would need labor support for a presidential run, but Bobby, seeing it as a point of personal integrity, would not budge. Joe once more lobbied Senator Lyndon Johnson, this time promising all sorts of things if he would put Jack onto the Senate Foreign Relations Committee. This time, the slippery Texas senator decided that it might not be a bad idea to have the persistent Joe Kennedy in his debt, so he went along with the idea. Then came the announcement that Jack Kennedy's best seller, *Profiles in Courage,* had won the Pulitzer Prize. There was some cynicism about the selection, especially since the book had not received a single nomination in the first round. Charges soon followed that Joe Kennedy had not only influenced the prize committee through his loyal friend Arthur Krock but had manipulated the book onto *The New York Times'* best-seller list in the first place. But the Kennedy machine was working too fast and the tentacles of Joe's money were so deep that it was practically impossible for anyone to keep up.

In 1958, Joe spent $1.5 million to ensure Jack's reelection as senator of Massachusetts. The landslide was considered an important step toward the presidency. By 1959, Joe Kennedy was bursting with pride. He told journalists that his son was more popular than Cary Grant or Jimmy Stewart. A reporter told his editor, "They confidently look forward to the day when Jack will be in the White House, Bobby will serve in the Cabinet as Attorney General, and Teddy will be the Senator from Massachusetts."[2]

The dream was easier said than done. It was a high-wire act that took many players to pull off. Former First Lady Eleanor Roosevelt openly opposed him, saying that perhaps a Catholic would be elected, but only if he could separate the issues of church and state, and she doubted Senator Kennedy could do that. She said he had yet to demonstrate the kind of courage he had written about in his book.

In October 1959, Bobby finally resigned his position as Senate counsel to take over Jack's presidential campaign. Flushed with confidence, he called for a meeting in Hyannis Port, where he dressed down his candidate brother for being so unorganized. One decision, made immediately, was to avoid any close association with Joe. It was a decision that the old ambassador immediately understood and applauded. Behind the scenes, he continued to be relentless. Joe had a knack for looking past titles such as state party chairman, congressman, or senator to find who the real power was in a given region or city. Sometimes it was a powerful politico—a state chairman, for example—but sometimes it was a key county finance chairman or a judge or newspaper publisher. Once that person was located, Joe dealt with the power brokers directly, man to man, including the famous Mayor Richard Daley of Chicago.

Kennedy's money was everywhere, and promises were made that could never be kept. FBI recording devices picked up information of donations from the chief Chicago mobster Sam Giancana and other mafiosi to the Kennedy campaign, all made through Joseph P. Kennedy.[3] Giancana, a clever Mafia leader who allowed more flamboyant racketeers to grab the headlines, would not be publicly recognized as the true power behind the Chicago rackets until long after his death. But Joe Kennedy knew the real underworld as well. When asked about Jack Kennedy's religion, Harry Truman intoned, "It's not the pope I worry about, it's the pop."[4]

The 1960 presidential election between Richard M. Nixon and John F. Kennedy was one of the closest in American history. That evening, Joe and Rose Kennedy hosted the whole family clan and friends at Hyannis Port. There were the candidate and his wife, Jackie; campaign manager Bobby and his wife, Ethel; younger brother Ted and Joan Bennett; Pat and her movie star husband, Peter Lawford; Eunice and Sargent Shriver; Jean and Steve Smith. There was Joe's old friend Father John Cavanaugh. After a grand feast at the ambassador's table, they moved to Bobby's nearby house to watch the election returns. But it was not turning out as the Kennedys had hoped. Joe and Jack paced back and forth across the compound, helplessly discussing the unfolding events. By two in the morning it became clear that four states—Michigan, Illinois, Minnesota, and California—held the balance of power.

At four o'clock the nation began to watch the political maneuverings in Illinois. It was becoming more and more likely that the whole decision would be made there. Precinct chairmen in the southern, Republican, rural part of the state had taken ballot boxes home with them to continue the count. Mayor Daley was holding back twice as many boxes in Chicago, waiting to see what the southern Illinois vote total would be. Jack Kennedy, exhausted by the tension, finally went to sleep. But he could not sleep more than an hour at a time.

Close to nine in the morning, Rose's niece Ann Gargan stopped by. "I've brought a message from your father," she said. "He says not to worry, you've got Illinois."

"Who says so?" Jack asked. "Did I miss it on TV?"

"No," she answered. "Your father says so."[5]

According to Gargan, Jack Kennedy grinned and cursed at the same time.

As promised by Joe Kennedy, who knew better than most that the big prizes do not come easily but kicking and screaming all the way, John F. Kennedy finally took the state of Illinois by a razor-thin margin and, with it, the national election. They had done it—the immigrant Irish family whose relatives were even then still living in the Old Country in cottages with thatched roofs and dirt floors. A Kennedy had been elected president.

A FAMILY IN DISARRAY

On a frigid inauguration day, January 1961, John Fitzgerald Kennedy placed his hand on a Fitzgerald family Bible and was sworn in as the thirty-fifth president of the United States. It was the first time in American history that both a mother and father were present at the inauguration of a son.

Following the inaugural parade, a reception was to be held for the families of the president and first lady. It would be hosted in the State Dining Room of the White House, while other groups of dignitaries would be received in the East Room. Inaugural balls would be attended later, but this was to be the moment for the Kennedys and Bouviers, the Lees and Auchinclosses. But Jackie, exhausted and not wanting to look tired for the cameras that night, was refusing to come downstairs from her private quarters.

One of Jackie's cousins spotted Joe standing by himself, looking diminished and oddly defeated, perhaps disappointed at being relegated to part of the herd. "I guess you must be extremely proud of your son today," the cousin said, sounding embarrassingly pedestrian.

"Oh yes, I guess it's quite an honor," Joe answered, shaking hands weakly.

Then the cousin asked Joe if there were some great vision for America that he held, something that his son might now realize. "He laughed at me as if I were naïve. Joe Kennedy's vision for America, I eventually realized, was simply to have his son President, to have the Kennedys at the summit of American political life. What vision he had was for a family, not a people." [6]

As planned, Jack Kennedy appointed his brother Bobby attorney general. Later, he appointed his sister's husband, Sargent Shriver, as the head of the newly created Peace Corps. It was nepotism on a breathless

Joseph P. Kennedy at his desk at the Columbia Trust Company, 1914. At twenty-four he was touted as the youngest bank president in the nation. He made fortunes in steel, motion pictures, liquor, and Wall Street. Kennedy's magic as a businessman was his timing. *Courtesy of the John F. Kennedy Library*

The Kennedys at Hyannis Port in 1948. From left to right standing, Jack, Jean, Rose, Joseph P. Kennedy Sr., Pat, Bobby, and Eunice. Teddy is in the front with a football. "The measure of a man's success in life," Joe wrote, "isn't the money he has made—it's the kind of family he has raised." *Courtesy of the John F. Kennedy Library*

Jack Kennedy, captain of PT Boat 109, became a World War II hero. His father, Joe, used his money and influence to promote the legend. *Courtesy of the John F. Kennedy Library*

The president and first lady at the Inaugural Ball, January 20, 1961. Jackie was stunned by her husband's unabashed philandering. A few months after this picture, the president and Jackie were greeting people in a receiving line, which included a young blonde procured for the president. Jackie turned furiously to one of her husband's staff. "Isn't it bad enough that you solicit this woman for my husband, but then you insult me by asking me to shake her hand!" *Abbie Rowe, White House photo, courtesy of the John F. Kennedy Library*

The president, FBI director J. Edgar Hoover, and Robert Kennedy in 1961. That December, Hoover told Bobby Kennedy that FBI listening devices had picked up conversations with top Mafia leaders. They were angry that campaign contributions made to Joe Kennedy in 1960 were not producing results. Joe Kennedy had a stroke that very week and never fully recovered. *Abbie Rowe, White House photo, courtesy of the John F. Kennedy Library*

Vice President Johnson, President Kennedy, and the first lady watch the flight of astronaut Alan Shepard on television. "History made him what he was," Jackie told historian Theodore White, "this lonely sick boy. His mother really didn't love him." *Cecil Stroughton, White House photo, courtesy of the John F. Kennedy Library*

Jack Kennedy and family at Hyannis Port, August 1962. Jacqueline Kennedy kept her children out of the limelight. The pictures of Caroline and John Jr. scampering around the Oval Office were atypical and taken when Jackie was out of the country. *Cecil Stroughton, White House photo, courtesy of the John F. Kennedy Library*

The president applauds his mother, Rose Kennedy, at an event in 1962. Joe and Rose Kennedy shared a longing for social acceptance. She once asked one of Jack's friends at Harvard, "When will the nice people of Boston accept us?" *Abbie Rowe, White House photo, courtesy of the John F. Kennedy Library*

FBI director J. Edgar Hoover, Attorney General Robert F. Kennedy, and Solicitor General Archibald Cox in the White House Rose Garden. Six months later the president was assassinated. "Why? What was the purpose?" Bobby was overheard saying. "The innocent suffer—how can that be possible and God be just?" *Cecil Stroughton, White House photo, courtesy of the John F. Kennedy Library*

The president's body lies in state at the Capitol. The family leaves after the ceremony. Caroline Kennedy, Jacqueline, and John F. Kennedy Jr. (Second row) Attorney General Robert F. Kennedy and sister Patricia Kennedy Lawford. (Third row) Brother-in-law Peter Lawford. *Abbie Rowe, White House photo, courtesy of the John F. Kennedy Library*

The Francis Nixon family (left to right): Donald and his wife; Francis and Hannah; Richard and his wife, Pat; and Edward. In his last speech from the White House, Nixon said of his mother, Hannah Milhous Nixon, "My mother was a saint."

Dorothy Ayer Gardner King holds her baby, Leslie Lynch King Jr., on his baptism day, September 1913. He would become the thirty-eighth president of the United States. *Courtesy of the Gerald R. Ford Library*

Leslie King and his family lived in this prestigious three-story house in Omaha, Nebraska, from 1913 to 1917. But King abused his wife. Fearing for herself and her baby, she fled to Michigan. *Courtesy of the Gerald R. Ford Library*

Gerald Ford's boyhood home in Grand Rapids, Michigan. Dorothy obtained a divorce from Leslie King and married a paint manufacturer. They lived a more humble life, but he was gentle and kind, and together they raised a president. *Courtesy of the Gerald R. Ford Library*

Gerald R. Ford Jr. with his father and half brothers Tom, Dick, and Jim Ford on the front steps of their Grand Rapids, Michigan, home, October 1927. His stepdad gave him a new name and a new life. *Courtesy of the Gerald R. Ford Library*

The Reagan sons, Neil and Ron, the future president. The father had a drinking problem and was once fired from a job on Christmas Eve, but the mother taught her boys that if one had faith, things would work out fine, regardless of the circumstances. *Courtesy Ronald Reagan Library*

This photo was taken for the Reagan family Christmas card in 1916. John Edward "Jack" and Nelle Reagan pose with their sons, Neil and Ronald Reagan (with Dutch-boy haircut). *Courtesy Ronald Reagan Library*

Prescott Bush on the links. His father-in-law, Bert Walker, helped organize the United States Golf Association and had the Walker Cup named after him. Prescott helped rewrite the rules for the game and in 1935 served as president of the association. *George Bush Presidential Library, Prescott Bush collection*

Barbara Pierce at age seven. She had a sometimes estranged relationship with her mother, Pauline, but she named her first daughter after her. *George Bush Presidential Library*

George H. W. Bush enlisted on his eighteenth birthday. He was the youngest aviator in history and won medals for his bravery in World War II. Shot down over the Pacific in 1944, he finished his mission in a crippled plane before bailing out. *George Bush Presidential Library*

George Bush and Barbara Pierce were married January 6, 1945. Barbara embraced her new family and wore her mother-in-law's wedding dress. *George Bush Presidential Library*

The Bushes and Walkers at Kennebunkport, Maine. George is standing next to his father, Prescott. Barbara is seated in the middle, next to Dottie (left). But Barbara has eyes only for her baby, Georgie. *George Bush Presidential Library, Prescott Bush collection*

Prescott and Dottie Bush celebrate his Senate victory. Prescott was so thrilled with serving in the Senate that he required his grandchildren to call him senator instead of grandpa. Men of the Bush family established their fortune first and then entered public life. *George Bush Presidential Library, Prescott Bush collection*

Prescott was a key figure in welcoming Dwight Eisenhower into the Republican Party and promoting his run for the presidency. The president often golfed with the senator. *George Bush Presidential Library, Prescott Bush collection*

Senator Prescott Bush and his son George H. W. Bush. "I had a very powerful father," George would say, "very much a leader, admired by everybody. I had a kind of—not really a competitive thing with him—but I wanted to get out on my own." *George Bush Presidential Library, Prescott Bush collection*

Two presidents and a first lady: George and Barbara Bush with their baby Georgie in New Haven, Connecticut, April 1947. *George Bush Presidential Library, Prescott Bush collection*

George H. Bush holds his son, George W., on an airstrip in Midland, Texas, 1949. Both men would love baseball, fly airplanes, attend Andover prep school, graduate from Yale, and be president of the United States. *George Bush Presidential Library*

George W. Bush with his father in Midland, Texas. The father was often gone from home. *George Bush Presidential Library*

George H. W. Bush in the oil fields. Once more, a Bush son traveled far from home and became a millionaire. A career in public life would follow. Although the sons were never verbally pressured, the lauded tradition was hard to miss. *George Bush Presidential Library*

Christmas 1955. George W. Bush is holding Neil on his lap. Jeb is to the left. The father founded Zapata Offshore the year before; it would provide the financial resources to allow him to run for office. *George Bush Presidential Library*

George H. holding Neil, George W., Jeb, and Barbara holding Marvin, 1956. When the boys became young men, the spotlight would turn to Jeb, the second son, who was expected to have a public career. Later, others would tout Neil, saying he should someday run for governor of Colorado. Marvin would build a successful investment banking career in the tradition of his grandfather. *George Bush Presidential Library*

Jeb and George W. after the 1959 family move to Houston, Texas. George was put in a private school and then sent on to a prep school in Massachusetts. When Bush Senior became successful, he was only returning to his roots after exile in the desert of West Texas, but Midland would always be home to George W., who was less impressed with the preppy life at Andover and Yale. *George Bush Presidential Library*

(From left) Doro, George H., Jeb, Marvin, George W., Neil, and Barbara. Second son, Jeb, whose arm is around his father, would be the first out of the gate. "There is no question in my mind that he will become a major political figure in the country," his father would say. "He is passionate in his caring and in his beliefs. He speaks well and at six-foot-four is an impressive man." *George Bush Presidential Library*

First Lady Barbara Bush. A 1994 Mother's Day poll declared her the woman most Americans would like to talk to on Mother's Day. In the year 2000, a CBS news poll found 63 percent of Americans had a favorable view of her and only 3 percent an unfavorable one. *George Bush Presidential Library*

President Bush talking with American troops heading into battle in Iraq. Later, when his president son ordered his own invasion of Iraq, he did not consult with his father. *George Bush Presidential Library*

George W. Bush with his father, President George H. Bush, and his nephew, George P. Bush, throwing out the opening pitch in Oriole Park at Camden Yards in Baltimore, Maryland, April 6, 1992. When asked how it felt to see his son elected president, the elder Bush answered with a question of his own. "You remember when your kid comes home with two A's—and you thought she was going to fail?" he said. "That's exactly what it's like." *George Bush Presidential Library*

George W. Bush standing over his father like a hunting trophy. Adam Bellow writes about the sons of powerful men: "They often feel the need to go on proving themselves and are haunted by the fear that nothing they do will ever be good enough. For them, success is a question of not just meeting expectations but of exceeding them, and not once but again and again." *Courtesy of Bettmann/Corbis*

Bill Clinton with his mother, Virginia Kelly. Raised by his grandparents, Clinton is one of three presidents whose father died before he was born. Many others died young or were absentee fathers. *Courtesy of the Clinton Presidential Library*

scale. Bipartisan laws would eventually be passed so it could never be done again. The founding fathers, it was joked, had not anticipated the Kennedys. Alice Roosevelt said that the world had seen nothing like them since the Bonapartes.

And Joe was still pushing for more, wanting Teddy to take his brother's old seat in the U.S. Senate. The problem was that, in 1961, young Ted was only twenty-nine. They would have to find a stand-in to fill the place temporarily. He would have to agree to step down when Teddy finally ran for the seat.

In April 1961, after the Bay of Pigs disaster, the president was discouraged. Joe Kennedy typically picked him up, stressing that the whole nation saw that the fault lay with the CIA and that, in fact, it was a good thing to be tested early. He would be a stronger president for the next crisis.[7] At the same time Jack received word from doctors that his father's health was failing. They feared a stroke but were unable to get the old man to take anticoagulants.

On December 11, Joe arrived at Palm Beach for the winter. Jack and Jackie and their two children were visiting. That very week, on the days of December 9, 11, and 21, FBI listening devices recorded conversations of top Mafia leaders discussing just what their money had bought for them in the Kennedy administration. The name of Joe Kennedy was mentioned repeatedly in their discussions.[8] J. Edgar Hoover sent Attorney General Robert Kennedy a memorandum with exact transcripts of the Mafia conversations attached. The gangsters had come to the conclusion that their money had not really bought them anything. They were angry with Joe and the Kennedy family.

On December 19, in the middle of this ongoing drama, Joe accompanied the president to the airport in his limousine. Caroline was sitting on her grandfather's lap. She and John, Jr., would be staying for Christmas, along with a host of grandkids. After seeing the president and first lady off to Washington, Joe took Caroline back to the house, played with her for a while and then left for a scheduled golf game at the Palm Beach Club on North Ocean Boulevard. Ann Gargan, Rose Kennedy's niece and a favorite of Joe Kennedy, was along.

On the sixteenth hole, Joe sat down, saying he was not feeling well. He was raced back to his compound, where Ann sounded the alarm. She was told not to call a doctor, to just let him rest. But after checking in on him and seeing his pale face, Rose finally called for help. Joe was rushed by his staff into the hospital, where tests showed that he had suffered a stroke on the left side of his brain.

Inexplicably, Rose played a round of golf and then left the club to go swimming before finally departing for the hospital to see her husband. She was told that his right side was now paralyzed. Described as thrombosis of the left cerebral hemisphere, the doctors explained that it almost certainly meant death.

The president, the attorney general, and Jean Kennedy Smith all flew to Florida on *Air Force One* to be at the side of the man who had made it all happen. Hour by hour, day by day, Joe Kennedy survived. His face was partially paralyzed, and he drooled and could not talk intelligibly.[9]

Early in his convalescence, Joe was often wheeled in for a breakfast with Rose. She would linger over her coffee and read the newspapers to him. One morning, bored by the routine and knowing that the two had no affection for each other, Ann Gargan slipped under the table and began imitating her aunt's gestures and facial inflections. Joe began laughing, apparently a dangerous thing for a man in his condition. It provoked a physical crisis, with Joe's laughter turning into weeping and almost causing him to fall out of his wheelchair.

Whether in Hyannis Port or Palm Beach, more and more Ann Gargan became his keeper, directing the nurses and therapists in their work. Contrary to popular historical accounts, staffers insisted that Rose almost never looked in on him. Rose, who still traveled frequently, packed her mourning clothes on every trip, fully expecting to receive the word that he was gone. She was prepared to be appropriately dressed for the news cameras when it came.

With his leadership gone, Rose Kennedy, who understood nothing of the budget, now pinched pennies. Hearing a television news report that the price of coffee was rising, she ordered that nursing and therapy staff be limited to one cup of coffee per shift. The charge nurse, confident that Rose would never actually visit the ambassador, moved a hot plate to the nurses' station, making unlimited coffee available to her personnel.[10]

When a grandson realized that a beloved staffer who had served the family for a lifetime was being dismissed without retirement, he was able to convince family members and the accountants to make some provision, but Rose was kept in the dark for fear that she would scuttle the plan.[11]

With their father no longer able to arbitrate between them, and perhaps grieving over the loss of his vibrancy from their lives, the Kennedy sisters turned on each other with a vengeance. Only Jean stayed out of it.

First Lady Jackie Kennedy made a special effort to physically touch the old man when she visited. Finding that someone had wrapped his gnarled, grotesque hand in a cloth, Jackie took it off and kissed and massaged the fingers, sending the signal that he was loved just the way he was. Staffers agreed that she seemed to bring him the most comfort.

The president, once again reminded of his own mortality, returned to his womanizing with a reckless, self-destructive abandonment. There were affairs with Pamela Turner, who was Jackie's press secretary, and Mary Pinchot Meyer, who was journalist Ben Bradlee's sister-in-law. There were the famous White House secretaries Fiddle and Faddle and a nineteen-year-old college sophomore who was working as an intern in the press office. Judith Campbell Exner was a mistress he shared with Mafia leader Sam Giancana. In Canada in 1961, the president and Jackie were greeting people in a receiving line that included a blonde recruited especially for the president's pleasure. Jackie turned furiously to Dave Powers, her husband's staffer in charge of procuring women. "Isn't it bad enough that you solicit this woman for my husband, but then you insult me by asking me to shake her hand!"[12]

But nothing stopped the compulsive behavior, and the stories from that period continue to surface. JFK once told columnist Joseph Alsop that he didn't expect to live much beyond forty-five years of age.[13] At least one historian described his destructive behavior as the equivalent of pinching himself to prove that he was still alive.

Still, the machinery that the father had set into motion continued to creak along, as if their ambition had a head and brain of its own. Ted Kennedy, the baby in the family, was still on track to run for the Senate in 1962. Bobby, worried about how such a race would affect the president's reputation and annoyed that his little brother had not done more to prepare himself for the role, was now speaking against the idea. At some point the public would have enough of the Kennedys' hubris, and when they turned on them, there would be no coming back.

In the summer of 1961, Ted took a tour of Latin America with an accompanying entourage of media that would flatter a presidential candidate. In Rio de Janeiro, toward the end of the tour, he hooked up with a young Brazilian beauty. The adoring media obediently looked the other way. Womanizing was nothing new for the family. The problem was that Ted would not bother to offer a crumb of discretion.

When worried White House staffers warned the president to back away from his brother, Jack replied, "He's going to win in Massachusetts bigger than I did. And besides, Dad is interested."[14] But Dad was unable to take the lead. The president himself, now head of the family, had to step into the fray.

Nepotism was not the only issue. Using the tactics that his father had so well refined, Jack began the work of cleaning up his little brother's messes. There was Ted Kennedy's cheating scandal at Harvard, for openers. In 1951, as a freshman, he had arranged for a friend to take his final exam in Spanish class. He had been expelled.[15] Without proper management, the story was destined for all the front pages of the nation's newspapers. Jack brought into the White House the Washington bureau chief of *The Boston Globe* to help devise the inoculation piece. The story would not mention the word "cheating" or "expelled" and would play heavily on Ted Kennedy's open admission, "What I did was wrong." In March 1962, JFK brought a political team into the White House to plan Teddy's candidacy. At one point the president asked if patronage—discreetly used, of course—would help. Rose, her political antennae intact, predicted a landslide.

In October, Jack Kennedy flew up to Hyannis Port, his marine helicopter landing on the lawn. His father, Joe, was wheeled out to see the arrival. The two huddled together, with Jack, of course, carrying the burden of the one-sided conversation. If the father could not easily communicate, by most accounts he was still there, inside his shell of a body, his blazing blue eyes flashing recognition, fear, and elation at any unfolding monologue.

When the visit ended and the helicopter lifted off, the president looked down for the last time at the receding figure of his father, sitting in his wheelchair on the front porch, a blanket covering him. Jack Kennedy turned to an aide and said, "He's the one who made all this possible, and look at him now."

THE END OF A DREAM

Ted Kennedy won his Senate election in a landslide. The dynasty was now complete. Joe Kennedy's family had achieved the unthinkable. His three sons were president, attorney general, and a U.S. senator respectively. His son-in-law Sargent Shriver was director of the Peace Corps. American history had never seen anything like it.

On the crisp morning of November 22, 1963, Rose Kennedy went to Mass as usual. Afterward, she and Joe were given a drive through the Massachusetts countryside, a chance to enjoy the brilliant colors of autumn. Joe was served lunch and then took a nap. Rose left for a game of gold. It was a perfectly ordinary day.

Strangely, the first radio reports of an assassination attempt on the president did not alarm Rose. She heard that someone had taken a shot at the president during his campaign stop in Dallas, Texas. Perhaps her famous self-denial had kicked in. She later told an interviewer that she had assumed the incident was not serious or someone would have called the house. Then the details began to make themselves clear. The phone calls finally came. First Bobby called, and then the newly sworn-in president, Lyndon B. Johnson.

By some accounts, it was not until the next day that they told Joe. Rose had hidden copies of the newspapers, wanting Eunice to tell him face to face. According to staffers, both Eunice and Ted broke into the room, with Eunice, babbling about an accident and heaven. Finally the two embraced Joe. "Dad, Jack was shot." [16] And then Eunice said flatly that he was dead. Joe was propped up and finally given a copy of *The New York Times.* He read the story, then let the pages of the paper fall to the floor. A nurse gave him a sedative.

The Kennedy public relations machine, which had long exaggerated the ambassador's health and alertness, now decided it was to its advantage to tilt the other way. "We have told him, but we don't think that he understands it," Rose said. [17]

Joe did not attend the funeral but watched it on television with Father John Cavanaugh, the former president of Notre Dame University and old friend who had been with the family on that dramatic election night three years before, when the Kennedy family had reached the brink and Jack Kennedy had narrowly won the presidency.

The death of this second son was a jolt that temporarily shook

Rose Kennedy's faith. She walked for miles along the cold beach, thinking and praying. Having exhausted herself, she now feared that she could not walk with the family procession to the cathedral without collapsing. She would join them at the service. Robert Kennedy was likewise bewildered by events. In many respects he mirrored his mother. Like Rose, he was a man of obsessive organization, and like Rose, he was a devout Catholic. He had tried to join his father and brother's womanizing fraternity, but it had been morally awkward for him and his forays had been limited. Now, joining Jackie at the White House, he went into the Lincoln Bedroom and collapsed, praying in sobs in a voice heard by staffers. Why? What was the purpose? "The innocent suffer—how can that be possible and God be just?"[18]

In 1968, when Eugene McCarthy embarrassed incumbent President Lyndon Johnson with his strong showing in the New Hampshire primary, the Kennedy family was stunned. The presidential nomination of the Democratic Party was suddenly thrown wide open. Robert would be starting late, but he had his brother's team available, mostly intact, and three generations of political experience working for him. According to John Davis, both Joe Kennedy and his son Ted argued against a run for the presidency, fearful of another assassination attempt.[19] Politically, because of the late start, the chance of victory was slim, but the family had proven that a slim chance was sometimes enough. Now serving as the U.S. senator from New York, Bobby could count on a strong start with the nation's most populous state behind him. There was also the family home-base bastion of Massachusetts. Their old nemesis, Hubert Humphrey, had been beaten before, and Eugene McCarthy was vulnerable. The upcoming California primary would be the test to settle the issue.

Before going to California, Bobby went in to see his invalid father. "I'm going to win this one for you, Dad."[20] In spite of his apparent early objections, Joe Kennedy committed $20 million to help his third son's drive for the White House. Rose Kennedy, along with most of the family clan, visited California to campaign for Bobby.

She was back in Hyannis Port on June 4, 1968, when she awakened to the news on television. "It's Bobby, it's Bobby!" she exclaimed. Another son had been assassinated. Rose gathered her wits about her and went to Mass, flashbulbs exploding in her face. After prayers she returned to the Kennedy compound and went in to see her husband.

They were alone for the first time in years. He was eighty now and still could not speak or walk, and his hearing was beginning to fail, as well. When his wife left, he signaled an assistant to turn on the television.

Rose was seen briefly in the kitchen, crying to herself. It was something the staff had not seen before, even through the ordeal of the first assassination. After a few minutes she went to her room and watched television alone.

A Mass was held at St. Patrick's Cathedral in New York City, where Senator Ted Kennedy delivered the most memorable lines of what would turn out to be a long career. "My brother need not be idealized," he said, "or enlarged in death beyond what he was in life, but to be remembered simply as a good and decent man, who saw wrong and tried to right it, saw suffering and tried to heal it, saw war and tried to stop it."[21] The body was put onto a train full of family and distinguished mourners and sent down to Washington for burial near his presidential brother at Arlington National Cemetery.

When the exhausted Kennedy clan returned to Hyannis Port, the daughters rushed into Joe's bedroom to report. "Daddy, Teddy was magnificent, absolutely magnificent!" And young Joe, the son of Robert F. Kennedy, who represented yet another generation? "Dad, he's got it! You should have seen him!" Young Joe had apparently greeted all one thousand mourners on the train to Washington. "Nobody put him up to it, Daddy, he did it on his own!"

One year later, in the summer of 1969, a group of young women who had worked with Robert Kennedy, calling themselves "the boiler room," met for a reunion on Chappaquiddick Island, Massachusetts. Shocked by the murder of their boss and stunned by the sudden end to their work together, they had come to reminisce, celebrate Bobby Kennedy's life, and talk of what might have been.

Senator Ted Kennedy showed up and left the party with a young lady, Mary Jo Kopechne. He later claimed that he had taken a wrong turn. In any case, the car had been driven off Dike Bridge with Kopechne trapped inside. That night, Ted Kennedy escaped the sinking car and returned to his motel room alone. Not until 9:45 the next morning did he finally report the accident to the police. Young Kopechne was found in the backseat of the car, her body upside down, her mouth open to gasp at the last pockets of air before she drowned.

Speculation swirled around the accident, and the Kennedy-

friendly media was beginning to come unraveled. Why had the senator delayed? Had he been inebriated? And if so, how could he have
swum across the channel?

At Hyannis Port, Ted Kennedy went in to meet with his father
alone. It could not have been a pleasant task. The old man listened,
nodded weakly, and closed his eyes. Rose would not speak to anyone
in the family or household staff. She met Teddy out on the lawn, by a
flagpole, so no one could eavesdrop on their conversation. No one
knows what was said between them.

THE PASSING OF A GENERATION

As the terrible aftermath of Chappaquiddick unfolded, with its in-
quests and attendant media circus, Joe Kennedy's life finally began
to wane. The dream had ended. And though many people felt that,
given enough money and enough time, Chappaquiddick could be
buried, Joe certainly knew that it would not happen in his lifetime, if
ever. He had experienced the finality of public judgment and likely
concluded that this second generation had fully vented itself. The
game was up.

In November 1969, his condition was serious enough that the
family began to return from all over the world to say good-bye. Pat
Lawford, now divorced from her movie star husband, arrived, followed
by Eunice and Sargent Shriver. Sarge was now the distinguished ambassador to France. Ted Kennedy, devastated that Joe no longer responded to his voice, curled up in a chair with a blanket, not leaving
his father's side. On November 15, Jackie Kennedy Onassis flew in
from Greece. Two days later, when Joe Kennedy finally slipped into a
coma, the whole clan was intact, including Bobby's widow, Ethel, and
Steve and Jean Smith. At 9 A.M. on November 18, the doctor reported
that his vital signs were dropping. The family was alerted that this was
the end. Ted still had not left the bedside.

Rose Kennedy's actions during the last months and days of her
husband's life are controversial. Historian Bonnie Angelo depicts Rose
as "popping in and out, trying to keep him interested, hoping to
brighten his day."[22] When he died, writes Angelo, "Rose wept."[23] But
the accounts of eyewitnesses, including attendant nurses and therapists,
insist that Rose almost never saw him. According to a staffer at the

Hyannis Port home, when Rose was told of his impending death, she went swimming.[24]

At 11 A.M., when all were certain of his immediate death, she was summoned. Rose walked into the room and put a rosary into her husband's hands. Eunice led in the Lord's Prayer, and, according to one account, during the actual prayer Joseph P. Kennedy died. He was eighty-one years old.

With the family broken and without leadership or strength of will, the funeral was a humble, modest event. There was no poignancy or pageantry befitting the remarkable legacy of the man. Rose had described him as the "architect of our lives," but his ambitious endeavors had had an impact far beyond his family and had helped shape the destiny of his nation.

After the passing of Joe, Rose would live another twenty-six years. She finally traveled to Wisconsin to find the truth about her daughter Rosemary. It was like rummaging through the attic, opening an old trunk and finding it filled with memories. From time to time, she brought her daughter back to visit at Hyannis Port and Palm Beach.

In 1972, her son-in-law Sargent Shriver was selected as the vice presidential running mate with George McGovern. Ironically, the decision would prove the old father right. He had feared Jack's winning the vice presidential spot on an Adlai Stevenson ticket, saying the defeat would ruin his career. Just so, the landslide loss for McGovern-Shriver had ended his son-in-law's public life.

Rose was ninety-three when a stroke on an Easter Sunday finally forced her to stop her amazing regimen of daily swimming and walks along the beach. She was reduced to a wheelchair, but, unlike Joe, she still had her voice. "I am one of the most fortunate people in the world," she declared at age ninety-five, "even though my life has been scarred by tragedy, I have never lost this feeling, God has held us all in his hand."[25]

Ted and Eunice visited her regularly, and though the houses deteriorated some, their mother's spirit seemed to be unquenchable. The press would often ask to see her, and she would make appearances, assuring them that she was still around. "I'm like old wine," she quipped. "They don't bring me out very often, but I'm well preserved."[26]

By the time Rose was 103 years old, she could no longer speak. On May 19, 1994, when Jackie Kennedy finally succumbed to cancer, the family decided not to tell her. Then, a few months later, Rose began to falter. In January 1995, the family gathered in Hyannis Port. On the afternoon of January 22, 1995, Rose Fitzgerald Kennedy died at the age of 104.

The funeral was conducted at St. Stephen's in north Boston, where she had been baptized long before. She was buried next to her husband in Holyhood Cemetery in Brookline, Massachusetts. Her only surviving son, Ted Kennedy, described her as "the most beautiful rose of all." [27] She had once said that life was a matter not of milestones but of moments, and she had certainly experienced her fair share.

If history has stripped away the glamour from the Kennedy legend, the fact of the family's meteoric rise to power and the engaging vision their sons and daughters offered the world is undeniable. Joe and Rose Kennedy, for all their flaws, raised sturdy young men and women who were instilled with grand ambition. Rose brought structure and organization to their early lives, a prerequisite for high achievers. She turned sibling rivalry into a positive force, fostering competition in a controlled environment. She refused to let her children play the victim, nor would she do so herself. Joe, meanwhile, taught teamwork and family loyalty. In any fight, business or political, the Kennedys could always count on one another. Joe was ambitious to the core, successfully instilling his winning doctrine into a new generation.

The combination proved extraordinary. From humble Irish origins, they produced sons and daughters whose leadership offered hope to millions of others. The rise to the top was hard fought and the price of success was devastating, but after the Kennedys, the American dream seemed within the reach of us all.

★

Part Five

THE BUSHES:
THE QUIET DYNASTY

SIXTEEN

About His Father's Business: Prescott Bush

Dad taught us about duty and service.
Mother taught us about dealing with life.[1]
—George H. W. Bush

The Bushes have been called the un-Kennedys, but they are much too indifferent to self-analysis to comment on such an observation. While several generations of Kennedys have made no secret of their ambition for social acceptance, the Bushes have been consistently disdainful of it. While Joe Kennedy amassed a fortune that would last a hundred years, not wanting his sons to have to repeat the same story, the Bushes have come close to great wealth several times in each generation and always backed away from it. Their respective children would insist on learning how to build anew from the bottom up, and usually in a different place, without the direct help of a father, although other relatives and friends are pointedly allowed by their arcane rules of the game.

With Joe Kennedy's manipulative power and media contacts, his son's war experiences were transformed into historic legend and became the inspiration for books and movies. Prescott Bush, the father and grandfather of presidents and patriarch of the Bush clan, "thought that old Joe Kennedy was unseemly in the way he courted the media."[2] His son, future president George H. W. Bush, was the youngest aviator in American history and risked his life again and again in deadly combat in World War II, finally being shot out of the skies and seemingly left to die in the Pacific. But at the end of the war he carefully put his medals in a box and never brought them out again.

During the presidential campaign of 1988, his heroics were cited by campaign biographies, and astonished journalists compared him to Kennedy's boy, saying that George H. W. Bush was the *real* war hero. But his mother was outraged, calling campaign headquarters and hotly admonishing him to rein in the errant staffers and journalists who were resorting to such personal promotion. "People aren't impressed by that sort of thing," she scolded.

Yet for all their understatement, the Bushes have become, as Michael Duffy of *Time* magazine aptly tagged them, "the quiet dynasty." With George W. Bush's reelection, they are arguably the consummate political family in American history. Until the arrival of the Bush family, no son of a president or presidential candidate had ever won election as a governor of a state. Many have tried. One of Grant's sons failed to make it work in California, as did one of FDR's boys. Teddy Roosevelt's son lost in New York. And another Roosevelt cousin, FDR, Jr., lost three times in that state. A son of William Howard Taft lost in Ohio, although a generation later one descendant finally made it. A son of Adlai Stevenson lost in Illinois. A son of Mondale and a son of Humphrey, both Democrats, lost in Minnesota, the most Democratic state in the nation at the time. It was the only state that Mondale's father had carried against Ronald Reagan in 1984, but the son lost it to an independent candidate. Joe P. Kennedy II made an attempt at the governorship of Massachusetts but backed down when the forces began to gather against him. In 2000, his cousin Kathleen Kennedy Townsend ran as a Democratic candidate for governor in Maryland, where Democrats outnumber Republicans two to one in voter registration, but lost anyway. Only twice in American history has the son or daughter of a president or presidential candidate ever been elected governor of a state: George W. Bush in Texas and John Ellis (Jeb) Bush in Florida.

A family member attending the first inauguration of George W. Bush, the second president in the family, quietly observed, "Two and counting." In a sense, the Bushes have fulfilled the dream that many had anticipated for the Kennedys. American history has seen nothing quite like the Bushes, and, as the family member correctly observed at the inauguration in 2000, the story is not quite over yet. Even after George W. Bush leaves office, his brother, Jeb, will still be out there.

Most of the recent conventional histories of the Bush family have followed a predictable line. The family is portrayed as a matriarchy, with the powerful personalities of Dorothy Bush, Barbara Bush, and Laura Bush marrying into the family, enriching each succeeding generation. Indeed, the Bushes themselves have increasingly come to this conclusion, with Jeb Bush telling an interviewer, "We have some strong women in our family."[3]

However, the great themes of the family originate with the early fathers. Dorothy "Dottie" Walker Bush, the mother and grandmother of presidents, for example, is credited with inspiring a sense of modesty and understatement among her children, with strict rules about not bragging or taking credit for their achievements, but that emphasis was virtually absent from her own parents' family. Dorothy's father, Bert Walker, was described by his children as a rowdy man who enjoyed his bourbon and willingly forfeited his Catholic faith to marry a pretty, blond Presbyterian named "Luli" Wear. "My grandfather was the worldliest man that ever lived, the very worldliest," said Nancy Bush Ellis.[4] Even during Prohibition, Bert Walker had his inexhaustible supply of liquor.

Yet the emphasis on strict rules of behavior appears quite vividly throughout a line of Bushes all the way back to James Smith Bush, an Episcopal priest born in 1825. A privately printed memoir from 1907 quoted James as teaching a family mantra: "Do the right thing." The Reverend James Bush also taught, "Give the credit to others," "Be loyal," and "Always, always, play fair."[5]

Likewise, the devotion to Christian teachings that is often attributed to Dorothy, who loved her Bible and read Francis Schaeffer and John Stott, can be seen all through the line of Bushes, right up to Prescott Bush.[6] Prescott faithfully read the family a lesson from the Bible each morning and once quietly walked out of a party because a crude aphorism was used from the stage. While circumspect about mixing his faith and his public career, Prescott's moral legalism could flare out into the open in dramatic ways, such as his public denouncement of Nelson Rockefeller's divorce in 1962.

If there is, as in the case of the Adamses, an iron chord of principled thinking and principled action running through the Bush family, there is also a rigid and peculiar pattern in how they chart their personal destinies. Anxiety over this tradition may be at the heart of the subterranean river of energy—or even anger—that races beneath this outwardly quiet and genteel family, as well as in the anomaly of George W. Bush, the evolved, extreme manifestation of both the paternal and maternal sides of the ancestral line.

The pattern was established early on. Each Bush son would make a break from his family and seek to find his own road in life. James's son, Samuel Prescott Bush—or S. P., as the family called him—left the New Jersey home of his father and went to Ohio. S. P.'s son, Prescott Bush, unwilling to take any financial help or a single favor from his father, immigrated to Saint Louis and then to Connecticut. His son, the first President George Bush, packed his family into a new red Studebaker and headed for Texas. The Studebaker was his only parting gift from his father. The job in Texas came from a family friend.

At times there was an undercurrent of ruthlessness in these generational breakaways. There were actions and words that left wounds. Occasionally, there were signs that the process broke down altogether, that fathers felt rejection and some of the sons felt pressured into playing a game they didn't want to play, maybe secretly hoping that the father would hold on to them and not let them go.

The break between S. P. and his son Prescott would be tense. Prescott's sense of humor would lead to antics that would publicly embarrass the family, and the father's reluctance to forgive the incidents immediately would be bitterly felt by the son. Although both would become eminently successful businessmen, Prescott would never once consult his accomplished father, whose wealth of experience had already blazed the trail. "The two men would see each other only occasionally."[7] By most accounts, when Prescott Bush married Dorothy Walker, his father did not even attend the wedding. And when S. P. finally died, leaving his estate to his five children, Prescott would not touch a dime. He gave his share to his two sisters. Bush men did things on their own.

Likewise, although after his passing Prescott Bush received many avowals of love from his sons, including George H. W. Bush, there was a tense undercurrent to those relationships. Prescott Bush was a no-nonsense disciplinarian who could be alternately harsh and gentle. "We were all terrified of Dad as boys," says his son Jonathan. Like most Bush men, Prescott was almost always gone, which did not seem to grieve his children. Jonathan saw his father as rigidly formal and described his father's absences as being "like the Fourth of July." He once spoke to his father's weary formalism: "I never heard him fart!" George

W. Bush, the grandchild who would become the second Bush president, described his grandfather as "scary."[8]

When George H. W. Bush ran for the Senate in Texas in 1964, his father, Prescott Bush, the investment banker who had become a U.S. senator, knew practically nothing of his own son's campaign or even the issues.[9] At Prescott's funeral his wife made a point of describing him as "giving advice only when sought."[10] Apparently, that wasn't very often. George H. W. Bush was himself perplexed by the relationship. "I had a very powerful father," he once admitted, "very much a leader, admired by everybody. I had a kind of—not really a competitive thing with him—but I wanted to get out on my own."[11]

A generation later, George W. Bush would have a similar relationship with his own father, living his own life, feeling no need to keep the elder Bush informed.[12] After graduating from Yale, the son trumped the father's educational journey by winning admission to Harvard to work on an MBA, but for weeks George W. withheld the exciting plans. His brother Jeb finally let their dad in on the news.

Yet George W. Bush was described by friends as being in awe of his father, even worshipful. When his father lost a political campaign, which happened several times, he would openly weep. If any hurt existed between these two men, it was rooted very deeply, never on public display, and probably never even conscious.

In the 1970s, George and Barbara were stunned to receive a phone call from twenty-year-old Jeb, announcing his marriage to Columba Garnica Gallo, a young Mexican woman who could not speak English and whom they had never even met. Such was the communication style of these Bush men. Zero. They were expected to strike out on their own and accomplish things, to lead their own lives, independent of the previous generation. The pronounced, ingrained expectations didn't cushion the blows—the sense of exclusion and rejection—that came with the territory.

What was at work was the drive to please the parent, to win approval by repeating the story that had been passed down with such pride, how the previous generation had shown initiative, how Prescott had refused even a dime of his inheritance, and how George H. W. Bush had declined a plush Wall Street job to start with a broom in Midland. And how at nineteen, he had rejected his weeping father's plea to continue his education and joined the navy to fight in World War II. "No sir, I'm going in."[13]

Such passion inevitably led to sibling rivalry. In 1994, when George W. Bush was winning the gubernatorial race in Texas, his brother Jeb was simultaneously losing his race for governor of Florida. During a phone call from the father, George W. Bush was overheard saying softly, "Why are you sad for him? Why aren't you happy for me?"[14]

When Bush called friends to say he was running for president in 2000, he made it clear that "it is not going to be a George Herbert Walker Bush Two, it is going to be a George W. Bush One."[15] It was a natural sentiment for a candidate who had to establish that he was a leader in his own right.

What was incomprehensible is that a few years later, when President George W. Bush invaded Iraq, he didn't call his father for counsel, even though the former president had been the commander in chief during the last war with Iraq. As a father he could presumably be trusted and was one of only a handful of people in the nation with access to the critical daily intelligence briefings. According to sources in the family, the father religiously read the intelligence reports, refining just what his advice would be when the call came, but, in the tradition of the Bush fathers, he would not break the rule of offering advice without solicitation.

When the calls finally came, they were filled with questions about the family and gossip about friends. The presidential son, upholding his end of the infuriating, prideful tradition, refused to ask for input. In spite of the necessary political posturing to the contrary, the nation assumed that the men, father-and-son presidents, were talking. It was a comfort to many that the son had such additional experienced counsel.

But no, the men in the Bush family didn't talk. They didn't need one another. When George W. was seven, he had not been told that his sister Robin was dying until it was over, until she was gone, giving him no chance even to say good-bye. "Why didn't you tell me?" he kept asking over and over in his grief. "Why didn't you tell me?"

Now he was a man, and he got it; he understood these things. In 1988, when his father had won the presidential election, he had been sent packing back to Texas. He had not expected nor wanted it to be any other way. Real men did their own thing, alone, without help. They didn't cut in on their father's action. Now the son was in the

White House and it was the senior Bush's turn to enjoy the bittersweet taste of internal family exile. George W. Bush went to war alone. The father could watch it on television like the rest of us. Such independent alpha male bravado was part of the drill. It had worked for generations of men in the Bush family. It was part of the chemistry that had made them great. But also, sometimes, it must have hurt like hell.

PRESCOTT BUSH:
OWING A DEBT TO SOCIETY

Like the Roosevelts, the Bush family can trace its heritage back to the *Mayflower*. Genealogist Gary Boyd Roberts determined that the Bushes are related to fifteen different American presidents. The point is that the Bushes have never made a big to-do about pedigree. It's where one is going, rather than where one has been, that matters. And where they go is all over the place.

Samuel P. Bush, the great-grandfather of George W. Bush, was one of the first adventurers. His father had been the Episcopalian minister in New Jersey, but S. P. would have none of it. He joined the Pennsylvania Railroad, arguably the Microsoft of its day, and headed out to the midwestern states. He eventually settled in Ohio, if you can call it settling, for S. P. was almost always gone from home.

Over time, frustrated inside the giant bureaucracy at the Pennsylvania Railroad, S. P. went to work for Buckeye Steel Castings, a local concern in Columbus. Buckeye made couplers for train cars but was in dire need of reorganization. Franklin Rockefeller, the younger, less talented brother of the famous John D. Rockefeller, made the rebuilding of Buckeye his personal project. He succeeded in raising the funds before finally concluding that he really didn't have the knack of running the thing. S. P., all agreed, was a natural leader and organizer, and in 1907 he was tapped to run the show, which he did for two decades.

S. P. Bush loved sports, especially the newly popular American football. He saw the competition as a great equalizer of men. A lowborn son of a laborer could mix it up with sons of the purest pedigree, and both would be governed by the mutual rules of the game and the ethic of good sportsmanship. Serving as an assistant coach, S. P. was in on the birth of the Ohio State University football program.

Samuel P. Bush was a stern father who was often away from home. His wife, Flora Sheldon Bush, who could claim a noble ancestry, hailed from a midwestern family of modest material wealth. She was tender and unassertive, a rarity for Bush women, and she struggled to keep her family of four children in line with S. P.'s rigid ideals.

Prescott Sheldon Bush, nicknamed Pres, who would be the father of a president, was the firstborn son, arriving on May 15, 1895. Three sisters followed. S. P. insisted that all his children, including Pres, attend public schools. He wanted them to experience a full range of American culture, but his great social experiment would not last.

Concluding that Pres lacked a sober commitment to self-improvement, S. P.'s parents sent him to St. George's Academy in Newport, Rhode Island. Pres felt lonely and abandoned during the first weeks, missing the constant in his life, his mother, Flora. However, the experience eventually proved to be so successful that the Bushes decided to send their daughters to a private school in Westover, Connecticut.

Pres loved sports and excelled at golf, returning to Columbus for a few weeks each summer, just long enough to become the schoolboy Ohio State champion. When the famous Hollywood star Douglas Fairbanks, Jr., took in a round of golf at the Watch Hill resort near St. George's Academy, Prescott was tapped to serve as his caddie. Impressed with the young man, Fairbanks later sent him tickets to a Broadway play. Inspired, Pres developed as a singer, which became a lifelong amateur pleasure. He joined various glee clubs and sang with the Silver Dollar Quartet, performing at various venues up and down the East Coast.

At St. George's, Pres Bush first seriously considered the idea of following his grandfather into the Episcopalian ministry. As a first step, he rejected the technical business school of his father and chose to follow his father and grandfather back to Yale University. Pres represented the third generation of Bushes at the eastern establishment school, with many more to come.

His beginnings at the university were awkward. His father was earning one of the higher salaries of any American CEO of his time, but he was a miser to his wife and children, demanding detailed reports of the most trivial expenditures. Pres was repelled by the arrogant sons of wealth and privilege at Yale and, burdened by his father's disposition and parsimony, couldn't match their lifestyle anyway. Nor could he find acceptance among the bright young students of the laboring classes. He later tried to align himself with alumni from this latter group, disingenuously suggesting that his father had only "a modest income." [16] But these less wealthy young men had broken the Yale barrier with their incisive scholarship, and Pres could not easily compete with them either.

Like other Bushes before and after, he succeeded by accommodating. He joined the Yale Glee Club and took to sports, especially baseball. By his senior year, he was batting in the cleanup position and was elected team captain. The ultimate break came in his junior year, when he was inducted into the famous Skull and Bones society.

Already romanticized by a popular American novelist and soon to be immortalized by F. Scott Fitzgerald, Skull and Bones was on its way to becoming the ultimate insider, secret American organization. By the year 2004, it could boast that both principal presidential nominees, John Kerry and George W. Bush, were Bonesmen and thus helped spawn a veritable industry of conspiracy theories.

In fact, as secret societies go, Skull and Bones, founded in 1832, was hardly a drop in the bucket compared to Freemasonry, which could claim most of the American presidents. When Pres Bush was tapped, Skull and Bones could claim only one, the Republican William Howard Taft, and membership in the secret society had not prevented Taft from being voted out of office for a second term, coming in third in a three-man race. Still, only fifteen Yale juniors were tapped for the honor, and the growing alumni list boasted an impressive roster of old WASP families, including the Harrimans, Rockefellers, Pillsburys, Vanderbilts, and Kelloggs. Pres seemed to have found a fit with the Bonesmen, where he forged bonds of friendship that would one day play a significant role in his life.

Prior to the United States' entry into World War I, Pres Bush joined thousands of other Ivy League students swept up in a wave of patriotic fervor. Bush, together with other Bonesmen, helped form the Yale Brigade, spending summers in training and preparation. When the United States finally entered the war, the brigade was sent into more intense preparation at Fort Sill, Oklahoma.

With America's entry into the war, S. P. Bush, Prescott's severe, hardworking father, helped convert Buckeye Steel in Columbus into a plant manufacturing 75mm guns. In 1918, in another quirky nod to Adams/Bush family parallels, S. P. Bush was asked to help run the Ordnance Small Arms and Ammunition Division of the newly formed War Industries Board. Patriotism and national security trumped earning money. The elder Bush packed his bags and moved to Washington, D.C. But Buckeye Steel prospered during the war, its sales increasing to $10 million a year.

Young Yale graduate Pres Bush, now a captain in the army, embarked for France as a part of the 158th Field Artillery Brigade. He was in the heart of fierce fighting in the terrible Meuse-Argonne offensive and was mired for months in the trenches of the world's most horrific war of attrition.[17] Young men were killed all around him, but Bush would never talk about the experience.

Elated at the declaration of armistice, Pres Bush celebrated with a comical letter home to his parents. His satirical account had him personally escorting the three Allied commanding generals around the front and personally deflecting an artillery shell intended for the generals by the wave of his combat knife. It was dry humor, and it was, unfortunately, taken literally by his unsophisticated midwestern mother at home. A proud Flora passed it on to the Columbus newspaper, which displayed the young Bush's heroics across its pages. Of course, it was all retracted, to the mortification of the family. The already remote, austere father became even further estranged from his son.

At the end of the war, the young Prescott Bush, looking for work, stopped by a Skull and Bones reunion at Yale University and met Wallace Simmons, the president of an enterprising hardware company in Saint Louis, Missouri. As S. P. Bush had abandoned the family home in New Jersey, Pres would leave Ohio and set out for new horizons of his own.

In Saint Louis, Pres Bush, war hero turned Simmons Hardware Company salesman, met Nancy Walker, daughter of a wealthy Missouri businessman. They were at the Walker home talking together when Nancy's vivacious eighteen-year-old younger sister came storming into the house. For a brief moment Pres and Dottie Walker locked eyes. She was sweating from a vigorous workout on the tennis court. The older sister, Nancy Walker, would never marry, but Prescott Bush would eventually win the hand of her younger sister, Dottie, the teenage tennis player. They would one day be the parents and grandparents of presidents.

DOROTHY WALKER:
MATRIARCH OF A CLAN

Perhaps no other figure in the recent Bush family history is more important to the development of their character and personalities than that of the energetic, self-confident Dottie Walker. It was Dottie's philosophical invocation of Proverbs 27:2, "Let another man praise thee and not thee, thyself," that so powerfully dictated the family ethic and so impacted the personality of her son George Herbert Walker Bush, the first president in the family. And it was Dottie's deep, evangelical-style Episcopal faith and take-no-prisoners personality that were manifested so dramatically in her famous president grandson, George W. Bush. Even while teaching moderation and the importance of fairness and the sin of self-importance, Dottie infused her children with heavy doses of competitiveness and laid on them the responsibility of doing no less than their very best in any undertaking. They might lose sometimes, but they had better have their tongues hanging out.

When Barbara Bush appeared a generation later, as a virtual second coming of Dottie Walker Bush and the inspiration of another Bush child to become president, she was, by her own admission, less the spiritual product of her own parents than that of her lively mother-in-law. Any way you tell the story of the Bush family, you cannot escape the importance of that young tennis player who walked in on Pres Bush and Nancy Walker that afternoon in Saint Louis. After Dottie, the Bush family would never be the same.

Born on July 1, 1901, Dorothy "Dottie" Walker was the daughter of a boisterous, wealthy Missouri businessman whom she adored. George Herbert Walker, known to his family and friends as "Bert," hailed from a wealthy family that owned a major stake in one of the leading dry goods wholesaler companies in the Midwest. They had a large, sprawling mansion in Saint Louis and spent their summers in the cool breezes of Kennebunkport, Maine, not far from the Atlantic coast where their ancestors had arrived in the seventeenth century.

The Walkers were staunch Catholics, and just to guarantee they stayed that way, they sent young Bert to Stonyhurst, a severe Jesuit boarding school in the United Kingdom. He took his valet along with him. Bert Walker acquitted himself easily as a scholar at Stonyhurst, but his real discovery was not in the textbooks. Bert excelled in the boxing ring and soon picked up the new sport of golf, then virtually unknown in the United States. As is often the case with golfers, the more he played, the more the endorphins kicked in. Young Bert Walker soon became addicted, playing every day. Planning on a career in medicine, he graduated from Stonyhurst and enrolled at the University of Edinburgh. But one year was enough. Though he could manage the academic load—everything seemed to come easily to this young man—he could not contain his boredom.

Returning to Saint Louis, Bert was expected to play his part in the family business. There was plenty of room for him. But he was restless. Golf was still a passion, and his boxing career became a curious success. As the son of a wealthy family with his own personal valet and nurse attendant at boxing matches, Bert was an unexpected crowd pleaser. There was no apparent torment in his life, yet he slugged his way past angry, violent street toughs and frontier muscle men to the Missouri state boxing heavyweight championship.

Rough, independent, and full of confidence, Bert Walker was not about to follow in his father's footsteps. As in the case of S. P. Bush, another Walker generation set out to chart its own course. Bert sold his share of the family business and launched G. H. Walker and Company, an investment banking firm in the American Midwest.

And when he met Lucretia "Luli" Wear, a staunch Presbyterian beauty, he dismayed his family by his willingness to depart from the family faith. Bert tried to arrange two wedding ceremonies as a compromise, but a priest was dispatched to warn that he would go to hell if he married the young Presbyterian. Bert responded wryly, "I'll go to hell if I *don't* marry her."[18] Distraught, his family refused to attend the wedding.

Willing to endure breathtaking risks, some of which he lost in spectacular fashion, G. H. Walker and Company was a resounding success. He bought summer homes on both oceans, including a sumptuous garden spot in Santa Barbara, California, and a rugged coastal outcropping in Kennebunkport, Maine, that was soon dubbed Walker Point.

Bert and Luli had four sons before Nancy and Dottie appeared, but the father was seldom home. It was an arrangement that suited the sons. "We had to box him, you know," one of the boys told an interviewer. "He fixed this room up like a boxing ring and he would take us in there and knock the hell out of us."[19] Apparently his verbal jabs were just as toxic. His sons toughed up physically but remained afraid of him. The ruthless, never-say-die tactics of the successful investment banker were emotionally devastating to the sons.

The Walker boys were not the only spontaneous targets of Bert's wrath. He could be exceedingly harsh and biting with Luli, criticizing her smallest misstep. She answered his tirades with a grace and calm that impressed her children, never fighting back, patiently explaining her actions, only later dealing with her private hurts alone with quiet times of Bible reading and prayer. Her children never remembered her saying a negative word about their father.

If the wife and boys had to pay the piper, Nancy and Dorothy, the two daughters, lived a life of American royalty, coddled and pampered by the very man who frightened their brothers. They toured Europe in the summer, dressed in the finest French silks, and were carried around Saint Louis in a fine coach and horses.

Dorothy, curiously following a long line of presidents' mothers before her, adored her father and picked up on his positive spirit. But Bert loved his bourbon, and that led to some embarrassing moments. One night his coarse behavior, normally reserved for his wife and sons, spilled out in public at the Saint Louis Club, drawing censure from the city's elite. Joyously contemptuous of the stuffed shirts, Bert Walker took his money and walked out of the club, starting his own, which almost immediately prospered, like everything else he did. Dottie forever shared her father's scorn of social conceit and acted out with her playmates the very lessons she would later ingrain in her children, namely that no one, simply because of his or her birth, deserves more respect than another.

No characteristic was more pronounced in father and daughter than Bert's powerful competitive drive. He taught his family to compete—and win. Dottie took the message to heart, becoming so talented on the tennis court that her brothers avoided playing her altogether. One afternoon, her brother Lou was coerced into a game but showed up too drunk to play. Furious, Bert announced that evening that his son would not be attending school the next year. He would be working, far away from home in a Pennsylvania steel mill. Early the next morning, the boy was put on the train out of town. Meanwhile, Dottie was soon sailing through the competition in Saint Louis, winning one tournament after another.

In 1919, Bert Walker joined the newly formed William Averell Harriman Company as president and chief executive officer. The family would move to New York City. The Harrimans had developed the Union Pacific railroad and were one of America's most prominent wealthy families. Bert had worked with the senior Harriman on projects over the years, but this new venture, spun off by one of the sons, would grow to become a giant worldwide concern, and Walker, the nimble financial adventurer from Saint Louis, would lead it into its glorious future.

As Walker was negotiating his role at the Harriman Company, Pres Bush was courting his youngest daughter back in Saint Louis. Bush was a twenty-five-year-old war veteran, a Yale graduate who had seen the world. Dottie was an eighteen-year-old sheltered beauty, whose worldly experience included luxury tours of Europe and a cloistered year at a finishing school for girls in Connecticut.

But then, as would oddly happen again in the saga of the Bush family history, there was an untimely death, an automobile accident, that accelerated events. S. P. Bush, somewhat estranged from his son, contacted him with the stunning news that Flora, Prescott's mother, had been killed by a runaway car. She had been an innocent pedestrian on the street. Pres raced home to the funeral. Dottie fretted, brokenhearted to see the man she loved in such despair.

So busy that he was almost never home, Bert Walker did not seem like the sort of man to let his daughter go without a fight. But Prescott Bush was a different man from most. The young Bush shared Walker's passion for golf. Bert would help organize the United States Golf Association and promote a plan for an international golf competition that would one day become the Walker Cup. Until presidents started appearing in the family, it was their greatest source of pride.

And Prescott was just as passionate. In 1926, he would serve as chairman of the USGA's Championship Committee and help rewrite the American rules of the modern game. In 1935, he would finally serve as president of the association, and at fifty-six years of age, he would shoot a sixty-six, winning the national senior golf championship. On the golf course Bert Walker could size up a man. What he saw of the young Prescott Bush impressed him greatly.

On August 6, 1921, almost two years after they met, Prescott Bush and Dorothy Walker were married in a ceremony at the Episcopal

Church of St. Ann in Kennebunkport, Maine. Dottie had some anxiety the night before. She would be forfeiting a likely professional career in tennis, and how could she possibly live so far from the family she loved? "Now Dorothy, darling," her mother tenderly counseled, "You're going to have a wonderful life." [20]

In fact, it must have begun as a shock to the young "daddy's girl," whose life had only recently been supervised by a French governess and who enjoyed gallivanting off to Europe for extended vacations. Pres stole her away to Missouri for a time and then to the remote hills of Kingsport, Tennessee, and finally, desperate in his career, back to Columbus, Ohio, for an ill-fated year of working on a business project with his father. They eventually ended up in Massachusetts, where Pres became a salesman for the Stedman Products Company. In two years' time, they had lived in four different cities.

Rapprochement with S. P. Bush had not worked. "He was very stern, always, that's how I remember him," a granddaughter would say. "And Pres was always so kind and gentle. They were different people—really different people." [21]

The good news for Dottie was that if Pres was unable to restore his relationship with his father, he seemed perfectly willing to adopt the Walker family as his own. The summer after their wedding, they returned to Kennebunkport, into the arms of Bert Walker and sons for a rousing time of dining, play, and competition.

In a moment that would grow with legend and capture her essence, Dottie Walker, though abundantly pregnant with her firstborn, didn't hesitate to take part in a family game of softball. She was standing in the batter's box at home plate when labor began, hit a home run, and ran all the bases before declaring, "Take me to the hospital." Prescott Bush, Jr., was born a few hours later.

Pres and Dottie would eventually have a family of five. The second child, George Herbert Walker Bush, born in 1924, would be followed by Nancy in 1926, Jonathan in 1931, and finally William, affectionately known in the family as "Bucky," in 1938.

In 1926, Prescott Bush was hired on at the W. A. Harriman Company. Dorothy was ecstatic. Her husband would be working at the same firm her father was running. And they would be living in Connecticut, just outside New York City. Trading on friendships from the old Skull and Bones network, Prescott went to work as an investment banker and never looked back. He had found his calling. In 1930, with the Depression wiping out the competition, the Harriman organization merged with the prestigious private banking firm of Brown Brothers. The newly formed conglomerate would be a major international powerhouse, and Prescott would be at the heart of many of its biggest projects.

As international bankers, Brown Brothers Harriman was all over the map, including, among other projects, the rebuilding of selected German industries after World War I. Europe was still in the throes of an ongoing depression. Deals with German industrialist Fritz Thyssen, the man who helped finance Hitler's Nazi Party and projects in Stalin's Soviet Union, would later provide fodder for conspiracy theorists. Actually, Thyssen was so outraged by anti-Semitism on the famous Kristallnacht (Night of Broken Glass), when Jewish shops across Germany were trashed by Nazi mobs, that he resigned all public positions in Germany and fled to Switzerland. Any exchange of greed for conscience was duly paid by Thyssen. He was captured by the Nazis and interned in a concentration camp till 1945, whereupon he was taken by the Allies and tried as the financier behind Hitler's rise to power.

Today, writers plumb these murky waters, looking for dark connections that will sensationalize the early investment projects of Brown Brothers Harriman, but the going is tough for true historians. For one thing, Averell Harriman, who later became governor of New York, was an ardent New Dealer and Democrat and was eventually at political loggerheads with Prescott Bush, a Republican.[22] They would have been unlikely conspirators. Harriman betrayed his own employee by fighting against him when he ran for the Senate. And Bush encouraged Dwight Eisenhower to run for president, thus thwarting Harriman's further political ambitions. As a candidate for the U.S. Senate from Connecticut, Bush drew unsolicited support from the infamous Communist baiter Joe McCarthy. Yet Prescott Bush was the man who finally stood up to McCarthy, an unthinkable act if there were any old skeletons lying around at Brown Brothers Harriman.

Prescott Bush, working tirelessly, committed to principle, and eventually trusted throughout Wall Street as a man of integrity, was an essential player in the formation of the Columbia Broadcasting System, one of America's first television networks, the Prudential Insurance Company, and Pan American Airways, then the world's most powerful commercial airline. Eventually, he would serve on the board of directors of all three, with many other companies knocking at the door. Pres and Dottie moved into a nine-bedroom home in Greenwich, Connecticut, with four servants, including a chauffeur to drive the children to their private schools. Everything in material wealth that Dottie had given up had come back to her.

In 1946, Prescott Bush was approached by Republican officials to run for Congress. He had seen many of his friends and colleagues involve themselves in public life, including Averell Harriman, who had served as ambassador to the Soviet Union for Franklin Roosevelt and was advising Truman, soon to be his secretary of commerce. The consensus of the partners at Brown Brothers Harriman was that a seat in Congress was beneath Bush, but if a seat in the Senate opened, they would get behind him.

In 1950, that seat opened, and Prescott Bush announced that he was running for the Senate. Dottie was not enthusiastic about the idea, but once the die was cast she and her children plowed into the effort with all that they had. Money came easily, but frustrating little fires kept flaring up during the campaign and Pres raced from one to the next, putting them out. Only two days before the election, fliers were distributed in Catholic churches across Connecticut, promoting an important exposé to be aired on Walter Winchell's popular radio news broadcast that night.

At six on the Sunday night before the election, when the local papers had all agreed to hold back any new sensational news that might "throw" the election, Walter Winchell took to the air, blasting Prescott Bush as county president of his local Birth Control League. It was not true, and Dottie did her best to handle the telephone calls coming in, but the salt was out of the shaker and nothing could get it back in again. That Tuesday, Pres Bush went down to defeat. Out of 862,000 votes, he lost by only 1,000. It was a bitter blow.

There is one quality in the Bush family that has stood them well in business and in public life. They don't go away. Stung by his first foray, Pres Bush tried again in 1952. This time he was unable even to win the nomination battle at the state GOP convention. Embarrassed and defeated, Pres had seemingly been dealt the death blow to any political ambitions. Only a month later a bizarre set of circumstances revived the dream. The Democratic senior senator for Connecticut died suddenly, and a special election would be called for in the fall. Pres Bush had his team in place and had done the careful wooing of delegates. In spite of bitter wrangling and a last-minute cabal to deny him the nomination, he was the winner at the Republican state convention.

The general election was not any easier. There was an unstated agreement among the partners at Brown Brothers Harriman: they would not attack one another publicly. Pres, in his own fastidious way, had carefully observed this dictum, gently defending Averell Harriman before Republican groups in his role for Democratic presidents Roosevelt and Truman and kindly offering a defense of his integrity when business colleagues complained. But when the Democrats gathered at their state convention in 1952, Harriman took center stage to blast Prescott Bush. It was a bitter betrayal, the cut made deeper by the hurtful rhetoric Harriman used. In the end, no meanness or last minute political high jinks could stem the general election tide of the Republican presidential nominee, General Dwight D. Eisenhower. The general's coattails carried Pres Bush on to victory in November. Watching the returns at an election party at home in Greenwich, Connecticut, Prescott Bush was overjoyed. Nothing that had ever happened to him could compare to the moment.

Hardworking and conscientious, Prescott Bush would forge a solid record as a U.S. senator. In 1956, during the Eisenhower administration, he would coauthor the Federal-Aid Highway Act, which created the intricate network of interstate highways that unite the nation today. And under John Kennedy he would coauthor the bill creating the Peace Corps.[23] Pleased with himself, Pres was allowed a rare dispensation by his wife, Dottie, the ever-vigilant vanity cop of the Bush family. Pres insisted that his own grandsons call him "Senator," rather than "Grandpa." And Dottie acquiesced.

Prescott Bush would live to see his second son lose two bids for the U.S. Senate, failing to qualify for the old-boys club that Prescott had so treasured. But in between, he would see him win an election to Congress and finally be appointed by Richard Nixon as the American ambassador to the United Nations. It was during his son's tenure at the United Nations that Prescott would begin to lose his ongoing battle with lung cancer. While Dottie stayed in their New York City apartment with George and Barbara, Pres was admitted to the nearby Memorial Hospital for Cancer and Allied Diseases, part of the Memorial Sloan-Kettering Cancer Center. He died on October 8, 1972. George Bush would say that they had lost a best friend. Exhausted and in great pain, saying that she wished she had gone home with her husband, Dottie nevertheless made all the funeral arrangements. It was her idea that her own sons not be pallbearers but rather the grandchildren, including George W., Jeb, Neil, and Marvin.

Dorothy Walker Bush would live another twenty years, long enough to see her son inaugurated the forty-first president. Like most fathers of presidents, Prescott Bush had been unaware of what was coming, but Dottie had kept her eye on the newest generation in the family and liked what she had seen. She would have a front-row seat onstage at the Capitol on that cold, wintry day in 1989.

For a few more summers, she would see the First Family romp across the lawn at Kennebunkport and take to the cold waters off the rocks at Walker Point. But she would never know that the cocksure, irreverent eldest son of the president, her grandson George W., would soon follow him into the White House. She had spent her life debunking the pompous and artificial. She had described self-aggrandizement or bragging or egocentricity as the "la dee da's." She was quick to cut short any arrogance at her dining table, from a full-grown child to one of her rapidly multiplying brood of great-grandchildren.

If someone had been able to tell her that she would one day be enshrined as the matriarch of one of the greatest political families in American history, that they would rival the Adamses and arguably transcend the Roosevelts and Kennedys, she would have interrupted them with her singsong voice, repressing and disbelieving the praise, almost superstitiously, lest it come back and hurt her. "La dee da!" she would say and shut her ears to the words. But she would live not quite long enough to be tempted.

———— ★ ————

SEVENTEEN

George and Barbara Bush: Raising a President

I was gone all the time, busy with my job
It was Barbara who really raised him.[1]
—George H. W. Bush

George H. W. Bush, the only president in American history to witness, in person, the inauguration of his own son as president, was born in Milton, Massachusetts, on June 12, 1924. He was Prescott and Dottie Bush's second son. Since their firstborn had been named after the father, this new son was given a name from the mother's side of the family. He was named George Herbert Walker Bush, after Dottie's irrepressible father, "Bert." The Walker sons, amused by the little boy who shared their "Pop's" name, started calling their nephew "Poppy." It was a moniker that stuck.

From the very beginning, young George Bush would be seen as a conciliator. He was two years old when his parents bought him a pedal car. Little George was ecstatic. And then in his moment of joy he hesitated, remembering his older brother and loyal playmate, Prescott Bush, Jr., or "Pressy." In a scene etched in family lore, little George offered to share his new treasure with his brother. "Have half, have half, have half," he insisted. The two would play together for hours, with George deferring to his elder brother when it was demanded. One game, practical during inclement weather, could be described as "baseball in a bedroom." The two boys would roll up their father's socks and bat them around the room, racing around the bases on their knees.

While Pres worked, Dottie raised the boys, and soon the family found itself absorbed into the greater Walker clan. Summers included annual visits to Kennebunkport, where the grounds were filled with Walker cousins. Each Christmas, they journeyed to Bert Walker's South Carolina plantation, where black servants in white gloves slipped into the children's bedrooms just before sunup to light the fireplaces and take the chill off the early morning. In the afternoon, the men went hunting.

But if Dottie was the principal figure in the raising of the children, the family philosophy was pure Bush. Dottie had always held an aversion to high-handed haughtiness. Even as a child she had rebuked a snobbish neighborhood queen bee who had tried to turn their playtime on the street into a social contest. The added generational emphasis of the Bushes must have been extraordinarily reaffirming. "We were taught that brotherhood was more important than winning an argument," said Bucky Bush.[2] In the spirit of James Bush, Poppy's great-grandfather, the children were told never to boast, unless it was about the accomplishments of another. When a teenage George began to pass Pressy in his tennis game, the older brother bragged about Poppy as if he were his son instead of a younger sibling.

Pressy and Poppy were sent to Greenwich Country Day School. Founded in 1925 by an impressive group of locals, including one of the Rockefeller wives, it had elementary-age schoolchildren learning Latin. The Bush boys, in the family tradition, were allowed to choose their own prep school. Pressy, the oldest, chose Phillips Academy Andover, following a friend who was already enrolled there. The motto at Andover could not have been more appropriate for the family, *Non sibi,* "Not for self." Andover had strict rules. One of the administrative tactics called for the early dismissal of a student or two, right at the beginning of the school year. Any minor infraction was suitable. It was intended to strike fear into the young people and ensure a more orderly student body the remainder of the term. At Andover, George Bush excelled in both sports and academics, making an impression as a young man who was fair but firm. His final year, he was elected class president.

On December 7, 1941, the nation was stunned by the Japanese surprise attack on Pearl Harbor. The United States was brought feverishly into World War II. Poppy Bush and others at Andover huddled together in their rooms, making plans, taking vows, determining to join the war effort as soon as possible.

During the Christmas break, as young men talked of war, George Bush went to a dance in Rye, New York, where he was introduced to a slender blonde named Barbara Pierce. After inviting her to dance, the band switched to a waltz, and George, too shy to try it, asked Barbara to sit it out with him. While the dance floor waited, the couple soon fell into deep conversation. By coincidence they ran into each other again the next night. This time George found the courage to ask her out. When he returned to Andover, he had Barbara on his mind. They corresponded faithfully till spring and then reconnected during a brief vacation time. The romance was on.

That June 1942, seventeen-year-old George Herbert Walker "Poppy" Bush graduated from Phillips Academy in Andover, Massachusetts. The whole family came to see the second son get his diploma, all of them expecting him to follow his older brother, Pressy, on to Yale University. The secretary of war, Henry L. Stimson, offered a stirring commencement speech but told the elite student body that there would be plenty of time to fight in the war, which would drag on for many years. Their country needed them to go on to college. As if he had previously been clued in to the sentiments of such remarks, Pres met with his son afterward to see if he had changed his mind about going to war. Would he be going on to Yale with Pressy?

"No sir," George said, "I'm going in."[3] Later in the day, with the family gathered around him, Prescott Bush broke into tears. It was the first time the children had seen their reserved, disciplined father cry. Two weeks later, fresh out of Andover, a high school graduate but determined to keep his vow to his fellow classmates, George H. W. Bush enlisted in the U.S. Navy Reserve as a seaman, second class. It was June 12, 1942, his birthday. He was now eighteen years old, and there was nothing more anyone could say or do to stop him. He had not followed Pressy to Yale; he had followed his father to war.

Much has been written about the World War II heroics of George H. W. Bush. Burdened by a tradition that disdained such self-glory, the details of the story languished for years until, as Ronald Reagan's vice president, he began contemplating his own run for the White House. Wanting to make sure that all the bases were covered, his press secretary, Pete Teeley, called for the official file and began to unravel his boss's story.

Receiving his wings on June 9, 1943, just shy of nineteen years of age, George Bush was the youngest aviator in American history. He flew slow, heavy TBF Avengers, the so-called flying turkeys because they were such easy targets for the enemy. These were not agile fighters that would engage the enemy. They were cumbersome, heavy bombers, and landing them on the makeshift aircraft carriers the navy was rushing into service was dangerous business. Pilots were trained to have nerves of steel, to let the enemy antiaircraft shoot away while they continued on undeterred to their targets.

Onboard the USS *San Jacinto,* a cruiser that had been awkwardly converted into an aircraft carrier, Poppy saw his share of mishaps and learned firsthand why he was in what many called the most dangerous service. Before the ship reached the Panama Canal, with the pilots constantly practicing their takeoffs and landings, more than half the planes on the carrier were involved in crashes, with numerous injuries and deaths. Outbound from Pearl Harbor, one Avenger, attempting to land on the short deck of the *San Jacinto,* wiped out a gun battery, sending parts of men skidding across the tarmac, including a man's leg.

"It landed right in front of me, quivering," Bush remembered. "We were all stunned—here was this body cut in two—and then one of the officers came along and yelled, 'Get this mess cleaned up!' So everybody went back to work."[4] It was the closest George Bush had come to death, and the random selection haunted him long after.

His first mission was over Wake Island, with George diving through miles of antiaircraft bursts to drop his bombs on the enemy. He returned safely, feeling an elation that would be hard for him to later describe, only to learn that his roommate, Jim Wykes, was not coming back at all. Bush maintained his reserve in front of his crew, but alone in his bunk he wept as he wrote a note to Wykes's parents.

In the summer of 1944, he was shot down and had to ditch his plane in the ocean. As he was unable to unload his 500-pound bombs, ditching was a tricky business. He had to finesse the Avenger into the turbulent waves with the tail hitting first and drag the plane to a slower speed. Even when the nose finally touched down, it was like smashing the plane into a brick wall. The three-man crew barely got away from the plane before it exploded.

George "Poppy" Bush had been lucky. In training, his landing gear had once failed to respond and his plane had skidded across the runway, sparks flying dangerously close to the gas tank, but again he had walked away untouched. Soon after his arrival in the Pacific, one of his best pilot friends had been blown out of the sky, right next to him. Bush had unnecessarily volunteered for the kinds of risky reconnaissance flights over Japanese positions that almost always eventually took the life of the pilot and crew. Mission after mission he had returned to the *San Jacinto* with more and more friends lost in the vast Pacific, their neatly made, empty beds standing as a vivid testimony that they had been there only a few hours before. He would land 116 times on the short runway of their carrier without a single mishap. The frightening water crash that summer was a stark reminder that he and his crew had no immunity. What was happening to their fellow aviators would eventually be visited on them as well. Their moment was coming.

On September 2, 1944, his squadron was sent into Chichi Jima, a little island south of Japan. They were supposed to take out a radio station on the island, part of a plan to interrupt Japanese communications in preparation for an American invasion of the Palau Islands. The squadron had gone in the day before and had picked up heavy flak from antiaircraft fire. The island would be even more prepared for this second attack.

That morning an old family friend and Yale graduate, William White, insisted on going along. George was uneasy, but the commander had given his okay. Leo Nadeau, his rear gunner, stayed behind to make room for the young man who wanted to finally see some action and make his parents at home proud of him. And so Leo Nadeau's life would be spared.

There was intermittent sunlight streaming through broken cloud cover as they soared out over the ocean toward their target. Bush had a negative thought cross his mind: "It would be a bad day to be shot down." He was the second plane in, and the Japanese were ready for them. There were black explosions filling the sky all around them and then a flash of light. The plane was jolted forward and suddenly enveloped in flames. The smoke filling the cockpit made it difficult to read the instruments, but he knew they were falling fast.[5]

True to the family motto of understatement, George Bush will often talk about how he and young Kennedy were seen as heroes in the Second World War because they were shot down or, in Kennedy's case, because his boat was cut to pieces. That was unfair; the real heroes were the men who had paid the ultimate price.

But it was what George Bush did next that made the navy take notice and has made his moment grow with the retelling. Instead of turning the plane out to the water and making an effort to save his own life, he insisted on finishing the bombing run. Diving at thirty degrees in his flaming, wounded Avenger, young George Bush delivered his payload, scoring hits on the radio station. Only then did he pull up and head out to sea. "To tell you the truth, I thought I was a goner."[6]

No one knows how his crewmates, John Delaney and William White, died. George Bush hit his head on the plane, ripped his chute on the tail, and barely had time to jump free before hitting the ocean. His rubber raft automatically opened. He swam over and crawled into it, but the drama was not over.

The raft was drifting toward the shore, where enraged Japanese soldiers were running along the beaches, hollering and shooting their guns. After the war, officers on this island chain would face war crimes trials for torturing and beheading young American aviators. *Life* magazine would do a story on the eccentric Japanese commander, Lieutenant General Yoshio Tachibana, a brutal warrior in the samurai tradition who immersed himself in the spirit of battle by filleting and eating his enemy captives.

George Bush's squadron circled once, scattering the Japanese on the beach with machine-gun fire and dropping medicine to the fallen hero. Then the planes turned for the long journey back to the *San Jacinto*. Bush could hear their drone disappear in the sky and knew that he was on his own in the middle of the vast Pacific. They could not afford to come back for him. His raft drifted inexorably toward shore.

"I thought, this is it, it's all over," he said in a later interview. "I was out there paddling for a couple of hours, with the wind blowing me back toward the shore, when this submarine rose up out of the waters. It was like an apparition. At first I thought, 'Maybe I'm delirious,' and then, when I concluded that it was a submarine all right, I feared that it might be Japanese. It just seemed to me too lucky and farfetched that it could be anything else."[7]

It was an American submarine. He was taken on board and adopted as part of the crew until he could be deposited in Honolulu thirty days later. At night, when they surfaced and he was given time on watch, he looked out into the inky sky, where the stars shone brilliantly, and thought about life and family and God. "Sometimes when there is disaster people will pray, 'Why me?' In an opposite way I had the same question: Why had I been spared and what did God have for me?"

He came to realize how rich in relationships he was and how important his family was to him. More and more, after his narrow escape, his thoughts turned to the name he had painted on his plane, "Barbara," and how he might have missed so many things in life had it all gone differently. Alone in the night, in the middle of the starlit Pacific Ocean, thousands of miles from home and family, George Bush began to long for the girl he loved.

BARBARA BUSH: AMERICA'S MOM

Barbara Bush, born in New York City on June 8, 1925, is one of the most popular figures in recent American history and the only woman since Abigail Adams who can claim to be both the wife and mother of presidents.[8] Most of her popularity stems from her no-nonsense personality which is direct, unpretentious, and refined with a marvelous but cunning, sometimes abrasive, wit. Like others in the family, she shuns self-analysis, which in the Bush tradition is seen as a close cousin to egocentricity. But because of that she, as well as her famous president son, can be remarkably revealing, counting on the rest of us to play fair and resist any interpretation.

Her autobiography was a lively, well-written best seller that offered a singular glimpse into the life of a woman who normally keeps her childhood a very private affair. As is the norm for the modern presidential mother, she adored her father, Marvin Pierce, who was employed by the McCall Corporation, publisher of the once popular *Collier's* magazine and still in business today with *Redbook,* as well as the flagship publication bearing its own name. Marvin commuted to and from New York City from the sleepy bedroom community of Rye, New York, riding on the same train that was taking Prescott Bush to and from Greenwich, Connecticut. In 1946, Marvin Pierce became the president of McCall.

Barbara obviously had issues with her mother, Pauline Robinson Pierce. She writes of her mother scolding her father over trivialities and resenting the financial support of his father. The great lesson she learned from her mother's life was, in Barbara's own words, "inadvertent."[9] She portrays Pauline as a woman who suffered bitterness unnecessarily, and Barbara, as a result, was determined to enjoy every moment of life. This was her triumph, her sweet revenge over a mother who hurt her. She would choose to be happy in spite of it.

Pauline Robinson, the mother in question, was the daughter of an Ohio Supreme Court justice. She was a gracious woman of the turn of the century but placed high importance on social standing and appearance. According to Barbara, her mother invested most of her effort and time in her eldest daughter, Martha, who appeared to have the talent and beauty that Pauline prized. Martha was attractive and well mannered and would go on to a career as a model, while Barbara developed early weight issues, had a proclivity for roughhousing with her father, and busied herself in a variety of unladylike sports. Later, the family's attention turned to a younger sibling, Scott, who had a cyst in his arm and was in and out of the hospital for several years with operations. When Barbara was sick with childhood diseases, a time when most children would be pampered and loved by a mother, she was cared for by a neighbor, at the neighbor's house, so little Scotty would not be exposed and further weakened.

According to her own narrative, Barbara sought attention any way she could get it, sometimes becoming a pest. An older brother once threatened to kill her if she didn't leave him alone. She hid out under the porch all day. As an adolescent she once took on a boyfriend whose only real qualification was that both her mother and older brother didn't like him.

Beneath the humor of Barbara Bush there is often a scar. "Eat up, Martha," she quotes her mother as saying. "Not you, Barbara!" In dance class she volunteered to be a boy just to avoid being the last girl chosen, until her mother caught on to the trick and squelched it.

In her teens, Barbara Pierce shot up to a leggy five feet eight, seemingly blossoming overnight into a slender, attractive young woman. Her clever personality, originally invented to divert attention away from her appearance, now combined with her new good looks to make her the life of the party. She threw herself into sports activities at Rye Country Day School, gaining a reputation as an athlete as well as the lead mischief maker. Posy Clarke, a childhood friend, noted, "She had more beaus than anyone. She was just extremely popular. She was just awfully good with people. She was like her father, who was a delightful man. She was confident. Very confident." [10]

By her junior year in high school, Barbara's mother, Pauline, decided that the party should come to an end. Her roguish daughter needed a bit of refinement. Barbara was sent away to Ashley Hall in Charleston, South Carolina, a finishing school for girls renowned for its award-winning academics. Barbara flourished, winning new friends and picking up the Rosalie McCabe Cup for general sportsmanship.

In the meantime, Barbara Pierce remained in contact with the old gang from Rye Country Day. During the fateful Christmas break of 1941, her junior year, she joined some friends at a formal dance. It was there that she met "the handsomest looking man you ever laid eyes on, bar none." [11] The man was young George Herbert Walker Bush. That night, Barbara's mother learned the identity of her new male friend and promptly checked out his pedigree. Barbara learned of her mother's inquiries and was incensed. Fearful that George might not meet Pauline's exacting standards, the couple kept their subsequent engagement quiet. When he joined the navy and left for combat, Barbara sent him a steady stream of letters, promising to remain faithful until his return. And young George painted her name on his torpedo bomber.

Christmas 1944 was an eventful time in the lives of George Bush and Barbara Pierce. After being shot down over the Pacific and disappearing for months, George returned stateside on extended leave and into the arms of family and friends. A quick end to the war seemed elusive. The Germans were falling back on the eastern front but had launched a counteroffensive in the Ardennes, scene of their earlier spectacular blitzkrieg victory against the French and British. This time American youth were dying. And the war in the Pacific seemed like an endless process of island hopping, with bloody, costly landings each time. Not willing to wait for a better time, George and Barbara seized the moment. They were married at the First Presbyterian Church in Rye, New York, on January 6, 1945.

Only days after the ceremony, the newlyweds were sent to a base in Virginia Beach, where George was to await reassignment to his old squadron in the Pacific. The future was bleak. Ten of the original fourteen pilots had been killed in combat, and George was faced with the prospect that if he were shot down again, he might be leaving behind a beautiful young widow.

Then came startling news. The United States had developed a nuclear bomb and, on President Truman's orders, it had been dropped in Japan. Within days a second bomb was used, and World War II came to an abrupt end. The naval base in Virginia exploded in pent-up celebration. "Pilots were running out in the streets and hugging each other," Bush remembers. "People everywhere were crying and laughing.

"Barbara and I slipped away to a little chapel. I remember thinking about all my buddies who had died, and I remember squeezing Barbara's hand and thanking God one more time for letting me live to see this day of peace." [12]

THE RISE OF A POLITICAL DYNASTY

With the war at an end, George picked up the trail blazed by three of the four generations before him, including that of his own father, and entered Yale University. He would play on the Bulldogs' varsity baseball team, winning a position as an all-star first baseman, and, like his father, he would be elected captain by his teammates. In a reprise of the Prescott Bush years, he would be tapped by Skull and Bones, and once again, a contact from that secret society would provide the spark for his postuniversity business adventure in Texas.

In love with her husband and seemingly fulfilled at last, Barbara went everywhere with George, keeping score at the baseball games and helping to organize his world. There in New Haven, Connecticut, on July 6, 1946, they had the first of six children, a baby boy. They named him George Walker Bush, but for years he would be known in the family as "Junior." He would become the forty-third president of the United States.

When George Herbert Walker Bush announced the move to Texas and his plans to pursue a career in the oil industry, Barbara was philosophical. She would let him make the decisions about his career. She would be supportive. "While he was out building a business," she recalled, "I was at home changing the babies' diapers and driving carpools. I was the disciplinarian, the enforcer, and he was the gentle father. It was sort of a bad cop/good cop routine." [13]

If George Bush was rarely home, his returning visits were long enough to keep Barbara busy. The babies kept coming one after the other. Pauline Robinson Bush was born December 20, 1949, John

Ellis "Jeb" Bush on February 11, 1953, Neil Mallon Bush on January 22, 1955, Marvin Pierce Bush on October 22, 1956, and Dorothy Walker Bush on August 18, 1959. It was a houseful. And the babies were not all. George's work meant that the family was constantly on the move from Texas to California and back again. In one terrible year in California, the family literally lived out of boxes, moving five different times.

Eventually, George Bush joined other investors and started his own oil company in Midland, Texas. The city on the prairie might have seemed stark and colorless to some, but the luxury of living in one place for a relatively long period of time was an extravagance that Barbara had never experienced in her life as a Bush.

Then came the shocking news that her mother had died in an automobile accident. Barbara Bush's relationship with her mother had been troubled, and that fact likely added to the shock of the announcement, for they would now remain unreconciled. When Barbara was welcomed into the Bush family, she had taken instantly to George's mother, Dottie. "She was the most wonderful woman," Barbara would say, "and had an extraordinary ability to see good in everyone without sounding insincere or like a Pollyanna."[14] Barbara may have used her newfound acceptance to send a message to her own mother. When she married George Bush, she wore Dottie's wedding dress.

As is so often the case in such relationships, Barbara earnestly counteridentified with the mother who had given her so much pain. If Pauline was a spendthrift, Barbara would pay every bill on time. If Pauline was prideful in her beauty, Barbara would one day flaunt her gray hair and plump figure to the nation, even calling attention to it by her cunning wit.

This ongoing contest with Pauline continued long after the mother was gone. Barbara had simply wanted her mother to love her unconditionally, the way she loved her own children, unrelated to how they looked or what they weighed or even how they acted. And if she felt she did not get such love from the woman who had given her birth, she won it from the whole nation by her extraordinary personality, earning widespread admiration and approval. The public was delighted with her the way she was, affirming what she always suspected: that her mother had been wrong and should have enjoyed the fact that she had a perfectly fine young daughter. Every survey and popular opinion poll justified Barbara. Most of the American people didn't want her to color a single strand of her gray hair. They loved her spunky, unconventional personality, which kicked the props out from underneath pompous people in public life.

Speaking of her husband, George H. W. Bush, John Ellis, a Bush cousin, would say, "He could go and do anything he wanted, anything he needed to do; he had an anchor. I don't know how many people are lucky enough to have a Barbara Bush as their wife. Everything gets done." [15]

Barbara, who was expecting their second child, was told not to return for her mother's funeral. It was a decision she would come to regret. Two months later, in the late fall of 1949, Barbara Bush gave birth to a baby girl. They named her Pauline Robinson Bush, after Barbara's mother.

There is a historical irony to this story, one that defies any real understanding. Students of Abraham Lincoln have often commented on his estranged relationship with his father and how he did not attend his father's funeral, and how, after his father's death, he finally named a newborn child Thomas Lincoln, after the man who had hurt him. But Abraham Lincoln could never bring himself to actually use the name, Thomas. He called the boy "Tad," instead. Barbara Bush had an estranged relationship with her mother and, through no fault of her own, did not attend her mother's funeral, but afterward gave her name to a newborn baby, Pauline Robinson Bush. And like the Lincolns, the Bushes would never use her real name. They called their baby "Robin."

Robin Bush was three years old when Barbara began to notice bruises on her body. She arranged for a doctor's appointment and soon after received a call. The doctor wanted to see both Barbara and her husband immediately. Their world was about to change forever. "Imagine being told one day by doctors that your little three-year-old girl has leukemia and will die within weeks." [16]

George Bush, the businessman, was solving big problems every day. In his "can-do" mode he could not immediately accept the finality of the Midland doctor's verdict. Repressing his panic, he called his uncle, Dr. John Walker, Dottie's brother, who just happened to be the president of Memorial Sloan-Kettering Hospital in New York City. They talked earnestly into the night, with Walker urging George and Barbara to bring Robin back east. But the situation did not look good.

Now began a six-month ordeal that would sorely test the mettle of both George and Barbara Bush. Robin was put on the most advanced cancer-treating drugs and therapies available. She was often in great pain. She grew weak, then recovered, then grew weaker still. Her parents rode an exhausting emotional roller coaster. Robin was shuttled in and out of the hospital. When the doctors were not treating her, she and her mother stayed with the Walkers in New York City, or sometimes in a room at Pres and Dottie's home in nearby Connecticut.

George Bush, the courageous young aviator who had defiantly tempted fate to complete his mission, did not have the stomach to look into the plaintive eyes of his suffering little girl. He returned to Midland to keep the business going and to care for Junior and little Jeb.

Barbara stayed in New York. She would not leave Robin's side. She read to her and touched her and tickled her. When the pain was unendurable, though she could do nothing about it, she crawled into bed and held Robin in her arms for hours. Adamantly, consistently, she laid down the rule that no visitor should cry or show the slightest sympathy in Robin's presence. Instinctively, she understood that Robin's life might come down to a single thread, her own will to live, and the mother did not want the slightest doubt or fear reflected back from other faces to her struggling child. Repressing her own agony deeply, Barbara's hair turned white in a matter of days.

This was the most cathartic moment in the life of Barbara Bush. Her own mother had died a few years before, so she would have been carrying some residual guilt. It attends the passing of any loved one, but especially when there are unresolved issues. Indeed, in her memoirs, Barbara often speaks of how mischievous and troublesome she was, wondering aloud if perhaps she were wrong and her mother right, inviting her readers to offer her some reassurance.

Barbara was now caring for Robin in the way that she had wanted to be loved and cared for by her mother. As a sick child, Barbara had been sent to neighbors to recover, lest her infection spread to Scott, the frail sibling. Barbara had never really complained. In fact, she implied that her neighbors were great people and she might have actually preferred being with them rather than with her irritating mother. But her actions with Robin belie such bravado. It is more likely that Barbara Bush, the little girl, sick with fever, alone in another house, with its own strange, creaking sounds at night, was aching for her mother's arms, wanting to be deserved and loved. What Barbara gave to Robin in six months of steadfast, hour-by-hour comfort, was what she had wanted herself. When she crawled into the hospital bed to hold her dying child in her arms, she was Pauline holding her suffering, abandoned Barbara. And till the end, she would not let her go.

On October 11, 1953, Pauline Robinson Bush, exhausted from the ordeal, her body destroyed by the very cancer-fighting drugs that the doctors had hoped would cure her, passed from this life.[17] Barbara Bush, who had not cried for six months, now collapsed, suffering from months of depression. Once the long-repressed weeping finally began, the tears flowed in torrents. "I felt I could cry forever."[18] Barbara insisted that in private her husband was her strength in these long months of grief. George Bush could not bring himself to talk about it publicly for forty years. He sought healing by keeping busy and keeping his wife busy. Publicly, at least, Barbara suffered alone.

The death of a child is said to be one of life's most stressing and unnatural events. In modern society it is often accompanied by the breakup of the marriage, and it has always been attended by disillusionment and a rethinking of life and its meaning. Confronted by the death of her younger brother, whom she had reared since the age of ten, Woodrow Wilson's first lady Ellen Wilson questioned her faith in a God who would "allow such horrible things to happen."[19] But the loss of Robin only brought George and Barbara closer together, and, if anything, it awakened their faith.

"There was no one for us to turn to but God," George Bush would say years later. "And I really learned how to pray. I would slip into our church sometimes when no one was there. I would ask God, 'Why? Why this innocent little girl?' "

There is another phenomenon associated with the loss of a child or sibling. Again and again, such a painful event is the precursor of a public career. William Herndon, Abraham Lincoln's law partner, was convinced that the loss of little Eddie Lincoln had prompted his friend's run for Congress. After the death of his son, Lincoln could not bear to face his wife and relive the pain. Public life, ironically, offered him the chance to be alone. And any fear of defeat at the polls was trivial when compared to the loss of a child. The same has been said of Andrew Jackson, who lost the Indian child he had adopted and raised as his own.

While almost all presidents in early American history lost a child early in their marriage, the phenomenon persists even into the modern era, when such deaths are less common among the general public. The Roosevelts, Eisenhowers, and Kennedys, for example, all lost young children. Eisenhower's son died in his father's arms. He was the same age as Robin Bush. Eisenhower biographers tend to pass over the event hurriedly. The Eisenhowers themselves did not talk of the incident and privately chose to celebrate the boy's birth rather than remember the day he had died. Each year, on September 24, their son's birthday, they sent one another notes and flowers of remembrance. In 1955, on that very anniversary day, Dwight David Eisenhower was struck down with his first heart attack. Years later, First Lady Mamie Eisenhower had her final stroke and passed away the night before her baby's birthday. Relatives said that it was no coincidence, that the loss of their three-year-old son had been the catalyst of many things in their life and that they had been changed profoundly by the experience. Mamie would say to a journalist that "giving up a baby is the hardest trial that a young couple may have to face." [20]

George H. W. Bush would write many speeches, letters, and memoranda over the years, but nothing would strike a chord with the public any more than a private letter he penned to his mother several years after the death of Robin:

There is about our house a need. The running, pulsating restlessness of the four boys as they struggle to learn and grow; their athletic chests and arms and legs; their happy noises as the world embraces them . . . all this wonder needs a counterpart. We need some starched crisp frocks to go with all our torn-kneed blue jeans and helmets. We need some soft blond hair to offset those crew cuts. We need a dollhouse to stand firm against our forts and rackets and thousand baseball cards. We need a cut-out star to play alone while the others battle to see who's "family champ." We even need someone who could sing the descant to "Alouette," while outside they scramble to catch the elusive ball aimed ever roofward, but usually thudding against the screens.

We need a legitimate Christmas angel—one who doesn't have cuffs beneath the dress.

We need someone who's afraid of frogs.

We need someone to cry when I get mad—not argue.

We need a little one who can kiss without leaving egg or jam or gum.

We need a girl.[21]

In 1959, the family moved to Houston, where George could better run his Zapata Oil Company. That August, their last child, Dorothy Walker Bush, a baby girl, was born.

The political rise of George Bush was stellar. He was elected Harris County, Texas, Republican chairman in 1962. He ran for the U.S. Senate in 1964 and went down to defeat in the Goldwater debacle. He ran for and won a seat in the U.S. Congress in 1966, then lost in a second try to follow his father into the Senate. He was ambassador to the United Nations in 1970, the first U.S. representative to the People's Republic of China in 1974, and director of the Central Intelligence Agency in 1976. In 1980, coming up short in his run for the presidency, he was tapped by Ronald Reagan as his running mate and elected vice president of the United States.

When he ran for president in 1988, his supporters touted his record as the greatest résumé in American history. Not since John Adams, they said, had one man held so many diverse and important positions. And the public responded, electing George Bush in a landslide. Little did they suspect that he would one day succeed John Adams in another, very unique category: both men would live to see their sons sworn in as presidents themselves. John Adams was ninety years old, too frail to make the arduous trip to Washington to actually witness the moment in person, but George Bush would stand a few yards away on the wooden inaugural platform and see the power pass from Bill Clinton, the man who had beaten him for reelection, back to his own son, George Walker Bush. Both men had tears in their eyes.

Barbara Bush would be supportive and often the pivot person for both men. During her husband's term in office, she accompanied him to sixty-eight countries, but her role as a First Lady and later as a first mom was never encroaching. Only once, in what some political pundits still insist was a calculated moment, did her biting wit flare into the open in defense of her husband. In 1984, with George Bush finding it difficult to be a gentleman and at the same time defend himself against what the family saw as the shrill attacks of his female Democratic vice presidential opponent, Geraldine Ferraro, Barbara Bush jumped into the fray, telling reporters that George's opponent could be characterized in one word that "rhymes with rich."[22] But her critiques were never directed at her own family. Even as she watched her husband, and later her son, take jobs and make policies contrary to her own instincts, she never wavered or objected publicly. "I've been brought up in a family where if your husband wanted you to do something, you'd do it, and gladly," she once said, then added defiantly, "I still think there's nothing wrong with that."[23]

Instead of overt public demonstration, she preferred to quietly promote her own favored universal causes, primarily in the fields of education and literacy. For much of her life, she had been a voracious reader. In later years, when illness strained her eyes, she refused to give up her great love of books, turning to unabridged audio versions of the latest releases. Inevitably, she began writing and quickly proved to be an imaginative and best-selling author, penning two unique family narratives from the perspective of the family dogs, and donating the profits to various national literacy groups. Her autobiography has outsold any other book ever written on the Bushes and established her as the gifted family scribe and historian.

During her son's campaign in the year 2000, Barbara became an unobtrusive confidante whose wisdom was widely respected. "I just feel a special relationship with my mother," George W. Bush once explained to journalists, "We're pretty much alike, people tell us. I don't mind a battle. I've got my father's eyes and my mother's mouth."[24]

———— ★ ————

EIGHTEEN

George W. Bush:
The Warrior President

Why are you sad for him? Why aren't you happy for me?[1]
—George W. Bush, to his father on the night
he was elected governor of Texas while his brother Jeb
was going down to defeat in the
gubernatorial election in Florida

His detractors describe him as angry and petulant. His admirers say he
is decisive and passionate. Both agree that George W. Bush is a fiercely
determined, stubborn man and that there is something at his very core
that is driving him. It is much too early to understand the forty-third
president. Sketches that can be done now are about as useful and relevant as profiles of John F. Kennedy or Lyndon Johnson were during
their lifetimes. Only now are historians culling the critical data that
will help us define those two presidents, and it will likely take many
years to truly understand George W. Bush. But for all we *don't* know
about him, for all the facts and anecdotes that will come with time,
what we *do* know paints a compelling picture.

The defining moment in his formative years was the death of his
sister Robin and not just her death, but the way in which this important and difficult event was handled by his parents. In 1953, while
three-year-old Robin was battling leukemia at Memorial Sloan-
Kettering Hospital in New York, seven-year-old George Bush was
waiting in Midland, Texas, with his little baby brother, Jeb. Barbara was
committed to the last months and hours of her daughter's life. Dottie
Walker, the indefatigable mother-in-law, was sufficiently worried
about the two children left behind in Texas, especially the baby, Jeb,
that she dispatched a nurse. Neighbors and friends would not be
enough.

The very month that Robin was diagnosed with leukemia, George Bush, the father, joined a business partner and launched his Zapata Oil Company. It would be an unmitigated success, but its early demands took him away from the family for extended periods. When the crisis first developed, Bush split time between New York, Midland, and business trips across the country. But unable to cope with his daughter's pain, the responsibilities with Robin were shifted more and more to his wife.

Back in Midland, young George, or Junior, as he was called, may have felt abandoned. His father's absences were a way of life, but the separation from his mother was something new and mysterious. And when his father was there, caring for him and the baby, Jeb, he may have caused more confusion than comfort. The Bushes had decided not to tell Junior of his sister's condition. Apparently still in denial, they thought that perhaps Robin would get better and the trauma of such an announcement would be unnecessary. Once they had taken such a course, there seemed to be no graceful way back. But it is unlikely that Junior would have missed the tension and pain in the air. Something was obviously going on. He had been told that Robin was sick. At a big summer reunion at Kennebunkport, where he longed to reconnect with the sibling he had missed, he had been warned not to play with her. It was a tormenting time for a young, inquisitive boy who had a vague notion that something was terribly wrong but could find no explanation. His myriad of questions was always dismissed with a cheerful assurance that there was nothing to worry about.

It was a curious time in the history of this remarkable family. There were two future presidents and a first lady, caught in a triad of pain and separation. Barbara Bush was in New York, suffering alone, single-handedly and courageously facing the loss of her child, desperately needing her husband. Meanwhile, George H. W. Bush was into and out of Midland, Texas, building the very business that would become his stepping-stone to a public life and all the while harboring a dark and painful secret from the little boy scampering about his feet. "There is nothing to worry about." And finally, there was seven-year-old George W. Bush, knowing that something was wrong. Probably, like most children, he was blaming himself. If ever they needed to talk, it was now. But they could not.

The day after Robin's death, George and Barbara were persuaded to play a game of golf with Prescott Bush. He thought it would offer relaxation and a diversion. It was the code of the white Anglo-Saxon Protestant: when trouble comes calling, keep a stiff upper lip. Barbara later admitted that she was numb, in shock over all that had happened.[2]

After a memorial service, they flew back to Midland, Texas, to finally bring home the awful truth about Robin. It would be a searing early memory for George W. Bush. "To this day, I am certain I saw her," he would write in his autobiography, "her small head rising barely above the back seat of my parents' green Oldsmobile as it drove up in front of Sam Houston Elementary."[3] Junior and a friend were walking along an outdoor covered walkway of Sam Houston Elementary School, carrying a bulky record player back to the principal's office.[4] When he saw his parents, he ran out to greet them. But Robin wasn't there.

"We felt devastated by what we had to tell him," Barbara says, "As I recall, he asked a lot of questions and couldn't understand why we hadn't told him when we had known for such a long time."[5]

If George and Barbara were circumspect about their loss, Junior, kept in the dark for so long and finally brought back into the circle, couldn't stop talking about it. In the grandstand at a football game he announced suddenly to his father that he wished he were Robin. When his father asked why, the boy said, "I bet she can see the game better from up there than we can here."[6] Later he asked if his sister had been buried lying down or standing up. He had just learned that the earth rotated on its axis, and if she spent part of her time standing on her head, well, that would be pretty neat.

According to all accounts, George W. Bush now became the family cheerleader, assuming a leadership role in dragging his heartbroken family out of its doldrums. Barbara overheard him telling neighborhood children that he couldn't come out to play; his mother needed him. He had been deprived of his mother for months during the crisis; now that he had her again, he would keep her.

Elsie Walker, Junior's second cousin, whose sister had died of polio, had always been very close to Junior and saw how deeply the sense of exclusion affected him. "He and I both saw our parents suffer enormously when we were very vulnerable. We both became clowns, trying to lift them out of their depression," she told an interviewer. "[I] always thought he was mad at the way they handled the death of Robin. G. W. didn't even know she was sick until she was dead."[7] He had not even been given the chance to say good-bye.

Years later, when Elsie Walker broached the idea with Barbara Bush, she was cut short: "Don't be so psycho-analytical."[8] But eventually, after Barbara had given it some thought, she was more reflective. In 1988, when her husband was running for president and her whole life was spilling out into the public view for scrutiny and appraisal, she told a reporter for *Texas Monthly,* "You have to remember that children grieve." And then she admitted that probably young George should have been told the truth immediately. "He felt cheated."[9]

Perhaps it is unrelated, perhaps it is an unconscious reaction, but George W. Bush would repay the favor often throughout his lifetime. Again and again, right up to and including his presidency, his parents would often be the last to know.

YOUTHFUL INDISCRETIONS

Barbara Bush would grieve the loss of Robin for many years, but her memories of perceived favoritism and neglect in her own childhood, and her awareness that Junior and baby Jeb were suffering collateral damage, must have startled her into action. There were other children in the family, and they needed her too. While she was processing her own issues with her parents, she was a mother, creating new issues for her children. She had to go on living.

There is every indication that Barbara and the firstborn George W. butted heads before their famous bonding took place. As the primary caregiver, it was Barbara the enforcer who was often called into the principal's office when her rambunctious eldest son was acting up. And it was Barbara the compassionate who wiped away the tears when her children hurt. George W. recalls, "The thing about my mother is that she could let you have it and then five minutes later be the most loving person in the world."[10] While her husband built his business, Barbara built the family. Soon Junior was at her side, her trademark wit and self-confidence manifesting itself in the son. A family friend would conclude, "It's like you cloned Barbara to get George."[11]

In 1959, the year Dorothy "Doro" Walker Bush was born, the family moved to Houston, Texas. The Zapata Oil Company was now booming. A family that had been rooted in wealth was now returning to it with a vengeance. The exile in west Texas was over. But if it was a comfortable fit for the father, like putting on an old pair of shoes, it was a bit jarring for the children, especially young George, whose whole life had been spent in Midland, Texas. Junior was on the very cusp of adolescence, and the move to Houston brought new pressures. He was sent to an upscale, elite private school near the Bush home, where at first he struggled academically. A part of him pined for the old life in Midland. Junior occasionally accompanied his father to Europe and South America on business trips. There was sometimes much at stake on these outings, but there were also sporadic downtime and wonderful moments together, which came at a critical time in the life of both father and son. It was a scene out of the lives of John Adams and his son John Quincy.

Later, when Junior was sent to Phillips Academy in Andover, Massachusetts, clearly following the trail his father had blazed before him, the culture shock was even more pronounced. Cut off from his friends and the Midland way of life, he employed his gifted, jocular personality to make new friends all around, but a part of him would never make the transition. He wasn't afraid—or so he blustered—but the elitist world from which his father had sprung was not a world of his choosing. At Andover, Junior was meeting the sons of America's wealthy establishment families. His father, with the new wealth from his successful oil company in Houston, was coming home, full cycle, to a lifestyle he had enjoyed in his youth. But the son, reared in Texas, found Andover and Yale a foreign culture.

At Andover, Junior would begin to employ a device that would serve him well throughout his life and be part of his mystifying rise to the presidency. He learned the art of lowering expectations, following it up in time with "doing better than expected." He further developed an ability to divert attention from his own perceived inadequacies, a technique borrowed from his mother and carried to new heights by the son. They were both principles he would see clearly in a political setting when his father entered public life, and they would both become weapons of choice that he would one day wield with a skill and subtlety that his talented father could not match. Coming in third place in an early presidential primary could be a win, if the expectations in the media's mind were low enough. If your opponents underestimated you, well, that made winning a little bit easier and less expensive.

His father and grandfather had been baseball stars at Yale; their pictures were on the walls with their respective winning teams. Junior, who had lived and breathed baseball as a youngster in Midland, had learned long ago that he could not compete with the previous generations. So he used his acid wit and contagious personality to co-opt the student body. At Andover and eventually at Yale, almost everyone was his friend and joined into his irreverent high jinks. This was the power of diversion. He became as popular as any athlete and at Andover even had his moments of glory on the baseball field, by so successfully downplaying his abilities that when he had a good game the results were magnified.

The summer before entering Yale University, he pretended to have no real desire to follow in his father's footsteps, telling a brother, "I really don't want to go to Yale. I just applied to please my dad." But when the acceptance letter came through, he displayed no more hesitation, packing his bags immediately to head back east.

And if his father had put off the Yale experience to fly torpedo bombers in World War II, the son seemed equally tempted by the unpopular war in Vietnam. Almost from his first day on campus, Junior talked about wanting to be a pilot. Indeed, after graduating from Yale he joined the Texas Air National Guard. Suspicions linger to this day that the father intervened to make it happen, to keep his son out of active duty in an unpopular war. But Bush men played by strict convention; Prescott himself had revised the old golf rules that allowed an opponent to block another golfer's shot at the cup. His father would not have interfered one way or the other. Nor would it have been necessary. The son could have simply called on anyone *except* his father, and by Bush rules it would have been fair. During a school break back in Houston, young George talked to the cigar-chomping commander of the 147th Fighter Wing of the Texas Air National Guard. "I want to be a fighter pilot because my father was," he said bluntly.[12]

It was not about Vietnam or patriotism, it was not even about giving something back, nor the Bush family ethic, it was about Dad. After graduating from Yale in May 1968, George W. Bush enlisted at Ellington Air Force Base near Houston, Texas. Before the year was over he was soaring through the heavens in an F-102 Delta Dagger.

The higher Junior climbed this mountain of expectation, following his father and grandfather and those who had climbed before, the greater the danger of falling and experiencing fatal injury. At Yale he was tapped to join Skull and Bones, but it never seemed to represent more than another notch in his gun, another thing his father had also done. The lure of a political life seemed to be the most intriguing aspect of the Bush tradition. Maybe his father's early defeats offered some unconscious encouragement. George W. was tempted to skip the millionaire part of the Bush story and go straight into public service. Off and on for years, he had audited various political careers besides his father's, taking time off during summers or later from his Guard duty to bury himself as a full-time worker in Senate campaigns for Ed Gurney of Florida and later Winton Blount of Alabama. It is not clear what he learned from these experiences, except that candidates can lose and it hurts big and they can win and it feels incredible. It was a colossal, emotional roll of the dice.

George W. Bush had joined the Texas Air National Guard in May 1968. By the fall of 1973, he had received his honorable discharge and seemed at a loss as to what to do.[13] He drifted from one idea and job possibility to the next, keeping one eye on his father's roller coaster, sometime victorious, sometimes hurtful and disappointing political career. His drinking began at Yale and, for a time, grew worse with each year. Later, his volunteer stints for political campaigns were often descents into debauchery with alcohol and promiscuity, which he described to an acquaintance as "non-stop booze and sex."[14] He seemed shiftless during this period, uncertain how he would accomplish the next difficult part of the climb, the millionaire part, the successful businessman part. "He had seven apartments in three different states, held three different jobs and had many girlfriends."[15]

By Christmas 1972, the mountaintop that George W. Bush was trying to reach seemed to become more elusive the higher he climbed. The Bush saga—those stories of Bush sons who had left the security of their fathers and struck out on their own and did spectacular things and became millionaires in their own right, followed by years of public service—were impressive bedtime tales for little boys. But they could drive grown men to drink.

There was at the time a sense that the Bush men were a declining breed. Prescott had stood in at an imposing six foot, four inches tall, his son a diminished six feet two, and young Junior was not even six feet. All three had been members of the prestigious Skull and Bones club, but in descending importance. Graduating from Yale was such a given that Junior's father didn't even go to his son's ceremony. The grandfather had been a talented baseball player who hit cleanup; the son was a national collegiate All-Star but admittedly no great slugger. The grandson was—well, he was a cheerleader. The grandfather had fought in the terrible Meuse-Argonne offensive in World War I. The son had been a certified war hero in World War II, his cardboard box of medals stashed under the bed, a wonder to his wide-eyed children, who occasionally touched them when he was out of town. But the grandson, Junior, who had flown jets in the Air National Guard, had not seen a minute of action in the Vietnam War. Each was arguably a more pastel version of the former, a diminishing force.

The most immediate point of reference for George W. was how each generation had built a successful career and how he would compare. His grandfather had been a millionaire extraordinaire at Brown Brothers Harriman before beginning his illustrious career in the U.S. Senate. His son George H. W. Bush had also miraculously built a financial base, and if it was not as solid, it had been accomplished in spectacular fashion as he rose from being a broom pusher at Dresser Industries to founding his own highly successful oil company. But he was just barely a millionaire, perhaps having sold out too soon for too little. The family still struggled financially from time to time. And his career in public service seemed to be an anemic version of his father's. Twice, George H. W. Bush had tried to win a seat in the U.S. Senate and failed. He had finally won the lesser job of congressman, the one that his father Prescott had felt was not important enough to interrupt his work to pursue. And with the Senate seemingly beyond reach, he had accepted the appointed position of U.N. ambassador. It was a consolation prize.

Yet if George Herbert seemed to be a downsized version of Prescott, the grandfather, George, Jr., by comparison, seemed to have no prospects at all. He was twenty-six years old, without much apparent interest in either work or marriage. No one in the family was expecting him to even enter the public service game. More and more, the spotlight of the family was shifting to the serious one, Jeb Bush, the second brother.

That Christmas, 1972, the family gathered in Washington. There were simmering problems just beneath the surface. Junior was a concern to his father, and fifteen-year-old Marvin was struggling at Andover and in a bit of trouble. When George W. Bush disappeared one night with Marvin in tow and the two later arrived home drunk, the tension finally erupted. Junior had driven into a neighbor's trash can and dragged it noisily down the street. The lights in the house went on, and Ambassador Bush was awake and ready. As events would have it, Jeb, the emerging favorite son, just happened to be the messenger, telling Junior that his dad wanted to talk to him in the study.

George W. Bush, his passion loosened by alcohol, was belligerent, the frustration of his life pouring out. "I hear you're looking for me," he said. "You want to go *mano a mano* right here?"[16]

There they stood, face-to-face, two future presidents of the United States, father and son, both at frustrating periods in their lives, in an astonishing personal confrontation. Jeb, knowing instinctively that this was about disappointment deeper than a night of excessive drinking, jumped between the two men, making the startling announcement to his father that Junior had been accepted at the Harvard Business School. He was going to get his MBA. The tension broke.

"Are you sure you want to do that, son?" the father asked, obviously relieved that he had miscalculated, that there was more to his firstborn than met the eye.

"No, I'm not going," Junior snapped. "I just did it to show you that I could."[17]

Actually, George W. Bush did go to Harvard and earned his MBA. Higher education was a comfortable place to hide when life was uncertain. But in the midst of that liberal eastern bastion he assumed the role of the conservative, redneck rebel. He found the political pack mentality stifling and hypocritical, and he was still nostalgic about his childhood in Midland, Texas. He flaunted his counterculture, wearing a Texas National Guard flight jacket to class and insisting on chewing tobacco, using a tin cup as a spittoon. Texas was never far from his mind. It symbolized more than his childhood roots. It was a badge of distinction from a father with whom he found it difficult to compete. "The difference between my father and me," he would one day declare to friends, "is that he went to Greenwich Country Day School and I went to Sam Houston Elementary."[18]

HEALING IN MIDLAND, TEXAS

That George W. Bush was conflicted, there is little doubt. He wept at each of his father's losses and selflessly devoted months, even years, of his life to help his father achieve his victories. His worship bordered on the ridiculous, and his faith in his father's perfection sometimes led to awkward political moments, such as his confrontation over his father's alleged adultery. "The answer to the big A," he announced to reporters in 1988, after grilling his dad, "is a big 'No.' " [19]

But there was anger too. He resented the austere, privileged world of his father, Andover, Yale, and Skull and Bones, a world that he had been thrust into. If he could never bring himself to target his father, he often needled surrogates. He saw Nicholas Brady, the consummate establishment figure who raised money for Skull and Bones and later served in the senior Bush cabinet as secretary of the Treasury, as a pompous snob. [20] And Brady openly despised the young Bush, feeling uncomfortable around him, feeling he didn't show due deference.

In 1975, in a reprise of his father's journey almost thirty years before, Junior headed back to Midland, Texas, to hopefully make his million in the oil industry. He arrived broke, at least by Bush standards, with only $15,000 in start-up funds left over from a family education trust. The plan was to establish his own company, become financially independent, and perhaps position himself on his own fast track to public service. West Texas had been a foreign adventure to the father; it would be a homecoming for the son. At least that was the plan.

In fact, Junior's first months in Midland were a bit disorienting. The old school and the old buildings and streets looked much smaller. And at first, even the culture seemed to have changed. Texas had not remained in a bubble for thirty years. His oil company, launched within the perfectly legitimate Bush rules of raising money from anyone but Dad, seemed to drill too many dry holes. In 1978, having for years toyed with the idea of skipping the millionaire part and going straight into political office, he preempted his younger brother Jeb by announcing a run for Congress.

The family was surprised by George W.'s decision, and Jeb was perhaps a little thrown. But after getting used to the idea, his father pulled out all the stops and called in all the favors. It was uncharacteristic, un–Bush-like, but it would set the pattern for future campaigns. Politics would be the one thing that a new generation of Bush fathers and sons would be allowed to do together.

George W.'s opponent attacked his education, his eastern connections, his family, his dad. "When it comes to the integrity of my father I will fight back," Junior stormed.[21] Nothing hurt as much as attacks on his family. On the last weekend, his opponent played a conservative religious card, alerting churches to the fact that Bush college volunteers were going to have a beer party after the election. In the end, George W.'s attempt to shortcut the family tradition and preempt his brother and perhaps even his own father failed.

In the middle of his campaign for Congress, he received a call for advice from Dad. The former U.N. ambassador and CIA director was thinking about running for president. What did Junior think?

It was not easy holding your own in the Bush family. The expectations that bore down on the Bush men could be at once inspiring and crushing. That other great American dynasty, the John Adams family, had seen the limits to such ambition. George Washington Adams, son and grandson of presidents, had been told by his father that he had not only one but two generations of honor to uphold. Young Adams died an alcoholic and a likely suicide at the age of twenty-eight.

At some point during these years of conflict, Junior's drinking led to something dark, at least in his mind, something that represented the closing of a door. George W. Bush apparently experimented with cocaine. He has never spoken about it publicly and so we can only speculate on if and when it happened. Actually, it would have little real impact on his later political career, but the fear that it might flare into the open would become at times an obsession. Privately, he brought the subject up often in his run for the presidency in 2000. From piecing together private conversations between George W. and various aides and friends, it is quite likely that it was not an ongoing problem, which makes it even more significant as a symbolic moment. Years later, in the heat of the 2000 campaign, he would be fearful that the Democratic Party would produce a witness, someone who may have been on the scene when it happened and would remember it wrong, claiming that they had seen him. And if they were to do so, he insisted, it would be a lie. No one had seen him.

A consensus in the media, he was told, concludes that "there *is* *something* [to the story] and you are just going to wait and see if there is any proof or if any one comes forward as a witness and if they don't, you are okay."

"That's it," Bush agreed.

"It could be a [big] story," an aide cautioned, "because one, you have denied it and two, your opponents might produce a witness."

"I haven't denied anything," George W. replied.[22]

For years, this incident released him from the terrible burden of family succession. He could never enter public life. The taint of having experimented with cocaine ruled it out. It may have been the reason why he had used it in the first place. Perhaps, at some deep level he was taking the option off the table and, with it, the pressure to achieve. In 1987, Supreme Court nominee Douglas Ginsburg withdrew his nomination when it was learned he had used marijuana. Cocaine, a much more dangerous drug with more severe legal penalties, would be the kiss of death to a political candidate. With the pressure gone, with the line of succession interrupted, George W. could relax. Things were out of his hands now.

In 1980, George H. W. Bush did not win the presidency, but he made a surprising effort, doing better than expected, and Ronald Reagan took him onto his ticket and into the White House as his vice president. Within the family, the spotlight shifted to Jeb, the younger brother. The mantle had passed by George, Jr.

Life in the backwaters of Midland, Texas, eventually proved to be a healing experience for George W. Bush. He had missed the place since the family move to Houston. Now, with the pressure off and his ambitions derailed, he would strive to carve out his own version of a normal life. He found his wife, Laura Welch, in the middle of his congressional campaign. And, even if he lost the election, he vowed, he would never lose Laura. His twin daughters, Jenna and Barbara, would be born there, the girls named after their maternal and paternal grandmothers. In Midland he would find faith, joining a group of men in a weekly Bible study. In 1986, after a rousing fortieth birthday party bash in Colorado Springs, Colorado, he would waken with an excruciating hangover, take a morning jog with friends, and announce that he would never drink another drop of alcohol again for the rest of his life.

Renewed and at peace with himself but bursting with the same raw energy that had always characterized his personality, a born-again version of George W. Bush came to Washington, D.C., in 1987, to help his father make a second run for the presidency.

In the first days of his work in Washington, George, Jr., announced that he would henceforth no longer be called "Junior" and he wanted family, friends, and staff to know it. From now on, he would be called "G. W." He was a new man. There would be no "George" in his name, no mistaking him for the father. The name would hold until he ran again for public office in Texas in 1994, when he would reinvent himself once more, this time for the history books. Then, with the family in exile after his father's defeat at the hands of Bill Clinton, he would feel sufficiently confident to reclaim the revered name. He would be called George W. Bush. It was a name that was neither subordinate nor in reaction to his father. The whole process was an obvious reflection of his life's struggle, an ongoing internal effort to establish his own identity, worthy of the name he had been given.

By 1987, G. W. was at peace with himself. Some family members were saying that he had "matured" and shaken off some of his demons. His preordained family plan was clearly back in play. Indifferent to the drama in Washington, he openly worked the phones to put together an investment team to buy the Texas Rangers baseball team. This would be his own version of the Zapata Oil Company, his own version of Brown Brothers Harriman, his Bush millionaire position before stepping into public life.

Meanwhile, Jeb Bush, his little brother, the man in the family spotlight, had acquitted himself quite well and was on track, having become a multimillionaire in Florida real estate and other business ventures and winning an appointment as state secretary of commerce. "There is no question in my mind that he will become a major political figure in the country," his father said. "He is passionate in his caring and in his beliefs. He speaks well and at six-foot-four is an impressive man." [23]

In 1988, when the Bush sons were interviewed for a book, Marvin was asked who was most likely of the new generation to pursue a career in public life. "Jeb is the studious one," he answered. "We have always thought that he would run for office some day."

"And what about George, the oldest?" he was asked.

"George?" he replied. "George is the family clown."[24]

Relaxed and relieved of any pressure, feeling good about himself, giving himself a new name, a new identity, off the bottle for more than a year, George W. Bush was just where he always liked to be—underestimated.

In 1992, after going down to defeat in a reelection bid against Bill Clinton, George Herbert Walker Bush retired from politics. It had been, he said, his last campaign. His political career had ended the way it had begun, with a tearful defeat. Jeb Bush, now positioned for a run for Florida governor, was surprised to learn that George W. was talking about a run for governor of Texas. George and Barbara both encouraged Jeb but warned George not to try. Barbara said he couldn't win and told the press that "Jeb is more like his father, if truth be known."[25] As the campaign heated up, Barbara found some affirmation in what was happening to her sons and their families. "They know it's ugly and they're still willing to do it," she said. "In a way, that sort of vindicates our life."[26]

Since Jeb seemed the most likely to pull it off, George and Barbara Bush spent almost twice as much time fund-raising in Florida as in Texas. Bush's cousin John Ellis later admitted, "Just about everyone in the family assumed that Jeb would win and George would lose."[27] George had always talked about being Willie Mays, Jeb about being president. But on election night 1994, Jeb Bush went down to defeat in Florida, and George W. Bush, the born-again family clown, was elected the governor of Texas.

George W. Bush was apparently a little disappointed with his father's response. When Bush, Sr., called to congratulate him, he seemed overwhelmed with grief for Jeb's loss. The former president told reporters, "The joy is in Texas: my heart is in Florida."[28]

On a cold day in January 2001, the Bush family gathered on a platform at the Capitol in Washington, D.C., before a crowd of thousands, with millions more watching on television around the world, as George W. Bush was sworn in as the forty-third president of the United States. He wore the cuff links that his father had worn in the White House and his grandfather had worn in the U.S. Senate.

Publicly, he would be identified more and more with his mother, the woman who had shaped his life and whose personality he shared. And that was good politics. Barbara Bush was a star. A 1994

Mother's Day poll commissioned by a leading women's magazine had declared her the woman most Americans would like to talk to on Mother's Day. In the year 2000, a CBS news poll found that 63 percent of Americans had a favorable view of her and only 3 percent an unfavorable one.

But many of the issues that had dominated George W.'s life were with his father. He almost never spoke to his friends about his mother, while his father constantly appeared in any conversation. After the inauguration, when George W. Bush first entered the Oval Office as president, he looked it over before hearing footsteps outside the door where his father and his new chief of staff, Andy Card, were approaching.

"Mr. President?" his father asked in a breaking voice.

"Mr. President?" the son shot back to his father. The men embraced and wept.

Yet the father could not hide his surprise. When asked how it felt, he answered with a question of his own. "You remember when your kid comes home with two A's—and you thought she was going to fail?" he said. "That's exactly what it's like." [29] After seeing his son win the White House he privately admitted to his own brother and sister that he had underestimated him.

The newly elected president, George W. Bush, moved his father's desk out of the Oval Office. It had served Bush, the father, and it had served Bill Clinton, but he was signaling that he was his own man. He ordered the White House staff to bring up JFK's desk.

At Kennebunkport that summer, in a grand and dramatic move, his father stood up and offered his president son the seat of honor at the head of the table. Family members who were there sensed that it was an important moment of respect for the father, a moment of heady symbolism in a family bound by its traditions. Prescott had been so impressed by serving in the Senate that he had required his grandchildren, including young Georgie, to call him "Senator." Now they had a second president. George and Barbara had taken to calling him "Quincy," as in John Quincy Adams, the other son who had succeeded a father to the White House. But George W. Bush brushed off his father's gesture, as if it were no big deal, saying, "Who cares?" Some family members were afraid that the father had felt hurt by the reaction.

It was now apparent that there had been a strong undercurrent running deep inside this firstborn son of this latest Bush generation. It had looked for a while that they were a family in decline, but that had been a deceptive snapshot taken too early. In fact, George, Sr., was a much more powerful and accomplished man than the father he had adored. And George W. Bush, who would win reelection as president, was, in many respects, a superior, more highly evolved Bush species than his father. Weak as a public speaker, lacking his father's gift at building networks, void of the interest in policy that is a prerequisite for presidents, he was nonetheless a superior strategist with ruthless self-discipline. He had worked almost unseen at the street level in campaigns for Ed Gurney in Florida, Winton Blount in Alabama, and Victor Ashe in Tennessee, and in virtually all of his father's many efforts in Texas and nationwide, learning and honing his craft as a politician. He had spent much of his frustrated life nervously coiled and ready to strike. When his moment had finally come, it had seemed to be a stunning ascent, from ground level to millionaire, governor, and president in ten years, but the rise had been more than a hundred years in the making.

There was a part of him that didn't want to take the head seat at the family table in Kennebunkport. Perhaps at some unconscious level, having achieved preeminence, he was signaling his disgust with the whole painful ordeal, something that would have sounded like sour grapes had it come from any other son. Perhaps he was rebelling against the Bush rite of passage that had so remarkably produced a senator, two governors, and two presidents but almost ruined his life. Maybe he was thankful that he had two daughters and no son to carry the burden of being a man in the Bush family.

Or perhaps he was only conflicted about taking the place of the man whose long shadow had hidden his life for so many years—a man he loved and raced against but had barely caught. If George W. Bush had surprised the family, well, maybe he had surprised himself a little too. In a campaign documentary, *Journeys with George,* Alexandra Pelosi asked him what he would do for the little guy if elected president. Good-naturedly, Bush replied, "I *am* the little guy. My brother is six foot three and I am only five feet eleven."[30] He was, of course, referring to Jeb and hearkening back to a time when he had seemingly been passed over.

"I'm the black sheep of the family," he had once told Queen Elizabeth at a reception. But he was now the leader of the free world and, perhaps even more significant, he had been offered the seat at the head of the family table in Kennebunkport, Maine.

─── ★ ───

A President in the Family:
How It Happens

You don't have to deserve your mother's love.
You have to deserve your father's.[1]
—Robert Frost

Many lessons can be gleaned by examining the lives of the presidents' parents and the relationships they shared with their extraordinary off-spring. Children seek the approval of the father figure in their life through *mimicry* or *completion*. *Mimicry* may mean rooting for the same baseball team, attending the same university, or entering the same profession. But *completion* takes place when a child does something the father figure has failed to do, to accomplish something left undone. Perhaps he or she becomes the first member of the family to earn a university degree, for example.

Theodore Roosevelt's father had attempted to win an appointment as the collector of the port of New York City, but the U.S. Senate turned him down. The son later won the appointment. Likewise, the son, embarrassed by his father's refusal to fight in the glorious Civil War, became immersed in everything martial. "My father was my hero," Theodore Roosevelt once said of the elder Roosevelt, "but I know that he was deeply disappointed by missing all the action." It led to heroics and his charge up Kettle Hill in San Juan, which in turn propelled him to national prominence and the presidency.

Once begun, this process labored on through yet another generation. Theodore Roosevelt's greatest disappointment was in not winning the Medal of Honor after his dramatic service in the Spanish-

American War. His sons spent their lives pursuing military glory, continually taking enormous risks, being wounded, and one of them dying in battle at the age of twenty. Representing the third generation to produce a son named Theodore Roosevelt, one of them finally brought home the Medal of Honor, which was awarded to him posthumously.

The father of Calvin Coolidge, as in the case of many other fathers of presidents, was a frustrated politician who barely made it to the state assembly. But he not only lived to see his son become president, he actually administered the oath of office to him.

Perhaps no story better illustrates all the elements discussed in these pages, including the need for completion, than the life of President Andrew Johnson. His grandfather saw the accumulation of four generations of family lands and homes disappear in a sheriff's sale to satisfy creditors. The president's father, Jacob Johnson, was landless, illiterate, and desperately poor. He worked at odd jobs in Raleigh, North Carolina, including a long stint as a humble porter at the local bank. Still, he won begrudging respect from the town's gentry, earning a reputation as "dependable," and was named the town's bell ringer.

In a dramatic moment etched in the history of Raleigh, three of the leading citizens were involved in a boating incident. Jacob Johnson, who was standing on the pier, dived into the water and one by one rescued the panicked boaters, hauling them from the bottom of a deep pond. A few hours later, exhausted by his efforts, the dependable Jacob Johnson climbed to the bell tower, pulled the rope one last time, and fell over dead. His wife, frightened and penniless, clung to his dead body and sobbed.

The third child in the family, Andrew, the future president, grew up dirt poor, often living off the largesse of the wealthy men whose lives his father had saved. His mother, Mary, was given odd jobs helping the rich. But however much Jacob Johnson's heroics had been appreciated, the social lines of demarcation were still clear. Andrew and his mother and siblings ranked little higher than the black slaves. The Johnson children often ran naked and were once beaten for taking a shortcut through the lawn of a "respectable" family.

It is hardly suprising that Andrew Johnson grew up a driven man. He would idealize his heroic father, taken from him when he was only three. Johnson would move to the hollows of eastern Tennessee, to an area even poorer than the Carolinas. He would organize the working class, take political power, and win election to Congress. Before he was finished, he would live in the governor's mansion and eventually the White House.

COMPLETION AND SADDAM HUSSEIN

Finally, there are the stories of the great political dynasties in American history, the Adams, Harrisons, Roosevelts, Tafts, Kennedys, and Bushes. The only two families to produce multiple presidents, the Adams and the Bushes offer classic examples of both mimicry and completion. The life of Adams, whose career chart is a replica of his father's, espoused an exaggerated version of his grandfather Deacon John's philosophy of purity through duty and service. It is as if the idea took on more potency with each of the three successive generations.

And in the Bush family there is the same dynamic. George W. Bush slavishly followed his father's career path while taking the family philosophy to an extreme. There were Andover, Yale, Skull and Bones, piloting airplanes, the oil business, baseball, becoming a millionaire on one's own, and, finally, public life. If mimicry could win fatherly approval, George W. would be classified as an overachiever. He copied his father's character traits, as well. There was, for instance, the disdain for self-analysis. There was the Bush penchant for integrity and discretion. "I think you could burn down the house in Kennebunkport," said cousin John Ellis, "and you'd be in less trouble than if you gave a bad quote to *The New York Times.*"[2]

And completion has no better champion than George W. Bush, whose ability to tie all the loose ends of his father's years as president rivals the story of John Quincy Adams. His father's greatest disappointment was his perceived lack of integrity in breaking a famous campaign promise "Read my lips: no new taxes." The son wiped the issue off the pages of history by continuously and insistently reducing taxes at every chance, establishing forever that the Bushes and tax cuts are synonymous and that the Bushes keep their promises.

The father's Texas credentials were constantly questioned. He was charged with living in Kennebunkport, Maine, while keeping only a hotel address in Houston to maintain his Texas voter registration. The son bought a ranch in steamy Waco, Texas, and put down roots, proving that Bushes are Texans. The father won the Persian Gulf War but left Saddam Hussein, the dictator of Iraq, in place. A few years later, the same dictator ordered the assassination of the father. The son came to power in the year 2001, and the next year he ended the reign of Saddam Hussein. Perhaps not to be overlooked is the fact that both of Hussein's sons were killed. This is called *completion.*

Charles Strozier, in his classic study *Lincoln's Quest for Union,* saw the loss of cohesion in an individual, in this case Lincoln himself, as generating rage. He warned that it could create an "affect storm," which he likened to a child's temper tantrum. This, he insisted, had been at work in Lincoln as a device to ward off further fragmentation. "For the group there are fascinating analogues to these characteristics of rage in the individual: the fury of war perhaps most accurately expresses the collective version of the temper tantrum."

Strozier saw Lincoln as resolving his personal conflicts with his father through public events. "In the idea of a house divided, Lincoln found a way of creatively enlarging his private concerns to fill the public space." [3] By fighting for the Union, Strozier feels, Lincoln was seeking accommodation with his father, his wife, and his dead mother.

Something similar may be at the core of George W. Bush and his war in Iraq. "Let us not forget," he said to us in an unguarded public moment, "this man tried to kill my father." Could George W. Bush have invaded Iraq to settle a score, to pick up the sword where it had been left lying on the battlefield, abandoned by his father more than ten years before? Was he seeking approval from his father by completing an unfinished task while simultaneously winning approval from Midland, Texas, peers, that important pack from his formative years, by doing what he knew they believed should have been done in the first place?

Like John Quincy Adams, the other son of a president to reach the White House, George W. Bush is a divisive personality to his American contemporaries, a hero to some and a villain to others. He is perhaps one of the most internationally despised figures in American history. But unlike John Quincy Adams, George W. Bush was reelected president, his work affirmed.

In the coming years, when the shrill voices of debate have passed, historians will have a better perspective to consider his decisions and how they impacted our lives for good or ill. It will be a difficult task to unravel it all, since we have taken certain turns in the road and will be unable to retrace our steps to know how it might have turned out differently. Surely, part of the process will be an understanding of the relationship between the two Bush presidents, father and son, and how each sought the approval of the other. This question can be a seductive puzzle in all families, but it takes on greater interest when society at large is impacted. The lives of President George Herbert Walker Bush and his president son will forever be entwined with the history of our nation and will be a classic study in relationships for years to come.

Adam Bellow writes about the sons of powerful men in his acclaimed study *In Praise of Nepotism:* "They often feel the need to go on proving themselves and are haunted by the fear that nothing they do will ever be good enough. For them, success is a question of not just meeting expectations but of exceeding them, and not once but again and again."[4] Robert Frost once observed, "You don't have to deserve your mother's love. You have to deserve your father's."[5]

GENTLE BUT FIRM

University studies offer the formula for raising high-achieving children. "Be gentle but firm" is the consensus.[6] A child must experience love from the parent, as well as some structure or discipline. It is exactly the combination that one can see in the parenting style that produced so many of these presidents. Yet it is missing in others.

The structure or firmness for the presidents was often provided through education, the military, or disciplined work. With some famous exceptions such as Abraham Lincoln, the educational advantages of the presidents have remained rather constant. Many early presidents were Harvard graduates, and while a university education is more available today, it is probably even more difficult for the common man of the twenty-first century to get into the most prestigious institutions, with the opportunities and contacts that such membership implies. And the insider knowledge that came from a savvy father of a John Tyler, William Howard Taft, or John Kennedy would not be available to the common man.

Quite a number of presidents hailed from the military: Washington, Jackson, the two Harrisons, Taylor, Pierce, Grant, Hayes, Eisenhower, and others. While heroics in battle are seen as examples of leadership qualities and as such are great selling points for a political campaign, they also fit the formula for high achievers, who must somehow acquire the discipline or structure to reach their goals. Some received the gentleness or love at home and found the discipline or firmness somewhere else.

Lincoln, whose combined formal education amounted to one year and whose brief military experience, fighting Indians on the frontier, was primarily a great camping exercise, nevertheless was exposed to a quaint, improvised version of the same formula. He was eight when his disciplined, hardworking father put an ax into his hands. And his education came at the feet of a gentle, nurturing mother, who encouraged her son to read.

But if discipline can come from outside the family, gentleness, at least in the case of these great men, must be found somewhere closer to home. It is not likely, however disciplined he may have been, that Gerald Ford would ever have risen to the presidency without his nurturing mother. Nor is this process dictated by gender. Often a father, such as George Herbert Walker Bush, may provide the "gentle" counterpoint to the mother's firmness, in this case Barbara Bush. Sometimes the roles are exchanged, with Joe and Rose Kennedy, for example, taking on different personae with their children at different times in their lives. Both could be extremely firm and at other times lovingly gentle. In some cases, such as those of Andrew Jackson and Bill Clinton, the president was essentially raised by grandparents or relatives.

Still, one keeps coming back to the inescapable conclusion that these presidents are the products of strong-willed mothers. This is the most pervasive common denominator. The fathers are often absent, through either death or career choices, which creates a vacuum that allows the mother an even stronger role. It is as if the whole study circles right back to the nineteenth-century poem of William Wallace that declares, "The hand that rocks the cradle, is the hand that rules the world." Behind many of these presidents were women who provided both qualities for their sons, the nurturing love and the structured environment that allowed for success. Many made their son feel as if he were the favorite. "I have found that people who know that they are preferred or favored by their mother," writes Sigmund Freud, "give evidence in their lives of a peculiar self reliance and an unshakeable optimism which often seem like heroic attributes and bring actual success to their possessors."[7]

In 1941, several months after the death of his mother, Franklin Delano Roosevelt returned to Hyde Park, where he and a staffer rummaged through some old boxes sent up from Washington. They were at the very beginning of a massive sorting project, preparing the way for what would become the Franklin D. Roosevelt Presidential Library. They came across an unusual box that no one recognized. Inside they found the president's baby shoes, his christening dress, a tenderly preserved lock of hair and all of his letters to his parents from Groton Academy and Harvard. The room seemed to be flooded with the presence of Sara Delano Roosevelt and her great love for her son. For the first time ever, his staff saw the president openly weep. They quietly slipped from the room to leave him alone with the thoughts of the woman who had cherished him as an infant and whose last letter to him had wistfully said, "I think of you night and day."

A Chronological List
of the Presidents' Parents
──── ★ ────

1. GEORGE WASHINGTON (1789–1797)

Augustine "Gus" Washington (1694–April 12, 1743). In a day of piety and powdered wigs, good breeding was essential. Augustine Washington could trace his lineage back to British gentry. While the family gave up such titles in the new country, Gus kept up business dealings in England, along with his new ventures in America. The demands of his business pursuits drew him away from home and family.

In all of his personal writings, George Washington makes only a few references to his father. In one account, George erroneously recalls that he was ten at the time of his father's death: he was actually eleven. Other references to Augustine are limited to the outer regions of familiarity, though George did remember him as tall, fair, strong, and kind.

History remembers Augustine Washington in a similar manner. Tales of great strength are passed down from his iron mining days, when he was said to be able to lift weight that would tax the limits of two men. On the other hand, George Washington's biographer James Thomas Flexner described Augustine as a "man who was restless, apprehensive, unsure, making deals which he subsequently denied making. He was often in the law courts."[1]

Mary Ball Washington (1708–August 25, 1789). Mary was Augustine's second wife. She lived in comfort with him but became a widow in her thirties and did not remarry. A single mother of growing children, she undoubtedly faced numerous challenges.

Whether because of her limited finances or her overly protective nature, Mary was reluctant after her husband's death to allow George, her firstborn, to travel overseas. Unlike his older half brothers, who studied in England, George received a minimal education at home while helping care for his siblings.

George's half brother Lawrence, fourteen years his senior, became influential in the upbringing of this president. The family could easily have secured a naval appointment for George, and according to Lawrence, such an appointment would have greatly profited the young man. However, Mary once again kept George close to home.

While her husband left provision for her needs, the practices of the time eventually left Mary dependent upon her children until her death. Even as George Washington suffered the hardships of winter with his troops at Valley Forge, he received letters from his mother complaining of his lack of concern and disregard for her comfort. According to Peter R. Henrigues in *George Washington Reconsidered,* her president son visited her in Fredericksburg before she died and confided to a sister, "I took a final leave of my mother, never expecting to see her more." [2]

George Washington Parke Custis, Washington's step-grandson, saw Mary Ball Washington as "the guide who directed your steps when they needed the guidance of age and wisdom, the parental affection which claimed your love, the parental authority which commanded your obedience." [3] Although critics sometimes view Mary Washington as overbearing, her determination and resolve as a mother helped her raise the man we now call the father of our country.

2. JOHN ADAMS (1797–1801)

John "Deacon" Adams, Sr. (February 8, 1690–May 25, 1761). John Senior, the father of our second president, exemplified moral character and a vigorous work ethic. He was raised in a strongly Puritan atmosphere.

John Senior was one of eight children born to Joseph Adams and Hannah Bass Adams. While attending school, he lived and worked on the family farm. In 1734, obeying his sense of duty, he joined the local militia. That same commitment to community continued into his adulthood, when he gained the sobriquet Deacon John through his service at the Congregational church. As a lieutenant in the militia, a selectman, a tax collector, and a constable, Deacon John became a pillar in his community. Adams recalls of his father that "no public business was transacted in Braintree without Deacon John's consent." [4] In addition to his farming and civic duties, Deacon John was a skilled leather crafter, putting in long hours of manual labor.

Deacon John sacrificed to send his son to Harvard, expecting him to become a minister. One year after graduation, John informed his father that rather than enter the ministry he would study law. Although John anticipated confrontation, he was pleased to receive his father's approval.

With his father's love and support, John indeed followed a path that would lead him to law and later the presidency. Unfortunately, Deacon John died early in John's public career, struck down by influenza at the age of seventy. "He was the honestest Man I ever knew," his presidential son would declare, "In wisdom, piety, benevolence and charity. In proportion to his Education and Sphere of Life, I have never seen his Superior."

Susanna Boylston Adams (March 5, 1708–April 21, 1797). Stemming from a line of doctors and raised in Brookline, Massachusetts, overlooking Boston, Susanna knew the privileges that education and wealth could afford. While she had many suitors, the strong-willed Susanna chose a cobbler from Braintree, eighteen years her senior.

Along with a notoriously fiery temper, the twenty-five-year-old bride brought sophistication and wealth to the family of John Adams when they married in the autumn of 1734. On October 19, 1735, Susanna Boylston Adams gave birth to John Adams, who would become the nation's second president.

In his prolific writings, John Adams surprisingly seldom refers to his mother, although their relationship appeared to be a fond one. Memories of quarrels between his parents are, however, reflected in his correspondence, and some believe that his passionate disposition and intellectual strength were likely inherited from Susanna.

At fifty-two, Susanna became a widow when Deacon John succumbed to influenza. Five years later, she married Lieutenant John Hall, whom she would also outlive. During her son's inauguration in Philadelphia, she lay weak in her bed, tended by her daughter-in-law Abigail Adams. She died on April 21, 1797, six weeks after her son took the oath of office.

3. THOMAS JEFFERSON (1801–1809)

Peter Jefferson (February 29, 1708–August 17, 1757). Peter claimed his inheritance at twenty-three when his father, Thomas Jefferson II, died, leaving him land, livestock, and servants. Peter settled in an uncharted area of Virginia and over the next ten years slowly gained prominence. But in October 1739, when he married Jane Randolph, his social standing rose dramatically.

Although Peter lacked a formal education, he valued learning; and he instilled that esteem in his third son, Thomas, sending him to study English at age five and Latin at age twelve. As Thomas grew older, he recognized the gaps in his father's education and was at times self-conscious about them. Yet he had great respect and admiration for Peter's strength, bravery, and sense of adventure. "My father's education had been quite neglected; but being of a strong mind, sound judgment, and eager information, he read much and improved himself." [5]

In addition to developing his tobacco plantation and serving his community, Peter Jefferson worked as a surveyor. Thomas would sit mesmerized by his father's tales of journeys through barely navigable country as his team surveyed and created maps that helped define much of Maryland, Pennsylvania, New Jersey, and North Carolina.

After frequent doctor's visits throughout the summer, Peter unexpectedly died from undetermined causes on August 17, 1757. At forty-nine, he left a generous inheritance to his wife and his eight children. Perhaps the bequests most appreciated by his son, Thomas, were his writing desk, his library, and his love for learning.

Jane Randolph Jefferson (February 20, 1720–March 31, 1776). Born in London, Jane Randolph is best known for her ancestry and the fact that her president son hardly mentions her in his prolific writings. At nineteen, Jane met Colonel Peter Jefferson, who was temporarily living in England. Though he was notably her inferior in social status, he won her hand, taking her back to Virginia where she became his bride on October 3, 1739. Within a few years, the young family moved to an uncleared plot of land. Although it began as a modest homestead, Jane would eventually name it the Shadwell plantation after her genteel birthplace. It was here that she gave birth to her third child and first son, Thomas Jefferson.

Jane was widowed when Thomas was fourteen. Some believe that Thomas may have transformed his grief at the loss of his father into blame of his mother. However, he remained in close proximity to her, returning home after completing his education and living with her till age twenty-seven. A few months before her son penned the Declaration of Independence, Jane Randolph Jefferson died of a sudden stroke. Although she never lived at her son's famous estate at Monticello, her small, shaded grave is nearby.

4. JAMES MADISON (1809–1817)

James Madison, Sr. (March 27, 1723–February 27, 1801). James Madison's carefree days of childhood came to an abrupt end when he was nine and his father died. At age eighteen, he came into his full inheritance, which included an 8,000-acre estate in Orange County, Virginia. From an early age James took much of the responsibility for the daily operation of the family's tobacco plantation.

In September 1749, at the age of twenty-six, James Madison married Nelly Conway, daughter of the wealthy warehouse owner to whom he shipped tobacco. Almost two years later, their first son, James Madison, was born. As James Senior's young family and his landholdings increased, so did his civic involvement. First, he served the Anglican church by overseeing alms to the poor; then he became a justice of the peace.

Following news of the Boston Tea Party, American colonists were torn between allegiance to the king and loyalty to the colonies. In December 1774, James Senior chose the side of the rebels and organized the Orange County Committee for Public Safety.[6] In preparation for war against the Crown, the committee mustered troops and assembled artillery. On May 9, 1775, James Senior wrote a letter to Patrick Henry, voicing the support of the Virginia settlement for the use of force against England.[7]

Nepotism was a force in Virginia. James Madison, Sr., was county lieutenant and so his son was appointed second in command. Together, they supported the Revolution. While the father eventually retired from his military career, he continued to open political doors for his son. Financially supported by his father during his service as a member of the Continental Congress, the future president was unhindered by the colony's insufficient provision for its delegation.

James Madison, Sr., died at seventy-seven, not seeing his son accept appointment as secretary of state under Thomas Jefferson. The great love and respect his son felt for him is evident in their personal correspondence. The president's letters to his father always began, "Honored sir," and closed, "Your dutiful son."

Eleanor "Nelly" Rose Conway Madison (January 9, 1731–February 11, 1829). Nelly Rose Conway was born in Port Conway, Virginia. The daughter of a successful planter who also owned a tobacco warehouse, at eighteen she became the bride of James Madison, one of her father's business associates.

James Senior and Nelly started their family in a modest wooden house against the backdrop of the Blue Ridge Mountains. James Madison, Jr., would be called Jemmy by his family in order to avoid confusion with the father. Nelly gave birth to twelve children, burying five before they reached maturity. Eventually, as the Madison family grew, a larger house was needed. It was completed in 1760; even it was modest compared with the remodeled version dubbed Montpelier by Jemmy.

As mistress of the growing estate, Nelly set an example of love and kindness for her children, guiding and nurturing them and encouraging her husband in his political pursuits. When her children were small, most of their playmates were the children of the family's slaves. The Madisons were known for their kind regard to those who served the family, making sure all were educated and received proper care. James learned reading, writing, and arithmetic at home. When he was eleven, Nelly and her husband placed him under the tutelage of Donald Robertson, an instructor at what was considered the finest school in the Virginia region. There he studied Latin and Greek, history, the sciences, and classical literature. When James was in college at Princeton and later in his travels, Nelly continued to send tokens of her love, from home-sewn shirts to fresh tubs of butter.

Nelly Madison was widowed at sixty-eight. While she suffered chronically in her later years from malaria, she was still a strong and gracious woman. The good-natured Nelly lived in a semiprivate apartment in the Montpelier mansion until her death at ninety-eight. Even in her late years it was said that she had fewer wrinkles than her seventy-seven-year-old son, who was considered the last of our founding fathers.

5. JAMES MONROE (1817–1825)

Spence Monroe (?–1774). Spence Monroe, a third-generation settler in the New World, was too poor to pay for college; he apprenticed with a carpenter. In England, carpentry was considered menial labor, beneath the dignity of a landowner. Yet much of the American frontier was still to be settled; with the high demand for skilled workers, English custom mattered little. Spence combined his fine carpentry skills and the meager production from his sandy-soiled plantation to adequately provide for his family. The historian Stuart Gerry Brown describes Spence as a "very worthy and respectable citizen."[8] Monroe married Elizabeth Jones in 1752 and settled in Westmoreland County, Virginia, where their first son, the future president James Monroe, was born on April 28, 1758.

Although there is no record of his receiving formal legal training, Spence Monroe became a circuit judge. His opposition to the Stamp Act and support of the colonies' boycott of English goods leagued him with George Washington and other Virginia revolutionaries.

Perhaps because Spence's education had been lacking, he sent eleven-year-old James to Campbelltown Academy, under the direction of Reverend Archibald Campbell of Washington Parish.[9] At sixteen, James began studying at William and Mary College.

Spence Monroe died while James was in his first year of college. Spence's brother-in-law, Judge Joseph Jones, was named guardian for the children and the executor of the estate, which passed in its entirety to James, the firstborn son. The future president continued studying at William and Mary until he, too, caught revolutionary fever; he dropped out of college, never to return, and joined the Continental Army in 1776.

Elizabeth Jones Monroe (?–?). Of Welsh descent, Elizabeth Jones was born in King George County, Virginia. No date of birth or death has been recorded. While history reveals little of this woman's life, the few available bits of information reflect warmly upon her character.

Elizabeth became the bride of Spence Monroe in 1752, bringing money with her. Both of her parents were wealthy, as was her esteemed brother, Judge Joseph Jones of Fredericksburg. Elizabeth was said to be better educated than most young women of the time and probably had a hand in furthering her firstborn son's education. One historian describes Elizabeth as "a very amiable and respectable woman, possessing the best domestic qualities, a good wife and a good parent." [10]

6. JOHN QUINCY ADAMS (1825–1829)

John Adams (October 19, 1735–July 4, 1826). John Quincy Adams's father was the first man to be both president and the father of a president.

At John Adams's birth, his parents agreed that their firstborn son would receive a college education. John enjoyed carefree days unburdened by his destiny, shooting marbles and flying kites and indulging in his passion for hunting. He was said to carry a gun to school, and besides bringing home books to study, he would often bring home fresh game for the dinner table.

His indifference to learning set him at odds with his father. However, he eventually accepted both the challenge and the responsibility. Under the tutelage of Joseph Marsh, one of the most respected teachers in the New England colonies, John became attentive to his studies and was accepted at Harvard.

John Adams's first employment was as a teacher for five- to fifteen-year-old boys and girls in Worcester, Massachusetts. He detested teaching, eventually finding daily refuge in the law offices of James Putnam. In 1758, he was admitted to the Massachusetts bar and began his law practice in Braintree.

At twenty-nine, with his fledgling practice and a small inheritance from his father, John Adams married Abigail Smith. Their first child was a daughter, Nabby. Their second was christened John Quincy Adams after his great-grandfather.

John was away on America's business through much of his children's youth. However, when John Quincy Adams was ten, his international education began as he accompanied his father to Paris. Residing in a flat with Benjamin Franklin, John pursued political matters while his son continued his studies in a local boarding school. It was a bonding experience for the two.

Work abroad continued, and in 1785, John Adams was appointed minister to England. This position was followed by two terms as

George Washington's vice president, and then his own term as president. When John Quincy was elected president, John Adams said, "No man who ever held the office of President would congratulate a friend on attaining it." On July 4, 1826, as the nation celebrated its fiftieth birthday, John Adams slipped into a coma and died at his Quincy residence. He was ninety years old.

Abigail Smith Adams (November 11, 1744–October 28, 1818). Considered a delicate child who was too ill to be sent to school, Abigail was taught to read by her mother, her elder sister, Mary, and her parson father; she was free to explore her father's extensive library. Her exuberant personality and quick wit set her apart from the other young women of Weymouth, Massachusetts.

When Abigail first met John Adams, she was intrigued by his directness. However, her interest went no further. When their paths crossed two years later, they recognized their passion, and finally, after three more years had passed while John established his law practice, they were married, on October 25, 1764.

As her husband was often traveling throughout the colonies or abroad, Abigail raised their children largely alone, and John Quincy became a source of strength and support. Because schools closed during the years of the Revolution, education took place at home where Abigail, zealous to see him succeed, became her son's primary tutor.

Perhaps Abigail Adams was born too early for her time. She had uncanny insight and social grace, both skills that benefit a politician. While her husband was in Philadelphia with the Continental Congress, Abigail quickly aligned herself with George Washington as he arrived to help defend Boston. With her political contacts and keen eye, Abigail was able to relay information to her husband which kept him abreast of the tenor of the city. Seldom encumbered by society's limits upon her as a woman, Abigail took John Quincy, then seven, to the top of Penn's Hill to witness the far-off Battle of Bunker Hill. With such a vantage point, she could vividly describe the "amazing roar of [the] cannon" in her correspondence with her husband.[11]

Abigail's international travel began in 1784 when she took leave of her family to travel with her husband to London. She is considered one of America's most accomplished first ladies and in retirement skillfully opened the door to help restore her husband's lost friendship with Thomas Jefferson. She was invaluable in the life of two presidents, her husband and her son. Outspoken in a day when women kept quiet, the life of Abigail Smith Adams marked a historical benchmark for women. Her death at the age of seventy-three from typhoid fever left John Adams, her "dearest friend," alone.

7. PRESIDENT ANDREW JACKSON (1829–1837)

Andrew Jackson (?–1767). Andrew Jackson, the father of the seventh president, left his farm in Antrim County, Ireland, in 1765. With his wife, Elizabeth, and their two young sons, he likely settled in Pennsylvania before moving on to a small plot of land on the border between North and South Carolina. After a few short years clearing land and planting crops, Andrew sustained an injury lifting a log and died, leaving his pregnant wife and two young sons alone.

Elizabeth "Betty" Hutchinson Jackson (?–1781). Two weeks after her husband's death, Elizabeth gave birth to her third son. In his father's memory, she christened him Andrew. According to some sources, she had hoped he would become a Presbyterian minister, but the Revolutionary War changed everything. Hugh, Elizabeth's oldest son, died during the war. Both Robert and thirteen-year-old Andrew were captured after a bloody encounter with the British. When the boys defied an order by a British officer to clean his muddy boots, he slashed them with his saber. Andrew was wounded on his face and hand; Robert's injury may have been fatal.

When Elizabeth learned that her boys were being held prisoner at a Camden prison camp, she negotiated with a militia captain for a prisoner exchange and won the release of her sons. Shortly afterward, however, Robert died, either from his infected sword wound or in the smallpox epidemic that was claiming lives throughout the colonies. Left with one son who was also fighting for his life, Elizabeth tended Andrew tenaciously.

Once she believed Andrew was out of danger, her compassion led her to aid other suffering young men. In the summer of 1781, Elizabeth joined the war effort and traveled to Charleston, where she provided care to American soldiers who were being held prisoner on British ships. In the confines of the ships, disease spread rapidly. After helping to nurse a family friend back to health from cholera, she succumbed to the illness and was buried in an unmarked grave with other victims. Elizabeth's final, tearful words to her son before leaving for Charleston were forever etched on his mind. "Andy, never tell a lie, nor take what is not your own, nor sue . . . for slander." [12]

8. PRESIDENT MARTIN VAN BUREN (1837–1841)

Abraham Van Buren (February 17, 1737–April 8, 1817). Martin Van Buren said little regarding his father. He noted that, admirably, his father had no enemies. Less admirably, his father had no money, as he managed to spend all that passed through his hands. Abraham was born of Dutch descent in Albany, New York, the fifth of nine children. He followed three generations of Van Burens who inhabited the settlement. Notwithstanding his birth order, upon his father's death Abraham inherited the family's farm, slaves, and Kinderhook tavern. He did not, however, inherit the means to successfully run the businesses.

At thirty-nine, the poor tavern owner was unappealing to most young women seeking some sense of security. However, he married Maria Van Hoes, a poor yet attractive widow ten years younger, with three children to feed. Together, Abraham and Maria had two daughters, followed by three sons, future president Martin being their firstborn. With eight children and a number of slaves to feed and clothe, resources were limited. Young Martin's education was limited to a rustic little village school. One brief success was Abraham's appointment as captain of the Seventh Regiment of the Albany County Militia. Finding himself unqualified as a military tactician, he quickly resigned. [13]

Whatever his shortcomings, Abraham's tavern became the local stop for all important visitors and provided Martin with a forum for public affairs that transcended the family's poor financial status. Abraham's renowned hospitality was a lesson for young Martin and a starting point for his political career. Abraham Van Buren would die at the age of eighty. His son, Martin, then a state senator, later became America's eighth president.

Maria Hoes Van Alen Van Buren (1747–February 16, 1818). [14] Born in Claverack, a Dutch village neighboring Kinderhook, Maria was the daughter of a respected family. At twenty, the attractive Maria married Johannes Van Alen. When Johannes died, she was left almost penniless with three young children. Determined to provide for her family, she married the forty-nine-year-old bachelor Abraham Van Buren. She had no dowry and three children to feed; he had a reputation for poor financial management but owned land and a local tavern and inn on the road between Albany and New York. They were married in 1776, even as the United States declared its independence.

Thanks to Abraham's benevolent attitude and Maria's resourcefulness, the tavern succeeded, but his propensity for loaning money to strangers, combined with an inability to collect a debt, left the family with little funds. Maria gave birth to two daughters and then three sons. In Martin, her firstborn son, she recognized promise. While Abe failed to see the value of an education for his children and wanted to put them to work, Maria persuaded her husband to allow Martin to attend school. Although he did not get the formal education afforded other presidents, Martin was given the modest foundation needed for his future career.

Their financial burdens notwithstanding, Maria's marriage to Abraham Van Buren grew into a union of great love and affection. Maria was seventy when her second husband died. She herself passed away within the year. Her son, for whom she had sacrificed, was then both a legislator and attorney general for the state of New York.

9. PRESIDENT WILLIAM HENRY HARRISON (1841)

Benjamin Harrison V (April 5, 1726–April 24, 1791). One of the signers of the Declaration of Independence, Benjamin Harrison blazed a political path for his son to follow. Born into wealth, he was charming and lived lavishly. "The Harrison family was one of the oldest in the colony and was highly respected; none could boast of more extensive and influential connections."[15] Benjamin's father already owned numerous plantations, but his wealth increased when he married Anne Carter, daughter of one of the wealthiest men in America. Benjamin Harrison V was born at the family plantation, Berkeley, which overlooked the picturesque James River in Charles County, Virginia.

Benjamin studied at William and Mary College but did not complete his education. In 1748, he married Elizabeth Bassett and, in the same year, began service in the House of Burgesses. What followed was a lifetime of public service, including stints in the Continental Congress and the Virginia House of Delegates, as a colonel in the militia, and as governor of the state of Virginia. His family holdings flourished and his wife Elizabeth had seven children. The youngest, William Henry Harrison, was, like his father, born in the family mansion.

Benjamin Harrison V succumbed to complications from gout and died at his Berkeley plantation on April 24, 1791. William Henry Harrison was forced to abandon his pursuit of a medical degree. The family was rich in land but had no cash to pay for his education. He embarked on a stellar military career and was elected president in 1841.

Elizabeth Bassett Harrison (December 13, 1730–1792). Although she was the wife of a prominent Virginia politician and a distant relative of Martha Washington, so little is known of Elizabeth Bassett Harrison that she is considered one of the "missing mothers of Virginia." [16] Elizabeth was born into a life of comfort at the Eltham plantation in New Kent County, Virginia. She was said to be quite beautiful, and, at eighteen, married Benjamin Harrison V, a prestigious landowner and rising political figure.

Over the next twenty-two years, she gave birth to seven children, four girls and three boys. As her husband was thoroughly involved in politics, she spent a great deal of time alone, guiding the development of her children. Each was said to have received the basics of education from tutors at the family estates. The Harrisons' lives were defined by comfort in spite of the political chaos around them. However, when William was nearly eight, the horrors of the Revolutionary War came to their doorstep. At her husband's summons, Elizabeth and her children hastily packed up and rushed out of their famous Berkeley mansion in an attempt to escape the advance of troops under the command of Brigadier General Benedict Arnold.[17] The family escaped, but furnishings, slaves, and cattle were abandoned to the Loyalist troops.

The Harrison family did not immediately return to Berkeley but rather took up residence in Richmond, where Benjamin would eventually serve as governor of Virginia. Elizabeth and her husband returned to the Harrison plantation at the completion of his term. Benjamin served as a legislator until his death. William continued to study medicine following his father's death, but joined the army before completing his studies. He was stationed at Fort Washington (Cincinnati), Ohio, at the time of his mother's death at the Berkeley plantation. Enterprising political campaigners would spread the word that William Henry Harrison was a man of the people, born and raised in a log cabin. In fact, the Harrisons were even then one of the nation's greatest political dynasties.

10. PRESIDENT JOHN TYLER (1841–1845)

John Tyler (February 28, 1747–January 6, 1813). A lawyer, a planter, and a politician, John Tyler, Sr., plowed a path for his son to follow. He was born into a life of privilege, the Tylers being one of the First Families of Virginia. At eighteen, he was a law student at William and Mary; he and his roommate, Thomas Jefferson, listened to the fiery oratory of their hero, Patrick Henry.[18] Soon both were consumed with the Revolutionary cause. After finishing his degree, Tyler quickly enlisted in the militia to further the cause of freedom.

In 1776, Tyler was wed to Mary Armistead, the young daughter of a prominent landowner. They moved to a Greenway, 1,900-acre plantation in Charles County, Virginia, and established a family of their own. The next year John left the militia and claimed a seat in the House of Delegates. Throughout his life, he was a forceful advocate for states' rights.

Tyler's sixth child, John Tyler, Jr., was born on March 29, 1790, and raised on the Greenway plantation. He was seven when his mother died. John Tyler, Sr., a judge and politician was suddenly thrust into the role of both father and mother to his eight children. His work as a stern statesman soon gave way to gentle love as a nurturing father. He was said to play lively fiddle music for hours under a willow tree to entertain his young family. Regaling them with his stories of the Revolution and sharing his love for literature, John Tyler forged a close relationship with his children, especially the young son who bore his name. He is often described as the future president's most influential teacher. Having taken on the role of an active, hands-on father, which was uncommon for the time, John Senior became guardian to more than twenty other, mostly orphaned, children who would also call the Greenway plantation home.

The family political philosophy sometimes manifested itself in remarkable ways. At age eleven, John Junior led a schoolroom revolt against a teacher, William McMurdo, who believed wholeheartedly that "the rod was one of the three R's."[19] After suffering enough of what they deemed abuse, John and his friends subdued McMurdo, bound him, and locked him in the schoolhouse. Upon being released by a passerby, McMurdo raced to John Senior, expecting his full support. To his dismay, it was not John Junior who received an immediate reprimand: John Senior "responded by reciting the Virginia state motto: 'Sic semper tyrannis' [Ever thus to tyrants] and sent McMurdo on his way."[20]

John Senior sent his son to study at nearby William and Mary as both he and his father before him had done. During his three terms as Virginia's governor (1809–1811), John Senior took his son as an aide, introducing him to many influential leaders, including Thomas Jefferson. John Senior was a public servant till the day he died and his son, who was then serving in the state legislature, would carry his name on to the White House.

Mary Armistead Tyler (1761–April 1797). The only daughter of a wealthy landowner, Mary Armistead gave the Tyler family a link to one of the great Virginia Colonial dynasties. Little else is known about her, although contemporaries remarked on her beauty. At the tender age of sixteen, Mary Armistead became the bride of a rising political figure, John Tyler. They were married in 1776 in Elizabeth City County, Virginia, and soon after they inherited the 1,900-acre family plantation known as Greenway.

Mary Tyler was said to have been quite shy, in contrast to her outspoken husband. Over the next twenty years, she gave birth to eight children, John Junior being her sixth. According to family lore, as her infant son sat in her lap, he reached toward the moon as if to pull down the shining orb. Proclaiming it a sign of his great aspirations, Mary announced, "This child is destined to be a president of the United States, his wishes fly so high."[21] But her influence on John's life was cut short: he was only seven when she died. "She who nurtured us in our infancy," the president wrote, "taught us to raise our little hands in prayer . . . and reared us to manhood in the love and practice of virtue—such a mother is of priceless value."[22]

11. PRESIDENT JAMES POLK (1845–1849)

Samuel Polk (July 5, 1772–November 5, 1827). Raised by an ambitious surveyor, Samuel Polk gleaned from his father the desire and skill necessary to succeed in the growing frontier. His education was rudimentary but sufficient to gain the attention of the beautiful daughter of James Knox. The two were wed on Christmas Day, 1794, in a double ceremony with Samuel's brother and his bride. Ten months later, future president James K. Polk was born, the first of ten children.

Samuel Polk demonstrated his stubborn nature on more than one occasion. Although he was a man of devout faith he did not share his wife's commitment to the Presbyterian Church. Without the father's public profession of faith, the Presbyterian minister would not baptize young James. Neither minister nor parishioner would bend, and the Polk family left the ceremony with the baptism incomplete. President James K. Polk would finally undergo Christian baptism on his deathbed at age fifty-three.

A resourceful man, Samuel Polk moved his young family from their home in North Carolina to Tennessee, where his father had gained numerous landholdings from government surveying and grants. There the family prospered. Samuel would soon own thousands of acres of land and more than fifty slaves. He would help found the Columbia newspaper and dabble in banking.

Samuel applied his famous stubborn streak to the raising of his James. First he trained his son in surveying, an occupation that had served both he and his father well. But James lacked the strength and constitution required to tramp through the rugged, undeveloped wilderness. Then Samuel secured a position for his son as a store clerk. But James lacked his father's merchandising spirit, and that experiment failed as well. Finally, James found academic success at a local Presbyterian academy. Samuel was relieved and steadfastly supported his son's academic advancement. When James pursued a legal career, his father became his first client. Charged with breach of the peace after losing his temper in an argument, Samuel Polk was fined one dollar and dismissed from the court.[23]

Samuel's drive and determination carried him through many enterprising opportunities and helped guide his son's steps. His health began failing in his late forties, and, with both mind and body weakened, he died at age fifty-five.

Jane Knox Polk (November 15, 1776–January 11, 1852). Jane Knox was born into a family that was dedicated, devout, and industrious. While she was still in her mother's arms, her father was whisked off to serve in the American Revolution. Jane was "a rigid Presbyterian, and a woman of keen intellect and high character."[24] She was descendant of the "father of Scotch Presbyterianism, [and it] was a legacy she didn't take lightly."[25]

On Christmas Day in 1794, Jane Knox became the bride of Samuel Polk. On November 2, 1795, the first of ten children was born. James Knox Polk would develop a close relationship with his mother. He accepted her faith and her sense of duty, and in the process may have failed to develop some of the manly features his father was expecting. Pleasure lacked purpose, in Jane's Presbyterian faith. As a result, she encouraged her son in his educational pursuits but especially in his devotion to God and Presbyterianism. It may be said that Jane's one disappointment was her son's decision to enter the law rather than the ministry. But she watched with veiled pride as her son was sworn in to the highest office in the land.

James K. Polk was in declining health when he left the White House, and his mother urged his Christian baptism. In a final act of independence and maybe to honor his father's memory, he acceded to a baptism but chose a Methodist ceremony rather than a Presbyterian. He died shortly afterward, at the age of fifty-three. Jane Knox Polk lived on two more years, becoming the first presidential mother to outlive her son.

12. PRESIDENT ZACHARY TAYLOR (1849–1850)

Richard Taylor (April 3, 1744–January 19, 1829). A planter, statesman, and lieutenant colonel in the Continental Army, Richard Taylor enjoyed the comforts of a wealthy colonial life, including an education at William and Mary College. During the war, Taylor met and married Sarah Dabney Strother, the beautiful daughter of a wealthy plantation owner. Richard was thirty-five, his bride eighteen. The couple took up residence on the Hare Forest plantation in Orange County, Virginia where three sons were born, the last one being future president Zachary Taylor.

When Lieutenant Colonel Richard Taylor returned home from the Revolutionary War, he was given a hero's welcome and the disappointing news that Virginia could not afford to pay monetary bonuses to their officers. As compensation, he was granted 8,000 acres in Kentucky, on the western edge of the newly formed United States. It was a remote and dangerous place, a frontier territory where the white man and Indian still clashed. Anxious to explore his new land, Richard quickly sold his Virginia holdings and ventured west. But Kentucky was nothing like the more civilized world they had left behind. The ease of plantation life gave way to a modest log cabin and the omnipresent terror of Indian raids. With the help of slave labor, Richard Taylor slowly carved out his own little paradise in the remote lands. His noted military record and growing social standing made him an influential player in the foundation of the state's government. He wrote and later revised a constitution. He served as legislator, presidential elector, justice of the peace, and county magistrate.

Zachary Taylor's pursuits were often an attempt to mimic his father. He, too, became a student of military strategy and pursued a military career. While the son's interests had not originally leaned toward public office, Zachary Taylor not only matched, but exceeded his father's achievements. He also became the last American president to own slaves. Shortly before Richard's death at eighty-four, his son Zachary complained in a letter to his sister of their father's "senile stubbornness."[26] Yet it was that very resolution that made Richard Taylor a formidable military leader, outstanding citizen and powerful father figure to young Zachary.

Sarah Dabney Strother Taylor (December 14, 1760–December 13, 1822). Born on a plantation west of Fredericksburg, Virginia, the young heiress became a well-educated woman for her day, thanks to her European tutors. On August 20, 1779, while the Revolutionary War raged on, she married Lieutenant Colonel Richard Taylor, a rising military leader of acceptable social standing seventeen years her senior. The historian Brainerd Dyer says of Sarah that "only a woman of courage, strength, and fortitude, a full match for her soldier husband, could have played the part in the strenuous pioneer life."[27]

The family first took up residence in a comfortable Virginia plantation. However, after the birth of two sons and near the end of her third pregnancy, her husband decided to follow his adventurous nature and move to the unsettled Kentucky frontier. Leaving the comforts of her genteel life behind, Sarah packed up her young brood and began their trek across the unknown path to Kentucky. Unfortunately, her "third pregnancy complicated the move. Her husband arranged for her to complete her confinement at Montebello, a plantation . . . owned by his cousin Valentine Johnson."[28] There, on November 24, 1784, Sarah gave birth to Zachary Taylor.

When she arrived with her husband and three young children, the unsettled countryside was far from peaceful. She established what sense of home she could in her new log cabin. She did not have to rough it for long. A new house was built on a creek, allowing easy transportation of goods. Soon, she enjoyed most of the refinements of good living that she and other women like her had left behind in Virginia.

The one missing element of civilized life was schools of higher learning. Using the knowledge that she had gained from her own English tutors, Sarah became her son's most consistent teacher. Zachary, far more interested in following in his father's military footsteps, proved a recalcitrant student. He would never be esteemed for his academic brilliance, but his strategic and tactical skill on the battlefield would earn him a reputation for military genius. Although Sarah was much younger than her husband, she preceded him to the grave, dying at the age of sixty-one long before her son attained the presidency.

13. PRESIDENT MILLARD FILLMORE (1850–1853)

Nathaniel Fillmore (April 19, 1771–March 28, 1863). Born in Bennington, Vermont, Nathaniel grew into a strong, handsome, blond youth with an adventurous spirit. He was twenty-five when he married sixteen-year-old Phoebe Millard, daughter of a prominent physician. But his optimism was soon dimmed by the challenges of farming in the rocky soil of Vermont. When approached by land agents offering stunning tracts in nearby New York, Nathaniel and his brother quickly grabbed the opportunity, sight unseen.

The Fillmore brothers moved their two families to their new homeland nestled deep within a forest. Location was not their greatest problem. Nor was the dense clay they unearthed once the land was cleared. Their greatest setback came with the realization that faulty surveying coupled with corruption among local government officials had left them with virtually nothing. Duped, tired, and poor, Nathaniel eventually became a tenant farmer, working the soil for landlords and taking their charity to survive.

Reduced to virtual servanthood, Nathaniel could see no way out for himself. The future of the family depended on helping his son break free. Millard Fillmore, the thirteenth president, was second of nine children born to Nathaniel and Phoebe. He was the oldest son and much depended on his success. Born on January 7, 1800, Millard arrived just before the loss of the family's New York property. At first, working a farm for a landlord demanded every waking hour of the whole family, and the strong, young Millard could hardly be spared. But eventually, Nathaniel was able to redistribute the family workload to free Millard for other projects. These were frustrated again and again. Poverty meant political and social impotence, and employers were quick to take advantage of the weakness. After many setbacks, Nathaniel's dreams for his son eventually prevailed. Millard secured an education, launched a career in law, won a seat in the New York State Assembly, then entered the U. S. Congress. In July 1850, with the death of Zachary Taylor, Vice President Millard Fillmore was sworn in as president.

Nathaniel Fillmore became the first father to be entertained by a son in the White House. As he stood next to his illustrious son, a guest posed the obvious question "How does one raise a son to become president?" When the guest departed, Nathaniel quietly "confided to a friend, 'If I could have the power of marking out the pathway in life for my son, it would never have led to this place, but I cannot help feeling proud of it now that he is here.' "[29]

Although Nathaniel Fillmore lacked the financial clout of so many other early presidential families, his dreams and hopes for his son helped guide the way. After a lifetime of strenuous work, Nathaniel Fillmore would live comfortably to the age of ninety-two, longer than any other father of a president.

Phoebe Millard Fillmore (1780–May 2, 1831). The young daughter of a prominent doctor, Phoebe said good-bye to comfort when she said "I do" to Nathaniel Fillmore. Handsome and robust, he had caught her eye, and they were wed when she was sixteen. Phoebe and Nathaniel soon moved to New York, where she gave birth to her first son on January 7, 1800. Desperately poor, with her family reduced to the status of tenant farmers, Phoebe managed to impart to Millard her great love for learning, teaching him to read and to write.

Some historians credit Phoebe with convincing her husband to secure a clerk's position for Millard in the office of their landlord, Judge Woods. When his mother surprised him with the news at the dinner table, Millard apparently cried openly, unable to contain his joy. The job was short-lived, but it gave her son his first glimpse of the world of law, and he quickly recognized the possibilities of life beyond their tenant shack. Phoebe Millard Fillmore, mother to nine children, was destined to spend her life in poverty and hardship. She would live to see her son admitted to practice law at the Court of Common Pleas and elected to the New York State legislature. But she would die young, still poor, unaware that she had shaped and inspired the life of an American president.

14. PRESIDENT FRANKLIN PIERCE (1853–1857)

Benjamin Pierce (December 25, 1757–April 1, 1839). Benjamin was the seventh of ten children born to Benjamin and Elizabeth Pierce, of Chelmsford, Massachusetts. The young boy was six when his father died suddenly, leaving him no inheritance and forcing his move into an uncle's home. Education gave way to work for young Pierce, who was only able to attend the local school three weeks each a year, spending the bulk of his time laboring on his uncle's farm.

When the Revolutionary War erupted, Benjamin Pierce was not far away. Nathaniel Hawthorne writes: "He immediately loosened the ox chain, left the plough in the furrow, took his uncle's gun and equipments, and set forth towards the scene of action." [30] In his nearly nine years of military service, Benjamin Pierce moved up in rank, fighting at Saratoga and Bunker Hill, and surviving the frigid, desperate conditions of Valley Forge. As head of the militia he earned the rank of brigadier general.

After the war, Benjamin worked surveying land in nearby New Hampshire. Taken with the possibilities, he quickly snatched up a small farm for one dollar an acre and turned his attention toward marriage and family. In 1787, Benjamin Pierce married Elizabeth Andrews, but she died eighteen months later giving birth to their surviving daughter, her namesake, Elizabeth.

During the next few years, Benjamin was occupied with raising a daughter and climbing the political ladder. He organized Hillsborough's militia, was a delegate to the Constitutional Convention, and served as a state legislator. On February 1, 1790, he married Anna Kendrick, a charming and extravagant young woman. They would have eight children together; Anna indulged Elizabeth as if she were her own. When their sixth child, Franklin, was born, Benjamin moved his growing family from their rustic log cabin to a striking mansion in Hillsborough's center. The house functioned also as a political office and a tavern, the latter serving to attract recruits to the former.

Somewhat self-conscious about his own lack of education, Benjamin valued education's power for his sons. Franklin first attended a local school. When his academic talent was recognized, he was sent eight miles away to Hancock Academy, a boarding school. One day, weary of schooling, Franklin returned home, announcing that he had already surpassed his father's educational achievements and it was enough. Benjamin listened in silence. After family dinner, he ordered Franklin to a wagon and drove back toward the Academy. Midway in the voyage, in the pouring rain, Benjamin stopped and ordered Franklin to walk the rest of the way. A wet, weary, and bedraggled Franklin Pierce arrived at Hancock Academy, ready to finish his education.

Benjamin served in the legislature for many years. He became the town sheriff and eventually was elected to two terms as governor of New Hampshire, from 1827 to 1829. Benjamin consistently encouraged and financed all of his son's educational pursuits and eventually relinquished his own office space to make room for his son's rising political career. Franklin was in the legislature while his dad was governor. This was the only such conjunction in New Hampshire history. In 1838, Benjamin's beloved wife died. Although she had become senile, and although Benjamin Pierce watched with joy the political career of his son, he missed his wife. Partially paralyzed, he died the following year at the age of eighty-two. His son, the future fourteenth American president, who had already risen in spectacular fashion, was then a U.S. senator from New Hampshire.[31]

Anna Kendrick Pierce (October 30, 1768–December 7, 1838). From Amherst, New Hampshire, Anna Kendrick grew up in an austere Puritan environment as a vivacious young woman who loved flashy clothes. When she moved to Hillsborough, she quickly caught the eye of the thirty-five-year-old widower Benjamin Pierce, a rising political figure and the single parent of a toddler. They were married on February 1, 1790, and she joined her husband and new daughter, Elizabeth, in a rustic log cabin near the Contoocook River. They would have eight children together.

Shortly after the birth of future president Franklin Pierce, the family moved to a mansion in the center of town. When her husband obtained a liquor license and opened a tavern in a portion of their home, Anna became the focus of gossip. Her love of bright, elaborate clothing attracted criticism and she soon began to experience bouts of depression and alcoholic binges. These were troubles that her famous son would battle throughout his own life. Franklin later told biographers that she was only "weak on the side of kindness and deep affection."[32] In her later years, before descending into the haze of senility, Anna took in her orphaned grandchildren. She died at the age of seventy.

15. PRESIDENT JAMES BUCHANAN (1857–1861)

James Buchanan, Sr. (1761–June 11, 1821). Born on the shores of Ireland, James Buchanan suffered the death of his mother and abandonment by his father at a young age. An uncle took him in and raised him. From his early years, James demonstrated a yearning for a better life. When an uncle, Joshua Russell, made the journey across the Atlantic to America, James began dreaming of such an adventure himself. Russell settled near Gettysburg, Pennsylvania, where he ran a local tavern. On July 4, 1783, James Buchanan boarded a vessel bound for the United States.

Shortly after his arrival he met the young Elizabeth Speer, a native Pennsylvanian, and his attachment to her strengthened his drive to succeed. Russell helped him get his start, and thanks to James's fiery dedication and perseverance, it did not take him long to get on his feet. He worked at the Stony Batter trading post as a clerk, saving and shrewdly investing. Within time, James bought the place, a one-hundred-acre tract that included cleared fields, an orchard, a few log cabins, and the store where he had gotten his start.

Shortly after acquiring the trading post, James married his Elizabeth and they took up residence in a log cabin on their new land. James Buchanan, Jr., was born on April 23, 1791. By their fifth year of marriage, James began to grow concerned about how rough and dangerous life was at the trading post. Goal-oriented, honest, and hardworking, he bought a three-hundred-acre estate known as Dunwoodie Farm outside Mercersburg, Pennsylvania; two years later, he purchased another parcel of land in the center of the small town and moved his family there.

James Senior was not playful nor was he at first interested in providing his son with a formal education, but he did diligently train James Junior in matters of business. The father could always account for every penny and was known for his fair treatment of customers. His reputation was rewarded with appointment as the local justice of the peace.

Over time, the family grew: the Buchanans would eventually have eleven children. Meanwhile, the father became convinced that the right kind of education could make a difference in his son's future and ensure financial security for the siblings. Ever ambitious, James decided that his son should practice law. The junior Buchanan was first sent to the Old Stone Academy and then, with the help and recommendation of the family's minister, Dr. John King, he was enrolled in Dickinson College in Carlisle, Pennsylvania. He was sixteen years old, already with junior status.

Once removed from the careful supervision of his industrious father, James Junior ran wild. Citing alcohol, cigars, and pranks, the administration sent home a stinging letter with the announcement that the boy had been expelled. Young James pleaded with Dr. King to help him again. Back in school, James acquitted himself admirably. Eventually, the elder Buchanan's disappointment turned to pride. James's career as a lawyer and politician prospered. In 1820 he was elected to the U.S. House of Representatives.

The following year, at the age of sixty, James Buchanan, Sr., was thrown from his open carriage when a frightened horse bolted. He died without a will. His lawyer son returned to their Mercersburg home and arranged the estate to assure the future of his siblings.

Elizabeth Speer Buchanan (1767–May 14, 1833). Born in Lancaster County, Pennsylvania, Elizabeth Speer was primarily self-educated, as were many women of her time. She carried her love for the Bible and poetry throughout her life, memorizing lengthy passages from John Milton and Alexander Pope. When she was sixteen, she met the young Buchanan, who had joined his tavern-owning uncle. At the time, she was living a rather lonely life in an isolated part of Pennsylvania where she kept house and cared for her widowed father and four brothers.

In 1788, at the age of twenty-one, she married James Buchanan. Just prior to their marriage, her husband had purchased a trading post, and the two moved into one of the small log cabins there. About a year later, their first child was born, a daughter named Mary. A year after Mary came her brother James Buchanan, Jr., on April 23, 1791. Shortly after his birth, the family suffered the tragic death of their infant daughter.

Elizabeth is given much credit for guiding her son both academically and socially. She would use her love of the written language and her quest for knowledge to challenge her children with questions of logic. While her husband hoped for a son who would become a lawyer, Elizabeth had dreams of James becoming a minister, and it was likely she who convinced her husband to release their son from his responsibilities in the store to pursue his academic interests.

Although James Buchanan did not follow his mother's plans for his life, she was nevertheless able to see his great political ascent. When he was named U.S. minister to Russia, she begged him not to go, warning that he would never see her again. True to her word, she died in Greensburg, Pennsylvania, while her son served his country far from home.

16. PRESIDENT ABRAHAM LINCOLN (1861–1865)

Thomas Lincoln (January 6, 1778–January 1851). He was six years old when the family was ambushed by Indians as they were working together to clear their land. His father was murdered before his eyes and he himself was being carried off into the forest when his brother felled his Indian captor with a single well-aimed shot. Thomas Lincoln's education was about survival. Over the next few years, he was passed from one relative to another, working in fields or for neighbors to earn his keep.

As a young man, Thomas was considered a rather successful farmer and a skilled carpenter; he had trained with the talented Joseph Hanks, uncle of his future bride. With his good nature and honest resolve, he gained the respect of his neighbors, serving in the militia and on a number of juries. Short and stocky but strong from years of physical labor, he was said to have a striking presence. In his late twenties, confident of his resources, he turned his attention toward marriage. His first proposal was refused. Undaunted, he turned his attention to the niece of his former teacher and, on June 12, 1806, he married Nancy Hanks. They lived in a succession of log cabins, moving to get closer to water or to find better soil or because of controversies over the title to their property.

Their first child, Nancy "Sarah" Lincoln, was born in a cramped cabin in Elizabethtown, Kentucky. Not long after, Thomas decided to move. He built a more comfortable one-room cabin on a 300-acre farm he called Sinking Spring.[33] It was there, in what is today Larue, Kentucky, that Abraham Lincoln was born on February 12, 1809. Two years later, a little boy named Thomas was born, but he died as a toddler.

When Abe was seven, the Lincolns moved across the Ohio River to Spencer County, Indiana. It was a time of great suffering. The frequent relocations had taken their toll, and Thomas Lincoln's decreasing physical energy and drive began to mark the family's sure decline. In 1818, "milk sickness" plagued the land. Free-roaming cows consumed white snakeroot plants, making their milk poisonous. Those who drank the milk were at risk of succumbing to the mysterious disease. Thomas's wife was stricken, and after seven days of suffering, she died. Thomas carefully built his wife's coffin and, with his mourning children at his side, he buried her in an unmarked grave.

Six months later, he left his children in Indiana and traveled back to Elizabeth, Kentucky, in search of a new wife. A year after his wife's death, he finally married his first love, Sarah Bush Johnston, in an arrangement of mutual need. She had personal debt that needed to be paid. He had children who needed to be raised.

Sarah brought into the marriage three children of her own and some luxuries, including a sturdy table and chairs, a bureau, a spinning wheel, feather beds, dishes, and matching cutlery.[34] She also brought the kindness and love that had been absent since Nancy's death.

Abraham's labor was called upon heavily. He often worked from dawn to dusk. When he was not needed at home, his father would hire him out to neighbors to supplement the family's income.

Thomas expected Abraham's undivided attention to his tasks, and he was known for using physical force to bring Abraham's focus from his books back to his farm work. In Abraham Lincoln's words, "My father taught me to work, but never taught me to love it."[35] Thomas grudgingly allowed Abraham to read in his spare time; the tradition persists that it was only at his stepmother's insistence that the young Lincoln found enough time for reading and study.

Until Abraham was twenty-two and his family moved to Coles County, Illinois, his father required that he turn over any money he earned. When Thomas moved the family again, Abe dutifully followed but soon left to begin charting his own course in life.

While Abraham Lincoln's feelings for his father were conflicted, he seemed unable to blame Thomas for any failure or unkindness. At the time of his father's fatal illness, Abraham was practicing law in Springfield, about seventy miles from the Lincoln home in Coles County. Yet after one visit he resisted all subsequent entreaties to come home to be at his father's side as he died. Nor did he attend the funeral. Shortly after his father's passing, Abraham asked that a marker be placed on Thomas's grave, a request that was ignored. Years later, as the nation's president-elect, he revisited his old home and walked to his father's grave, this time insisting to his entourage that he himself would arrange a proper gravestone. It was a promise that Honest Abe would not keep.

Nancy Hanks Lincoln (February 5, 1784–October 5, 1818). The life of Nancy Hanks was not one of ease. Her young, unmarried mother had fled from her Virginia home to West Virginia, where she gave birth to Nancy. Until her teen years, Nancy was raised by her grandparents. Her mother was once set for trial for the charge of fornication, but the family moved again and the trial was avoided. Eventually, Nancy's mother married and bore legitimate children; the danger of prosecution passed. But the trail of hostile gossip from neighbors and acquaintances would follow her wherever she went for the rest of her life, and a similar cloud hovered over Nancy Hanks.

Following the death of her guardian grandfather, the untutored but intelligent Nancy was taken in by her mother's sister. It would be a life-changing relationship. Nancy's aunt taught her to read the Bible, which offered her a lifetime of solace and escape from her misery. And with her aunt's teaching, she soon became a skilled seamstress. It was during this period of her life that Nancy met Thomas Lincoln, a somewhat successful farmer and an accomplished cabinetmaker. They were married in 1806. She was twenty-two.

Their first daughter was born in a log cabin nine months later. She was named Nancy but the family called her Sarah. Two years later, a second child was born, a boy named Abraham.

Nancy followed her husband through several unsuccessful land purchases and failed farming attempts. With each move, they seemed to lose a bit more. In her final and fatal move, she accompanied her husband to Indiana, where he carelessly built a three-sided dwelling that barely protected her and her children from the rigors of their first winter.

The next year they moved into a new one-room log cabin, but while it provided greater protection from the harrowing winters and encroaching wildlife, the family endured many hardships and the cabin could not wall out disease. Finally, after two difficult years, "milk sickness" swept the Indiana countryside, claiming many lives. The condition was caused by drinking the milk of cows that had foraged on poisonous plants.

Nancy's uncle and aunt had moved to Indiana to join the Lincolns. There was much joy as the family worked together to build a cabin, but the milk sickness took them first. Nancy exhausted herself nursing her family, but in the end she lost them both. They were buried near a creek on a deer run near her cabin. Then, still in her mid-thirties, Nancy succumbed to the same fate.

Her constant admonition to her young son Abraham had been to learn all he could, and some suggest that it partly explains his unrelenting hunger for books. Following her death, he helped his father fashion her coffin, whittling the pegs that held the planks in place, and then stood by Thomas's side as the mother of America's greatest president was buried in an unmarked grave.

Sarah Bush Johnston Lincoln (December 13, 1788–April 12, 1869).[36] Lincoln's stepmother was born in Hardin County, Kentucky. When Sarah was two, her parents and her eight brothers and sisters moved to Elizabethtown, where she was raised.

According to legend, thirteen years later Thomas Lincoln asked for her hand in marriage and she rejected him, marrying instead one Daniel Johnston, a poor man who was eventually appointed the county's jailer. The couple lived with their three children in a corner of the jail, and Sarah cleaned and cooked for the inmates.

Daniel Johnston died in 1816, leaving Sarah with personal debt and no home. She moved into a small cabin that she later purchased and lived there with her three children in what comfort she could provide. When she once again met Thomas Lincoln, ten years her senior, she recognized the opportunity that lay before her. While it may have been more than a marriage of convenience, their union on December 2, 1819, took care of her debt, provided a father to her children, and offered a much-needed mother for the suffering Lincoln home in the Indiana woods.

Although poor, Sarah had a few personal belongings that became treasured items in remote Pigeon Creek. These belongings, which included a solid table, a beautiful walnut bureau, matching silverware, and a spinning wheel, were loaded on a covered wagon and the new family set out to join the Lincoln children, who had been left alone for six months in Indiana.

Of all the Lincoln children, Abraham took to his stepmother most favorably. It is said that he ran into her full skirts and clung to her legs. Sarah's kindness toward her stepson provided an emotional anchor throughout his difficult youth.

According to tradition and family testimony, Sarah insisted that Abraham seek every educational opportunity. Indiana offered no public education for its youth, but among Sarah's possessions were her books. She encouraged her stepson to read, and Abraham responded by virtually memorizing some of the classics she had brought with her. In spite of the rigorous manual labor needed for survival on the frontier, with his stepmother's encouragement young Abe learned to calculate, as well.

Until Abraham was twenty-two, at his father's insistence, he turned over all of his earned money. Deciding that his only chance for a life of his own was to make a complete break, Abraham Lincoln announced he was leaving home. And although he loved his stepmother more than anyone else in the world, he decided that he must greatly reduce his visits to her as well.

When Thomas Lincoln died in 1851, Abraham was finally able to reconnect with his beloved stepmother. He ensured that she would be cared for by giving her a forty-acre plot of land. In her later years, suffering from arthritis, Sarah nevertheless continued to live an energetic life. She remained at her Goosenest Prairie home until her death at the age of eighty on April 12, 1869. She lived through Abraham's presidency and grieved along with his broken country at his assassination.

17. PRESIDENT ANDREW JOHNSON (1865–1869)

Jacob Johnson (April 1778–January 4, 1812). Clearly one of the poorest of presidential fathers, Jacob Johnson was a good man who, according to historian Harold Gullan, "died too soon." [37] His amiable and hardworking nature garnered the respect of the townspeople in Raleigh, North Carolina, where he struggled to eke out an existence.

While Jacob received offers to work on the prominent area plantations, he preferred the chatter and camaraderie of his friends in town, accepting various menial tasks to provide his income. Jacob worked as janitor for the bank, town constable, caretaker for the Presbyterian Church, and town bell-ringer. During his service to the state militia, his friends honored him as their captain.

Among other jobs, Jacob Johnson worked at the local tavern, Casso's Inn, where he met his future wife, Mary McDonough. Like the man she would wed, Mary was illiterate but resourceful and hardworking. The couple married in 1801, combining their small incomes, taking on any task that would bring even a little amount of money.

Ten years into their marriage, on a frigid December day in 1811, Jacob accompanied a group of prominent men on a local fishing trip. According to accounts, Jacob provided food for the outing as well as cleaning the day's catch. In a careless moment, one of the men would change forever the lives of the Johnson family. Colonel Tom Henderson, editor of the *Raleigh Star,* began to playfully rock the canoe that he and two other men were using. The canoe capsized, dumping the three men into the icy water. One man struggled to shore but the other could not swim. In a state of panic, he grabbed Henderson, and together they sank to the bottom. All stood by, aghast. Without hesitation, Jacob dove into the icy water and rescued them both. It was a heroic moment and it saved the lives of the two men, but it would cost him his own. Exhausted, unable to change quickly from his wet clothes, facing frigid temperatures, he became ill. Not long after, ringing the bell for a funeral, he collapsed; he died shortly thereafter, leaving his wife and children alone.

Andrew Johnson, the youngest child and future president, was three years old. All he had of his father was an obituary written by Colonel Henderson on January 12, 1812 for the *Raleigh Star.*

> Died, in this city on Saturday last, Jacob Johnson, who for many years occupied a humble but useful station. He was the city constable, sexton and porter to the State Bank. In his last illness he was visited by the principal inhabitants of the city, by all whom he was esteemed, none lament him, except perhaps his own relatives, more than the publisher of this newspaper, for he owes his life on a particular occasion to the kindness and humanity of Johnson.[38]

Mary "Polly" McDonough Johnson (1783–1856). "Polly the weaver" was petite, poor, and illiterate. As a servant at the local tavern, she did washing and mending for the more prominent families in town. But Polly was attractive and an accomplished seamstress; she could spin and weave her own fabric and she knew how to work hard. It was at Peter Casso's Inn in Raleigh, North Carolina, that she met her husband, Jacob, her social equal. Their union did not ease their financial situation, but they were no longer alone in their poverty.

Mary was eighteen when she became Jacob Johnson's bride. She soon gave birth to her first child, a daughter who would not survive infancy. Two sons followed, Andrew, the younger, was born on December 29, 1808, in a log cabin on the Casso Inn property. Andrew was three when his father died of an illness contracted after rescuing two other men from drowning in icy water.

Mary was now a struggling young widow. Perhaps out of loneliness, perhaps out of her desperate financial need, or perhaps seeking a father for her young sons, she became the wife of Turner Dougherty. What meager benefit she gained from the marriage couldn't have made up for its deprivations. According to one historian, "Her first husband was a good man who died too soon, her second a wastrel who lived too long."[39]

The family had always been too poor for school. The children were needed to work. When Andrew was fourteen and his brother eighteen, Mary arranged for their apprenticeships with James Selby, a tailor in Raleigh. They quickly learned the trade. Andrew was apparently the more talented. Two years into service to Selby, the two boys found themselves in trouble. They had thrown rocks at an elderly woman's house and were on the run for fear of arrest. Selby ran an advertisement in the local newspaper, offering ten dollars for the capture and return of Andrew Johnson. The boys hid out in Carthage, North Carolina, and eventually Andrew convinced his mother and stepfather to move the family to Greeneville, Tennessee. There, at the age of seventeen, Andrew Johnson opened a tailor shop. It was a small beginning that would lead to bigger things. In Tennessee, Andrew organized the local working class and launched a political career that took him to the governor's mansion and eventually the White House.

During one bitter political campaign, rumors began swirling around the legitimacy of his birth. Andrew apparently bore some physical resemblance to a Judge John Haywood, for whom his mother had worked as a washerwoman. No marriage certificate could be found. Johnson returned to North Carolina, produced the legal documents to end the accusations, and redeemed his mother's honor.

Mary Johnson lived on a farm purchased by her son; when she died, he was serving as governor of Tennessee. Despite abject poverty, Mary raised a young man who overcame great personal odds, turned his disadvantages into political equity, and rose to become the seventeenth president of the United States. Gerald F. terHorst, press secretary to Gerald Ford, would write, "Success in American politics is rarely determined by time of birth, place of upbringing, family name, or private wealth. The basic requirement is the possession of certain personal attributes that are in public demand at an hour of public need."[40]

18. PRESIDENT ULYSSES S. GRANT (1869–1877)

Jesse Root Grant (January 23, 1794–June 29, 1873). Jesse Root Grant was a harsh, quarrelsome figure, an outspoken abolitionist while most of his friends and neighbors were tolerant of slavery. Yet he was elected mayor of Bethel, Ohio, and appointed postmaster of Covington, Kentucky.

Born in Westmoreland County, Pennsylvania, near the city of

Greensburg, Jesse was the second of five children. He was ten years old when his mother died; his father, unable to handle the responsibility of his children, dispersed them into various apprenticeships. As luck would have it, Jesse's first apprenticeship was in Youngstown, Ohio, with George Tod, an Ohio Supreme Court judge. Tod taught Jesse to read, sent him to a local school for six months, and allowed him access to his immense library, thus inspiring a lifelong passion for education. Jesse's son Ulysses S. Grant described his father as an avid reader with an unquenchable thirst for learning. "When he got through with a book," Ulysses recalled, "he knew everything in it."

The judge encouraged Jesse to take an active role in planning a future. Together, they established goals that would result in a secure family, retirement, and wealth. The old judge helped secure the sixteen-year-old an apprenticeship at a Kentucky tannery. Through hard work and enterprise, Jesse learned how to turn a handsome profit by tanning leather cheaply and selling the finished product for a higher price. He swiftly developed a knack for negotiations.

Jesse's political views eventually encroached on his livelihood and forced a move from Kentucky. He wrote an open editorial for *The Castigator,* an antislavery newspaper, and publicly announced that he "would not own slaves and I will not live where there are slaves." Adhering to his life plan and political convictions, Jesse moved to Point Pleasant, Ohio, where he started his own tannery yard, built a house, and married Hannah Simpson. On April 27, 1822, the young couple had their first of six children, a boy, who would become president. He remained nameless for almost a month, his mother wanting to name him Albert. They finally settled on Hiram Ulysses but the boy, apparently humiliated by the initials HUG, would later change his name to Ulysses Simpson.

With an expanding business, Jesse purchased property in Georgetown, Ohio, where he built a two-room, two-story house and a tannery, adding on twice to complete the house in 1828. Incredibly proud of his young son, Jesse boasted to all who would listen that his "Ulyss" was destined for greatness. Ulysses suffered under such expectations. Even his slightest mistakes became fodder for ridicule from friends and relatives. An often repeated anecdote has an eight-year-old Ulysses asking his father to buy a horse. Jesse agreed, deciding to use the opportunity to teach the important art of negotiation. Jesse carefully explained how Ulysses should deal with the merchant. But when the time came, Ulysses respectfully told the seller, "My father says I am to offer you first twenty dollars. Then if you don't accept it, I am to offer you twenty-two and a half. If you don't take that, I am only to give you twenty-five at the most." The seller, of course, agreed to the highest price, and Ulysses became the talk of the town, much to Jesse's chagrin.

Since Jesse had only a few months of formal education, he insisted that his firstborn son have the best education money could buy.[41] Ulysses started school at the age of five and continued in subscription schools until his tenth year, when he attended Maysville (Kentucky) Seminary and later the Presbyterian Academy in Ripley, Ohio. In 1838, without speaking with Ulysses, Jessie secured an appointment for his son to the U.S. Military Academy at West Point. Ulysses was reluctant to go, fearing that he would fail, but his father insisted.

As Ulysses became an adult, Jesse's meddlesome nature was often met by his son's equally stubborn resolve. Upon graduation from West Point, Ulysses stunned his father by refusing an army commission. Jessie tried to use his political connections to get the resignation rescinded but failed in the attempt. The Mexican War brought young Grant back into action, but afterward he quit the army again. When, after years of chiding from his father, Ulysses finally returned to the army to support the Union in the great Civil War, Jesse was still not satisfied. He should command a regular army, the father insisted, and not settle for command of the Twenty-First Illinois Infantry Volunteers. He was in the army to win the war, Ulysses replied tersely, not to advance a career.

Ulysses' successes in the military increased his public exposure and with it came a plethora of public criticism. Jesse often felt inspired to defend his son. Embarrassed and troubled by his father's public statements, which although well intentioned were usually counterproductive, Ulysses demanded that his father stop. In a letter dated September 1862, Ulysses struck at the core, "I have not an enemy in the world who has done me so much injury as you in your efforts in my defense. I require no defenders and for my sake let me alone." Military advisers warned Ulysses against sending his father any information regarding troop movements. Jesse would often inadvertently leak such news to journalists.

Meanwhile, Jesse Grant's tanneries and leather goods stores in Ohio, Kentucky, Illinois, and Wisconsin thrived and he amassed a small fortune. At his retirement in 1866, he distributed $150,000 to his children; Ulysses declined, saying that he had not earned the money and so would not feel right in taking it.

When Ulysses S. Grant was promoted as a possible candidate for president, his unrelenting father became a leading supporter, ignoring his son's protests that he had no such ambition and using his political connections to advance the idea. As a Grant campaign staff emerged, Jesse was ordered to take a backstage role. It was feared that the elder Grant would damage his son's chances. But Jesse could not sit still. He addressed a Chicago convention of Civil War veterans and later attended the 1868 Republican National Convention. More meddlesome still, Jesse planted "insider accounts" with major newspapers and befriended journalists who helped and sometimes hurt his son's campaign.

Throughout Ulysses S. Grant's first term in office, his father was often an uninvited White House guest, offering unsolicited advice to those close to the president. Only Ulysses was able to rein him in, thus straining an already difficult father-son relationship. On March 4, 1873, Jesse attended his son's second inauguration. After the ceremony, he slipped and fell on a set of icy steps. Returning home to recover, he promised reporters that he would be back soon to offer the sage advice his son so desperately needed. But, on June 29, 1873, Jesse Root Grant died in Covington, Kentucky, at the age of seventy-nine. Ulysses was inconsolable. Friends' efforts to comfort him were only met with a chilly silence.

Hannah Simpson Grant (November 23, 1798–May 11, 1883). Hannah Simpson was raised on a prosperous farm in Berks County, Pennsylvania, one of four children. Her father, John Simpson, was a kind, Christian man dedicated to his wife and family. Although Hannah's mother died when she was three years old, John was sensible and in no hurry to find a wife. When he finally made his choice several years later, he found a highly refined woman who fully supported his decision to educate his daughters. Hannah attended the local school and developed an extensive reading library.

After the War of 1812, John moved to a six-hundred-acre farm just outside Point Pleasant, Ohio. Deeply Calvinistic, the family was untroubled by Hannah's spinsterhood. She was approaching age twenty-three, long past the prime marrying age for the period. But when a brash Jesse Root Grant confided to John Simpson that he was looking for a wife and that he needed to be married within the year, John began to think of marriage for his daughter. Jesse Root Grant found favor with the educated Simpsons. His love of learning and his life goals fell into line with John's values. Even his verbose personality seemed to complement Hannah's shy and silent nature. He often commented that he did enough talking for the both of them, and most observers agreed.

Jesse left the naming of his firstborn son completely to Hannah. He was nameless for over a month, while Hannah considered the name Albert, though she eventually settled on Hiram to please her father, who thought the boy needed a biblical name, and Ulysses to please her stepmother, who thought that a Greek hero's name would destine the boy for greatness. Jesse never took to the name Hiram Ulysses Grant, opting instead to call the boy Ulyss. Eventually, all of Hannah's searching for the appropriate name went for naught. When a family friend, Representative Thomas L. Hamer, arranged the appointment at West Point for her son, he mistakenly enrolled him as Ulysses S. Grant, assuming his middle name was Simpson after his mother's maiden name. This suited the new cadet just fine as he did not like the initials "H.U.G." stamped on his trunk. He began signing himself Ulysses S. Grant, while classmates just called him U.S. or Uncle Sam.

When Ulysses was growing up, many of the neighbors were concerned about his quiet mother's treatment of him. She often let her infant crawl around the stables, ignoring the great risk of his being trampled. Instead of seeking medical attention when he was sick, she gave him castor oil and put him to bed until he was well. Her ultimate belief was that every day was a gift from God, whose will would ultimately be done. She instilled in her son a benign acceptance of fate.

Ulysses and his mother had a special bond. They had similar personalities. She shunned public attention and spoke only in private conversations. The greatest insights into this unique woman can be gleaned from letters to or about her. Jesse wrote that "her steadiness, firmness, and strength of character have been the stay of the family through life." [42] Ulysses' letters home from West Point are equally tender: "I seem alone in the world without my mother. . . . I cannot tell you how much I miss you. I was so often alone with you, and you so frequently spoke to me in private, that the solitude of my situation here . . . is all the more striking. It reminds me the more forcibly of home, and most of all, dear Mother, of you. . . . Your kindly instructions and admonitions are ever present with me."[43] She died in 1883; two years later, her son, the Civil War hero and former U.S. president Ulysses S. Grant, died as well.

19. PRESIDENT RUTHERFORD BIRCHARD HAYES (1877–1881)

Rutherford Hayes (January 4, 1787–July 20, 1822). The red-haired little boy was nicknamed Ruddy and he was his father's pride. His father was a farmer and blacksmith; believing his son too weak for physical labor, he found him a job as a clerk for his brother-in-law's store in Wilmington, Vermont. There he met Sophia Birchard and was taken by her rosy cheeks and cheery optimism. On September 13, 1813, the couple married. Ruddy was then partner in the Noyes and Mann store, but business suffered during the War of 1812. Ruddy was captain of the militia, but much to Sophia's relief, he did not need to fight.

This was perhaps their only reprieve from sadness. Their first son, to be named Rutherford Birchard Hayes, was born dead. Sophia was familiar with grief, as she had lost her father when she was thirteen and her mother five years later, yet she did not slip into the depression that gripped her husband. Racked by grief, Ruddy struggled forward only with the constant encouragement of his wife.

Ready to leave a Vermont that held bad memories and diminishing opportunities, Ruddy uprooted his family and joined other pioneers on the Cumberland Trail. After a forty-day journey, the family arrived in Delaware, Ohio. They would not find extravagant wealth but they would live in a beautiful brick house in the center of town and own a lucrative farm that yielded abundant crops and a productive orchard. Ruddy opened some businesses of his own and invested in a small distillery. The venture proved profitable, but his temperate wife did not approve.

When typhoid fever swept through the region, the whole family was hit by the epidemic. Young daughter Sarah Sophia died first; then

Ruddy fell ill, dying three days later at the age of thirty-five. His son was born eleven weeks later and was named Rutherford Birchard Hayes in his memory and in that of the family's firstborn who never drew breath. Rutherford B. Hayes was one of three presidents born after the death of their father. (The others were Andrew Jackson and Bill Clinton.)

Sophia Birchard Hayes (April 15, 1792–October 30, 1866). Born and raised in Wilmington, Vermont, Sophia was of English descent. Her father was a farmer and merchant but he died of consumption when Sophia was only thirteen. It would be the first heartbreak of many. And yet, bolstered by her Presbyterian doctrine, she found hope in nearly every moment of despair, and her sunny optimism inspired those around her. Sophia's devout faith was augmented by her love of reading. For Sophia, the popular *Pilgrim's Progress* was second only to the Bible. The two books combined to help shape her strong moral code. She excelled academically, and unlike many women of her day, was able to attend a district school.

After the death of her father, Sophia's mother remarried, but it was a doomed relationship that ended quickly in divorce. Sophia suffered her next great loss at eighteen, when her mother succumbed to spotted fever. But six months after her mother's death, the resilient nineteen-year-old married Rutherford Hayes, an enterprising young merchant. Financially, the marriage prospered, but their personal life was often marked by sadness. In 1814, their first child, who was to be named Rutherford Birchard Hayes, was stillborn. Typically, Sophia helped her husband through the loss. In the next few years, their home was blessed with two healthy, happy children, Lorenzo and Sarah Sophia.

Rutherford's business pursuits were generally successful. However, in the aftermath of war, everyone in Vermont suffered. He persuaded Sophia that Ohio held more promise for the young family, and she, with some sadness at leaving her relatives and birthplace behind, agreed to move on. With their comfortable belongings filling three wagons, the family set off for Ohio. The family eventually moved into a beautiful brick house in the center of the small town of Delaware, where their next daughter, Fanny, was born. Their happiness lasted for five more years before tragedy struck once more. During the summer of 1822, fever swept through the Ohio region. Everyone in the Rutherford home fell ill, including Sophia, who was in her last months of pregnancy. First, she lost her beautiful little Sarah Sophia, and three days later, her husband died.

Eleven weeks later on October 4, 1822, still weakened with fever, Sophia gave birth to a baby boy. She named him Rutherford Birchard Hayes in memory of both his father and his brother. Her losses were still not over. Three years after the death of her husband and daughter, Lorenzo fell through thin ice while skating and drowned. Sophia was left with her son, whom she called Rud, and his older sister, Fanny.

Although it was common for widows to remarry, Sophia pledged never to do so. Perhaps she recalled the unhappy circumstances surrounding her widowed mother's remarriage. In addition, Sophia's devotion to her late husband superseded any desire that she had for a husband's strength and support. To support herself, she rented out the family farm, receiving a third of the crop and half of the fruit from the productive orchards.

Sophia's bachelor brother Sardis Birchard lived with them for a short time, lending his support to his grieving sister. Although he moved on, traveling the world, seeing his business ventures succeed, he would return to Ohio, bringing gifts to the family. He also paid for his nephew's education.

Sophia's losses had been so profound that she could not bear the thought of losing anything more. She was obsessively fearful for her son and overprotective in her care. Rud was seldom out of his mother's sight; he was not allowed to play with other children until he was nine years old, and then only under close scrutiny. Rutherford was taught to read, write, and calculate by his mother and she taught him lessons on morality and religion. Rud was essentially raised in a woman's world, playing with dolls instead of toy soldiers.

When Rud was fourteen, Sophia finally agreed to a public education. Like many of the presidents' mothers, she hoped her son would become a minister. A woman with a strong mind, Sophia applauded the work of the Women's Christian Temperance Union and approved of Sarah Polk's prohibition of liquor in the White House, but she was worried by Rud's interest in public affairs, fearing that it might lead her son into politics. When he studied law, she was saddened but consoled herself with the thought that law was a respectable profession, which need not necessarily lead to public life. In 1852, Rud married Lucy Ware Webb, a well-educated, religious woman, much like his mother.

When the Civil War broke out, Sophia watched her son march away. Within months, families all around her were mourning their dead. With her past losses haunting her, Sophia spent much of the conflict on her knees, praying for Rud's safe return. Despite being wounded several times on West Virginia battlefields, Rutherford B. Hayes came home an honored war hero and a major general of volunteers.

Sophia Birchard Hayes died at age seventy-four in Columbus, Ohio. The very profession she had feared for her son had claimed him. He was serving as a U.S. congressman when she passed away. Two years later, he became governor of Ohio, and eventually he was elected our nineteenth president. But he would carry with him into the White House the principles and devout faith she cherished. Like first lady Sarah Polk, whom his mother had so admired, Lucy Hayes would bar liquor from the White House; she is remembered as "Lemonade Lucy."

20. JAMES A. GARFIELD (1881)

Abram Garfield (December 28, 1799–May 3, 1833). Abram Garfield was born in Worcester, New York, to Thomas Garfield, a man who could trace his lineage all the way back to the Puritans who left England and settled in Massachusetts in 1630. Abram was probably literate, but by most accounts he had little if any formal education. He relied instead on his physical strength. He was as strong as an ox and he was known throughout Ohio as a champion wrestler.

He and his future bride, Eliza Ballou, met as children in Worcester but as he grew into adolescence his eyes were first set on her older sister, Mehitabel. In 1814, Eliza's father moved the family to Muskingum, Ohio; five years later, Abram followed, hoping to find Mehitabel and marry her. He was too late. She had married another. A neighbor watching this drama unfold predicted that the visitor from New York would fall in love with Eliza and they would be married within three months. The neighbor proved right. Abram and Eliza were married on February 3, 1820.

Abram worked hard as a foreman on his own canal-digging enterprise and enjoyed a burst of success. But a second canal project was a losing venture, draining all the profits he had gained in his previous work. Abram then tried his hand at farming. He built a small log cabin, where James A. Garfield would be born on November 19, 1831. Just eighteen months after that, a forest fire threatened the Garfields' cabin and all they owned. Abram worked like a demon to battle the disaster, caught a severe cold afterward and died at the age of thirty-three.

Four decades later, Eliza described Abram to his son: "Your father was five feet eleven inches tall, large head, broad shoulders and chest, high forehead, blue eyes, light complexion, as beautiful a set of teeth as any man ever had . . . cheeks very red, lips tolerably full, but to me very handsome . . . fond of his friends, everybody liked him, his judgments very good, more than common."[44]

According to Eliza, Abram's dying thoughts turned to his sons. "Eliza," he said on his deathbed, "I have brought these four young saplings into these woods. Take care of them."[45] The youngest of those saplings, James, who had not yet seen his second birthday, would grow to become president. Former president Rutherford B. Hayes would write that "no man ever started so low that accomplished so much in all our history."[46]

Eliza Ballou Garfield (September 21, 1801–January 21, 1888). On her father's side, Eliza Ballou descended from fierce Huguenot stock, while her mother was English. The heritage is noteworthy for she would be plagued by adversity throughout her life. Eliza spent her early childhood in Richmond, New Hampshire. She was six when her father died, leaving her mother the solitary breadwinner for a family of four children. In time, each child assumed his or her responsibility. Eliza passed on educational opportunities to learn the trade of a weaver and help put food on the table. Exceptionally bright, she used the only textbook available, the large family Bible, to learn how to read and write. Her sunny disposition helped her pass the long hours of monotonous work as a weaver and led her to develop an extraordinary personal repertoire of hymns. It was said that she could sing forty-eight consecutive hours without repeating a song.[47]

After moving with her family to Ohio, she was reacquainted with a family friend, the handsome Abram Garfield, whom she wed on February 3, 1820. The young couple moved to Newburgh and Independence, where they had relatives with established homes to share. The tribulations of pioneer farming took their toll; both newlyweds succumbed to ague, a form of malaria. In the first eight years of their marriage they did not own their own home. Nagging health problems forced them to live with relatives.

Eventually, Abram found work building a portion of the Ohio and Erie Canal, while Eliza gave birth to four children: Mehitabel, Thomas, Mary, and James Ballou. She also fed and tended to the twenty men working on the canal project with her husband. Their youngest child, James Ballou, died suddenly in 1829 at the age of two. Eliza found it difficult to reconcile herself to his death, and prayed that she and Abram would have another son.

The family of six moved to Tuscarawas County, Ohio, in April 1827, when Abram secured a contract working on another section of the canal. As the venture failed, the Garfield family moved to fifty acres of land near a stream off the Chagrin River in Orange Township, Ohio. Abram built a log cabin with the help of relatives and neighbors. After close to ten years of marriage, it would be the first home the family had ever owned. It was here that Eliza's prayers were answered: James Abram Garfield was born in the cabin on November 19, 1831. Just as it seemed their luck had turned, a forest fire threatened; and Abram overtaxed himself battling the blaze. Weakened from the effort, he caught a severe cold that led to his premature death.

A lesser woman would have succumbed to the overwhelming task of raising four children under the age of ten alone in the harsh wilderness. Buttressed by her strong faith and fierce independence, Eliza brought up her young family unaided, still managing to impress upon them high standards of morality and intellectual worth. The elder son, Tom, was taught how to plow and the two girls how to weave. Tenuously, the family survived. The younger son, James Abram Garfield, was special from the day he arrived. Eliza made grand plans for him, having the girls walk him a mile and half to a rural schoolhouse to learn the three R's. By the age of three, James was reading his mother lengthy passages from the Bible. He grew big and strong like his father and was known to be quite adept with his fists.

Eliza married Alfred Belding in 1842; he filed for divorce six years later and the divorce became final in 1850. Furious at his mother's second marriage, Tom left home. The marriage also caused a great disturbance to James in his adolescent years. He now had to share his mother's attention and follow another man's rules. In January 1881, at the age of forty-nine, Garfield would write in his diary of Belding's death, "After this long silence, ended in death, it is hard for me to think of the man without indignation."[48]

At age sixteen, James left his mother and their cabin and walked to the shores of Lake Erie to find a job as a sailor. He was rebuffed by a blustery ship's captain and instead found work on the Ohio & Erie Canal. When his stint in the rough-and-tumble world of canal work ended abruptly he returned home, a much humbler son. James graciously accepted his mother's suggestion to enroll at the Geauga Seminary and Eliza spent her life savings of seventeen dollars to make it happen. From 1851 to 1854 James studied at the Western Reserve Eclectic Institute, finally finishing his academic career at Williams College in Massachusetts, graduating second in his class in 1856.

James Garfield returned to the Western Reserve Eclectic Institute (later Hiram College) in Ohio as a classics professor, and within a year was made its president. Garfield served the Union Army in the Civil War beginning in 1861; at thirty, he became a brigadier general. Two years later, after showing courage at the Battle of Chickamauga, he was promoted to major general of volunteers. In 1862, he was elected to Congress and took his seat in December 1863.

Of all James's success, nothing made Eliza prouder than her son's fine service in Congress for nearly eighteen years. Later, she became the first mother to be present at her son's inauguration. It seemed as if the great pain of her early life had been swept away by the sheer joy of her son's ascendancy. But one final trial awaited her. On July 2, 1881, James was mortally wounded by a mentally unstable, disgruntled office seeker. While our twentieth president lay struggling for life, he summoned enough strength to pen a short note to his mother, assuring her that he would only need some time and patience to recover and sending his love to the entire family. But James Garfield was wrong. Despite the best medical attention of the day, he died of infection and internal hemorrhaging on September 19, 1881. His mother would live on another five years.

21. PRESIDENT CHESTER ALAN ARTHUR
(1881–1885)

Reverend William Arthur (1796–October 27, 1875). William Arthur was a tall, fiery Baptist preacher with a childhood limp and an unwavering honesty, who delivered his message throughout the Vermont countryside in a strong Irish brogue.

Education was valued in his parents' home; William had graduated from Belfast College before leaving Ireland for Quebec, where he took a job as a teacher. In 1821, he met Malvina Stone and the two eloped. They would have nine children, including the son who became president. Shortly after the wedding, William decided to make some changes both in location and profession. The couple moved to Vermont, where he took a clerk's position in a law office. Their life had lacked comfort on his modest teacher's income, but now a promising career in law lay ahead.

There came an unexpected turn of events. Always interested in religion, William attended a Baptist revival, where he experienced a conversion that completely altered his life. In 1827, he left the practice of law and became a licensed Baptist minister. His took his first church a year later, but his blunt, opinionated demeanor was often offensive, making him more suited to the life of an itinerant preacher. His longest tenure in a parish would be only five years. Nonetheless, the urgency of his message and the absolute confidence of his beliefs attracted a following.

After four daughters, Chester Alan Arthur was born on October 5, 1829, in a parsonage in North Fairfield, Vermont. Critical of the senior Arthur's enthusiasm, a religious neighbor recounted years later how his grandmother had been helping with the birth. "And think of it," she said, reproachfully, "when I announced the boy to Elder Arthur he danced up and down in the room."[49] Named after the doctor who delivered him, Chester Alan Arthur would become the nation's twenty-first president.

The Arthurs lived humbly, a large family subsisting on what was collected in the church offering plates. They would lose a two-year-old son and an eighteen-year-old daughter, but their faith would remain certain. Perhaps the minister's greatest influence on his son was as a staunch abolitionist: William helped found the New York Antislavery Society. William also encouraged his son's academic pursuits. While he could not pay for his son's tuition, he was able to arrange for a job as a principal of a school that met in their church basement. Chester was able to work at the school while pursuing his law degree. After launching his law career, Chester was able to provide for his parents' needs. In 1863, William retired from the ministry and returned to teaching, running a boarding school and helping train young college-bound men. During these years, thanks to his son's financial help, he was able to serve as an editor for a number of books and publications and finally to write his own book on etymology.

His wife, Malvina, died in 1869 and William remarried, a decision that was resented by the children. In 1871, President Grant appointed the son, Chester, as the collector of the port of New York. Four years later, William's health took a sharp turn for the worse; he was suffering from stomach cancer. Chester traveled back to his father's Newtonville home to be at his side, but with William drifting in and out of consciousness there was little he could do. Soon after he returned to New York, his father died. William was seventy-nine. Perhaps the minimalist lifestyle of Chester's childhood explains the extravagant nature of the Arthur presidency. While Chester accepted his father's beliefs regarding the fair treatment of all citizens, he never shared his religious fervor or his modest lifestyle.

Malvina Stone Arthur (April 29, 1802–January 16, 1869). One of her grandfathers was Major Uriah Stone, a hero of the French and Indian War, but when Malvina was still a child, her father, George Washington Stone, moved the family to Quebec, Canada. The Stones were devoutly religious. George was a Methodist minister and Malvina's uncle, Elder John Stone, was a Baptist evangelist. They were living fifteen miles into Canada, just across the Vermont state line, when she met and fell in love with William Arthur, a young teacher from Ireland. In 1821, the couple eloped; they soon returned to the United States to begin a life of their own. Ambitious to provide for his wife and their new family, William abandoned teaching in favor of a career in law. But one night at a Baptist revival changed all that. Uncle John preached that night; William Arthur was not only deeply moved but converted on the spot and soon after announced he would be a preacher.

William Arthur's new calling led the family from hamlet to hamlet across the Vermont countryside. Parish life provided for basic needs but left little for extras. But Malvina faithfully supported her husband and their home was graced with nine children. On October 5, 1829, after the birth of four daughters, their son Chester was born. The family was thrilled to have a boy.

Malvina Stone Arthur died at the age of sixty-six, when Chester was working as a lawyer in New York. Years after Malvina's death, while the country waited to see whether President Garfield would recover from an assassination attempt, opponents suggested that the vice president had been born on Canadian soil and was thus ineligible to become president. Many family documents had been destroyed by fire, but eventually, the nation accepted Malvina's correspondence as proof of Chester's Vermont birth. When President Garfield finally succumbed to septicemia, Malvina's words from the grave assured her son's rightful place in American history, and Chester became the twenty-first president.

22. & 24. PRESIDENT GROVER CLEVELAND
(1885–1889, 1893–1897)

Richard Falley Cleveland (June 19, 1804–October 1, 1853). Richard was born the fifth of six children in Norwich, Connecticut, to William Cleveland and Margaret Falley Cleveland. They were a devoutly religious family, descended from a long line of deacons and clergy, including some of great prominence.[50] As a dutiful son, Richard Falley Cleveland accepted his family heritage, spending his early years studying theology. A thin, pale young man with a brilliant intellect, he graduated from Yale with honors in 1824 and accepted a teaching position at Princeton, even while pursuing his advanced theological studies.

As a student he had met Ann Neal, the daughter of a well-to-do book publisher; they were married in Baltimore on September 10, 1829. Ann would face a dramatic economic change. For many years, Richard, Ann, and their nine children would exist on a mere $600 a year. Richard was pastor of a church in Windham, Connecticut, for two years before accepting a position at the Presbyterian Church in Caldwell, New Jersey. Here in the rural hills of New Jersey, their fifth child, Stephen Grover Cleveland was born. Named after the pastor who had preceded Richard in Caldwell, he eventually dropped his first name and became known as Grover Cleveland.

In the home of the Clevelands, frugality was a way of life and piety was held in the highest esteem. Strict obedience to parents was part of the code. As the Cleveland household grew, the father searched for a better way to provide for his expanding family. In late 1850, the American Home Missionary Society offered him the position of New York district secretary at a salary of almost $1,000 per year. It seemed like a small fortune to the struggling family, but Richard suffered from gastric ulcers, and the new position, which would entail constant travel over unpaved roads in all kinds of inclement weather, was believed to be a threat to his health.

The family moved to Utica, New York, where Richard accepted a pastorate in a small church. Tragically, his first sermon at his new parish would also be his last. His unexpected death at the age of forty-nine left Ann an impoverished widow with seven children still at home. At just sixteen, the mature and responsible Grover soberly took on permanent responsibility for his mother and unmarried sisters.

Reverend Richard Cleveland left nothing of material wealth to his poor family, but his reputation for speaking the truth somehow transferred. Even Grover Cleveland's detractors and enemies conceded he was a man of remarkable honesty; he even admitted to a youthful liaison with a woman when the whole affair might have been covered up.[51] In his excellent study of Cleveland, the historian Allan Nevins notes, "Character is not made overnight. When it appears in transcendent degree it is usually the product of generations of disciplined ancestry, or a stern environment or both."[52] In his years of preaching hundreds of sermons in little churches across the Northeast, unbeknownst to the Reverend Richard Cleveland his most important auditor and beneficiary had been the little boy sitting on the front pew.

Ann Neal Cleveland (February 4, 1806–July 19, 1882). Grover Cleveland, the first Democrat elected to the White House after the Civil War, was born to devout Presbyterian parents in Caldwell, New Jersey, on March 18, 1837. Young Ann Neal was the daughter of a prosperous Baltimore publisher and grew up accustomed to fine china, parties, and beautiful silk gowns. It is a wonder she ever fell for the thin, somber-faced intellectual, Richard Falley Cleveland. Richard had little to offer materially, but he had graduated from Yale with honors, and his religious training at Princeton was well under way when they met. Richard Falley Cleveland mustered all his courage to propose to the twenty-three-year-old society girl, and they were wed on September 10, 1829.

The couple moved to Windham, Connecticut, where Richard accepted his first pastorate. Ann naively brought her necessities with her to the parsonage—fine silk gowns, colorful jewelry, and a Negro maid. But the ladies of the church rebuked her worldliness and Ann graciously relinquished her possessions, sending them all back home, including her maid. Richard preached diligently at a succession of small congregations; his slim ministerial wage was barely enough for Ann and their nine children.

Without regret, Ann dutifully turned her attention to raising young champions. She threw much of her effort into her fifth child, Grover Cleveland, who found an exceptional place in her heart. In the isolated country village of Caldwell, New Jersey, the Cleveland children were excluded from the normal frivolity of childhood and instead memorized huge chunks of dogmatic writings.[53] Ann's strictness in raising her children produced well-disciplined, highly determined, responsible adults.

When Richard died at the age of forty-nine, the whole family felt the pain of responsibility. Sixteen-year-old Grover went to work, teaching and eventually going into law before launching a public career. Throughout the years, even during times of stressful transition, Grover faithfully provided for his mother and sisters. She died at age seventy-six, with her son in the middle of a successful election campaign for governor of New York.

Grover was a bachelor when he was first elected president and became the first president to be married in the White House. Fortunately, his mother died before hearing the torrid gossip about Grover siring an illegitimate son. Although the paternity of the child could not be proven and the mother had had several lovers, Cleveland paid for the boy's education and expenses. The event would have broken his mother's Puritan heart. Despite the controversy, Grover Cleveland was elected to two terms as president and his love for his mother and all she stood for gave him great strength. Upon his mother's death, he commented, "Do you know if Mother were alive I would feel so much safer . . . I have always thought her prayers had much to do with my success." [54]

23. PRESIDENT BENJAMIN HARRISON (1889–1893)

John Scott Harrison (October 4, 1804–May 25, 1878). John Scott Harrison has the unique distinction of being both the son and the father of a U.S. president. For a time, it appeared that he himself was destined for public life, but after a short stint in the U.S. Congress, he acquired a clear distaste for politics and opted for farming.

John Scott was born in Vincennes, Indiana, while his famous father, William Henry Harrison, was serving as the governor of the Indiana Territory. John Scott was the fifth of ten children and the only one of the Harrison sons to live to see his father inaugurated as president. [55] The family seemed to be wholly identified with their famous father. After his death in the White House, the Harrison daughters began dying as well. Within five years of the death of President William Henry Harrison, nine of his ten children were dead. Only John Scott remained.

Graduating from Cincinnati College, John Scott was valedictorian of his class. When his father left to serve as minister to Colombia for President John Quincy Adams, John Scott took on the responsibility of overseeing the family estate in North Bend, Ohio. It was an arrangement that suited both father and son.

In 1824 John Scott married Lucretia Knapp Johnson, who gave him three children, but died in 1830. John Scott quickly found a new wife, Elizabeth Irwin, whom he wed in 1831. They had ten children, including Benjamin Harrison, our twenty-third president.

John's father, William Henry Harrison, deeded him five hundred acres which became known as the Point. This estate was the childhood home of Benjamin Harrison. Though the family was quite far from any schools, John personally saw to his children's education by building a one-room log schoolhouse and hiring tutors. [56] The Harrisons owned land, but with so many mouths to feed, they sometimes fared poorly. Every child was expected to pitch in and do his share of chores around the farm.

John Scott somehow managed to scrape together enough funds

for his two oldest sons, Irwin and Benjamin, to go to college. Benjamin attended Farmer's College and then graduated from Miami University in Oxford, Ohio, in 1852. Upon his son's graduation, John gave Benjamin unfortunate news: he had overextended himself and had to mortgage most of the estate. Benjamin would not go to law school; instead he would work as a law clerk in a Cincinnati firm.

John Scott was elected to the U.S. House of Representatives. After failing to win reelection, he never grieved his retirement from public life. During these years, father and son experienced a brief estrangement over differing political views. John Scott transferred his allegiance to the newly formed American Party, while his son Benjamin was climbing in the ranks of the Republican party, adhering to its strong antislavery platform. Eventually, the two men were able to transcend their differences and hold to opposing views as gentlemen, without putting their relationship as father and son at risk. Benjamin Harrison went on to fame as a Civil War officer, finally brevetted as a general in 1865.

John Harrison eventually recognized his son's talent for the political game and his growing respect within the party establishment. He was soon encouraging and advising his son's rise, proud to see him reclaiming the family heritage. Benjamin ran for governor of Indiana in 1876 and lost. Two years later, John Scott Harrison died in North Bend, Ohio. He was seventy-three. Bizarrely, grave robbers stole his body. They were never brought to justice.

Benjamin went on to the Senate and the White House, becoming the twenty-third American president.

Elizabeth Irwin Harrison (July 18, 1810–August 15, 1850). Elizabeth Irwin was a devout Presbyterian who birthed ten children; her second son, Benjamin Harrison, became president. She came from a distinguished family. Elizabeth's Scottish grandfather was the founder of a prosperous mill in Pennsylvania. Her own father, Captain Archibald Irwin, moved the family to the promising new state of Ohio.

Elizabeth was twenty-one when she met the serious-minded lawyer John Scott Harrison. John, a widower with three children of his own, was the son of President William Henry Harrison and a member of a political dynasty. They were married on August 12, 1831, and lived on the Harrison family compound in North Bend, Ohio, where their son Benjamin was born. Elizabeth believed that children should be raised to fear the Lord and do what was wise and prudent. She exhorted Benjamin and his older brother in a letter upon their departure for school: "I pray for you daily that you may keep from sinning and straying from the path of duty."[57]

She would die at the age of forty, during childbirth, only five days before her famous son's seventeenth birthday, never imaging that having married into a great presidential family, she herself had also given birth to a president. She did not see him become a lawyer, or a Civil War hero, or a general; she did not see him win election to the Senate or be inaugurated president of the United States. And Benjamin Harrison would say that he felt the loss.

25. WILLIAM MCKINLEY (1897–1901)

William McKinley Sr. (November 15, 1807–November 24, 1892). William McKinley, Sr., was born in Mercer County, Pennsylvania, to hardworking parents of Scottish-Irish-English and Puritan descent. Both of his grandfathers fought in the Revolutionary War and were devout and pious men.

As the second in a family of fourteen children, William had little time to attend school. But by the age of sixteen, he managed to achieve the equivalent of a grade school education. And a lack of academic opportunity did not prevent him from being well-read. It may have actually ignited a passion for learning in his own children. William, Sr., worked twelve-hour shifts in a foundry, but somehow found time to read the Bible, Shakespeare, and Dante.[58]

William, Sr., followed in his father's and grandfather's footsteps, becoming a manager of furnaces used in the production of iron. The workdays were extremely long and physically demanding but McKinley men were stoic and never complained. In time, his patience paid dividends and he became a partner in an iron manufacturing firm.

Most of the raising of the McKinley children was left to his wife, Nancy, while William worked the long hours to provide for the family. The McKinleys were devout Methodists. "Whatever you be," he told his children, "you will be a credit to your family and to your God."[59]

William would see his seventh child and namesake become a member of congress and later governor of Ohio. In the summer of 1892, William, Jr., was an unsuccessful candidate for president. His father died a few months later, four years before William McKinley, Jr., was elected to the highest office in the land.

Nancy Allison McKinley (April 22, 1809–December 12, 1897). Nancy Allison McKinley, daughter of hardworking Scottish farmers, was born in a simple log cabin on the Ohio frontier. Her parents placed great importance on their children's education and made great sacrifices to move the family to the town of Lisbon where the children could attend school. It was in Lisbon that Nancy met the stocky, hard-working William McKinley. They were married on January 6, 1829.

While William carved out a living in the steel business, Nancy devoted herself entirely to her children and her faith. Some neighbors credited her with running the local Methodist church single-handedly. On January 29, 1843, the seventh of her nine children was born in Niles and she proudly named the robust infant after his father. Convinced that young William had promise, she set her heart on his becoming a bishop. To give her son every advantage, Nancy moved to nearby Poland, where William could get a better education, while her husband stayed to work in Niles, visiting his family on Sundays. Nancy instilled in William the proper behavior for an aspiring bishop.

William McKinley, Jr., respected his mother's ambition for his life. He neither drank intoxicating beverages nor used foul language. He briefly attended Allegheny College but then enlisted as a private in the Union Army, returning home a major of volunteers. After the war, William studied law and at the age of twenty-four opened his own practice. Serving as a prosecutor, a congressman, and then as governor of Ohio, William McKinley was soon on the fast track to the presidency.

But William's wife was an epileptic and her seizures made public appearances impossible. More and more, Nancy became actively involved in her son's aspirations. During the presidential campaign of 1896, crowds of visitors would gather every Sunday to watch as William McKinley called on his mother, escorting her to church. The onlookers would recall seeing William and his mother rocking side by side on her front porch.[60] This tenderness toward his mother and wife won McKinley a place in the electorate's heart. In 1896, William McKinley won his party's nomination and went on to win the general election by one of the largest majorities of the popular vote since 1872.[61]

William McKinley had not become the Methodist bishop his mother had hoped, but Nancy saw him become president. Dependent on her prayers and inspired by their conversations, McKinley set up a special wire from the White House to her home in Ohio so they could talk to each other daily. When she fell ill, he was inconsolable and took his presidential train to Ohio to be at her side. She died at the age of eighty-eight. Less than four years later, William McKinley, too, lay dead, the victim of an assassin's bullet.

26. PRESIDENT THEODORE ROOSEVELT
(1901–1909)

Theodore Roosevelt, Sr. (September 22, 1831–February 9, 1878). "My father, Theodore Roosevelt, was the best man I ever knew. He combined strength and courage with gentleness, tenderness, and great unselfishness." So wrote President Theodore Roosevelt in his autobiography.[62] Roosevelt, Sr., unquestionably had one of the most profound impacts of any presidential parent upon a son. He was born in New York City, one of six children, to hardworking businessman Cornelius Van Schaak Roosevelt and his wife, Margaret. Instead of attending college, Roosevelt, Sr., joined his father and older brother in a family business that imported and sold plate glass.

While traveling in the summer of 1850, he met Martha "Mittie" Bulloch, the strikingly beautiful daughter of a wealthy plantation owner, and fell head over heels. Three years later they were married in grand style. Theodore moved his new bride into a four-story brownstone in New York City. Within the first year of marriage their first daughter was born. Then on October 27, 1858, came the son who would bear not only his father's name but so much of his nature.

Love abounded in the Roosevelt home, and there never seemed to be an idle moment. Besides working long hours at his successful glass company, Theodore Roosevelt, Sr., engaged in countless philanthropic activities. He had a gift for loosening the purse strings of his affluent friends to help fund multiple charities to assist the poor and homeless.

Theodore and Martha were known as charming hosts, throwing parties for the rich and influential of New York City.

To placate his wife, a Confederate sympathizer, he hired a substitute to fight in his place for the Union Army. Still, he did more than his fair share to contribute to the welfare of all soldiers. He conceived of the idea of the allotment—a small voluntary deduction from a soldier's pay that would be sent home to dependents, and lobbied for it to be provided for by law.

Though his busy schedule often kept him away from home, he always managed to take time for his children. When Theodore Roosevelt, Jr., suffered asthma attacks his father would sweep him up in his arms and carry him around. It was his father's firm decree that to reach his fullest success, the boy must make his body as strong as his mind. Young Theodore took the message to heart, engaging in a strict regimen of weightlifting and strenuous exercise.

To teach the family the splendors of history, Theodore, Sr., took them all on a year-long tour of Europe. After a two-day father-son hiking expedition inspecting Saxon ruins, young Theodore confided to his diary that his father's full attention made them "the happiest days that I have ever spent."[63]

With his affluence, Theodore, Sr., ensured that his son would have what he never attained, a college degree. In the spring of 1867, the son left for Harvard. The father had a brief stint in politics but the corruption appalled him. The son would spend much of his career cleaning it up. Theodore, Sr., died of stomach cancer before seeing his son graduate from Harvard, but his portrait would one day hang in the White House. Years later, Theodore, Jr.'s, sister recalled that the president said, "He never took any serious step or made any vital decision for his country without thinking first what position his father would have taken on the question."[64]

Martha Bulloch Roosevelt (July 8, 1835–February 14, 1884). Martha "Mittie" Bulloch was petite and frail, yet stunningly beautiful. Her father was a wealthy Georgian gentleman farmer who died when she was but a child. Her mother, an engaging Southern lady, filled the vacuum by smothering her with love. Mittie seemed almost too perfect for any male suitor, but in the spring of 1850, a worthy young man of good character and fine reputation visited the Bulloch estate. Theodore Roosevelt, father of the future president, was smitten with the grace of the fifteen-year-old beauty. For three years they exchanged a torrent of love letters, culminating in a lavish wedding on December 22, 1853.

Mittie came to married life somewhat unprepared. Her early life of luxury had demanded little of her. As a wife, she was seemingly deficient in performing traditional household duties, including the managing of finances, but her gift of love and laughter made up the difference. After the birth of her first daughter, Mittie's mother and older sister quickly stepped in to help manage the home and prepare for a second pregnancy.

On October 27, 1858, Theodore Roosevelt was born. Teddy's frequent bouts of asthma made him something of a bookworm. A selfless mother, Mittie often sat up all night comforting him during his frequent illnesses.

Mittie's eccentricities were the subject of conversation in the family. She made a fetish of cleanliness, could not keep appointments, and constantly battled "sick headaches." But nothing tainted her image in the eyes of her loving children and husband. None of the family referred to her simply as Mother—she was "Darling beloved little Mother," a phrase coined by young Teddy.[65]

After the death of Theodore Roosevelt, Sr., the grief seemed too much for Mittie to bear. At times she mustered some of her trademark optimism and rallied sufficiently to cheer on her son as he plunged headfirst into New York politics.

The year 1884 was filled with tragedy. Mittie caught a cold that developed into typhoid fever and killed her. Theodore, Jr.'s wife, Alice, died later that same afternoon from an unsuspected case of kidney disease. She was only twenty-two. Both women died in the same house, with future president Theodore Roosevelt rushing up and down the stairs from one deathbed to the next, helpless as the two most important women in his life slipped away from him.

27. WILLIAM HOWARD TAFT (1909–1913)

Alphonso Taft (November 5, 1810–May 21, 1891). Born in West Townshend, Vermont, Alphonso was the only child of Peter Rawson Taft and Sylvia Howard Taft. They were third-generation immigrant farmers from England, but Alphonso decided early in life that farming was not for him. Fortunately, his parents encouraged his pursuit of an education. He attended local schools in Vermont until he was sixteen, then enrolled in Amherst for two years before returning to West Townshend, where he was tutored while he worked to save the money for higher education. Eventually, Alphonso Taft graduated from Yale with honors.

Migrating west, Alphonso began a law practice in bustling Cincinnati, Ohio. There he married his first wife, Fanny Phelps. Soon his new bride gave him two sons, but tragedy struck; Fanny died suddenly of "congestion of the lungs." Pouring his energy into his work, Alphonso built a prosperous law practice and became one of the most influential citizens in the state. A trip to Washington, D.C., made a lasting impression and gave rise to a national political career that spanned the decades. In 1848 he was elected to the city council. He served as U.S. attorney general and secretary of war under President Ulysses S. Grant, made an unsuccessful bid for the governorship of Ohio in both 1875 and 1879, and served as minister to Austria-Hungary and Russia.

Alphonso held nothing dearer than his beloved second wife, Louisa Maria, and his children. While Alphonso could be domineering, he was also gentle, and all of his sons admired him. He demanded the best from his children and they seemed to respond without bitterness. All five sons earned law degrees and all distinguished themselves in their father's eyes.

Though he would not live to see his son's greatest accomplishments, Alphonso Taft would have been pleased with his legacy. William H. Taft became the twenty-seventh president of the United States and later served on the Supreme Court. His grandson Robert Taft and his great-grandson Robert Taft, Jr., were U.S. senators; his grandson Charles Taft was a tireless civic and social reformer and founder of the World Council of Churches; his great-great-grandson Bob Taft would be elected governor of Ohio. Alphonso Taft passed away in San Diego, California, on May 21, 1891. William Howard Taft wrote admiringly of the man who had raised him: "a man never had . . . a dearer kinder more considerate father." [66]

Louisa Torrey Taft (September 11, 1827–December 8, 1907). The four Torrey girls took after their liberal and enthusiastic mother. Louisa was the dark-haired beauty of the group. She was fiercely independent and held that women could chart their own destinies. This mind-set might have frightened other parents of the mid-1800s, but Louisa's forward-thinking mother and doting, prosperous, Republican father tolerated her radical ideas. The Torrey girls received a liberal arts education, with Louisa and her favorite sister Delia going on to Mount Holyoke Female Seminary for further training. The rigid rules at Mount Holyoke only slightly tempered Louisa's exuberant, free spirit.

When she was twenty-six, Louisa visited her aunt in New Haven, Connecticut, where she met a Yale graduate named Alphonso Taft. He was a widower with two young sons and a promising law practice in Cincinnati. The tall, kind Mr. Taft seemed sufficiently liberal-minded to suit her. After a one-month engagement they wed on December 26, 1853. This bright couple forged a union that would produce a president of the United States, two senators, and a governor.

Though modern in her opinions, Louisa was focused on her children. "I do not believe we can love our children too much," she would say. "It seems to me there can be no stronger motive for improvement than the thought of the influence on our children. It is what we are and not what we do in reference to them which will make its impress on their lives."[67] On September 15, 1857, she delivered a robust baby boy named William Howard Taft.

With her children grown and her husband a member of President Grant's cabinet, Louisa gracefully took on the role of a politician's wife in Washington. Her life had its share of sorrows. One of her sons died as an infant, and a stepson was committed to a sanatorium. But her beloved husband's death in 1891 was the hardest of all.

Louisa found joy in supporting Will's budding political career, even accompanying him as an emissary of President Theodore Roosevelt to the Vatican in Rome. She died just two months before her eightieth birthday. Her legacy would live on in the many fine sons she raised. She once shared with family and intimates her fears about Will: she worried that if he were to be president he would have to endure the worst kind of malice and hatred. Less than a year after her passing, her son William Howard Taft would be elected president.

28. PRESIDENT WOODROW WILSON (1913–1921)

Joseph Ruggles Wilson (February 28, 1822–January 21, 1903). Born to James and Anne Adams Wilson in Stuebenville, Ohio, Joseph grew to be both strikingly handsome and strong-minded. His father was financially successful in the newspaper business both in Ohio and Pennsylvania during Joseph's formative years. His mother was a devout woman. Joseph gleaned both the power of the pen and the power of prayer from his parents.

Marked as the scholar in the family early in his life, Joseph attended Jefferson College where he was graduated as valedictorian in 1844. In 1846, he took a divinity degree from Princeton. Although ordained by the Presbyterian church, Joseph returned to a teaching position in Steubenville.

While teaching, Joseph met Janet "Jesse" Woodrow, a student at a nearby school. The two were married on June 7, 1849, a few weeks before Joseph's ministerial ordination. Following their marriage, Joseph joined the faculty at Jefferson College as a professor of rhetoric; later he held a professorship of chemistry and natural science at Hampden-Sydney College in Virginia.

In 1855, he took a pastorate in Staunton, Virginia, and so began a lifelong career of scholarship and ministry. It was in Staunton on December 28, 1856, that their first son, Thomas Woodrow Wilson, was born.

About a year later, Joseph moved to a church in Augusta, Georgia. Like his new parishioners, Joseph approved wholeheartedly of slavery, believing that he had doctrinal evidence to support the secession of the southern states, the war, and slavery itself.

During the Civil War, Joseph converted the Augusta churchyard into a military camp, which served as both an emergency hospital and a prison camp for Union soldiers. He also helped organize the Presbyterian Church of the Confederate States of America.

Joseph Wilson was probably the strongest influence on his son's character and intellect.[68] He accepted nothing but excellence. Having been a professor of rhetoric, Joseph worked to hone Woodrow's speaking skills. He required him to use a dictionary to learn the precise meanings of words. When the two traveled together, Joseph would give his son written tests on their experiences, tutoring Woodrow to improve his writing in both clarity and economy. Joseph was Woodrow's "teacher, role model, playmate, and confidant."[69]

The father and son relationship were so entwined that they drew the attention of Sigmund Freud, who with William C. Bullitt coauthored a book on their relationship. "His passionate love of his father was the core of his emotional life."[70] Joseph continually challenged and sometimes overrode Woodrow's life decisions.

In the fall of 1873, Woodrow went off to the college of his father's choosing for the express purpose of becoming a minister. The anxiety that resulted from the separation from his parents weakened Woodrow physically. He had never had his father's physical strength or endurance, and the stress worsened his stomach conditions. He returned home with his academic career unfinished, only to find his father involved in denominational power struggles within the Presbyterian church. In 1874, the family moved to North Carolina.

Woodrow Wilson continued his education at Princeton and later the University of Virginia, his father all the while trying to persuade him to become a minister. Woodrow seemed, at times, to buckle under the pressures of his father's expectations. Eventually his health broke and he was forced to return home; he finished his education from his parents' home, earning a law degree in absentia from the University of Virginia.

Joseph continued to influence his son during each career move. And Woodrow never seemed to view his father's influence as intrusive. In 1885, Woodrow dedicated his first book, *Congressional Government,* to his father, "the patient guide of his youth, the gracious companion of his manhood, . . . his best instructor and his most lenient critic."[71]

In 1888, Jesse Wilson died. Joseph had lost his wife and Woodrow had lost his mother, yet father and son now entered a strained and distant period. When Joseph's health began failing in 1902, he moved into his son's home near Princeton University. His final days were painful and he died at the age of eighty, when his son was serving as president of Princeton.

Janet "Jessie" Woodrow Wilson (December 20, 1830–April 15, 1888). Jesse Woodrow was born in Carlisle, England. When she was five, her family immigrated to Ontario; they later moved to Ohio, where her father, the Reverend Thomas Woodrow, led a Congregational church.

Reverend Woodrow recognized Jesse's quiet intelligence and encouraged her academic pursuits. While attending the Female Seminary, she met a teacher from a nearby school. Joseph Wilson was noted for his academic excellence and his desire to preach. She could hardly help her attraction to him. He was remarkably handsome and possessed both academic and spiritual strength, all of which she admired.

Joseph Wilson and Jesse Woodrow married on June 7, 1849, in a ceremony performed by her proud father. While her husband worked on his teaching career and his ministry, Jesse provided a loving home. Her first two children were girls. On December 28, 1856, a third child, Thomas Woodrow Wilson, was born. Jesse called him Tommy. He would carry both family names into the White House. One more baby boy completed the family. Jesse was a loving mother; she read to her children and worked diligently to protect them during the turbulent years of the Civil War. By this time, the Wilsons were living in the deep South. Her husband was a strong supporter of secession and white supremacy, while Jessie's relatives still resided in the free state of Ohio. Such bitter differences divided other families, but the Woodrows and Wilsons maintained strong family ties throughout the war years and after.

Jesse was liberal with her emotions and affection within the family, but she was reserved in her role as a minister's wife. People sometimes criticized her "aloofness." Like so many mothers of presidents, Jesse hoped that her son would one day step into the pulpit, but while her husband actively promoted the idea, Jesse simply encouraged Woodrow, regardless of his choices.

In his freshman year of college, young Thomas Woodrow Wilson decided to drop his first name, Thomas. Taking no offense, his mother wrote, "My darling Woodrow, I am going to make a desperate effort to call you Woodrow from this time on. . . . I have learned to love the name we have called you ever since your baby-hood . . . But 'Tommy' is certainly an unsuitable name for a grown man."[72]

While Joseph's love for his son was often harsh or judgmental, Jesse's love was unconditional. One of her daughters described her as "the most beautiful and gentle person in the world; her eyes always seemed to shine with tenderness and laughter, and there was no limit to her understanding."[73] While Woodrow was away at school, Jessie's health began to decline, but she continued to write letters of support and comfort. In 1888, with her son serving as an associate professor at Bryn Mawr College, fifty-seven-year-old Jesse Woodrow Wilson died in Clarksville, Tennessee.

29. PRESIDENT WARREN G. HARDING (1921–1923)

George Tyron Harding II (June 12, 1843–November 19, 1928). George—"Tyron," as he would be known—was a colorful figure, the third of ten children born to Charles Alexander and Mary Anne Harding in Blooming Grove, Ohio. The Hardings were originally Puritan fishermen who fled England and immigrated to Braintree, Massachusetts, before settling in Ohio. In the running of a farm, every son was needed for work, but Charles Harding was just successful enough to spare Tyron and allow him to pursue an education. Tyron first went to a school run by his aunt. At the age of fourteen he matriculated at Liberia College, where he earned his bachelor's degree in 1860. For a time, Tyron taught at a country school near Gilead, Ohio, but teaching did not hold his interest. He was distracted by Phoebe Dickerson, a young beauty who lived nearby. He hastily enrolled in the school she was attending. After a secret engagement, they eloped on May 7, 1864.

Phoebe returned to her parents' home while Tyron left to fight for the Union cause in the last days of the Civil War. One notable story that became part of the family lore was young Harding's encounter with Abraham Lincoln. On furlough in Washington, D.C., he and two of his fellow soldiers boldly walked into the White House, requesting a meeting with Abraham Lincoln. After waiting about an hour, the trio was ushered into Lincoln's study, where the president personally thanked them for their service to the Union and jovially shook their hands.[74] Tyron bragged about this moment for the rest of his life and it undoubtedly impressed his young son Warren.

Tyron Harding's career in the Union Army ended abruptly when he contracted typhoid fever. He was honorably discharged and sent home to Phoebe; they lived with his parents until he recovered. Tyron resumed teaching and built Phoebe their first home. It would be the birthplace of Warren G. Harding. Tyron and Phoebe would have seven more children over the next fourteen years.

Tired of teaching, Tyron Harding decided to become a doctor. He was mentored by a Blooming Grove physician and attended one term at the Homeopathic College in Cleveland, Ohio. Life as a physician did not bring the wealth and honor he expected. His meager income as a country doctor was supplemented by dealings as a trader, speculator, and real estate investor. Most of these enterprises were risky and impractical and left him in deeper debt, but there was one stroke of success. Harding became part owner of the newspaper *The Marion Star.* His son would one day become the sole proprietor of the paper and use it as a stepping-stone to a political career.

As his son, Warren, rose in politics. Tyron Harding shamelessly enjoyed the limelight and power. Never shy about receiving his son's financial support, Tyron was quick to trade on the famous family name for any advantage. After Phoebe's death in 1910, he married Eudora Kelley, a widow twenty-five years his junior. His lack of personal ambition and money led to their divorce five years later. Perhaps out of boredom, he courted and married a woman twenty-six years younger, whom he had employed to assist him in his office. The two eloped in August 1912 and Tyron doctored their marriage license to show a mere six-year age gap.[75]

Warren Harding's untimely death made Tyron the first father of a president to outlive his son. As the Teapot Dome Scandal and numerous other humiliations destroyed the reputation of his son's presidency, Tyron retreated from the publicity he had once embraced. He died at the age of eighty-five on November 19, 1928, in Santa Ana, California.

Phoebe Dickerson Harding (December 21, 1843–May 20, 1910). Phoebe Dickerson Harding would start her young life with controversy and adventure. The attractive, vivacious farm girl from central Ohio met and fell in love with her neighbor, George Tyron Harding II. Like so many other nineteen-year-olds of the time, Tyron had plans to volunteer to fight the rebels. But the thought of leaving his beloved Phoebe behind worried him. Tyron and Phoebe devised a plan. Young Harding visited the neighboring Dickerson girls, secretly stealing Phoebe and her sister away on a wagon ride that led straight to the local Methodist preacher's house. There the two lovers were wed on a spring day in 1864, with Phoebe's sister as the witness.

Tyron Harding enlisted with the Union Army, while Phoebe kept their marriage a secret, living on her family's farm in the rural hamlet of Blooming Grove, Ohio. A few short months later, when Tyron was discharged with typhoid fever, the wedding was announced to their stunned parents.

Phoebe wasted no time becoming pregnant and on November 2,

1865, gave birth to her first son, Warren Gamaliel Harding. He would become the twenty-ninth president of the United States. Some critical biographers have described Warren G. Harding as the least qualified man ever to live in the White House.[76] Some have faulted Phoebe's free-spirited nature, her lack of discipline and permissiveness as a mother. In her later years, Phoebe embraced the Seventh Day Adventist faith. She lived to see her son become lieutenant governor of Ohio. But she passed away at the age of sixty-six, more than a decade before her son would reach the White House and long before the scandals that would discredit the Harding name.

30. CALVIN COOLIDGE (1923–1929)

John Calvin Coolidge (March 31, 1845–March 18, 1926). In his autobiography, Calvin Coolidge expressed his admiration for his father: "I was extremely anxious to grow up to be like him."[77] John Calvin Coolidge was honest, decent, frugal, and the embodiment of old-fashioned virtue. Born in Plymouth Notch, Vermont, he was educated at the local public schools before attending the Black River Academy in Ludlow, Vermont. He worked for nine years on his father's farm before going to work as a schoolteacher, storekeeper, and businessman-entrepreneur.

In 1868, John Coolidge married the twenty-two-year-old Victoria Josephine Moor, who would bear him two children, John Calvin and Abigail. Sadly, tuberculosis would claim Victoria's life when young Calvin was twelve. Five years later, Abigail also died, leaving a great void in the lives of the Coolidge men.

John Coolidge was well known for his inventiveness and common sense. He could build a buggy or nurse a sick farm animal to health. Along with his skills as a handyman and farmer, John became a successful businessman and then launched into public service, holding many positions in Vermont government: superintendent of schools, deputy sheriff, road commissioner, representative to the Vermont House, and (for one term) state senator.

His young son assisted him in a wide variety of projects. The two grew so close that young Coolidge's departure for Amherst College was a painful separation. Calvin constantly wrote home to his father and was pleased when old John finally found a companion to ease the loneliness. Caroline Athena Brown and John Coolidge were wed in 1891, during Calvin's freshman year.

Upon graduation, Calvin entered law and politics in Northampton, Massachusetts. Slowly, he climbed the political ladder from councilman in Northampton to Republican governor of Massachusetts to vice president of the United States. Throughout Calvin's political career, John was there to experience his son's successes. The two were together at the Coolidge farm when Calvin received word that President Warren G. Harding, supposedly recovering from a heart attack, had taken a turn for the worse and died. Late at night, by the light of a gas lamp, John Calvin Coolidge invoked his authority as a notary to swear his son into office as the thirtieth president of the United States. This father and son who had bonded early in life would once again rely on each other's strength to rise to the challenges the nation put before them. John became something of a celebrity while his son was in office, graciously entertaining the hordes of well-wishers who descended on his Vermont home. After suffering both a heart attack and prostate cancer, he passed away on March 18, 1926, just shy of his eighty-first birthday.

Victoria Moor Coolidge (March 14, 1846–March 14, 1885). Victoria Josephine was named after two famous empresses, though her beginnings were far more humble. She was of Scottish ancestry, perhaps with some Native American blood. Born to poor farmers in the hamlet of Pinney Hollow, Vermont, she spent her early childhood moving with her family before settling in the area of Plymouth Notch. Like John, she attended public school and then the Black River Academy, where the two met. They wed on May 6, 1868. Victoria was twenty-two.

The newlyweds had a promising future. John ran the store attached to their cottage. He was smart and could provide a host of services to the community, from building buggies and performing veterinary work to plumbing and carpentry. On July 4, 1872, Victoria proudly brought into the world a son, and three years later a baby girl.

But happiness was to elude this young family. Victoria died of tuberculosis on her thirty-ninth birthday. Twelve-year-old Calvin and nine-year-old Abigail were left; five years later, Abigail died of appendicitis. Some historians believe that these losses produced the taciturn and peculiar Coolidge personality.[78]

Though Calvin had few years with his mother, he wrote wistfully of that time. "There was a touch of mysticism and poetry in her nature which made her love to gaze at the purple sunsets and watch the evening stars."[79] Although he lived without her most of his life, she was never far from his thoughts. At his death, he was still carrying her picture in a pocket watch near his heart.

31. HERBERT HOOVER (1929–1933)

Jesse Clark Hoover (September 2, 1846–December 13, 1880). Born in West Milton, Ohio, Jesse Hoover was from a family of pioneers and risk takers. In 1854, his father joined the westward expansion, moving the family from Ohio to Iowa in a covered wagon and eventually settling on a farm near the small village of West Branch.

Early in life, Jesse discovered an interest and skill in tearing down and rebuilding the mechanical equipment on his father's farm. The same talent would mark his sons and grandsons, who became engineers and inventors. When he was old enough to strike out on his own, Jesse left the farm to become a blacksmith. In 1870, he married his old schoolmate Hulda Randall Minthorn. It was a happy marriage that produced three children. Theodore Jesse Hoover arrived a year after the wedding ceremony; shortly after midnight on August 11, 1874, the future president Herbert Clark Hoover was born. Bursting with pride, Jesse compared his new son to the popular President Grant, then in his second term, declaring that there was another General Grant in the world. Mary, the last child in the family, arrived two years later.

Always industrious, with a sunny disposition, Jesse prospered as a blacksmith. In 1878 he sold his business, netting a healthy $1,000 profit, and with the proceeds launched a retail business, selling everything from sewing machines to farm equipment. The future seemed bright. The Hoover family moved into a comfortable two-story house in West Branch proper and became more involved with their Quaker congregation and community. Jesse served as town assessor and councilman.

And then suddenly, on December 13, 1880, thirty-four-year-old Jesse Clark Hoover died of rheumatism of the heart. The town was heartbroken at his unexpected death. An obituary in the *West Branch Local Record* described him as "ever happy and cheerful himself, he always had a kind word for all."[80] Herbert Hoover was only six years old. Hulda was devastated but turned to God to help her survive as a widow with three children.

Hulda Minthorn Hoover (May 4, 1848–February 24, 1883). When Herbert Hoover ran against Al Smith for the presidency, some Republicans thought that his mother's birthplace was a fact better left unrevealed. Born on an Ontario farm, Hulda Minthorn was legally a Canadian and thus a source of embarrassment to campaign managers. Campaign biographies of Hoover tended to downplay her remarkable role in his life. Hulda was a progressive pioneer woman who valued her college education. A Quaker minister and an early leader in the Temperance movement, she was a powerful maternal example of a leader.

The Minthorns were Quakers who moved from Canada to West Branch, Iowa, when Hulda was eleven years old. Hulda's parents fully supported her pursuit of an education, and she was a talented student at the University of Iowa. It was not until the death of her father that she returned home to help her mother, teaching school in West Branch until, at the age of twenty-two, she married Jesse Clark Hoover.

After his death, she began to assert herself as a community leader. She became an ordained minister of the Society of Friends and an outspoken member of the community. One of Herbert's memories of her included spending all day at the polls attempting to convince men to vote themselves dry during an anti-liquor campaign.

Personally convinced of the value of a proper education, Hulda refused to touch her husband's life insurance money, managing it and investing it instead for her children's education. Soon after her husband's death, the Hoovers lost their house, but Hulda hired herself out as a seamstress and preached wherever there was an open door, managing somehow not only to keep the family afloat but also to save enough additional money to educate her children.

On a cold, rainy February night, exhausted and sweating after preaching for a congregation, Hulda Hoover insisted on walking the several miles home to be with her children. A few days later, she fell ill with pneumonia. Worried for her children and trying to live, Hulda could not fight off the illness. Like her beloved husband, Hulda

Minthorn Hoover died at thirty-four. Herbert Hoover, the future president, had not yet turned eight.

32. FRANKLIN D. ROOSEVELT (1933–1945)

James Roosevelt (July 16, 1828–December 9, 1900). When Franklin D. Roosevelt spoke of his father he said, "He was the most generous and kindly of men and always liberal in outlook."[81] The father of America's twenty-third president was born in Hyde Park to affluent parents. His father, Isaac, was a graduate of Princeton and the Columbia School of Physicians and Surgeons, but spent little time practicing medicine. He later went on to study law, became a wealthy entrepreneur, and retired to the life of a country squire, devoting much of his time to his beloved Dutch Reformed Church.

Although James rebelled against his restrictive upbringing, he attended and graduated from Harvard Law School. After a brief stint as an attorney he became a financier and returned to the life of a country gentleman, much like his father before him. At age twenty-five, James married his first wife, Rebecca Brien Howland. They had one son together, with the aristocratic double appellation of James Roosevelt Roosevelt, but they simply called him Rosy.

James, like many other rich men of his day, sidestepped the tumultuous American Civil War by hiring a substitute to serve in his place. But there was no insulation against the rumblings on the world's financial markets. The Panic of 1873 thwarted two new business ventures in railroads and coal mining, a significant financial setback. And Rebecca Roosevelt died at the age of forty-eight.

On October 7, 1880, fifty-two-year-old James Roosevelt married a beautiful twenty-six-year-old socialite, Sara Delano. Their son, Franklin Delano Roosevelt, was born in 1882. Though James suffered a debilitating heart attack when young Franklin was only eight, he spent a fair amount of time with his son, teaching him how to swim, sled, skate, fish, hunt, and ride. Franklin accompanied his parents on eight trips to Europe and absorbed a knowledge of forestry, farming, and land management by riding alongside his father as James oversaw the estate. By Thanksgiving, 1900, James was seriously ill, and a few days later, with his two sons and Sara at his side, he passed away.

Sara Delano Roosevelt (September 21, 1854–September 7, 1941). On the Hudson River, encompassed by acres of meandering gardens, stands a stately home called Algonac. On this palatial estate was born a strong-willed girl who would dramatically shape her son's destiny. Sara Delano Roosevelt would produce the future thirty-second president of the United States and would become one of the most influential of presidential mothers.

Sara was born into a wealthy, aristocratic family. Her father, Warren Delano, was a swashbuckling entrepreneur who made a fortune in the opium trade in China, then lost it all and won it back again. Warren fathered a total of eleven children; Sara, or Sallie, was right in the middle. She grew up with all the proper training for a society lady and excelled at almost every undertaking, craving new experiences and enjoying exotic cultures. No ordinary life would satisfy young Sara, but she finally met her match in James Roosevelt, a friend of her father's, whose intellectual prowess and sense of propriety matched her own. Though he was twenty-six years her senior, they were married, and on January 30, 1882, Sallie had her only child, a splendid baby boy weighing in at a healthy ten pounds.

The child, Franklin Delano Roosevelt, immediately became Sara's single obsession and lifelong project. He was pursuing his education at Harvard when his father died. Sara bought a house nearby so the mother and son could spend their weekends together. Franklin's mother successfully vetoed any girlfriends until he asserted himself, announcing his marriage to Eleanor Roosevelt, a distant cousin with the same family name.

Though infuriatingly proper and civil, Eleanor and Sara lived constantly at odds, vying for power within the triad. But when Franklin was struck with polio, they rallied to give him support, temporarily overcoming their resentment of each other. Eventually, as Franklin defied them both, restarting a public career that would eventually lead to the White House, Sara finally acquiesced to her son's destiny, and in the process, along with daughter-in-law Eleanor, became a public figure in her own right.

33. HARRY S. TRUMAN (1945–1953)

John Anderson Truman (December 5, 1851–November 2, 1914). When asked by a reporter whether his father, a poor farmer, had been a success in life, Harry S. Truman replied testily, "He was the father of a president of the United States, and I think that is success enough for any man."[82] If Harry S. Truman's good sense came from his mother, his love of politics came from his father. John was a likable man of character, cheerful and eager to please. Born to Anderson Shipp Truman and Mary Jane Holmes Truman in Platte County, Missouri, on December 5, 1851, he was one of five children with little opportunity for education or advancement. He grew to only five feet, four inches tall, but his pugnacity fostered a reputation for fistfights.

When John proposed to Martha Young he had little to offer. For a time he ran a mule-trading business in Lamar, Missouri, but business failures kept his little family on the move from town to town. Even then, John carved out time for politics. He often took young Harry to political meetings, including the 1900 Democratic National Convention, held in nearby Kansas City. John served as a delegate to the Missouri State Democratic Convention in 1908.

When Harry was a teenager, John took a risky gamble in grain futures and lost his life savings and his inherited farm. It was the low point for a man who had lived in poverty much of his life. John was reduced to working as a night watchman for a grain elevator. The family's financial collapse shattered Harry's dreams of college. In 1905, John Truman grudgingly succumbed to his in-laws' generosity, returning to Grandview, Missouri, to run their farm. During these difficult years, Harry worked side by side with his father, creating a bond that would strengthen them both. More and more John came to depend on his son's common sense. And John sufficiently recovered in spirit to confide to his son that setbacks will come in life but should never be seen as permanent. "Never, never give up," he would say.[83]

Eventually, John Truman's years of political work were rewarded. He was appointed road overseer for Jackson County, Missouri. Characteristically, he accepted the position determined to excel. When he single-handedly insisted on removing a boulder blocking a road he suffered a severe hernia. He underwent surgery to have it repaired, but never fully recovered. John Anderson Truman died of cancer on November 2, 1914, at the age of sixty-two. His son was at his side.

Martha Young Truman (November 25, 1852–July 26, 1947). No one could have guessed that this simple, spirited girl from Missouri would be the best ally her son would have as he was thrust into the presidency in the final months of World War II. In her nineties, flying into Washington on the president's private airplane on Mother's Day, she took in the crowd of well-wishers at the airport and announced, "Oh, fiddlesticks, if I'd known there was going to be all this fuss, I wouldn't have come."[84] It was the beginning of a long love affair between the unpretentious Martha Truman and the American public.

Martha Young was born on a farm outside Kansas City, Missouri, in 1852. She was the next-to-last of nine children in the family of a successful farmer, Solomon Young. Suspected of supporting the Confederacy in the Civil War, the family was forced into temporary exile in the South. As she grew older, Martha studied at the Baptist Female College in bustling Kansas City. Most girls her age felt the pressure to be married, but independent "Mat," an avid reader, was in no rush to experience the drudgery of life as a farmer's wife. It took a persistent suitor, nicknamed "Peanuts" because of his short stature, to win her heart. Martha Young and John Anderson Truman were married in the Youngs' parlor on December 28, 1881.

Tragically, their first child was stillborn, but on May 8, 1884, they produced a healthy baby boy, Harry S. Truman. Another son would follow, and then a daughter, but Harry always had a special place in his mother's heart. She taught him his alphabet early, and by age five he was reading the family Bible. While other boys fished and hunted, Harry stayed inside with a book propped up against his knees. One year Martha gave him an expensive set of books entitled *Great Men and Famous Women,* which became his favorite reading and a source of inspiration.

After the death of his father, Harry stepped up to run the family farm, acquitting himself quite handily, leaving only when the crisis of World War I intruded and his National Guard unit was called to active duty. During the war Harry reached the rank of colonel, returning to Missouri a hero and marrying his sweetheart, Elizabeth Virginia Wallace.

Over the years, Harry S. Truman visited his mother virtually every Sunday. As he rose in politics he sometimes missed a day, but the tradition persisted even after he was elected to the U.S. Senate. When reporters asked what she thought of her son's sudden elevation to the nation's highest office, Martha humbly replied, "If he'd been voted in I'd be out waving flags, but right now it doesn't seem right to be very happy." [85] Thirty minutes after the Japanese surrendered, Harry was on the phone to his aging mother getting her reaction. "I'm glad Harry decided to end the war." [86]

In February 1947, Martha Truman fell, fracturing her hip. President Truman flew to Missouri, where he set up a temporary White House for twelve days to be near her side. Pneumonia set in and Martha died on July 26, 1947, at the age of ninety-four. Days later, a portrait of Martha Young Truman was hung in the White House. She was gone but not forgotten.

34. DWIGHT DAVID EISENHOWER (1953–1961)

David Jacob Eisenhower (September 23, 1863–May 10, 1942). Dwight D. Eisenhower wrote in his diary, "I loved my Dad." [87] But biographers suggest that it was not an easy task. David Eisenhower was austere, harsh, and emotionally distant, a man who inspired fear more than love. "Father was the breadwinner, Supreme Court and Lord High Executioner." [88]

David Jacob Eisenhower, father of the thirty-fourth president, was born in Elizabethville, Pennsylvania, to one Jacob Eisenhower, a successful farmer and devout Mennonite who expected his son to follow in his footsteps. Jacob moved his family across the country with three hundred other Mennonite families, establishing a colony in Dickinson County, Kansas. As David became a teenager, he rebelled against the long hours and monotony of farming, longing for a different life and studying engineering. Jacob considered farming the God-ordained task of man. Any other ambition represented rebellion against the Almighty. David persisted, attending the small Lane University in Lecompton, Kansas, where he fell in love with the bubbly, vivacious Ida Stower. They were married in 1885 and David was forced to end his formal education to provide for a new family.

David Eisenhower's business skills were poor. A wedding gift of

160 acres was quickly mortgaged, the money invested in a partnership and the opening of a general store. But within two short years the newlyweds were bankrupt. David set out alone to look for work in Texas. He found employment as an engine-wiper for the railroads, earning the respectable sum of ten dollars a day. He sent for Ida and their two young sons to join him. There in Denison, Texas, in a rented one-room shack, his third son, Dwight David Eisenhower, future leader of the free world, was born.

But the pull of Kansas was too great. When Ida's brother offered David a job as a mechanic at a creamery in Abilene, the family returned to the Midwest. Some family sources suggest that the new job represented a financial step down for David, but living near family provided stability for Ida. They had three boys and more would come. There was no longer room for them in a small cottage. In Kansas, generous relatives helped the Eisenhowers build a bigger house on a small farm, but the new, more expensive life demanded extra work. While his wife organized the operation, David Eisenhower ran the work detail like a military commander. Chores began when the father rose at five in the morning. Tardiness or failure was subject to corporal punishment, usually a whipping with a supple tree branch. In his autobiography, *At Ease,* Dwight devotes seventeen pages to his mother, giving his father short shrift. A shocking story of the father's rage and severe beating of Dwight's brother Edgar paints a vivid picture of David Eisenhower's temper.[89] The boy had skipped school. David was an autocratic and stern father, yet his reputation for integrity would be honored by his sons.

In 1916, David accepted a job that would offer the family security. He was hired as a mechanic for the Abilene Gas and Electric Company. He stayed with the company until retirement, advancing from mechanic to plant manager. Able at last to provide well for Ida in their later years, he would nonetheless have no inheritance for his sons, a fact that embarrassed him greatly. He lived to see Pearl Harbor and to see his son, Dwight, serve as a personal assistant to the famous General Douglas McArthur in the Pacific theatre. But he died the month before his son was appointed commanding general of the European Theater of Operations.

Ida Stover Eisenhower (May 1, 1862–September 11, 1946). Ida seemed to have a gift for finding joy in the midst of misery. She would need it, for her childhood and early marriage were less than ideal. She was born in 1862 near the Shenandoah Valley; her earliest memories were of losing her mother and the family farm to the ravages of the Civil War. Ida and her seven brothers were sent to live with her maternal grandparents, a strict and severe couple. As the lone girl, young Ida was responsible for the cooking. If she burned the food, a harsh punishment was waiting.[90]

Ida's father passed away several years later, leaving each child with a small inheritance. The brothers set out to make their fortune in Kansas, but Ida had a different dream. Convinced that she could advance herself with an education, she worked her way through high school by cooking and cleaning for nearby families. Her strict and devout grandfather insisted that she read only the Bible at home, so Ida turned it into a massive intellectual and spiritual exercise, committing more than 1,356 verses to memory.[91] After graduating from high school, she joined her brothers in Topeka, where she learned of a nearby college in Lecompton. Soon after enrolling, Ida set eyes on a somber quiet fellow of German descent, David Jacob Eisenhower. Though they were opposites in personality, their common faith and mutual attraction were strong. They were married on September 23, 1885.

Ida would give birth to seven boys, among them the future president Dwight David Eisenhower, born on October 14, 1890, in Denison, Texas. One son would die in infancy, but the others would all grow into fine young men. Times were tough for the family. Legal problems and unpaid debts constantly plagued her husband. A modest job offer lured the Eisenhowers back to Kansas, to the comfortable town of Abilene. There, for the first several years, they struggled in a cramped cottage. But Ida kept her joy, trusting in the comforting words of her Bible. And eventually things changed. They bought a small farm with a barn, fruit trees, cows, and chickens. Here Ida's organization and ability to manage effectively paid off. In a matter of months, she had her boys efficiently running the small farm, producing all the necessities of life. Humming hymns as she worked, Ida was the more dominant of the two parents, but she did everything with such joy that no one seemed to mind.

Though a pacifist and heartbroken at Dwight's decision to enter West Point, she supported her son and was careful never to interfere with his choices. During World War II, Dwight Eisenhower rose to become the commander of the entire Allied effort and was transformed into a hometown hero. When asked by a reporter whether she was proud of her son, she genuinely asked, "Which one?"[92] She was equally proud of all her children. Each was successful in his chosen career. Arthur became a banker, Edgar a lawyer, Roy a pharmacist, Earl an engineer and journalist, and Milton, the youngest, who would be mentioned as a presidential possibility himself, became an extraordinary educator and administrator, building Johns Hopkins University into one of the nation's leading institutions.

Ida lived to see Dwight, her third son, accept the surrender of the Axis in World War II and be hailed an American hero in ticker-tape parades in New York and Washington, but she died before he was elected president. It probably didn't matter. He was already a great success in her view. All that mattered to Ida was that her boys grew to be God-fearing men of integrity. This she saw to fruition with great joy and dignity. She was eighty-four years old when she died peacefully in her sleep.

35. JOHN FITZGERALD KENNEDY (1961–1963)

Joseph Patrick Kennedy (September 6, 1888–November 18, 1969). Joseph Patrick Kennedy, son of Patrick Joseph "P. J." Kennedy, was born in Boston, Massachusetts. His father was an importer of wine and spirits and a leading figure in the local Democratic party. In the fall of 1908, Joe fulfilled his parents' wish by enrolling in Harvard. Nine years after first meeting Rose Fitzgerald, the daughter of the popular Boston mayor John Francis Fitzgerald, he married her. They had nine children, including President John Kennedy, U.S. Attorney General and U.S. Senator Robert Kennedy, and U.S. Senator Edward Kennedy. Their daughter Eunice would marry Sargent Shriver, first director of the Peace Corps, ambassador to France, and the 1972 Democratic vice-presidential nominee.

Joe Kennedy's early relationship with his children was distant but respectful. He had high expectations for his sons, telling them that "second best is a loser."[93]

Joe Kennedy was the nation's youngest bank president. Before his amazing business career was over he would make a fortune on Wall Street in shipbuilding, in the movie industry, and in liquor importing.

His infidelities, including a famous liaison with the movie actress Gloria Swanson, the most glamorous woman of the day, set a pattern for his sons.[94] Despite his failures as a husband and father, Rose would label him "the architect of our lives."[95]

Kennedy was an active member of the Democratic party and in 1934 President Franklin D. Roosevelt appointed him chairman of the Securities and Exchange Commission. In 1937 he was appointed U.S. ambassador to Great Britain. Joe was an isolationist who disapproved of Roosevelt's growing involvement in Europe; he resigned in 1940. His views were so out of sync with the nation that any further political ambition was dashed.

Pain was no stranger to the Kennedys. Kennedy's eldest son, Joe (1915–1944), was killed while serving in the armed forces in World War II; their daughter Kathleen (1920–1948) died in a plane crash. After the war, Joe concentrated on helping the political careers of his three surviving sons. John Fitzgerald Kennedy became president but was assassinated in 1963. Robert Kennedy served as attorney general under his brother and as U.S. senator from New York before he, too, was murdered, in 1968. Edward Kennedy became a U.S. senator from Massachusetts. Joseph P. Kennedy's oldest daughter, Rosemary, was mentally handicapped. Joe agreed to a lobotomy, drastically worsening her condition. This he kept a secret from his family. In December 1961, Joe suffered a paralyzing stroke from which he never recovered. He died eight years later, on November 18, 1969.

Rose Fitzgerald Kennedy (July 1890–January 22, 1995). Born to John "Honey Fitz" Fitzgerald and Josephine Mary Hannon Fitzgerald, Rose began her life on the campaign trail. She possessed her father's political charisma and her mother's abiding religious faith. Honey Fitz was a congressman and later the popular mayor of Boston. Young Rose often stood smiling beside him at ribbon cuttings and other ceremonial occasions, charming the crowd. The dark-haired beauty, gifted with a bright mind, graduated from high school at the age of fifteen. She studied abroad in Europe, where she gained her famous high-society polished look. Upon returning to Boston, she devoted herself to teaching catechism to slum children.

Rose's real destiny was motherhood. On October 7, 1914, nine years after her first dance with the fiery, red-haired Irishman Joe

Kennedy, the two wed. Twenty-five-year-old Joe had just become the youngest bank president in Massachusetts, and this helped persuade Rose's parents to give their blessing to the union. Big money and big business were soon pouring into Joe's hands, taking him away from his family and leaving Rose to raise the children.

On May 20, 1917, the Kennedys were blessed with a second son, John F. Kennedy. Rose's program for all her children included attending mass every day, taking them on historical field trips to Plymouth Rock, and teaching them right and wrong. Rose worked very hard at bringing up winners, just as hard as her husband worked at amassing his millions and at philandering. Even in her times of greatest pain, the loss of her children, she seemed never to complain. Her composure after JFK's assassination attested to her strength and faith.

Rose Kennedy actively campaigned for her sons throughout their political careers. And throughout her life she supported numerous philanthropic causes. She was an American icon of motherhood with grace and beauty who lived to the astounding age of 104 years, passing away on January 22, 1995, in Hyannis Port, Massachusetts.

36. PRESIDENT LYNDON BAINES JOHNSON
(1963–1969)

Sam Ealy Johnson, Jr. (October 11, 1877–October 22, 1937). Sam Ealy Johnson, Jr., was born in Buda, Texas, to Sam Johnson, Sr., and Eliza Bunton Johnson. Sam was a notably bright child with a quick mind and an amazing memory. When he was eleven, the family moved to the banks of the Pedernales River, where the town of Johnson City, Texas, would one day be established by Sam's nephew James. As a teenager, Sam was determined to get an education to better himself and leave the drudgery of farm life. Money for schooling was scarce and Sam was the fifth of nine children. So he learned to be a butcher and barber to help pay the small fees for attending public school. When doctors diagnosed him with a nervous stomach, forcing him to drop out, he devoted himself to his own private regimen of study, eventually passing the Texas state teacher's examination.

After two years of teaching, Sam was restless. He tried his hand at farming before finally discovering a more practical use for his persuasive personality. He ran for the Texas State House of Representatives and won. While serving his second term in the legislature, Sam married the beautiful Rebekah Baines. In 1908, the same year Lyndon Baines Johnson was born, Sam sought his third legislative term. An unfortunate financial collapse caused by the decline of the cotton market forced him to leave politics for ten years. During this hiatus, he earned a living as a rancher, real estate agent, and land speculator; he soon regained prosperity. Young Lyndon, though most definitely a "mama's boy," resembled his father in many ways—he was precocious, ambitious, competitive, and determined. Sam could not help but make everything a competition. In the morning he would shake Lyndon awake before sunrise and holler "Get up, Lyndon, every boy in town already has gotten an hour start on you and you will never catch up." [96] Sam returned to the legislature in 1917. His most notable achievements were the historic preservation of the Alamo and the "Johnson Blue Sky Law." [97]

In July 1937, Sam suffered a massive heart attack. He died at home that fall, at the age of sixty. Lyndon Johnson would outdo his father's political career with public service that spanned more than three decades, culminating in the presidency of the United States.

Rebekah Baines Johnson (June 26, 1881–September 12, 1958). Growing up in McKinney, Texas, Rebekah Baines was exceptionally bright; in a different time, she might have had political ambitions of her own, but instead she channeled her ambition and drive into her son, who would become our thirty-sixth president.

From the moment Rebekah opened her tiny blue eyes she would be her daddy's girl. Tracing his heritage to Scotland, Joseph Baines came from a long line of highly educated Baptist preachers. He taught his beloved Rebekah to read at an early age. She attended Baylor University and worked as a freelance writer for several newspapers in the Austin area. Proudly, Rebekah watched her father be appointed Texas secretary of state, but he died before reaching his lifelong goal of running for Congress.

Shortly before his death, Joe had introduced his daughter to a young state legislator by the name of Sam Johnson. Crushed by the loss of her father, mentor, and guide, she ran into the comforting arms of her new friend. Sam was an earthy, clever man with a boisterous laugh and a promising career as a rancher and politician. Rebekah, refined and beautiful, with her blue eyes and blond hair, seemed an unlikely match for the rough-hewn rancher. But they were wed on August 20, 1907. A year later, Rebekah would give birth to Lyndon Baines Johnson. Seeing her baby for the first time, Rebekah would understand "the deep purposefulness and true nobility" that had shone in her own father's eyes.[98] From that moment on, little Lyndon became her life's focus.

Life on a remote farm near the Pedernales River was a challenge, but Rebekah would somehow provide the resources a future president would need. By his second birthday she had taught him the alphabet, and by the time he was three he was reciting Longfellow. She poured her love of culture and education into all five of her children, but she worshiped her firstborn. Throughout his life, Rebekah was a constant support and actively encouraged his pursuit of politics. When he was elected to Congress, she wrote proudly that "today my faith is restored. How happy it would have made my precious noble father to know the first born of his first born would achieve the position he so desired . . . how dear you are."[99] She lived to see him ascend to majority leader of the Senate, but she died in Austin, Texas, in 1958, five years before Lyndon Johnson became president.

37. RICHARD MILHOUS NIXON (1969–1974)

Francis Anthony Nixon (December 3, 1878–September 4, 1956). In his early teenage years, Frank Nixon left lonely Vinton, Ohio, and set out on his own. Sporadic schooling in his tumultuous childhood made finding a steady occupation difficult. Frank tried his hand as a carpenter, a painter, a farmer, and even as a railway motorman. In 1907, he traveled to Southern California. He worked the rail line that went from Los Angeles to Whittier. Surprisingly, this brash, energetic young Irishman won the heart of a quiet beauty, Hannah Milhous. Seven years Hannah's senior, Frank was opinionated, boisterous, and lavish in his love of this simple, sheltered Quaker girl. Hannah and Frank were wed on June 25, 1908, only four months after they met.

During their first year of marriage things seemed promising; Frank had a job as a field hand at the Jordan Ranch just east of Whittier. The small flimsy cottage that came with the job would be Frank and Hannah's first home together. But financial worries seemed to plague

Frank, and his inability to accept advice made things worse. His father-in-law set him up in a small orange farm, but the project failed. He then moved to the new community of Yorba Linda to grow lemons, but again failed miserably, inflaming his hurt pride. Finally he and Hannah eked out a living running a gas station and market.

Frank's exuberant charm could be offset by a raging temper. Neighbors heard him yelling loudly at his boys.[100] Hannah, never confrontational, only offered the gentle criticism that "he could be very undiplomatic."[101] In Frank's later years, his charm faded and a meanness and bitterness set in that Hannah quietly endured. In 1947, he retired to a relative's farm near York, Pennsylvania. Some wondered if he was reaching out to his son, who was nearby, forging a political career in Washington, D.C. Frank lived to see his son elected the vice president of the United States. But in 1956, after being bedridden for months and in declining health, Frank Nixon slipped away. He would miss his son's mercurial rise and fall from power, his opening to China, and the important role he would play in world history.

Hannah Milhous Nixon (March 7, 1885–September 30, 1967). Richard Nixon tearfully proclaimed his mother as a saint on his final day as president.[102] Though Hannah would not live to see her son take up the highest office in the land, her kindness gave him a soft place to land during his sometimes harsh childhood.

Born into a serene family of devout Quakers in Jennings County, Indiana, Hannah had an idealistic upbringing. Her gentle-spirited father, Franklin Milhous, a prosperous fruit farmer, decided to pack up the family and head west to promises of fertile land in California. Twelve-year-old Hannah quickly settled into a new Quaker community on the West Coast. She enjoyed her studies at Whittier Academy and her regular attendance at Whittier Friends Church. On a cold Valentine's Day in 1908, her plans to pursue a career as a teacher took a backseat to the dashing but temperamental Francis Anthony Nixon. Despite her parents' misgivings and concern over Frank's ability to earn a living, they were married on June 25, 1908.

Richard M. Nixon was born in a humble white bungalow on January 9, 1913, in Yorba Linda, California. He was the second of five children, all boys. Hannah emphasized the importance of education, teaching Richard to read before he began school. Her kindness and encouragement of his dreams forged a strong bond between the two. Along with rearing her rambunctious brood, she was up at dawn each day to ensure that the family grocery store was ready for business. Hannah endured Frank's unpredictable temper and doomed business investments, but her greatest pain came from the ravages of tuberculosis, which took her oldest son, Harold, and her second youngest son, Arthur. Richard Nixon was devoted to his mother to the end. She passed away on September 30, 1967, at the age of eighty-two. The following year her son was elected president.

38. PRESIDENT GERALD FORD (1974–1977)

Leslie Lynch King (July 25, 1886–February 18, 1941). Gerald Ford was thirteen when he learned about Leslie Lynch King, a multimillionaire who had made a fortune as a wool merchant. He married Gerald's mother, Dorothy Gardner, on September 7, 1912. Unfortunately, their marriage was difficult and short-lived. King abused his wife, who reportedly fled with her infant son, Leslie Lynch King, Jr., to her parents' home in Grand Rapids, Michigan. Leslie and Dorothy were divorced within three years of their wedding.

Poor business practices reportedly cost King his fortune, but when he introduced himself to his teenage son, he did not seem broke. Leslie had traveled to Grand Rapids to pick up a new Lincoln. While in Michigan, he tracked his son to a local restaurant, where the young man worked as a waiter. King introduced himself as Gerald's father and asked the stunned boy to take a lunch break. The two ate together, and at the end of their meal, Leslie King gave his son twenty-five dollars. Gerald was in his last year of study at Yale when his biological father, suffering from asthma, died in Tucson, Arizona, unaware of the historic and healing role his president son would one day play for the nation.

Gerald Rudolph Ford, Sr. (December 9, 1890–January 26, 1962). Gerald Rudolph Ford's father was killed in a train accident when Gerald was fourteen. The boy dropped out of school after eighth grade to start work in a paint store, where he successfully learned the trade that eventually enabled him to open the Ford Paint and Varnish Company.

On February 1, 1916, Gerald married Dorothy Gardner King, a

beautiful young woman whom he had met at church. With their marriage, he instantly became a father to her young son from her troubled first marriage, not only accepting the boy as his own but giving him his own name, Gerald Rudolph Ford, Jr. The boy would become the thirty-eighth president. Gerald, Sr., was a civic leader and member of many organizations and orders. His integrity earned more than just the respect of his Grand Rapids community. During the Depression, when other businesses were folding, the DuPont Corporation extended credit to Gerald and the Ford Paint and Varnish Company. Customers knew they could count on Ford to stand behind his product, and DuPont believed they could trust him with an impressive line of credit even though the bank had foreclosed on his house. Rather than lay off his employees, Ford lowered every worker's wage, including his own, to five dollars per week until the economy improved and could support better wages.

Ford was a strong Republican and a man who lived his faith. Both he and his wife continued to serve their community and to teach their sons values of family and faith. Dorothy Ford often said of her husband, "If Dad would give as much time to the paint business as to public affairs, we'd be rich." [103] Ford had three strict rules for his four sons: tell the truth, work hard, and show up for dinner on time. Gerald Ford died at the age of seventy-two after a fall on a patch of ice brought on a heart attack.

Dorothy Ayer Garner Ford (February 27, 1892–September 17, 1967). Born in Harvard, Illinois, she was educated at a girls' finishing school, then attended college. However, she was swept away by the dashing young Leslie King after her first year of school and married him on September 7, 1912. Their marital bliss was cut short on their honeymoon, when a gentleman tipped his hat to the new Mrs. King. The jealous Leslie began slapping his wife. Bouts of abuse continued, followed by repentant moments that brought them back together. Their son, Leslie Lloyd King, Jr., was born on July 14, 1913, and sixteen days later, after being threatened by her husband with a butcher knife, Dorothy fled with her new baby to her parents' home in Grand Rapids, Michigan.

Dorothy was noted for her strong faith in a loving and caring God, faith that carried her through the heartbreak. Little was said about the reasons behind her failed marriage, but she found solace in her family's home. There she met the enterprising young Gerald Ford. He was quiet but ambitious. Because of her tumultuous past, Dorothy was not anxious to risk another marriage. Yet when she was confident that Gerald would provide a good home and be a good father to her son, she consented.

Her judgment proved sound. Gerald established a reputation for integrity and he loved his sons, especially the little adopted baby from Dorothy's first marriage. While Gerald was building a prominent business, Dorothy took care of their home. Remembering her own trials and hardships as a young bride, she devoted much of her life to helping others in need.

Much of her life revolved around Grace Episcopal Church. It was there that she met her second husband. It was there that the two were happily married. And in 1967, it was there, while she sat in her regular pew waiting for services to commence, that Dorothy Ford suffered a fatal heart attack. In 1974, Leslie Lynch King, Jr., the little baby born into a troubled, abusive home, became president of the United States and helped heal the nation after the division of the Watergate years.

39. JAMES EARL CARTER, JR.
(1977–1981)

James Earl Carter, Sr. (September 12, 1894–July 23, 1953). Thirty years after the Civil War, William Archibald Carter and his wife, Nina, celebrated the birth of their fourth child. (They would eventually have five children.) In true Southern fashion, the boy was called by his middle name, Earl. He spent the first nine years of his life in Arlington, Georgia, the town of his birth. Then tragedy struck: his father was shot and killed by a business partner. In 1904, the family moved to Plains, Georgia, to be closer to a supportive uncle. The move was to change Earl's life. It was a small, dusty town but Earl determined to conquer it. With his uncle providing moral support, he was able to complete the tenth grade at Riverside Academy in Gainesville, Florida. The family could trace its lineage to the 1700s and in all those years, no other Carter had ever achieved as much academically.

Thirsty for adventure, seventeen-year-old Earl took a job as a cowboy in Texas. After two years, he had saved enough money to move back to Plains to launch the first of many successful businesses, an ice house. With the profits he started a laundry and dry-cleaning business. His entrepreneurial career was interrupted by World War I; despite poor eyesight, he rose to the rank of lieutenant in the Quartermaster Corps. Returning to Plains, he continued his investments, opening a grocery store on Main Street and taking out a line of credit to purchase acreage.

In 1921, he met and fell in love with Lillian Gordy, a student nurse at the local private hospital. They met at a dance and although Earl was sure of "Lilly," she needed some time. Her boss, Dr. Sam Wise, who would one day serve as the attending physician at Jimmy Carter's birth, told Lillian that Earl had more ambition than anyone in town and that he would undoubtedly be a success in life. After a constant stream of notes and flowers, Earl prevailed, only to insist that Lillian finish her schooling before they married, on September 27, 1923. Earl was twenty-nine and Lillian was twenty-five. Earl had hoped that a potato crop would pay for the reception and honeymoon, but the yield was poor and the celebrations were postponed. On October 1, 1924, at seven in the morning, the new couple welcomed the birth of the first of four children, James Earl "Jimmy" Carter, Jr. He became the first president to have been born in a hospital.

Earl Carter continued to prosper. By 1927, he had generated enough profits to pay off his loan, increase his landholdings to 700 acres, and offer loans to other Sumter County farmers. Eventually, most farmers in the area came to Earl for help and his land holdings grew to a sizable 4,000 acres. Living in rural Georgia in those days was not easy. There was no electricity or indoor plumbing for the Carters. But using advanced crop rotation and diversification, newly effective insecticides, and the latest agricultural machinery, Earl was able to succeed when others around him were falling to the ravages of the Great Depression.

As his affluence grew, Earl did not neglect his family or civic duties. Since his wife was often absent, helping neighbors deliver children or tending to other medical needs, he was the parent who dealt with the children. He took them to school, to church, and to social events and even helped with their homework. He served on the Sumter County School Board and was an early director of the Rural Electrification Administration. Earl was a member of the Plains Baptist

Church, the local Lions Club, the Americus Elks, and the American Legion.

Earl and his firstborn, Jimmy, were very close. "He was the center of my life," the future president would say, "and the focus of my admiration. My daddy was the dominant personality in our family." He described his father as his only friend. When Jimmy was a teen, Earl offered him a deal. If his boy did not start smoking until after he turned twenty-one, Earl would give him his gold watch. Jimmy, alone in the family, hated smoking and never took it up. But the father's favor had a barb in its tail: Earl held his namesake to a higher standard than he did the other children. Jimmy's sister Gloria Carter insisted that no matter how well Jimmy did, Earl would always insist he could have done better.

When Jimmy was graduated from high school in 1941, Earl was supportive of his dream to attend the U.S. Naval Academy at Annapolis. While his son attended classes at Georgia Southwestern College in Americus and Georgia Institute of Technology, Earl discussed with a local congressman the idea of an appointment to Annapolis. In 1943, Jimmy was admitted to the Naval Academy. Meanwhile, Earl was elected Sumter County's representative in the House of Representatives of the Georgia General Assembly. Politically, the father and son disagreed. "He was quite conservative, and my mother was a liberal," Jimmy Carter would explain. "Although in our family we never thought much about such labels." [104]

At the time of his election to state office, Earl Carter was already suffering from the ravages of pancreatic cancer. He died at his home on July 22, 1953. Only then did the family learn of his considerable charity, especially toward his own tenant farmers. Returning from the funeral, Jimmy Carter made a life-altering resolution to resign from the Navy. He told his sister, "I want to be a man like my father." Responding to a call from Lillian at age twenty-eight, Jimmy returned to Plains, Georgia, to manage his father's farm and peanut brokerage business.

Bessie Lillian Gordy Carter (August 15, 1898–October 30, 1983). James Jackson Gordy and Mary Ida Nicholson had eight children of their own, with Lillian—"Lilly"—somewhere in the middle. When an aunt died, James and Mary happily took in her two children and when a grandfather died they welcomed his widow. The Gordy home fairly bulged, with thirteen children and other relatives.

They were all fortunate that James Jackson Gordy, known as Jim Jack, always seemed to have a comfortable job. Most prominently, he was the postmaster of Richland, Georgia, for twenty-one years and held positions as revenue officer and later as U.S. deputy marshal. During tough economic times, the Gordys could count on the relative security of Jim Jack's government jobs. Although he enjoyed politics, Gordy wasn't interested in holding office; instead, he assisted worthy candidates. Many of his liberal ideas affected Lillian. He believed in a woman's right to an education, considering his daughters the intellectual equals of any man. Although he lived in the Deep South, he believed in racial justice and equality. He believed that it was the government's responsibility to improve the quality of life and to care for its citizens. Jim Jack enthusiastically supported a plan to have government-funded free rural mail. In 1918, with World War I raging, he supported his daughter's aspiration to become a nurse. But when the war came to an abrupt end, all nurse training programs were phased out. Lillian was heartbroken, but Jim Jack turned to Dr. Sam Wise, an old family friend who was building a private hospital in Plains, Georgia, and as a favor to Jim Jack agreed to take his daughter on as a trainee.

In Plains, Lillian met the man she would marry, James Earl Carter, Sr. They were engaged in 1923 but Earl insisted that Lillian finish her nurse's training before the wedding. For six months Lillian worked as a trainee in Atlanta, Georgia, where she received the requisite advanced training. During the separation, Earl placed weekly phone calls and visited twice, keeping the home fires burning. On September 26, 1923, they were married. Earl was twenty-nine. Lillian was twenty-five. James Earl Carter, Jr., was born on October 1, 1924; he would be the first of four children, and he grew up to become the president of the United States.

Earl and Lillian were a power couple before their time. Lillian earned a decent living as a surgical and private-duty nurse, while Earl's investments prospered. Their financial security allowed Lillian to take on poor patients in need. She became a virtual doctor to the indigent of Sumter County. With Lillian often gone for days at a time, Earl and a succession of nannies took on the extra duties of raising the children.

"My childhood world was really shaped by black women," Jimmy Carter would say. Lillian would later regret some of her choices, saying that Earl "had been a more affectionate father than I had been a mother." But her family would be proud of her.[105]

Working tirelessly for the poor of the community, Lillian knew nothing of Earl's business. When he died, in July 1953, she was unprepared to manage his enterprises. The Georgia state legislature asked the widow to finish her husband's term. She quickly demurred, declaring herself unqualified to represent people who had elected a man of conservative views, while her own were defiantly liberal. Then, she was wholly unprepared to manage the farm and peanut warehouse business. With so many employees' lives at stake, Lillian felt a solemn responsibility to act, but there was only one person capable of helping her pick up the pieces and make it all work. Lieutenant Jimmy Carter, Jr., resigned from the Navy and a promising career working on the nation's first atomic submarine. He returned to Plains to help his mother run the family business.

Shortly after her husband's death, Lillian descended into a deep depression, which required months of treatment. Her family rallied around her. When she learned of the need for a house mother at Auburn University, they encouraged her to take the job, believing that the busy life of a fraternity would help bring healing. She worked for the fraternity for over seven years. But her return to Plains brought renewed grief and stifling boredom. Looking for a cause to support, she attended the 1964 Democratic Convention and became the cochair of the Lyndon Johnson presidential campaign committee in Americus, Georgia. The action only inspired a greater desire for civic duty.

When Lillian was sixty-eight, she saw a public service announcement for the Peace Corps. She laughingly told her children she was signing up. But what began as a flight of fantasy eventually became reality. She formally joined the organization in 1966, studied Marathi and Hindi at the University of Chicago, and traveled to Vikhroli, India. The posting lasted for two years, with Lillian writing glowing letters home to her children. "I didn't dream that in this remote corner of the world. . . . I would discover what life is really all about. Sharing yourself with others and accepting their love for you is the most precious gift of all."[106]

During Jimmy Carter's presidential campaign, Lillian became an international figure. She made more than 600 speeches to show her support and privately counseled her son behind the scenes. Lillian Carter won the hearts of America with her blunt, straight-talking style. When Jimmy was elected, she attended the inaugural proceedings, thoroughly enjoying her role as the nation's "First Mother." And she would visit the White House often. In February 1977, she returned to India as a representative of the United States for the funeral of President Fakhruddin Ali. Carter described his mother as "an extrovert, very dynamic, inquisitive in her attitude about life, compassionate towards others."[107] She died of cancer in 1983. She was eighty-five.

40. PRESIDENT RONALD REAGAN
(1981–1989)

John Edward "Jack" Reagan (July 13, 1883–May 18, 1941). John Reagan, known to all as Jack, was born in Fulton, Illinois, to John and Jennie Reagan. His parents were ordinary people, the father employed at a grain elevator. Both parents died of tuberculosis within days of each other, leaving six-year-old Jack, his sister, and their brother orphans. The three children were immediately separated. The brother and sister went to live with their uncle, William Reagan, while Jack was sent alone to Bennett, Iowa, to live with his aunt Margaret and her husband, Orson G. Baldwin.

It was while living with the Baldwins that Jack had his first taste of salesmanship, working as a clerk in his uncle's store. At the age of sixteen, he returned to Fulton and entered the work force full-time as a salesman for J. W. Broadhead Dry Goods Store. A second-generation Irish-American Catholic, Jack fell in love with Nelle Clyde, a petite, optimistic Protestant. Jack was already demonstrating a weakness for alcohol, but Nelle seemed to think she could love him out of the illness and married him anyway in a Catholic ceremony on November 8, 1904. Jack's sales work led the couple from one small Illinois town to another; they finally settled in Tampico in 1906. There, Jack became involved in community affairs, serving as a city councilman. On February 6, 1911, a second son, Ronald Wilson Reagan, was born. In 1914, Jack was on the move again. Over a four-year period they lived in Chicago, Galesburg, and Monmouth before finally returning to

Tampico. The Great Depression may not have affected the Roosevelts, the Kennedys, the Bushes, or the Carters, but Jack Reagan was devastated. After he lost a job one Christmas Eve, Jack's days as a salesman were finished.

As a liberal Democrat, Jack Reagan worked diligently on Franklin Delano Roosevelt's presidential campaign and afterward was rewarded with a position in the Works Progress Administration in Dixon, Illinois, providing food and food scrip to families, and finding jobs for the unemployed. But poor health forced him to quit.

When Ronald Reagan's acting career began to flourish, he sent money to support his parents. After signing a contract with Warner Bros., he purchased a house for them in California, and Jack took a studio job, managing his son's fan mail for twenty-five dollars a week. Despite Jack's weakness for alcohol, he was a noted storyteller and an honest man, both gifts he passed on to his son. The senior Reagan instilled in his boys an "abhorrence of religious and racial bigotry." [108] He would not allow them to view movies that glorified bigotry or hatred. As a traveling salesman, he slept in his car on a cold winter's night rather than stay at the town's only hotel, which refused minorities.

When Ronald Reagan ran for president in 1980, the Kremlin leaked stories about Jack's alcoholism, hoping they would weaken Ronald's election chances. Jack Reagan was mercifully deceased. In his autobiography, *Where's the Rest of Me?*, Reagan refers to his father as "a man who might have made a brilliant career out of selling but he lived in a time—and with a weakness—that made him a frustrated man." [109]

One of the highlights of Jack's relationship with his son was attending the premiere of his first significant film, *Knute Rockne— All American*. The event was held in South Bend, Indiana, home of the Notre Dame University Fighting Irish football team. Ronald Reagan introduced his father to his all-time favorite movie star, Pat O'Brien. The elder Reagan and O'Brien, both Irishmen who loved the bottle, hit it off immediately, becoming drinking buddies for the final weeks of Jack's life. He died suddenly of heart failure.

Throughout his life, Ronald Reagan continued to glory in the movie role of the Gipper. Till the very end, when he was completely overtaken by Alzheimer's disease, he would speak of the football player he personified in the film. And he would often quote the line "Win one for the Gipper." Ronald Reagan would go on to the governorship of California, the White House and a role in ending the Cold War, but he could not let go of his last link to the man who had raised him and to a time when the father had been unabashedly proud of the son.[110]

Nelle Wilson Reagan (July 24, 1883–July 25, 1962). Nelle Wilson was born into a large, loving family in Fulton, Illinois, the youngest of seven children. Like her future husband, Jack, she received a minimal education, but unlike Jack, she was an optimistic young person, devout in her faith and compassionate toward others, making it a practice to visit any acquaintance who was ill or in prison. At twenty-three, she was working as a salesclerk alongside Jack Reagan. It was already apparent that Jack was struggling with alcohol, but Nelle knew no defeat or sadness; strong in her conviction that alcoholism was an illness not a moral failing, she responded to her colleague with open friendship.

Nelle Wilson and Jack Reagan became husband and wife in a Catholic ceremony in 1904. Their marriage would not be easy, however, being marked by her husband's uncontrollable drinking binges and their constant moves. Nelle turned to her faith for strength and hope. An accomplished seamstress, she worked to help stretch the family's means in difficult times, and she tutored her young sons, Neil and Ronald, to help them in school.

Born in 1908, son John Neil was baptized in the Catholic church. But as her marriage worsened, Nelle reverted to the Protestant faith of her childhood. By the time of Ronald's birth on February 6, 1911, Nelle was the spiritual leader in the home and her youngest son was raised according to her lights. Nelle often drew on support from her family, staying with a sister or brother during difficult periods, but she continued to support Jack and taught her children to love and respect him: "We should remember how kind and loving he was when he wasn't affected by drink."[111] Regardless of where they lived or where her husband worked, Nelle's benevolence and optimism continued unabated. Ronald was taught "that all things work together for good to them that love God." Either as a distraction or as a complement to their daily routine, Nelle organized drama recitals and plays in the small towns where they lived. It was young Ronald Reagan's first taste of the theatre.

When Reagan began to draw a salary from his radio broadcasts, he sent money home to support his parents. Nelle was finally able to quit working. Until they moved into a California home purchased by Ronald in 1939, Nelle had never lived in a house that she could call her own. She died in California in 1962, at the age of seventy-seven, when her Ronald was a rising television personality. Greatly affected by his mother's death, that year Reagan retired from his work as a spokesman for General Electric, left the board of the Screen Actors Guild, and switched his membership from the Democratic party to the Republican. Two years later, his nationally televised speech in behalf of the Republican presidential nominee catapulted him into national prominence.

41. GEORGE HERBERT WALKER BUSH
(1989–1993)

Prescott Sheldon Bush (May 15, 1895–October 8, 1972). The first of a long line of public servants in the Bush family, Prescott Sheldon Bush set an example for his children and influenced the nation with his high-minded idealism. "My father was the real inspiration in my life," said presidential son George Herbert Walker Bush. "He was strong and strict, but full of decency and fairness."[112] Born in Columbus, Ohio, Prescott was the oldest son of four children of Samuel Prescott Bush and Flora Sheldon. S. P., as the father was called, had left an early career with the Pennsylvania Railroad to make his fortune in steel. Prescott saw the effects of hard work by watching his father climb from a mechanical engineer to a twenty-year reign as president of Buckeye Steel. S. P. also encouraged health and athleticism, as one of the first assistant coaches of the Ohio State University football team.

Prescott, or Pres as he was called, resumed a family tradition, interrupted by his father, of earning a degree at Yale University. He excelled in sports, academics, singing, and debate. His popularity secured him a position in the secret Skull and Bones Society. After graduating from Yale, Prescott joined the army, where he served as captain in the 158th Field Artillery Brigade during World War I.

Like his father before him, Pres set out on his own, moving to St. Louis, where he began a career in sales. In a business career that spanned decades, Pres became a partner at the prestigious New York firm of Brown Brothers Harriman, eventually serving on the board of directors of the Columbia Broadcasting System, Prudential Insurance Company, the Pennsylvania Water and Power Company, and Pan American Airways.

He married the first girl he fell in love with, Dorothy Walker. They would have five children together, four boys and a girl. The second son, George Herbert Walker Bush, was born in Milton, Massachusetts, on June 12, 1924, and would grow up to become the forty-first president. Prescott was a man who understood the importance of the father within the family dynamics. George Bush recalled that his parents practiced "an old-fashioned way of bringing up a family with generous measures of both love and discipline." [113]

Subscribing to a philosophy that one must take care of the family first and then enter public life, Pres Bush used his vast network of friends and his money to launch a public career. In 1947 he was named chairman of the Connecticut State Finance Committee of the Republican party. By the end of the next year, he served as a delegate-at-large to the Republican National Convention. In 1950, the Republicans nominated Pres for the U.S. Senate. He lost to William Benton by approximately 1,000 votes but ran again two years later and won. President Eisenhower named Pres on a list of ten best candidates for the 1960 Republican presidential nomination. In 1972, with his second son serving as United Nations Ambassador, Prescott Sheldon Bush died of lung cancer at the age of seventy-seven.

Dorothy Walker Bush (1901–November 19, 1992). Dorothy Walker was the daughter of George Herbert Walker, a successful businessman who cofounded the largest private investment house in the history of Wall Street. An avid sportsman, he originated golf's Walker Cup and served as the president of the U.S. Golf Association. Walker demanded athletic excellence from all his children, including Dorothy. She was raised to develop her own skills in basketball, golf, baseball, swimming, and tennis. In 1918, she was the runner-up in the Women's National Tennis Tournament. Her competitive spirit can easily be linked to her father's need to be the best.

If sports ruled, education was a close second. Dorothy's family enrolled her in a private school in St. Louis, Missouri, and then sent her on to one of the nation's renowned finishing schools, Miss Porter's in Farmington, Connecticut. As usual in those times, great importance was placed on a "proper" marriage. In the summer of 1919, Prescott Bush announced his engagement to Dorothy. They were married at the church of St. Ann in Kennebunkport, Maine, on August 6, 1921. Dorothy reared all of her five children to respect good-natured competition. According to her family, when she was nine months pregnant with her first child, Prescott, Jr., she was participating in a friendly softball game. She hit a home run, went into labor, and was rushed to the hospital.

Known as Dottie within the family, she instilled a sense of humility and perspective in the family. Braggarts were cut down to size. Her famous son George was on the receiving end of her advice even into the White House. After a severe stroke, ninety-one-year-old Dorothy Walker Bush died in 1992, only days after George was defeated by Bill Clinton. The president would say, "My mother's kindness, and discipline, and values inspired me all my life." [114]

42. PRESIDENT WILLIAM J. CLINTON
(1993–2001)

William Jefferson Blythe (February 27, 1918–May 17, 1946). "Few American presidents have had so little idea of their family's past as William Jefferson Clinton." [115] Even his biological father's date of birth is controversial. Many official reference books and military records give the date as February 21, 1917. The Clinton Library declares that he was born on February 27, 1918. [116] Blythe was born near Sherman, Texas, to a large family. The sixth of nine children, he was in his early teens when his father was stricken with colon cancer. William dropped out of school and took a job at a local dairy to help provide for their family. (The circumstances are eerily like those of other presidential fathers.) He was unable to meet the family's financial needs; the bank foreclosed on their farm, and the Blythes moved into a rental apartment.

Over the next few years, Billy Blythe entered into a series of marriages that resulted in children and divorces. He met Virginia Cassidy at a hospital in Shreveport, Louisiana. His girlfriend had been suffering from appendicitis and he was there to comfort her, but when Virginia, a student nurse, walked into the room he quickly transferred his affections to her. The couple was married before a justice of the peace two months later, on September 3, 1943, and a few weeks after that he was bound for the Mediterranean on an Army troopship. World War II took him to Africa and Italy, where he worked to repair heavy equipment. In December 1945, with his service complete, Bill Blythe was honorably discharged and returned to his young bride.

Bill earned his living in sales, first auto parts and then heavy equipment. They purchased a home in a Chicago suburb. With Bill on the road throughout the Illinois region, a pregnant Virginia temporarily stayed with her parents. On May 17, 1946, Bill was on his way to pick up his wife when, near Sikeston, Missouri, a front tire blew, sending his car reeling. It rolled twice and landed in a ditch. Bill Blythe was apparently thrown from the vehicle. While his injuries consisted of a "scratch on his forehead and a bump on the back of his head," he landed facedown in standing water.[117] His body was found two hours after the accident. The cause of death was drowning.

On August 19, 1946, eight months after his father's return from the service, William Jefferson Blythe IV was born by cesarean section. His name would later be changed to Bill Clinton and he would become the forty-second American president.

Virginia first learned of her husband's previous marriages during her son's campaign when eager journalists reconstructed the family histories. By then she had no reason to doubt his true love for her or his honesty. In *The Comeback Kid: The Life and Career of Bill Clinton,* Clinton's own words describe his father's impact on his life and career: "Most kids never think about when they might die. I thought about it all the time because my father died at twenty-nine, before I was born."[118]

Roger Clinton (July 25, 1909–November 8, 1967). Roger Clinton was born in Arkansas, one of five children. His first marriage, to Ina Mae Murphy, lasted fifteen years, ending in 1948 with charges of abuse. Roger first met Virginia Kelley Blythe during her days as a nursing student, but there had been no relationship. When they met again, years later, in 1947, he was still married to Ina Mae. But Virginia missed that fact and also chose to ignore the stories of his drinking, gambling, fighting and womanizing.[119] They were married on June 19, 1950.

The problems that had plagued Roger in his first marriage and throughout his life did not vanish with a new exchange of vows. After selling his Buick dealership in 1952, he moved his family to Hot Springs, Arkansas. There, he quickly gambled away any chance for a better life. "Roger's beatings, verbal abuse, and drunken, jealous rages were common and chronic." [120] When Bill was fourteen, he was finally big enough and strong enough to intervene on his mother's behalf. [121] But the cycles of abuse followed by repentance continued. On May 15, 1962, Roger and Virginia were divorced. On August 6, 1962, they were remarried.

Diagnosed with cancer in 1965, Roger began to make some changes. While enduring radiation treatments at Duke Medical Center, he began to communicate with Bill. His stepson would drive from Georgetown on the weekends to see him, and in between visits, he would write words of encouragement. "Write me more," Bill suggested, reaching out to his stepfather. "People—even some of my political enemies—confide in me." [122] At the end, Bill Clinton and his mother kept vigil day and night for the failing Roger Clinton. Their stormy lives together were finally calmed. Liquor, gambling, and violence were gone, and at fifty-eight, Roger Clinton died.

Virginia Dell Cassidy Blythe Clinton Dwire Kelley (June 6, 1923–January 6, 1994). She was born and raised in Hope, Arkansas. Her mother, Edith, provided in-home care, and her mild-mannered father, Eldridge, was an iceman. The tender care Edith gave her patients seemed in direct contrast to the abuse she rained down on her daughter. People in the small town were accustomed to Edith's heavy makeup, just as Virginia became accustomed to her mother's heavy-handed discipline. Neither Edith nor Eldridge trusted the other's fidelity, so their daughter's childhood was less than stable. In spite of the struggles in her home, the intelligent young Virginia excelled in school while serving as a waitress at the Checkerboard Cafe. Her goal was simply to complete high school and leave her small town in search of something better.

As a young woman, Virginia moved to Shreveport, Louisiana, where she studied nursing at the Tri-State Hospital. It was as a student nurse that she walked into a patient's room one day and met Bill Blythe for the first time. He was comforting his girlfriend, who had appendicitis. Bill and Virginia began a relationship that within weeks led to her first marriage.

Soon after they exchanged vows, Bill was shipped overseas, stationed in Africa and later Italy, but mercifully away from the front lines of World War II. Meanwhile, the young bride finished her nurse's training and then returned to Hope to live with her parents. Bill received his honorable discharge on December 7, 1945, but died five months later in a freak automobile accident. Eight months after that, on August 19, 1946, Virginia's baby, William Jefferson Blythe, was delivered by cesarean section.

Once more Virginia moved in with her parents. Forty-five-year-old Edith accepted the role of grandmother with more love and enthusiasm than she had the role of mother. And, perhaps to get out of the house, Virginia began dating again. One boyfriend, Roger Clinton, lived in nearby Hot Springs but was the owner of a Buick dealership in Hope. The fact that he was a married man supposedly escaped Virginia, but her mother was livid.[123] At one point, lonely and on the hunt, Virginia moved to New Orleans to become a nurse-anesthetist, leaving her young son in her parents' care and enjoying the nightlife of the Big Easy.

On June 19, 1950, in a ceremony not attended by her parents or her young son, Virginia Blythe became the bride of Roger Clinton. Roger and Virginia and her son, Bill Blythe, moved into a house in Hot Springs. Their marital bliss was short-lived. Roger's alcoholic binges generally precipitated physical abuse. Several recorded instances reflect the dangerous environment. In one notorious instance, police were called to the house after Clinton fired a gun at his wife. The bullet lodged in the wall, between Virginia and her young son. Abuse was always followed by repentance, and each time, Virginia would cave in. In 1962, the couple divorced and then remarried. Shortly after this last reconciliation, Bill Blythe changed his name to Bill Clinton. Virginia remained married to Roger until his death of colon cancer in 1968. After that, there would be two more marriages. One was to Jeff Dwire, a hairdresser in Hot Springs. He, too, had a questionable past, but the two remained married until he died in 1974. And there was a final marriage to Richard Kelley, a food broker.

In January 1993, when her son stood on a platform to take the presidential oath of office for the first time, Virginia Kelley already knew that she had breast cancer. But she would not allow it to darken the joyous event. A year later, she was dead. She had faced many challenges and struggles throughout her life, but from the very beginning she had recognized her son's great potential for leadership and had lived to see her instincts proven right.

43. GEORGE WALKER BUSH (2001–)

George Herbert Walker Bush (June 12, 1924–). The second son of Prescott Sheldon Bush and Dorothy Walker, George Herbert Walker Bush lived his early life in privilege. When he was still an infant, his family moved to the exclusive suburb of Greenwich, Connecticut. In the midst of the Great Depression, Bush enjoyed the privileges that came with wealth. He was driven to school by his father's chauffeur, Alec. Bush attended the Greenwich Country Day School and played on the baseball, football, soccer, and tennis teams. At age thirteen, Bush was enrolled at the Phillips Academy, an all-boys college-preparatory school in Andover, Massachusetts. He excelled in extracurricular activities, becoming the senior class president, captain of the baseball and soccer team, manager of the basketball team, president of the Society of Inquiry, and an editor of the school paper.

Inspired by the surge of patriotism following Pearl Harbor, young Bush joined the Navy on his eighteenth birthday and became the youngest aviator in American history. He flew in fifty-eight combat missions and logged 1,228 flight hours in just thirty-nine months. He was one of only four pilots in his squadron to survive the war. On a dangerous mission in 1944, as his plane descended to its target, it was struck by antiaircraft fire. Despite the risks and with the plane in flames, Bush continued to his target, dropped his payload, and made it back out to sea. He was twenty years old.

Arriving home on Christmas Eve, 1944, George Bush married his nineteen-year-old sweetheart, Barbara Pierce. Within two months of receiving his naval discharge, George Bush enrolled in Yale's accelerated program, in which veterans could earn their degrees in two and a half years. During this time, Barbara became pregnant with their first child, George Walker Bush. He was born on July 6, 1946. Although the boy did not share his father's full name, family and friends often referred to him as Junior.

After his graduation and following a long family tradition before him, George H.W. sought to make his own fortune, independent of his father's help. He and Barbara decided to risk their future in search of "black gold" in the Texas oil business. During the next twenty years, the family would move into twenty-eight different houses in seventeen cities across the country before settling to some degree of permanence in Midland, Texas. During these years the family added another child, Pauline Robinson Bush, called Robin by her family. She died of leukemia in 1953, two months before her fourth birthday. By 1959, George, Sr.'s, oil business was booming. The family moved to Houston to be near the action for offshore drilling opportunities.

While in Houston, George H.W. began developing his public life. He became the Harris County Republican party chairman and failed in two bids to follow his father into the U.S. Senate. He was elected to the U.S. House of Representatives, appointed ambassador to the United Nations, and served as chairman of the Republican National Committee, the U.S. representative to China, and director of the Central Intelligence Agency. By 1980 he was Ronald Reagan's vice president.

In 1988, George H. W. Bush was elected the forty-first American president. His measured tone helped seal the end of the Cold War and the unraveling of the Soviet empire. In 1995, when his son, George W. Bush, was inaugurated as the governor of Texas, George H.W. offered him a special gift with a simple note attached. "Dear George, these cufflinks are my most treasured possession. They were given to me by Mom and Dad on June 9 . . . in 1943 when I got my Navy wings at Corpus Christi. I want you to have them now. . . . You are ready for this huge challenge. You'll do just fine. You'll be strong, honest, caring governor. . . . You have given us more than we ever could have deserved. . . . We love you. Devotedly, Dad."[124] In January 2001, George Walker Bush took the presidential oath of office himself and followed his father into the White House.

Barbara Pierce Bush (June 8, 1925–). Barbara Pierce Bush is the only woman who has seen both her husband and her son take the oath of office as president of the United States. Her charismatic common-sense nature has not only impacted three presidencies—those of Reagan, George H. W. Bush, and George W. Bush—but has won the hearts of the American public.

She was born into a moderately wealthy home; her father, Marvin Pierce, made his money in publishing, most notably as the president of *McCall's* in New York. Raised in the upscale suburb of Rye on Long Island Sound, Barbara was the third of four children. Her mother, Pauline Robinson, was a daughter of an Ohio Supreme Court justice. A gracious woman of the turn of the century, Pauline placed high importance on social standing and appearance. From Barbara's perspective, she gave most of her time to her eldest daughter, Martha, since Barbara lacked the graces that Pauline prized. Martha was attractive and well-mannered, while Barbara developed early weight issues and had a proclivity for roughhousing with her father and playing a variety of unladylike sports. In her teens, Barbara shot up to a leggy five foot eight, blossoming overnight into a slender, attractive young woman. She thoroughly enjoyed her time at the Rye Country Day School, where she excelled in sports and mischief-making. She was sent to Ashley Hall, a finishing school for girls in Charleston, South Carolina.

During a fateful Christmas break in her junior year, she accompanied old friends from Rye Country to a formal dance. It was there that she met young, handsome George Herbert Walker Bush. They were married on January 6, 1945. A year and half later they had the first of six children, George Walker Bush. He would become the forty-third president.

When her husband graduated from Yale in 1948, the couple moved to west Texas to start a new life. On October, 11, 1953, her three-year-old daughter, Robin, died of leukemia. George W. took his mother's emotional well-being personally. After the death, Barbara was overtaken with grief. "I felt I could cry forever."[125] With the father often gone, George W. helped pull his mother out of her despair. She recalled a turning point when she overheard seven-year-old George talking with his friends, politely explaining that he would not be able to play with them that day because he needed to cheer up his mother. George W. and his mother clearly share the same self-confidence. A family friend would conclude, "It's like you cloned Barbara to get George."[126]

As a first lady and a "first mom," she has been supportive but not encroaching. Even as she watched her husband take jobs and make policies that did not fall in line with her own beliefs, she did not voice her objections publicly. Instead of overt, public demonstrations, she prefers quietly to promote universal causes, primarily in education and literacy. She has published numerous best-selling books, donating much of the profits to national literacy groups. During her son's campaign, Barbara became an unobtrusive confidante whose wisdom was widely respected.

—— ★ ——

Appendix A:
The Presidents' Ancestry and Background

THE PRESIDENTS' ANCESTRY

George Washington	English
John Adams	English
Thomas Jefferson	Scottish, English, Welsh
James Madison	English
James Monroe	Scottish
John Quincy Adams	English
Andrew Jackson	Scotch-Irish
Martin Van Buren	Dutch
William Henry Harrison	English
John Tyler	English
James K. Polk	Scotch-Irish
Zachary Taylor	English
Millard Fillmore	English
Franklin Pierce	English
James Buchanan	Scotch-Irish
Abraham Lincoln	English
Andrew Johnson	English, Scottish, Irish
Ulysses S. Grant	English, Scottish
Rutherford B. Hayes	Scottish, English

James Garfield	English, French
Chester Arthur	Scotch-Irish, English
Grover Cleveland	English, Irish
Benjamin Harrison	English
William McKinley	Scotch-Irish
Theodore Roosevelt	Dutch, Scottish, French, Irish
William Howard Taft	English
Woodrow Wilson	Scotch-Irish, English, Scottish
Warren G. Harding	English, Scottish, Irish, Dutch
Calvin Coolidge	English, Scottish, Welsh
Herbert Hoover	Swiss-German, English
Franklin D. Roosevelt	Dutch, French
Harry Truman	English, Irish, German
Dwight Eisenhower	Swiss-German
John F. Kennedy	Irish
Lyndon Johnson	English, Scottish, German
Richard M. Nixon	Scotch-Irish, English, Irish, German
Gerald R. Ford	English
Jimmy Carter	English, Scotch-Irish
Ronald Reagan	Irish, English, Scottish
George H. W. Bush	English
Bill Clinton	English
George W. Bush	English

PRESIDENTS' PARENTS BORN OUTSIDE THE UNITED STATES

Andrew Jackson	His mother and father were born in Ireland.
James Buchanan	His father was born in County Donegal, Ireland.
Chester Arthur	His father was born in County Antrim, Ireland.
Thomas Jefferson	His mother was born in London, England.
Woodrow Wilson	His mother was born in Carlisle, England.
Herbert Hoover	His mother was born in Ontario, Canada.

---— ★ —---

Appendix B:
Professions of the Presidents' Parents

PRESIDENTS WHO WERE
PREACHER'S CHILDREN

PRESIDENT	FATHER OF PRESIDENT
Chester Arthur	William Arthur was a Baptist clergyman.
Grover Cleveland	Richard Cleveland was a Congregational clergyman.
Woodrow Wilson	Joseph Wilson was a Presbyterian clergyman.

PRESIDENTS WHO WERE SONS
OF GOVERNORS

PRESIDENT	FATHER OF PRESIDENT
William Henry Harrison	Benjamin Harrison served as governor of Virginia, from November 30, 1781, to November 20, 1784.
John Tyler	John Tyler served as governor of Virginia from December 12, 1808, to January 15, 1811.

Franklin Pierce   Benjamin Pierce served two terms as
                              the constitutional executive of New
                              Hampshire, 1827–1828 and
                              1829–1830.

THE TWO PRESIDENTS WHO WERE SONS
OF PRESIDENTS

John Quincy Adams, the sixth president, was the son of John Adams,
  the second president.
George Walker Bush, the forty-third president, was the son of George
  Herbert Walker Bush, the forty-first president.

—— ★ ——

Appendix C:
Presidents' Birth Order

PRESIDENTS WHO WERE ONLY SONS

Three presidents were the only children of their parents' marriages, but in each case they had half brothers:

Calvin Coolidge	was an only son but had one sister.
Gerald Ford	had three younger half brothers from his mother's second marriage.
Franklin D. Roosevelt	had one fully grown half brother from his father's first marriage.
William J. Clinton	had one younger half brother from his mother's second marriage.

PRESIDENTS WHO WERE FIRSTBORN
IN THEIR FAMILIES

John Adams
James Madison
James Monroe
James K. Polk
Ulysses S. Grant
Warren G. Harding

Calvin Coolidge
Harry S. Truman
Lyndon Baines Johnson
Gerald R. Ford
Jimmy Carter
William Jefferson Clinton
George Walker Bush

PRESIDENTS WHO WERE MIDDLE CHILDREN

George Washington	was the fifth child in a family of ten.
Martin Van Buren	was the third child in a family of five.
Abraham Lincoln	was the second child in a family of three.
Chester Arthur	was the fifth child in a family of nine.
Herbert Hoover	was the second child in a family of three.

PRESIDENTS WHO WERE THE "BABIES" OF THEIR FAMILIES

Andrew Jackson
William Henry Harrison
Andrew Johnson
Rutherford B. Hayes
James A. Garfield
Franklin Delano Roosevelt
Ronald Reagan

PRESIDENTS WHO WERE SONS OF THEIR FATHER'S SECOND MARRIAGE

George Washington	Son of Mary Ball
Franklin Pierce	Son of Anna Kendrick
Benjamin Harrison	Son of Elizabeth Ramsey Irwin
William H. Taft	Son of Louisa Maria Torrey
Franklin D. Roosevelt	Son of Sara Delano

Appendix D:
Ages of Presidents at the Death
of Their Parents

AGES OF PRESIDENTS AT THE DEATH
OF THEIR FATHER

Three fathers of presidents died before the births of their sons. These were the fathers of Andrew Jackson, Rutherford B. Hayes, and William Jefferson Clinton. Two fathers of presidents survived their sons. These were the fathers of Warren G. Harding and John F. Kennedy.

Andrew Jackson	Born after his father's death
Rutherford B. Hayes	Born after his father's death
William Jefferson Clinton	Born after his father's death
James A. Garfield	1 year, 170 days
Andrew Johnson	3 years, 6 days
Herbert Hoover	6 years, 124 days
George Washington	11 years, 49 days
Thomas Jefferson	14 years, 126 days
James Monroe	16 years
Grover Cleveland	16 years, 197 days
William Henry Harrison	18 years, 74 days
Franklin Delano Roosevelt	18 years, 313 days
Theodore Roosevelt	19 years, 105 days

William Jefferson Clinton	21 years, 8 days (stepfather)
John Tyler	22 years, 283 days
John Adams	25 years, 207 days
Gerald R. Ford	27 years, 219 days (father)
Jimmy Carter	28 years, 296 days
Lyndon Baines Johnson	29 years, 56 days
James Buchanan	30 years, 49 days
Ronald Reagan	30 years, 101 days
Harry S. Truman	30 years, 179 days
James K. Polk	32 years, 3 days
William Howard Taft	33 years, 248 days
Martin Van Buren	34 years, 124 days
Franklin Pierce	34 years, 129 days
Zachary Taylor	41 years, 56 days
Abraham Lincoln	41 years, 339 days
Richard M. Nixon	43 years, 239 days
Benjamin Harrison	44 years, 278 days
Chester A. Arthur	46 years, 22 days
Woodrow Wilson	46 years, 23 days
George Herbert Walker Bush	48 years, 119 days
Gerald R. Ford	48 years, 196 days (stepfather)
William McKinley	49 years, 299 days
James Madison	49 years, 348 days
Ulysses S. Grant	51 years, 63 days
Dwight D. Eisenhower	51 years, 147 days
Calvin Coolidge	53 years, 257 days
John Quincy Adams	59 years, 358 days
Millard Fillmore	63 years, 80 days
Warren G. Harding	Survived by father
John F. Kennedy	Survived by father

AGES OF PRESIDENTS AT THE DEATH
OF THEIR MOTHER

John Tyler	7 years
Herbert Hoover	9 years, 196 days
Abraham Lincoln	9 years, 235 days
Calvin Coolidge	12 years, 253 days

Andrew Jackson	14 years
Benjamin Harrison	16 years, 360 days
William Henry Harrison	19 years
Theodore Roosevelt	25 years, 110 days
Woodrow Wilson	31 years, 197 days
Millard Fillmore	31 years, 107 days
Thomas Jefferson	32 years, 352 days
Franklin Pierce	34 years
Martin Van Buren	34 years, 73 days
Zachary Taylor	38 years, 19 days
Chester Arthur	39 years, 103 days
James Buchanan	42 years, 21 days
Rutherford B. Hayes	44 years, 26 days
Warren G. Harding	44 years, 199 days
Grover Cleveland	45 years, 123 days
Andrew Johnson	47 years, 46 days
Lyndon Baines Johnson	50 years, 16 days
William Howard Taft	50 years, 84 days
William Jefferson Clinton	50 years, 140 days
John Quincy Adams	51 years, 109 days
Ronald Reagan	51 years, 131 days
Gerald R. Ford	54 years, 65 days
Richard Nixon	54 years, 264 days
William McKinley	54 years, 317 days
Dwight D. Eisenhower	55 years, 332 days
George Washington	57 years, 184 days
Jimmy Carter	59 years, 29 days
Franklin Delano Roosevelt	59 years, 220 days
Ulysses S. Grant	61 years, 14 days
John Adams	61 years, 169 days
Harry S. Truman	63 years, 79 days
James Monroe	68 years
George Herbert Walker Bush	68 years, 160 days
James Madison	77 years, 332 days
James K. Polk	Survived by mother
James A. Garfield	Survived by mother
John F. Kennedy	Survived by mother

——— ★ ———
Appendix E:
Deaths of Children and
Siblings of Presidents

PRESIDENTS WHO LOST A CHILD OR A SIBLING BEFORE THEIR INAUGURATION

John Adams	Took office in 1797
Siblings:	Elihu Adams died March 18, 1776.
Children:	Suzanna Adams died February 4, 1770.
Thomas Jefferson	Took office in 1801
Siblings:	Jane Jefferson died October 1, 1765.
	Elizabeth Jefferson died February 1774.
	Peter Jefferson died November 29, 1748.
	Jefferson (son) born and died March 9, 1750.
Children:	Jane Randolph Jefferson died September 1775.
	Jefferson (son) born May 28, 1777 died June 14, 1777.
	Lucy Elizabeth Jefferson died April 15, 1781.
James Madison	Took office in 1809
Siblings:	Ambrose Madison died October 1793.
	Catlett Madison died March 18, 1758.
	Nelly Conway Madison died in 1802.
James Monroe	Took office in 1817
Children:	J. S. Monroe died September 28, 1801.

John Quincy Adams	Took office in 1825
Siblings:	Abigail Adams died August 15, 1813.
	Susanna Adams died February 4, 1770.
	Charles Adams died November 30, 1800.
Children:	Louisa Catherine Adams died in 1812.
Andrew Jackson	Took office in 1829
Siblings:	Hugh Jackson, died May 29, 1779.
	Robert Jackson, died August 6, 1781.
Martin Van Buren	Took office in 1837
Siblings:	Abraham Van Buren died October 3, 1836.
William H. Harrison	Took office in 1841
Siblings:	Ann Harrison died in 1821.
	Benjamin Harrison died in 1799.
	Lucy Harrison died in 1809.
	Carter Bassett Harrison died April 18, 1808.
	Sarah Harrison died in 1812.
John Tyler	Took office in 1841
Siblings:	Anne Contesse Tyler died June 12, 1803.
	Elizabeth Armistead Tyler died in 1824.
James Polk	Took office in 1841
Siblings:	Franklin Ezekiel Polk died January 21, 1831.
	Marshall Tate Polk died April 12, 1831.
	John Lee Polk died September 28, 1831.
	Naomi Tate Polk died August 6, 1836.
	Samuel Wilson Polk died February 24, 1839.
Zachary Taylor	Took office in 1849
Siblings:	Hancock Taylor died March 20, 1841.
	William Taylor died June 3, 1808.
	Elizabeth Lee Taylor died April 22, 1845.
	Emily Taylor died November 30, 1842.
Children:	Sarah Knox Taylor died September 15, 1835.
	Octavia Pannel Taylor died July 8, 1820.
	Margaret Smith Taylor died October 22, 1820.
Millard Fillmore	Took office in 1850
Siblings:	Almon Hopkins Fillmore died January 17, 1830.
	Darius Ingraham Fillmore died March 9, 1837.
	Phoebe Maria Fillmore died July 2, 1843.

Franklin Pierce   Took office in 1853
   Siblings: Benjamin Kendrick Pierce died August 1,
                    1850.
                  Nancy Pierce died August 27, 1837.
                  John Sullivan Pierce died March 13, 1824.
                  Harriet Pierce died November 24, 1837.
                  Charles Grandison Pierce died June 15, 1828.
   Children: Franklin Pierce died February 5, 1836.
                  Frank Robert Pierce died November 14,
                    1843.
                  Benjamin Pierce died January 6, 1853.

James Buchanan   Took office in 1857
   Siblings: Mary Buchanan died in 1791.
                  Jane Buchanan died in 1839.
                  Maria Buchanan died in 1849.
                  Sarah Buchanan died in 1825.
                  Elizabeth Buchanan died in 1801.
                  Harriet Buchanan died in 1840.
                  John Buchanan died in 1804.
                  William Speer Buchanan died December
                    19, 1826.
                  George Washington Buchanan died
                    November 13, 1832.

Abraham Lincoln   Took office in 1861
   Siblings: Nancy Sarah Lincoln died January 20, 1828.
                  Thomas Lincoln died in 1813.
   Children: Edward Baker Lincoln died February 1, 1850.

Andrew Johnson   Took office in 1865
   Siblings: Johnson (daughter) died in infancy.
   Children: Charles Johnson died April 4, 1863.

Ulysses S. Grant   Took office in 1869
   Siblings: Samuel Simpson Grant died September 13,
                    1861.
                  Clara Rachel Grant died March 6, 1865.

Rutherford B. Hayes   Took office in 1877
   Siblings: Hayes (son) born and died August 4, 1814.
                  Lorenzo Hayes died January 20, 1825.
                  Sarah Sophia Hayes died October 9, 1821.

	Fanny Arabella Hayes died July 16, 1856.
Children:	Joseph Thompson Hayes died June 24, 1863.
	George Crook Hayes died May 24, 1866.
	Manning Force Hayes died August 28, 1874.

James A. Garfield   Took office in 1881
Siblings: James Ballou Garfield died January 8, 1829.
Children: Eliza Arabella "Trot" Garfield died
December 3, 1863.
Edward Garfield died October 25, 1876.

Chester Arthur   Took office in 1881
Siblings: Jane Arthur died April 15, 1842.
George Arthur died March 8, 1838.
Children: William Lewis Arthur died July 7, 1863.

Grover Cleveland   Took office in 1885
Siblings: Richard Cecil Cleveland died October 22,
1872.
Lewis Frederick Cleveland died October 22,
1872.

Benjamin Harrison   Took office in 1889
Siblings: William Henry Harrison died September 15,
1829.
Archibald Irwin Harrison died December 16,
1870.
Mary Jane Irwin Harrison died September 14,
1867.
Anna Symmes Harrison died August 26, 1838.
John Irwin Harrison died October 25, 1839.
James Friedlay Harrison died January 3, 1848.
James Irwin Harrison died August 25, 1850.

William McKinley   Took office in 1897
Siblings: David Allison McKinley died September 18,
1892.
Anna McKinley died July 29, 1890.
James McKinley died October 11, 1889.
Children: Katherine McKinley died July 25, 1875.
Ida McKinley died August 22, 1873.

Theodore Roosevelt   Took office in 1901
Siblings: Elliott Roosevelt died August 14, 1894.

William H. Taft	Took office in 1909
Siblings:	Peter Rawson Taft died June 4, 1889.
	Mary Taft died in infancy in 1848.
	Alphonso Taft, Jr., died March 2, 1851.
	Alphonso Taft II died June 21, 1852.
	Samuel Davenport Taft died April 8, 1856.
Warren G. Harding	Took office in 1921
Siblings:	Mary Clarissa Harding died October 29, 1913.
	Eleanor Priscilla Harding died November 9, 1878.
	Charles Alexander Harding died November 9, 1878.
Calvin Coolidge	Took office in 1923
Siblings:	Abigail Gratia Coolidge died March 6, 1890.
Franklin D. Roosevelt	Took office in 1933
Siblings:	James Roosevelt died May 27, 1927.
Children:	Franklin Roosevelt died November 8, 1909.
Dwight D. Eisenhower	Took office in 1953
Siblings:	Roy Jacob Eisenhower died June 17, 1942.
	Paul A. Eisenhower died March 16, 1895.
Children:	Dwight Doud Eisenhower died January 2, 1920.
John F. Kennedy	Took office in 1961
Siblings:	Joseph Patrick Kennedy died August 12, 1944.
	Kathleen Kennedy died in a plane crash, 1948.
Children:	Kennedy (daughter: stillborn) died in 1956.
Lyndon B. Johnson	Took office in 1963
Siblings:	Josefa Hermine Johnson died December 25, 1961.
Richard M. Nixon	Took office in 1969
Siblings:	Harold Samuel Nixon died March 7, 1933.
	Arthur Burdg Nixon died August 10, 1925.
George H. W. Bush	Took office in 1989
Children:	Pauline Robinson "Robin" Bush died October 11, 1953.
George W. Bush	Took office in 2001
Siblings:	Pauline Robinson "Robin" Bush died October 11, 1953.

—— ★ ——

Appendix F:
Deaths of Parents Before
and After Presidents

PRESIDENTS' FATHERS WHO DIED
BEFORE THE BIRTH OF THEIR SON

Andrew Jackson Born March 15, 1767, father died in March of 1767.

Rutherford B. Hayes Born October 4, 1822, father died August 20, 1822.

William Jefferson Clinton Born August 19, 1946, father died May 17, 1946.

PRESIDENTS' FATHERS WHO DIED
AFTER THEIR SONS

Warren G. Harding Died August 2, 1923; George T. Harding died November 19, 1928.

John Fitzgerald Kennedy Died November 22, 1963; Joseph P. Kennedy died November 18, 1969.

PRESIDENTS' MOTHERS WHO DIED
AFTER THEIR SONS

James K. Polk   Died June 15, 1849; Jane Polk died
                                 January 11, 1852.

James A. Garfield   Died Sept. 19, 1881; Eliza Garfield died
                                 January 21, 1888.

John Fitzgerald Kennedy   Died Nov. 22, 1963; Rose Kennedy
                                 died January 22, 1995.

———— ★ ————

Appendix G:
Parents Who Lived to See the
Inaugurations of Their Sons

PARENTS, BOTH FATHER AND MOTHER,
WHO LIVED TO SEE THEIR SON
INAUGURATED PRESIDENT

Only three presidents had both a living father and mother when they took office, Grant, Kennedy, and George W. Bush. Only two had both parents present at the inauguration, Kennedy and Bush.

Ulysses Simpson Grant was inaugurated on March 4, 1869; his father, Jesse Root Grant, who attended the ceremony, died on June 29, 1873; his mother, Hannah Simpson Grant, who did not attend, died on May 11, 1883.

John Fitzgerald Kennedy was inaugurated on January 20, 1961; his father, Joseph Patrick Kennedy, and his mother, Rose Fitzgerald Kennedy, both attended the ceremony. President Kennedy was assassinated on November 22, 1963; his father died on November 18, 1969; his mother died on January 22, 1995.

George Walker Bush was inaugurated on January 20, 2001; his father George Herbert Walker Bush, and his mother, Barbara Pierce Bush, both attended the ceremony.

FATHERS WHO LIVED TO SEE THEIR SON INAUGURATED PRESIDENT

Four fathers, in addition to those of Ulysses S. Grant, John F. Kennedy, and George W. Bush, lived to see their sons take office as president:

John Quincy Adams was inaugurated on March 4, 1825; his father John Adams, died on July 4, 1826.

Millard Fillmore took office on July 10, 1850; his father, Nathaniel Fillmore, died on May 28, 1863.

Warren Gamaliel Harding was inaugurated on March 4, 1921; his father, George Tryon Harding, died on November 19, 1928.

Calvin Coolidge took office on August 3, 1923; his father, John Calvin Coolidge, died on March 18, 1926.

MOTHERS WHO LIVED TO SEE THEIR SON INAUGURATED PRESIDENT

Eleven mothers, in addition to those of Ulysses S. Grant, John F. Kennedy, and George Herbert Walker Bush, lived to see their sons take office as president:

George Washington was inaugurated on April 30, 1789; his mother, Mary Ball Washington, died on August 25, 1789.

John Adams was inaugurated on March 4, 1797; his mother, Susanna Boylston Adams, died on April 17, 1797.

James Madison was inaugurated on March 4, 1809; his mother, Nelly Rose Conway Madison, died on February 11, 1829.

James Knox Polk was inaugurated on March 4, 1845; his mother Jane Knox Polk, died on January 11, 1852.

James Abram Garfield was inaugurated on March 4, 1881; his mother, Eliza Ballou Garfield, died on January 21, 1888.

William McKinley was inaugurated on March 4, 1897; his mother, Nancy Allison McKinley, died on December 12, 1897.

Franklin Delano Roosevelt was inaugurated on March 4, 1933; his mother, Sara Delano Roosevelt, died on September 7, 1941.

Harry S. Truman took office on April 12, 1945; his mother, Martha Ellen Young Truman, died on July 26, 1947.

Jimmy Carter was inaugurated on January 20, 1977; his mother Lillian Gordy Carter, died on October 30, 1983.

George Herbert Walker Bush was inaugurated on January 20, 1989; his mother Dorothy Walker Bush, died on November 19, 1992.

William Jefferson Clinton was inaugurated on January 20, 1993; his mother, Virginia Kelley, died on January 6, 1994.

———— ★ ————
Appendix H:
Fathers of Presidents
Who Remarried

The fathers of eleven presidents remarried. Five of them remarried after the birth of their president sons.

Millard Fillmore was 31 years and 114 days old when his mother, Phoebe Millard Fillmore, died on May 2, 1831. His father remarried Eunice Love on May 2, 1834.

Abraham Lincoln was 9 years and 235 days old when his mother, Nancy Hanks Lincoln, died on October 5, 1818. His father married Sarah Bush Johnston on December 2, 1819.

Warren Gamaliel Harding was 44 years and 198 days old when his mother, Phoebe Elizabeth Dickerson Harding, died on May 20, 1910. His father married Eudora Adella Kelley Luvisi on November 23, 1911; was divorced from her in 1916; and married Mary Alice Severns on August 11, 1921.

Calvin Coolidge was 12 years and 253 days old when his mother, Victoria Josephine Moor Coolidge, died on March 14, 1885. His father married Caroline A. Brown on September 9, 1891.

Gerald Rudolph Ford was 2 years old when his father, Leslie Lynch King, and his mother, Dorothy Ayer Gardner King, were divorced, in 1915. His father married Margaret Atwood on January 5, 1919.

Ford remained with his mother, who married Gerald Rudolph Ford on February 1, 1916.

Five presidents were the sons of their fathers' second marriages. They were George Washington, Franklin Pierce, Benjamin Harrison, William Howard Taft, and Franklin Delano Roosevelt.

One president, William Jefferson Clinton, was the son of his father's fifth marriage.

NOTES

——— ★ ———

As in my previous book on presidents' children, I drew from my own unpublished interviews and conversations with five presidents and five first ladies, covering six different presidents' families. In each case, I kept the notes, audiotapes, and—on one occasion—the videotape of these interviews. Quite often the subject of family and children was raised, and the comments and attitudes elicited were of immense value in understanding this subject.

I am especially grateful to the authors who have blazed the trail before me and have helped shorten my own journey. Although this is the first book devoted to the parents of the presidents, there have been many that have focused exclusively on either the fathers or the mothers. Doris Faber's book *Mothers of American Presidents,* Bonnie Angelo's work on *First Mothers,* and Harold Gullan's books *Faith of Our Mothers* and *First Fathers,* as well as Jeff C. Young's volume *The Fathers of American Presidents* were all helpful.

As in my last volume on presidents' children, I decided to use modern terms for places and things and modern spellings as well. For example, the White House was called the executive mansion until the time of Rutherford B. Hayes and only officially became the White House under Theodore Roosevelt, yet I refer to it by its current name throughout the book. Likewise, the term *first lady* was not in use until the 1870s. The Blue Room was once the Elliptical Saloon. I took such literary license to ease the narrative for the reader only when it did not affect the major events and issues of history.

ONE: HOW THE PRESIDENTS' PARENTS SHAPED THEIR SONS AND INFLUENCED THE NATION

1. William H. Herndon and Jesse W. Weik, *Herndon's Life of Lincoln* (New York: Fawcett Publication, 1961), p. 47.

2. Dale Atkins, *I'm Okay, You're My Parents* (New York: Henry Holt, 2004), p. 15.

3. Webb Garrison, *The Lincoln No One Knows* (Nashville: Rutledge Hill Press, 1993), p. 7.

4. Doris Faber, *The Presidents' Mothers* (New York: St. Martin's Press, 1968).

5. Attributed to Woodrow Wilson. Ibid., p. 144.

6. Jan Pottker, *Sara and Eleanor: The Story of Sara Delano Roosevelt and Her Daughter-in-Law, Eleanor Roosevelt* (New York: St. Martin's Press, 2004), p. 63.

7. Ibid.

8. Richard Nixon, *RN: The Memoirs of Richard Nixon* (New York: Grosset and Dunlap, 1978), p. 133.

9. Jeffrey Kluger, "The Power of Love," *Time,* January 19, 2004, p. 63.

10. Ishbel Ross, *An American Family: The Tafts—1678 to 1964* (The World Publishing Company, Cleveland, 1964), p. 188.

11. Jack Bauer, *Zachary Taylor: Soldier, Planter, Statesman of the Old Southwest* (Baton Rouge, La.: Louisana State University Press, 1985), p. 63.

12. Doris Kearns Goodwin, *The Fitzgeralds and the Kennedys: An American Saga* (New York: St. Martin's Press, 1987), p. 479.

13. Harry S. Truman, *Memoirs: Years of Trial and Hope* (New York: Doubleday and Company, 1956), p. 17.

14. Author's conversation with Ronald Reagan, 1992.

15. Author's interview with Dr. Thomas Schwartz of the Illinois State Historical Association.

16. Author's interview with Kerry Little, October 2004.

17. Merrill D. Peterson, *Thomas Jefferson and the New Nation: A Biography.* (New York: Oxford University Press, 1970), p. 35.

18. Author interview with Jeb Bush, May 1987.

19. Francis Bacon, *Essays, Civil and Moral, The Harvard Classics* (Cambridge, Mass.: Cambridge Press, 1909), p. 14.

20. Doug Wead, *All the Presidents' Children* (New York: Atria, 2003).

TWO: A MAGNIFICENT OBSESSION: GEORGE WASHINGTON'S PARENTS

1. Douglas Southall Freeman, *George Washington: A Biography.* Vol. 1, *Young Washington* (New York: Scribner's, 1948).

2. Jeff C. Young, *The Fathers of American Presidents: From Augustine Washington to William Blythe and Roger Clinton* (Jefferson, N.C.: McFarland, 1997), p. 7.

3. Thomas A. Lewis, *For King and Country: The Maturing of George Washington 1748–1760* (New York: HarperCollins, 1993), p. 7.

4. Noemie Emery, *Washington: A Biography* (New York: G. P. Putnam's Sons, 1976), p. 20.

5. Young, *The Fathers of American Presidents,* p. 6.

6. John Rodehamel, *The Great Experiment: George Washington and the American Republic* (New Haven, Conn.: Yale University, and San Marino, Calif.: Huntington Library, 1998), p. 2.

7. Freeman, *George Washington,* p. 14.

8. James Thomas Flexner, *George Washington: The Forge of Experience* (New York: Little, Brown, 1965), p. 15.

9. Emery, *Washington,* p. 31.

10. Attributed to Ralph K. Andrist, cited in George Nordham, *George Washington's Women* (Philadelphia: Dorrance & Co., 1977), p. 40.

11. Joseph Nathan Kane, Janet Podell, and Steven Anzovin, *Facts About the Presidents* (New York: H. H. Wilson, 2001), p. 4.

12. Emery, *Washington,* pp. 25–26.

13. Ibid., p. 25.

14. Flexner, *George Washington,* p. 11.

15. Kane, Podell, and Anzovin, *Facts About the Presidents,* p. 4.

16. Flexner, *George Washington,* p. 11.

17. Nordham, *George Washington's Women,* p. 29.

18. Washington's birthday was actually February 11, 1732. A reform calendar twenty years later changed the dates. Ibid., p. 12.

19. George Washington Parke Custis, *Recollections and Private Memoirs of Washington* (New York: Derby & Jackson, 1860), p. 16.

20. Cited in Nordham, *George Washington's Women,* p. 40.

21. Lewis, *For King and Country,* p. 7.

22. Gail Snyder concludes that Mary's refusal to allow Washington to pursue a career in the British Navy caused him to move out altogether and live permanently with Lawrence. Gail Snyder, *George Washington* (Philadelphia: Mason Crest Publishers, 2003), p. 29.

23. Flexner, *George Washington,* p. 19.

24. www.philaprintshop.com/frchintx.html.

25. Some historians believe that Mary was genuinely worried for his safety. Laura Aline Hobby, *Washington the Lover* (Dallas, Tex.: Southwest Press, 1932), p. 38.

26. Nordham, *George Washington's Women,* p. 2.

27. Ibid., p. vii.

28. Emery, *Washington,* p. 294.

29. Harold I. Gullan, *Faith of Our Mothers: The Stories of Presidential Mothers from Mary Washington to Barbara Bush* (Grand Rapids, MI: William B. Eerdmans Publishing Co., 2001).

30. *Adams Family Correspondence,* vol. 1, p. 216, as cited by David McCullough, *John Adams* (New York: Simon & Schuster, 2001), p. 28.

31. McCullough, *John Adams,* p. 28.

32. Paula Felder, ed., *George Washington's Relations and Relationships in Fredericksburg, Virginia* (Fredericksburg, Va.: Historic Publications of Fredericksburg, 1981), p. 33.

33. Interview with James C. Rees, executive director of the Mount Vernon Ladies' Association, July 2004.

34. Interview with Dawn Bonner of the Mount Vernon Ladies' Association.

35. Nordham, *George Washington's Women,* p. 39.

36. Ibid.

THREE: JOHN ADAMS AND THE FIRST AMERICAN DYNASTY

1. L. H. Butterfeld, ed., *Diary and Autobiography of John Adams* (Cambridge, Mass.: Harvard University Press, 1961), vol. 3, pp. 257–258.

2. Peter Shaw, *The Character of John Adams* (New York: W.W. Norton & Company, 1976), p. 3. Shaw states that Henry Adams arrived in 1638, as does David McCullough, *John Adams* (New York: Simon & Schuster, 2001), p. 29. Paul C. Nagel, in *John Quincy Adams: A Public Life, A Private Life* (New York: Knopf, 1998), p. 4, states that John Quincy Adams liked to tell everyone about his ancestors having arrived in America in 1632.

3. McCullough, *John Adams,* p. 30.

4. Samuel Willard, *John Adams, A Character Sketch* (Danville, N.Y., Instructor Publishing Co., The University Association, 1898), p. 12.

5. McCullough, *John Adams,* p. 32.

6. Ibid., p. 30.

7. Nagel, *John Quincy Adams,* p. 5.

8. Shaw, *The Character of John Adams,* pp. 3–4 (quoted from *The Adams Papers: Diary and Autobiography of John Adams*).

9. L. H. Butterfield et al., eds., *The Adams Papers: Diary and Autobiography of John Adams,* 4 vols. (Cambridge, Mass.: Belknap Press of Harvard University, 1962), vol. 2, pp. 103, 116; John Adams to Abigail Adams, August 4, 1776, and May 12, 1780, in L. H. Butterfield et al., eds., *Adams Family Correspondence,* 4 vols. (Cambridge, Mass.: Belknap Press of Harvard University, 1963–), vol. 2, p. 75; vol. 3, p. 342; Edmund S. Morgan, *The Meaning of Independence: John Adams, George Washington, Thomas Jefferson* (Charlottesville, Va.: University of Virginia Press, 1976), p. 8; and John Ferling, *John Adams: A Life* (New York: Henry Holt and Company, 1992), p. 175.

10. Nagel, *John Quincy Adams,* p. 5.

11. Ferling, *John Adams: A Life,* p. 101.

12. Paul C. Nagel, *The Adams Women: Abigail and Louisa Adams, Their Sisters and Daughters* (New York: Oxford University Press, 1987), p. 18.

13. McCullough, *John Adams,* p. 30.

14. Ferling, *John Adams: A Life,* p. 173.

15. McCullough, *John Adams,* p. 33.

16. Ibid.

17. Ferling, *John Adams: A Life,* p. 12.

18. Ibid.

19. Ibid., p. 31.

20. Joseph J. Ellis, *Passionate Sage: The Character and Legacy of John Adams* (New York: W. W. Norton, 1993), p. 202.

21. McCullough, *John Adams,* p. 31.

22. Shaw, *The Character of John Adams,* p. 5.

23. Ibid.

24. Ferling, *John Adams: A Life,* p. 14.

25. Butterfield et al., eds., *The Adams Papers: Diary and Autobiography of John Adams,* vol. 3, pp. 257–258 (punctuation added).

26. Shaw, *The Character of John Adams,* p. 4.

27. Adams to Skelton Jones, March 11, 1809, in *Works of John Adams,* vol. 9, p. 611. Adams Family Papers, Massachusetts Historical Society and to Jonathan Mason, October 27, 1820, Adams Papers, Reel 124; and Shaw, *The Character of John Adams,* pp. 46–47.

28. McCullough, *John Adams,* p. 34.

29. Ibid., p. 63.

30. Ibid., p. 35.

31. Shaw, *The Character of John Adams,* p. 8.

32. Ferling, *John Adams: A Life,* p. 16.

33. Ibid.

34. Ibid., 1, 43, 27, 26, 264.

35. Ibid., p. 262.

36. Ibid., p. 263; and Shaw, *The Character of John Adams,* p. 9.

37. McCullough, *John Adams,* p. 37.

38. Robert J. Taylor et al., eds., *Papers of John Adams* (Cambridge, Mass.: Massachusetts Historical Society, 1977–), vol. 1, pp. 12–13.

39. Butterfield et al., eds., *The Adams Papers: Diary and Autobiography of John Adams,* vol. 3, p. 263.

40. Ferling, *John Adams: A Life,* p. 17.

41. Ibid.

42. Ibid.

43. L. H. Butterfield, ed., *The Adams Papers: The Earliest Diary of John Adams* (Cambridge, Mass.: Belknap Press of Harvard University Press, 1966), p. 38.

44. McCulloch, *John Adams,* p. 43.

45. Shaw, *The Character of John Adams,* p. 32.

46. McCullough, *John Adams,* p. 45.

47. Shaw, *The Character of John Adams,* p. 6.

48. Ibid. (McCullough, in *John Adams,* p. 46, says that it was Cicero whom Adams started to read, who is, of course, the same man.)

49. McCullough, *John Adams,* p. 57.

50. Ibid., p. 44.

51. L. H. Butterfeld, ed., *Diary and Autobiography of John Adams* (Cambridge, Mass.: Harvard University Press, 1961), vol. 1, p. 53.

52. Shaw, *The Character of John Adams,* p. 33.

53. Jeff C. Young, *The Fathers of American Presidents: From Augustine Washington to William Blythe and Roger Clinton* (Jefferson, N.C.: McFarland, 1997), p. 10.

54. Shaw, *The Character of John Adams,* p. 12.

55. Butterfield et al., eds., *The Adams Papers: Diary and Autobiography of John Adams,* vol. 3, p. 256, cited in Shaw, *The Character of John Adams,* p. 45.

56. McCullough, *John Adams,* p. 58.

57. Mary Ann Wilcox, *Women Forgotten in Time* (Baltimore, Md.: Publish America, 2003), p. 9.

58. Ellis, *Passionate Sage,* p. 203.

59. Shaw, *The Character of John Adams,* p. 50.

60. Ibid., p. 51.

61. Butterfield et al., eds., *The Adams Papers: Diary and Autobiography of John Adams,* vol. 1, p. 276.

FOUR: SACRIFICED ON THE AMERICAN ALTAR

1. Paul C. Nagel, *Descent from Glory: Four Generations of the John Adams Family* (New York: Oxford University Press, 1983), p. 3.

2. Carol Berkin, *Founding Fathers, Vol. 1, Rebels with a Cause: John Adams.* The History Channel.

3. Edith B. Gelles, *Portia: The World of Abigail Adams* (Bloomington, Ind.: Indiana University Press, 1992), p. 24.

4. Ibid.

5. L. H. Butterfield, "Abigail Adams," in *Notable American Women 1607–1950: A Biographical Dictionary,* ed. Edward T. James et al. (Cambridge, Mass.: Harvard University Press, 1971), p. 6.

6. Paul C. Nagel, *John Quincy Adams: A Public Life, A Private Life* (Cambridge, Mass.: Harvard University Press, 1997), p. 6.

7. Paul C. Nagel, *The Adams Women: Abigail and Louisa Adams, Their Sisters and Daughters* (New York: Oxford University Press, 1987), p. 8.

8. John E. Ferling, *John Adams: A Life* (Knoxville: University of Tennessee Press, 1992), p. 31.

9. The calendars changed during this time. I am using the date from what would be called the "new style" calendar.

10. Nagel, *John Quincy Adams,* p. 9.

11. Nagel, *The Adams Women,* p. 45.

12. Lynne Withey, *Dearest Friend: A Life of Abigail Adams* (New York: Touchstone Books, 1981), p. 6. (Ferling, *John Adams,* p. 31, says they owned four slaves.)

13. R. B. Bernstein, ed., *The Wisdom of John and Abigail Adams* (New York: Metrobooks, 2002), pp. 78–79.

14. Nagel, *The Adams Women,* p. 12.

15. Gelles, *Portia,* p. 72.

16. Nagel, *The Adams Women,* p. 10.

17. Ibid.

18. Withey, *Dearest Friend,* p. 4.

19. David McCullough, *John Adams* (New York: Simon & Schuster, 2001), p. 55.

20. Nagel, *The Adams Women,* p. 13.

21. Ferling, *John Adams,* p. 57.

22. Bennett Champ Clark, *John Quincy Adams: "Old Man Eloquent"* (Boston: Little, Brown, 1932), pp. 17–18.

23. Lynn Hudson Parsons, *John Quincy Adams* (Madison, Wis.: Madison House Publishers, 1998), pp. 12–13.

24. Ferling, *John Adams,* p. 123.

25. Jack Shepherd, *Cannibals of the Heart: A Personal Biography of Louisa Catherine Adams and John Quincy Adams* (New York: McGraw-Hill Book Company, 1980), p. 18.

26. L. H. Butterfield et al., eds., *The Adams Family Correspondence,* 4 vols. (Cambridge, Mass.: Harvard University Press, 1963, 1973), vol. 1, p. 183, February 3, 1775; cited by Gelles, *Portia,* p. 31.

27. Withey, *Dearest Friend,* p. 65.

28. Shepherd, *Cannibals of the Heart,* p. 18.

29. Ibid., p. 19.

30. Gelles, *Portia,* p. 35.

31. McCullough, *John Adams,* p. 181.

32. Gelles, *Portia,* p. 32.

33. Ibid.

34. Ferling, *John Adams,* p. 135.

35. Ibid.

36. Peter Shaw, *The Character of John Adams* (Chapel Hill, N.C.: University of North Carolina Press, 1976), p. 95.

37. Ibid., p. 137.

38. Ibid., p. 177.

39. Ferling, *John Adams,* p. 186.

40. Gelles, *Portia,* p. 61.

41. Shaw, *The Character of John Adams,* p. 108.

42. Ibid., p. 107.

43. McCullough, *John Adams,* p. 179.

44. Clark, *John Quincy Adams,* p. 19.

45. John Adams, *Diary of John Adams,* vol. 2, p. 276, as cited by McCullough, *John Adams,* p. 182.

46. John Adams, *Diary of John Adams,* vol. 2, pp. 275–276, as cited by McCullough, *John Adams,* p. 182.

47. McCullough, *John Adams,* p. 182.

48. Ibid., p. 183.

49. Ibid, pp. 368, 183.

50. Samuel Willard, *John Adams, A Character Sketch* (Danville, N.Y.: Instructor Publishing Co., The University Association, 1898), p. 115.

51. John Adams, *Diary of John Adams,* vol. 2, pp. 286–287 as cited by McCullough, *John Adams,* p. 186.

52. Shaw, *The Character of John Adams,* p. 109; L. H. Butterfield, ed., *Diary and Autobiography,* vol. 4, p. 7

53. Alfred, Lord Tennyson, "Ulysses."

54. L. H. Butterfield, ed., *Adams Family Correspondence,* vol. 3, p. 91; and McCullough, *John Adams,* p. 206.

55. Paul C. Nagel, *Descent from Glory,* p. 25.

56. Butterfield, *Adams Family Correspondence,* vol. 3, p. 268; and McCullough, *John Adams,* p. 226.

57. Shaw, *The Character of John Adams,* p. 33.

58. Ibid., p. 143.

59. Mercy Otis Warren, *History of the Rise, Progress, and Termination of the American Revolution,* vol. 2, ed. Lester H. Cohen (Indianapolis, Ind.: Liberty Foundation, 1989), p. 675; and McCullough, *John Adams,* p. 594.

60. Doug Wead, *All the Presidents' Children* (New York: Atria, 2003), p. 312.

FIVE: A PRIVATE GRIEF

1. Doug Wead, *All the Presidents' Children* (New York: Atria, 2003), p. 311.

2. Stagg, ed., *Papers of James Madison,* vol. 16 (Charlottesville: University Press of Virginia, 1989), p. 448, as cited by David McCullough, *John Adams* (New York: Simon & Schuster, 2001), p. 476.

3. JA to JQA, March 31, 1797, Adams Papers, Massachusetts Historical Society; and McCullough, *John Adams,* p. 476.

4. Stewart Mitchell, ed., *New Letters of Abigail Adams, 1788–1801* (Boston: Houston Mifflin, 1947), p. 178; McCullough, *John Adams,* p. 502.

5. R. A. Brown, *Presidency of John Adams* (Lawrence: University Press of Kansas, 1975), p. 174; McCullough, *John Adams,* p. 567.

6. JA to AA, March 5, 1797, Adams Papers, Massachusetts Historical Society; McCullough, *John Adams,* p. 468.

7. Ibid., p. 481.

8. Ibid.

9. Ibid., p. 482.

10. You can read the entire story in Wead, *All the Presidents' Children,* pp. 304–312.

11. Mitchell, *New Letters of Abigail Adams,* p. 261; and McCullough, *John Adams,* p. 555.

12. Edith B. Gelles, *Portia: The World of Abigail Adams* (Bloomington: Indiana University Press, 1992), p. 87.

13. Mary Jefferson Eppes: Lester J. Cappon, ed., *The Adams-Jefferson Letters* (Chapel Hill: University of North Carolina Press, 1959), p. 270; and McCullough, *John Adams,* p. 582.

14. Mary Jefferson Eppes, cited in Cappon, *The Adams-Jefferson Letters,* p. 273; McCullough, *John Adams,* p. 583.

15. McCullough, ibid.

16. Ibid., pp. 584–585.

17. Alexander Biddle, ed., *Old Family Letters Copied from the Originals for Alexander Biddle* (Philadelphia: Lippincott, 1892), p. 62; McCullough, *John Adams,* p. 588.

18. Biddle, *Old Family Letters,* p. 137; McCullough, *John Adams,* p. 591.

19. Biddle, *Old Family Letters,* p. 137.

20. McCullough, *John Adams,* p. 600.

21. Cappon, *Adams-Jefferson Letters,* p. 284; McCullough, *John Adams,* pp. 602–603.

22. L. H. Butterfield, ed., *Letters of Benjamin Rush,* vol. 2 (Princeton, N.J.: American Philosophical Society, 1951), p. 1110; McCullough, *John Adams,* p. 603.

23. Paul C. Nagel, *The Adams Women: Abigail and Louisa Adams, Their Sisters and Daughters* (New York: Oxford University Press, 1987), p. 155.

24. Ibid., p. 156.

25. Abigail Adams, letter to John Adams, March 31, 1776, ed. L. H. Butterfield, *Adams Family Correspondence,* vol. 1. (Cambridge, Mass.: Harvard University Press, 1963), p. 370.

26. McCullough, *John Adams,* p. 640.

27. Shepherd, Jack. *Cannibals of the Heart: A Personal Biography of Louisa Catherine and John Quincy Adams* (New York: McGraw-Hill Book Company, 1980), p. 341.

28. McCullough, *John Adams,* p. 635.

29. Ibid., p. 640.

30. "The Diary of George Whitney," Adams Papers, no. 475, Massachusetts Historical Society; McCullough, *John Adams,* p. 645.

31. Ibid., p. 646.

32. John Marston to John Quincy Adams, July 8, 1826, Adams Papers, no. 476, Massachusetts Historical Society; McCullough, *John Adams,* p. 647.

33. Ibid., p. 634.

34. You can read the whole story in Wead, *All The Presidents' Children,* pp. 10–17.

35. R. B. Bernstein, ed., *The Wisdom of John and Abigail Adams* (New York: Metrobooks, 2002), pp. 34–35.

36. Bennett Champ Clark, *John Quincy Adams: "Old Man Eloquent"* (Boston: Little, Brown, 1932), p. 314.

37. Ibid.

38. Ibid., p. 315.

39. Ibid., p. 316.

40. Ibid.

41. Ibid., p. 317.

42. Ibid., p. 319.

43. Charles Francis Adams, ed. *Familiar Letters of John Adams and His Wife Abigail Adams* (New York: Hurd & Houghton, 1976), p. 267.

SIX: FORGED IN A CRUCIBLE: ABRAHAM LINCOLN AND HIS FATHER

1. A. Lincoln to J. L. Scripps, senior editor of the *Chicago Press & Tribune,* cited in William H. Herndon and Jesse Weik, *Herndon's Life of Lincoln* (Greenwich, Conn.: Fawcett Publications, 1960), p. 45.

2. The author found the works of David Herbert Donald and Michael Burlingame to be the most reliable, but even an approximate retelling of Lincoln's early life is speculation. Many thanks are owed to Dr. Thomas Schwartz of the Illinois State Historical Association.

3. J. G. Holland, *The Life of Abraham Lincoln* (Springfield, Mass.: Republican Press, 1866), p. 18.

4. Louis A. Warren, *Lincoln's Youth: Indiana Years Seven to Twenty-one* (New York: Appleton Century Crofts, 1959), p. 67.

5. Carl Sandburg, *Abraham Lincoln: The Prairie Years and the War Years,* 6 vols. (New York: Harcourt, Brace and World, 1926–1939), vol. 1, p. 133.

6. Ibid., vol. 1, p. 135

7. Ibid., vol. 1, p. 136

8. Ibid.

9. Ibid., vol. 1, p. 169.

10. David Herbert Donald, *Lincoln* (New York: Simon & Schuster, 1995), p. 22.

11. Louis Warren, *Lincoln for the Ages* (New York: Doubleday, 1960), p. 43.

12. Donald, *Lincoln,* p. 22.

13. Sandburg, *Abraham Lincoln,* vol. 1, p. 7.

14. Webb Garrison, *The Lincoln No One Knows* (Nashville, Tenn.: Rutledge Hill Press, 1993), p. 7.

15. A famous statement from Dennis Hanks to William Herndon, June 13, 1865.

16. This story is attributed to Dennis Hanks in Herndon and Weik, *Herndon's Life of Lincoln.* Almost all Lincoln biographers mention it, but most only in passing. Carl Sandburg softens this testimony, implying that it was a singular event and that Abe was poised on a fence, making it easy to knock him over, but he offers no source for this abbreviated version. Donald and Burlingame do not dwell on the story, nor curiously does Strozier, though none of them excludes it.

17. In Herndon and Weik, *Herndon's Life of Lincoln,* and cited by many authors; see Jeff C. Young, *The Fathers of American Presidents: From Augustine Washington to William Blythe and Roger Clinton* (Jefferson, N.C.: McFarland, 1997), p. 76.

18. Herndon and Weik, *Herndon's Life of Lincoln,* p. 64.

19. Both sides of this debate are famously developed in Louis A. Warren, *Lincoln's Parentage and Childhood* (New York: Century, 1926), and William E. Barton, *The Lineage of Lincoln* (Indianapolis: Bobbs-Merrill, 1929).

20. Sandburg, *Abraham Lincoln,* vol. 1, p. 6.

21. David Anderson, *Abraham Lincoln* (New York: Twayne Publishers, 1970), p. 27. As recently as 1828, however, the son shared the father's Jacksonian views; p. 28.

22. H. Donald Winkler, *The Women in Lincoln's Life* (Nashville, Tenn.: Rutledge Press, 2001), p. 5.

23. See Warren, *Lincoln's Youth;* David Herbert Donald, *Lincoln.*

24. Sandburg, *Abraham Lincoln,* vol. 1, p. 10.

25. Dale Carnegie, *Lincoln the Unknown* (New York: Dale Carnegie and Associates, 1932), p. 20.

26. Sandburg, *Abraham Lincoln,* vol. 1, p. 7.

27. Ida M. Tarbell, *The Early Life of Abraham Lincoln* (New York: A. S. Barnes and Company, 1974).

28. Ibid., p. 105.

29. Cited in Jan Morris, *Lincoln: A Foreigner's Quest* (New York: Simon & Schuster, 2000), p. 33.

30. Holland, *The Life of Abraham Lincoln,* p. 25.

31. Benjamin Thomas, *Abraham Lincoln: A Biography* (New York: Knopf, 1952), p. 37.

32. Sandburg, *Abraham Lincoln,* vol. 1, p. 7.

33. Ibid., vol. 1, p. 11.

34. Carnegie, *Lincoln the Unknown,* p. 20.

35. Harold I. Gullan, *Faith of Our Mothers: The Stories of Presidential Mothers from Mary Washington to Barbara Bush,* p. 96.

36. Sandburg, *Abraham Lincoln,* vol. 1, p. 111.

37. Young, *The Fathers of American Presidents,* p. 78.

SEVEN: NANCY HANKS: A MOTHER OF MYSTERY

1. William H. Herndon and Jesse Weik, *Herndon's Life of Lincoln* (Greenwich, NT: Fawcett Pub., 1960), p. 322.

2. Jan Morris traces this tradition back through the Hanks lineage and sees it as part of the tradition of Welsh women; Jan Morris, *Lincoln: A Foreigner's Quest* (New York: Simon & Schuster, 2000), p. 27.

3. H. Donald Winkler, *The Women in Lincoln's Life* (Nashville, Tenn.: Rutledge Press, 2001), p. 6.

4. J. G. Holland, *The Life of Abraham Lincoln* (Springfield, Mass.: Republican Press, 1866), p. 23.

5. Doris Faber, *The Mothers of American Presidents* (New York: Penguin, 1968), p. 171.

6. Ibid.

7. Dale Carnegie, *Lincoln the Unknown,* p. 13.

8. Harold I. Gullan, *Faith of Our Mothers: The Stories of Presidential Mothers from Mary Washington to Barbara Bush,* p. 89; and Stern, *The Life and Writings of Abraham Lincoln,* p. 7.

9. Descriptions of Nancy Hanks vary wildly. "Small and dark": Philip Van Doren Stern, *The Life and Writings of Abraham Lincoln* (New York: Random House, 1940), p. 7.

10. Jeff C. Young, *The Fathers of American Presidents: From Augustine Washington to William Blythe and Roger Clinton* (Jefferson, N.C.: McFarland, 1997), p. 74.

11. Holland, *The Life of Abraham Lincoln,* p. 24.

12. Ibid., p. 7.

13. Ibid., p. 26.

14. Carl Sandburg, *Abraham Lincoln: The Prairie Years and the War Years,* 6 vols. (New York: Harcourt, Brace and World, 1926–1939), vol. 1, p. 35.

15. Carnegie, *Lincoln the Unknown,* p. 22.

16. Ibid.

17. Sandburg, *Abraham Lincoln,* vol. 1, p. 32.

18. Ibid., p. 416.

19. Ibid., p. 32.

20. J. Edward Murr to Albert J. Beveridge, New Albany, Ind., November 21, 1924, Beveridge Papers, Library of Congress, Washington, D.C.; Herndon to Chas. Hart, Springfield, Ill., December 28, 1866; and Herndon to Ward Hill Lamon, Springfield, February 25, 1870, Lamon Papers, Henry E. Huntington Library.

21. Dennis Hanks was actually the illegitimate nephew of Elizabeth Sparrow; David Herbert Donald, *Lincoln* (New York: Simon & Schuster, 1995), p. 26.

22. Cited in Ralph Geoffrey Newman, ed., *Abraham Lincoln, His Story in His Own Words* (New York: Doubleday, 1975), p. 13.

23. Carnegie, *Lincoln the Unknown,* p. 23.

24. Emanuel Hertz, *The Hidden Lincoln* (New York: Viking, 1938), pp. 279–281; and Herndon and Weik, *Herndon's Life of Lincoln,* p. 27.

25. "My early history": A. Lincoln to J. L. Scripps of the *Chicago Press & Tribune,* cited in Herndon and Weik, *Herndon's Life of Lincoln,* p. 45.

26. Donald, *Lincoln,* p. 27.

27. Charles Strozier, *Lincoln's Quest for Union* (Philadelphia: Paul Dry Books, rev. ed., 2001), p. 22.

28. Sandburg, *Abraham Lincoln,* vol. 1, p. 40.

29. Holland, *The Life of Abraham Lincoln,* p. 28.

30. Sandburg, *Abraham Lincoln,* vol. 1, p. 41.

31. Holland, *The Life of Abraham Lincoln,* p. 24; and Winkler, *The Women in Lincoln's Life,* p. 11.

EIGHT: A WONDERFUL STEPMOTHER: LESSONS IN LOVE

1. William H. Herndon and Jesse Weik, *Herndon's Life of Lincoln* (Greenwich, CT: Fawcett Pub., 1960), p. 375.

2. Dale Carnegie, *Lincoln the Unknown* (Garden City, NY: Dale Carnegie and Associates, 1932), p. 25.

3. Herndon and Weik, *Herndon's Life of Lincoln,* p. 28.

4. David Herbert Donald, *Lincoln* (New York: Simon & Schuster, 1995), p. 28.

5. Actually, there are other versions of this, including the idea that she borrowed the book for him from his teacher Andrew Crawford. J. G. Holland, *The Life of Abraham Lincoln* (Springfield, Mass.: Republican Press, 1866), p. 32.

6. Donald, *Lincoln,* p. 29.

7. Mrs. Thomas Lincoln's statements to William Herndon, as cited in Donald, *Lincoln,* p. 29.

8. Herndon and Weik, *Herndon's Life of Lincoln,* p. 13.

9. Ibid., p. 364.

10. Carl Sandburg, *Abraham Lincoln: The Prairie Years and the War Years,* 6 vols. (New York: Harcourt, Brace and World, 1926–1939), vol. 1, p. 50.

11.   Herndon and Weik, *Herndon's Life of Lincoln,* p. 377.

12.   Charles Strozier, *Lincoln's Quest for Union* (Philadelphia: Paul Dry Books, rev. ed., 2001),p. 22.

13.   Sandburg, *Abraham Lincoln,* vol. 1, p. 108.

14.   Ibid., p. 144.

15.   Ibid., p. 61.

16.   A. Lincoln to J. L. Scripps of the *Chicago Press & Tribune,* cited in William H. Herndon and Jesse Weik, *Herndon's Life of Lincoln* (Greenwich, Conn.: Fawcett Publications, 1960), p. 45.

17.   Afterward, Lincoln made arrangements to help his parents live on their land without fear of eviction.

18.   Stephen B. Oates, *With Malice Toward None* (New York: Harper & Row, 1992), p. 4.

19.   J. G. Randall, *Mr. Lincoln* (New York: Dodd, Mead & Co., 1957), p. 7.

20.   Donald, *Lincoln,* p. 27.

      David Donald offers a poignant description of this last meeting. Ibid., p. 271.

NINE: JAMES ROOSEVELT: AN AMERICAN ARISTOCRAT

1.   Jan Pottker, *Sara and Eleanor: The Story of Sara Delano Roosevelt and Her Daughter-in-Law, Eleanor Roosevelt* (New York: St. Martin's Press, 2004), p. 32.

2.   Ibid., p. 33.

3.   Ibid.

4.   Jeff C. Young, *The Fathers of American Presidents: From Augustine Washington to William Blythe and Roger Clinton* (Jefferson, N.C.: McFarland, 1997), p. 160.

5.   Pottker, *Sara and Eleanor,* p. 39.

6.   Joseph P. Lash, *Eleanor and Franklin* (New York: Norton, 1971), p. 114.

7.   Actually, various sources say that James returned in 1848. William DeGregorio, *The Complete Book of U.S. Presidents* (New York: Gramercy Books, 2001), p. 480.

8.   Young, *The Fathers of American Presidents,* p. 165.

9.   "A Notable Social Event: The Wedding of Miss Astor and Mr. Roosevelt," *The New York Times,* November 19, 1878, p. 1.

10.   Pottker, *Sara and Eleanor,* p. 47.

11.   Young, *The Fathers of American Presidents,* p. 165.

12.   Peter Collier and David Horowitz, *The Roosevelts: An American Saga* (New York: Simon & Schuster, 1994), p. 49.

13.   Pottker, *Sara and Eleanor,* p. 44.

14.   Ibid., p. 9. Actually, Sara qualified as a member of the Daughters of the American Revolution, the Society of Colonial Wars, Americans of Royal Descent, and most of the other organizations so important to the socialites of the Industrial Age and the so-called Gilded Age that followed.

15.   Geoffrey C. Ward, *Before the Trumpet: Young Franklin Roosevelt, 1882–1905* (New York: Harper & Row, 1985), p. 116.

16.   Young, *The Fathers of American Presidents,* p. 164.

17.   Ibid., p. 163.

18.   Michael Beschloss, *The Conquerors* (New York: Simon and Schuster, 2002). Later in 2004, a team of scholars reviewing 240,000 pages of declassified documents concluded that the U.S. government had known of German plans regarding the extermination of the Jews as early as 1942, which would be almost as the decisions were made. "Scholars: U.S. Gave Tips on Holocaust Low Priority in '42." *USA Today,* May 14, 2004, p. 3a.

19.   Pottker, *Sara and Eleanor,* p. 61.

20.   Lash, *Eleanor and Franklin,* p. 146.

21.   Ward, *Before the Trumpet,* p. 124.

22.   Doris Kearns Goodwin, *No Ordinary Time* (New York: Simon and Schuster, 1994), p. 77.

23.   Collier, *The Roosevelts: An American Saga,* p. 108. According to Kenneth Davis, he was first passed over in 1901. Kenneth Davis, *FDR: The Beckoning of Destiny, 1882–1928: A History* (New York: Putnam, 1972), p. 155.

24.   Sara Delano Roosevelt to FDR, November 20, 1890. The Roosevelt Correspondence Col-

lection, The Franklin D. Roosevelt Presidential Library, 4079 Albany Post Rd., Hyde Park, New York.

TEN: SARA ROOSEVELT: A FORMIDABLE PRESENCE

1. Cited in Jan Pottker, *Sara and Eleanor: The Story of Sara Delano Roosevelt and Her Daughter-in-Law, Eleanor Roosevelt* (New York: St. Martin's Press, 2004), p. 195.

2. Ibid., p. 7.

3. Ibid., p. 8.

4. Ibid., p. 11.

5. The family lived on an estate named Rose Hill. It was 85 miles downriver from Canton. Ibid., p. 19.

6. Ibid., p. 23.

7. See the biography of Stanford White by Marjorie Dorfman at www.pagewise.com; also, http://dede.essortment.com/stanfordwhiteb_rbyy.htm.

8. Pottker, *Sara and Eleanor,* p. 29.

9. Bonnie Angelo, *First Mothers: The Women Who Shaped the Presidents* (New York: Harper-Collins, 2001), p. 3.

10. There are some differing accounts on this. Bonnie Angelo writes that she "continued to nurse him a year longer than the usual practice." While Jan Pottker states flatly that she nursed him "a full year." Angelo, *First Mothers,* p. 5; and Pottker, *Sara and Eleanor,* p. 63.

11. Angelo, *First Mothers,* p. 5.

12. Peter Collier, *The Roosevelts: An American Saga* (New York: Simon & Schuster, 1994), p. 102.

13. FDR to James Roosevelt, June 7, 1890, in Elliott Roosevelt, ed., *FDR: His Personal Letters* (New York: Duell, Sloan & Pearce, 1947), vol. 1, p. 16.

14. Cited in Angelo, *First Mothers,* p. 6.

15. Ibid., p. 7.

16. Pottker, *Sara and Eleanor,* p. 81.

17. Geoffrey C. Ward, *Before the Trumpet: Young Franklin Roosevelt, 1882–1905* (New York: Harper & Row, 1985), p. 194.

18. Pottker, *Sara and Eleanor,* pp. 86–87.

19. Author's correspondence with Bob Clark, archivist at the Franklin D. Roosevelt Presidential Library.

20. Pottker, *Sara and Eleanor,* p. 91.

21. Collier, *The Roosevelts: An American Saga,* p. 108.

22. Angelo, *First Mothers,* p. 16.

23. Joseph P. Lash, *Eleanor and Franklin* (New York: Norton, 1971), p. 109.

24. Ibid.

25. Ibid., p. 115.

26. Ibid., p. 135.

27. Pottker, *Sara and Eleanor,* p. 182.

28. Eleanor Roosevelt, *This Is My Story* (New York: Garden City Publishing, 1937), p. 18.

29. Lash, *Eleanor and Franklin,* p. 110.

30. Ibid.

31. Ibid., p. 130.

32. Ibid., p. 139.

33. *The Washington Post,* February 21, 1980.

34. Lash, *Eleanor and Franklin,* p. 162.

35. Ibid.

36. Ibid.

37. Cited in Collier, *The Roosevelts: An American Saga,* p. 159.

38. Ibid.

39. Ibid., p. 255.

ELEVEN: FDR'S BREAK WITH MOTHER

1. Doris Faber, *The Mothers of American Presidents* (New York: Penguin, 1968), p. 98.
2. Joseph P. Lash, *Eleanor and Franklin* (New York: Norton, 1971), pp. 474–480.
3. Ibid., pp. 248–249.
4. Conrad Black, *Roosevelt: Champion of Freedom* (New York: Public Affairs, 2003), p. 185.
5. S. D. Roosevelt, Sara Roosevelt, Isabel Leighton, and Gabrielle Forbush, *My Boy Franklin* (New York: Ray Long and Richard R. Smith, Inc., 1933), p. 4.
6. Cited in Doris Kearns Goodwin, *No Ordinary Time* (New York: Simon & Schuster, 1994), p. 275.
7. Peter Collier, *The Roosevelts: An American Saga* (New York: Simon & Schuster, 1994), p. 252.
8. For a fascinating, detailed study of Sara's day-to-day life, see *The House at Hyde Park*. Sara kept a small notebook of her writings, beginning the year before she married. It was discovered three years after her death and is now in the Roosevelt Family Archives. One day's entry reads, "How to wash silk knit articles." Clara and Hardy Steeholm, *The House at Hyde Park, Together with Sara Delano Roosevelt's Household Book* (New York: Viking Press, 1950).
9. Cited in Goodwin, *No Ordinary Time,* p. 272.
10. Ibid., pp. 270–271.
11. Maurine Beasley, Holly Shulman, and Henry Beasley, eds., *The Eleanor Roosevelt Encyclopedia* (Westport, Conn.: Greenwood Press, 2001), pp. 317–318.
12. Jan Pottker, *Sara and Eleanor: The Story of Sara Delano Roosevelt and Her Daughter-in-Law, Eleanor Roosevelt* (New York: St. Martin's Press, 2004), p. 332.
13. Black, *Roosevelt, Champion of Freedom,* p. 660.
14. Cited in Pottker, *Sara and Eleanor,* p. 328.
15. Lash, *Eleanor and Franklin,* p. 643.

TWELVE: THE RUTHLESS ASCENT OF JOSEPH P. KENNEDY

1. Harold Gullan, *First Fathers: The Men Who Inspired Our Presidents* (Hoboken, N.J.: Wiley, 2004), p. 219.
2. Robert Dallek, *Kennedy,* pp. 5–6.
3. Actually, as many as 9,000 may have died. Thomas Maier, p. 26. Others cite statistics showing that only 20 percent died during the worst year. It is still a staggering number. Peter Collier and David Horowitz, *The Kennedys: An American Drama* (New York: Summit, 1984), p. 8.
4. Thomas Maier, *The Kennedys: America's Emerald Kings* (New York: Basic Books, 2003), p. 33.
5. Doris Kearns Goodwin, *The Fitzgeralds and the Kennedys* (New York: Simon & Schuster, 1987), p. 227.
6. Ibid., p. 228.
7. Collier and Horowitz, *The Kennedys: An American Drama,* p. 15.
8. Goodwin, *The Fitzgeralds and the Kennedys,* p. 229.
9. Collier and Horowitz, *The Kennedys: An American Drama,* p. 7.
10. Ibid., p. 36.
11. This story seems to grow with the telling. Collier and Horowitz hold that it was a $300 investment that grew to $5,000. Ibid., p. 27. A more recent Kennedy biography lists a $600 investment growing to $10,000. Robert Dallek, *Kennedy,* p. 17.
12. Ibid., p. 19.
13. Ibid., p. 20.
14. Ibid.
15. www.bethlehempaonline.com/schwab_bio.html.
16. Collier and Horowitz, *The Kennedys: An American Drama,* p. 33.
17. Apparently Kennedy was engaging in practices that other gentlemen on Wall Street considered unethical. See Thomas J. Whalen, *Kennedy and Lodge: The 1952 Massachusetts Senate Race* (Boston: Northeastern University Press, 2001), p. 71.
18. Goodwin, *The Fitzgeralds and the Kennedys,* p. 392.
19. Ibid., p. 304.

20. http://home.hiwaay.net/~oliver/gsquotes.htm.

21. Collier and Horowitz, *The Kennedys: An American Drama,* p. 47.

22. The cardinal's office denies this meeting and says that it was not on the cardinal's schedule. It comes from Swanson's memoirs, and most Kennedy biographies include it.

23. Gloria Swanson, *Swanson on Swanson* (New York: Random House, 1980), p. 394.

24. Ted Schwarz, *Joseph P. Kennedy* (Hoboken, N.J.: Wiley, 2003).

25. Joseph P. Kennedy, *I'm for Roosevelt* (New York: Reynal and Hitchcock, 1936).

26. Michael R. Beschloss, *Kennedy and Roosevelt* (New York: Norton, 1980), p. 157.

27. Peter Collier and David Horowitz, *The Roosevelts: An American Saga* (New York: Simon and Schuster, 1994), p. 291.

28. "The Nine Kennedy Kids Delight Great Britain," *Life,* April 11, 1938.

29. Collier and Horowitz, *The Kennedys: An American Drama,* p. 90.

30. Conrad Black, *Roosevelt, Champion of Freedom* (New York: Public Affairs, 2003), p. 439.

31. Collier and Horowitz, *The Kennedys: An American Drama,* p. 114.

32. Dallek, *Kennedy,* p. 60.

33. Collier and Horowitz, *The Kennedys: An American Drama,* p. 113.

34. Ibid, p. 88.

35. Cited in John H. Davis, *The Kennedys: Dynasty and Disaster, 1848–1948* (New York: McGraw-Hill, 1984), p. 86.

THIRTEEN: SURVIVOR: THE MOTHER OF JOHN F. KENNEDY

1. Theodore H. White Papers, JFK Library, as cited in Robert Dallek, *Lone Star Rising: Lyndon Johnson and His Times, 1908–1960* (New York: Oxford University Press, 1991), p. 70.

2. Bonnie Angelo, *First Mothers: The Women Who Shaped the Presidents* (New York: Harper-Collins, 2001), p. 154.

3. Rose Fitzgerald Kennedy, *Times to Remember* (New York: Doubleday & Company, 1974), p. 11.

4. Robert Dallek, *Kennedy,* p. 19.

5. Angelo, *First Mothers,* p. 118.

6. Ibid., p. 70.

7. John H. Davis, *The Kennedys: Dynasty and Disaster, 1848–1948* (New York: McGraw-Hill, 1984), p. 52.

8. Doris Kearns Goodwin, *The Fitzgeralds and the Kennedys* (New York: Simon & Schuster, 1987), p. 353.

9. www.brainyquote.com/quotes/authors/r/rose_kennedy.html.

10. Peter Collier and David Horowitz, *The Kennedys: An American Drama* (New York: Summit, 1984), p. 33.

11. Ibid., p. 44.

12. Dallek, *Kennedy,* p. 7.

13. www.brainyquote.com/quotes/authors/r/rose_kennedy.html

14. Goodwin, *The Fitzgeralds and the Kennedys,* p. 367.

15. www.brainyquote.com/quotes/authors/r/rose_kennedy.html.

16. Collier and Horowitz, *The Kennedys: An American Drama,* p. 57.

17. Kennedy, *Times to Remember,* p. 57.

18. Goodwin, *The Fitzgeralds and the Kennedys,* p. 353.

19. Theodore H. White Papers, JFK Library, as cited in Robert Dallek, *Lone Star Rising,* p. 70.

20. Goodwin, *The Fitzgeralds and the Kennedys,* p. 353.

21. JFK Library, transcript of a CBS television interview.

22. Goodwin, *The Fitzgeralds and the Kennedys,* p. 635.

23. Collier and Horowitz, *The Kennedys: An American Drama,* p. 44.

24. Angelo, *First Mothers,* p. 141.

25. Goodwin, *The Fitzgeralds and the Kennedys,* p. 643.

26. www.brainyquote.com/quotes/authors/r/rose_kennedy.html.

27. Ibid.

28. Ibid.

FOURTEEN: THE RISE OF CAMELOT

1. Joseph P. Kennedy, *I'm for Roosevelt* (New York: Reynal and Hitchcock, 1936), p. 3.

2. Peter Collier and David Horowitz, *The Kennedys: An American Drama* (New York: Summit, 1984), p. 55.

3. John H. Davis, *The Kennedys: Dynasty and Disaster, 1848–1948* (New York: McGraw-Hill, 1984), p. 71.

4. Robert Dallek, *Kennedy,* p. 28.

5. Ibid., p. 38.

6. Collier and Horowitz, *The Kennedys: An American Drama,* p. 121.

7. Dallek, *Kennedy,* p. 106.

8. Ibid., p. 47.

9. Seymour Hersh, *The Dark Side of Camelot* (Boston: Little, Brown, 1997).

10. Dallek, *Kennedy,* p. 58.

11. Victor Lasky, *J.F.K.* (New York: Macmillan, 1963), p. 75.

12. Doris Kearns Goodwin, *The Fitzgeralds and the Kennedys* (New York: Simon & Schuster, 1987), p. 688.

13. Ibid., p. 693.

14. Joan and Clay Blair, Jr., *The Search for JFK* (New York: Putnam, 1974), p. 356.

15. Collier and Horowitz, *The Kennedys: An American Drama,* pp. 172–173.

16. Cited in Robert Dallek, *Kennedy,* p. 118.

17. Ralph G. Martin and Ed Plaut, *Front Runner, Dark Horse* (Garden City, N.Y.: Doubleday, 1960), p. 136.

18. Dallek, *Kennedy,* p. 126.

19. Collier and Horowitz, *The Kennedys: An American Drama,* p. 195.

20. Dallek, *Kennedy,* p. 85.

21. Collier and Horowitz, *The Kennedys: An American Drama,* p. 258.

FIFTEEN: SHATTERED DREAMS

1. Peter Collier and David Horowitz, *The Kennedys: An American Drama* (New York: Summit, 1984), p. 258.

2. Harold Martin, "The Amazing Kennedys," *The Saturday Evening Post,* September 7, 1957, p. 49.

3. John H. Davis, *The Kennedys: Dynasty and Disaster, 1848–1948* (New York: McGraw-Hill, 1984), pp. 239–240.

4. David McCullough, *Truman* (New York: Simon & Schuster, 1992), p. 970.

5. Doris Kearns Goodwin, *The Fitzgeralds and the Kennedys* (New York: Simon & Schuster, 1987), p. 806.

6. Ibid., pp. 265–266.

7. Ted Schwarz, *Joseph P. Kennedy* (Hoboken, N.J.: Wiley, 2003), p. 422.

8. Davis, *The Kennedys,* p. 402.

9. According to some sources, the old man could occasionally communicate verbally and did so with his president son as they prepared for Ted Kennedy's run for the Senate. But such moments were rare and a struggle. Laurence Leamer, *The Kennedy Men* (New York: Perennial, 2002), p. 669.

10. Ibid., p. 429.

11. Schwarz, *Joseph P. Kennedy,* p. 427.

12. Cited as a confidential source in Robert Dallek, *Lone Star Rising: Lyndon Johnson and His Times, 1908–1960* (New York: Oxford University Press, 1991), p. 477.

13. Ibid.; Dallek, *Kennedy,* pp. 154–155.

14. Leamer, *The Kennedy Men,* p. 666.

15. Dallek, *Kennedy,* p. 499.

16. Schwarz, *Joseph P. Kennedy,* p. 433.

17. Dallek, *Kennedy*, p. 697.
18. Cited in ibid., p. 697.
19. Davis, *The Kennedys*, p. 536.
20. Ibid., p. 564.
21. Ibid., p. 562.
22. Bonnie Angelo, *First Mothers: The Women Who Shaped the Presidents* (New York: Harper-Collins, 2001), p. 151.
23. Ibid.
24. Schwarz, *Joseph P. Kennedy*, p. 436.
25. Angelo, *First Mothers*, p. 154.
26. www.brainyquote.com/quotes/authors/r/rose_kennedy.html.
27. Angelo, *First Mothers*, p. 153.

SIXTEEN: ABOUT HIS FATHER'S BUSINESS: PRESCOTT BUSH

1. George H. W. Bush with Victor Gold, *Looking Forward* (New York: Bantam, 1987), p. 14.
2. Attributed to Nancy Ellis, sister of George H. W. Bush, cited in Peter Schweizer and Rochelle Schweizer, *The Bushes: Portrait of a Dynasty* (New York: Doubleday, 2004), p. xiv.
3. Author's interview with Jeb Bush, May 1987.
4. Schweizer and Schweizer, *The Bushes*, p. 38.
5. Cited in Mickey Herskowitz, *Duty, Honor, Country* (Nashville, Tenn.: Rutledge Hill Press, 2003), p. 20.
6. Author's interview with Dorothy Bush, January 1988.
7. Schweizer and Schweizer, *The Bushes*, p. 23.
8. Harold Gullan, *First Fathers: The Men Who Inspired Our Presidents* (New Jersey: John Wiley and Sons, 2004), p. 262.
9. Author's interview with Peter Schweizer, June 2004.
10. Schweizer and Schweizer, *The Bushes*, p. 214.
11. Jeff C. Young, *The Fathers of American Presidents: From Augustine Washington to William Blythe and Roger Clinton* (Jefferson, N.C.: McFarland, 1997), p. 227.
12. Author's interview with George W. Bush, September 1997.
13. Schweizer and Schweizer, *The Bushes*, p. 69.
14. Ibid., p. xii.
15. Author's conversation with George W. Bush, September 1997.
16. Schweizer and Schweizer, *The Bushes*, p. 12.
17. Fitzhugh Green, *George Bush: An Intimate Portrait* (New York: Hippocrene Books, 1989), p. 3.
18. Schweizer and Schweizer, *The Bushes*, p. 27.
19. Ibid., p. 31.
20. Ibid., p. 35.
21. Ibid., p. 37.
22. www.multied.com/Bio/people/Harriman.html
23. Mickey Herskowitz, *Duty, Honor, Country*, p. 6.

SEVENTEEN: GEORGE AND BARBARA BUSH: RAISING A PRESIDENT

1. Peter Schweizer and Rochelle Schweizer, *The Bushes: Portrait of a Dynasty* (New York: Doubleday, 2004), p. 98.
2. Ibid., p. 54.
3. Ibid., p. 69.
4. Author's interview with George H. W. Bush, February 1982.
5. Parts taken from the author's book *George Bush: Man of Integrity* (Eugene, Oreg.: Harvest House, 1988), pp. 39. From taped interviews with George Herbert Walker Bush.
6. Author's interview with George H. W. Bush, February 1982.
7. Ibid.
8. Abigail Adams died in 1818; her son John Quincy became president seven years later.

9. Barbara Bush, *Barbara Bush: A Memoir* (New York: Scribner, 1994), p. 9.

10. Pamela Kilian, *Barbara Bush: Matriarch of a Dynasty* (New York: Thomas Dunne Books, St. Martin's Press, 2002), p. 19.

11. Author's interview with Barbara Bush, June 1987.

12. Author's interview with George H. W. Bush, February 1982.

13. Author's interview with Barbara Bush, June 1987.

14. Barbara Bush, *Barbara Bush,* p. 19.

15. Schweizer and Schweizer, *The Bushes,* p. 99.

16. Author's interview with George H. W. Bush, July 1986.

17. The drugs were eating holes in Robin's stomach, and the doctors had decided to operate. She did not survive the operation.

18. Harold Gullan. *Faith of Our Mothers: The Stories of Presidential Mothers from Mary Washington to Barbara Bush* (Grand Rapids, MI: William B. Eerdmans Publishing Co., 2001), p. 357.

19. Doug Wead, *All the Presidents' Children* (New York: Atria, 2003), p. 78.

20. Ibid., p. 81.

21. Barbara Bush, *Barbara Bush,* p. 48.

22. Gullan, *Faith of Our Mothers,* p. 358.

23. Kilian, *Barbara Bush,* p. 34.

24. Gullan, *Faith of Our Mothers,* p. 358.

EIGHTEEN: GEORGE W. BUSH: THE WARRIOR PRESIDENT

1. Peter Schweizer and Rochelle Schweizer, *The Bushes: Portrait of a Dynasty* (New York: Doubleday, 2004), p. xii.

2. Barbara Bush, *Barbara Bush: A Memoir* (New York: Scribner, 1994), p. 45.

3. George W. Bush and Karen Hughes, *A Charge to Keep* (New York: William Morrow, 1999), p. 14.

4. There are differing accounts of this. According to Barbara Bush, he was headed back to his classroom, while classmates say he was headed the other way. Bill Minutaglio, *First Son: George W. Bush and the Bush Family Dynasty* (New York: Three Rivers Press, 2001), p. 45; and Barbara Bush, *Barbara Bush,* p. 45.

5. Barbara Bush, *Barbara Bush,* p. 45.

6. Ibid., p. 46.

7. Schweizer and Schweizer, *The Bushes,* p. 109.

8. Ibid., p. 109.

9. "Good-bye to Robin," *Texas Monthly,* February 1988.

10. Harold Gullan, *First Fathers: The Men Who Inspired Our Presidents* (Hoboken, N.J.: Wiley, 2004), p. 351.

11. Ibid., p. 358.

12. Schweizer and Schweizer, *The Bushes,* p. 191.

13. For a report on the missing months of George W.'s service, see Josh White, "Why Bush Stopped Flying in the Guard Is Unclear," *The Washington Post,* February 22, 2004.

14. Author's conversation with confidential source 1988.

15. Schweizer and Schweizer, *The Bushes,* p. 193.

16. Author's interview with Neil Bush, 1999.

17. Ibid.

18. Author's conversation with George W. Bush, 1998.

19. Author's conversation with George W. Bush, 1988.

20. Ibid.

21. Schweizer and Schweizer, *The Bushes,* p. 264.

22. This remarkable conversation is confirmed by two sources.

23. Schweizer and Schweizer, *The Bushes,* p. 424.

24. Author's interview with Marvin Bush, 1988.

25. Schweizer and Schweizer, *The Bushes,* p. 414.

26. Ibid., p. 415.

27. Ibid., p. 425.

28. Ibid., p. 426.

29. Ibid., p. 540.

30. Aaron Lubarsky and Alexandra Pelosi, *Journeys with George* (New York: Warner Home Video, February 2004).

EPILOGUE: A PRESIDENT IN THE FAMILY: HOW IT HAPPENS

1. Robert Frost, cited on www.Quoatationsshop.com/poets/frost.html.

2. Peter Schweizer and Rochelle Schweizer, *The Bushes: Portrait of a Dynasty* (New York: Doubleday, 2004), p. xii.

3. Charles Strozier, *Lincoln's Quest for Union* (Philadelphia: Paul Dry Books, rev. ed., 2001), p. 233.

4. Adam Bellow, *In Praise of Nepotism* (New York: Doubleday, 2003), p. 508.

5. Robert Frost, ibid.

6. www.cyfc.unm.edu/Documents/H/N/HN1053.html.

7. Sigmund Freud, translated by A. A. Brill, *Interpretation of Dreams* (New York: Gramercy Books, 1996), p. 87.

A CHRONOLOGICAL LIST OF THE PRESIDENTS' PARENTS

1. James Thomas Flexner, *Washington: The Indispensable Man* (Boston: Little, Brown, 1974), p. 4.

2. Don Higginbotham, *George Washington Reconsidered* (Charlottesville, Va.: University Press of Virginia, 2001), p. 260.

3. Harold I. Gullan, *Faith of Our Mothers: The Stories of Presidential Mothers from Mary Washington to Barbara Bush* (Grand Rapids, Mich.: William B. Eerdmans, 2001), p. 12.

4. Jeff C. Young, *The Fathers of American Presidents: From Augustine Washington to William Blythe and Roger Clinton* (Jefferson, N.C.: McFarland, 1997), p. 8.

5. Gullan, *Faith of Our Mothers,* p. 13.

6. Young, *The Fathers of American Presidents,* p. 19.

7. Ibid.

8. James Monroe, *The Autobiography of James Monroe,* ed. Stuart Gerry Brown (Syracuse University Press, 1959), p. 21.

9. William A. DeGregorio, *The Complete Book of U.S. Presidents* (New York: Gramercy Books, 2001), p. 75.

10. Ibid., p. 21.

11. Doris Faber, *The Mothers of American Presidents* (Penguin, 1968), p. 153. This is probably an exaggeration. Most sources place her ten miles from the scene and able to barely hear the distant rumble of cannon.

12. Ibid., p. 226

13. Young, *The Fathers of American Presidents,* p. 38.

14. She was actually baptized on January 6, 1747, and thus some historians give the year of her birth as 1746.

15. Freeman Cleaves, *Old Tippecanoe: William Henry Harrison and His Time* (Newton, CT: Political Biography Press., 1939), p. 1.

16. Gullan, *Faith of Our Mothers,* p. 62.

17. DeGregorio, *The Complete Book of U.S. Presidents,* p. 139.

18. Oliver Perry Chitwood, *John Tyler, Champion of the Old South* (Newton, Conn.: American Political Biography Press, 1939 and 2000), p. 3.

19. Gullan, *Faith of Our Mothers,* p. 56.

20. Young, *The Fathers of American Presidents,* p. 48.

21. DeGregorio, *The Complete Book of U.S. Presidents,* p. 151.

22. Gullan, *Faith of our Mothers,* p. 65.

23. Charles Grier Sellers, *James K. Polk: Jacksonian* (Princeton, N.J.: Princeton University Press, 1957), p. 61.

24. Eugene Irving McCormac, *James K. Polk: A Political Biography* (Berkeley, California: University of California Press, 1922), p. 1.

25. Ibid.

26. Young, *The Fathers of American Presidents,* p. 56.

27. Brainerd Dyer, *Zachary Taylor* (New York: Barnes & Noble, 1946), p. 2.

28. Jack K. Bauer, *Zachary Taylor: Soldier, Planter, Statesman of the Old Southwest* (Baton Rouge: Louisiana State University Press, 1985), p. 2.

29. Young, *The Fathers of American Presidents,* p. 61.

30. Nathaniel Hawthorne, *The Life of Franklin Pierce* (New York: MSS Information Corporation, 1970), p. 8.

31. Roy Frank Nichols, *Franklin Pierce: Young Hickory of the Granite Hills* (Philadelphia: University of Pennsylvania Press, 1958), p. 421.

32. Ibid., p. 10.

33. Gullan, *Faith of Our Mothers,* p. 90.

34. Ibid., p. 93.

35. Ibid., p. 84.

36. The birthdate of Lincoln's stepmother is much in question. This date comes from Betty Elliot at the Lincoln Log Cabin Site.

37. Gullan, *Faith of Our Mothers,* p. 98.

38. Hans L. Trefousse, *Andrew Johnson: A Biography* (New York: W. W. Norton, 1989), p. 20.

39. Gullan, *Faith of Our Mothers,* p. 97.

40. Jerald F. terHorst, *Gerald Ford and the Future of the Presidency* (New York: Third Press, 1974), p. 27.

41. Ulysses S. Grant, *Ulysses S. Grant: Memoirs and Selected Letters,* ed. Mary Drake McFeely and William S. McFeely (New York: Library of America, 1990), p. 22.

42. Gullan, *Faith of Our Mothers,* p. 108.

43. Ibid., p. 109.

44. James A. Garfield, *The Diary of James A. Garfield,* ed. Harry J. Brown and Frederick D. Williams, vol. 1 (Lansing: Michigan State University Press, 1967), p. ix.

45. Faber, *The Mothers of American Presidents,* p. 161

46. Garfield, *The Diary of James A. Garfield,* p. 48.

47. Faber, p. 159.

48. Ibid., p. xiv.

49. Thomas C. Reeves, *Gentleman Boss: The Life of Chester Alan Arthur* (New York: Alfred A. Knopf, 1975), p. 5.

50. The first of Richard's American ancestors had emigrated from England to Plymouth in 1635 as an indentured servant.

51. Young, *The Fathers of American Presidents,* p. 105.

52. Allan Nevins, *Grover Cleveland: A Study in Courage* (New York: Dodd, Mead & Company, 1948), p. 5.

53. Faber, *The Mothers of American Presidents,* p. 226.

54. Ibid.

55. Young, *The Fathers of American Presidents,* p. 107.

56. Ibid., p. 108.

57. Ibid., p. 228.

58. Ibid., p. 116.

59. Ibid., p. 114.

60. Faber, *The Mothers of American Presidents,* p. 222.

61. Official White House Web site on presidents, http://www.whitehouse.gov/history/presidents/.

62. Theodore Roosevelt, *Theodore Roosevelt: An Autobiography* (New York: Macmillan, 1914), p. 7.

63. Young, *The Fathers of American Presidents,* p. 122.

64. Ibid., p. 125.

65. Faber, *The Mothers of American Presidents,* p. 149.

66. Young, *The Fathers of American Presidents,* p. 127.

67. Faber, *The Mothers of American Presidents,* p. 134.

68. DeGregorio, *The Complete Book of U.S. Presidents,* p. 410.

69. Young, *The Fathers of American Presidents,* p. 135.

70. Ibid., p. 134.

71. Ibid., p. 140.

72. Gullan, *Faith of Our Mothers,* p. 168.

73. Eleanor Wilson McAdoo, *The Woodrow Wilsons* (New York: Macmillan, 1937), p. 3.

74. Young, *The Fathers of American Presidents,* p. 144.

75. Ibid., p. 147.

76. Faber, *The Mothers of American Presidents,* p. 220.

77. Harold I. Gullan, *First Fathers: The Men Who Inspired Our Presidents* (Hoboken, N.J.: John Wiley, 2004), p. 181.

78. Faber, *The Mothers of American Presidents,* p. 217.

79. Ibid., p. 219.

80. Young, *The Fathers of American Presidents,* p. 158.

81. Ibid., p. 160.

82. Ibid., p. 172.

83. Ibid., p. 169.

84. Faber, *The Mothers of American Presidents,* p. 84.

85. Ibid., p. 95.

86. Ibid.

87. Young, *The Fathers of American Presidents,* p. 173.

88. Ibid.

89. Dwight Eisenhower, *At Ease: Stories I Tell to Friends* (New York: McGraw-Hill, 1988), p. 179.

90. Faber, *The Mothers of American Presidents,* p. 68.

91. Ibid., p. 69.

92. Ibid., p. 79.

93. Ibid., p. 59.

94. Young, *The Fathers of American Presidents,* p. 185.

95. Ibid.

96. Faber, *The Mothers of American Presidents,* p. 42.

97. Young, *The Fathers of American Presidents,* p. 194.

98. Faber, *The Mothers of American Presidents,* p. 41.

99. Ibid., p. 46.

100. Ibid., p. 29.

101. Ibid.

102. Ibid., p. 19.

103. Bud Vestal, *Jerry Ford, Up Close: An Investigative Biography* (New York: Coward, McCann & Geogheagan, 1974), p. 49.

104. Author's interview with Jimmy Carter, 1981.

105. Gullan, *First Fathers: The Men Who Inspired Our Presidents,* p. 255.

106. Gullan, *First Fathers: The Men Who Inspired Our Presidents,* p. 316.

107. DeGregorio, *The Complete Book of U.S. Presidents,* p. 618.

108. Young, *The Fathers of the American Presidents,* p. 220.

109. Ronald Reagan, *An American Life* (New York: Simon & Schuster, 1990), p. 23.

110. In the author's last conversation with Ronald Reagan in 1992, he once more told stories about the exploits of the Gipper. Author's interview with Ronald Reagan, 1992.

111. Gullan, *First Fathers,* p. 259

112. Author's interview with George Herbert Walker Bush, 1988.

113. Ibid.

114. Ibid.

115. Nigel Hamilton, *Bill Clinton: An American Journey Great Expectations* (New York: Random House, 2003), p. 3.

116. See Joseph Nathan Kane, Janet Podell, and Steven Anzovin, *Facts About the Presidents* (New York: H. H. Wilson, 2001), p. 499, for the February 21 date. The Clinton Library has determined that the correct date is February 27, 1917. Correspondence with Linda Dixon at the Clinton Library. Chelsea Clinton was also born on February 27.

117. Ibid., p. 232.

118. Charles E. Allen and Jonathan Portis, *The Comeback Kid: The Life and Career of Bill Clinton* (New York: Birch Lane Press, 1992), p. 42.

119. Young, *The Fathers of American Presidents,* p. 230.

120. Ibid., p. 236.

121. Bill Clinton, *My Life* (New York: Alfred A. Knopf, 2004), p. 45.

122. Ibid, p. 237.

123. Hamilton, *Bill Clinton,* p. 38.

124. Cited in Gullan, *First Fathers,* p. 283.

125. Gullan, *First Fathers,* p. 357.

126. Ibid., p. 358.

Bibliography

——— ★ ———

MANUSCRIPT COLLECTIONS AND CORRESPONDENCE

Note: "MHS" refers to the Massachusetts Historical Society.

Adams, Charles Frances. Diary entry, April 28, 1829. Adams Family Papers, MHS.

———, ed. *Letters of John Adams Addressed to His Wife.* 1841.

Adams, George Washington. Letter to Louisa Catherine Adams, September 30, 1817. Adams Family Papers, MHS.

Adams, John. Interview from 1822. In Josiah Quincy, *Memoir of the Life of Josiah Quincy, Jr., of Massachusetts, 1744, 1775,* 2nd ed., Boston, 1874.

———. Letter to Skelton Jones, March 11, 1809, *Works of John Adams,* vol. 9, and to Jonathan Mason, October 27, 1820. Adams Papers, reel 124.

———. Letter to Abigail Adams, March 5, 1797. Adams Papers, Massachusetts Historical Society.

———. Letter to George Washington Adams, September 3, 1810, and May 10, 1811. Adams Family Papers, MHS.

Adams, Louisa Catherine. Letter to John Quincy Adams, April 11, 1804. Adams Family Papers, MHS.

————. Letter to John Quincy Adams, May 29, 1804. MHS. Also in Shepherd, *Adams Chronicles.*

Adams Papers, No. 475, *The Diary of George Whitney.*

Blair, D.C., and Francis Preston. Letter to former President Martin Van Buren, March 30, 1849.

Bush Presidential Library, College Station, Texas.

Carr, Hetty. Letter to Dabney S. Carr, March 13, 1826. Carr-Cary Papers, University of Virginia, Charlottesville, Va.

Coolidge, Grace. Letters, Coolidge Collection, Forbes Library, Northampton, Mass.

Congress of the United States. *U.S. Statutes at Large.* Library of Congress.

Congressional Globe, 27th Congress, 1st session, vol. 10, Appendix.

Flick, Alexander C. History of the State of New York. New-York Historical Society, vol. 2.

Ford, Gerald R. Inaugural speech. August 9, 1974. Gerald R. Ford Library, Ann Arbor, Mich.

Harris, Gibson W. Letter to Abraham Lincoln, November 7, 1860. Abraham Lincoln Papers, Library of Congress.

Harrison, General. Letter to Carter Bassett Harrison, November 27, 1794. Harrison Papers, vol. 1, pp. 21–22, Library of Congress.

Harrison, W. H., Jr. Letters to James Findlay, March 21 and May 22, 1832. *Publications of the Historical and Philosophical Society.*

Hayes, Rutherford B. *Diary and Letters of Rutherford B. Hayes,* Ohio Archeological and Historical Society, vol. 4. p. 24, July 7, 1881.

————. Letter to Rachel Jackson, Fort Strother, December 29, 1813.

————. Letter to John Coffee, April 24, 1815. Library of Congress.

Herndon, to Charles Hart. Springfield, Ill., December 28, 1866. Lamon Papers, Henry E. Huntington Library, San Marino, Calif.

Herndon, to Ward Hill Lamon. Springfield, Ill., February 25, 1870. Lamon Papers, Henry E. Huntington Library, San Marino, Calif.

Jefferson, Thomas. Letter to John Adams, November 7, 1819. Ford, 12:134, 135.

Lincoln, Abraham. Address at New Salem, Ill., March 9, 1832. Library of Congress.

Lincoln, Robert T. Letter to J. G. Holland, Chicago, June 6, 1865. In Rufus Rockwell Wilson, ed., *Intimate Memories of Lincoln.* Elmira, N.Y.: Primavera Press, 1945.

Marston, John. Letter to John Quincy Adams, July 8, 1826. Adams Papers, no. 476. MHS.

Murr, J. Edward. Letter to Albert J. Beveridge, New Albany, Ind., November 21, 1924. Beveridge Papers. Library of Congress, WDC.

Nichols, Josiah. Letter to Andrew Jackson, December 26, 1825. Jackson Papers, University of Tennessee, Knoxville, Tenn.

Nixon, Richard. Farewell address. August 8, 1974. Richard Nixon Library, Yorba Linda, Calif.

Randolph, Thomas Mann. Letter to Thomas Jefferson, March 20, 1802. MHS.

Royall, Anne. *Letters from Alabama* 1830.

Senate of the United States, 22nd Congress, 1st Session, March 20, 1832.

Van Buren, John. *Biographical Directory of the American Congress.*

Van Buren, Martin. Letter to John Van Buren, March, 1830 and June 25, 1830. Van Buren Papers, Library of Congress.

PERSONAL INTERVIEWS AND CONVERSATIONS

Anderson, Claudia. Supervisory Archivist, LBJ Presidential Library and Museum, July 2004.

Aucella, Frank. Executive Director, Woodrow Wilson House, June 2002.

Barrie, Diane. Archivist, Ronald Reagan Library and Museum, July 2004.

Bittinger, Cyndy. Executive Director, Calvin Coolidge Memorial Foundation, June 2002.

Bohanan, Robert. Deputy Director, Jimmy Carter Library, July 2004.

Bonner, Dawn. Mount Vernon Ladies' Association, July 2004.

Brittingham, Selma. Ulysses S. Grant Boyhood Home, July 2004.

Bush, Barbara. June 1987.

Bush, Dorothy. January 1988.

Bush, George H. W. February 1982; July 1986; 1988.

Bush, George W. September 1997; June 13, 1998; August 1998; December 21, 1998.

Bush, Jeb. May 1987.

Capps, Jennifer. Curator, President Benjamin Harrison Home, July 2004.

Capps, Mike. Chief of Interpretation, Lincoln Boyhood National Memorial, July 2004.

Card, Nan. Manuscript Curator, Rutherford B. Hayes Presidential Center, June 2002.

Cardwell, Dr. John. Psychologist, New York City; President and CEO of EVAXX, Inc., July 2004.

Carter, Debbie. Archivist, George Bush Presidential Library and Museum, July 2004.

Carter, Jimmy. 1981.

Clark, Bob. Archivist, Franklin D. Roosevelt Presidential Library, July 2004.

Clark, Elaine. Curator, Andrew Johnson National Historic Site, June 2002.

Cochran, Joshua. Archive Technician, Gerald R. Ford Library, July 2004.

Dixon, Linda. Clinton Presidential Library, August 2004.

Elliot, Betty. Lincoln Log Cabin Site, September 2004.

Finan, Patrick. Library Director, William McKinley Memorial Library, July 2004.

Geeslin, Phyllis. Director, President Benjamin Harrison Home, July 2004.

Gable, Dr. John A. Executive Director, Theodore Roosevelt Association, June 2002.

Gilpin, Melinda. Site Manager, Harding Home, June 2002 and October 2004.

Graham, Nicholas. Reference Librarian, Massachusetts Historical Society, June 2002.

Henderson, Ray. Chief of Interpretations, William Howard Taft National Historic Site, July 2004.

Hogan, Margaret. Assistant Editor, Adams Papers, Massachusetts Historical Society, July 2004.

Holden, Florence. Franklin Pierce, Pierce Manse, July 2004.

Holtzapple, John. Polk Home Director, July 2004.

Houston, Tina. Chief Archivist, LBJ Library and Museum, August 2002.

Hunter, Helen Taft Manning, July 18, 2002.

Joyce, Christine Crumlish. Curator of Education, Sherwood Forest Plantation, June 2002.

Kapsch, Joan. Interpreter, James Garfield National Historic Site, August 2002.

Lee, Meghan. Archivist, Richard Nixon Library and Birthplace, July 2004.

Little, Kerry. MS, Licensed Mental Health Counselor, July 2004.

McNitt, Bill. Archivist, Gerald Ford Library, June 27, 2002.

Molano, Linda. Theodore Roosevelt Association, June 2002.

Moore, Anne. Librarian, President Benjamin Harrison Home, June 2002.

Mullin, Marsha A. Chief Curator, Ladies Hermitage Association, 2001.

Pisano, Frank. Reference Librarian, William McKinley Memorial Library, July 2004.

Pitzer, K. *Guiding Children*. Children, Youth & Family Consortium, January 1991.

Pulfer, Laura. Columnist with Cincinnati Enquirer, August 2002.

Reagan, Ronald. 1992.

Rees, James C. Executive Director, Mount Vernon Ladies' Association, June 2004.

Schnurr, Marie. Aurora Historical Society, Millard Fillmore House, July 2004.

Schwartz, Dr. Thomas. Illinois State Historian, July 2004.

Schweizer, Peter, June 2004.

Shaffer, Roger. Canyonville Academy, June 2002.

Slaymaker, Sam. Executive Director, James Buchanan's Wheatland, July 2004.

Sowell, Randy. Archivist, Harry S. Truman Library, July 2004.

Thompson, Mary. Research Specialist, Mount Vernon Ladies' Association, July 2004.

Townsend, Tim. Historian, Lincoln Home National Historic Site, July 2004.

Tyler, Harrison. President's grandson, director of Sherwood Forest and Tyler family historian, April 27, 2002, and July 2004.

Tyler, Kay. Managing Director, Sherwood Forest Plantation, July 2004.

Voelkel, David. Assistant Director and Curator, James Monroe Museum, July 2002.

Walsh, Tim. Director, Hoover Presidential Library and Museum, June 2002.

Weinkamer, Debbie. Researcher/Educator, James A. Garfield National Historic Site, July 2004.

Woodward, Hobson. Research Assistant, Massachusetts Historical Society, July 2004.

Works, John. President and CEO, Thomas Jefferson Heritage Society, June 2002.

BOOKS

Abels, Jules. *In the Time of Silent Cal.* New York: G. P. Putnam's Sons, 1969.

Abrahamsen, David. *Nixon vs. Nixon: An Emotional Tragedy.* New York: Signet, 1978.

Adams, Andrew N. *A Genealogical History of Henry Adams of Braintree and His Descendants; also John Adams, of Cambridge, Mass., 1632–1897.* Rutland, Vt.: Privately printed, 1898.

Adams, Charles Francis. *Three Episodes of Massachusetts History.* 2 vols. Boston: Houghton Mifflin, 1893.

Adams, Cindy, and Susan Crimp. *Iron Rose.* Dearborn, Mich.: Dove Books, 1995.

Adams, James Truslow. *The Adams Family.* Boston: Little, Brown, 1930.

Adams, John Quincy. *Diary.* New York: Longmans, Green, 1928.

———. *Diary of John Quincy Adams.* Boston: Belknap Press of Harvard University, 1982.

Adams, Samuel Hopkins. *Incredible Era: The Life and Times of Warren Gamaliel Harding.* Boston: Houghton Mifflin, 1939.

Adler, Bill, ed. *The Kennedy Wit.* New York: Citadel, 1964.

Aitken, Jonathan. *Nixon: A Life.* Weidenfeld & Nicholson, 1993; Washington, D.C.: Regenery, 1993.

Alden, John R. *George Washington: A Biography.* Baton Rouge: Louisiana State University Press, 1996.

Aldrich, Gary. *Unlimited Access: An FBI Agent Inside the Clinton White House.* Washington, D.C.: Regnery, 1996.

Allen, Charles F., and Jonathan Portis. *The Comeback Kid: The Life and Career of Bill Clinton.* New York: Birch Lane Press, 1992.

Alsop, Joseph. *FDR, 1882–1945: A Centenary Remembrance.* New York: Viking, 1982.

Alsop, Stewart. *Nixon and Rockefeller: A Double Portrait.* Garden City, N.Y.: Doubleday, 1960.

Ambrose, Stephen E. *Eisenhower.* 2 vols. New York: Simon & Schuster, 1983, 1984.

———. *Nixon: The Education of a Politician, 1913–1962.* New York: Simon & Schuster, 1987.

Ammon, Harry. *James Monroe: The Quest for National Identity.* New York: McGraw-Hill, 1971.

———. *James Monroe: The Quest of National Identity.* Charlottesville: University Press of Virginia. 1990.

Andersen, Christopher. *The Day John Died.* New York: William Morrow, 2000.

Anderson, David. *Abraham Lincoln.* New York: Twayne Publishers, 1970.

Anderson, Donald F. *William Howard Taft: A Conservative's Conception of the Presidency.* Ithaca, N.Y.: Cornell University Press, 1973.

Anderson, Dwight G. *Abraham Lincoln: The Quest for Immortality.* New York: Alfred A. Knopf, 1982.

Anderson, Judith Icke. *William Howard Taft: An Intimate History.* New York: W. W. Norton, 1981.

Anderson, Martin. *Revolution: The Reagan Legacy.* Stanford, Calif.: Hoover Press, 1990.

Anderson, Nancy S., and Dwight C. Anderson. *The Generals: Ulysses S. Grant and Robert E. Lee.* New York: Alfred A. Knopf, 1988.

Anderson, Patrick. *The President's Men: White House Assistants of FDR, HST, DDE, JFK, and LBJ.* New York: Doubleday, 1968.

Angelo, Bonnie. *First Mothers: The Women Who Shaped the Presidents.* New York: HarperCollins, 2001.

Angle, Paul M., and Earl Schenk Miers, eds. *The Living Lincoln.* New York: Barnes and Noble, 1992.

Annin, Robert E. *Woodrow Wilson: A Character Study.* New York: Dodd, Mead, 1924.

Anson, Robert Sam. *Exile: The Unquiet Oblivion of Richard M. Nixon.* New York: Simon & Schuster, 1984.

Anthony, Carl Sferrazza. *America's First Families.* New York: Touchstone, 2000.

Anthony, Katherine. *Dolley Madison*. Garden City, N.Y.: Doubleday, 1949.

Asbell, Bernard. *The F.D.R. Memoirs: A Speculation on History*. New York: Doubleday, 1973.

Atkins, Dale. *I'm Okay, You're My Parents*. New York: Henry Holt, 2004.

Baber, Adin. *Nancy Hanks of Undistinguished Families*. Privately printed, 1960.

Bacon, Francis. *Essays, Civil and Moral, The Harvard Classics*. Cambridge, Mass.: Cambridge Press, 1909.

Bailey, Thomas A. *Presidential Greatness: The Image and the Man from George Washington to the Present*. New York: Appleton-Century, 1966.

Baker, Leonard. *The Johnson Eclipse*. New York: Macmillan, 1966.

Baker, Ray Stannard. *Woodrow Wilson: Life and Letters*. 8 vols. New York: Doubleday, Dornan & Co. 1927–1939.

Barber, James B. *U. S. Grant: The Man and the Image*. Carbondale: Southern Illinois University Press, 1986.

Barber, James David. *The Presidential Character*. New York: Prentice-Hall, 1972, 1992.

Barnard, Harry. *Rutherford B. Hayes and His America*. Indianapolis: Bobbs-Merrill, 1954.

Bartlett, J. Gardner. *Henry Adams of Somersetshire, England, and Braintree, Mass.: His English Ancestry and Some of His Descendants*. New York: Privately printed, 1927.

Barton, William E. *Abraham Lincoln*, vols. 1 and 2. Indianapolis: Bobbs-Merrill, 1925.

———. *The Lineage of Lincoln*. Indianapolis: Bobbs-Merrill, 1929.

———. *The Women Lincoln Loved*. Indianapolis: Bobbs-Merrill, 1927.

Barzman, Sol. *The First Ladies*. New York: Cowles, 1970.

Basler, Roy P., ed. *The Collected Works of Abraham Lincoln,* vols. 1–3. New Brunswick, N.J.: Rutgers University Press, 1953.

Bates, Samuel A., ed. *Records of the Town of Braintree, Massachusetts, 1640–1793*. Bowie, Md.: Heritage Books, 1991.

Bauer, Jack K. *Zachary Taylor: Soldier, Planter, Statesman of the Old Southwest*. Baton Rouge: Louisiana State University Press, 1985.

Beasley, Maurine, Holly Shulman, and Henry Beasley, eds. *The Eleanor Roosevelt Encyclopedia*. Westport, Conn.: Greenwood Press, 2001.

Bell, Jack. *The Johnson Treatment.* New York: Harper & Row, 1965.

Bemis, Samuel Flagg. *John Quincy Adams and the Union.* New York: Knopf, 1956.

Bennett, William J. *The Death of Outrage: Bill Clinton and the Assault on American Ideals.* New York: Simon & Schuster, 1998.

Bent, Silas. *Old Rough and Ready.* New York: Vanguard, 1946.

Bergeron, Paul H. *The Presidency of James K. Polk.* Lawrence, Kans.: University Press of Kansas, 1987.

Bernard, Harry. *Rutherford B. Hayes and His America.* New York: Russell & Russell, 1967.

Bernard, Jesse. *The Future of Motherhood.* New Jersey: Penguin, 1975.

Bernstein, R. B., ed. *The Wisdom of John and Abigail Adams.* New York: Metrobooks, 2002.

Berquist, Laura, and Stanley Tretick. *A Very Special President.* New York: McGraw-Hill, 1965.

Beschloss, Michael. *The Conquerors.* New York: Simon & Schuster, 2002.

———. *Kennedy and Roosevelt.* New York: Norton, 1980.

Beveridge, Albert J. *Abraham Lincoln,* vol. 1. Boston: Houghton Mifflin, 1928.

Biddle, Alexander, ed. *Old Family Letters Copied from the Originals for Alexander Biddle.* Philadelphia: Lippincott, 1892.

Binkley, Wilfred E. *American Political Parties.* New York: Knopf, 1962.

Bishop, Jim. *FDR's Last Year.* New York: Morrow, 1974.

Blair, Joan, and Clay, Jr. *The Search for JFK.* New York: Putnam, 1974.

Blum, John Morton. *Woodrow Wilson and the Politics of Morality.* Boston: Little, Brown, 1956.

Bober, Natalie S. *Thomas Jefferson: Man on a Mountain.* New York: Atheneum, 1988.

Boller, Paul F., Jr. *Presidential Anecdotes.* New York: Oxford University Press, 1981.

Bonnell, John Sutherland. *Presidential Profiles: Religion in the Life of America's Presidents.* Philadelphia: Westminster Press, 1971.

Booraem, Hendrik. *The Road to Respectability: James A. Garfield and His World, 1844–1852.* Cranbury, N.J.: Bucknell University Press, 1988.

———. *Young Hickory, The Making of Andrew Jackson.* New York: Taylor, 2001.

Bourne, Miriam Anne. *First Family: George Washington and His Intimate Relations.* New York: Norton, 1982.

Bourne, Peter G. *Jimmy Carter: A Comprehensive Biography from Plains to Post-Presidency.* New York: Scribner's, 1997.

Bowen, Catherine Drinker. *John Adams and the American Revolution.* Boston: Little, Brown, 1950.

Bowers, Claude G. *The Young Jefferson, 1743–1789.* Boston, Houghton Mifflin, 1945.

Boyarski, Bill. *Ronald Reagan: His Life and Rise to the Presidency.* New York: Random House, 1981.

Bradlee, Benjamin C. *Conversations with Kennedy.* New York: W. W. Norton, 1975.

Brands, H. W., ed. *The Selected Letters of Theodore Roosevelt.* New York: Cooper Square Press, 2001.

———. *TR, The Last Romantic.* New York: Basic Books, 1997.

Brant, Irving. *James Madison.* 6 vols. Indianapolis: Bobbs-Merrill, 1941–1961.

Breeden, Robert L., chief ed. *The Presidents of the United States of America.* Washington, D.C.: White House Historical Association, 1978.

Brendon, Piers. *Ike: His Life and Times.* New York: Harper & Row, 1986.

Brinkley, Douglas. *The Unfinished Presidency.* New York: Viking, 1998.

Brockett, L. P. *Life and Times of Abraham Lincoln.* New York: Bradley, 1865.

Broder, David. *The Party's Over.* New York: Harper & Row, 1972.

Brodie, Fawn. *Richard Nixon: The Shaping of His Character.* New York: W. W. Norton, 1981.

———. *Thomas Jefferson: An Intimate History.* New York: Norton, 1974.

Brodsky, Alyn. *Grover Cleveland: A Study in Character.* New York: St. Martin's Press, 2000.

Brookhiser, Richard. *Founding Father: Rediscovering G. Washington.* New York: Free Press, 1996.

Brooks, Stewart M. *Our Murdered Presidents: The Medical Story.* New York: Frederick Fell, 1966.

Brown, Harry J., and Frederick D. Williams, eds. *The Diary of James A. Garfield,* vol. 1, Lansing: Michigan State University Press, 1967.

Brown, R. A. *Presidency of John Adams.* Lawrence: University Press of Kansas, 1975.

Brown, Stuart Gerry, ed. *James Monroe's Autobiography,* Syracuse, N.Y.: Syracuse University Press, 1959.

Bruce, David K. *Sixteen American Presidents.* New York: Bobbs–Merrill, 1962.

Bruni, Frank. *Ambling Into History: The Unlikely Odyssey of George W. Bush.* New York: HarperCollins, 2002.

Bryant, Traphes, and Frances Spatz. *Dog Days at the White House: The Outrageous Memoirs of the Presidential Kennel Keeper.* New York: Macmillan, 1975.

Bulloch, Joseph G. *A History of the Genealogy of the Families of Bulloch, Stobo, Etc.* Savannah, Ga., 1892.

Bundy, Jonas Mills. *The Life of General James A. Garfield.* New York: A. S. Barnes, 1880.

Burleigh, Ann Husted. *John Adams.* New Rochelle, N.Y.: Arlington House, 1969.

Burlingame, Michael. *The Inner World of Abraham Lincoln.* Chicago: University of Illinois Press, 1994.

Burner, David. *Herbert Hoover: A Public Life.* New York: Alfred A. Knopf, 1979.

Burnham, Sophy. *The Landed Gentry: Passions and Personalities Inside America's Propertied Class.* New York: Putnam, 1978.

Burns, James MacGregor. *John Kennedy: A Political Profile.* New York: Harcourt, Brace, & World, 1959.

———. *Roosevelt: The Lion and the Fox.* New York: Harcourt, Brace, & World, 1956.

Burt, Nathaniel. *First Families: The Making of an American Aristocracy.* Boston: Little, Brown, 1970.

Bush, Barbara. *Barbara Bush: A Memoir.* New York: Scribner's, 1994.

Bush, George H. W. *All the Best: My Life in Letters and Other Writings.* New York: Simon & Schuster, 1998.

———, with Victor Gold. *Looking Forward: An Autobiography.* New York: Bantam, 1988.

Bush, George W., and Karen Hughes. *A Charge to Keep.* New York: William Morrow, 1999.

Butterfield, Lyman H., et al., eds. *The Adams Papers: Diary and Autobiography of John Adams, vol. 1, 1755–1770.* Cambridge, Mass.: Belknap Press of Harvard University, 1962.

————, ed., *The Adams Papers: The Earliest Diary of John Adams*. Cambridge, Mass.: Belknap Press of Harvard University Press, 1966.

————, et al., eds. *John Adams to Abigail Adams, Aug. 4, 1776, and May 12, 1780.* 4 vols.; *Adams Family Correspondence*. Cambridge, Mass.: Harvard University Press, 1963.

————, ed. *Letters of Benjamin Rush,* vol. 2. Princeton, N.J.: American Philosophical Society, 1951.

Butterfield, Lyman H., Marc Fridlaender, and Mary Jo Kline, eds. *The Book of Abigail and John: Selected Letters of the Adams Family*. Cambridge, Mass.: Harvard University Press, 1975.

Caldwell, Robert A. *James A. Garfield*. New York: Dodd, Mead, 1931.

Canfield, Cass. *The Iron Will of Jefferson Davis*. New York: Harcourt Brace Jovonovich, 1978.

Canliffe, Marcus. *George Washington: Man and Monument*. Boston: Little, Brown, 1958.

Cannon, James M. *Time and Chance: Gerald Ford's Appointment with History*. New York: HarperCollins, 1994.

Cannon, Lou. *President Reagan: The Role of a Lifetime*. New York: Simon & Schuster, 1989.

————. *Reagan*. New York: Putnam, 1982.

Cappon, Lester J., ed. *The Adams-Jefferson Letters*. Chapel Hill: University of North Carolina Press, 1959.

Cardigan, J. H. *Ronald Reagan: A Remarkable Life*. Kansas City: Andrews McMeel, 1995.

Carnegie, Dale. *Lincoln the Unknown*. Garden City, New York: Dale Carnegie and Associates, 1932.

Caro, Robert A. *The Years of Lyndon Johnson: The Path to Power*. New York: Knopf, 1982.

Caroli, Betty Boyd. *Inside the White House*. New York: Canopy Books, 1992.

Carter, Jimmy. *Keeping Faith: Memoirs of a President*. New York: Bantam Books, 1982.

Carter, Lillian, and Gloria Carter Spann. *Away from Home*. New York: Simon & Schuster, 1977.

Carter, Rosalynn. *First Lady from Plains*. Boston: Houghton Mifflin, 1984.

Catton, Bruce. *Grant Moves South*. Boston: Little, Brown, 1960.

————. *Grant Takes Command*. Boston: Little, Brown, 1969.

————. *U. S. Grant and the American Military Tradition.* Boston: Little, Brown, 1954.

Charnwood, Lord. *Abraham Lincoln.* Garden City, N.Y.: Garden City Publishing, 1917.

Chessman, G. Wallace. *Theodore Roosevelt and the Politics of Power.* Boston: Little, Brown, 1969.

Chidsey, Donald Barr. *And Tyler Too.* New York: Thomas Nelson, 1978.

Childs, Marquis. *Eisenhower: Captive Hero.* New York: Harcourt, Brace, & World, 1958.

Chinard, Gilbert. *Honest John Adams.* Boston: Little, Brown, 1933.

Chitwood, Oliver Perry. *John Tyler, Champion of the Old South.* Newton, Conn.: American Political Biography Press, 1939, 2000.

Churchill, Allen. *The Roosevelts: American Aristocrats.* New York: Harper & Row, 1978.

Clark, Bennett Champ. *John Quincy Adams: "Old Man Eloquent."* Boston, Mass.: Little, Brown, 1932.

Clark, Champ, and the Editors of Time-Life Books. *The Civil War: Decoying the Yanks.* Alexandria, Va.: Time-Life Books, 1984.

Clark, Harrison. *All Cloudless Glory: The Life of George Washington from Youth to Yorktown.* Washington, D.C.: Regnery Publishing, 1995.

Cleaves, Freeman. *Old Tippecanoe.* Newtown, Conn.: American Political Biography Press, 1939.

Clinton, Bill. *My Life.* New York: Alfred A. Knopf, 2004.

Clinton, Roger, with Jim Moore. *Growing Up Clinton.* New York: Summit, 1995.

Cochran, Bert. *Harry Truman and the Crisis Presidency.* New York: Funk & Wagnall's, 1973.

Cole, Donald B. *Martin Van Buren and the American Political System.* Princeton, N.J.: Princeton University Press, 1984.

Collier, Edward A. *History of Old Kinderhook.* New York: Putnam, 1914.

Collier, Peter, and David Horowitz. *The Kennedys: An American Drama.* New York: Summit, 1984.

————. *The Roosevelts: An American Saga.* New York: Simon & Schuster, 1994.

Colum, Mary. *Life and the Dream.* Garden City, N.Y.: Doubleday, 1947.

Conwell, Russell H. *The Life, Speeches and Public Services of James A. Garfield.* Portland, Maine: Stinson & Co., 1881.

Cook, Blanche Wiesen. *Eleanor Roosevelt,* vol 1. New York: Viking, 1992.

Coolidge, Calvin. *The Autobiography of Calvin Coolidge.* New York: Cosmopolitan, 1929.

Cormier, Frank. *LBJ: The Way He Was.* New York: Doubleday, 1977.

Costello, William. *The Facts About Nixon.* New York: Viking, 1960.

Cramer, Jesse Grant. ed. *Letters of Ulysses S. Grant to His Father and Youngest Sister.* New York: Putnam, 1912.

Craven, Avery Odelle. *The Coming of the Civil War.* New York: University of Chicago Press, 1942.

Cresson, William Penn. *James Monroe.* New York: Archon, 1971.

Cronkite, Walter. *A Reporter's Life.* New York: Alfred A. Knopf, 1996.

Crowley, Monica. *Nixon off the Record.* New York: Random House, 1996.

Cunliffe, Marcus. *George Washington: Man and Monument.* Boston: Little, Brown, 1958.

Cunningham, Nobel E., Jr. *In Pursuit of Reason: The Life of Thomas Jefferson.* Baton Rouge: Louisiana State University, 1987.

Current, Richard N. *The Lincoln Nobody Knows.* New York: McGraw-Hill, 1958.

Curtis, George Ticknor. *Life of James Buchanan: Fifteenth President of the United States.* New York: Harper and Bros., 1883.

Curtis, James C. *Andrew Jackson and the Search for Vindication.* Boston: Little, Brown, 1976.

————. *The Fox at Bay: Martin Van Buren and the Presidency, 1837–41.* Lexington: University of Kentucky Press, 1970.

Custis, George Washington Parke. *Recollections and Private Memoirs of Washington.* New York: Derby and Jackson, 1860.

Cutler, John Henry. *"Honey Fitz": Three Steps to the White House.* Indianapolis: Bobbs-Merrill, 1962.

Dallas, Rita, with Jeanire Ratcliff. *The Kennedy Case.* New York: G. P. Putnam's Sons, 1973.

Dallek, Robert. *Lone Star Rising: Lyndon Johnson and His Times, 1908–1960.* New York: Oxford University Press, 1991.

————. *An Unfinished Life: John F. Kennedy, 1917–1963.* Boston: Little, Brown, 2003.

Daniel, Margaret Truman. *Souvenir.* New York: McGraw-Hill, 1956.

Daniels, Jonathan. *The Man of Independence.* Philadelphia: Lippincott, 1950.

Davis, Burke. *Old Hickory: A Life of Andrew Jackson.* New York: Dial, 1977.

———. *To Appomattox.* New York: Rinehart, 1959.

Davis, Elizabeth Harbison. *I Played Their Accompaniments.* New York and London: D. Appleton-Century Company, 1940.

Davis, John H. *The Kennedys: Dynasty and Disaster, 1848–1948.* New York: McGraw-Hill, 1984.

Davis, Kenneth. *FDR: The Beckoning of Destiny, 1882–1928: A History.* New York: Putnam, 1972.

Davis, Kenneth S. *Soldier of Democracy: A Biography of Dwight D. Eisenhower.* Garden City, N.Y.: Doubleday, 1945.

Davis, Patti. *Angels Don't Die: My Father's Gift of Faith.* New York: HarperCollins, 1995.

Davison, Kenneth E. *The Presidency of Rutherford B. Hayes.* Westport, Conn.: Greenwood, 1972.

Deaver, Michael. *A Different Drummer: My Thirty Years with Ronald Reagan.* San Francisco: HarperCollins, 2001.

DeGregorio, William. *The Complete Book of U.S. Presidents.* New York: Gramercy, 2001.

Dineen, Joseph F. *The Kennedy Family.* Boston: Little, Brown, 1959.

Divine, Robert A., ed. *Exploring the Johnson Years.* Austin: University of Texas Press, 1981.

Doenecke, Justus. *Presidencies of James A. Garfield and Chester A. Arthur.* Lawrence, Kans.: Regents Press of Kansas, 1998.

Donald, David Herbert. *Lincoln.* New York: Simon & Schuster, 1995.

Donovan, Frank. *Eisenhower: The Inside Story.* New York: Harper and Brothers, 1956.

———. *The Women in Their Lives: The Distaff Side of the Founding Fathers.* New York: Dodd, Mead, 1966.

Donovan, Robert J. *Tumultuous Years: The Presidency of Harry S. Truman.* New York: Norton, 1982.

Downes, Randolph, *The Rise of Warren Gamaliel Harding, 1865–1920.* Columbus: Ohio State University Press, 1970.

D'Souza, Dinesh. *Ronald Reagan: How an Ordinary Man Became an Extraordinary Leader.* New York: Free Press, 1997.

Dublin, Louis J., Alfred Lofka, and Mortimer Spiegelman. *Length of Life.* New York: Ronald Press, 1948.

Duffy, Michael, and Dan Goodgame. *Marching in Place: The Status Quo Presidency of George Bush.* New York: Simon & Schuster, 1992.

Dugger, Ronnie. *On Reagan: The Man and His Presidency.* New York: McGraw-Hill, 1983.

Duke, Jan Taylor. *Kenmore and the Lewises.* Fredericksburg: Kenmore Association, 1965.

Dumbauld, Edward. "Jefferson and Adams' English Garden Tour" in *Jefferson and the Arts: An Extended View,* ed. William Howard Adams. Washington D.C.: National Gallery of Art, 1976.

Duncan, Kunigunde. *Earning the Right to Do Fancy Work: An Informal Biography of Ida Eisenhower.* Lawrence: University of Kansas Press, 1953.

Dyer, Brainerd. *Zachary Taylor.* Baton Rouge: Louisiana State University Press, 1946.

East, Robert A. *John Adams.* Boston: Twayne, 1979.

Eaton, David W. *Historical Atlas of Westmoreland County.* Richmond, Va.: Dietz Press, 1942.

Eckenrode, H. J. *Rutherford B. Hayes.* New York: Kennikat, 1963.

Edwards, Anne. *Early Reagan: The Rise to Power.* New York: William Morrow, 1990.

Eisenhower, Dwight D. *At Ease: Stories I Tell to Friends.* New York: McGraw-Hill, 1988.

Eisenhower, John S. D. *Strictly Personal: A Memoir.* New York: Doubleday, 1974.

Eisenhower, Julie Nixon. *Special People.* New York: Simon & Schuster, 1977.

Eisenhower, Milton S. *The President Calling.* New York: Doubleday, 1974.

Eisenhower, Susan. *Breaking Free: A Memoir of Love and Revolution.* New York: Farrar Straus Giroux, 1995.

Ellett, Katherine T. *Young John Tyler.* Richmond, Va.: Dietz Press, 1976.

Ellis, Joseph J. *American Sphinx: The Character of Thomas Jefferson.* New York: Alfred A. Knopf, 1996.

————. *Passionate Sage: The Character and Legacy of John Adams.* New York: W. W. Norton, 1993.

Emery, Noemie. *Washington: A Biography.* New York: G. P. Putnam's Sons, 1976.

Evans, Rowland, and Robert Novak. *Lyndon B. Johnson: The Exercise of Power.* New York: New American Library, 1966.

Faber, Doris. *The Mothers of American Presidents.* Penguin, 1968.

Faber, Harold, ed. *The Kennedy Years.* New York: Viking, 1964.

Farley, James A. *Jim Farley's Story: The Roosevelt Years.* New York: McGraw-Hill, 1948.

Farrell, John J. *Millard Fillmore, 1800–1874.* Dobbs Ferry, N.Y.: Oceana, 1971.

Faulkner, Leonard. *The President Who Wouldn't Retire: John Quincy Adams, Congressman from Massachusetts.* New York: Coward-McCann, 1967.

Fay, Bernard. *George Washington: Republican Aristocrat.* Boston: Houghton Mifflin, 1931.

Felder, Paula, ed. *George Washington's Relations and Relationships in Fredericksburg, Virginia.* Fredericksburg, Va.: Historic Publications of Fredericksburg, 1981.

Ferling, John E. *The First of Men: A Life of George Washington.* Knoxville: University of Tennessee Press, 1988.

———. *John Adams: A Life.* Knoxville: University of Tennessee Press, 1992.

Ferrell, Robert H., ed. *Off the Record: The Private Papers of Harry S. Truman.* New York: Harper & Row, 1980.

———. *Truman: A Centenary Remembrance.* New York: Viking, 1984.

Fick, Paul M. *The Dysfunctional President.* New York: Birch Lane Press, 1995.

Fitzgerald, Carol B. *Rutherford B. Hayes.* Westport, Conn.: Meckler, 1991.

Fitzpatrick, John, ed. *The Autobiography of Martin Van Buren,* vol 1. Reading, Mass.: Perseus Books, 1973.

Flammonde, Paris. *The Kennedy Conspiracy.* New York: Meredith, 1969.

Fleming, Thomas. *The Man from Monticello: An Intimate Life of Thomas Jefferson.* New York: William Morrow, 1969.

Flexner, James T. *George Washington: A Biography.* 4 vols. Boston: Little, Brown, 1965–1972.

————. *George Washington: The Forge of Experience, 1732–1775*. Boston: Little, Brown, 1963.

————. *Washington the Indispensable Man*. Boston: Little, Brown, 1974.

Flynn, John T. *Country Squire in the White House*. New York: Doubleday Doran, 1955.

Foner, Eric, and Olivia Mahoney. *A House Divided: America in the Age of Lincoln*. New York: W. W. Norton, 1990.

Foote, Shelby. *The Civil War, A Narrative: From Sumter to Perryville*. New York: Random House, 1958.

Ford, Gerald R. *A Time to Heal*. New York: Harper & Row, 1979.

————, and J. R. Stiles. *Portrait of the Assassin*. New York: Simon & Schuster, 1965.

Ford, Paul Leicester. *The True George Washington*. Philadelphia: Lippincott, 1898.

Fowles, Jib. *Starstruck*. Washington, D.C.: Smithsonian Institution Press, 1992.

Frank, Sid, and Arden Davis Melick. *The Presidents: Tidbits and Trivia*. New York: Random House, 1988.

Frantz, Joe B. *Texas: A Bicentennial History*. New York: W. W. Norton, 1976.

————. *Thirty-Seven Years of Public Service: The Honorable Lyndon B. Johnson*. Austin, Tex.: Shoal Creek Publishing, 1974.

Fraser, Kennedy. *Ornament and Silence: Essays on Women's Lives*. New York: Alfred A. Knopf, 1997.

Freeman, Cleaves. *Old Tippecanoe: William Henry Harrison and His Time*. New York: Scribner's, 1939.

Freeman, Douglas Southall. *George Washington: A Biography*, vol. 1. *Young Washington*. New York: Scribner's, 1948–1954.

————. *Lee's Lieutenants*, vol. I, New York: Scribner and Sons, 1942.

————. *Washington*. New York: Scribner's, 1995.

Freidel, Frank. *Franklin D. Roosevelt*. 4 vols. Boston: Little, Brown, 1952–1973.

Freud, Sigmund, and William C. Bulitt. *Woodrow Wilson: A Psychological Study*. New York: Houghton Mifflin, 1966.

Fuess, Claude. *Calvin Coolidge: The Man from Vermont*. Boston: Little, Brown, 1940.

Furman, Bess. *White House Profile: A Social history of the White House, Its*

Occupants and Its Festivities. Indianapolis and New York: Bobbs-Merrill, 1951.

Gallen, David. *Bill Clinton as They Know Him: An Oral Biography.* New York: Marlowe, 1996.

Gara, Larry. *The Presidency of Franklin Pierce.* Lawrence: University Press of Kansas, 1991.

Gardner, Joseph L., and Julian P. Boyd, eds. *Thomas Jefferson: A Biography in His Own Words,* vol. 1. Princeton, N.J.: Princeton University Press, 1970.

Garraty, John Arthur. *Woodrow Wilson: A Great Life in Brief.* Westport, Conn.: Greenwood, 1977.

Garrison, Webb. *The Lincoln No One Knows.* Nashville, Tenn.: Rutledge Hill Press, 1993.

————, and Beth Wieder. *A Treasury of White House Tales.* Nashville, Tenn.: Thomas Nelson, 2002.

Gelles, Edith B. *Portia: The World of Abigail Adams.* Bloomington: Indiana University Press, 1992.

Gibson, Barbara, with Caroline Latham. *Life with Rose Kennedy.* New York: Simon & Schuster, 1971.

Gibson, Barbara, and Ted Schwarz. *Rose Kennedy and Her Family: The Best and Worst of Their Lives and Times.* New York: Birch Lane Press, 1995.

Gilbert, Robert. *The Mortal Presidency.* New York: HarperCollins, 1992.

Gilman, Daniel C. *James Monroe,* rev. ed. Boston: Houghton Mifflin, 1898.

Glad, Betty. *Jimmy Carter: In Search of the Great White House.* New York: Norton, 1980.

Goebel, Dorothy Burne. *William Henry Harrison: A Political Biography.* Indianapolis: Historical Bureau of the Indiana Library and Historical Department, 1926.

Goldhurst, Richard. *Many Are the Hearts: The Agony and the Triumph of Ulysses S. Grant.* New York: Reader's Digest Press, 1975.

Goldman, Eric F. *The Tragedy of Lyndon Johnson.* New York: Knopf, 1969.

Goodwin, Doris Kearns. *The Fitzgeralds and the Kennedys.* New York: Simon & Schuster, 1987.

————. *No Ordinary Time.* New York: Simon & Schuster, 1994.

Gould, Lewis L. *Presidency of William McKinley*. Lawrence: Regents Press of Kansas, 1980.

Graff, Henry F., ed., *The Presidents: A Reference History*. New York: Simon & Schuster, 1997.

Graff, Robert, Robert Bennett Ginn, and Roger Butterfield. *FDR*. New York: Harper & Row, 1963.

Graham, Billy. *Just As I Am*. New York: HarperCollins, 1997.

Grant, Ulysses S. *Memoirs and Selected Letters*. New York: Library of America, 1990.

Grant, Ulysses S., III. *Ulysses S. Grant: Warrior and Statesman*. New York: Morrow, 1968.

Grayson, Benson Lee. *Unknown President: The Administration of Millard Fillmore*. New York: University Press of America, 1981.

Green, Fitzhugh. *George Bush: An Intimate Portrait*. New York: Hippocrene, 1989.

Green, John Robert. *The Presidency of Gerald R. Ford*. Lawrence: University of Kansas Press, 1995.

Greenstein, Fred I. *The Hidden-Hand Presidency: Eisenhower as Leader*. New York: Basic Books, 1982.

Gullan, Harold I. *Faith of Our Mothers: The Stories of Presidential Mothers from Mary Washington to Barbara Bush*. Grand Rapids, Mich.: William B. Eerdmans, 2001.

———. *First Fathers: The Men Who Inspired Our Presidents*. Hoboken, N.J.: John Wiley and Sons, 2004.

Gurian, Michael. *Mothers, Sons and Lovers: How a Man's Relationship with His Mother Affects the Rest of His Life*. Boston, Mass.: Shambhala, 1994.

Gurko, Leo. *The Angry Decade*. New York: Dodd, Mead, 1947.

Hagdorn, Hermann. *The Roosevelt Family of Sagamore Hill*. New York: Macmillan, 1964.

Hall, Gordon Langley. *Mr. Jefferson's Ladies*. Boston: Beacon Press, Boston, 1966.

Hamby, Alonzo L. *Man of the People: A Life of Harry S. Truman*. New York: Oxford University Press, 1995.

Hamilton, Holman. *Three Kentucky Presidents: Lincoln, Taylor, Davis*. Lexington: University Press of Kentucky, 1978.

———. *Zachary Taylor: Soldier in the White House*. 2 vols. Indianapolis: Bobbs-Merrill, 1941, 1951.

Hamilton, Nigel. *Bill Clinton: An American Journey: Great Expectations.* New York: Random House, 2003.

Hamilton, Nigel. *JFK: Reckless Youth.* New York: Random House, 1992.

Handlin, Oscar and Lilian. *Liberty in Expansion, 1760–1850.* New York: Harper & Row, 1989.

Harwood, Richard, and Haynes Johnson. *Lyndon.* New York: Praeger, 1973.

Hatfield, J. H., and Mark Crispin Miller. *Fortunate Son: George W. Bush and the Making of an American President.* New York: Soft Skull Press, 2001.

Hawthorne, Nathaniel. *Life of Franklin Pierce.* New York: MSS Information Corporation, 1970.

Hayden, Horace E. *Virginia Genealogies.* Washington, D.C.: Rare Book Shop, 1931.

Hechler, Ken. *The Truman White House: The Administration of the Presidency, 1945–1953.* Lawrence: University of Kansas Press, 1980.

Hecht, Marie B. *John Quincy Adams: A Personal History of an Independent Man.* New York: Macmillan, 1972.

Heckscher, August. *Woodrow Wilson.* New York: Scribner's, 1991.

Hedley, John Hollister. *Harry S Truman: The Little Man from Missouri.* Woodburn, New York: Barron's Educational Series, 1979.

Heiskell, S. G. *Andrew Jackson and Early Tennessee History.* Nashville, Tenn.: Best Books, 1920.

Herndon, William H. *Life of Lincoln.* Reading, Mass.: Perseus Books, 1973.

———, and Jesse Weik, *Herndon's Life of Lincoln.* Greenwich, Conn.: Fawcett Publications, 1960.

———, and Jesse William Weik. *Herndon's Lincoln.* Scituate, Mass.: Digital Scanning, Herndon Lincoln Publishing, 1999.

Hersh, Seymour. *The Dark Side of Camelot.* Boston: Little, Brown, 1997.

Herskowitz, Mickey. *Duty, Honor, Country.* Nashville, Tenn.: Rutledge Hill Press, 2003.

Hertz, Emanuel. *The Hidden Lincoln.* New York: Viking, 1938.

———. *Lincoln Talks: A Biography in Anecdote.* New York: Viking Press, 1939.

Hess, Stephen. *America's Political Dynasties.* New York: Doubleday & Company, 1966.

Higginbotham, Don. *George Washington Reconsidered.* University Press of Virginia, 2001.

Higgins, Eva. *William McKinley: An Inspiring Biography.* Canton, Ohio: Daring, 1989.

Higham, Charles. *Rose: The Life and Times of Rose Fitzgerald Kennedy.* New York: Pocket Books, 1995.

Hillman, William. *Mr. President.* New York: Farrar, Strauss, 1952.

Hilty, James W. *Robert Kennedy: Brother Protector.* Philadelphia: Temple University Press, 1997.

Hinshaw, David. *Herbert Hoover: American Quaker.* New York: Farrar, Straus, 1950.

Hitchcock, Caroline Hanks. *Nancy Hanks.* New York: Doubleday & McClure, 1899.

Hobby, Laura Aline. *Washington the Lover.* Dallas, Tex.: Southwest Press, 1932.

Holland, J. G. *The Life of Abraham Lincoln.* Springfield, Mass.: Republican Press, 1866.

Holman, Hamilton. *Zachary Taylor: Soldier in the White House.* Indianapolis: Bobbs-Merrill, 1951.

Hoogenboom, Ari. *Rutherford B. Hayes, Warrior and President.* Lawrence: University of Kansas Press, 1995.

Howar, Barbara. *Laughing All the Way.* New York: Stein and Day, 1977.

Howe, George F. *Chester A. Arthur, A Quarter-Century of Machine Politics.* New York: Dodd, Mead, 1934.

Hoyt, Edwin P. *James Buchanan.* Chicago: Reilly and Lee, 1966.

———. *Martin Van Buren.* Chicago: Reilly and Lee, 1964.

Hugh, Russell Frazer. *Democracy in the Making: The Jackson-Tyler Era.* Indianapolis: Bobbs-Merrill, 1938.

Hughs, Rupert. *George Washington.* New York: Morrow, 1922.

Hyams, Joe. *Fight of the Avenger: George Bush at War.* New York: Harcourt Brace Jovanovich, 1991.

Ide, Arthur Frederick. *The Father's Son: George W. Bush, Jr.* New York: Minuteman Press, 1998.

Irving, Washington. *Life of Washington.* New York: Putnam, 1856.

James, Edward T., et al., eds. *Notable American Women 1607–1950: A Biographical Dictionary.* Cambridge, Mass.: Harvard University Press, 1971.

James, Marquis. *The Border Captain.* Indianapolis: Bobbs-Merrill, 1933.

————. *The Life of Andrew Jackson*. Indianapolis: Bobbs-Merrill, 1938.

Jeffers, H. Paul. *Theodore Roosevelt, Jr.: The Life of a War Hero*. Novato, Calif.: Presidio, 2002.

Jenkins, Roy. *Truman*. New York: Harper & Row, 1980.

Johnson, Gerald W. *Andrew Jackson: An Epic in Homespun*. New York: Minton, Balch, 1927.

Johnson, Lyndon Baines. *The Vantage Point*. New York: Holt, Rinehart & Winston, 1971.

Johnson, Rebekah Baines. *A Family Album*. New York: McGraw-Hill, 1965.

Johnson, Sam Houston. *My Brother Lyndon*. New York: Cowles, 1969.

Jordan, Judith V., Alexandra Kaplan, Jean Baker Miller, Irene P. Stiver, and Janet L. Surrey. *Women's Growth in Connection: Writings from the Stone Center*. New York: Guilford Press, 1991.

Kagan, Jerome. *The Nature of the Child*. New York: Basic Books, 1984.

Kane, Joseph Nathan. *Facts About the Presidents*. New York: H. W. Wilson, 1981.

————, Janet Podell, and Steven Anzovin. *Facts About the Presidents*. New York: H. H. Wilson, 2001.

Kaplan, David A. *The Accidental President: How 413 Lawyers, 9 Supreme Court Justices and 5,963,110 Floridians Give or Take a Few Landed George W. Bush in the White House*. New York: William Morrow, 2001.

Kaplan, Louie J. *Oneness and Separateness*. New York: Touchstone, 1978.

Kearns, Doris. *Lyndon Johnson and the American Dream*. New York: Harper & Row, 1976.

Keckley, Elizabeth. *Thirty Years a Slave, and Four Years in the White House*. New York: G. W. Carleton, 1868.

Kelley, Brent P., and Arthur M. Schlesinger, Jr., eds. *James Monroe: American Statesman*. New York: Library Binding, 2000.

Kelley, Virginia Clinton, with James Morgan. *Leading with My Heart: My Life*. New York: Simon & Schuster, 1994.

Kelly, Frank K. *The Martyred Presidents and Their Successors*. New York: Putnam, 1967.

Kennedy, Joseph P. *I'm for Roosevelt*. New York: Reynal and Hitchcock, 1936.

Kennedy, Rose Fitzgerald. *Times to Remember.* New York: Doubleday, 1974.

Ketcham, Ralph. *James Madison: A Biography.* New York: Macmillan, 1971.

Kilian, Pamela. *Barbara Bush: A Biography.* New York: St. Martin's Press, 1992.

———. *Barbara Bush: Matriarch of a Dynasty.* New York: Thomas Dunne Books, St. Martin's Press, 2002.

Kleeman, Rita S. Halle. *Gracious Lady: The Life of Sara Delano Roosevelt.* New York: Appleton-Century, 1935.

Klein, Carole, *Mothers and Sons.* New York: Houghton Mifflin, 1984.

Klein, Philip S. *President James Buchanan.* University Park: Pennsylvania State University Press, 1962.

Klein, Will S. *Kinderhook, N.Y., The Village Beautiful,* Privately printed, 1911.

Knollenberg, Bernhard. *George Washington: The Virginia Period, 1732–1775.* Durham, N.C.: Duke University Press, 1964.

Koch, Adrienne, and William Peden, eds. *Selected Writings of John and John Quincy Adams.* New York: Alfred A. Knopf, 1946.

Koegh, James. *This Is Nixon.* New York: G. P. Putnam's Sons, 1956.

Kornitzer, Bela. *The Great American Heritage: The Story of the Five Eisenhower Brothers.* New York: Farrar, Straus, 1955.

———. *The Real Nixon: An Intimate Biography.* New York: Rand McNally, 1960.

Kucharsky, David. *The Man from Plains: The Mind and Spirit of Jimmy Carter.* New York: Harper & Row, 1976.

Kuhn, William T. *Memories of Old Canton.* Canton: privately printed, 1937.

Kunhardt, Philip B. Jr., Philip B. Kunhardt, III, and Peter W. Kunhardt. *Lincoln.* New York: Knopf, 1992.

Lamon, Ward Hill. *Recollections of Abraham Lincoln, 1847–1865.* Lincoln: University of Nebraska Press, reprinted from A. C. McClurg & Co., 1895.

Langhorne, Elizabeth. *Monticello: A Family Story.* Chapel Hill, N.C.: Algonquin Books, 1987.

Lash, Joseph P. *Eleanor and Franklin.* New York: Norton, 1971.

———. *Eleanor Roosevelt: A Friend's Memoir.* Garden City, N.Y.: Doubleday, 1964.

Lasky, Victor. *J.F.K.* New York: Macmillan, 1963.

Lathem, Edward C., ed. *Meet Calvin Coolidge: The Man Behind the Myth.* Brattleboro, Vt.: Stephen Greene, 1960.

Latner, Richard B. *The Presidency of Andrew Jackson: White House Politics, 1829–1837.* Athens: University of Georgia Press, 1979.

Leamer, Laurence, *The Kennedy Men.* New York: Perennial, 2002.

——. *The Kennedy Women: The Saga of an American Family.* New York: Villard, 1994.

——. *Make-Believe: The Story of Nancy and Ronald Reagan.* New York: Harper & Row, 1983.

Lee, Alton R. *Dwight D. Eisenhower: Soldier and Statesman.* New York: Nelson-Hall, 1981.

Leech, Margaret. *In the Days of McKinley.* New York: Harper & Bros., 1959.

——, and Harry Brown. *The Garfield Orbit.* New York: Harper & Row, 1978.

Leman, Kevin. *The New Birth Order Book.* Grand Rapids, Mich.: Fleming H. Revell, 1985.

Leonard, Lewis A. *Life of Alphonso Taft.* New York: Hawke, 1920.

Levin, Phyllis Lee. *Abigail Adams, A Biography.* New York: St. Martin's Griffin, 2001.

Levin, Robert E. *Bill Clinton: The Inside Story.* New York: S.P.I. Books/Shapolski, 1992.

Lewis, David, and Darryl Hicks. *The Presidential Zero-Year Mystery.* Plainfield, N.J.: Haven, 1980.

Lewis, Lloyd. *Captain Sam Grant.* Boston: Little, Brown, 1950.

——. *Letters from Lloyd Lewis Showing Steps in His Research for His Biography of U. S. Grant.* Boston: Little, Brown, 1950.

Lewis, Thomas A. *For King and Country: The Maturing of George Washington, 1748–1760.* New York: HarperCollins, 1993.

Limbaugh, David. *Absolute Power: The Legacy of Corruption in the Clinton-Reno Justice Department.* Washington, D.C.: Regnery, 2001.

Link, Arthur S. *Wilson.* 5 vols. Princeton, N.J.: Princeton University Press, 1947–1965.

——, et al. *The Papers of Woodrow Wilson.* Princeton, N.J.: Princeton University Press, 1966.

Link, Paxson. *The Link Family, 1417–1951.* Privately printed, 1951.

Little, Nina F. *Some Old Brookline Houses.* Brookline, Mass.: Historical Society, 1949.

Lomask, Milton. *Andrew Johnson: President on Trial*. New York: Farrar, Straus, 1960.

Longmore, Paul K. *The Invention of George Washington*. Berkeley: University of California Press, 1988.

Looker, Earle. *The White House Gang*. New York, Chicago, London, and Edinburgh: Fleming H. Revell, 1929.

Lossing, Benson J. *Mary and Martha: The Mother and the Wife of George Washington*. New York: Harper, 1886.

Lynch, Dennis Tilden. *An Epoch and a Man: Martin Van Buren and His Times*. Port Washington, N.Y.: Kennikat Press, 1971 (originally published 1929).

———. *Grover Cleveland: A Man Four-Square*. New York: Horace Liveright, 1932.

Lyon, Peter. *Eisenhower: Portrait of a Hero*. Boston: Little, Brown, 1974.

Lyons, Eugene. *Herbert Hoover: A Biography*. New York: Doubleday, 1964.

Maddox, Bob. *A Preacher in the White House*. Nashville: Baptist Press, 1980.

Maier, Thomas. *The Kennedys: America's Emerald Kings*. New York: Basic Books, 2003.

Malone, Dumas. *Jefferson and His Time*. 6 vols. Boston: Little, Brown, 1948–1981.

Manchester, William. *The Death of a President*. New York: Harper & Row, 1987.

———. *The Glory and the Dream,* vols. 1 and 2. Boston: Little, Brown, 1974.

Maraniss, David. *First in His Class: The Biography of Bill Clinton*. New York: Simon & Schuster, 1995.

Marcus, Eric. *Why Suicide*. New York: HarperCollins, 1996.

Martin, Ralph G., and Ed Plaut. *Front Runner, Dark Horse*. Garden City, N.Y.: Doubleday, 1960.

Martin, William Emmon. *Martin Van Buren*. Washington, D.C.: privately printed, 1835.

Mayo, Bernard, ed. *Thomas Jefferson and His Unknown Brother Randolph*. Charlottesville: University of Virginia, 1942.

Mazlish, Bruce. *In Search of Nixon*. New York: Basic Books, 1972.

———, and Edwin Diamond. *Jimmy Carter: An Interpretive Biography*. New York: Simon & Schuster, 1979.

Mazo, Earl. *Richard Nixon: A Political and Personal Portrait.* New York: Harper & Bros., 1959.

———, and Stephen Hess. *Nixon: A Political Portrait.* New York: Harper & Row, 1968.

McAdoo, Eleanor Wilson. *The Woodrow Wilsons.* New York: Macmillan, 1937.

McCann, Kevin. *Man from Abilene.* New York: Doubleday, 1952.

McCormac, Eugene Irving. *James K. Polk: A Political Biography.* Berkeley: University of California Press, 1922.

McCormick, Eugene I. *James K. Polk.* New York: Russell, 1965.

McCoy, Charles A. *Polk and the Presidency.* Austin, Tex.: Haskell House, 1977.

McCoy, Donald R. *Calvin Coolidge: The Quiet President.* New York: Collier-Macmillan, 1967.

McCoy, Drew R. *The Last of the Fathers: James Madison and the Republican Legacy.* New York: Cambridge University Press, 1984.

McCullough, David. *John Adams.* New York: Simon & Schuster, 2001.

———. *Mornings on Horseback.* New York: Simon & Schuster, 1981.

———. *Papers of James Madison,* vol. 16. Charlottesville: University Press of Virginia, 1989.

———. *Truman.* New York: Simon & Schuster, 1992.

McDonald, Forrest. *The Presidency of Thomas Jefferson.* Lawrence: University Press of Kansas, 1976.

McElroy, Richard L. *James A. Garfield: His Life and Times.* Canton, Ohio: Daring, 1986.

McElroy, Robert. *Grover Cleveland: The Man and the Statesman: An Authorized Biography.* New York: Harper & Bros., 1923.

McElroy, William L. *William McKinley and Our America.* Canton, Ohio: Stark County Historical Society, 1996.

McFeely, William S. *Grant: A Biography.* New York: W. W. Norton, 1974, 1981.

McGrath, Jim, ed. *Heartbeat: George Bush in His Own Words.* New York: Scribner's, 2001.

McKinley, Silas Bent, and Silas Bent. *Old Rough and Ready: The Life and Times of Zachary Taylor.* New York: Vanguard, 1946.

McNeese, Tim. *George W. Bush: First President of the New Century.* Greensboro, N.C.: Morgan Reynolds, 2001.

McPherson, James M. *Abraham Lincoln and the Second American Revolution*. New York: Oxford University Press, 1991.

———. *To the Best of My Ability: The American Presidents*. London: Dorling Kindersley, 2000.

McReynolds, B. S. *Presidential Blips*. University City, Calif.: B. S. Book Publishing, 1998.

Mee, Charles L., Jr. *The Ohio Gang: The World of Warren G. Harding*. New York: M. Evans, 1981.

Meyer, Bertrand. *Les Dames de L'Elysée*. Paris: Librairie Académique Perrin, 1987.

Meyers, Joan, ed. *John Fitzgerald Kennedy . . . As We Remember Him*. New York: Atheneum, 1965.

Miller, Alice. *The Drama of a Gifted Child*. New York: Basic Books, 1997.

Miller, Hope Ridings. *Scandals in the Highest Office*. New York: Random House, 1973.

Miller, Merle. *Lyndon: An Oral Biography*. New York: G. P. Putnam's Sons, 1980.

———. *Plain Speaking: An Oral Biography of Harry S. Truman*. New York: Berkley, 1973.

Miller, Nathan. *FDR: An Intimate History*. New York: Doubleday, 1983.

———. *Theodore Roosevelt: A Life*. New York: William Morrow, 1992.

Miller, Richard Lawrence. *Truman: The Rise to Power*. New York: McGraw-Hill, 1986.

Miller, William, and Frances Spatz Leighton. *Fishbate*. Englewood Cliffs, N.J.: Prentice Hall, 1977.

Mills, Judie. *John F. Kennedy*. New York: Franklin Watts: 1988.

Minutaglio, Bill. *First Son: George W. Bush and the Bush Family Dynasty*. New York: Three Rivers Press, 2001.

Mitchell, Elizabeth. *W: Revenge of the Bush Dynasty*. New York: Hyperion, 2000.

Mitchell, Stewart. *New Letters of Abigail Adams, 1798–1801*. Boston: Houghton Mifflin, 1945.

Montgomery, Ruth. *Hail to the Chiefs*. New York: Coward-McCann, 1970.

———. *Mrs. LBJ*. New York: Holt, Rinehart & Winston, 1964.

Moore, Charles. *The Family Life of George Washington.* Boston: Houghton Mifflin, 1926.

Moore, Jim, and Rick Inde. *Clinton: Young Man in a Hurry.* New York: Simon & Schuster, 1992.

Moore, Virginia. *The Madisons: A Biography.* New York: McGraw-Hill, 1979.

Morgan, Edmund S. *The Meaning of Independence: John Adams, George Washington, Thomas Jefferson.* Charlottesville: University of Virginia Press, 2004.

Morgan, H. Wayne. *McKinley and His America.* Syracuse, N.Y.: Syracuse University Press, 1963.

Morgan, Robert J. *A Whig Embattled: The Presidency Under John Tyler.* Lincoln: University of Nebraska Press, 1954.

Morgan, Ted. *FDR: A Biography.* New York: Simon & Schuster, 1985.

Morrell, Martha McBride. *Young Hickory: The Life and Times of President James K. Polk.* New York: Dutton, 1949.

Morris, Edmund. *Dutch: A Memoir of Ronald Reagan.* New York: Random House, 1999.

———. *Rise of Theodore Roosevelt.* New York: Coward, McCann, 1979.

Morris, Jan. *Lincoln: A Foreigner's Quest.* New York: Simon & Schuster, 2000.

Morris, Kenneth E. *Jimmy Carter: American Moralist.* Athens: University of Georgia Press, 1996.

Morris, Roger. *Partners in Power.* New York: Henry Holt, 1996.

———. *Richard Milhous Nixon.* New York: Henry Holt, 1990.

Morrison, Elting E., ed. *The Letters of Theodore Roosevelt,* vol. 1, *The Years of Preparation, 1868–1900.* Cambridge, Mass.: Harvard University Press, 1951.

Morse, Frances Rollins, ed. *Henry and Mary Lee: Letters and Journals.* Boston: Privately printed, 1926.

Moser, Harold D., ed.-in-chief. *The Papers of Andrew Jackson: 1804–1813,* vol. 2. Knoxville: University of Tennessee Press, 1984.

Mulder, John M. *Woodrow Wilson: The Years of Preparation.* Princeton, N.J.: Princeton University Press, 1987.

Myers, Elizabeth P. *Benjamin Harrison.* Chicago: Reilly and Lee, 1969.

Nagel, Paul C. *The Adams Women: Abigail and Louisa Adams, Their Sisters and Daughters.* New York: Oxford University Press, 1987.

————. *Descent from Glory: Four Generations of the John Adams Family.* New York: Oxford University Press, 1983.

————. *John Quincy Adams: A Public Life, A Private Life.* New York: Alfred A. Knopf, 1998.

Nash, George H. *The Life of Herbert Hoover: The Engineer.* New York: Norton, 1983.

Nathan, Richard P. *The Plot That Failed: Nixon and the Administrative Presidency.* New York: Wiley, 1975.

Neal, Steve. *The Eisenhowers: Reluctant Dynasty.* Garden City, N.Y.: Doubleday, 1978.

Nevins, Allan. *Grover Cleveland: A Study in Courage.* New York: Dodd, Mead, 1948.

————, ed. *Polk: Diary of a President, 1845–1849.* New York: Capricorn, 1968.

Newman, Ralph Geoffrey, ed. *Abraham Lincoln: His Story in His Own Words.* New York: Doubleday, 1975.

Nichols, Edward J. *Zach Taylor's Little Army.* Garden City, N.Y.: Doubleday, 1963.

Nichols, Roy Franklin. *Franklin Pierce: Young Hickory of the Granite Hills.* Newtown, Conn.: American Political Biography Press, 1931.

Niven, John. *Martin Van Buren: The Romantic Age of American Politics.* New York: Oxford University Press, 1959.

Nixon, Richard. *The Challenges We Face.* New York: McGraw-Hill, 1960.

————. *RN: The Memoirs of Richard Nixon.* New York: Grosset and Dunlap, 1978.

Noonan, Peggy. *What I Saw at the Revolution: A Political Life in the Reagan Era.* New York: Random House, 1990.

Nordham, George. *George Washington's Women.* Philadelphia: Dorrance & Co., 1977.

Oates, Stephen B. *With Malice Toward None.* New York: Harper & Row, 1992.

Olcott, Charles S. *The Life of William McKinley.* 2 vols. Boston: Houghton Mifflin, 1916.

Olsen, Paul. *Sons and Mothers.* New York: Fawcett Crest, 1981.

Osborn, George. *Woodrow Wilson: The Early Years.* Baton Rouge: Louisiana State University Press, 1968.

Paletta, Lu Ann, and Fred L. Worth. *The World Almanac of Presidential Facts.* New York: World Almanac, 1988.

Parmet, Herbert S. *George Bush: The Life of a Lone Star Yankee.* New York: Scribner's, 1997.

———. *Jack: The Struggles of John F. Kennedy.* New York: Dial, 1980.

———. *Richard Nixon and His America.* Boston: Little, Brown, 1990.

Parrish, T. Michael. *Richard Taylor: Soldier, Prince of Dixie.* Chapel Hill: University of North Carolina Press, 1992.

Parry, Jay A., and Andrew M. Allison. *The Real George Washington.* Washington, D.C.: National Center for Constitutional Studies, 1991.

Parsons, Lynn H. *John Quincy Adams.* Madison, Wis.: Madison House Publishers, 1998.

Parton, James. *Andrew Jackson.* New York: Johnson Reprint Organization, 1860.

Peabody, James B., ed. *John Adams: A Biography in His Own Words.* New York: Newsweek Books, 1976.

Pemberton, William E. *Exit with Honor: The Life and Presidency of Ronald Reagan.* Armonk, N.Y.: M. E. Sharpe, 1997.

Perkins, Frances. *The Roosevelt I Knew.* New York: Viking, 1946.

Perling, J. J. *Presidents' Sons.* New York: Odyssey Press, 1947.

Perling, John E. *John Adams: A Life.* Knoxville: University of Tennessee Press, 1992.

Perret, Geoffrey. *Ulysses S. Grant: Soldier and President.* New York: Random House, 1997.

Peskin, Allan. *Garfield.* Kent, Ohio: Kent State University Press, 1978.

Peterson, Merrill D., ed. *James Madison: A Biography in His Own Words.* New York: Newsweek Books, 1974.

———. *Lincoln in American Memory.* New York: Oxford University Press, 1994.

———. *Thomas Jefferson and The New Nation: A Biography.* New York: Oxford University Press, 1970.

Peterson, Norman L. *The Presidencies of William Henry Harrison and John Tyler.* Lawrence: University Press of Kansas, 1989.

Pittman, Mrs. H. D., ed. *Americans of Gentle Birth.* Baltimore: Genealogical Publishing, 1970.

Poen, Monte M. *Strictly Personal and Confidential: The Letters Harry Truman Never Mailed.* Boston: Little, Brown, 1982.

Polk, William Harrison. *The Polk Family and Kinsmen.* Louisville, Ky.: privately printed, 1912.

Pottker, Jan. *Sara and Eleanor: The Story of Sara Delano Roosevelt and Her Daughter-in-Law, Eleanor Roosevelt.* New York: St. Martin's Press, 2004.

Pringle, Henry F. *The Life and Times of William Howard Taft,* vols. 1 and 2. Hamden, Conn.: Archon Books, 1939.

———. *Theodore Roosevelt: A Biography.* New York: Harcourt Brace Jovanovich, 1956.

Pryor, Sara Agnes. *The Mother of Washington and Her Times.* New York: Macmillan, 1902.

Pusey, Merlo. *Eisenhower the President.* New York: Macmillan, 1956.

Putnam, Carleton. *Theodore Roosevelt: The Formative Years, 1858–1886.* New York: Scribner's, 1958.

Quaife, Milo M., ed. *The Diary of James K. Polk During His Presidency, 1845–1849.* 4 vols. Chicago: McClurg, 1910.

Quinn, Sandra L., and Sanford Kanter. *America's Royalty: All the Presidents' Children.* Westport, Conn., and London, England: Greenwood, 1983, 1995.

Radcliffe, Donnie. *Simply Barbara Bush.* New York: Warner, 1989.

Randall, J. G. *Mr. Lincoln.* New York: Dodd, Mead, 1957.

Randolph, Sarah N. *The Domestic Life of Thomas Jefferson,* 1871; reprinted New York: Ungar, 1958.

Randolph, Wassell. *William Randolph I of Turkey Island, Henrico Co., VA, . . . and His Immediate Descendants.* Memphis, Tenn.: Seebode Mimeo, distributed by Dossitt Library, 1949.

Rayback, Robert J. *Millard Fillmore: Biography of a President.* Buffalo, N.Y.: Stewart, 1959.

Reagan, Ronald. *An American Life.* New York: Simon & Schuster, 1990.

———. *Reagan: In His Own Hand.* New York: Free Press, 2001.

———. *Speaking My Mind.* New York: Simon & Schuster, 1989.

———, with Richard G. Hubler. *Where's the Rest of Me? The Autobiography of Ronald Reagan.* New York: Karz, 1965, 1981.

Reeves, Richard. *A Ford, Not a Lincoln.* New York: Harcourt Brace Jovanovich, 1975.

———. *President Kennedy: Profile of Power.* New York: Simon & Schuster, 1993.

———. *Running in Place: How Bill Clinton Disappointed America.* Kansas City: Andrews McMeel, 1996.

Reeves, Thomas C. *Gentleman Boss: The Life of Chester Alan Arthur.* New York: Alfred A. Knopf, 1975.

———. *A Question of Character: A Life of John F. Kennedy.* New York: Free Press, 1991.

Remini, Robert V. *Andrew Jackson and the Course of American Empire, 1767–1821.* New York: Harper & Row, 1977.

———. *The Life of Andrew Jackson.* New York: Harper & Row, 1988.

———. *Martin Van Buren and the Making of the Democratic Party.* New York: Columbia University Press, 1959.

Renehan, Edward J., Jr. *The Lion's Pride: Theodore Roosevelt and His Family in War and Peace.* New York: Oxford University Press, 1998.

Rice, Arnold S., ed. *Herbert Hoover: 1874–1964.* Dobbs Ferry, N.Y.: Oceana Publications, 1971.

Richardson, Albert Deane. *A Personal History of U.S. Grant.* Hartford, Conn., 1868.

Richardson, James D. *A Compilation of the Messages and Papers of the Presidents: 1789–1879,* vol. 4. Washington D.C., 1897.

Rixey, Lilian. *Bamie: Theodore Roosevelt's Remarkable Sister.* New York: McKay, 1963.

Robinson, Corinne Roosevelt. *My Brother, Theodore Roosevelt.* New York: Scribner's, 1921.

Robinson, Edgar Eugene. *The Roosevelt Leadership, 1933–1945.* New York: J. B. Lippincott, 1955.

Rodehamel, John. *The Great Experiment; George Washington and the American Republic.* New Haven: Yale University, and San Marino, Calif.: Huntington Library, 1998.

Roosevelt, Eleanor. *This Is My Story.* New York: Garden City Publishing, 1937.

Roosevelt, Elliott, ed. *F.D.R.: His Personal Letters.* New York: Duell, Sloan & Pearce, 1947.

———. *Rendezvous with Destiny: The Roosevelts of the White House.* New York: Putnam, 1975.

———, and James Brough. *An Untold Story: The Roosevelts of Hyde Park.* New York: G. P. Putnam's Sons, 1973.

Roosevelt, Nicholas. *Theodore Roosevelt: The Man as I Knew Him.* New York: Dodd, Mead, 1967.

Roosevelt, Sara, Isabel Leighton, and Gabrielle Forbush. *My Boy Franklin*. New York: Ray Long and Richard R. Smith, 1933.

Roosevelt, Theodore. *Theodore Roosevelt: An Autobiography*. New York: Macmillan, 1914.

Roosevelt, Mrs. Theodore, Jr. *Day Before Yesterday: The Reminiscences of Mrs. Theodore Roosevelt, Jr.* Garden City, N.Y.: Doubleday, 1959.

Rosebloom, Eugene H. *A History of Presidential Elections*. New York: Macmillan, 1964.

Ross, Ishbel. *An American Family: The Tafts—1678 to 1964*. Cleveland and New York: World Publishing Company, 1964.

———. *The Life of Mrs. Ulysses S. Grant*. New York: Dodd, Mead, 1959.

———. *Sons of Adam, Daughters of Eve: The Role of Women in American History*. New York: Harper & Row, 1969.

Ross, Shelley. *Fall from Grace,* New York: Ballantine, 1988.

Russell, Francis. *The Shadow of Blooming Grove: Warren G. Harding in His Times*. New York and Toronto: McGraw-Hill, 1968.

Rutland, Robert A. *James Madison: The Founding Father*. New York: Macmillan, 1987.

Rutland, Robert Allen. *The Presidency of James Madison*. Lawrence: University Press of Kansas, 1990.

Ryan, Patrick. *George W. Bush*. United States Presidents. Edina, Minn.: Abdo, 2001.

Salinger, Pierre. *With Kennedy*. New York: Doubleday, 1966.

Sandburg, Carl. *Abraham Lincoln: The Prairie Years and the War Years*. 6 vols. New York: Harcourt, Brace, & World, 1926–1939.

Schachner, Nathan. *Thomas Jefferson: A Biography*. New York: Appleton-Century-Crofts, 1961.

Schlesinger, Arthur M., Jr. *The Age of Jackson*. Boston: Little, Brown, 1946.

———. *A Thousand Days: John F. Kennedy in the White House*. Boston: Houghton Mifflin, 1965.

———, ed. *History of American Presidential Elections, 1789–2000*. n.y.p.

Schriftgiesser, Karl. *The Amazing Roosevelt Family, 1613–1942*. New York: Funk, 1942.

Schwartz, Ted. *Joseph P. Kennedy*. Hoboken, N.J.: John Wiley and Sons, 2003.

Schweizer, Peter, and Rochelle Schweizer. *The Bushes: Portrait of a Dynasty.* New York: Doubleday, 2004.

Seager, Robert, II. *And Tyler Too: A Biography of John and Julia Gardiner Tyler.* New York: McGraw-Hill, 1963.

Seale, William. *The President's House.* Washington, D.C.: White House Historical Association/National Geographic/Harry Abrams, 1986.

Seigel, Beatrice. *George and Martha Washington at Home in New York.* New York: Four Winds Press, 1989.

Seigenthaler, John. *James K. Polk, 1845–1849.* New York: Times Books, 2003.

Sellers, Charles Grier, Jr. *James K. Polk, Jacksonian.* Princeton, N.J.: Princeton University Press, 1957.

Severance, Frank H., ed. *Millard Fillmore Papers,* vol. 1. New York: Krans, 1970.

Shaw, Peter. *The Character of John Adams.* Chapel Hill: University of North Carolina Press, 1976.

Shepherd, Jack. *The Adams Chronicles.* Boston: Little, Brown, 1975.

———. *Cannibals of the Heart: A Personal Biography of Louisa Catherine and John Quincy Adams.* New York: McGraw-Hill, 1980.

Sherwood, Robert. *Roosevelt and Hopkins.* New York: Harper & Row, 1948.

Shipton, Clifford, ed. *Sibley's Harvard Graduates.* Boston: Belknap Press, 1996.

Sidey, Hugh. *John F. Kennedy, President.* New York: Atheneum, 1963.

———, and Fred Ward. *Portrait of a President.* New York: Harper & Row, 1975.

Sievers, Harry J. *Benjamin Harrison,* vols. 1 and 2, New York: University Publishers, 1952, 1959. Vol. 3, Indianapolis: Bobbs-Merrill, 1968.

Silver, Thomas. *Coolidge and the Historians.* Durham, N.C.: Carolina Academic Press, 1982.

Silverstein, Olga, and Beth Rashbaum. *The Courage to Raise Good Men.* New York: Viking, 1994.

Simon, John Y., ed. *The Papers of Ulysses S. Grant,* vol. 1, *1837–1861.* Carbondale: Southern Illinois University Press, 1967.

Simpson, Brooks D. *Ulysses S. Grant: Triumph over Adversity, 1822–1865.* Boston and New York: Houghton Mifflin, 2000.

Sinclair, Andres. *The Available Man: Warren Gamaliel Harding.* New York: Macmillan, 1965.

Smith, Amanda, ed. *Hostage to Fortune: The Letters of Joseph P. Kennedy.* New York: Viking, 2001.

Smith, Elbert B. *The Presidencies of Zachary Taylor and Millard Fillmore.* Lawrence: University Press of Kansas, 1988.

Smith, Gene. *High Crimes and Misdemeanors: The Impeachment and Trial of Andrew Johnson.* New York: Morrow, 1977.

———. *The Shattered Dream: Herbert Hoover and the Great Depression.* New York: William Morrow, 1970.

———. *When the Cheering Stopped: The Last Years of Woodrow Wilson.* New York: William Morrow, 1964.

Smith, Jean Edward. *Grant.* New York: Simon & Schuster, 2001.

Smith, Margaret Bayard. *The First Forty Years of Washington Society.* New York: Scribner's, 1906.

Smith, Merriman. *A White House Memoir.* New York: Norton, 1972.

Smith, Page. *John Adams.* 2 vols. New York: Doubleday, 1962.

———. *Thomas Jefferson: A Revealing Biography.* New York: McGraw-Hill, 1976.

Smith, Richard Norton. *An Uncommon Man: The Triumph of Herbert Hoover.* New York: Simon & Schuster, 1984.

Smith, Theodore Clark. *James Abram Garfield, Life & Letters,* vol. 1. New Haven, Conn.: Yale University Press, 1925.

Snyder, Charles M. *The Lady and the President: The Letters of Dorothea Dix and Millard Fillmore.* New York: University Press of America, 1981.

Snyder, Gail. *George Washington.* Philadelphia: Mason Crest, 2003.

Sobel, Robert. *An American Enigma.* Washington, D.C.: Regnery, 1998.

Sorensen, Theodore C. *Kennedy.* New York: Harper & Row, 1965.

———. *The Kennedy Legacy.* New York: Macmillan, 1969.

Spielman, William Carl. *William McKinley: Republican Stalwart.* New York: Exposition Press, 1954.

Stagg, John C. A., ed., *Papers of James Madison,* vol. 16. Charlottesville: University Press of Virginia, 1989.

Steeholm, Clara and Hardy. *The Home at Hyde Park, Together with Sara Delano Roosevelt's Household Book.* New York: Viking, 1950.

Stefoff, Rebecca. *William Henry Harrison.* Ada, Okla.: Garrett Educational, 1990.

Steinberg, Alfred. *The First Ten: The Founding Presidents and Their Administrations.* Garden City, N.Y.: Doubleday, 1967.

———. *The Man from Missouri: Life and Times of Harry S. Truman.* New York: G. B. Putnam's Sons, 1962.

———. *Sam Johnson's Boy: A Close-up of the President from Texas.* New York: Macmillan, 1968.

Stern, Philip Van Doren. *The Life and Writings of Abraham Lincoln.* New York: Random House, 1940.

Stewart, James B. *Blood Sport: The President and His Adversaries.* New York: Simon & Schuster. 1996.

Stinnett, Robert B. *George Bush: His World War II Years.* Washington, D.C.: Brassey's, 1992.

Stratton, Joanna L. *Pioneer Women: Voices from the Kansas Frontier.* New York: Simon & Schuster, 1981.

Strode, Hudson, ed. *Jefferson Davis: Private Letters, 1823–1889.* New York: Harcourt, Brace & World, 1966.

Stroud, Kandy. *How Jimmy Won. The Victory Campaign from Plains to the White House.* New York: Morrow, 1977.

Strozier, Charles. *Lincoln's Quest for Union.* Philadelphia, Pa.: Paul Dry Books, revised edition, 2001.

Stryker, Lloyd Paul. *Andrew Johnson: A Study in Courage.* New York: Macmillan, 1929.

Styron, Arthur. *The Last of the Cocked Hats: James Monroe and the Virginia Dynasty.* Norman: University of Oklahoma Press, 1945.

Sumner, William Graham. *Andrew Jackson.* Boston: Houghton Mifflin, 1883.

Swanson, Gloria. *Swanson on Swanson.* New York: Random House, 1980.

Taft, Horace Dutton. *Memories and Opinions.* New York: Macmillan, 1942.

Tanner, Robert. *Stonewall in the Valley.* New York: Doubleday, 1976.

Tarbell, Ida M. *The Early Life of Abraham Lincoln.* New York: A. S. Barnes, 1974.

Tartan, Beth, and Elizabeth Hedgecock Sparks. *Miss Lillian and Her Friends.* Modern American Library, 1977.

Taylor, James M. *Garfield of Ohio: The Available Man.* New York: W. W. Norton, 1970.

Taylor, Robert J., et al., eds. *Papers of John Adams.* Cambridge, Mass.: 1977.

Taylor, Tim. *The Book of Presidents.* New York: Arno Press, 1972.

terHorst, Jerald F. *Gerald Ford and the Future of the Presidency.* New York: Third Press, 1974.

Thomas, Benjamin P. *Abraham Lincoln: A Biography.* New York: Alfred A. Knopf, 1952.

————. *Portrait for Posterity.* New Brunswick, N.J.: Rutgers University Press, 1947.

Thomas, Lately. *The First President Johnson.* New York: William Morrow, 1968.

Thompson, Josiah. *Six Seconds in Dallas.* New York: Bernard Geis, 1967.

Thompson, Robert, ed. *A Collation and Co-ordination of the Mental Processes and Reactions of Calvin Coolidge, as Expressed in His Address and Messages, and Constituting a Self-Delineation of His Character and Ideals.* Chicago: Donahue, 1924.

Trefousse, Hans L. *Andrew Johnson: A Biography.* New York: W. W. Norton & Company, 1989.

Tribble, Edwin, ed. *A President in Love: The Courtship Letters of Woodrow Wilson and Edith Bolling Galt.* Boston: Houghton Mifflin, 1981.

Truman, Harry S. *Memoirs: Years of Trial and Hope.* New York: Doubleday, 1956.

Truman, Margaret. *Harry S Truman.* New York: Morrow, 1973.

Tugwell, Rexford G. *Grover Cleveland.* New York: Macmillan, 1968.

Tyler, Lyon G. *The Letters and Times of the Tylers.* Reading, Mass.: Perseus, 1970.

Tyrell, R. Emmett. *The Impeachment of William Jefferson Clinton.* Washington, D.C.: Regnery, 1997.

Unger, Irwin, and Debi Unger. *LBJ: A Life.* New York: Wiley, 1999.

Vestal, Bud. *Jerry Ford, Up Close: An Investigative Biography.* New York: Coward, McCann & Geogheagan, 1974.

Vidal, Gore. *Great American Families.* New York: Norton, 1977.

Walker, Jane C. *John Tyler, A President of Many Firsts.* Blacksburg, Va.: McDonald and Woodward, 2001.

Walker, Martin. *The President We Deserve.* New York: Crown, 1996.

Walworth, Arthur. *Wilson and His Peacemakers: American Diplomacy at the Paris Peace Conference.* New York: Norton, 1986.

Ward, Geoffrey C. *Before the Trumpet: Young Franklin Roosevelt, 1882–1905*. New York: Harper & Row, 1981.

——. *First Class Temperament: The Emergence of Franklin Roosevelt*. New York: Harper & Row, 1989.

Warren, Louis A. *Lincoln for the Ages*. New York: Doubleday, 1960.

——. *Lincoln's Parentage and Childhood*. New York: Century, 1926.

——. *Lincoln's Youth: Indiana Years, 1816–1830*. New York: Appleton-Century-Crofts, 1959.

Warren, Mercy Otis. *History of the Rise, Progress, and Termination of the American Revolution Interspersed with Biographical, Political, and Moral Observations,* vol. 2. Ed. Lester H. Cohen. Indianapolis: Liberty Foundation, 1989.

Washburn, Mabel Thacher. *Ancestry of William Howard Taft*. New York: Frank Allaben Genealogical Company, 1908.

Washburn, Robert. *Calvin Coolidge, His First Biography*. New York: Small Maynard, 1923.

Wead, Doug. *All the Presidents' Children*. New York: Atria, 2003.

——. *George Bush: Man of Integrity*. Eugene, Ore.: Harvest House, 1988.

——, and Bill Wead. *Reagan: In Pursuit of the Presidency*. Plainfield, N.J.: Haven Books, 1980.

Weatherford, Doris. *A History of the American Suffragist Movement*. Santa Barbara, Calif.; Denver, Colo.; and Oxford, England: Moschovitis Group, 1998.

Weisberger, Bernard A. *America Afire: Jefferson, Adams and the Revolutionary Election of 1800*. New York: HarperCollins, 2000.

Welch, Richard E., Jr. *The Presidencies of Grover Cleveland*. Lawrence: University Press of Kansas, 1988.

Whalen, Richard J. *The Founding Father: The Story of Joseph P. Kennedy*. Washington, D.C.: Regnery Gateway, 1993.

Whalen, Thomas J. *Kennedy and Lodge: The 1952 Massachusetts Senate Race*. Boston: Northeastern University Press, 2001.

White, Theodore. *Breach of Faith: The Fall of Richard Nixon*. New York: Atheneum, 1975.

White, Theodore H. *The Making of the President, 1960*. New York: Atheneum, 1961.

White, William Allen. *A Puritan in Babylon: The Story of Calvin Coolidge*. New York: Macmillan, 1938.

Whitney, David C. *American Presidents*. New York: Doubleday, 1978.

Wicker, Tom. *Kennedy Without Tears.* New York: William Morrow, 1964.

Wilcox, Mary Ann. *Woman Forgotten in Time.* Baltimore, Md.: Publish America, 2003.

Willard, Samuel. *John Adams: A Character Sketch.* Danville, N.Y.: Instructor Publishing Co., The University Association, 1898.

Williams, Charles Richard. *The Life of Rutherford Birchard Hayes: Nineteenth President of the United States.* 2 vols. Columbus: Ohio State Archaeological and Historical Society, 1928.

Williams, T. Harry, ed. *Hayes: Diary of a President, 1873–1881.* New York: McKay, 1964.

Wills, Garry. *Nixon Agonistes.* Boston: Houghton Mifflin, 1970.

———. *Reagan's America: Innocents at Home.* New York: Doubleday, 1987.

Wilson, Daniel Munro. *Three Hundred Years of Quincy, 1625–1925.* Quincy, Mass.: City of Quincy, 1926.

Wilson, James Grant. *Presidents of the United States, 1789–1914.* New York: Scribner's, 1914.

Wilson, Joan Hoff. *Herbert Hoover: Forgotten Progressive.* Boston: Waveland Press, 1975, reprint 1992.

Winkler, H. Donald. *The Women in Lincoln's Life.* Nashville, Tenn.: Rutledge Press, 2001.

Winston, Robert W. *Andrew Johnson: Plebian and Patriot.* New York: Henry Holt, 1928.

Wise, David. *The Politics of Lying, Government Deception, Secrecy, and Power.* New York: Random House, 1973.

Wister, Owen. *Roosevelt: The Story of a Friendship, 1880–1919.* New York: Macmillan, 1930.

Witcover, Jules. *Marathon: The Pursuit of the Presidency, 1972–1976.* New York: Viking, 1977.

Withey, Lynne. *Dearest Friend: A Life of Abigail Adams.* New York: Touchstone, 1981.

Wofford, Harris. *Of Kennedys and Kings.* New York: Farrar, Straus, and Giroux, 1980.

Woodward, Bob. *The Agenda: Inside the Clinton White House.* New York: Simon & Schuster, 1994.

Woodward, W. E. *Meet General Grant.* New York: Liveright, 1928.

Wooten, James. *Dasher: The Roots and Rising of Jimmy Carter.* New York: Summit, 1979.

Wright, Mike. *What They Didn't Teach You About the American Revolution*. Novato, Calif.: Presidio, 1999.

Young, Jeff C. *The Fathers of American Presidents: From Augustine Washington to William Blythe and Roger Clinton*. Jefferson, N.C.: McFarland, 1997.

Zilg, Gerald Colby. *DuPont: Behind the Nylon Curtain*. New York: Prentice-Hall, 1974.

ARTICLES

Associated Press. Newswire, May 16, 2001.

Barak, Barry. "Team Player Bush: A Yearning to Serve." *Los Angeles Times,* November 22, 1987.

Barnes, Lorraine. "Lyndon's Mother." *Austin American,* November 19, 1955.

Bedard, Paul. "George 'McKinley' Trades up to a 'Theodore' Bush." *U.S. News & World Report,* January 14, 2002.

Benedetto, Richard. "Bush Relays Message from the Heart." *USA Today,* June 21, 2002. *Newsweek.* "Bush Down Home." June 18, 2001.

Beschloss, Michael. "The Curse of the Famous Scion." *Newsweek,* August 14, 1995.

Birnbaum, Jeffrey H. "The Making of a President 2001." *Fortune,* November 12, 2001.

Blumenfeld, Amy, and Richard Jerome. "When Dad Is President." *People,* June 18, 2001.

Bly, Nellie. *The New York World,* October 28, 1888.

Borger, Gloria. "Practicing the Art of Secrecy." *U.S. News & World Report,* March 18, 2001.

————. "Same Old, Same Old." *U.S. News & World Report,* January 21, 2002.

Boston Evening Transcript. September 21, 1933.

Carlson, Margaret. "A Pillow Away from the President." *Time,* December 31, 2001–January 7, 2002.

Carney, James, and John F. Dickerson. "A Work in Progress." *Time,* October 22, 2001.

Carpenter, Elizabeth. "Rebekah Baines Johnson." *Houston Post,* June 20, 1954.

Carroll County Independent (Center Ossippee, N.Y.), November 9, 1995.

Chicago Inter Ocean, May 20–21, 1875.

Cincinnati Daily Gazette, November 2, 1830.

Collier's Weekly, August 20, 1938.

Dagostino, Mark. "Insider." *People,* July 22, 2002.

Dickerson, John F. "Meet the President as the Cutup in Chief." *Time,* February 18, 2002.

Dionne, E. J., Jr. "Conservatism Recast: Why This President's Reach Could Be Monumental." *The Washington Post,* January 27, 2002.

Donaldson, Sam. "Home front" book reviews. *Washington Monthly,* April 1986.

Duffy, Michael, and Nancy Gibbs. "The Bush Dynasty." *Time,* August 7, 2000.

Elie, L. Eric. "Chip Carter Working on the Fringe of Politics." *The Atlanta Journal-Constitution,* May 16, 1988.

Ellis, Sam. "When George W. Bush Was the Stickball King." *Boston Globe,* June 20, 1999.

Fitzgerald, Mark. "NNA Convention Celebrates First Amendment Rights." National Newspapers Association, October 12, 1991.

Fournier, Ron. "Crises Transform Bush Presidency." Associated Press, as reported in *The Orlando Sentinel,* January 20, 2002.

Friendship Force. Press Release. Atlanta, Georgia, May 1, 2000.

Goodpasture, Albert V. "The Boyhood of President Polk." *Tennessee Historical Magazine,* April 1921.

Higgins, Marguerite. "Rose Fitzgerald Kennedy." *McCall's,* May 1961.

Houston Post, December 15, 1980.

Illinois State Journal, June 30, 1936.

Illinois State Register, June 28, 1926.

Kaiser, Robert G., and David B. Ottaway. "Saudi Leader's Anger Revealed Shaky Ties." *The Washington Post,* February 10, 2002.

Kleiner, Carolyn. "Breaking the Cycle." *U.S. News & World Report,* April 29, 2002.

Kluger, Jeffrey. "The Power of Love." *Time,* January 19, 2004.

Korda, Michael. "Reagan." *The New Yorker,* October 6, 1997.

Kulman, Linda. "Who Owns History?" *U.S. News & World Report,* April 29, 2002.

"The Nine Kennedy Kids Delight Great Britain." *Life,* April 11, 1938.

"Behind the Main Event." *Life,* June 18, 1971.

"Rose Kennedy at 100." *Life,* March 1990.

"The New Kennedy Generation." *Life,* July 1997.

Life, October 30, 1992.

Loftus, Mary. "The Other Side of Fame." *Psychology Today,* May–June 1995.

Los Angeles Times, August 13, 1938.

Martin, Harold. "The Amazing Kennedys." *The Saturday Evening Post,* September 7, 1957.

McCullough, David. "Mama's Boys." *Psychology Today,* October 1983.

McKee, Rose. "Senator Johnson's Mother." *Austin American,* September 13, 1958.

"Nixon Spoke of Break-in at Embassy, Newly Released Tapes Reveal." *Miami Herald,* February 26, 1999.

New York Herald, December 11, 1841.

New York Herald, May 22, 1874.

New York Herald Tribune, July 26, 1926.

New York Herald Tribune, January 19, 1945.

"A Notable Social Event: The Wedding of Miss Astor and Mr. Roosevelt." *The New York Times,* November 19, 1878.

The New York Times, September 13, 1933.

The New York Times, July 13, 1935.

The New York Times, January 19, 1889.

The New York Times, April 30, 1933.

The New York Times, March 25, 1935; April 4, 1935; November 20, 1935; December 23, 1935.

The New York Times, December 7, 1967.

New York World. May 26, 1884.

Newsweek, July 10 and July 24, 1944.

Obituary. *The New York Times,* March 14, 1901.

Obituary of Andrew Johnson. *The New York Times,* August 1, 1875.

"The President Requests . . ." *People,* July 25, 1994.

"What a Difference a Year Makes." *People,* January 21, 2002.

Reeves, Richard. "The Danger in the Limelight." *U.S. News & World Report,* July 26, 1999.

Roberts, Paul. "The Psychology of Parenting." *Psychology Today,* May–June 1996.

"Rose Kennedy: The Legend and the Legacy." *Ladies' Home Journal Special,* March 1994.

Sanger, David. "Bush Relishes Reactions to His Rallying Cry." *The New York Times,* as reported in *International Herald Tribune,* February 18, 2002.

The Saturday Evening Post, July 2, 1938.

The Saturday Evening Post, August 26, 1948. *The Presidents* Indianapolis: Curtis Publishing, 1989.

"Lyndon Johnson's Mother." *The Saturday Evening Post,* May 8, 1965.

"What I Have Learned." *The Saturday Review,* September 10, 1966.

Scott, Walter. "Personality Parade." *Parade,* April 22, 2001.

Smiley, Jane, Andrew J. Cherlin, and Peggy Orenstein. "Mothers Can't Win." *The New York Times Magazine,* April 5, 1998.

Smith, Evan. "George Washington: What His First Stint There Taught Him About Loyalty." *Texas Monthly,* June 1999.

Taylor, Stuart. "Before the Bar of History." *Newsweek,* December 10, 2001.

"Good-bye to Robin." *Texas Monthly,* February 1988.

Thompson, Bill. "Belated Recognition of Gerald Ford's Courage." Knight-Ridder/Tribune News Service, May 25, 2001.

Time, August 29, 1938.

Time, July 4, 1938.

Time, December 31, 2001–January 7, 2002.

Notebook. *Time,* January 2002.

"Scholars: U.S. Gave Tips on Holocaust Low Priority in '42." *USA Today,* May 14, 2004.

"His Mother's Story of LBJ." *U.S. News & World Report,* February 15, 1965.

"The Secret Skill of Leaders." *U.S. News & World Report,* January 14, 2002.

U.S. News & World Report, February 25–March 4, 2002.

Washington Evening Star, September 25, 1868.

"10 Days in September, Epilogue, There Is No Doubt In My Mind, Not One Doubt." *The Washington Post,* February 3, 2002.

"10 Days in September, Epilogue, With World's Eyes on Him, Bush Stresses Results." *The Washington Post,* February 3, 2002.

The Washington Post, February 21, 1980.

The Washington Post, February, 10, 2002.

Washington Star, April 28, 1981.

Washington Sunday Herald. The New York Times, April 12, 1912.

Welch, William M. "Bush: Stimulus Plan Mostly Tax Cuts." *USA Today,* October 5, 2001.

Willing, Richard. "Research Downplays Risk of Cousin Marriages." *USA Today,* April 4, 2002.

Zakaria, Fareed. "Spend It Now, Mr. President." *Newsweek,* May 20, 2002.

Zuckerman, Mortimer B. "A Man on a Mission." *U.S. News & World Report,* March 18, 2002.

INTERNET SOURCES

Adams, John—Diaries online.

American Civil War Overview, Chapter XII, The Trans-Mississippi: The Red River Campaign, www.civilwarhome.com/redriver; www.toledo_bend.com/srala/area/mansfield

www.americanhistory.si.edu/presidency/3a4.html

americanpresident.org/KoTrain/Courses/WHH/WHH_Family_Life.htm

Biographical Directory of the U.S. Congress

bioguide.congress.gov/scripts/biodisplay.pl?index=M000293

Carter, Jimmy. A website quoting an informal book written by Jimmy Carter for a family reunion.

www.uftree.com/UFT/WebPages/jholcomb/JECalif.RTER/d0/i0000818.htm

Contemporary Authors Online. The Gale Group, 2001. Reproduced in Biography Resource Center. Farmington Hills, Mich.: The Gale Group, 2001.

Cooper, John S. "Charles Francis Adams: Unsung Hero," Suite101.com. www.suite101.com/article.cfm/presidents_and_first_ladies/40724. June 2, 2000.

Cooper, John S. White House Heroes, Part II. www.suite101.com/article.cfm/presidents and first ladies

Dorfman, Marjorie. Biography of Stanford White. www.pagewise.com and http://dede/essortment.com/stanfordwhiteb_rbyy.htm.

Fiore, Faye and Geraldine Baum. www.latimes.com/news/la-042302 sisters.story

French and Indian War: http://www.philaprintshop.com/frchintx
.html

Hoover.nara.gov website

Learning Network Website http://www.infoplease.com/spot/ken
nedybio.html

Nichols, John. "Republican Feminist": Recalling a Better Reagan,"
Common Dreams News Center, http://www.commondreams.org/
views01/0809-03.htm

Official White House Website on Presidents

Rayner, B.L. Life of Thomas Jefferson, Online: edited by Eyler Robert
Coates, Sr., 1997. Eyler Robert Coates, Sr.

Taft, Charlie. Quoted in the Taft Memorial Program of Christ Church
Cincinnati, at christchurchcincinnati.org/newweb1/programs_or
ganizations/taft_memorial_program.htm

Taft.edu website

Texas Handbook, www.angelfire.com/va3/valleywar/people/taylor

www.taylor-barry-roots.com/civilwar/RichardTaylor

Whitehouse.gov website

Women's International League for Peace and Freedom; www.wilpf
.org/history

www.bethlehempaonline.com/schwab_bio.html–The Master Hustler

www.brainyquote.com/quotes/authors/r/rose_kennedy.html–

www.cyfc.unm.edu/Documents/H/N/HN1053.html

www.home.hiwaay.net/~oliver/gsquotes.htm

www.multied.com/Bio/people/Harriman.html

www.spartacus.schoolnet.co.uk/USAsuffrage.htm

www.suite101.com/article.cfm/4996/91157

www.whitehouse.gov/history/firstladies/im25.html

www.worldwar1.com/dbc/roosev.ht

PUBLIC TELEVISION

Burns, Ken. *Thomas Jefferson*. The American Lives Film Project, 1996,
PBS. Distributed by Warner Home Video, Burbank, Calif.

Byker, Carl, and David Mrazek. *Woodrow Wilson, A Passionate Man*.
WGBH Educational Foundation and Community Television of
Southern California, 2002.

CBS television interview, transcription. JFK Library.

Grubin, David, and Geoffrey C. Ward. *Theodore Roosevelt,* PBS Video. WGBH Education Foundation, Boston, 1996.

Kunhardt, Philip B., Jr., Philip B. Kunhardt, III, Peter W. Kunhardt. *The American President,* PBS film, 2000. Burbank, Calif.: Warner.

———. *Echoes From the White House.* New York and Washington: A Four Score Production, with WNET and WETA, distributed by PBS, 2001.

Lubarsky, Aaron, and Alexandra Pelosi. *Journeys with George.* New York: Warner Home Video, February, 2004.

The History Channel: Carol Berkin, Professor of History, CUNY; Founding Fathers, vol. 1, Rebels with a Cause: John Adams.

Ward, Geoffrey C. *Thomas Jefferson, A Film by Ken Burns.* Burbank, Calif.: PBS and AOL Time Warner, 1996.

Acknowledgments

⸺ ★ ⸺

My heartfelt thanks to Jillian Manus, my literary agent, who makes everything happen for me and who is one of the most talented persons I have met. And to the extraordinary editorial supervisor on this project, Emily Bestler, vice president of Atria Books, who has twice helped craft a work of history into something far more compelling. Sarah Branham again brought much needed editorial strength to the work and gave this book its title.

For more than twenty-five years, Mary Achor has helped me research and write books. I can hardly imagine doing a project without her. She wrote the first draft of the Adams chapters and helped turn a ten-year research project into three fascinating years of writing. And once again, Mindy Herbert served as the director of this project, assembling the pieces from tape recorded interviews, information from dozens of museums, presidential libraries, associations and presidential homes. Sue Motter Johnson and my daughter-in-law, Amy Wead combined to research and write drafts on the chronology. Both were indispensable.

There are a number of family and mental health counselors, doctors and psychologists who offered opinions from their wealth of experience, among them Dr. John Cardwell, psychologist, New York City; president and CEO of EVAXX, Inc., and Kerry Little, MS, licensed mental health counselor and adjunct professor at City College, in Fort Lauderdale, Florida. Practicing psychologist Dr. Chet

Sunde and Dale Pollard, Ed.D., Educational Psychology from Oklahoma State University, were especially helpful in plumbing the depths of the Lincoln parents. Steven Carson, chairman of the White House conference on presidential children and an authority on the histories of the great dynastic families, the Roosevelts and Kennedys, was an excellent resource and sounding board. Dr. Thomas Schwartz, Illinois State Historian and Lincoln authority, was especially helpful.

Always, I am indebted to many helpful employees at the Library of Congress. A special thanks to Claudia Anderson, LBJ Presidential Library and Museum; Diane Barrie, Ronald Reagan Library and Museum; Robert Bohanan, Jimmy Carter Library; Selma Brittingham, Ulysses S. Grant Boyhood Home; Jennifer Capps, President Benjamin Harrison Home; Mike Capps, Lincoln Boyhood National Memorial; Debbie Carter, George Bush Presidential Library and Museum; Joshua Cochran, Gerald R. Ford Library; Linda Dixon, Clinton Presidential Library; Betty Elliot, Lincoln Log Cabin Site; Patrick Finan, William McKinley Memorial Library; Phyllis Geeslin, President Benjamin Harrison Home; Ray Henderson, William Howard Taft National Historic Site; Margaret Hogan, The Adams Papers, Massachusetts Historical Society; Florence Holden, Franklin Pierce, Pierce Manse; John Holtzapple, Polk Home; Meghan Lee, Richard Nixon Library and Birthplace; Frank Pisano, William McKinley Memorial Library; James C. Rees, Executive Director, Mount Vernon Ladies' Association; Marie Schnurr, Aurora Historical Society; Millard Fillmore House; Sam Slaymaker, James Buchanan's Wheatland; Randy Sowell, Harry S. Truman Library; Mary Thompson, Mount Vernon Ladies' Association; Tim Townsend, Lincoln Home National Historic Site; Harrison Tyler, Sherwood Forest and Tyler family historian; Kay Tyler, Sherwood Forest Plantation; Debbie Weinkamer, James A. Garfield National Historic Site; Hobson Woodward, Massachusetts Historical Society.

Finally, I owe a very deep debt of love and gratitude to my wife, Myriam. She helped me understand what was happening in many of these families and how to bring the lesson home for the rest of us. And thanks to my children and their spouses, Shannon, Janeen, Scott, Amy, Joshua, Chloe, and Camille, who have patiently allowed their father to tell them these stories and offer their insights back. For more than a decade they have encouraged me in the researching and writing of this ongoing series on America's first families.

INDEX

———— ★ ————